# Lecture Notes in Computer Science 6908

Commenced Publication in 1973
Founding and Former Series Editors:
Gerhard Goos, Juris Hartmanis, and Jan van Leeuwen

## Editorial Board

A Min Tjoa   Gerald Quirchmayr   Ilsun You
Lida Xu (Eds.)

# Availability, Reliability and Security for Business, Enterprise and Health Information Systems

IFIP WG 8.4/8.9 International Cross Domain
Conference and Workshop, ARES 2011
Vienna, Austria, August 22-26, 2011
Proceedings

 Springer

Volume Editors

A Min Tjoa
Vienna University of Technology
Institute of Software Technology and Interactive Systems
Favoritenstr. 9/188, 1040 Vienna, Austria
E-mail: amin@ifs.tuwien.ac.at

Gerald Quirchmayr
University of Vienna, Multimedia Information Systems
Liebiggasse 4, 1010 Vienna, Austria
E-mail: gerald.quirchmayr@univie.ac.at

Ilsun You
Korean Bible University, School of Information Science
16 Danghyun 2-gil, Nowon-gu, 139-791 Seoul, Korea
E-mail: isyou@bible.ac.kr

Lida Xu
Old Dominion University, Information Technology and Decision Sciences
2076 Constant Hall, Norfolk, VA 23529, USA
E-mail: lxu@odu.edu

ISSN 0302-9743                                    e-ISSN 1611-3349
ISBN 978-3-642-23299-2                            ISBN 978-3-642-23300-5 (eBook)
DOI 10.1007/978-3-642-23300-5
Springer Heidelberg Dordrecht London New York

Library of Congress Control Number: 2011934288

CR Subject Classification (1998): H.4, H.5, K.6.5, E.3, K.4

LNCS Sublibrary: SL 3 – Information Systems and Application, incl. Internet/Web
and HCI

*Typesetting:* Camera-ready by author, data conversion by Scientific Publishing Services, Chennai, India

Printed on acid-free paper

Springer is part of Springer Science+Business Media (www.springer.com)

# Preface

The Cross-Domain Conference and Workshop on Multidisciplinary Research and Practice for Business, Enterprise and Health Information Systems is focused on the relevance of availability, reliability and security within the domain of information systems.

The idea of organizing cross-domain scientific events originated from the IFIP president Leon Strous at the IFIP 2010 World Computer Congress in Brisbane which was echoed with acceptance by many IFIP activists in further discussions at this occasion. This scientific event concentrates on the many aspects of availability, reliability and security for information systems as a discipline bridging the application fields and the well-defined computer science field.

This leads us to the consideration of the many important issues of massive information sharing and integration (MISI) which will (in our opinion) dominate scientific work and discussions in the area of information systems in the second decade of this century.

The organizers of this event who are engaged within IFIP in the area of Enterprise Information Systems (WG 8.9) and Business Information Systems (WG 8.4) very much welcome the cross-fertilization of this event by the collocation with the Workshop on Security and Cognitive Informatics for Homeland Defense on a topic where application factors must be regarded as the most essential. Therefore we are very much convinced that homeland security can only be successful if we do not neglect the bridging nature of this field between application aspects and computer science aspects. The cross-domain viewpoint is an inherent characteristic of this area.

The papers presented at this conference were selected after extensive reviews by the Program Committee and associated reviewers. Special emphasis was placed on applications in the area of electronic health organized as a special track. We would like to thank all PC members and the reviewers for their valuable advice, and the authors for their contributions.

July 2011

A Min Tjoa
Gerald Quirchmayr
Lida Xu
Ilsun You

# Organization

## General Chair

Günther Müller                University of Freiburg, Germany

## Program Co-chairs

| | |
|---|---|
| Mukesh Mohania | IBM Research India, India |
| Gerald Quirchmayr | University of Vienna, Austria and University of South Australia |
| A Min Tjoa | Vienna University of Technology, Austria |

## Publicity Co-chairs

| | |
|---|---|
| Ladjel Bellatreche | LISI/ENSMA, France |
| Lida Xu | Old Dominion University, USA |

## Program Committee

| | |
|---|---|
| Ladjel Bellatreche | LISI/ENSMA, France |
| Smriti Bhagat | Rutgers University, USA |
| Christian Bizer | Freie Universität Berlin, Germany |
| Zhongli Ding | Google |
| John Doucette | University of Waterloo, Canada |
| Sabine Graf | Athabasca University, Canada |
| Martin Hentschel | ETH Zurich, Switzerland |
| Christian Körner | Technical University Graz, Austria |
| Jens Lehmann | University of Leipzig, Germany |
| Scott T. Leutenegger | University of Denver, USA |
| Anirban Mondal | India |
| Mukesh Mohania | IBM Research India, India |
| Peter Mork | MITRE, USA |
| Goran Nenadic | University of Manchester, UK |
| Axel Polleres | National University of Ireland, Ireland |
| Wenny Rahayu | La Trobe University, Australia |
| Josef Schiefer | UC4, USA |
| Il-Yeol Song | Drexel University, USA |
| ChunQiang Tang | Thomas J. Watson Research Center, USA |

| | |
|---|---|
| A Min Tjoa | Vienna University of Technology, Austria |
| Peter van Rosmalen | Open University of the Netherlands, The Netherlands |
| Kyu-Young Whang | Korea Advanced Institute of Science and Technology, Korea |
| John Zeleznikow | Victoria University, Australia |

## Conference Special Track eHealth

### eHealth Track Chair

| | |
|---|---|
| Thomas Neubauer | Vienna University of Technology, Austria |
| Peter Birner | Medical University of Vienna, Austria |

### eHealth Track Committee

| | |
|---|---|
| Rashid L. Bashshur | University of Michigan Health System, USA |
| Olivier Bodenreider | National Library of Medicine |
| Asuman Dogac | Middle East Technical University, Ankara, Turkey |
| John A. Doucette | University of Waterloo, Canada |
| Stefan Fenz | Vienna University of Technology, Austria |
| Stanley Finkelstein | University of Minnesota, USA |
| Yang Gong | University of Missouri, USA |
| Tyrone Grandison | IBM Almaden Research Center |
| Trisha Greenhalgh | University of London, UK |
| Katharina Kaiser | Vienna University of Technology, Austria |
| Klaus Kuhn | Munich University of Technology, Germany |
| Stan Matwin | University of Ottawa, Canada |
| Luciano Milanesi | CNR-bioinformatics, Italy |
| Henning Müller | University of Applied Sciences Western Switzerland |
| Goran Nenadic | University of Manchester, UK |
| Christopher Nugent | University of Ulster, UK |
| Rob Procter | University of Edinburgh School of Informatics, UK |
| Roy Rada | University of Maryland, USA |
| Andrey Rzhetsky | University of Chicago, USA |
| Stefan Schulz | Medical University of Graz, Austria |
| Hiroshi Takeda | Jikei Institue, Japan |
| Philipp Tomsich | Theobroma Systems Design und Consulting GmbH, Austria |
| Xinwen Zhang | Huawei America Research Center at Santa Clara, CA, USA |

# International Workshop on Security and Cognitive Informatics for Homeland Defense (SeCIHD)

**General Chair**

Ilsun You                        Korean Bible University, Republic of Korea

**General Vice Chair**

Jinshu Su                        National University of Defense Technology
Moin Uddin                       Delhi Technological University, India

**Program Chair**

Marek R. Ogiela                  AGH University of Science and Technology
                                 Institute of Automatics, Poland

**Publicity Chair**

N.S. Raghava                     Delhi Technological University, India

**Program Committee**

Anirban Basu                     Tokai University, Japan
Pascal Bouvry                    Luxembourg University, Luxembourg
Jorg Cassens                     Norwegian University of Science and
                                 Technology, Norway
Aniello Castiglione              University of Salerno, Italy
Fumiharu Etoh                    ISIT, Japan
Tomasz Hachaj                    Pedagogical University in Krakow, Poland
Zhang Jie                        Nanyang Technological University, Singapore
Rahul Katarya                    Delhi Technological University, India
Hoon Ko                          Institute of Engineering-Polytechnic of Porto,
                                 Portugal
Gabriele Lenzini                 SnT - University of Luxembourg, Luxembourg
Fang-Yie Leu                     Tunghai University, Taiwan
Lidia D. Ogiela                  AGH University of Science and Technology,
                                 Poland
Dhananjay Singh                  National Institute for Mathematical Sciences,
                                 Korea
James Stanier                    University of Sussex, UK
Chul Sur                         Kyushu University, Japan
Miroslaw Trzupek                 AGH University of Science and Technology,
                                 Poland
Baokang Zhao                     National University of Defense Technology,
                                 China
Toshihiro Yamauchi               Okayama University, Japan
Kangbin Yim                      Soonchunhyang University, Republic of Korea

# Table of Contents

# Workshop

## International Workshop on Security and Cognitive Informatics for Homeland Defense

# Benefits of Federated Identity Management - A Survey from an Integrated Operations Viewpoint

Jostein Jensen

Norwegian University of Science and Technology, Department of Computer and
Information Science, Norway
jostein.jensen@idi.ntnu.no

**Abstract.** Federated Identity Management is considered a promising
approach to facilitate secure resource sharing between collaborating partners. A structured survey has been carried out in order to document the
benefits of adopting such systems from a user and business perspective,
and also to get an indication on how Integrated Operations in the oil and
gas industry can benefit from identity federations. This has resulted in a
set of benefit categories grouping existing claims from researchers. The
literature indicates that adoption of Federated Identity Management in
Integrated Operation seems like a good idea, however, there are several
challenges that need to be solved.

## 1 Introduction

Federated Identity Management (FIdM) is a promising approach to facilitate
secure resource sharing between collaborating partners in heterogeneous (IT)
environments. Such resource sharing is the essence of the ideas of Integrated
Operations in the oil and gas industry, as outlined in the next section (section
2). Federation technologies *"provide open, standardised and secure methods for a
service provider to identify users who are authenticated by an identity provider"*
[30]. Further, identity federations facilitate delegation of identity tasks across
security domains [21].

There are different perspectives on Identity Management (IdM) [3], where the
first is the traditional way of doing IdM, and the next two are alternatives for
Federated Identity Management:

- **Isolated IdM** is the way IdM is commonly done today. Each company establishes, uses and maintains a local user repository where credentials are
  stored and used for authentication purposes to access company internal resources.
- **Centralised IdM** is one architectural model to realise Federated Identity
  Management. User data is registered in a central repository. User authentication is performed by this central entity, which issues identity assertion
  upon a successful authentication process. These assertion, or security tokens,
  can then be used to access distributed services across company borders.

A M. Tjoa et al. (Eds.): ARES 2011, LNCS 6908, pp. 1–12, 2011.

– **Distributed IdM** is the opposite of the previous alternative. Each collaborating company or service provider keeps a local user repository. Authentication is performed locally, but the issued security token can be used to prove identity, and as such get access to, distributed services across company borders.

This illustrates the point that FIdM is about inter-organisation and inter-dependent management of identity information rather than identity solutions for internal use, and that it has emerged with the recognition that individuals frequently move between corporate boundaries [9]. The federation model enables users of one domain to securely access resources of another domain seamlessly, and without the need for redundant user login processes [5]. According to Balasubramaniam et al. [6] an Identity Management solution consists of the following functionality attributes: 1) Identity provisioning, 2) Authentication and authorisation, 3) Storage, management, 4) query/retrieve and indexing of identity information, 5) Certification of identity and credentials, 6) Single-sign-on/single-sign-off, 6) Audit capabilities.

Smith [30] has observed that the predictions of rapid acceleration in the industrial uptake of FIdM technology have not been fulfilled. This is despite the fact that the technological building blocks have been developed for years, and that the technology is relatively mature and well understood. This paper presents partial results of a research project to understand why FIdM processes and tools have not been widely adopted in industry, and what should be done to increase the adoption rate, and/or if there is an actual industrial need for it at all. A company's management need to be convinced of the benefits, challenges and cost of adopting a technology before they make the investment. So as a starting point, we wanted to identify what benefits of deploying FIdM have been reported in scientific literature. The following research questions were stated in this respect, and will be answered in this paper:

**RQ1:** What are the reported benefits of adopting Federated Identity Management from a user perspective?
**RQ2:** What are the reported benefits of adopting Federated Identity Management from a business perspective?
**RQ3:** How can an Integrated Operations scenario benefit from using Federated Identity Management?

The last question is related to the case for the ongoing research project, which is an Integrated Operation (IO) scenario in the Norwegian oil & gas sector. This scenario is presented in the following section. Section 3 presents how the research leading to the the presented results was carried out, while section 4 presents a list of benefit categories obtained by analysing the literature, as well as a discussion on how an IO scenario can benefit from FIdM. Section 5 discuss our results before the paper is concluded and directions for further work are given in section 6.

## 2    The Integrated Operations Scenario

In mid 1990, oil and gas companies operating on the Norwegian Continental Shelf (NCS) started developing and deploying mechanisms for simple remote operation of offshore installations. In 2002, the Norwegian Oil Industry Association (OLF) initiated a project group to look into this development, and consider the potential benefits and consequences of such initiatives. This resulted in a report [19] describing future scenarios and visions for oil and gas operations in the North Sea. Prior to the remote management initiatives, there had been a distinct separation between onshore and offshore installations. Now, OLF saw that there was an increasing amount of data being made available and shared real-time. With new processes and tools these data could be utilised in decision support processes that would change the way work was organised. They envisioned that the workload between offshore and onshore installations would be changed, and virtual teams would emerge. The operations would be more integrated, and thus the term Integrated Operations (IO) emerged.

The concept of Integrated Operations has been refined and widely deployed in the companies operating on the NCS. Land-based operation centers monitor and control large portions of the daily oil and gas production. However, the current focus has been on intra-organisational collaboration, meaning that systems (more or less) only allow interaction between humans and systems within a single company. One of the visions in the OLF report referred to was, on the other hand, also to enable inter-organisational collaboration where partners (see Figure 1 for an overview of IO participants) could share information and knowledge seamlessly across company borders.

In 2008 a new OLF report was released: Reference Architecture of IT systems for OLF's IO G2 [1]. This report sketched the reference architecture for a common service platform supporting inter-organisational collaboration. The enhanced collaborative capacity has been seen as the next generation of IO systems and as such is referred to as IO gen 2. A Service Oriented Architecture (SOA) has been proposed to facilitate this collaboration.

The OLF architecture report [1] lists various governing principles for the future IO architecture, including those shown in Table 1.

## 3    Method

A structured literature review approach inspired by Kitchenham [17] was used as research method leading to the results presented in this paper. The focus has been on performing the search phase with rigor. The aim of this systematic survey was to identify scientific literature that could provide answers to our research questions listed in the previous section.

### 3.1    Identification of Research

The starting point for the survey was a research protocol where the research questions and the search strategy were defined. A rigorous and comprehensive search was key to identify relevant scientific literature.

**Table 1.** Extract of principles governing the IO gen 2 architecture

| Principle | Comment |
|---|---|
| Loose coupling between systems | Systems should be independent of changes in other systems |
| A service provider and a service consumer must be able to interact with each other | Reachability is an essential prerequisite for service interaction. |
| Conform to open standards | |
| Roles and corresponding responsibilities must be defined | Roles and responsibilities must be described to see who needs what in the patterns |
| Access should be role and asset based | Users need to be allocated a role for an asset (e.g. an oil field) so that it is possible to see what access is allowed against that asset for that person. |
| Authentication should be at the local company | Authenticated at his or her own company, for use anywhere. |
| Build on existing infrastructure | |
| A service should be reusable | Designed to be used by multiple customers, and also to be used in different contexts (within the scope if its intended use) |

We used the following online databases for scientific literature to search for studies:

- IEEE Xplore[1]
- ACM Digital Library[2]
- Compendex[3]
- SpringerLink[4]

For each of these databases we used the following search phrase: *"federated identity management"*. The total amount of papers after this search was 684. Papers were then filtered based on title and abstract after the search, and duplicate publications were removed. All papers clearly not relevant for this study were taken out of the reading list. This process led to 113 remaining papers. The last selection of papers were read in the full, and text indicating benefits of using Federated Identity Management was extracted. This resulted in a total of 30 primary studies considered within the frame of this paper.

---

[1] http://ieeexplore.ieee.org/Xplore/dynhome.jsp
[2] http://portal.acm.org/dl.cfm
[3] http://www.engineeringvillage2.org/
[4] http://www.springerlink.com

# 4   Results

This section presents the results after analysing all citations reported as benefits of using FIdM. The reported benefits were first split in two categories: those reporting benefits from a user perspective, and those reporting benefits from a business perspective. A further analysis led to categories of benefits as summarised in Table 2.

**Table 2.** Benefit categories from a user and business perspective

| User perspective | Business perspective |
| --- | --- |
| Increased privacy protection | Reduced cost |
| Better security | Improved data quality |
| Improved usability | Increased security |
|  | Simplified/Improved user management |
|  | Reduced complexity for service providers |
|  | Facilitate cooperation |

## 4.1   Benefits from a User Perspective

In this section benefits of using FIdM from a user perspective are reflected, and indicates answers to RQ1.

**Increased Privacy Protection.** Several researchers agree that the use of FIdM can increase the ability to protect personal privacy. Ahn et al. [3] [2] even say that *"The main motivation of FIM* [FIdM] *is to enhance user convenience and privacy "* , which is also supported by Gomi et al. [13]. Both Landau et al. [18] and Bertino et al. [8] claim that FIdM technology can facilitate users to control their personal data, and what is being sent to a service provider. Requirements related to minimal disclosure of information can be fulfilled. Squicciarini et al. [32] say that: *Federated identity management systems [...] enable organizations to provide services to qualified individuals; and empower them with control over the usage and sharing of their identity attributes within the federation.*

**Better Security.** FIdM may lead to improved security for users. According to Wolf et al. [33] users are released from remembering several credentials due to the single sign-on feature facilitated by FIdM systems. Madsen et al. [20] argue that the reduced number of authentication operations will make it practical for users to choose different and stronger passwords at their Identity Providers. This is also supported by Bhargav-Spantzel et al. [9]. Fewer and stronger authentication events will also help to minimise the risk of ID theft [8].

With the FIdM model, credentials do not need to be sent to/via Service Providers. It is sufficient to send asserted claims [20]. As such the credentials are better protected [18] [26].

**Improved Usability.** Users can benefit from increased simplicity with FIdM solutions [18] [26]. It is especially the Single-sign-on (SSO) feature that is emphasised in this respect, and Madsen et al. [20] highlight this feature as the archetypical example of a federated application. With SSO users can log in once and access different resources at different service providers [28] [22] [21] [16], without needing to remember multiple ways of authenticating at each site [18] and potentially by only remembering one password [14].

Seamless access to resources, and the elimination of redundant user login processes leads to improved user experience [4]. Satchell et al. [24] add that instead of having several identities at different service providers, FIdM allows all these to be gathered under one umbrella. This does *"not only provide users with vital cohesion but contributes to digital environments that are easily traversable spaces"*. Scudder and Jøsang [26] also state that identity federations release users from the burden of managing an increasing number of online identities.

From this we can deduce that users can experience improved usability since multiple services can be *accessed as a unified whole* [18].

## 4.2   Benefits from a Business Perspective

This section presents reported benefits of FIdM with respect to a business perspective, and as such indicates answers to RQ2.

**Reduced Cost.** Several statements from researchers indicate that introduction of FIdM can lead to reduced cost with respect to identity management for an organisation [22] [18] [11]. Madsen et al. [20] claim that the administrative costs of account maintenance for service providers can be reduced, and Ahn et al. [3] say that FIdM allows businesses to share the identity management cost with its partners. Bertino et al. [8] explain the cost saving a bit more: Costs and redundancy is reduced *because organisations do not have to acquire, store and maintain authorisation information about all their partners' users.* Also Kang and Khashnobish say that the redundancy problem in user administration may be solved with FIdM, while Smith [30] claims that multiple corporations in theory can share a single [FIdM] application, and that the consolidation can result in cost savings.

**Improved Data Quality.** Since identity data is essential to make correct access control decisions it is paramount that they are correct and up to date. FIdM can help improve the overall quality of this data. Bertino et al. [8] argue that identity information can be made available on demand and with low delay in a distributed environment in a FIdM scenario. They also claim that the user data will be more up-to-date and consistent compared to a scenario where user data is stored and maintained several places. Hoellrigl et al. [15] and Han et al. [14] present similar views. Both groups claim that the strength is that the administrative burden of user management is moved from the service provider to the Identity Provider. As such, redundancy and information inconstancies in identity information can be avoided [15], and the exchange of user's identity information can be optimised.

**Increased Security.** There are several security aspects that are facilitated by FIdM solutions. Bertino et al. [8] claim that a federation prevents the problem of 'single point of failure'. However, this assumes that a distributed IdM model is followed. Speltens and Patterson [31] call it the 'true holy grail' of Federation, that applications become fully claims aware, and that access control decisions are based on claims. In such a situation the 'minimal disclosure' of information principle can be satisfied in that only required data needed to access a service have to be transmitted to a business partner [8]. Further, a claims based system can facilitate fine-grained authorisation [23]. Also Satchell et al. [24] highlight that FIdM facilitates the assignment of access rights and privileges, and Sharma et al. [27] add that it facilitates possibilities for detailed audit trails. Finally, Balasubramaniam et al. [6] give a general comment that FIdM will lead to min-imisation of privacy and security violations.

**Simplified/Improved User Management.** Federated Identity management can simplify the complex process of managing user accounts [18]. User manage-ment tasks can be decentralised among identity and service providers [3] [2] [13], without being worried that the work of managing user identities and attributes is doubled [12]. There is a clear link between this point and *Improved Data Quality* and *Increased Security*. User account provisioning [4] is simplified, and with a holistic view of users' identity data, deprovisioning of user accounts is also better facilitated [33].

**Reduced Complexity for Service Providers.** By separating identity man-agement tasks from the service providers, they can focus fully on delivering high quality services, while at the same time reducing the complexity [4] [5]. Identity management tasks can be outsourced to a separate IdP.

**Facilitate cooperation.** In the literature on FIdM there are several researchers arguing that federated solution will facilitate cooperation. Sharma et al. [27] say that FIdM technologies will allow companies to share applications without needing to adopt the same technologies for directory services and authentication. Similarly Brossard et al. [10] state that enterprises can offer services across domain bound-aries to users and other services not controlled or defined internally. The technol-ogy offers an opportunity to create new business relationships and realise business goals at a lower cost [24]. The typical usecase is cross-domain single-sign-on [5], where a user's identity information can be used across multiple organisations [34] [25]. FIdM help share this information in a protected way based on contractual and operational agreements [8]. Sliman et al. [29] add to the above that final au-thorisation decisions can be kept at the end application or service, even though user data is stored and authentication is performed in a remote location.

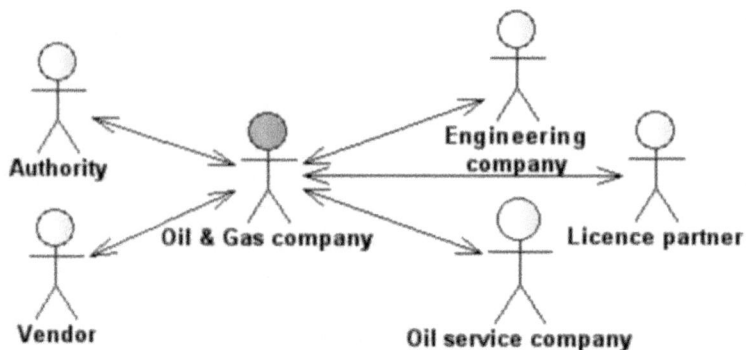

**Fig. 1.** Collaborating actors. Adapted from [1].

### 4.3   Benefits from an IO Perspective

As presented in section 2, Integrated Operation is all about inter-organisational resource sharing and collaboration, in a complex environment. In the following we give a brief view on how IO can benefit from adopting a FIdM model (RQ3).

Figure 1 shows part of the complexity associated with implementing IO; there are several actors involved. Examples of collaborative events include, vendors who may need remote access to the equipment they have delivered in order to read status reports and plan maintenance, and authorities who need access to drilling reports to monitor the production [1].

Today, isolated IdM models are realised by the IO actors. As such, e.g. the Oil and Gas company needs to provision a local user identity to the Vendor representative before he can remotely access equipment in the production environment. This raises several questions, such as: What are the procedures to keep user data up-to-date? What are the procedures when the vendor representative quits his job or changes position? What is the time delay before this is registered at the Oil and Gas company so that they can remove or update access rights?

The whole IO scenario seems as a good match for implementing the ideas of Federated Identity Management, especially considering the reported benefits from a business perspective. Independent of the chosen federation model (see section 1) user data will be registered once. This will *simplify the user management* process, which has the important effect that the *quality and correctness of user data* is always as good as they are collected at the primary source, and synchronisation issues are eliminated. This again is key to maintain a *high security level* in that access is given based on updated data. Instead of spending resources on managing external users, the IO actors can focus on maintaining dynamic access policy sets, and improve the granularity of access constraints based on identity attributes/claims.

With the large number of IO actors it is an unrealistic scenario that all of them will invest in identical infrastructure related to Identity Management. However, selecting a FIdM model using standardised protocols and interfaces will *facilitate cooperation* and make system integration less difficult.

Most communication will go through the Oil and Gas Company, meaning that they will experience most of the overhead related to the current Isolated IdM model. *Cost savings* may thus be considerable for these companies, while the economic incentive to move to a FIdM model might not be as large for the other actors.

In addition to this, FIdM may also facilitate the realisation of the architectural principles for IO as outlined in Table 1 . Systems and services can be loosely coupled, and identity and authentication services will be decoupled from functionality services. FIdM facilitates communication and interaction between service providers and service consumers in that identity data is sent in a standardised way designed for distributed systems. Access may be role based, but can also be made at more granular levels based on claims. Next, the distributed FIdM model is designed for keeping identity data at the local company, and performing local authentication of users.

## 5 Discussion

A lightweight version of Kitchenham's guide to structured surveys has been used to obtain the results presented in this paper. We have been less strict in the paper selection phase (as there have only been one researcher involved) and data synthesis phase (papers were read, raw data collected and grouped once, without iteration) than what is recommended to pass the strict requirements of the guide. Further, the search phrase we used may prevent us from identifying an exhaustive literature list on the topic; there might e.g. be papers talking about identity federations without mentioning our exact search phrase. Yet, we argue that the process is sufficient to answer the stated research questions, as it allows to get a representative view on existing research on the topic.

Next, it is important to be aware of the fact that the benefit categories listed in this paper are a result of analysing claims from researchers in the field. These claims must to a large extent be considered as expert opinions, which are not necessarily backed up by existing research. E.g. several researchers mention cost savings as a possible benefit of FIdM, however, none of the cited papers report from case studies where real cost savings are presetend.

This being said, FIdM seems like a promising approach to support inter-organisational collaboration, and there seems to be a good match between the reported benefits and the architectural principles for IO in the Oil and Gas sector. However, there are considerable challenges still to be solved, and which might hinder adoption. Trust among the participants in a Federation is one [26]. Baldwin et al. [7] point to the fact that stakeholders might have different assumptions and risk appetite, and as such different requirements with respect to the level of assurance associated with identity claims. These trust challenges are related to people, processes and technology. According to Scudder and Jøsang [26] the degree of needed trust does not foster large-scale federations. Smith [30] raises the issue of liability. What will happen if one of the federation partners fails to follow a proper process for identification of their employees? Another aspect of implementing FIdM is the consequences of single-sign-on functionality if a digital identity is stolen, or a password compromised [21]. In such cases not only internal resources are compromised, but also potentially those of the federation partners. There are also technological challenges. Wolf et al. [33] point to complexity with respect to standardisation of FIdM protocols and data formats among the collaborators, and that this is essential to reach the goal. These challenges indicate that RQ3 can not be answered by looking at the reported benefits alone. A deeper analysis to answer this question, and a cost benefit analysis, should be done after all challenges are considered, and a risk assessment has been carried out.

## 6    Conclusion and Further Work

In this paper we report benefits of adopting Federated Identity Management systems from a user and business perspective, and a high-level view on perspectives of adopting FIdM in an Integrated Operations environment. Our conclusion is that there is a good match between the benefits of adopting FIdM and the architectural principles suggested for IO. However, we have also mentioned considerable challenges of adopting FIdM, and more research is needed to facilitate adoption in an industrial setting.

As part of a larger ongoing work on FIdM to facilitate IO, similar work as presented in this paper will be carried out with respect to documentation of reported challenges in the near future. The combined results will be used as input to a large case study including the stakeholders on different levels (management, IT operations, system users), from the various actors shown in Figure 1. This case study will result in empirical evidence as to what the enablers for FIdM adoption are, and whether it is realistic in an IO setting or not.

**Acknowledgment.** This work is supported by grant 183235/S10 from the Norwegian Research Council, and the GoICT project.

## References

1. Reference architecture of it systems for olfs io g2. Tech. Rep. OLF report, OLF (2008)
2. Ahn, G.J., Lam, J.: Managing privacy preferences for federated identity management (2005)
3. Ahn, G.J., Shin, D., Hong, S.P.: Information assurance in federated identity management: Experimentations and issues. In: Zhou, X., Su, S., Papazoglou, M.P., Orlowska, M.E., Jeffery, K. (eds.) WISE 2004. LNCS, vol. 3306, pp. 78–89. Springer, Heidelberg (2004)
4. Almenarez, F., Arias, P., Marin, A., Diaz, D.: Towards dynamic trust establishment for identity federation (2009)
5. Arias Cabarcos, P., Almenarez Mendoza, F., Marin-Lopez, A., Diaz-Sanchez, D.: Enabling saml for dynamic identity federation management. In: Wozniak, J., Konorski, J., Katulski, R., Pach, A. (eds.) Wireless and Mobile Networking. IFIP Advances in Information and Communication Technology, vol. 308, pp. 173–184. Springer, Boston (2009)

6. Balasubramaniam, S., Lewis, G.A., Morris, E., Simanta, S., Smith, D.B.: Identity management and its impact on federation in a system-of-systems context. In: 2009 3rd Annual IEEE Systems Conference, pp. 179–182 (2009)
7. Baldwin, A., Mont, M.C., Beres, Y., Shiu, S.: Assurance for federated identity management. J. Comput. Secur. 18(4), 541–572 (2010)
8. Bertino, E., Martino, L., Paci, F., Squicciarini, A., Martino, L.D., Squicciarini, A.C.: Standards for web services security. In: Security for Web Services and Service-Oriented Architectures, pp. 45–77. Springer, Heidelberg (2010)
9. Bhargav-Spantzel, A., Squicciarini, A.C., Bertino, E.: Establishing and protecting digital identity in federation systems (2005)
10. Brossard, D., Dimitrakos, T., Gaeta, A.: Aspects of general security & trust. In: Dimitrakos, T., Martrat, J., Wesner, S. (eds.) Service Oriented Infrastructures and Cloud Service Platforms for the Enterprise, pp. 75–102. Springer, Heidelberg (2010)
11. Chadwick, D.: Federated identity management. In: Aldini, A., Barthe, G., Gorrieri, R. (eds.) Foundations of Security Analysis and Design V. LNCS, vol. 5705, pp. 96–120. Springer, Heidelberg (2009)
12. Elberawi, A.S., Abdel-Hamid, A., El-Sonni, M.T.: Privacy-preserving identity federation middleware for web services (pifm-ws). In: 2010 International Conference on Computer Engineering and Systems (ICCES), pp. 213–220 (2010)
13. Gomi, H., Hatakeyama, M., Hosono, S., Fujita, S.: A delegation framework for federated identity management (2005)
14. Han, J., Mu, Y., Susilo, W., Yan, J.: A generic construction of dynamic single sign-on with strong security. In: Jajodia, S., Zhou, J. (eds.) Security and Privacy in Communication Networks. Lecture Notes of the Institute for Computer Sciences, Social-Informatics and Telecommunications Engineering, vol. 50, pp. 181–198. Springer, Heidelberg (2010)
15. Hoellrigl, T., Dinger, J., Hartenstein, H.: A consistency model for identity information in distributed systems. In: 2010 IEEE 34th Annual Computer Software and Applications Conference (COMPSAC), pp. 252–261 (2010)
16. Kang, M., Khashnobish, A.: A peer-to-peer federated authentication system. In: Sixth International Conference on Information Technology: New Generations, ITNG 2009, pp. 382–387 (2009)
17. Kitchenham, B.: Procedures for performing systematic reviews. Tech. Rep. TR/SE-0401, Keele University (2004)
18. Landau, S., Le Van Gong, H., Wilton, R.: Achieving privacy in a federated identity management system. In: Dingledine, R., Golle, P. (eds.) FC 2009. LNCS, vol. 5628, pp. 51–70. Springer, Heidelberg (2009)
19. Lilleng, T., et al.: Edrift på norsk sokkel - det tredje effektiviseringsspranget. Tech. Rep. OLF report, OLF (2003)
20. Madsen, P., Koga, Y., Takahashi, K.: Federated identity management for protecting users from id theft (2005)
21. Maler, E., Reed, D.: The venn of identity: Options and issues in federated identity management. IEEE Security & Privacy 6(2), 16–23 (2008)
22. Ranga, G., Flowerday, S.: Identity and access management for the distribution of social grants in south africa (2007)
23. Rieger, S.: User-centric identity management in heterogeneous federations. In: Fourth International Conference on Internet and Web Applications and Services, ICIW 2009, pp. 527–532 (2009)
24. Satchell, C., Shanks, G., Howard, S., Murphy, J.: Beyond security: implications for the future of federated digital identity management systems (2006)

25. Schell, F., Dinger, J., Hartenstein, H.: Performance evaluation of identity and access management systems in federated environments. In: Mueller, P., Cao, J.N., Wang, C.L. (eds.) Scalable Information Systems. Lecture Notes of the Institute for Computer Sciences, Social-Informatics and Telecommunications Engineering, vol. 18, pp. 90–107. Springer, Heidelberg (2009)

26. Scudder, J., Jøsang, A.: Personal federation control with the identity dashboard. In: de Leeuw, E., Fischer-Hübner, S., Fritsch, L. (eds.) Policies and Research in Identity Management. IFIP Advances in Information and Communication Technology, vol. 343, pp. 85–99. Springer, Heidelberg (2010)

27. Sharma, A.K., Lamba, C.S.: Survey on federated identity management systems. In: Meghanathan, N., Boumerdassi, S., Chaki, N., Nagamalai, D. (eds.) Recent Trends in Networks and Communications. CCIS, vol. 90, pp. 509–517. Springer, Heidelberg (2010)

28. Shim, S.S.Y., Geetanjali, B., Vishnu, P.: Federated identity management. Computer 38(12), 120–122 (2005)

29. Sliman, L., Badr, Y., Biennier, F., Salatge, N., Nakao, Z.: Single sign-on integration in a distributed enterprise service bus. In: International Conference on Network and Service Security, N2S 2009, pp. 1–5 (2009)

30. Smith, D.: The challenge of federated identity management. Network Security (4), 7–9 (2008)

31. Speltens, M., Patterson, P.: Federated id management - tackling risk and credentialing users. In: ISSE/SECURE 2007 Securing Electronic Business Processes, pp. 130–135. Vieweg (2007)

32. Squicciarini, A.C., Czeskis, A., Bhargav-Spantzel, A.: Privacy policies compliance across digital identity management systems (2008)

33. Wolf, M., Thomas, I., Menzel, M., Meinel, C.: A message meta model for federated authentication in service-oriented architectures. In: 2009 IEEE International Conference on Service-Oriented Computing and Applications (SOCA), pp. 1–8 (2009)

34. Zuo, Y., Luo, X., Zeng, F.: Towards a dynamic federation framework based on saml and automated trust negotiation. In: Wang, F.L., Gong, Z., Luo, X., Lei, J. (eds.) Web Information Systems and Mining. LNCS, vol. 6318, pp. 254–262. Springer, Heidelberg (2010)

# A Security Policy Model for Agent Based Service-Oriented Architectures

Eckehard Hermann

Department of Secure Information Systems,
Upper Austria University of Applied Sciences, Austria
eckehard.hermann@fh-hagenberg.at

**Abstract.** During the last years service oriented architectures (SOA) have gained in importance, when looking at today's implementation of business processes. A SOA is a loosely coupled system of services, where a service is implemented by an agent. The protection of information and data objects and their well-directed flow are essential for the success of enterprises, which also applies to the communication inside a SOA. To guarantee an approved protection of data objects and to prevent an illegal information flow, approved security policy models are chosen that are suitable for the considered use case. The Limes Security Model [1] is based on a not necessarily symmetric, not necessarily reflexive and not necessarily transitive conflict of interest relation. The model is introduced for pure subject/object relationships, where agents are not taken into account. The current paper extends the Limes Security Model by the support of agents, suitable for the use in a SOA.

**Keywords:** security models, service-oriented architectures, principal agent theory, information flow control.

## 1 Introduction

Service oriented architectures (SOA) have gained in importance by the implementation of business processes as a dynamic and loosely coupled system of services. In [8] Burbeck defines the term *service-oriented* for

> architectures that focus on how services are described and organized to support their dynamic, automated discovery and use [...] to work easily, flexibly, and well together, services must be based on shared organizing principles that constitute a service-oriented architecture (SOA), the architectural concept behind Web services.

Such kinds of services are used in business-to-business scenarios, where the services communicate with each other by sending and receiving messages via a request/response protocol. A client invokes a service by sending a request and providing the necessary data that the service needs to process in order to preparing and sending the response. A service is implemented by an agent, a program that acts on behalf of a person or an organization [2] at runtime. The described

A M. Tjoa et al. (Eds.): ARES 2011, LNCS 6908, pp. 13–25, 2011.
© IFIP International Federation for Information Processing 2011

situation is a typical outsourcing scenario, where a client outsources one or more tasks to a service instead of implementing them himself. As described by Pratt and Zeckhausen in [9]

> Whenever one individual depends on the action of another, an agency relationship arises. The individual taking the action is called the agent.

The problem described by Pratt and Zeckhausen in [9] is based on an asymmetric relationship, because of an informational advantage of the agent compared to the client. In many cases the client (application) provides data of some sort of critical nature to the agent. The problem lies in the uncertainty of the client, not knowing whether the agent might misuse this data. To guarantee an approved protection of the client data and to prevent an illegal information flow, an approved security policy model has to be chosen that is suitable for the considered use case. The security policy model defines the rules and policy that have to be implemented by any kind of read and write access of all the participants to prevent provable an illegal information flow.

The current paper gives an introduction to the Limes Security Model, discusses the problems, where the model is applied to agents and presents an extension of the Limes Security Model by the support of agents, suitable for the use in service oriented architectures.

## 2   State of the Art

### 2.1   Agent Based Service-Oriented Architectures

A service-oriented architecture is a loosely coupled system of services. Resources are made available as independent services, with a high degree of abstraction of the underlying platform [10], which can be dynamically integrated into new applications. Resources are made available as independent services, which can be dynamically integrated into new applications.

A service is characterized by its abstract set of functionality that it provides and which is implemented by an agent, a program that acts on behalf of a person or an organization [2]. For the rest of this paper agents are defined according to the characterization of [2]. An agent

- is a computational resource,
- has an owner that is a person or organization,
- may realize zero or more services,
- may request zero or more services. [2]

### 2.2   Security Models

Different security policy models like the one from Bell and LaPadula, are a formalization of a military security model in [5] or they address the integrity of data objects in commercial transactions, as stated by Clark and Wilson [6]. In 1989 Brewer and Nash presented their Chinese Wall Security Policy model

(CWSP model) that is based on conflict of interest classes [3] and nearly one year later Lin showed some limitations of the CWSP model and presented in [4] a modified version, called the Aggressive Chinese Wall Security Policy model (ACWSP model).

**The Chinese Wall and the Aggressive Chinese Wall Security Policy model.** As part of the Chinese Wall Security Policy model Brewer and Nash defined in [3] a hierarchically arranged filing system, where, like Loock and Eloff summarized in [7], on the lowest level, individual items of information are considered, each concerning a single corporation. At the intermediate level, all objects, which concern the same corporation are grouped together and form the company dataset. And on the highest level all company datasets are grouped, whose corporations are in competition. The highest level is called the conflict of interest classes [3]. If a subject intends to access an object, access is only granted if the object requested

- is in the same company dataset as an object already accessed by that subject or
- belongs to an entirely different conflict of interest class [3].

Lin showed in [4] that Brewer and Nash implicitly assume that the conflict of interest is an equivalence relation. He showed that the conflict of interest is a binary relation but not in general an equivalence relation. Lin assumed that the conflict of interest relation is symmetric but non-reflexive and non-transitive, except under special conditions.[4]

Let us recollect some of our earlier considerations [1]: Because each organization defines its own security policy, symmetric conflict of interest classes are not the default in the real world of business. When an organization $A$ defines a conflict with organization $B$, it should be independent of the definition of conflicts that $B$ creates on its own behalf.

*Example 1.* Let $O = \{$Company A, Opensource Community$\}$ and let CIR = "in conflict with". Let the Company A be "in conflict with" the Opensource Community because the business model of the Company A depends on licensing their software, which would imply the protection of their own knowhow against competitors. If CIR were symmetric and Company A would be "in conflict with" the Opensource Community, it would imply that the Opensource Community is "in conflict with" Company A, which is obviously not the case. [1]

## 3   Related Work

In the recent past security policy models for web services environments or Workflow Management Systems have been developed by Hung et al or by Hsiao and Hwang. Hung et al extended the CWSP model in [12] into specifying and implementing conflict of interest assertions in WS-Policy for Web Services enabled environments. Hsiao and Hwang implemented the CWSP model into a Workflow Management Systems in [11].

Debasish and Bijan described in [13] an AAA (Authentication, Authorization and Accounting) security model of service oriented computational grids. The model is not a provable formalized model. It has been modeled and implemented by using a token based authentication, based on Kerberos or a PKI and implementing XML Signature and XML Encryption for integrity and privacy.

Wu et al adopt in [14] the Chinese Wall policies to address the problems of insecure information flow inside a cloud and to resolve the conflict-of-interest issues for service providers in clouds.

The Limes security model, introduced in [1], extends the CWSP model and is based on a not necessarily symmetric, not necessarily reflexive and not necessarily transitive conflict of interest relation.

## 4   The Limes Security Model

The Limes Security Model as defined in [1] works on the assumption that an object does only stay in conflict with an object and does not stay in conflict with a subject. This concludes that the information flow between objects has to be controlled, which can be done by controlling the write accesses of the subjects. A conflict of interest is not necessarily symmetric, not necessarily reflexive and not necessarily transitive. Each object is able to express its individual conflict of interest by the definition of its own time depending Conflict Function and Conflict Of Interest List. In [1] the Conflict Function and Conflict Of Interest List are defined as follows:

**Definition 1.** *Let $S$ be a set of subjects and let $O$ be the set of all known objects. $O_t \subseteq O$ is the set of all available objects at instant of time $t \in \mathbb{N}$.*

**Definition 2 (Conflict Function).** *For each instant of time $t \in \mathbb{N}$, all objects $i, j \in O_t$ and each instant of time $l \in \mathbb{N}$ with $l \leq t$ and where $l$ is the instant of time, where a read access to object $i$ has been performed, let $_iCIL_l^t$ be the Conflict Of Interest List and let $_iNCL_l^t$ be the Non Conflict Of Interest List of the object $i$ depending on the read access to the instant of time $l$ with the following properties [1]:*

- $_iCIL_l^t \cup {}_iNCL_l^t = O_t$.
- $_iCIL_l^t \cap {}_iNCL_l^t = \{\}$.
- $i \in {}_iNCL_l^t$.
- *If $j \in {}_iNCL_l^t$, then at instant of time $t$ the object $i$ is not in conflict with object $j$ in relation to the read access at instant of time $l$.*
- *If $j \in {}_iCIL_l^t$, then at instant of time $t$ the object $i$ is in conflict with object $j$ because of the read access at instant of time $l$.*

*A function $f_i^t : O_t \times \mathbb{N} \to \mathbb{Z} \cup \{\infty\}$ is called Conflict Function of object $i$ if $f_i^t$ has the following property:*

$$f_i^t(j, l) = \begin{cases} < 0, & \text{if } _iCIL_l^t = \{\}, \\ 0, & \text{if } j \in {}_iNCL_l^t \wedge {}_iCIL_l^t \neq \{\}, \\ > 0, & \text{if } j \in {}_iCIL_l^t. \end{cases} \tag{1}$$

All data that is owned by an individual object or subject, is grouped together and defines the dataset of the individual object or subject. If a subject performs a read access to an object, we assume that it reads the whole dataset of the object. If the subject performs a write access to an object, we assume that it writes its own dataset completely into the dataset of the object.

Each subject owns its own Read Access History, containing the information about the sources of the data in its own dataset and the instance of time, when the data has been read from the individual objects. The Read Access History $_sH^t$ is the set of tuples $(j, t')$ of objects $j \in O_t$ that have been read accessed by the subject $s \in S$ in the past and the instant of time $t' \in \mathbb{N}$ of the individual read access.

In addition to the Read Access History of the subjects, each object also owns a history, called the Dataset Actuality of the object. The Dataset Actuality $_iA^t$ of an object $i \in O_t$ is the set of tuples $(j, t')$. The objects $j \in O_t$ have been read accessed by a subject $s \in S$ in the past and the read dataset has been written to the object $i$. $t'$ is the instance of time the read access has been performed at $j$. The Dataset Actuality contains the information about the sources and actuality of the data contained by the dataset of $i$. In addition to the Dataset Actuality each object owns an Actuality Function as defined by Definition 3.

**Definition 3 (Actuality Function).** *For each instant of time $t \in \mathbb{N}$ and all objects $i, j \in O_t$ let $t' \in \mathbb{Z}$ be the instant of time, where the read access at object $j$ has been made and where the read dataset has been written to $i$ later. The function $a_i^t : O_t \to \mathbb{Z}$ is called the Actuality Function of $i$, if $a_i^t$ has the following property [1]:*

$$a_i^t(j) = \begin{cases} t', & \text{if } (j, t') \in {}_iA^t, \\ -1, & \text{otherwise.} \end{cases} \tag{2}$$

*Example 2.* Figure 1 $(a.)$ shows the instant of time $t$ of an example, where the subjects $s_1$ and $s_2$, pictured as circles, have not accessed any of the objects $o_1$ and $o_2$, which are pictured as rectangles. Therefore the Read Access Histories of the subjects and the Dataset Actualities of the objects are empty.

If a subject performs a read access to an object, it adds the dataset of the object to its own dataset. Additionally it merges its own Read Access History with the Dataset Actuality of the object in a way that its own Read Access History contains the entries of both histories afterwards. The entry with the more recent instance of access time is selected in case of a collision. Additionally the subject adds the currently accessed object with the current time to its Read Access History.

Figure 1 $(b.)$ shows the instant of time $t + 1$, where the subject $s_1$ performs a read access operation to object $o_1$. As part of the read access the dataset of $o_1$ is added to the dataset of $s_1$ and a tuple consisting of the instance of time $t + 1$ and $o_1$ is added to the Read Access History of $s_1$.[1]

If a subject performs a write access to an object, it writes its dataset into the dataset of the object. Additionally the Read Access History of the subject is merged with the Dataset Actuality of the object in a way that the Dataset

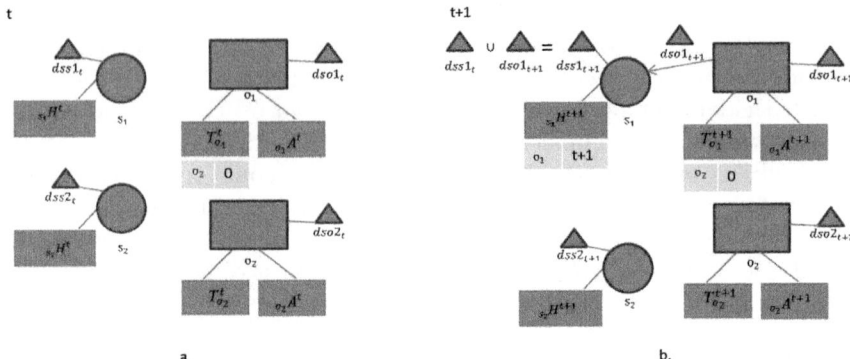

**Fig. 1.** Initial situation at instant of time $t$ ($a.$) and read access at instant of time $t + 1$ ($b.$) [1]

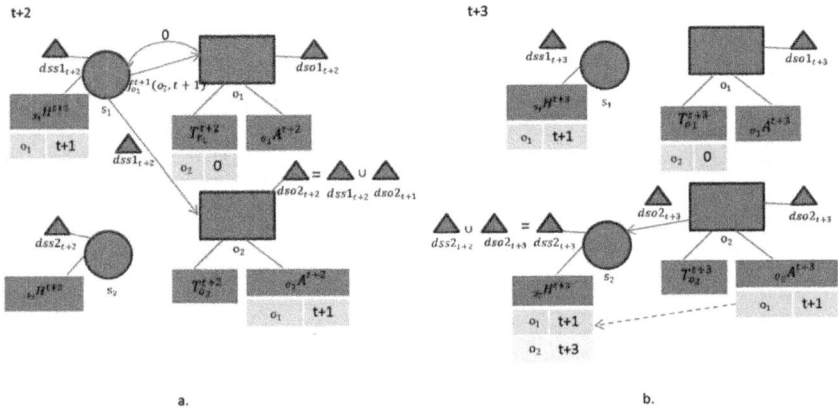

**Fig. 2.** Write access at instant of time $t + 2$ ($a.$) and read access at instant of time $t + 3$ ($b.$) [1]

Actuality of the object contains the entries of both histories afterwards. The entry with the more recent instance of access time is selected in case of a collision.

Before a subject performs a write access, it invokes the Conflict Function of all the objects enlisted in its own Read Access History. The write access is denied, if one of the objects signals a conflict with the intended write access.

Figure 2 ($a.$) shows the instant of time $t + 2$, where the subjects $s_1$ performs a write access to object $o_2$. Before it writes its dataset to $o_2$, $s_1$ has to invoke all the Conflict Functions of the objects enlisted in its own Read Access History. In addition to the merging of the dataset of $s_1$ into the dataset of $o_2$, a merging of the Read Access History of $s_1$ with the Dataset Actuality of $o_2$ is performed and written to the Dataset Actuality of $o_2$.[1]

Figure 2 ($b.$) shows the instant of time $t + 3$, where subject $s_2$ performs a read access to $o_2$. As part of the read access, a merging of the Dataset Actuality of $o_2$ with the Read Access History of $s_2$ is performed and written to the Read Access

History of $s_2$. After the Read Access History of $s_2$ is refreshed with a tuple of $o_2$ and the instant of time of the current read access, it contains the complete information about the sources and actuality of the data contained by the dataset dss2 of $s_2$.[1]

## 5    An Agent Based Extension of the Limes Security Model

The Limes Security Model is introduced for pure subject/object relationships. In the use cases considered by the Limes Security Model objects only stay in conflict with objects and do not stay in conflict with a subject. In such scenarios the information flow between objects has to be controlled, which can be done by controlling the write accesses of the subjects. Agents in the sense of [2] are not taken into account. Agents implement services and can be accessed like objects and on the other hand may request services and act like subjects. Because of this ability objects and agents can stay in conflict with an agent and an agent can stay in conflict with other objects and agents. This implies that not only the write accesses of an agent have to be taken into account, but also the read accesses.

An agent combines the characteristics of both a subject and an object.

**Definition 4.** *Let the set of all agents $SA$ be the set of all subjects that are objects, i.e. $SA := O_t \cap S$*

This means that an agent owns not only its dataset, but also a Read Access History if it acts like a subject and a Conflict Function and a Dataset Actuality in the case it is accessed like an object (shown for the agent $x$ in Figure 3 $(a.)$). Because each agent has only one dataset, the Read Access History and the Dataset Actuality have to contain the same information. This is a prerequisite if both contain the complete information about the sources and actuality of the data contained by the agents dataset. If the agent acts as a subject, it has to synchronize its Read Access History with its Dataset Actuality and vice versa in case the agent is accessed like an object. Therefore it is obvious to define one

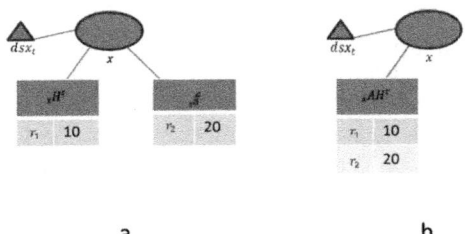

a.                                   b.

**Fig. 3.** Agent with Dataset Actuality (if considered to act like an object) and Read Access History (if considered to act like a subject) $(a.)$ and with Dataset History $(b.)$

history, the Dataset History. It is used as the Read Access History if the agent
acts like a subject and as the Dataset Actuality in the case, where it is accessed
like an object (shown for the agent $x$ in Figure 3 $(b.)$). The Dataset History
contains the complete information about the sources and actuality of the data
contained by the dataset of the agent.

**Definition 5 (Dataset History of an agent)**
   *For each instant of time $t \in \mathbb{N}$ and each agent $x \in SA$ let $_xAH^t$ with the
property*

$$\forall \, j \in O_t : \; \forall \, t_1, t_2 \in \mathbb{N} : \big((j, t_1) \in \, _xAH^t \land (j, t_2) \in \, _xAH^t\big) \implies t_1 = t_2$$

*be the Dataset History of the agent $x$. The Dataset History is the set of tuples
$(j, t')$ of the object or agent $j$ that have been read accessed by the agent $x$ in the
past, or where the dataset has been read and has been written to $x$ afterwards
and the instant of time $t'$ of the individual read access to $j$.*

   *If $(j, t') \in \, _xAH^t$ then $t'$ is the instant of time, where the last read access to
object or agent $j$ has been performed and where the read dataset has been written
to $x$ afterwards.*

In addition to the Dataset History each agent owns a Dataset History Function
as defined by Definition 6.

**Definition 6 (Dataset History Function of an agent).** *For each instant of
time $t \in \mathbb{N}$ and each agent $x \in SA$ and all objects and agents $j \in O_t$ the value
$t' = \, _xAH^t$ is the instant of time, where the read access to object $j$ has been
performed and where the read dataset has been added to the dataset of $x$ later.
The function $d_x^t : O_t \to \mathbb{Z}$ is called the Dataset History Function of $x$, if $d_x^t$ has
the following property:*

$$d_x^t(j) = \begin{cases} t', & if \ (j, t') \in \, _xAH^t, \\ -1, & otherwise. \end{cases} \tag{3}$$

*If $x$ is accessed like an object $d_x^t(j)$ is also termed as $a_x^t(j)$. If $x$ acts like a subject
$d_x^t(j)$ is also termed as $h_x^t(j)$.*

## 5.1   Access Limitations of an Agent

Because of its object behavior, an agent can remain in conflict with different
objects or agents. Before an agent is granted read access to an object or agent it
has to be clarified if the object (or agent) itself or one of the objects (or agents)
in the Dataset Actuality of the accessed object (or the Dataset History of the
accessed agent) is in conflict with the accessing agent.

   Definition 7 defines in  4 the condition under which a read access is granted
and additionally the sanitization of the Dataset History of the accessing agent.

**Definition 7 (Read access of an agent).** *For each instant of time $t \in \mathbb{N}$, all objects $i \in O_t$, all agents $x \in SA$ and for all $r \in O_t$ with $a_i^t(r) \geq 0$ a read access from $x$ to $i$ is granted at instant of time $t$ if and only if:*

$$(f_r^t(x, a_i^t(r)) \leq 0) \wedge (f_i^t(x, t) \leq 0) \tag{4}$$

*If $x$ performs a read accesses to $i$ and (4) is fulfilled then let $D \subseteq O_t \times \mathbb{N}$ with*

$$D := \{(i, d_x^t(i)) \mid d_x^t(i) \geq 0\} \cup \{(r, d_x^t(r)) \mid d_x^t(r) \geq 0 \wedge a_i^t(r) > d_x^t(r)\}$$

*be the set of tuples in $_xAH^t$ that have to be removed from $_xAH^t$ because $x$ receives from $i$ as part of its dataset more recent data from the object $r$ than $x$ already owns in its own dataset. Also, let $M \subseteq O_t \times \mathbb{N}$ with*

$$M := \{(i, t)\} \cup \{(r, a_i^t(r)) \mid (d_x^t(r) \geq 0 \wedge a_i^t(r) > d_x^t(r)) \vee d_x^t(r) = -1\}$$

*be the set of tuples of objects $r$, where $x$ receives from $i$ as part of its dataset more recent data from the object $r$ than $x$ already owns in its own dataset and the instances of access times, when these objects have been read accessed, and when $i$ has been accessed with the current instant of time $t$. If $x$ performs a read access to $i$ at instant of time $t$, then $_xAH^{t+1}$ is defined as*

$$_xAH^{t+1} := (_xAH^t \setminus D) \cup M.$$

Definition 8 defines in  5 the condition, under which a write access is granted and additionally the sanitization of the Dataset History of the accessing agent and of the Dataset Actuality of the accessed object.

**Definition 8 (Write access of an agent).** *For each instant of time $t \in \mathbb{N}$, all objects $r \in O_t$, all agents $x \in SA$ and for all $i \in O_t$ with $d_x^t(i) \geq 0$ a write access from $x$ to $r$ is granted if and only if:*

$$(f_i^t(r, d_x^t(i)) \leq 0) \wedge (f_x^t(r, t) \leq 0) \tag{5}$$

*If $x$ performs a write access to $r$ and (5) is fulfilled then $_xAH^{t+1}$ is defined as*

$$_xAH^{t+1} := {}_xAH^t \setminus \{(i, d_x^t(i)) \mid d_x^t(i) \geq 0 \wedge f_i^t(r, d_x^t(i)) < 0\}.$$

*Let $D \subseteq O_t \times \mathbb{N}$ with*

$$D := \{(x, a_r^t(x)) \mid a_r^t(x) \geq 0\} \cup \{(i, a_r^t(i)) \mid d_x^t(i) \geq 0 \wedge a_r^t(i) \geq 0 \wedge d_x^t(i) > a_r^t(i)\}$$

*be the set of tuples in $_rA^t$ that have to be removed from $_rA^t$, because $r$ receives from $x$ as part of the dataset from $x$ more recent data from object $i$ than $r$ already possesses in its own dataset. Also, let $M \subseteq O_t \times \mathbb{N}$ with*

$$M := \{(i, d_x^t(i)) \mid d_x^t(i) \geq 0 \wedge a_r^t(i) \geq 0 \wedge d_x^t(i) > a_r^t(i)\}$$
$$\cup \{(i, d_x^t(i)) \mid d_x^t(i) \geq 0 \wedge a_r^t(i) < 0\} \cup \{(x, t)\}$$

be the set of tuples of objects $i$, where $r$ receives as part of the dataset from $x$ more recent data from the object $i$ than $r$ already owns in its own dataset and the instances of access times, when these objects have been read accessed. If $x$ performs a write access to $r$ at instant of time $t$ and (5) is fulfilled then $_rA^{t+1}$ is defined as

$$_rA^{t+1} := (_rA^t \setminus D) \cup M.$$

### 5.2  Illegal Information Flow

Similarly to the Limes of a subject, defined in [1], the Limes of an agent describes the borderline between the objects (and agents), where an agent is allowed to perform a read or write access, and those objects (and agents), where the agent is not allowed to perform a read or write access. The Limes of an agent is the set of objects (and agents) that the agent is currently not allowed to read or write access because of a conflict of interest.

**Definition 9 (Limes For Write Access of an agent).** *For each instant of time $t \in \mathbb{N}$ and all agents $x \in SA$ let the Limes For Write Access $_xLW^t \subseteq O_t$ of $x$ at instant of time $t$ be defined as*

$$_xLW^t := \{j \in O_t \mid \exists\, i \in O_t :\ (d_x^t(i) \geq 0 \wedge f_i^t(j, d_x^t(i)) > 0) \vee f_x^t(j, t) > 0\}.$$

**Definition 10 (Limes For Read Access of an agent).** *For each instant of time $t \in \mathbb{N}$ and all agents $x \in SA$ let the Limes For Read Access $_xLR^t \subseteq O_t$ of $x$ at instant of time $t$ be defined as*

$$_xLR^t := \{j \in O_t \mid \exists\, i \in O_t :\ (a_j^t(i) \geq 0 \wedge f_i^t(x, a_j^t(i)) > 0) \vee f_j^t(x, t) > 0\}.$$

**Definition 11 (Illegal Information flow).** *For each instant of time $t \in \mathbb{N}$ and each agent $x \in SA$ and all objects or agents $j \in\ _xLW^t$ and all objects or agents $i \in\ _xLR^t$ an illegal information flow takes place, if $x$ performs a write access to $j$ or $x$ performs a read access to $i$ at instant of time $t$.*

**Theorem 1.** *For each instant of time $t \in \mathbb{N}$ and all agents $x \in SA$ and all objects or agents $i, j \in O_t$ implementing their Conflict Function according to Definition 2, there will be no illegal information flow between $i$, $j$ or $x$, if $x$ only performs a read or write access according to Definitions 7 and 8, and if $x$ is only read or write accessed according to Definitions 7 and 8.*

*Proof.* Assumption 1: There has been an illegal information flow from object or agent $i$ to object or agent $j$ because of a read access to $i$ and a following write access to $j$ by agent $x$, although the objects and agents have implemented their Conflict Function according to Definition 2 and the read and write accesses of $x$ have been performed according to Definitions 7 and 8.

Conforming to Definition 11 an illegal information flow from $i$ to $j$ happens, when $x$ performs a write access to $j$ in case $j \in\ _xLW^t$, which is true after the read access of $x$ to $i$ or in general after a read access to $i$, where the read dataset has been written to $x$ later and if $f_i^t(j, d_x^t(i)) > 0$.

If $d_x^t(i) \geq 0 \wedge f_i^t(j, d_x^t(i)) > 0$. From $d_x^t(i) \geq 0$ follows that $d_x^t(i)$ is the instant of time of the last read access of $x$ to $i$ or in general the last read access to $i$, where the read dataset has been written to $x$ later.

From Definition 2 and $f_i^t(j, d_x^t(i)) > 0$ follows that $i$ is in conflict with $j$. Definition 11 specifies that a write access is only allowed if for every $i \in O_t$ with $d_x^t(i) \geq 0$ the Conflict Function delivers a result $f_i^t(j, d_x^t(i)) \leq 0$. This contradicts the assumptions that the objects and agents have implemented correctly their Conflict Function according to Definition 2 and the read and write accesses have been performed according to Definitions 7 and 8.

Assumption 2: There has been an illegal information flow from agent $x$ to object or agent $j$ because of a write access to $j$ by agent $x$ although the objects and agents have implemented their Conflict Function according to Definition 2 and the write access of $x$ has been done according to Definition 8.

By Definition 11 an illegal information flow from $x$ to $j$ happened, because of the write access of $x$ to $j$ if $j \in {}_xLW^t$, which is the case if $f_x^t(j, t) > 0$. It follows that $x$ is in conflict with $j$. Definition 11 defines that a write access is only allowed if the Conflict Function of $x$ delivers a result $f_x^t(j, t) \leq 0$. This contradicts the assumptions that $x$ has implemented its Conflict Function according to Definition 2 and the write access has been executed according to Definition 8.

Assumption 3: There has been an illegal information flow from object or agent $i$ to agent $x$ because of a read access to $i$ by agent $x$ although the objects and agents have implemented their Conflict Function according to Definition 2 and the read access of $x$ has been executed according to Definition 7.

By Definition 11 an illegal information flow from $i$ to $x$ happened, because of the read access of $x$ to $i$ if $i \in {}_xLR^t$, which is the case if $f_i^t(x, t) > 0$. It follows that $i$ is in conflict with $x$. Definition 11 defines that a read access is only allowed if the Conflict Function of $i$ delivers a result $f_i^t(x, t) \leq 0$. This contradicts the assumptions that $i$ has implemented its Conflict Function according to Definition 2 and the read access has been executed according to Definition 7.

# 6 Conclusion and Future Works

Service-oriented architectures have gained in importance by the implementation of business processes as a dynamic and loosely coupled system of services. In [9] Pratt and Zeckhausen discuss a problem that is based on an asymmetric relationship because of an informational advantage of the service compared to the client. The problem lies in the uncertainty of the client, not knowing whether the agent might misuse his data. To guarantee an approved protection of the client data and to prevent an illegal information flow, an approved security policy model has to be chosen that is suitable for the considered use case.

The Limes Security model introduced in [1] acts on the assumption that a conflict of interest is not necessarily symmetric, not necessarily reflexive and not necessarily transitive. It is introduced for pure subject/object relationships, where agents are not considered. An agent combines the characteristics of both a subject and an object. In the current paper, the Limes Security model has been extended to prohibit an illegal information flow in an agent based service-oriented architecture. In any kind of access the complete dataset of an object, subject or agent is read or written, which probably is a limitation for some possible use cases. For the future work this point has to be dicussed in-depth. Additionaly a prototype implementation of the security policy model and a performance evaluation needs to be conducted.

**Acknowledgement.** The author thanks Prof. Dr. Fuss for his openness to discussion on mathematical questions and Prof. Dr. Grimm and Dipl-Inf. Dieter Kessler for there support in the preparation of this paper.

# References

1. Hermann, E.: The Limes Security Model for Information Flow Control. In: FARES Workshop of the Sixth International Conference on Availability, Reliability and Security (ARES 2011), Vienna, Austria, Aug 22-26 (accepted, 2011)
2. Booth, D., Haas, H., McCabe, F., Newcomer, E., Champion, M., Ferris, C., Orchard, D.: Web Services Architecture, W3C Working Group Note, February 11 (2004), http://www.w3.org/TR/ws-arch/
3. Brewer, D.F.C., Nash, M.J.: The Chinese Wall Security Policy. In: IEEE Symposium on Security and Privacy, Oakland, pp. 206–214 (1989)
4. Lin, T.Y.: Chinese Wall Security Policy-An Aggressive Model. In: Proceedings of the Fifth Aerospace Computer Security Application Conference, December 4-8, pp. 286–293 (1989)
5. Bell, D., LaPadula, L.: Secure Computer Systems: Mathematical Foundations. MITRE Corporation, Bedford, MA, Technical Report MTR-2547, Vol. I (1973)
6. Clark, D., Wilson, D.: A Comparison of Commercial and Military Security Policies. In: IEEE Symposium on Security and Privacy, pp. 184–194 (1987)
7. Loock, M., Eloff, J.H.P.: A new Access Control model based on the Chinese Wall Security Policy Model. In: Proceedings of the ISSA 2005 New Knowledge Today Conference, Information Security South Africa (ISSA), pp. 1–10 (2005)
8. Burbeck, S.: The Tao of E-Business Services. IBM Developer Works (2000), http://www-128.ibm.com/developerworks/libraryws-tao
9. Pratt, J.W., Zeckhausen, R.J., *Principals and Agents: The Structure of Business*, Harvard Business School Press, Boston, 1985
10. Ricci, A., Buda, C., Zaghini, N.: An Agent-Oriented Programming Model for SOA & Web Services. In: 5th IEEE International Conference on Industrial Informatics, Vienna (2007)
11. Hsiao, Y.-C., Hwang, G.-H.: Implementing the Chinese Wall Security Model in Workflow Management Systems. In: Proceedings of the International Symposium on Parallel and Distributed Processing with Applications (ISPA 2010), pp. 574–581. IEEE Computer Society, Washington, DC (2010)

12. Hung, P.C.K., Qiu, G.-S.: Implementing Conflict of Interest Assertions for Web Services Matchmaking Process. In: 2003 IEEE International Conference on E-Commerce Technology (CEC 2003), Newport Beach, California, USA (2003)
13. Debasish, J., Bijan, B.B.: Security Model of Service Oriented Computational Grids. In: 2006 Annual IEEE India Conference, New Delhi, September 15-17 (2006)
14. Wu, R., Ahn, G.-J., Hu, H., Singhal, M.: Information flow control in cloud computing. In: 6th International Conference on Collaborative Computing: Networking, Applications and Worksharing (CollaborateCom), Chicago (2010)

# A Risk-Based Evaluation of Group Access Control Approaches in a Healthcare Setting

Maria B. Line, Inger Anne Tøndel, and Erlend Andreas Gjære

SINTEF ICT, Trondheim, Norway
{maria.b.line,inger.a.tondel,erlendandreas.gjare}@sintef.no

**Abstract.** This paper focuses on access control approaches usable for information sharing through large screens where several individuals are present at the same time. Access control in this setting is quite different from traditional systems where a user logs on to the system. The paper outlines a number of possible approaches to access control, and evaluates them based on criteria derived from risk analyses of a planned coordination system for the perioperative hospital environment. It concludes that future work should focus on extending the location-based approach with situation awareness, and add support for using pop-ups or handheld devices for sharing of the most sensitive information.

**Keywords:** Access control, privacy, health care, information security.

## 1  Introduction

There are a number of systems available whose main purpose is to inform the public about status and status changes. Examples are screens showing incoming flights at airports, or overviews of meeting room occupancy at hotels. In these example systems the information on the screen is unlikely to be sensitive, and thus there is no need to control information visualization. But imagine such information displays being used in healthcare or in other businesses where some status information should be considered internal.

In this paper we focus on access control solutions for wall-mounted screens that show status information in a perioperative hospital environment (before, during and after surgery). This environment is characterized by multidisciplinary teams, the need to react to unanticipated events, and utilization of expensive resources. Planning and coordination are difficult but important in such a setting [1]. To improve coordination, wall-mounted screens visualizing progress and current status can be placed at waiting rooms, wards, operating rooms, recovery rooms etc. where health care personnel is likely to see them. As a result it becomes easier to understand how the patient care is progressing and adapt own behaviour.

Access control in systems communicating via large public wall-mounted displays is quite different from traditional access control where a single user logs on to a system. First, it is difficult to know at a given point of time who is able to view the information on screen. In the perioperative environment, there

A M. Tjoa et al. (Eds.): ARES 2011, LNCS 6908, pp. 26–37, 2011.
© IFIP International Federation for Information Processing 2011

can be a number of health care personnel having access to the location of a screen, in addition to patients, their next-of-kin, and other types of personnel such as cleaners or technicians. Still, if we were able to know who were present, it is not a straight-forward task to determine how this knowledge should affect what information to display. Access policies are normally defined on a single-user level, while the coordination system may just as well have none or several users to consider in its decisions on what to display. Second, the information - though it may be sensitive - is displayed because it is needed for a purpose. What to display in a given situation must be based on proper trade-off decisions between privacy on one hand and efficiency and patient safety on the other. This calls for access control solutions that are dynamic and context-aware, and that fit the way of work in the perioperative domain. To further complicate matters, there is in general no time for users to login to the system, as information should be available by just by taking a quick look at the screen.

In our previous work [1] we have decided on a strategy in order to overcome these challenges, termed flexible de-identification. With *flexible* we mean that decisions on what to display should not be static but adapted to the situation and current context. *De-identification* leads to solutions that go beyond the more traditional consideration of whether to display identifying information or not. Instead we assume that information needs not be at the highest level of granularity to be useful for coordination purposes.

In this paper we focus on providing flexible access control, while de-identification is left out[1]. We do not consider access to information by single users, but instead how to determine access rights for a dynamically changing group of individuals. This group is likely to consist of personnel with different professions and different needs and rights for information, who - though they work together - will have different opinions as to what information gives meaning and is useful. We present several approaches to access control in this setting. Our main contribution is a preliminary evaluation of these approaches based on criteria derived from a risk analysis of a the COSTT system[2] - a planned coordination system for the perioperative hospital environment.

The paper is organized as follows: Section 2 outlines relevant approaches for access control. Section 3 explains the method used to perform the risk analyses and to deduce evaluation criteria. Section 4 gives the results of the risk analyses, explains the evaluation criteria and applies them in order to evaluate the different access control approaches. Section 5 discusses the validity of the evaluation result, and suggests directions for future research, before section 6 presents our concluding remarks.

---

[1] See Gjære et al. [2] for more information on de-identification solutions for this kind of systems.

[2] Developed by the Co-operation Support Through Transparency (COSTT) research project. http://www.costt.no

## 2   Relevant Approaches to Access Control

Access control related to shared disiplays have been given some attention from researchers, and proposed solutions include using special types of glasses to allow different people to see different types of information [3] and using visualizations (e.g. colors) instead of text to present the most sensitive information [4] (similar to our de-identification approach). Available research on how to determine access rights of dynamically changing groups of users is however sparse. We are only aware of one publication [5] that addresses this issue to some extent. This publication lists three different approaches that can be used in combination. The first approach is *aggregation* where the access rights of a group correspond to the sum of the access rights of the individuals in the group. As a result, larger groups are likely to get access to more resources than smaller groups. The second approach is *maximum/minimum* where the individual with the highest/lowest access rights determines access rights for the whole group. Third, the *group structure* approach computes access rights based on the structure of the group, e.g. ensures that at least two users with a certain access level are needed in order to gain access to a specific resource.

Current access control solutions developed for healthcare are mainly based on Role Based Access Control [6] where users are granted access based on their profession [7][8]. A study of an up-and-running Electronic Patient Record system at a Norwegian hospital [9] identified the need for access control solutions more tailored to the needs of health care personnel. Solutions should be better able to handle dynamic events, workflow and collaboration.

Dynamic context-aware access control solutions have been suggested in various forms, some also specifically addressing health care (e.g. Hu et al. [10]). We will not go into specifics on the different models, but rather point to parameters that can be used when creating more dynamic access control solutions in a health care setting. Hu et al. mention time, location, trust-level of authentication, relationship to patient, and specialist area. Most of these are also mentioned by Alam et al. [11], who add device type, duration, purpose, number of accesses, user consent, presence of the patient, delegation and emergency situations to the list. Risk and benefit are also factors that can be taken into account in access control decisions. Examples of access control solutions that include the concept of risk is the work of Cheng et al. [12], Dimmock et al. [13] and Diep et al. [14].

Below we present the main access control approaches considered in this paper. It is assumed that we have technology available for authenticating and locating users[3].

**Location-based:** Only the screen's location applies, which means that all screens have a given default view that can not be affected by persons being present. Access control to the screen is managed through physical access control; people being allowed to be at a certain location are also allowed to see all information displayed on the screen at the given location.

---

[3] The purpose of locating users will NOT be surveillance of all their movements and actions.

**Minimum [5]:** A group's access rights will correspond to the lowest level of access rights present in the group. This will clearly ensure patients' privacy, as nobody in the group will see more information than they are allowed to. However, the usefulness may be low, as the persons with higher levels of access rights will not always see all information meant for them.

**Maximum [5]:** A group's access rights will correspond to the highest level of access rights present in the group. This will ensure usefulness, as all health care workers will see all the information meant for them. However, the patient's privacy may be compromised.

**Group structure [5]:** The access level is decided by computations on the group structure. An average value is calculated based on who is present, including weighting of who is closest to the screen and considerations of how many is present with limited access rights vs. wide access rights.

**Facilitator:** One of the users in the group acts as a facilitator. The facilitator is authenticated, and makes decisions as to whether to include new users into the group and which information is needed/appropriate based on the users present.

**Situation aware:** The system is aware of the situation in which it operates, e.g. it combines information on type of patient and diagnosis with time of day and an understanding of whether this is an emergency or normal operation. Situational awareness is then used to decide access rights of the group.

**Possible extensions: Pop-up window and handheld devices:** All the suggested approaches can be extended with solutions that grant individual users access to more information. This can be done by utilizing small pop-up windows where e.g. surgeons can authenticate themselves and get access to more details shown in a limited part of the screen, or get the information sent to a handheld device. Getting access to information in a pop-up window limits the reading access for other people being within proximity, information is only readable for the one/those standing really close to the screen. Sending information to a handheld device further reduces the risk of confidentiality breaches.

## 3   Method

In this work, we use the results of two risk analyses of the planned COSTT system to identify criteria that the access control solution need to fulfil, and use these criteria to evaluate and compare the alternative access control approaches. The main motivation for using risk analysis in this respect is twofold. First, the results of the risk analyses are already available and provide valuable insight into the environment in which the access control solution will be put to use. Second, access control aims to protect (some of) the system assets by reducing risks, but may also introduce new risks. Performing a risk analysis is a good way to identify both the assets and the risks towards these assets. We recognise that using risk analysis of systems to evaluate access control policies is uncommon. Still, we uphold that the results of a risk analysis are useful for performing a preliminary evaluation of alternatives in order to decide which should be further investigated and evaluated.

Two risk analyses have been performed, and both were carried out in two stages: 1) Asset identification[4]: "What are the most valuable assets in the COSTT system? What do you want to protect?", and 2) Risk identification and ranking: "What are the most important risks for COSTT? What are you most afraid of happening?". In each stage the participants were given five minutes to write down their answers to the questions posed. Both stages were summarized by organizing the brainstorming results into groups that the participants agreed upon. The risk identification stage also included ranking of the risks. Each participant was given three votes they could use to prioritize risks. The risks were then ranked according to votes in total.

The COSTT project group was used as participants. Together they represent a broad spectrum of specialist areas; IT, sociology, medicine, and technology management. The first risk analysis was performed at the stage where the system itself existed only as a concept and many decisions that would affect the outcome had not been made yet. The purpose of this preliminary analysis was to get an initial sense of what are the key risks as perceived by the project team. The second risk analysis of the future COSTT system was performed 10 months after the first one. The system itself still existed only as a concept but some research, including literature studies and empirical studies, had been performed. The purpose this time was to see if the results would differ a lot from earlier, and to identify the major changes, if any.

## 4   Results

In this section we present the results of the risk analyses, and use these results as a basis for identifying evaluation criteria. Then we show to what extent the identified access control approaches are able to meet the criteria.

### 4.1   Results of the Risk Analyses

The findings from the first risk analysis represent a starting point and a snapshot of the project status at that point of time. The second risk analysis revealed the same results, but both broader and in more depth. One of the main differences, was the ranking of the risks related to sensitive information and access control; as the participants increased their understanding of what the COSTT system will be, they also increased their worries of sensitive information leakage, while they decreased their worry of the access control mechanisms not being strong enough. We choose to present the results from the latter only, because that is sufficient in order to cover all identified issues.

Table 1 presents all assets and risks identified. Note that the categories of assets and risks are not considered to be mutually exclusive. The participants themselves sorted the input from their brainstorming process and gave names to the categories of information. The assets mainly include types of information available in the system; both to be displayed on the screen and underlying

---

[4] Inspired by the asset identification method described by Jaatun and Tøndel [15].

**Table 1.** Identified assets and risks

| Category | Assets |
|---|---|
| Patient information | Identification, medical data, secret relations, irrelevant health history |
| Employee information | Name, role, actions, personal data |
| Location data | Position for all tagged persons, info about rooms, movements |
| Aggregated/reasoned data | Efficiency of employees, process statistics, surveillance of procedures |
| Deviations | Unwanted incidents, info on operations, system errors in hospital |
| Usefulness | Utility value by using the COSTT system |

| Category | Risks |
|---|---|
| Poor quality of data (9) | Drawing wrong conclusions on what info means, inaccurate catching of events, misinterpretation of events, coordination trouble due to erroneous data, patient injury |
| Surveillance of employees (6) | Management monitoring efficiency of employees, wrong/incomplete statistics on employees, employees feel they are being monitored, public negative exposure of some employees |
| Sensitive personal information (6) | Info displayed to persons not concerned, deduction of patient having a sensitive diagnosis, unintended access to sensitive info, hacking/data theft, info is taken out from the hospital |
| Unintended/erroneous use (5) | Location tag theft, active bypassing of access control lists in other systems, bypassing physical access control, unhealthy changes in work processes, employees working against the system or refusing to use it, conflicts due to low efficiency |
| Patient (2) | Patients choosing a different hospital, theft of patient data, patient info known to public press |
| Access control (1) | Limitations hide important data when it should be available, bugs giving illegitimate access |
| Wrong focus (1) | Fussbudget, loss of efficiency, debates on prioritizing, critical questions due to insignificant errors |
| Relatives (0) | Creating unnecessary feelings, unhappy relatives calling frequently on health personnel |
| Public (0) | Negative newspaper headlines |

information needed to make the system work properly. Also, parameters that can be deduced from information in the system are considered valuable assets. The risks span from concerns of the underlying sensors not being able to catch events to breaches of both patients' and employees' privacy. The numbers listed in parenthesis in the column of categories indicate the prioritizing done by the process participants. In the table, the risks are presented in prioritized order.

## 4.2   Identification of Evaluation Criteria

In the process of identifying evaluation criteria, we focused on the highest ranked risks. The criteria are referred to as C1, C2 etc., which constitutes a mapping to table 2 where they all are summed up.

**Poor quality of data:** The main risk was considered to be poor quality of data. As shown in table 1, this is mainly a concern about the underlying system not being able to catch and/or interpret events correctly. In the COSTT project, the coordination information that is to be displayed on the screens are built by capturing events in other information systems [16]. Simple events (e.g. access to the medical record of patient A by a given health care personnel) are combined into composite events (e.g. cardiology assesment of patient A has been performed), and it is these composite events that will be displayed on the screens. It is however important to be aware of the uncertainty involved in the event enrichment process. As an example, access to medical record of patient A can indicate that the health care personnel that accessed the record is performing an examination of the patient, but it can also be that the health care personnel is preparing for the examination. Thus, events in the COSTT system will be associated with a quality attribute that is a measure of the validity of the event [16]. This quality attribute should ideally influence the access control decision, as presenting information that is correct is an important part of the information security of any system (integrity). This is reflected by the data quality awareness criteria (C1).

**Surveillance of employees:** The next highest ranked risk was that of surveillance of employees. This covers the employees' fear of being monitored and the possibility for management to misuse registered data about their employees to measure efficiency or other statistics. Data registered for the purpose of COSTT may not give the complete and correct picture of employees' actions, which means that it should be used with high caution, if at all, for management purposes. Thus it is relevant to consider whether the solutions increase the need for surveillance, e.g. by requiring location information (C2). Employee surveillance is also related to what information is published on the screens (further addressed for the risk of sensitive personal information).

**Sensitive personal information:** The third highest ranked risk is that of displaying sensitive personal information in ways that makes the information available to unauthorised persons. It is important that solutions are able to maintain privacy of both patients and employees, and strive towards the ideal solution where everybody gets access to what they need - and no more. This is reflected by the privacy preserving criteria (C3).

**Unintended/erroneous use:** The risk related to sensitive personal information should also be considered together with the risk of unintended/erroneous use (rated fourth) and also the much lower prioritized risk related to access control. The concern that access control does not support the work flow is reflected in all these three risks. Failure in this respect can lead to active bypassing of access control due to important information not being available (C4). To meet this challenge it is important to consider dynamic and/or user controlled access control solutions that is able to fit into the way people work. It is also important to consider the effort required from users in order to use the systems in a secure manner (C5), as expectations on user involvement may require changes in work processes in itself in addition to requiring time and effort from the users. This

**Table 2.** Identified criteria based on risk analysis

| Nr | Criteria | Explanation |
|---|---|---|
| C1 | Data quality awareness | The ability of the solution to take the data quality into account in the access control decisions. |
| C2 | Minimisation of employee surveillance | The need for use of employee surveillance techniques, e.g. for monitoring the location of employees. |
| C3 | Privacy preservation | The ability to restrict sensitive/private information to those that are authorized for access. |
| C4 | Availability ensurance | The ability to ensure that information important for safe and efficient treatment of patients are available when needed. This can e.g. be ensured by using dynamic approaches able to adapt to the situation , or to ensure that users can override the access control decision. |
| C5 | Workload reduction | The ease of use for users. Solutions that rely on user cooperation will require some time and effort on behalf of the users. |
| C6 | Complexity | The more complex the access control mechanism is the higher risk of mistakes that may render the access control solution vulnerable. |

influences the perceived system efficiency and is likely to have an impact on the employees' attitudes towards the system; employees working against the system or refusing to use it. Risks related to access control can also increase with complexity (C6). With complex access control solutions it is easier to make mistakes e.g. during implementation or during policy specification.

### 4.3   Evaluation of Access Control Approaches

Table 3 summarises the evaluation of the suggested access control approaches with respect to the evaluation criteria. A '+' indicates a positive score while a '-' indicate a negative score. A score of '-/+' indicates that the approach is able to meet the criteria to some extent, but not fully. A '?' is used in situations where the evaluation result will depend on trade-offs made when defining access control policies. A '*' is used to illustrate that the score depends on the mechanism used to determine who is present.

The *location-based* approach is in many ways the most simple approach. Its ability to meet the needs of COSTT is however dependent on how easy it is to determine beforehand which information should be available in given locations. As several of the envisioned locations (e.g. corridors and examination rooms) are likely to be accessed by a number of different groups of users, we envision that it will be difficult to make such pre-set trade-offs that are able to meet the criteria for both privacy and availability.

The *minimum* approach is unlikely to meet the availability requirements of the users in need for most information. The same way, the *maximum* approach will probably result in too many privacy breaches, as everybody will get access to whatever information should be available to the one present with the highest access rights. Considering group structure is likely to perform better than using

**Table 3.** Evaluation of access control approaches with respect to the selected criteria

| Approach | C1 qual. | C2 surv. | C3 priv. | C4 avail. | C5 workl. | C6 compl. |
|---|---|---|---|---|---|---|
| Location-based | - | + | ? | ? | + | + |
| Minimum | - | - | + | - | +* | + |
| Maximum | - | - | - - | + | +* | + |
| Group structure | - | - | ? | ? | +* | - |
| Facilitator | - | + | -/+ | + | - | + |
| Situation aware | ? | + | ? | ? | + | - |
| Extension: Pop-up/handheld | - | -/+ | + | + | - | + |

the minimum/maximum access rights, but is complex and its success depends on the ability to make proper trade-offs between the access rights of the highest and lowest ranked users present.

Relying on a *facilitator* seems to be a solution that could fit COSTT well, as it is able to meet the majority of criteria to some extent. The privacy achieved will be dependent on whether we can trust the facilitator to make good decisions as to what information to display in given situations. In a study of clinicians' experiences related to privacy and security of health information systems [17] Fernando and Dawson noticed that most clinicians used measures such as lowering their voices and omitting to ask relevant questions in order to protect privacy and security when residing in a shared workplace. At the same time they found that privacy and security implementations on electronic health information systems often took time from patient care, and were therefore considered to hamper patient care. Sharing of passwords was mentioned in this study, as well as in a study by Vaast [18]. In his study he also found that physicians were concerned that employees on wards were overwhelmed with work and therefore were likely to forget to close programs or patient charts. To be able to reach a conclusion as to whether the facilitator approach is adequate in the COSTT setting, more research is needed on the situation in which the COSTT system will operate when it comes to the work process and the general attitude of the employees.

Making the access control solution more *situation aware* is also likely to improve the trade-off between privacy and availability, but at the cost of complexity. This is the only approach that has the potential to meet the data quality awareness criterium.

The *pop-up/handheld extension* also seems promising, and is able to meet the majority of criteria. By implementing this extension one is able to introduce more flexibility and user involvement without sacrificing privacy. It should however not be used as the only approach.

To sum up, none of the access control approaches studied is able to meet all evaluation criteria. However, the ones that seem most promising are either using the facilitator role or using an access control solution that is situation aware. Alternatively, one of the more simple automatic approaches, e.g. the location-based approach, can be combined with the pop-up/handheld extension.

## 5   Discussion

The preliminary evaluation performed is based on a risk analysis of the COSTT system at an early stage and with participants from the project group. At this stage the project participants are the ones most likely to have the best understanding of how the COSTT system will work and what are the main challenges and risks. The results of the risk analysis would however be more reliable if it had included project-external representatives as well.

Basing the preliminary evaluation on the results of a risk analysis is useful in that the evaluation criteria will be risk-based and likely to reflect the top issues. The criteria derived are however high level and have not been evaluated by the intended users of the system. It is also not possible from this initial evaluation to state how the different access control approaches will perform in real life. User evaluations are needed in order to assess how the alternative approaches are able to fit the work processes of the perioperative domain. In particular we suspect that the facilitator-based approach, though getting good scores in the evaluation, will fail in this respect.

In the evaluation of the alternative access control approaches, we have studied the approaches individually and evaluated how they perform related to the identified criteria. It is however possible to combine several of the approaches into a final solution and in this way achieve a solution that better fits the needs of COSTT. To illustrate, screens in waiting rooms may have a preset access level (location-based approach) while screens at other locations may have a maximum access level that is determined by their location but where the group structure, the general situation or a facilitator determines the access level at a given point of time. It is also possible to use the extension suggested where individual employees can get access to more information by utilizing pop-up windows or handheld devices. The preliminary evaluation of the approaches suggests that future work looks into combinations of the location-based approach, the facilitator approach, the situation aware approach and the pop-up/handheld extension approach. The location-based approach is a simple one with the possibility of offering good baseline security. The facilitator approach is able to meet the majority of the criteria. The situation aware approach is the only one able to meet the data quality criterium, and has the potential to also perform well on most of the other criteria. The pop-up/handheld extension approach has good scores on both the privacy and availability criteria.

As the location-based approach is in many ways the most feasible solution, we plan to use this solution as a starting point and look into how it can be combined with risk-based access control approaches in order to add situation awareness. Making proper trade-offs between the risk of privacy breaches and the risk that information is not available is central to the success of the COSTT solution. Risk-based access control solutions can utilise knowledge of the screens' location in order to determine the probability of privacy breaches, as well as the availability requirements for an information item. Other context information, like the time of day and who is likely to be present, can influence the risk evaluation as well. This way, the combined solution will likely perform better on the criteria related to privacy (C3) and availability (C4). In addition, the quality of the information can be taken into account (criterion C1). Though the facilitator approach gets quite high scores on the criteria used in our evaluation, we believe that this solution will not be usable for this type of systems, as it requires quite a lot of interaction with the users. Instead we recommend using handheld devices in combination with large wall-mounted screens in cases where highly sensitive information is needed (to better meet criteria C3 and C4).

# 6    Conclusion

The main contribution of this paper is a preliminary evaluation of several approaches to access control for public screens used in a perioperative setting. The evaluation criteria used are derived from a risk analysis of the COSTT system. In the evaluation, the facilitator based and the situation aware approaches received high scores, and so did the possible extension of using pop-up windows or handheld devices to get access to additional information. Of the simpler and most feasible approaches, the location-based approach turned out to be the best candidate. As none of the approaches were able to perform well on all evaluation criteria, the results motivate to look further into combining access control approaches. As there are major usability concerns with the facilitator approach in this setting, we recommend focusing on extending the location-based approach with situation awareness, and add support for pop-ups or handheld devices.

**Acknowledgments.** Thanks to the COSTT project group for participating in the risk analyses. Thanks also to Torstein Nicolaysen for his work in a related MSc thesis, and to Åsmund A. Nyre, Arild Faxvaag, Andreas Seim and Warren Sandberg for reading and commenting on this paper during the writing process. This work has been performed as part of the COSTT project that is supported by the Norwegian Research Council's VERDIKT program (grant no. 187854/S10).

# References

1. Faxvaag, A., Røstad, L., Tøndel, I.A., Seim, A.R., Toussaint, P.J.: Visualizing patient trajectories on wall-mounted boards - information security challenges. In: Adlassnig, K.-P., Blobel, B., Mantas, J., Masic, I. (eds.) MIE. Studies in Health Technology and Informatics, vol. 150, pp. 715–719 (2009)
2. Gjære, E.A., Tøndel, I.A., Line, M.B., Andresen, H., Toussaint, P.: Personal health information on display: Balancing needs, usability and legislative requirements. In: MIE. Studies in Health Technology and Informatics (to be published, 2011)
3. Shoemaker, G.B.D., Inkpen, K.M.: Single display privacyware: augmenting public displays with private information. In: Proceedings of the SIGCHI Conference on Human Factors in Computing Systems, CHI 2001, pp. 522–529 (2001)
4. Tarasewich, P., Campbell, C.: What are you looking at. In: The First Symposium on Usable Privacy and Security, SOUPS 2005 (2005)
5. Bullock, A., Benford, S.: An access control framework for multi-user collaborative environments. In: GROUP 1999: Proceedings of the International ACM SIG-GROUP Conference on Supporting Group Work, pp. 140–149 (1999)

6. ANSI, American National Standard for Information Technology - Role Based Access Control. ANSI INCITS 359-2004 (2004)
7. Appari, A., Johnson, M.E.: Information security and privacy in healthcare: Current state of research. Forthcoming: International J. Internet and Enterprise Management (2009)
8. Ferreira, A., Cruz-Correira, R., Antunes, L., Chadwick, D.: Access control: how can it improve patients' healthcare? Studies in Health Technology and Informatics 127, 65–76 (2007)
9. Røstad, L., Edsberg, O.: A study of access control requirements for healthcare systems based on audit trails from access logs. In: ACSAC 2006: Proceedings of the 22nd Annual Computer Security Applications Conference, pp. 175–186 (2006)
10. Hu, J., Weaver, A.C.: Dynamic, context-aware access control for distributed healthcare applications. In: Proceedings of the First Workshop on Pervasive Security, Privacy and Trust, PSPT (2004)
11. Alam, M., Hafner, M., Memon, M., Hung, P.: Modeling and enforcing advanced access control policies in healthcare systems with SECTET. In: 1st International Workshop on Model-Based Trustworthy Health Informaton Systems, MOTHIS 2007 (2007)
12. Cheng, P.-C., Fohatgi, P., Keser, C.: Fuzzy MLS: An experiment on quantified risk-adaptive access control. IBM Thomas J. Watson Research Center, Tech. Rep. (January 2007)
13. Dimmock, N., Belokosztolszki, A., Eyers, D., Bacon, J., Moody, K.: Using trust and risk in role-based access control policies. In: Proceedings of the Ninth ACM Symposium on Access Control Models and Technologies, SACMAT 2004, pp. 156–162 (2004)
14. Diep, N.N., Hung, L.X., Zhung, Y., Lee, S., Lee, Y.-K., Lee, H.: Enforcing access control using risk assessment. In: European Conference on Universal Multiservice Networks, pp. 419–424 (2007)
15. Jaatun, M.G., Tøndel, I.A.: Covering your assets in software engineering. In: Third International Conference on Availability, Reliability and Security, pp. 1172–1179 (2008)
16. Wienhofen, L.W.M., Landmark, A.D.: Poster: Representing events in a clinical environment - a case study. In: The 5th ACM International Conference on Distributed Event-Based Systems, DEBS 2011 (to be published, 2011)
17. Fernando, J.I., Dawson, L.L.: The health information system security threat lifecycle: An informatics theory. International Journal of Medical Informatics 78(12), 815–826 (2009)
18. Vaast, E.: Danger is in the eye of the beholders: Social representations of Information Systems security in healthcare. The Journal of Strategic Information Systems 16(2), 130–152 (2007)

# Usage Control Enforcement - A Survey

Åsmund Ahlmann Nyre

Department of Computer and Information Science,
Norwegian University of Science and Technology,
Trondheim, Norway
nyre@idi.ntnu.no

**Abstract.** Sharing information allows businesses to take advantage of hidden knowledge, improve work processes and cooperation both within and across organisations. Thus there is a need for improved information protection capable of restricting how information is *used*, as opposed to only accessed. Usage Control has been proposed to achieve this by combining and extending traditional access control, Digital Rights Management and various encryption schemes. Advances in usage control enforcement has received considerable attention from the research community and we therefore believe there is a need to synthesise these efforts to minimise the potential for overlap. This paper surveys the previous efforts on providing *usage control* enforcement and analyses the general strengths and weaknesses of these approaches. In this paper we demonstrate that there are several promising mechanisms for enforcing usage control, but that reliable empirical evidence is required in order to ensure the appropriateness and usability of the enforcement mechanisms.

## 1   Introduction

Despite almost daily reports of security flaws and breached security, Internet users continue to share information at an increasing rate. Basically about anything from personal habits to sensitive corporate secrets, using a wide variety of communication channels. The fundamental problem is however that current security systems are unable to enforce any restrictions on the access, use or distribution of information once it has been transferred from one system to another. Hence, the sender involuntarily looses any control of the information and must resort to trusting the receiver to not misuse information. It is this problem that has lead to serious concerns about users privacy on the Internet, and the music and film industry's concern about intellectual property rights violations, and corporations concern about sensitive information misuse.

Usage control have been proposed as a means to remedy this problem by extending common security mechanisms beyond single systems such as PCs, servers or entire corporate systems. The idea is to provide a model for expressing and enforcing restrictions on how the information is to be *used* . Current mechanisms such as access control, Digital Rights Management, confidentiality and privacy protection all attempt to restrict information in one way or the other. The focus

A M. Tjoa et al. (Eds.): ARES 2011, LNCS 6908, pp. 38–49, 2011.

of usage control is to create an holistic approach to restricting information, such that it may be used for any of the purposes listed above.

The purpose of this review is to identify and analyse existing mechanisms for usage control enforcement in order to identify shortcomings and possible improvements.

The remaining parts of the paper is organised as follows. First, in Section 2 the research method employed is outlined and discussed. Next, in section 3 we provide a brief introduction to usage control. We review enforcement mechanisms in Section 4 and in Section 5 we report on the testing and evaluation that has been conducted . Section 6 includes our analysis and discussion of the enforcement mechanisms. Related work is outlined in Section 7, before our final conclusions are given in Section 8.

## 2   Research Method

The research method employed in this review is inspired by the recommendations by Kitchenham and Charters [15] regarding systematic literature reviews in software engineering, however with softer requirements regarding rigour.

This review will address the following research questions:

RQ1.  What usage control enforcement mechanisms have been proposed and how do they relate to each other?

RQ2.  What evidence exists supporting their appropriateness?

The purpose of this review is therefore to synthesise the previous research efforts on usage control and distributed enforcement strategies to identify open issues and prevent duplication of work. To this end, we also investigate the supporting evidence of appropriateness.

The papers subject to the review were selected based on search through the main online portals of scientific publications. These portals were: IEEE Xplore, ACM Digital Library, Scopusand SpringerLink. Potential papers were selected based on a search for "usage control" and "enforcement" in title, keywords and abstracts, for each of the portals listed above. The search capabilities of these portals vary considerably, hence minor modifications have been conducted. Most notably for SpringerLink, the amount of results returned made it necessary to conduct a nested search of the two phrases.

The search strategy clearly results in several irrelevant papers being potential subject to the review. Additional criteria were therefore specified to ensure only relevant papers be included in the actual review. These criteria are referred to as inclusion and exclusion criteria, indicating both a positive definition and a negative definition of what the review should and should not contain. Published peer-reviewed papers were included in the review if meeting any of the following criteria:

– Papers presenting mechanisms for enforcement of usage control models.
– Papers reporting on testing and experience of use with such mechanisms.

The criteria may be met by only parts of the paper, thus it need not be the main focus of the paper to be included. Papers meeting one or more of the of the following criteria were excluded:

– Position papers identifying threats and challenges to usage control.
– Papers focusing solely on subsets of usage control, such as access control and digital rights management.

Note that inclusion criteria was given a higher order than exclusion criteria, such that any paper satisfying both were included in the review.

From each of the included papers, the following content was extracted and analysed:

– The main idea of the model (RQ1.).
– The main strengths and limitations of the approach (RQ1.).
– The supportive evidence of its appropriateness (RQ2.).

While the data extraction part is mainly about documenting previous efforts, the analysis part was intended to look beyond specific claims to make more general assessments of the quality and usability of the proposed enforcement mechanisms.

## 3    Usage Control

The UCON (Usage Control) model was proposed by Park and Sandhu [27] to alleviate many of the shortcomings of existing access control mechanisms, particularly for distributed assets. The authors focus on three important parts of the model, which are *Authorizations*, *oBligations* and *Conditions*, resulting in what they denote the $UCON_{ABC}$ model. The main elements of this model are

**Subject.** an entity with a set of attributes (subject attributes) either holding or exercising rights on an object.
**Object.** an entity with a set of attributes (object attributes) that a subject hold or exercise a right on.
**Right.** a privilege held by a subject to perform certain functions on an object.
**Authorization.** a functional predicate to be evaluated in order to decide whether the subject is allowed to perform the requested rights on the object.
**oBligation.** a functional predicate to verify requirements a subject has to perform before or during a usage exercise.
**Condition.** a functional predicate to verify the requirements for the environment or system to be present before or during a usage exercise.

The family of models have later been expanded and detailed using various formalisms. A survey by Lazouski et al. [20] provide a good overview of these efforts. One of the main concepts of UCON is the view on continuous enforcement (see Figure 1). Contrary to common access control mechanisms, UCON assumes authorisations to be an ongoing activity such that misbehaviour may result in real-time revocation of rights. Park and Sandhu defined 16 basic UCON models based on the different steps in Figure 1.

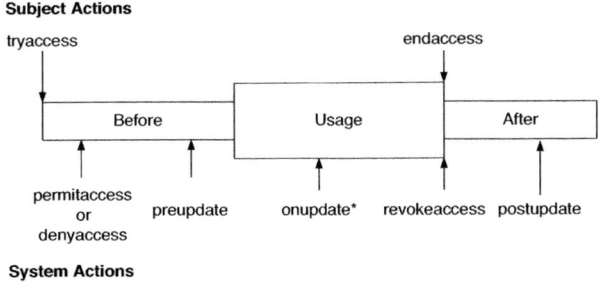

**Fig. 1.** UCON model with continuity of enforcement and mutability of properties[32]

# 4    Enforcement Mechanisms

In this section we describe the identified usage controlled enforcement mechanisms. We have separated them into three main categories which are proactive enforcement, reactive enforcement and trust-based enforcement. Although these categories are not mutually exclusive, they are often treated separately.

## 4.1    Proactive Enforcement

In this section we elaborate on the mechanisms that are mainly focused on preventing policy violation through proactive security measures. We categorise the mechanisms into three groups of client-side enforcement: trusted computing-based enforcement, hardware-based enforcement and software-based enforcement. Finally we also provide a category for server-side enforcement. Note that some of the approaches falls into several categories, but are placed in the one that best describe the focus of the mechanism.

*Trusted computing.* Trusted computing has been introduced as one of the main building blocks to enforce usage control policies on remote client devices. Although there are many that assume the use of trusted computing or a trusted platform, we include here only the approaches where trusted computing is essential to the mechanism.

Sandhu et al. propose a Trusted Reference Monitor (TRM) residing in user space to enforce policies [31,33]. A hardware-based Trusted Platform Module (TPM) is envisioned to provide a root of trust that together with a Public Key Infrastructure (PKI) may be used to attest cooperating platforms. The protocol between applications and TRM, as well as between different TRMs is based on challenge-response. Any request is followed by a challenge from the receiver. The requester subsequently attest the platform, application or environment through the means of a digital signature. Abie et al. propose a somewhat similar strategy based on a TPM to enforce usage policies on digital objects [1,2]. Self-enforcing objects (SEOs) are used as a secure container to transfer objects and policies and are also capable of enforcing the attached policy autonomously on any trusted platform.

A practical example of such an enforcement mechanism is given by Kyle and Brustolini [19]. UCLinux is a Linux Security Module that provides attestation, sealing and usage control support. Applications is provided access to the file if they are part of the trusted computing base and the file metadata contain a hash of the application. If the application is deemed trusted, UCLinux will handle any usage control enforcement to the application itself. Untrusted applications will however not be able to read nor write to the file. Alam et al. propose a similar enforcement mechanism [3] but also describe the concept of platform attestation [4]. Prior to releasing information to an authorised requester, the system verifies through a WS-Attestation procedure that the receiving platform will behave properly. A prototype implementation indicates an introduced delay of approximately five seconds, compared to not having such attestation.

*Hardware enforcement.* Hardware UCON Engine (HUE) [25] is another enforcement mechanism based on trusted computing that unlike most mechanisms does not rely on a built-in Trusted Platform Module (TPM). Instead, HUE is designed as a secure co-processor with a designated software stack to provide integration with the operating system. While obviously more flexible and efficient than TPM-based systems, the downside is that it the tailor-made hardware is not commercially available.

*Software-based enforcement.* The RightsEnforcer [24] is a product for enforcing simple usage control restrictions such as limiting the ability to view, print, copy and store. The mechanism is integrated in an e-mail client such that whenever a usage controlled object is sent to a receiver, the RightsEnforcer encrypts the content and sends the terms of use to a centralised RightsServer. The receiver is forced to use the RightsEnforcer to be able to decrypt the content and therefore the policy is always enforced.

Brustolini et al. propose a simplified version where policies are specified through allowing or denying specific operations (open, copy, print, etc.) on digital objects [6,9]. The system comprises a kernel level security module for SELinux, a web browser plugin and a modified web server that offers the ability to post information objects to a web service. Upon uploading documents, users are given the option to specify any usage restrictions. When downloading content from the service, the client warns the user of unacceptable policies.

A somewhat similar strategy is employed by Kumari et al. to provide usage control enforcement for web applications [18]. The solution is based on a web browser plugin that intercepts requests for enforcement enabled web applications and subsequently enforces the obtained policy. They demonstrate the feasibility of the approach through a modified social network application that generates policies whenever a content request is made by a user. Users can tag friends with a trust level in intervals from 0 to 1 and similarly tag content with a sensitivity on the same scale. A permission $p$ is then computed as the product $p(t, s) = t(1 - s)$ where $t$ is the trust value of the subject and $s$ the sensitivity of the content. These permissions are grouped into permission classes in five intervals such that the users may define which permission classes are allowed to perform events such as "view", "copy", etc. Any request not originating from the browser plugin is treated as permission class 0 (minimum permissions). Although currently not implemented, the authors argue that to prevent users from evading enforcement, some TPM based mechanism should be in place to guarantee that the browser plugin is not hijacked by other malicious plugins.

*Server-side.* An enforcement architecture for server-side enforcement is given in [14]. The focus of the approach is to enforce post usage obligations on possibly remote systems. Obligations may be placed on the system or on the subject (of usage) and relates to either controllable or uncontrollable objects as seen by the system. Katt et al. argue that system obligations on controllable objects, denoted trusted obligations, do not need a fulfilment check, since the system is assumed to be trusted. However for any other untrusted obligations, the system translates the obligations into a sequence of system operations including a condition at the end. Thus, if the condition holds, the obligation is assumed to be fulfilled. In the event that the obligation is not fulfilled (e.g. a file is not deleted), the system will issue any necessary compensating action as specified in the policy.

Layered UCON (L-UCON) provides partial (or layered) usage of resources. Since digital resources often are provided in a layered fashion (e.g. the varying pixel resolution of images), L-UCON provides the user with the ability to negotiate both content and policies with the content owner. Hence, the content owner may adjust a policy based on for example the usage purpose stated by the user.

Gheorghe et al. [11] utilise the Message Service Bus of Service-Oriented Architectures (SOA) to enforce business and regulatory usage control policies on messages exchanged between services. Since all messages are placed on the service bus, messages may easily be intercepted and validated for compliance with stated policies. However, policies are assumed to be fairly static and message level usage policies are not handled by the architecture.

## 4.2 Reactive Enforcement

Reactive security measures may be seen as an acceptance of failure, since security breaches cannot be prevented, penalties are our only options. While they do seem weaker at first glance, the main reason for utilising reactive measures is lack of control. It is difficult to prevent policy violations from occurring when the enforcer has no or limited control over the target device. Since detecting such violations after the fact are in many cases easier, reactive enforcement may provide a powerful complement to any proactive enforcement. In the following we survey some of the main efforts on reactive enforcement of usage control policies.

*Audit-based enforcement.* The approach taken by Corin et al. is not to prevent policy violation but to ensure that users are held accountable for their actions through a proper auditing process [8]. Time stamping and signature mechanisms are used to establish evidence of communication and to bind a usage policy to the communicated objects. Then, whenever an auditing process is started by any of the communicating parties, the other parties are obliged to provide evidence that their usage is in accordance with the policies agreed upon. The communication protocol with timestamps assures that honest parties do have such evidence.

Pretschner et al. [28] argue that many high-level obligations may not be controllable by the content provider. They therefore separate between controllable and uncontrollable obligations, and further introduce the weaker notion of *observable* obligations. Unobservable obligations are weakened and adapted until they become observable, and hence subject to monitoring and auditing. Therefore, rather than controlling obligations fulfilment, the content owner can observe (indications of) policy violations. Examples include watermarking content to detect unauthorised redistribution. Pretschener et al. [28] lets the server (content provider) employ traditional access control first to determine applicable rules and authorisations. In the next step, the consumer is provided with the set of provisional actions that must be taken prior to access and the obligations that must be fulfilled during or after usage of the content. Subsequently the consumer must provide evidence that the provisional actions have been taken and that he has committed himself to the obligations and compensations. Compensations, or sanctions as they are termed, is also proposed formally in [5]. The authors show how a system may violate certain rules in a policy and still be compliant with the policy through fulfilling a set of sanctions. The sanctions are specified for a rule in the policy and therefore also known to the user prior to a policy violation. APPLE (A Posteriori PoLicy Enforcement) is based on the same principles but utilises Auditing Authorities to automatically check the policy adherence of users [10]. The Authorities either selects documents or objects they have become aware of, or selects one randomly. While some policy violations may go undetected, the authors argue that the possibility of being caught and held accountable will in some cases deter significant violations [10].

Cederquist et al. [7] attempt to handle the problem of administrative policies in usage control. That is, who is authorised to specify and change the policy guarding a specific piece of information. In a fully decentralised system based on discretionary policies this is next to impossible, especially since it may be difficult to assess who is the owner of data after multiple changes by others. The solution by Cederquist et al. is to require that users are accountable for their actions. Such that if Alice changes a policy regarding a document before sending it to Bob, then Alice is held accountable for the change. In the event that the change is unauthorised, Bob will be able to prove that he is not to blame for the unauthorised change. Thus, the basic action required on the receiver side is to ensure that the sender is accountable. The authors also point out that as a consequence, users may perform deliberate policy infringements while accepting full responsibility for it.

*Monitoring.* Hilty et al. [12,30] propose an active monitoring approach where the client-side monitoring component signals to a server-side enforcement mechanism whenever obligations have been fulfilled. Hence, if information some information should be deleted within 30 days, the monitoring component signals to the provider at time of deletion and ends the monitoring of the information

object. In the event that the information is not deleted, the monitoring component signals a policy violation to the provider.

### 4.3   Trust-Based Enforcement

Trust has been extensively studied in computer science and have numerous application areas. Here we describe how trust assessments may be used for enforcement purposes.

Krautsevich et al. proposes to use trust management as means to grant usage privileges to users [17]. The idea is to utilise trust relationships and trust
propagation between users and content providers to determine a usage control
decision between parties that are mutually untrusted. Hence a user A with a
credential issued by some other user or provider B may be given usage rights to
a resource controlled by C if C trusts B.

Nyre and Jaatun also propose a trust-based enforcement strategy, but in their
case the trust denotes whether the content receiver may be trusted to adhere to
the usage policy [26]. Further, they specify a method to compute the probability
that the receiver will enforce the policy and use this probability for content
dissemination decisions.

## 5   Testing and Evaluation

To answer the second research question, we aimed to determine what evidence
are provided to support the appropriateness of the proposed enforcement mechanisms. Here we describe the quantitative testing and evaluation of the enforcement mechanisms we have described. We do not consider qualitative self-
assessments as evidence of appropriateness.

*Performance analysis.* Performance analysis is the predominant form of testing
strategy employed and primarily aimed at identifying latency introduced by the
enforcement mechanisms.

In [11] the introduced round-trip latency said to be around 5000 $\mu m$ of which
the policy decision takes about 22 $\mu m$. Although the policy decision time is
insignificant compared to the round-trip time, the lack of a neutral benchmark
makes it difficult to assess wether the entire round-trip time is acceptable or
not. Similar shortcomings are found in [13] where the read and write speeds
are analysed for files of varying sizes and in [4] where the attestation request is
said to introduce a a latency of about five seconds. Since these values are not
benchmarked to a system without the implemented enforcement mechanism, it
is difficult to assess the appropriateness.

Djalaliev et al. do provide a benchmark of regular HTTP and TLS traffic and
show that the modified TLS used for attestation only introduces an increase
in CPU usage of about 20% [9]. The latency analysis demonstrates that usage
controlled file retrieval introduces a penalty varying from 100% to 30% with
increasing file sizes.

The UCLinux implementation in [19] is analysed to find the system boot latency and general usage latency. General usage latency was simulated through measuring the time needed to compile a Linux kernel since this involves several different file operations. The tests show that the boot process takes 9% longer to complete on UCLinux compared to regular Linux, whereas the file operations require some 10% more time to complete.

*Usability testing.* Brustoloni et al. [6] conduct an end-user test of their proposed system. The test seems to support their claim that performance is not significantly affected and that user awareness of unacceptable policies are considerably improved. However, there are only ten participants in the test all of which are students and only 50% have a computer science or engineering background despite the fact that the test has been designed with such professionals in mind. Further, the test seems to have no reference group and hence comparison of awareness is only done with the test group, something which could potentially bias the result. Although there is nothing to suggest that the enforcement mechanism is inappropriate, we find the low participation and the limited procedure not convincing enough for the mechanism to be deemed appropriate.

## 6    Analysis and Discussion

In this section we attempt to analyse and generalise the strengths and limitations of the enforcement mechanisms we have described so far since space limitations prevent us from dwelling into the details of each solution.

Virtually all mechanisms for usage control assume the existence of a trusted module to ensure that enforcement cannot be evaded, yet none have discussed to any extent the practical problems of establishing and maintaining a trust infrastructure based on Trusted Computing Modules. Particularly since other considerably less complex security infrastructures, such as Public Key Infrastructures, have experienced only limited success [22]. Although the benefit of usage control may be easier to identify, most of the reasons for PKI failure described in [22] also apply to Trusted Computing. Perhaps a property-based approach to Trusted Platform Module could alleviate some of the complexity of using binary hashes of applications [16]. We do however agree that TPMs and Trusted Computing-based approaches are the only means of guaranteeing enforcement on remote devices.

There are cases in which enforcement guarantees are not necessarily required, particularly in closed systems such as business environments where the predominant threat is end-users' lack of awareness. In such circumstances, perhaps a more lightweight approach could be adopted that is technically infeasible for the average user to circumvent, but without the cost of a hardware-based trust infrastructure. It seems that the RightsEnforcer [24] is the only approach investigating along these lines.

Allowing policy violation may seem like a contradiction for a policy enforcer. Massacci [23] argues that enforcement should be *reasonable*, and therefore should allowed to be circumvented in cases where there is a just cause. If users are accountable for their action, they may only be required to justify why the violation (e.g. authorisation given orally) such that penalties may be given in retrospect. Most of the audit-based approaches do offer the violation capability, but at the same time rely on previously described compensations to be carried out. Which in essence means that only exceptions that are identified in the policy are handled by the enforcer, and therefore the rigour of the policy is not reduced.

The perhaps most striking issue we have come across is the lack of empirical evidence of the enforcement mechanisms' appropriateness. This may be due to the fact that usage control enforcement is a relatively new research field and that formal models and prototypes showing technical feasibility is a prerequisite to be able to perform proper end-user tests. However, from the effort listed here we conclude that the formal and technical basis should be well in place to allow for more user centric enforcement strategies that properly balance the usability and the security provided.

## 7   Related Work

There have been some reviews conducted previously. From the digital rights management perspective, Liu et al. [21] have conducted a survey on DRM technology but does not treat the more general case of usage control. The review by Pretschner et al. [29] is also on DRM technology, but is more focused on alternative use of such technology including privacy and business information protection. Four different DRM technologies are analysed and compared to a set of general usage control enforcement capabilities. The idea is to see whether DRM can be used for all regular consumer side enforcement. While the evaluated systems do vary to some degree, their main limitation is the lack of enforcement after rendering. In this paper, we consider enforcement of much more expressive policies than the simple content protection mechanisms of most commercially available products and services.

A recent survey by Lazouski et al. [20] does however target usage control in general. The centre of gravity is the UCON model proposed by Park and Sandhu [27] such that other initiatives are described based on how they relate to this model. Formal models, architectures, enforcement strategies and implementations are discussed and some of the open challenges outlined. Contrary to this paper, enforcement is not considered throughly.

## 8   Conclusion

This paper has identified existing approaches to usage control enforcement as identified in research question RQ1. Despite the relatively short period of time since the term and concept of Usage Control was coined, there has been considerable efforts in establishing proper enforcement mechanisms. While formal models and prototype implementations have been, and still are necessary to demonstrate the technical feasibility of usage control enforcement, more effort is required in obtaining reliable empirical data on the usefulness and usability of these approaches. Therefore we are currently unable properly address research question RQ2 to judge particular approaches as more appropriate than others.

## References

1. Abie, H., Spilling, P., Foyn, B.: A distributed digital rights management model for secure information-distribution systems. International Journal of Information Security 3(2), 113–128 (2004)
2. Abie, H., Spilling, P., Foyn, B.: Rights-carrying and self-enforcing information objects for information distribution systems. Information and Communications Security, 546–561 (2004)
3. Alam, M., Seifert, J., Li, Q., Zhang, X.: Usage control platformization via trustworthy SELinux. In: Proceedings of the 2008 ACM Symposium on Information, Computer and Communications Security, pp. 245–248 (2008)
4. Alam, M., Zhang, X., Nauman, M., Ali, T.: Behavioral attestation for web services (BA4WS). In: Proceedings of the 2008 ACM workshop on Secure Web Services, pp. 21–28 (2008)
5. Brunel, J., Cuppens, F., Cuppens, N., Sans, T., Bodeveix, J.: Security policy compliance with violation management. In: Proceedings of the 2007 ACM Workshop on Formal Methods in Security Engineering, pp. 31–40 (2007)
6. Brustoloni, J.C., Villamarín-Salomón, R., Djalaliev, P., Kyle, D.: Evaluating the usability of usage controls in electronic collaboration. In: Proceedings of the 4th Symposium on Usable Privacy and Security, pp. 85–92 (2008)
7. Cederquist, J., Corin, R., Dekker, M., Etalle, S., den Hartog, J., Lenzini, G.: Auditbased compliance control. International Journal of Information Security 6(2), 133–151 (2007)
8. Corin, R., Galindo, D., Hoepman, J.H.: Securing data accountability in decentralized systems. In: On the Move to Meaningful Internet Systems 2006: OTM 2006 Workshops, pp. 626–635 (2006)
9. Djalaliev, P., Brustoloni, J.C.: Secure web-based retrieval of documents with usage controls. In: Proceedings of the 2009 ACM Symposium on Applied Computing, pp. 2062–2069 (2009)
10. Etalle, S., Winsborough, W.H.: A posteriori compliance control. In: Proceedings of the 12th ACM Symposium on Access Control Models and Technologies, pp. 11–20 (2007)
11. Gheorghe, G., Mori, P., Crispo, B., Martinelli, F.: Enforcing ucon policies on the enterprise service bus. In: Meersman, R., Dillon, T., Herrero, P. (eds.) OTM 2010. LNCS, vol. 6427, pp. 876–893. Springer, Heidelberg (2010)
12. Hilty, M., Pretschner, A., Basin, D., Schaefer, C., Walter, T.: Monitors for usage control. In: Trust Management, pp. 411–414 (2007)
13. Hu, H., Li, H., Feng, D.: L-ucon: Towards layered access control with ucon. In: Proceedings of the International Conference on Computational Science and Engineering, vol. 2, pp. 823–829 (August 2009)
14. Katt, B., Zhang, X., Breu, R., Hafner, M., Seifert, J.: A general obligation model and continuity: enhanced policy enforcement engine for usage control. In: The ACM Symposium on Access Control Models and Technologies, pp. 123–132 (2008)
15. Kitchenham, B., Charters, S.: Guidelines for performing systematic literature reviews in software engineering. EBSE Technical Report EBSE-2007-01, Keele University and University of Durham (2007)

16. Korthaus, R., Sadeghi, A., Stüble, C., Zhan, J.: A practical property-based bootstrap architecture. In: Proceedings of the 2009 ACM Workshop on Scalable Trusted Computing, pp. 29–38 (2009); ACM ID: 1655114
17. Krautsevich, L., Lazouski, A., Martinelli, F., Mori, P., Yautsiukhin, A.: Usage control, risk and trust. In: Katsikas, S., Lopez, J., Soriano, M. (eds.) TrustBus 2010. LNCS, vol. 6264, pp. 1–12. Springer, Heidelberg (2010)
18. Kumari, P., Pretschner, A., Peschla, J., Kuhn, J.: Distributed data usage control for web applications: a social network implementation. In: Proceedings of the First ACM Conference on Data and Application Security and Privacy, pp. 85–96 (2011)
19. Kyle, D., Brustoloni, J.: Uclinux: a linux security module for trusted-computingbased usage controls enforcement, pp. 63–70 (2007)
20. Lazouski, A., Martinelli, F., Mori, P.: Usage control in computer security: A survey. Computer Science Review 4(2), 81–99 (2010)
21. Liu, Q., Safavi-Naini, R., Sheppard, N.P.: Digital rights management for content distribution. In: Proceedings of the Australasian Information Security Workshop Conference on ACSW Frontiers 2003, vol. 21, pp. 49–58 (2003)
22. Lopez, J., Oppliger, R., Pernul, G.: Why have public key infrastructures failed so far? Internet Research 15(5), 544–556 (2005)
23. Massacci, F.: Infringo ergo sum: when will software engineering support infringements? In: Proceedings of the FSE/SDP Workshop on Future of Software Engineering Research, pp. 233–238 (2010)
24. Matson, M., Ulieru, M.: The 'how' and 'why' of persistent information security. In: Proceedings of the International Conference on Privacy, Security and Trust, pp. 1–4 (2006)
25. Nauman, M., Ali, T.: Hue: A hardware ucon engine for ne-grained continuous usage control. In: The IEEE International Multitopic Conference, pp. 59–64 (2008)
26. Nyre, A.A., Jaatun, M.G.: A probabilistic approach to information control. Journal of Internet Technology 11(3), 407–416 (2010)
27. Park, J., Sandhu, R.: The UCON$_{ABC}$ usage control model. ACM Transactions on Information Systems Security 7(1), 128–174 (2004)
28. Pretschner, A., Hilty, M., Basin, D.: Distributed usage control. Communications of the ACM 49(9), 39–44 (2006)
29. Pretschner, A., Hilty, M., Schutz, F., Schaefer, C., Walter, T.: Usage control enforcement: Present and future. IEEE Security & Privacy 6(4), 44–53 (2008)
30. Pretschner, A., Massacci, F., Hilty, M.: Usage control in service-oriented architectures. In: Trust, Privacy and Security in Digital Business pp. 83–93 (2007)
31. Sandhu, R., Zhang, X., Ranganathan, K., Covington, M.J.: Client-side access control enforcement using trusted computing and pei models. Journal of High Speed Networks 15(3), 229–245 (2006)
32. Zhang, X., Park, J., Parisi-Presicce, F., Sandhu, R.: A logical specification for usage control. In: Proceedings of the 9th ACM Symposium on Access Control Models and Technologies, pp. 1–10 (2004)
33. Zhang, X., Seifert, J.P., Sandhu, R.: Security enforcement model for distributed usage control. In: IEEE International Conference on Sensor Networks, Ubiquitous and Trustworthy Computing, SUTC 2008, pp. 10–18 (2008)

# Discovery and Integration of Web 2.0 Content into Geospatial Information Infrastructures: A Use Case in Wild Fire Monitoring

Manuela Núñez-Redó, Laura Díaz, José Gil,
David González, and Joaquín Huerta

Institute of New Imaging Technologies, University Jaume I, Castellón, Spain
{nunezm,laura.diaz,jose.gil,gonzaled,huerta}@uji.es

**Abstract.** Efficient environment monitoring has become a major concern for society to guarantee sustainable development. For instance, forest fire detection and analysis is important to provide early warning systems and identify impact. In this environmental context, availability of up-to-date information is very important for reducing damages caused. Environmental applications are deployed on top of Geospatial Information Infrastructures (GIIs) to manage information pertaining to our environment. Such infrastructures are traditionally top-down infrastructures that do not consider user participation. This provokes a bottleneck in content publication and therefore a lack of content availability. On the contrary mainstream IT systems and in particular the emerging Web 2.0 Services allow active user participation that is becoming a massive source of dynamic geospatial resources. In this paper, we present a web service, that implements a standard interface, offers a unique entry point for spatial data discovery, both in GII services and web 2.0 services. We introduce a prototype as proof of concept in a forest fire scenario, where we illustrate how to leverage scientific data and web 2.0 content.

**Keywords:** VGI, SDI, Geospatial Information Infrastructures, Web 2.0, Open Search.

## 1 Introduction

Analyzing the Earth's behavior requires a multidisciplinary approach and the assessment of a broad range of thematic areas [1] [2]. Geospatial information is essential for addressing related challenges. The amount of scientific geospatial data collected has increased significantly due to advances in data-capturing technologies. Geospatial Information Systems (GIS) have become indispensable tools for organizing and exploiting this geospatial content for environmental sciences, and providing a framework for multidisciplinary analysis [3].

In this domain, we find multiple geospatial standards for data encodings and service interfaces. The combination of these standards allows for establishing Geospatial Information Infrastructures (GIIs), also known as Spatial Data Infrastructures (SDIs) [4]. These multi-participatory infrastructures allow administration and other official providers to publish environmental information.

A M. Tjoa et al. (Eds.): ARES 2011, LNCS 6908, pp. 50–68, 2011.

However, GIIs are dynamic and require continuous maintenance. Still, GII complex deployment mechanisms limit the possible contributions of expert users suffering from a low-rate of user motivation regarding participation and content management [6][7]. Recent natural disasters such as the Indian and Chilean tsunamis, forest fires in Greece and California or the earthquake in Haití have demonstrated that difficulties still exist inefficiently exploiting geospatial resources in GII. The difficulties stem from the absence of sufficient available resources and a lack of collaboration and interrelation between different geospatial infrastructures and components.

In contrast, we are witnessing the consolidation of a new generation of the World Wide Web, in which the main feature is user participation. Tim O'Reilly (2005) popularized the evolving nature of the web by introducing the term 'Web 2.0.' The Web is now a collaborative environment where the increasing number of web-based social networks has turned users into active providers [11] [31], motivated to provide a massive amount of information [30]. This user-generated content [16] is mostly geo-georeferenced to the user location, leading to huge amounts of geo-referenced information available in practically any domain [32]. For example, the photos uploaded by the public on Flickr during the California wildfires in 2007. These photos provided a quicker overview of the situation than information coming from official channels, such as mapping agencies.

This information provides a complementary view to the scientific data and shows the social impact of environmental events like forest fires. Furthermore, due to advanced devices that allow users to capture and share data from the field, there is a massive source of geo-information available at near real time. This humans-as-sensors paradigm [17] provides a new means of providing data in its context, which is fundamental to the vision of a spatially enabled society [14]. To leverage this new source of information, has to be integrated, in the context of the GIIs, to enrich scientific information with social and local knowledge.

However, the integration of these sources of information in GII poses new research challenges. Environmental applications need to retrieve this valuable information. This means to deal with the different search interfaces of each web 2.0 service and its heterogeneous capacities.

To address these issues, we propose a more scalable solution, which aims at improving the interoperability of the heterogeneous nature of the multiple Web 2.0 services available.

Our proposal materializes in a middleware component that provides a homogeneous search interface to improve the discover ability over social networks and crowd sourcing platforms. This middleware is a discovery service that implements the OpenSearch Geo-Time standard interface specification. Although some of the Web 2.0 services already expose an OpenSearch interface to increase interoperability, they do not offer the spatio-temporal query capacity, which is crucial for most of the environmental scenarios. The realization of our proposal, called Web 2.0 Broker (W2.0B), offers a common entry point to retrieve and aggregate web 2.0 content according to spatial and temporal criteria.

The remainder of this paper is structured as follows: Section 2 defines the overall context of geospatial information infrastructures, volunteered geographic information and geospatial discovery. Section 3 defines the Open Search specification. We present the architecture in Section 4, the prototype (Section 5), and conclude the paper with a discussion and an outlook towards future work (Section 6).

## 2  Background and Related Work

Geoscience research is a multidisciplinary field that demands heterogeneous data and a multitude of expert profiles such as technologists and remote sensing specialists [1] [2] [8]. These experts collect and manage data to run scientific models and produce information. On the other hand web 2.0 Services and crowdsourcing platforms have demonstrated how ordinary citizens, encouraged by technological advances, are also able to generate and publish high scale spatial information at near real time offering a complementary vision to monitor our environment. In this section, we briefly reflect on standard based approaches to share geospatial content and approaches to leverage both sources of information to enrich environmental monitoring.

### A.  Geospatial Information Infrastructures

A trend involves deploying geospatial and environmental applications on service-oriented architectures (SOA) [9]. One of the goals of SOA is to enable interoperability among existing technologies and provide an interoperable environment based on reusability and standardized components.

GIIs enable end-users to share geospatial content in a distributed manner following an SOA approach. They play a key role in supporting users and providers in decision-making where they can discover, visualize, and evaluate geospatial data at regional, national and global levels [4].

International Initiatives describe the overall architecture and best practices to design and implement GIIs. Content is managed by means of regulated and standardized service types. Adopted as a European directive in February 2007, INSPIRE sets out a legal framework for the European GII, regarding policies and activities with environmental impact [5]. It defines a network based on discovery, view, download, transformation and invocation services. The technical level provides a range of interoperability standards available for the integration of information systems [12].

In this context many authors address questions concerning the increasing number of people participating in crowdsourcing platforms while GIIs traditionally face problems to attract users. GII researchers have called for a user-driven model [60] [61] [62], which relates to the hybrid GII that incorporates user generated content. Combining scientific knowledge and public information is not new, according to [58] . [59] develope the "citizen panels" in the 1970's involving experts and citizens to allow everybody to participate. In the context of municipal activities, [57] also proposed to capture and utilize the "city knowledge" from those close to a particular phenomenon with the richest geospatial knowledge. Another example is the management of natural resources in the Amazon where there is a need for user participation to integrate their local knowledge [63].

### B.  Web 2.0 Services and volunteered geospatial information

With the emergence of Web 2.0, ordinary citizens have begun to produce and share Geographic Information (GI) on the Internet. These Web 2.0-based activities show that users are willing to engage more actively in the production and provision of contents. This gives rise to a new phenomenon, which has been referred to as "neogeography" [15] [18], "cybercartography" [30], or "voluntary geographic information" (VGI) [17] [21].

VGI provides a massive source of information that cannot be ignored. This information can complete gaps in official data including cheap and big scale up to date information. Research has related these collaborative services, paying special attention to the trust and credibility [23] [25], quality, and reliability as compared to official data, [22] [26] constraints and user motivation [14] [24].

In our scope we consider VGI as a complement to official data. Scientists will be provided with discovery mechanisms to retrieve appropriate VGI that will complement the social aspect with their scientific information.

The use of a hybrid approach that integrates bottom-up and top-down methodologies has already been demonstrated [27], with the purpose of integrating user generated information, scientific tools and official information in the same geospatial infrastructure. In this context merging the top-down SDI model with VGI infrastructures has already been described [13] [17] [28] [29].0 [7] [20] describe a publication service to hide complex standards and assist users in publishing content directly into standard geospatial data services. This direct user publication raises issues about data consistency and quality in GII. A Second approach is the retrieval of data directly from crowdsourcing services. In this context we propose a Discovery Service that deploys on an INSPIRE-based infrastructure that offers a standard and unique entry point to retrieve Web 2.0 resources according to spatial and temporal criteria that can be integrated with official environmental information to produce a richer and more up to date system [14].

We have performed a survey of the multiple Web 2.0 Services available, with the aim of selecting those where spatial and temporal queries were reliable. The service selection is the following: Twitter a social networking and micro-blogging service. Its users can send and read text-based posts of up to 140 characters, so-called "tweets", which are publicly visible by default. Flickr is an online application that allows uploading, storing and organizing photographs. It enables the creation and retrieval of the pictures. YouTube allows sharing videos that can be geo-referenced. OpenStreetMap and Geonames are both explicit VGI platforms. Meteoclimatic is a weather resource and Wikipedia is an open free web enclyclopedia.

*C. Geospatial content discovery*

Within GIIs, metadata and catalogue services are key to discover content properly [54] [55]. In this context most of the issues arise because metadata creation and publication is a complex and arduous task that has to be done manually [53]. On the contrary, the ease of content production and publication in Web 2.0 Services makes vast amounts of VGI available. As a result, social networks are immense online repositories with geo-referenced content. However, attempts at providing spatial and temporal-based search engines over VGI are relatively scarce [33]. Despite the popularity of Web 2.0 services, there has not been many integrated and interoperable approaches that allow users to search for content regardless of the nature of the underlying services [37]. One of the reasons may be found in the diversity and heterogeneity of these types of services and their interfaces.

The process of searching over multiple services becomes a tedious task because they provide different data encodings, geo-referencing and proprietary application programming interface (API).

In order to overcome this heterogeneity the use of a common interface, following a standard specification, would increase interoperability. Walsh [35] points out the need to pay attention to discovery interfaces widely spread in other information communities different from the established catalogues services in the geospatial domain [36]. Several Web 2.0 services, like Flickr, expose basic discovery capacities through the Open Search specification allowing for a common technique to run term-based queries. In this sense, our approach extends this to the design a mechanism that allows users to search using the OpenSearch (OS) specification [38] by also adding spatial-temporal criteria to retrieve content over different social networks and services.

## 3  The Open Search Specification

Web 2.0 services expose their own API to be accessed, using specific encodings formats and schemas. This constitutes a technical barrier for discovering content in a homogeneous way.

To overcome this problem our proposal is materialized in a discovery web service, the so-called Web 2.0 Broker. The W2.0B implements the OpenSearch specification with the Geo and Time extension [51], adopted by the Open Geospatial Consortium and the geospatial community as a standard de facto.

OS specification offers an interface based on minimal input, which can be extended, among others, with spatial or temporal criteria. OS has rapidly become a successful search specification over web repositories, which are increasingly adapting it to demonstrate their search interfaces in a standard and simple way. In this section we describe the OpenSearch Geo-Time specification and how we have adopted it as the interface for our discovery service to allow users to perform spatio-temporal queries over social networks.

### A.  Keyword-based discovery

OS defines a service interface for minimal search and retrieval capabilities. The simplicity of OS for search fits into the basic search interfaces that identified many Web 2.0 services. An OpenSearch-enabled service exposes an interface for client applications to send simple HTTP GET requests providing specific query parameters. As a result, responses are often encoded in lightweight data formats such as GeoRSS [39], Atom [40] or KML [41].

The OpenSearch specification has only one mandatory query parameter called "searchTerms" allowing client applications to retrieve information related to one or more keywords. Other query parameters like those supporting results pagination ("count", "startIndex", "startPage") are optional. The W2.0B implements this interface to broadcast keywords-based search over a selected pool of Web 2.0 services. Each service must be described by its Description Document, a file whose aim is, to describe the search engine of the target service. This description could vary from one to another, but there are several mandatory parameters like the root node called *OpenSearchDescription*, *shortName* that contain a brief human-readable title to identify this search engine, *Description* which is a text explanation of the search engine and the URL with the location to execute a search request.

### B. Spatial and Temporal-based discovery

More advanced search criteria are necessary in our environment-monitoring scenario. Specific search profiles are described by extending the OpenSearch specification. The OGC OpenSearch Geo Temporal specification [51], defines a list of query parameters to enable spatial and temporal filtering. This extension is built upon the basic OpenSearch specification, so all mandatory and optional query parameters previously mentioned are also available. The spatial and temporal extensions define spatial and time specific, optional query parameters. The "geo:box" parameter filters are the result of a  rectangular area. The "geo:lat", "geo:lon" and "geo:radius" parameter filters results from a circular area around a point. The "geo:geometry" parameter defines a geographic filter by means of an arbitrary geometry. The "geo:name" parameter allows filtering by place name. The "time:start" and "time:end" allow the definition of a temporal range for valid results.

The W2.0B implements the OS Geo-Time specification. Therefore, we increase the interoperability of the selected crowdsourcing platforms because now client applications can run spatio-temporal queries in these services by using OS-Geo-Time as unique interfaces. Table 1 shows the current status of the W2.0B prototype. The colored cells show the service currently offered where the rows show the web 2.0 services where the query is propagated and the columns shows the operations, available in the OS Geo- Time specification, implemented to query the Web 2.0 services. Regarding the response formats, Atom, the format recommended by [51], KML and MIMETEXT KML[43] are supported.

**Table 1.** Search Parameters implemented in the W2.0B applicable to  Web 2.0 services

| | | Base OS params | | | | Geo Extension | | | | Time Ext | | Data Formats | | |
|---|---|---|---|---|---|---|---|---|---|---|---|---|---|---|
| | | Search Terms | Count | Start Index | Start Page | bbox | Lon,lat,radius | geometry | Name/location | start | end | KML | KML/MIMEXT | ATOM (+GeoRSS) |
| | Twitter | | | | | | | | | | | | | |
| | OpenStreetMap | | | | | | | | | | | | | |
| | Meteoclimatic | | | | | | | | | | | | | |
| Web 2.0 Service | YouTube | | | | | | | | | | | | | |
| | Flickr | | | | | | | | | | | | | |
| | Geonames | | | | | | | | | | | | | |
| | RSS (Geonames) | | | | | | | | | | | | | |
| | Wikipedia | | | | | | | | | | | | | |
| | **Multiquery** | | | | | | | | | | | | | |

## 4   System Architecture

In this section we elaborate on the architecture of the proposed approach. Our main goal is to extend traditional GII architecture with a middleware component that offers a standard interface to retrieve and integrate web 2.0 content.

The W2.0B offers the functionality to perform a spatio-temporal search of VGI in multiple Web 2.0 services for its integration with official environmental information available in the infrastructure. In this way the vast amount of VGI becomes another data source in GIIs to complement scientific data. The integration is performed at the client side since the W2.0B provides common data encoding.

Figure 1 shows a simplified overview of the INSPIRE technical architecture which basically extends a classical three-layered SOA. This architecture is composed (top-down) of the application layer, service layer and content layer. The next subsections will describe each of these layers and the components that describe our contribution.

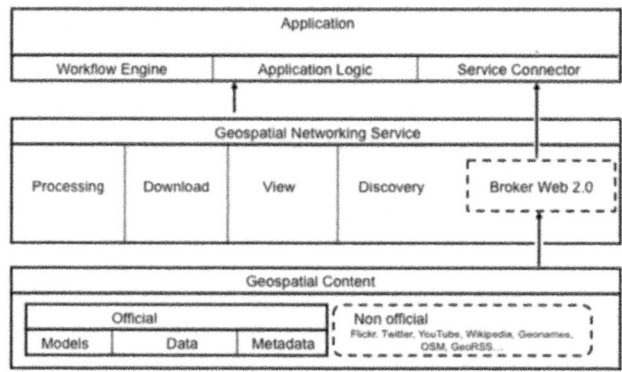

**Fig. 1.** Classical three-tier GII architecture (extracted from [10]) extended with a new channel connecting to VGI sources

## A.  Application Layer

Whereas traditional applications offer access to the content via the Geospatial Networking Service layer (Figure 1), this architecture offers an additional entry point to the W2.0B. This functionality is part of the Service Connector module, since it is the component in charge of connecting to the available middleware.

In this layer users are presented with a friendly interface to perform queries according to keyword and spatial-temporal criteria. Both standard catalogues and the W2.0B can be used to retrieve results. In the case of the W2.0B, this query will be transmitted and the results transformed to a well-known common data encoder to be presented in this layer using geospatial Web Mapping technology.

## B.  Geospatial Networking Service Layer

A classical GII provides discovery, access and processing services that, implement the OGC standards, such as Catalogue Services (CS-W), Web Mapping Service (WMS), Web Feature Service (WFS), and Web Processing Service (WPS), providing access to the geospatial content. In our research we propose to extend this layer with a new discovery service that, by implementing the OpenSearch Geo-Time interface, acts as a search engine to access Web 2.0 content.

W2.0B allows searching for VGI data through its standard OS Geo-Time interface and through a specific API. Client that have two ways to connect on the one hand, through its Java API which facilitates the development of client applications implemented in JAVA or accessing the OS standard interface.

*C. Content Layer*

We focus on the integration of both official and non official sources. Specifically, we focus on the retrieval of the content provided by Web 2.0 Services. These non-official resources are especially relevant due to the fact that users provide real time information, local knowledge and social impact to enrich the official environmental information.

Table 1 shows the set of crowdsourcing platforms being queried by the W2.0B. The content provided by these platforms differs in nature, for instance, geo-tagged photographs are shared through Flickr [45], short text messages shared via Twitter [48], or videos uploaded to Youtube [50], encyclopedic descriptions in Wikipedia [49], place names using Geonames [46], tagged vector geometries in OpenStreetMap [47] or information about weather stations provided by Meteoclimatic [56]. Due to the substantial availability of resources in crowdsourcing platforms a big part of the retrieved results are not related to the target scenario and they represent somehow "noise" that has to be eliminated for an appropriated assessment. Although it is out of the scope of this current investigation to assess data quality, section 7 overviews a preliminary discussion and outlines open questions that remain for future research.

# 5  Web 2.0 Broker: Open Search Service

W2.0B implements the function to search different social networks and Web 2.0 Services. A collection of social media services, with geo-referencing capabilities, has been analyzed (Table I), and only those that support, to some degree, geospatial and temporal filtering functions through their public API have been selected as target repositories [44].

Although some Web 2.0 services implement the OpenSearch specification (Flickr, Wikipedia, Youtube OpenStreetMap), some of them do not offer the OpenSearch-Geo-Time search interface. The W20B overcomes this limitation by offering spatial and temporal criteria queries to these services.

*A. Web 2.0 Broker –Design*

Figure 2 shows the component diagram of the W20B. It illustrates its modular design and how the components are linked to each other. Below, we will elaborate more on each component and its functionality.

At the top of Figure 2 we can see how the W2.0B implements the OS Geo-Time specification to provide discovery capabilities over heterogeneous VGI resources.

The *OS Core* component deals with the interpretation of the query in the standard OS format. It retrieves the query and forwards it to the Search Engine component. Only the SearchTerms input parameter from the specification is mandatory, but other criteria can be specified. The accuracy of results is improved either by adding spatial

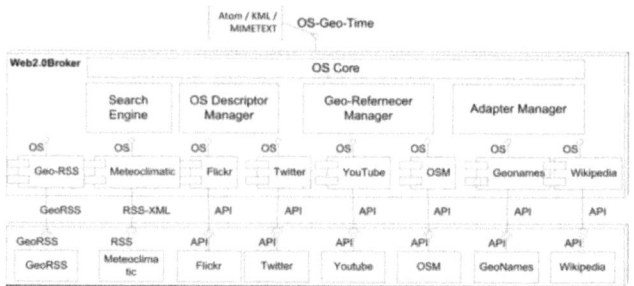

**Fig. 2.** W2.0B components diagram

filtering with the bbox, location or lon, lat and radius parameters, or adding time criteria by setting up the start and end parameters as we will see in the discussion section.

The *Search Engine* component contains the logic to map the query and the specified search criteria to then perform the concrete operations offered by the different web 2.0 services. It will broadcast the query to the different search engines and adapters that the client has selected. The supported query can add spatial constraints to the queries sent to the Web 2.0 services that natively support geographic search capabilities through their own API. For instance, users can search for resources that are restricted to a given area of interest represented as a polygonal geometry.

The *OS Descriptor Manager* dynamically generates the service description document [38] specifying how the different services must be queried. This document, mandatory by the specification, is generated by each service adapter. Its function is to advertise the set of accepted query parameters and supported response formats. This allows both calls from outside and within a client application to understand the discovery interfaces supported by services and how to build valid OpenSearch-styled queries.

The *Geo-reference Manager* component deals with the management of geospatial content. In terms of spatial search accuracy and performance, the W20B relies on the spatial search capabilities provided by the services queried and the content available, for instance, only a few tweets are actually geo-referenced. In this case, the Geo-reference Manager follows a methodology to extract the location from the user profile by using the Geonames service to extract the location of a place name found in the content.

The *Adapter Manager* component is the manager of a set of specific adapters for each service. It plays a mediating role between service-specific APIs and the OpenSearch query.

The W2.0B clients control the search procedure by selectively activating one or more services. The Adapter Manager delegates on the selected adapters which adapt the query to the specific APIs. The manager will aggregate the results. Furthermore, since these social networks and media services offer specific discovery interfaces, they also provide different response formats.

Table 1 shows the specific capabilities of each adapter in terms of the OpenSearch Geo-Time features. Capabilities supported by W2.0B were shaded in the corresponding cell(s). These capabilities are limited by the functionality offered natively by each specific API. For example, some services allow filtering by bounding box and others by centre and radius. In all cases, KML and Atom extended with GeoRSS are provided as standard geographic formats in the response. In addition, the nature of each service leads to different constraints and requirements in terms of discovery. For instance, Flickr's resources can be queried over time while Twitter's resources are only discoverable during a narrow time frame. Indeed, these open issues pose new challenges in the field of social mining.

However, not all the web 2.0 services have an API from which the data is accessed. For instance wheather information extracted from Meteoclimatic or environmental news from European media sites are analyzed and interpreted to add them information sources. For the time being, the RSS information that is retrieved is related to Fire News and MODIS Hotspots of the last seven days, and it is gathered from European Forest Fire Information System (EFFIS)[52] sources through the European Commission's Joint Research Centre (JRC).

This component also allows the integration of the custom search engine with the most popular web browsers such as Internet Explorer, Firefox and Opera. This custom search engine refers to the Multiquery adaptor which offers a multiple search of each service provided by the W2.0B (Table 1). To do so, we add auto-discovery by adding to the search client a HTML tag which points to the corresponding OpenSearch description document. This tag activates the "search engine manager" of the browsers to offer the possibility of adding Web 2.0 broker as a new Search Engine as we can see in Figure 3.

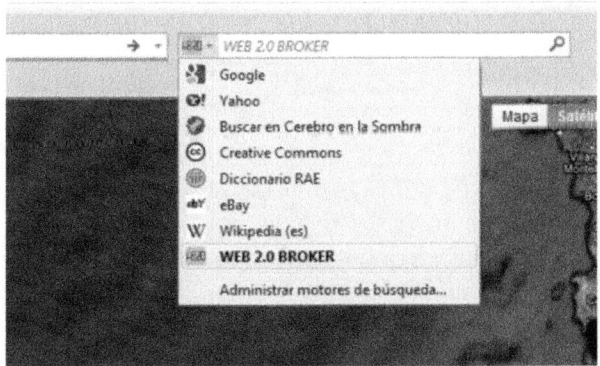

**Fig. 3.** Web 2.0 Broker search engine added in a common browser

This broker architecture configuration is flexible  as new adapters may be added without altering the broker's discovery interface from the client perspective. In doing so, clients and adapters are independent, loosely coupled components where each one evolves separately, enhancing the system scalability as a whole [34].

### B.   Web 2.0 Broker implementation

The W2.0B has been designed as a middleware component with a standard interface to be re-used in different scenarios. OpenSearch Geo-Time is the standard of choice to implement the W2.0B in order to increase interoperability when accessing multiple Web 2.0 services. In this section we illustrate how the W2.0B works when it is invoked. Figure 4 shows a sequence diagram illustrating the workflow of how the different components are invoked when running a query. The W2.0B receives a OS GeoTime styled query such as the following:

*http://elcano.dlsi.uji.es:8082/broker.jsp?service=service&q={searchTerms}&per_page={count?}&page={startPage}&format={responseFormat}&name={geo:name}&lon={geo:lon?}&lat={geo:lat?}&radius={geo:radius?}&bbox={geo:box?}&start={time:start}&end{time:end}&format=datformat*

This adapter injects the query parameters into the specific Flickr API discovery methods and carries out the query. Optional query parameters may be encoded in the URL itself for results pagination, language selection, and character encoding.

First of all, as shown in Figure 4, search clients retrieve the required descriptors via OS Descriptor Manager component.

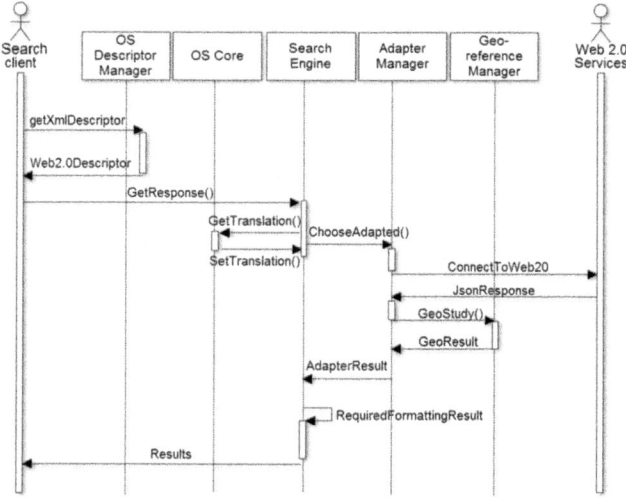

**Fig. 4.** Web 2.0 Broker sequence diagram

Once the descriptor is loaded, the client is able to build and send the OS query. When the query is received, the OS Core interprets it and the Search Engine propagates the query to the Adapter Manager. Afterwards, the adapter manager connects and queries each service by means of the specific adapter.

At this point, the Geo-Reference component becomes important as it is in charge of several geospatial features such as extracting coordinates from a placenames, as well as the inverse functionality, or getting the center coordinates and radius from a bounding box based on the Haversine formula, implemented in this module.

The Adapter Manager aggregates the retrieved results and the Search Engine component generates the response to be derived to the client.

# 6 Prototype: Use Case in Forest Fire Monitoring

Forest fire disasters are increasingly frequent events around the globe. The growing severity of fire disasters is a consequence of increased vulnerability of the natural environment. Forest fires are not only an environmental problem; as a social concern a forest fire is reflected in the social networks. People use social networks in Internet to reveal their perception and feeling. Therefore, it is possible to find pictures, videos, real-time information, NGO reports, and scientific papers in Internet that describe fires, the post-fire consequences and even events regarding vegetation recovery. Our purpose is to include this web 2.0 content to complement data coming from the "official sources" at global, national or regional level.

To demonstrate the added value of our solution to the scientific workflow we will describe a scenario and how the solution is integrated into it. We focus on assisting scientific users in the data collection step so that the user can compare the official information with Web 2.0 content to refine the output and help in the decision making. The central functioning of the W2.0B as middleware can be best illustrated with a practical example.

For demonstration purposes we have designed and developed a web client application to access the W2.0B. This client, developed with Google Web Toolkit technology, offers a user-friendly interface to facilitate users' access to the functionality of the W2.0B in a simple and visual way.

## A. Forest Fire monitoring scenario

Forest fire monitoring is a complex scenario that involves many phases and procedures. To illustrate our prototype we focus on the post fire monitoring phase, i.e., once the fire has taken place, how it will be monitored to evaluate its environmental and social impact. In our scenario the chosen geographical area is the region of Ibiza, one of the Balearic Islands in Spain. In order to monitor the status of the detected fire, the user accesses the web client that provides a map viewer. This map viewer is able to visualize data coming from SDI services. In this context we add some layers to the map coming from the Data Services of EFFIS to overview some official information in the fire warning index or HotSpots as is shown in Figure 5.

For the first prototype, W2.0B encompasses the adapters for a selection of services: Twitter, Flickr, YouTube, OpenStreetMap, Wikipedia and Geonames. Different levels of expertise and quality can be found in crowd sourcing platforms. In our scenario different queries demonstrated that the most relevant information was retrieved from Youtube, Twitter and Flickr services.

The web client offers a simple and an advanced user interface to the user to specify the search criteria and build the query. Users can add spatial temporal criteria by setting the area of interest by selecting a rectangle in the map or by point and radius information; users can also set the time period by what the results are valid.

**Fig. 5.** Screenshot of the EFFIS layer with hotspots of the last seven days

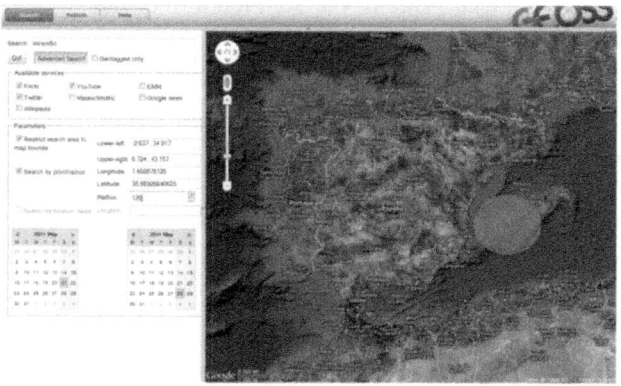

**Fig. 6.** Screenshot of the area selected by the user

In our scenario the user restricts the area of interest to the island of Ibiza, Spain and fills out the time constraint in order to retrieve information about fires during a one week time period beginning on May 21st.

According to the parameters available in the OS Geo and Time specification, the OS query set to the W20B is as follows:

*http://elcano.dlsi.uji.es:8082/broker.jsp?service=fck,twi,ytb&q=incendio&format= kml&bbox=2.637,34.917,6.724,1.450&lon=1.450&lat=38.993&radius=120&start= 2011-05-21&end=2011-05-28*

When the W2.0B receives the query sent by the search client, it is broadcasted to the web 2.0 services that were specified in the query. Users are able to select different web 2.0 services at once to be queried. This increases the amount of retrieved information. In our case we specify "service=fck,twi,ytb"  which means that the

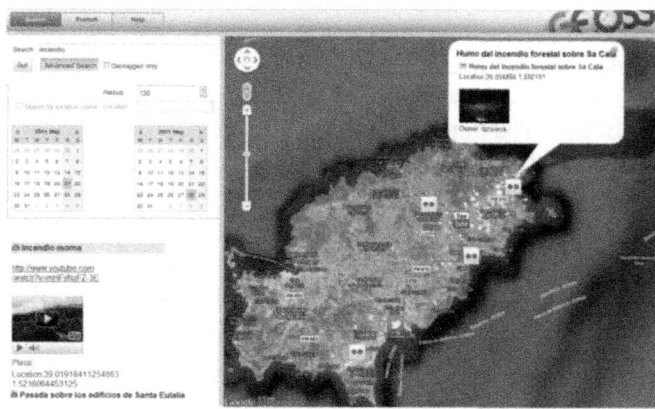

**Fig. 7.** Screenshot of W20B results

W2.0B queries the services Flickr, Twitter and Youtube. Figure 7 shows some of the retrieved results, which in this case are returned in KML format to be visualized in the map.

Figure 8 shows an example of a photograph of the fire in Ibiza. Some other retrieved results are videos about the fire from YouTube, and user comments expressing current concerns or describing other events at near real time from Twitter.

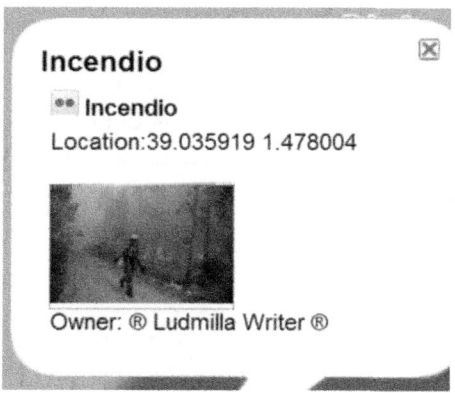

**Fig. 8.** VGI Data extracted from Flickr through W2.0B

## 7 Discussion and Conclusions

The implemented prototype illustrates the current work on the W2.0B. Practically speaking, we have developed a mechanism to collect and aggregate VGI from multiple platforms.

To increase interoperability and scalability this mechanism offers a standard entry point to query multiple web 2.0 services to be integrated [44] and implements a mechanism to use a simple query interface to integrate a set of Web 2.0 Services and improve data accessibility. Based on this previous research we propose a web service, the Web 2.0 Broker. The functionality of this service is to access the Web 2.0 Services functions (search interface, geographic content data type) through a unique entry point implementing a common simple query interface: OpenSearch Geo and Time extension.

OpenSearch (OS) defines a minimal interface to query a search engine that is extensible by adding extra parameters to define other filtering criteria. Such extensions include the time and geo-extension [42] [51] allowing the use of spatial and temporal filters: bounding box, circle, polygon, place name and valid period of time.

OS and its geo and time extensions are proposed as the query interface to access spatial content, both for Web 2.0 Services and SDI services. The Web 2.0 Broker is able to receive OS queries, propagate them to a set of Web 2.0 Services and return the results encoded in standard data formats such as GeoRSS, GeoJSON, KML or ATOM.

As a first assessment of the results retrieved in the previous section, using spatial and time criteria, we have performed a preliminary study that may be used as a starting point for future work. Table 2 shows some statistics of the results retrieved in three of the services. Three queries have been built and sent; the first one (identified as OS row) contains only the term criteria (fire) with the basic Opens Search parameters, the second one (OS GEO) using spatial criteria and the third one (OS GEO TEM) also adds time criteria. Regarding the location information, the retrieved results are handled by the Geocoding Manager of the W2.0B to extract the coordinates when missing, especially in the case of Twitter.

Relevance and accuracy in the content is achieved thanks to the addition of spatial and time criteria to the query. This is also reflected in Table 2.

**Table 2.** Findings of the W2.0B comparative study of Open Search Extension in three services

| | | Content Information | | | Location | | |
|---|---|---|---|---|---|---|---|
| | | Non relevant | Related to other fire | Related to use case fire | Given by Web 2.0 service | Extracted from W2.0B | None |
| Flickr[1] | OS | 97% | 3% | 0% | 100% | 0% | 0% |
| | OS GEO | 92% | 7% | 1% | 100% | 0% | 0% |
| | OS GEO TEM | 8.69% | 0% | 91,3% | 100% | 0% | 0% |
| Youtube[2] | OS | 34% | 64% | 2% | 92% | 6% | 2% |
| | OS GEO | 2% | 96% | 2% | 2% | 98% | 0% |
| | OS GEO TEM | 0% | 1% | 99% | 50% | 50% | 0% |
| Twitter[3] | OS | 29% | 70% | 1% | 0% | 0% | 100% |
| | OS GEO | 14% | 53% | 33% | 3% | 83% | 14% |
| | OS GEO TEM | 12% | 30% | 54% | 3% | 93% | 4% |
| [1] 100 results [2] 50 results [3] 100 results | | | | | | | |

The Web 2.0 Broker aggregates Web 2.0 adapters that translate an original OS query to the concrete syntax of each Web 2.0 Service API. This approach implies the development of OS adapters for each Web 2.0 Service instead of using the proprietary search tools of each Web 2.0 resources. Its advantage is that potential calibration mechanisms can be encapsulated in well-defined components, which directly connect and use the specific Web 2.0 service APIs. However, the search criteria based on the OS needs to be mapped into the specific Web 2.0 service API and this means that we could lose accuracy in certain parts of a query. This may have an impact on the numbers of VGI items retrieved and therefore further research has to be performed.

The wild fire examples illustrate the complexity of VGI data integration where VGI publication patterns differ depending on the considered types of phenomena and the associated geospatial, temporal and event criteria.

The potential of the massive VGI availability monitoring, which is the state of the environment to validate global models with local knowledge, has yet to be fully exploited.

Our work indicates that VGI can be complementary and can provide high-scale value-added information at low cost. Furthermore, this approach could be used to enrich crisis management models inputs or to refine their output results. Further developments of the Web 2.0 Broker are ongoing to improve the means to harness VGI to integrate it into GII and to leverage its full potential.

**Acknowledgments.** This work has been partially supported by the European FP7 Project nr. 226487 called EuroGEOSS.

# References

[1] Craglia, M., Goodchild, M.F., Annoni, A., Câmara, G., Gould, M., Kuhn, W., Mark, D.M., Masser, I., Maguire, D.J., Liang, S., Parsons, E.: Next generation Digital Earth. A position paper from the Vespucci Initiative for the Advancement of Geographic Information Science. International Journal of Spatial Data Infrastructure Research 3, 146–167 (2008)

[2] Goodchild, M.F.: Geographic information science: the grand challenges. In: Wilson, J.P., Fotheringham, A.S. (eds.) The Handbook of Geographic Information Science, pp. 596–608. Blackwell, Malden (2008)

[3] Ramamurthy, M.K.: A new generation of cyberinfrastructure and data services for earth science education and research. Advances in Geosciences, 69–78, June 6 (2006)

[4] Masser, I.: GIS Worlds: Creating Spatial Data Infrastructures. ESRI Press, Redlands (2005)

[5] INSPIRE EU Directive: Directive 2007/2/EC of the European Parliament and of the Council of 14 March 2007 establishing an Infrastructure for Spatial Information in the European Community (INSPIRE). Official Journal of the European Union, L 108/1 50, April 25 (2007)

[6] Coleman, D.J., Georgiadou, P.Y., Labonte, J.: Volunteered geographic information: the nature and motivation of produsers. International Journal of Spatial Data Infrastructures Research: IJSDIR 4, 332–358 (2009)

[7] Díaz, L., Granell, C., Gould, M., Huerta, J.: Managing user generated information in geospatial cyberinfrastructures. Future Generation Computer Systems 27(3), 304–314 (2011)

[8] Schade, S., Craglia, M.: A Future Sensor Web for the Environment in Europe. In: EnviroInfo Conference, Berlin, Germany (2010)

[9] Papazoglou, M., Van den Heuvel, W.-J.: Service oriented architectures: approaches, technologies and research issues. The VLDB Journal 16(3), 389–415 (2007)

[10] Aalst, W.M.P., van der Beisiegel, M., van der Hee, K.M., Konig, D., Stahl, C.: An SOA-based architecture framework. International Journal of Business Process Integration and Management 2(2), 91–101 (2007)

[11] Alameh, N.: Chaining Geographic Information Web Services. IEEE Internet Computing 7(5), 22–29 (2003)

[12] Mykkänen, J., Tuomainen, M.: An evaluation and selection framework for interoperability standards. Information and Software Technology 50(3), 176–197 (2008)

[13] Budhathoki, N.R., Bertram, B., Nedovic-Budic, Z.: Reconceptualizing the role of the user of spatial data infrastructure. GeoJournal 72, 149–160 (2008)

[14] Coleman, D.J.: Volunteered Geographic Information in Spatial Data Infrastructure: An Early Look At Opportnities And Constraints. In: GSDI 12 World Conference, Singapore (October 2010)

[15] Turner, A.: Introduction to Neogeography. O'Reilly Short Cuts series. O'Reilly Media, Sebastopol (2006)

[16] O'Reilly, T.: What Is Web 2.0: Design Patterns and Business Models for the Next Generation of Software (2005)

[17] Goodchild, M.F.: Citizens as voluntary sensors: spatial data infrastructure in the world of Web 2.0. International Journal of Spatial Data Infrastructures Research 2(437), 24–32 (2007)

[18] Goodchild, M.F.: NeoGeography and the nature of geographic expertise. Journal of Location Based Services 3(2), 82–96 (2009)

[19] Bishr, M., Kuhn, W.: Geospatial information bottom- up: A matter of trust and semantics. In: Fabrikant, S., Wachowicz, M. (eds.) The European Information Society: Leading the Way with Geo-information, pp. 365–387. Springer, Berlin (2007)

[20] Díaz, L., Schade, S.: GEOSS Service Factory: Assisted Publication of Geospatial Content. Accepted to the 14th AGILE International Conference on Geographic Information Science (AGILE 2011), Utrecht, The Netherlands (April 2011)

[21] Tulloch, D.L.: Many many maps: Empowerment and online participatory mapping. First Monday (2007)

[22] Coote, A., Rackham, L.: Neogeographic Data Quality – Is it an issue? Paper presented at the, Annual Conference of the Association for Geographic Information, AGI (2008)

[23] Harvey, F.: Developing geographic information infrastructures for local government: the role of trust. The Canadian Geographer 47(1), 28–36 (2003)

[24] Elwood, S.: Volunteered geographic information: future research directions motivated by critical, participatory, and feminist GIS. GeoJournal 72(3-4), 173–183 (2008)

[25] Flanagin, A.J., Metzger, M.J.: The credibility of volunteered geographic information. GeoJournal 72(3-4), 137–148 (2008)

[26] Shade, S., Luraschi, G., De Longueville, B., Cox, S., Díaz, L.: Citizens as sensors for forest fires: Sensor Web Enablement for Volunteered Geographic Information. In: Brovelli, M.A., Dragicevic, S., Li, S., Veenendaal, B. (eds.) ISPRS Workshop on Pervasive Web Mapping, Geoprocessing and Services XXXVIII-4/W13 (WebMGS 2010), Como, Italy, pp. 1682–1777 (August 2010) ISSN 1682-1777

[27] Jankowski, P.: Towards participatory geographic information systems for community-based environmental decision making. Journal of Environmental Management 90, 1966–1971 (2009)

[28] Craglia, M.: Volunteered Geographic Information and Spatial Data Infrastructures: when docparallel lines converge? In: Specialist Meeting on Volunteered Geographic Information, Santa Barbara, December 13-14 (2007)

[29] Gould, M.: Vertically interoperable geo-infrastructures and scalability. In: Specialist Meeting on Volunteered Geographic Information, Santa Barbara, December 13-14 (2007)

[30] Belimpasakis, P., Saaranen, A.: Sharing with people: a system for user-centric content sharing. Multimed. Syst. 16, 399–4216 (2010)

[31] Boll, S.: MultiTube–Where Multimedia and Web 2.0 Could Meet. IEEE Multimed. 14(1), 9–13 (2007)

[32] Editorial, N.: A place for everything. Nature 453(2), 2 (2008)

[33] Tsai, F.S.: Web-based geographic search engine for location-aware search in Singapore. Expert Systems with Applications 38, 1011–1016 (2011)

[34] Nuñez, M., Díaz, L., Granell, C., Huerta, J.: Web 2.0 Broker: a tool for massive collection of user information. Accepted to European Geosciences Union (EGU) General Assembly 2011 (EGU 2011), Vienna, Austria (April 2011)

[35] Walsh, J.: On Spatial Data Search. Terradue White Paper (2007), http://www.terradue.com/images/T2-Research-07-003-OnSearch.pdf

[36] Nogueras-Iso, J., Zarazaga-Soria, F.J., Béjar, R., Álvarez, P.J., Muro-Medrano, P.R.: OGC Catalog Services: a key element for the development of Spatial Data Infrastructures. Computers & Geosciences 31(2), 199–209 (2005)

[37] Naaman, M.: Social multimedia: highlighting opportunities for search and mining of multimedia data in social media applications. Multimed. Tools Appl. (in press), doi:10.1007s/11042-010-0538-7

[38] Clinton, D.: OpenSearch 1.1 Draft 4 specification (2010), http://www.opensearch.org

[39] GeoRSS (2011), http://www.georss.org/Main_Page

[40] Nottingham, M., Syare, R.: The Atom Syndication Format. RFC 4287 (2005), http://tools.ietf.org/html/rfc4287

[41] OGC KML: OpenGIS Keyhole Markup Language (KML) Implementation Specification, Version 2.2.0. Open Geospatial Consortium Inc. (Open GIS Consortium Inc.) (2008), http://www.opengeospatial.org/standards/kml

[42] Turner, A.: The OpenSearch Geo extension, draft 2 (2010)

[43] Abargues, C., Beltrán, A., Granell, C.: MIMEXT: a KML extension for georeferencing and easy share MIME type resources. In: Geospatial Thinking, pp. 315–334. Springer, Heidelberg (2010)

[44] Fonts, O., Huerta, J., Díaz, L., Granell, C.: OpenSearch-geo: The simple standard for geographic search engines. In: Proceedings IV Jornadas SIG Libre (2009)

[45] Flickr.com (2011), http://www.flickr.com

[46] Geonames (2011), http://www.geonames.org

[47] Open Street Maps (2011), http://www.openstreetmaps.org

[48] Twitter (2011), http://twitter.com

[49] Wikipedia (2011), http://www.wikipedia.org

[50] YouTube (2011), http://youtube.com

[51] Gonçalves: OpenSearch Geo –Time extension. OpenGIS (2010)

[52] http://effis.jrc.ec.europa.eu/data

[53] Díaz, L., Martín, C., Gould, M., Granell, C., Manso, M.A.: Semi-automatic Metadata Extraction from Imagery and Cartographic data. In: International Geoscience and Remote Sensing Symposium (IGARSS 2007), pp. 3051–3052. IEEE CS Press, Barcelona (2007)

[54] Craglia, M., Kanellopoulos, I., Smits, P.: Metadata: where we are now, and where we should be going. In: Proceedings of 10th AGILE International Conference on Geographic Information Science 2007, Aalborg University, Denmark (2007)

[55] Nogueras-Iso, J., Zarazaga-Soria, F.J., Béjar, R., Álvarez, P.J., Muro-Medrano, P.R.: OGC Catalog Services: a Key element for the development of Spatial Data Infrastructures. Computers and Geosciences 31(2), 199–209 (2005)

[56] Meteoclimatic, http://www.meteoclimatic.com/

[57] Carrera, F., Ferreira, J.: The Future of Spatial Data Infrastructures: Capacitybuilding for the Emergence of Municipal SDI. International Journal of Spatial Data Infrastructures Research 2, 49–68 (2007)

[58] Jankowski, P.: Towards participatory geographic information systems for community-based environmental decision making. Journal of Environmental Management 90, 1966–1971 (2009)

[59] Dienel, P.: Contributing to social decision methodology: citizen reports on technological projects. In: Social Decision Methodology for Technological Projects. Theory and Decision Library, Series A. Kluwer Academic Publishers, Dordrecht (1989)

[60] Williamson, I.: SDIs—setting the scene. In: Developing Spatial Data Infrastructures: From Concept to Reality, pp. 3–16. CRC Press, Boca Raton (2003)

[61] Masser, I.: GIS worlds: Creating spatial data infrastructures, 1st edn. ESRI Press, Redlands (2005)

[62] Budhathoki, N.R., Nedovic-Budic, Z.: Expanding the SDI knowledge base. In: Onsrud, H. (ed.) Research and Theory in Advancing Spatial Data Infrastructure, pp. 7–32 (2007)

[63] Fonseca, C.R., Ganade, G., Baldissera, R., Becker, C.G., Boelter, C.R., Brescovit, A.D., Campos, L.M., Fleck, T., Fonseca, V.S., Hartz, S.M., Joner, F., Käffer, M.I., Leal-Zanchet, A.M., Marcelli, M.P., Mesquita, A.S., Mondin, C.A., Paz, C.P., Petry, M.V., Piovezan, F.N., Putzke, J., Stranz, A., Vergara, M., Vieira, E.M.: Towards an ecologically sustainable forestry in the Atlantic Forest. Biological Conservation 142, 1144–1154 (2009)

# The Problem of Conceptual Incompatibility
## Exploring the Potential of Conceptual Data Independence to Ease Data Integration

Simon McGinnes

Trinity College Dublin, Dublin 2, Ireland
simon.mcginnes@tcd.ie

**Abstract.** Application interoperability and data exchange are desirable goals, but conventional system design practices make these goals difficult to achieve, since they create heterogeneous, incompatible conceptual structures. This conceptual incompatibility increases system development, maintenance and integration workloads unacceptably. Conceptual data independence (CDI) is proposed as a way of overcoming these problems. Under CDI, data is stored and exchanged in a form which is invariant with respect to conceptual structures; data corresponding to multiple schemas can co-exist within the same application without loss of integrity. The use of CDI to create domain-independent applications could reduce development and maintenance workloads and has potential implications for data exchange. Datasets can be merged without effort if stored in a conceptually-independent manner, provided that each implements common concepts. A suitable set of shared basic-level archetypal categories is outlined which can be implemented in domain-independent applications, avoiding the need for agreement about, and implementation of, complex ontologies.

**Keywords:** Data integration, domain-independent design, conceptual data independence, archetypal categories.

## 1 Introduction: The Problem of Conceptual Incompatibility

The present massive proliferation of databases, web pages and other information resources presents a data integration problem. There is a need to use data in a joined-up way, but mechanisms are lacking that allow easy data integration in the general case; it is often hard to combine data resources. A prime reason for this is that different datasets typically have incompatible conceptual structures. Common practice in information systems (IS) design leads each organisation or software vendor to create its own idiosyncratic data structures that are incompatible with those created by others; commercial pressures can have the same effect. Standard conceptual structures are normally used only in limited circumstances, when imposed by enterprise software platforms, legislative requirements or other external constraints. In the rush to create ever-more comprehensive and powerful IS, the increasing problem of heterogeneous, incompatible conceptual structures has been left for future technology to solve.

A M. Tjoa et al. (Eds.): ARES 2011, LNCS 6908, pp. 69–81, 2011.

## 1.1   Why Do Current Methods of Integration Not Solve the Problem?

Developers have historically faced two issues with regard to integration of systems that have distinct conceptual data structures: physical incompatibility and conceptual incompatibility. Thankfully, many technologies now exist to resolve the first issue, by physically interconnecting heterogeneous platforms; these include RPC, CORBA and web services. Programs can also be linked simply by exchanging files using a common format such as XML. However, progress on physical compatibility has exposed the deeper second issue of conceptual or semantic compatibility: the problem of reconciling implicit conceptual models.

If we wish to use several data resources in an integrated way, they must share both a common vocabulary and a common conceptual framework. This fundamental and unavoidable principle of semiotics [1] may be understood by analogy to human communication: if two people wish to exchange information effectively they must speak the same language, but they must also possess shared concepts. Conceptual compatibility thus runs deeper than mere language; for people to communicate they must interpret words identically, or nearly so, and there is no guarantee that this will be the case. Meaning is essentially personal and subjective, affected by context, culture, and so on.

Getting two programs to exchange data involves a similar problem. A common, recognisable vocabulary must be used by both sides, and the two programs must also have been programmed with common concepts, so that they can act on the data appropriately. Computers cannot yet understand data in the sense that a human does, but they can be programmed to deal sensibly with specific items of data provided that the data is of a known type; this is what we mean when we say that a program "understands" a particular concept. In practice, however, most IS share neither vocabulary nor concepts. It would be surprising if they did, given they ways they are developed and the rarity with which standard conceptual structures are applied. For this reason, linking real-world IS that have heterogeneous conceptual schemas is rarely a simple matter.

In trivial cases it can seem straightforward to map the conceptual models of distinct systems to one another. For example, two programs which manage data about customers might well use similar data structures and common terms such as *name, address* and *phone number*. But semantic complexity lurks even in apparently straightforward situations. Is a customer a person or an organisation? Are business prospects regarded as customers, or must we already be trading with someone for them to be considered a customer? What about ex-customers? Many such questions can be asked, highlighting the inconvenient truth that most concepts are more complex than they seem, when one scratches the surface, and certainly far more complicated and esoteric than the trivial example quoted above. Uniting separately-developed conceptual structures can be challenging even for expert developers working with systems in closely-related domains [2]; it can be difficult to discern what data structures are intended to signify and what unstated assumptions have been made.

Another approach to data integration involves the use of automated schema matching, and tools for this purpose have been developed with some success [3]. But there is an inherent limit to the ability of automated matching strategies to operate reliably in the general case. Software cannot easily call upon context, domain expertise and general knowledge to understand and disambiguate the meaning of conceptual structures [4]. Again, the analogy of human understanding is relevant. When conversing with others, we draw upon our prior knowledge to understand what is meant. A person without prior knowledge has no hope of understanding what somebody else says. This analogy suggests that automated schema matching strategies must first overcome the grand challenge of accumulating and applying general knowledge before they can be expected to extract the semantics in arbitrary schemas with sufficient reliability [5].

In summary, semantic issues make it difficult, as a rule, to match conceptual models between IS—especially since most IS have idiosyncratic designs and complex conceptual structures that are based on unstated assumptions [6]. Conceptual incompatibility therefore presents a major barrier when we attempt to link IS. And this ignores the scalability problem, that integrating systems typically requires a good deal of interface code which must be crafted, onerously, by hand.

Conceptual incompatibility is also a problem for end users [7]. It means that we must adopt a different mental model of reality each time we use a different program. For example, consider how the concept *person* is treated in different software products from the same vendor. In Microsoft Word, people are represented merely as "users". In Microsoft Project, people are considered from a management perspective as "resources". In Microsoft Outlook people are considered as "contacts". Although these different treatments refer to the same underlying entity (a person), they are in fact three quite distinct mental concepts, each with its own meaning and implications.

The same applies to most software applications: each application takes a unique perspective on reality to suit its own purpose. The user is left to mentally reconcile the various perspectives. This is at best confusing, since the concepts may be overlapping or orthogonal, and applications rarely spell out precisely what they mean by any given term. It can also be a problem for developers, who often lack understanding of the domain concepts in applications [8].

## 2 Standardisation of Conceptual Structures

The reliance on post-hoc system integration implicitly facilitates the trend towards growth in conceptual incompatibility. By allowing heterogeneous applications to proliferate, we are effectively supporting the development of incompatible conceptual structures. This is a major concern [9]; "the Semantic Web should not sit on the Tower of Babel" [10]. Some means is needed of limiting heterogeneity or at least of facilitating the job of reconciling heterogeneous conceptual structures.

An alternative to the idea of reconciling data structures is to design IS such that they conform *ab initio* to standard conceptual structures. The use of standardised conceptual structures could have benefits for a software industry which is experiencing uncontrolled growth in conceptual incompatibility and its associated costs. This is an idea with some support, and many competing standards, formats and ontologies have been developed over the years for use in different application domains.

Parallels can be drawn with the development of other industries. For example, in the early railway industry, locomotives and track were crafted individually, resulting in a variety of incompatible gauges and coupling mechanisms [11]. At first, the absence of standards was unimportant, because railways were not linked. But when integration of the network became important, the existing ad hoc design practices soon became a barrier to progress. Standards were needed, addressing not just infrastructure but also more fundamental concepts such as *time* [12]. Competing standards faced resistance and controversy. For example, broad gauge was regarded as technically superior, but lost out to standard gauge in some regions after decades of competition.

Table 1 lists other spheres in which integration has led to the need for standards, often despite conflict and opposition. In all of these domains, growth led to increasing interconnection and this in turn created a need for standardisation. In retrospect, the inevitability of such standards is obvious, given the need for interoperability, and the alternative is unthinkable. Nevertheless, the adoption of standards is often painful because it requires that some or all participants give up their own solutions. We argue that the software industry has yet to fully confront this issue with regard to conceptual structures.

A common argument against standardisation is that a single solution cannot possibly be the best technical choice for every situation. Yet many IT standards have emerged despite superior competition. SQL became the standard database query language, despite the existence of languages considered more powerful and easier to use [13]. TCP/IP is dominant despite widespread promotion of the OSI standard [14]. The QWERTY keyboard layout remains the standard despite the development of more ergonomic layouts [15].

In all of these cases, adopting standards has provided widespread benefits despite the pain involved for those with vested interests. We suggest that the IS field could obtain similar benefits by standardising conceptual structures. Implementation of standard conceptual structures could make interoperation more straightforward, perhaps even offering the ability to integrate information resources in a plug-and-play fashion. The alternative is a future of information islands, multiple interfaces, frequent schema translation operations, with attendant complexity and opportunities for conceptual confusion.

**Table 1.** Examples of Standards

| Sphere | Examples of standards |
| --- | --- |
| Finance | Accounting conventions |
|  | International payment systems |
| Law | Legal harmonisation within the European Union |
|  | International double taxation treaties |
| Electricity | Adoption of AC with standard frequency and voltage |
|  | Use of standard electrical connectors |
| Electronic media | VHS (despite alleged technical inferiority to Betamax) |
|  | Blu-Ray |

Much current thinking on data integration centres on tagging, using technologies such as the Semantic Web, RDF, linked data, ontologies and microformats [16]. The hope is that tagging will allow applications to exchange and process data without intervention. "We're not that far from the time when you can click on the web page for the meeting, and your computer, knowing that it is indeed a form of appointment, will pick up all the right information, and understand it enough to send it to all the right applications" [17].

How feasible is this? Referring to the discussion in Section 2, this kind of interoperability would require both a shared vocabulary and a shared conceptual framework. That means that each piece of data must be named in a recognisable way (vocabulary) and its name must refer to some shared meaning (concept). Organisations wishing to exchange tagged data must therefore agree on a common terminology, which they can map to their proprietary data structures, and they must also agree on common concepts, which they can code into their applications. For an application to possess a concept means that the application recognises what to do with data pertaining to that concept. Asking two software applications to exchange data in the absence of common concepts is rather pointless, since the receiving application can do little with the data except store it.

Microformats offer an illustration. They provide a common terminology (hRecipe, hCard, etc.) and also a series of common, if rather simplistic, concepts that applications can be programmed to share. The development of microformats is perhaps a pragmatic reaction against large-scale ontology development, the seemingly never-ending effort to create universal "conceptual models of everything" [18]. Microformats offer the potential for quick wins because they are intended as simple, uncontroversial conceptual model snippets. They are couched at an "everyday" level of generality and therefore easy to understand [19]. By definition, microformats ignore most of the complexity of real-life conceptual structures. In particular, they neglect the relationships between concepts, which is where most conceptual complexity lies. This is what allows developers to use microformats so readily.

But, while it is easy to envisage agreement on simple, well-known concepts such as recipes and appointments, it is in the nature of conceptual structures to quickly become complex. Efforts to create reusable, generic structures can soon result in hard-to-understand abstractions that are less useful for any particular application. Microformats remain useful while they remain simple and disconnected from one another, but when there is a need for integration to reflect the real-world relationships between concepts, the complications associated with larger-scale ontologies quickly arise [20].

In summary, it remains difficult to agree on standards for the domain-specific concepts found in much enterprise data, particularly when IS are viewed as a source of competitive advantage and best practice in IS design begins with idiosyncratic conceptual structures. Historically, previous efforts at conceptual standardisation have encountered similar problems for similar reasons [21].

## 2.1 Ontologies as a Potential Solution to Conceptual Incompatibility

Ontologies are a current focus of attention in conceptual standardisation. *Domain* (industry-specific) ontologies are now available or in development, each created more or less in isolation to suit the needs of a particular business area. Domain ontologies are normally incompatible with one another and lack common concepts. As a result, matching two arbitrary domain ontologies can be challenging. In contrast, *upper* ontologies are more wide-ranging; so as to encompass a range of application domains they typically include broad and generic abstractions. One approach to ontology matching makes use of this by mapping domain ontologies to one another using the high-level abstractions in upper ontologies [22].

Ontologies offer a potential source of common conceptual structures and may therefore present a solution to the problem of conceptual incompatibility. They can be used to integrate applications in two primary ways. One is by acting as a design blueprint, so that applications are constructed to share a common conceptual model. This automatically renders applications compatible provided that they do not introduce extensions or subtle variations in semantics to suit their own needs. It is therefore possible that conceptual incompatibility could be resolved, if all applications were built to conform to a single upper ontology, linked in turn to an agreed set of domain ontologies, if the ontologies in question remained relatively static. However, the task would be enormous, even if everyone could agree on a single set of ontologies to suit all purposes. Given that reality can be modelled in an infinite variety of ways, this seems unlikely. As one researcher succinctly put it, "knowledge cannot be standardised, since each day more sprouts" [23]. Others have observed that it might be more practical to have a flexible means of interpreting concepts at runtime rather than a conceptual language that is rigidly defined a priori.

The other way in which ontologies can be used to integrate applications is for each application to use its own conceptual structure or ontology, as at present, but to match up the distinct ontologies, so allowing translation and exchange of data. This is in effect the commonly-used approach. However, it seems unlikely that this approach can provide a lasting solution to the problem of integration on a large scale. It does not address the fundamental problem of conceptual fragmentation; as in schema matching, ontology matching is labour-intensive and fully-automated matching is currently infeasible in the general case.

# 3   Conceptual Data Independence

Below we propose an alternative solution to the problem of conceptual incompatibility. Our solution is based on conceptual data independence (CDI), which refers to the storage of data in a format that is invariant with respect to conceptual structures. A primary benefit of CDI is that it reduces the knock-on effects of changes to conceptual structures, so that development and maintenance costs can be reduced. However, CDI also offers the prospect of easier data integration. Below we give a brief explanation of CDI and how it can be achieved, and then discuss how it can assist in the data integration task. The scheme outlined below is not presented as the only or best way of implementing CDI, but as an example for illustrative purposes. We hope that it will stimulate discussion on alternative ways of achieving CDI and their respective advantages.

An aim of CDI is to avoid the need to modify applications whenever underlying conceptual structures change. This suggests that applications and databases should be designed using software structures which are independent of conceptual structures. For example, to store data about customers, one would have to construct a database structure without referring to the concept *customer*, or anything like it. This requirement contradicts current design practice, since one would normally expect to store data about customers in a "Customers" table or equivalent.

A step in the right direction is to find some invariant aspect of customers to use as a data structuring mechanism. The idea of a role is helpful here. If customers are people, then the concept *customer* is a role that people play. Roles are, by definition, transient and overlapping—we play them from time to time. The idea of a person is also a concept, but a less volatile and more universal one. Accordingly, it may help to base our data structure on the concept *person* rather than the role *customer* [24].

In general, mental concepts may be divided into roles and non-roles. Non-roles can be recorded as invariant knowledge whilst roles may be better recorded as variant or volatile data. This idea is represented in the conceptual structures shown in Figure 1. The first structure shows concepts *customer* and *supplier*. In the second, substitution of these concepts with more general ones (*person* and *organisation*) transforms the role into a relationship.

The distinction between variant and invariant knowledge is not a very rigorous one. However, there can be practical value in distinguishing concepts, which are relatively permanent, from roles, which are relatively impermanent. For example, without negotiation there is unlikely to be universal agreement on what a customer is and how a customer is defined. But it is possible to assume agreement that people exist, and this agreement is all that is needed to allow the most basic level of data exchange. Once again, the analogy of human communication is helpful; two individuals can converse effectively if they can safely assume that common basic-level concepts are shared (such as the idea of a person or a place) even if they have slightly different ideas about how these things might be defined in detail.

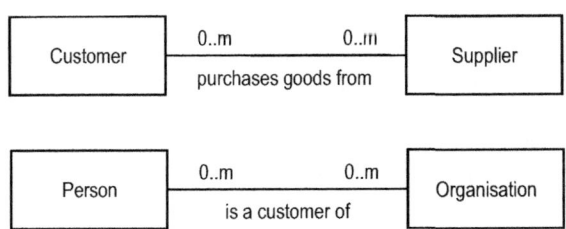

**Fig. 1.** Conceptual structure representing a role as a relationship

A more complex example follows. Consider a software application that handles information about product types, suppliers, stores, customers and the purchases that customers make. In a classically-designed database, the process of normalisation would lead to a separate table representing each entity type. A possible solution is illustrated in Figure 2.

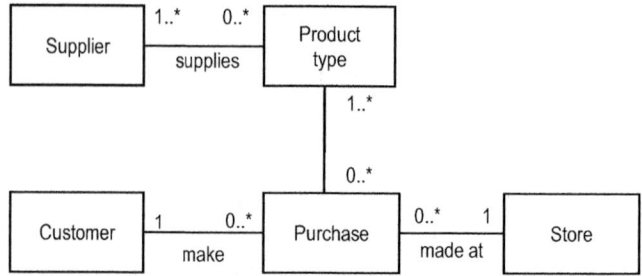

**Fig. 2.** Normalised conceptual structure

We can simplify the structure as before by replacing the entity types with more general categories. To do this, we observe that customers are people, stores are places, suppliers are organisations, purchases are activities, and product types are categories. The result is illustrated in Figure 3. We now have a more general model with potentially wider applicability. Role-based concepts like *customer* and *supplier* have been replaced by more generic categories and encapsulated in relationships.

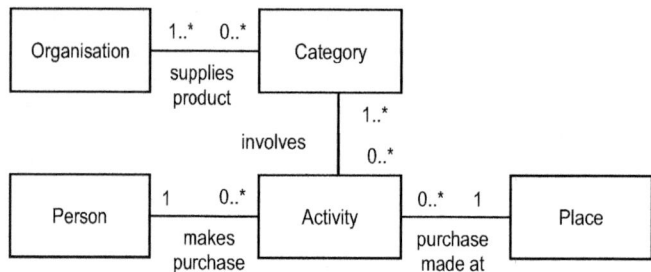

**Fig. 3.** Roles replaced with archetypal categories

Of course, this model is still subject to volatility, because the relationships are likely to alter over time. If these relationships were implemented in a database structure they would "fossilize" a particular snapshot of the conceptual structure, and make it hard to modify or extend later on. One way of avoiding that is to represent the entity types and relationships as data, using a structure similar to the one shown below.

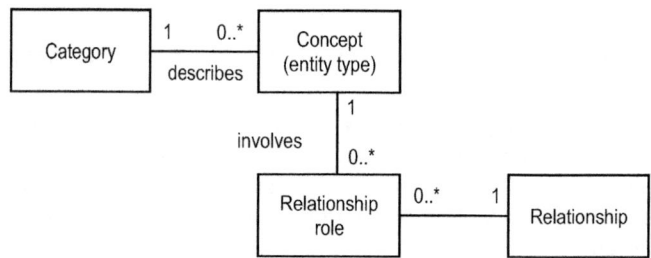

**Fig. 4.** Concepts and relationships represented as data (for clarity, provision for storage of attributes is omitted)

This provides a structure which is effectively a meta-model; it is designed to store conceptual models as data. We refer to a conceptual model stored in this manner as a *soft schema*. Soft schemas can be stored using any appropriate means, including in databases or as XML. The corresponding data described by each conceptual model can also be stored in a variety of ways, but XML is an obvious candidate, as shown in the example below.

```
<customer category="person">
 <name>Joanne Wall</name>
 <id>2012</id>
 <address>43 Tows Str</address>
</customer>
<customer category="person">
 <firstname>Maurice</firstname>
 <lastname>Smith</lastname>
 <id>2002</id>
 <address>3 Yannou Street</address>
 <phone>2273034397</phone>
</customer>
```

**Fig. 5.** Data fragment

Note that this XML fragment exhibits CDI, because it does not conform to any particular conceptual structure. In effect, each instance of data carries its own conceptual structure. The example shows two data instances, and although both refer to the same concept (*customer*), the concept is defined differently in each instance. In a conventional database or application, this would be evidence of a failure of data integrity, and would probably cause the application to fail. But in a system with CDI, it merely reflects the fact that the conceptual structure has evolved over time, or is contingent on context, or data has been merged from heterogeneous applications, or some other circumstance. In other words, such differences in conceptual structure between data instances are natural and entirely to be expected. Any software application which uses this data would be required to cope smoothly with the difference in structure between the two instances.

With appropriate management software (analogous to database management software) domain-level semantic constraints can be enforced including referential integrity, subject to the constraint that data relating to multiple schema versions must be able to co-exist. It is envisaged that this layer of systems software would mediate between the data storage and applications which access it, in much the same way that database management software does.

This ability to store data instances corresponding to multiple schemas alongside one another provides a unique advantage. Because the architecture is not specific to any particular conceptual structure, it allows for the storage of data pertaining to any conceptual structure, and therefore any application domain. The logical consequence is that data could be stored for any *and all* domains using a single datastore. In other words, a single datastore could concurrently hold data corresponding to any number of distinct schemas. By implication, a single application could consult this datastore, responding in real time to the embedded conceptual structures to provide suitable functionality across multiple domains. We refer to applications with this property as *domain independent* [25]. The potential for domain-specific design in such an application would be reduced and the consistency of application design would be increased, relative to current practice. This may or may not be an advantage and is a subject for further research. We note also in passing that the functions of such an application could easily be incorporated into an operating system or other system software.

## 4   Archetypal Categories as a Basis for Integration

The example above refers to a number of basic-level concepts which are considered relatively invariant. They include *people, places, organisations, activities,* and *categories.* This is not an arbitrary list of concepts; it stems from research into the cognitive aspects of conceptual modelling and system design [26]. The list also includes *documents, physical objects, conceptual objects* and *systems.* These basic-level concepts are termed *archetypal categories.*

According to one view of cognition, meaning is generated in the brain by unconscious feature-driven classification of perceptual inputs on the basis of similarity and associative recall. While it had been thought that the brain's neural networks were structurally indifferent to categories, evidence suggests that the mind has evolved to give preference to certain concepts in particular; examples from different studies include people, activities, tools and locations. It has been proposed that human memory tends to converge on such basic-level concepts, which are neither highly specific nor particularly generic [19]. Physical evidence from brain imaging studies also suggests that we may possess a limited number of hard-wired semantic regions into which perceptions are routed [27], corresponding again to categories pitched at a basic, everyday level [28]. We suggest that IS could exploit the familiarity of these innate categories by storing and presenting data in terms of them. Further, we suggest that their use would make data exchange easier.

Ontologies typically include thousands of classes, but only a subset correspond to basic-level concepts. For example, the ontology SUMO contains the hierarchy *sentient agent → cognitive agent → human → internet user* [29]. The class *internet user* is a role, and the classes *sentient agent* and *cognitive agent* are abstract; this leaves *human* as the only basic-level concept (essentially identical to our *person*). In a similar vein, *animal* might be more easily understood than *organism,* and *man* easier to deal with than *hominid.* In our list of archetypal categories *person* and *organisation* could be replaced by the more general concept *party,* but again this would not be pitched at a basic level and would therefore not be so understandable.

It should now be apparent how CDI and archetypal categories can offer a solution to the problem of conceptual incompatibility, allowing the exchange of conceptually-incompatible data. IS could use a small vocabulary of archetypal categories, reflecting the mind's basic-level concepts. This would provide the common conceptual framework required for meaningful exchange of information [1]. If data is expressed in terms of a small list of shared archetypal categories, it can be understood by both parties in the exchange even if no concepts per se are shared.

The example in Figure 5 is a simple illustration of this principle. Both instances of *customer* refer to the archetypal category *person*. To deal with the data, the receiving application would need to "understand" what people are and how to handle data about people—without expecting any particular conceptual structure attached to instances of the category *person*. The receiving application would thus not need to share a conceptual model or ontology with the sending application. The same argument applies for data corresponding to the other archetypal categories: places, organisations, documents and so on. Implementation of this simple set of archetypal categories in the context of domain-independent applications could therefore offer a convenient "middle road", allowing data to be exchanged meaningfully without the need for complex shared conceptual models or ontologies.

## 5 Conclusion and Further Work

To summarise, the argument for conceptual data independence is as follows. Interoperability between applications and easy exchange of data are desirable goals, but heterogeneous design makes them difficult to achieve. Standard design practices create ad hoc, incompatible conceptual structures. This was acceptable when there were relatively few applications and change was infrequent. However, as a result of the creation of many applications and increasingly rapid business change, conceptual incompatibility is causing an unacceptable increase in system development, maintenance and integration workloads.

The idea behind CDI is that data is stored and exchanged in a form that is invariant with respect to conceptual structures; each instance of data carries its own conceptual structure, which can be interpreted at runtime. This implies that data corresponding to multiple schemas can co-exist within the same datastore or application. When used in application design, CDI therefore has potential to reduce development and maintenance workloads substantially, because applications do not have to be domain-specific. In effect, one application with CDI could fulfil the function of many of today's domain-specific, non-CDI applications; the result could be a substantial reduction in cost and delay. CDI also has implications for data exchange; any two datasets can be merged without effort if they are stored in a conceptually-independent manner, provided that both use a common set of concepts. The use of archetypal categories provides such a set of common concepts which can easily be implemented in multiple domain-independent applications, because it does not rely on agreement about, and implementation of, complex ontologies.

Research is proceeding into the use of CDI. One project has produced a proof-of-concept software prototype which demonstrates how the need to modify software applications can be avoided as conceptual structures evolve [25]. Work is in progress on usability testing. Next, it is planned to proceed with the development of a fully-featured domain-independent application in order to test the impact of CDI on system maintenance and data integration. Overall, CDI represents a fundamentally different approach to information system construction; further empirical and theoretical research will be needed to explore the significant possibilities that it affords.

# References

1. Liebenau, J., Backhouse, J.: Understanding Information: An Introduction. Macmillan, Basingstoke (1990)
2. Sowa, J.F.: The Challenge of Knowledge Soup. Vivo Mind Intelligence, Inc. (2004)
3. Rahm, E., Bernstein, P.A.: A survey of approaches to automatic schema matching. The International Journal on Very Large Data Bases 10, 334–350 (2001)
4. Hauser, L.: Searle's Chinese box: debunking the Chinese room argument. Minds and Machines 7, 199–226 (1997)
5. Kalfoglou, Y., Hu, B.: Issues with Evaluating and Using Publicly Available Ontologies. In: Chen, C. (ed.) Handbook of Software Engineering and Knowledge Engineering (2006)
6. Taylor, P.: Adhocism in software architecture-perspectives from design theory. In: Proceedings of International Conference on Software Methods and Tools, SMT 2000, pp. 41–50 (2000)
7. Klein, M.: Combining and relating ontologies: an analysis of problems and solutions. In: Workshop on Ontologies and Information Sharing, IJCAI, vol. 1 (2001)
8. Eick, S.G., Graves, T.L., Karr, A.F., Marron, J.S., Mockus, A.: Does code decay? Assessing the evidence from change management data. IEEE Transactions on Software Engineering 27, 1–12 (2001)
9. Fonseca, F.T., Martin, J.E.: Toward an Alternative Notion of Information Systems Ontologies: Information Engineering as a Hermeneutic Enterprise. Journal of the American Society for Information Science and Technology 56, 46–57 (2005)
10. Fensel, D.: Spinning The Semantic Web: Bringing the World Wide Web to Its Full Potential. MIT Press, Cambridge (2005)
11. Miller, R.C.B.: railway. com. Institute of Economic Affairs, London (2005)
12. Bartky, I.R.: Selling the True Time: Nineteenth-century Timekeeping in America. Stanford University Press, Stanford (2000)
13. Siau, K.L., Chan, H.C., Wei, K.K.: Effects of query complexity and learning on novice user query performance with conceptual and logical database interfaces. IEEE Transactions on Systems, Man and Cybernetics, Part A 34, 276–281 (2004)
14. Maathuis, I., Smit, W.A.: The battle between standards: TCP/IP Vs OSI victory through path dependency or by quality? In: The 3rd Conference on Standardization and Innovation in Information Technology, pp. 161–176 (2003)
15. David, P.A.: Clio and the Economics of QWERTY. The American Economic Review 75, 332–337 (1985)
16. Craighead, C.W., Patterson, J.W., Roth, P.L., Segars, A.H.: Enabling the benefits of Supply Chain Management Systems: an empirical study of Electronic Data Interchange (EDI) in manufacturing. International Journal of Production Research 44, 135–157 (2006)
17. Hendler, J., Berners-Lee, T., Miller, E.: Integrating Applications on the Semantic Web. Journal of the Institute of Electrical Engineers of Japan 122, 676–680 (2002)
18. Khare, R., Çelik, T.: Microformats: a pragmatic path to the semantic web. In: Proceedings of the 15th International Conference on the World Wide Web, pp. 865–866. ACM, Edinburgh, Scotland (2006)
19. Pansky, A., Koriat, A.: The Basic-Level Convergence Effect in Memory Distortions. Psychological Science 15, 52–59 (2004)
20. Heath, T., Motta, E.: Ease of interaction plus ease of integration: Combining Web 2.0 and the Semantic Web in a reviewing site. Web Semantics: Science, Services and Agents on the World Wide Web 6, 76–83 (2008)

21. Graham, I., Spinardi, G., Williams, R., Ivebster, J.: The dynamics of EDI standards development. Technology Analysis & Strategic Management 7, 3–20 (1995)
22. Musen, M.A., Lewis, S., Smith, B.: Wrestling with SUMO and Bio-ontologies. Nature Biotechnology 24, 21 (2006)
23. Guzman-Arenas, A., Olivares-Ceja, J.M.: Measuring the understanding between two agents through concept similarity. Expert Systems With Applications 30, 577–591 (2006)
24. Wieringa, R., de Jonge, W., Spruit, P.: Roles and dynamic subclasses: a modal logic approach. In: Proceedings of European Conference on Object-Oriented Programming (1994)
25. Kapros, E.: Multi-component Evaluation of an Adaptive User-interface for a Generic Application. In: Workshop on Experience, Usability, and Functionality, Irish HCI Conference 2009, September 17-18 (2009)
26. McGinnes, S., Amos, J.: Accelerated Business Concept Modeling: Combining User Interface Design with Object Modeling. In: Harmelen, M.V., Wilson, S. (eds.) Object Modeling and User Interface Design: Designing Interactive Systems, pp. 3–36. Addison-Wesley, Reading (2001)
27. Mason, M.F., Banfield, J.F., Macrae, C.N.: Thinking About Actions: The Neural Substrates of Person Knowledge. Cerebral Cortex 14, 209–214 (2004)
28. Eysenck, M.W., Keane, M.: Cognitive Psychology: A Student's Handbook. Psychology Press, UK (2005)
29. Niles, I.: Mapping WordNet to the SUMO Ontology. In: Proceedings of the IEEE International Knowledge Engineering Conference, pp. 23–26 (2003)

# Health Care Reform and the Internet

Patricia MacTaggart[1] and Stephanie Fiore[2]

[1] Lead Research Scientist,
The George Washington University,
Department of Health Policy,
Washington, DC, United States of America
Patricia.mactaggart@gwumc.edu
[2] Research Assistant,
The George Washington University,
Department of Health Policy,
Washington, DC, United States of America
Stephanie.fiore@gwumc.edu

**Abstract.** U. S. health care delivery and administration systems have undergone transformations that create an evolving demand for health information technology (health IT) infrastructure. The successes of both U.S. Health Care reform and the use of the Internet for Health Information Technology rely on consumer/patient "trust" that information will remain private and secure and recognizing the interdependence of policy choices. Each decision is a balance between ease of use, privacy and security concerns of consumers/patients, practicality, costs and political will. Currently, U.S. stakeholders ranging from the federal government to private companies are working collaboratively to structure this balance. The U.S. opportunities and challenges of implementing a complete health IT picture in our current Health Reform and legal environment provides experiences for other countries to consider as health IT continues to develop internationally.

**Keywords:** Health Information Technology (health IT) Health Information Exchange (HIE), Health Insurance Exchange (HIE), privacy of protected health information (PHI), security.

## 1 Introduction

Health care delivery and administration systems are undergoing transformations that are dependent on and creating an expansive demand for health information technology (health IT). These transformations include monitoring diseases and health related activities at an individual and population level, coordinating care across providers and specialties, treating patients outside of the traditional face-to-face encounters, and tracking patient data through secure and reliable systems. In addition, consumers and providers expect access to real time information at the point of clinical care. Administratively, payment and data collection methodologies demand consideration of various insurance coverage types, demographics, use of quality metrics and reporting, and the use of performance incentives.

A M. Tjoa et al. (Eds.): ARES 2011, LNCS 6908, pp. 82–88, 2011.

The use of the Internet and broad adoption of health IT is growing at various rates across the U.S. and other countries, and there is a need to establish international standards and guidance. Decisions must be made balancing ease of use, privacy and security concerns of consumers/patients, practicality, costs and political will. The overall goal is determining the safest, most efficient methods for health IT implementation within an appropriate legal framework specific to each country, while also developing and adhering to standards that can be applied nationally as well as internationally.

## 2 Background

Health Information Technology "tools" help providers, consumers, vendors and stakeholders achieve efficient care and service delivery. Consistency and collaboration in policy development and implementation for use between regulatory agencies, participants (physicians, other providers and patients), and stakeholders is necessary to fully utilize the Internet and health IT to reach the U.S national goals of better health, better care and lower costs. [1]

One of the first steps is for patients and providers to understand the terminology of the changing health IT environment. Every day, new terms and acronyms are created in the U.S. alone, and their meanings change over time. For example, in the U. S., electronic health records (EHRs) go across health organizations, while electronic medical records (EMRs) are within one medical facility. More importantly, U.S. providers receive "meaningful use" incentive payments for appropriate functional use of certified EHRs, but not EMRs. The national legal basis for much of U.S. Health Care Reform can be found in the American Recovery and Reinvestment Act[2] (ARRA) and the Affordable Care Act[3] (ACA). Each Act created a HIE, but the HIEs are not the same. ARRA HIEs are Health Information Exchanges with a focus on clinical information, while ACA HIEs are Health Insurance Exchanges with a focus on coverage, or payment system, Exchanges. Both use the internet and require a secure infrastructure. Both are consumer centric; however, they are not the same.

Next, it is important that patients and providers acknowledge that use of the Internet expands faster and safer movement of data, but also magnifies potential risks. Health data protection can be enhanced through encryption, role-based access and authentication when appropriately applied. In the U.S. and other countries, electronic health (e-health) information, absent of privacy and security safeguards, is at risk of disclosure through human error such as laptop thefts and inadvertent data posting on the Internet, disregard of personal information, and breaches. Additional internet challenges include cloud computing and mobile devices that collect PHI, such as smart phones, tabulate computers, laptops, and PDAs. Many devices and systems have security capability, but with an emergent system and security rules, these options are not adequately pursued. The potential impact of privacy and security breaches not only involves invasion of privacy and finances, but also the risk of flawed medical decisions with life threatening results.

In response, security countermeasures to minimize and hopefully avoid risks are being implemented at various levels in U.S. systems and standards. They include physical access controls (locks on doors and computers), administrative controls (security and privacy training, authorization, and auditing) to technical controls (use of authentication, encryption and firewalls). (*See Figure 1*). The security process must address all the countermeasures and allow for cross-checks.  At a granular level, systems must reason if an individual seeking access is permitted to view data, and if not, what is the procedure to ensure access if denied? In the internet environment, how does the system validate that the individual is the individual he/she indicates he/she is?  If the individual is authorized to receive demographic data but not clinical, what are the policies and procedures in place to assure how authorization is granted and overseen?   Since the data is transported, how does it remain secure during transport as well as at rest? And lastly, what is the audit trail and who is responsible for managing the process?

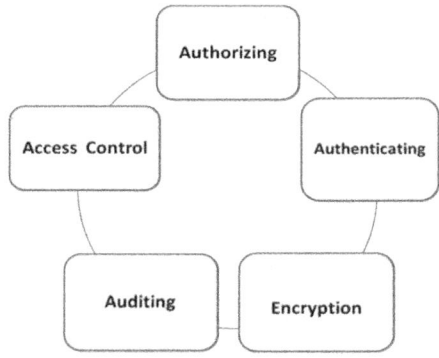

**Fig. 1.** Security Countermeasures for Protecting Health Information

## 3   Privacy and Security Themes

As expected with any field dealing with consumer's personal information, there are numerous policy and operational issues related to privacy and security in health IT. Some concerns are based on perceptions and others on reality, but to the consumer the potential impact is the same.  Current key critical privacy and security themes being addressed in U.S. policies and standards are identified as follows:

*A.   Adequacy and Appropriateness of Current U.S. Privacy and Security Laws in an e-Health Environment*

Privacy and security of health information is not a new set of concepts.  In the United States, diverse federal and state laws and regulations exist that seek to address privacy and security such as HIPAA Privacy and Security Rules, Privacy Act of 1974, 42 CFR Part 2: Confidentiality of Alcohol and Drug Abuse Patient Records Regulations[4], Family Educational Rights and Privacy Act (FERPA)[5], Gramm-Leach-Bliley Financial Act[6], Federal Information Security Management Act of 2002 (FISMA)[7] and Genetic Information Nondiscrimination Act of 2008 (GINA)[8]. U.S. policy makers must examine if existing laws and regulations are appropriate and necessary for the evolving e-health environment.  For example, 42

CFR Part 2 regulations, related to confidentiality of alcohol and drug abuse patient records, was developed prior to a time when chemical dependency was considered a part of health care services.

While the examples are U.S. specific, the issues are the same for any country. For example, Canada's Personal Information Protection and Electronic Documents Act (PIPEDA) and the European Union's Directive on Data Privacy (EU Directive) are both known for their strict regulations and potential burdens that limit flow of patient and consumer information. Privacy and security laws need to be reviewed to determine what is missing, what is no longer relevant and what amendments may be necessary due to the transformation of health care and evolution to "e-everything".

A public demand for enforcement when breaches occur will dictate further development, clarifications and modifications to existing language. Two changes that have already had significant positive impact in the U.S. are: 1) changes by Drug Enforcement Administration (DEA) related to two-factor authentication for prescribing controlled substances that make e-prescribing more viable and 2) Meaningful Use and Certification Criteria Stage 1 Privacy and Security measurements and provider attestation of a security risk assessment.

## B. Consent

There are significant legal and consumer related considerations related to consent. For example, the U.S. HIPAA Privacy Act sets forth rules governing the use and disclosure of protected health information (PHI) by "covered entities" defined as health plans, health care clearinghouses, and health care providers who transmit health information in electronic form in connection with a covered transaction, such as submitting a health care claim to a health plan[9]. HIPAA[10] establishes the national minimum compliance framework, but states within the U.S. can and have expanded the legal provisions in areas of concern to their constituents. In addition, implementation and enforcement varies across states. Consent implementation issues relate to when and how often consent must be granted, the use of verbal or written consent, and the ability of patients to consent to the inclusion or exclusion of their personal health information. . In the U.S, legal requirements related to consent vary by the patient's age (adult or child), status (youth or emancipated adult), location of service (school or medical facility), type of service (behavioral health or substance use treatment) and purpose (secondary use of data or treatment). In addition, U.S policies include additional parameters related to disclosure and re-disclosure related to substance use treatment.

Consent implementation issues are further complicated when certain services can be categorized different ways, such as pharmaceuticals used for behavioral health could be categorized as either a pharmaceutical or a mental health service. The consent requirements vary depending on the categorization.

## C. Use of Data for Treatment

Data must be "near real-time," actionable, valid and credible to be of value to providers. Data that does not easily and quickly provide accurate information has limited value. Factors that affect the transformation of data into actionable information include the security of the data in storage and transmission, standardization of terminology and transmission systems, use of structured versus unstructured (free-text) data, access controls and the potentiality of "gaps" in vital data because of legal or consumer barriers that may result in liability concerns.

## D.  Use of Data Beyond Treatment

Additional and broader patient concerns arise related to secondary use of data for functions other than clinical care.  This includes public health purposes such as epidemiological monitoring, administrative functions and quality improvement efforts. For example, access to eligibility and enrollment into public or private health care coverage is important for appropriate cost-covered treatment in the U.S. and can decrease the administrative burden on consumers.  It can can also be useful for focusing quality improvement efforts and measuring quality results.  The existing U.S. policy issue is whether the data must be de-identified when used for a secondary purpose.

## E.  Identity Management

A sensitive privacy and security issue currently being debated in the U.S. is the use of a national unique patient identifier.  Concerns include increased patient privacy risks related to the ability to secure information about individual, fears of personal data tracking, implementation related issues (connecting to existing records), and cost when other alternatives might meet most of the needs.  However, the cost of not implementing a national patient identifier has also had an impact as significant dollars and time are spent on identifying correct patient data.

From an emergency care perspective, efficient information access saves money by reducing unnecessary testing and admissions, but more importantly it aids physician care decisions. Ensuring that accurate information about the specific individual is easily accessed is very important. This is a critical policy area where the solution is a balance between accessibility to critical information while avoiding inappropriate access or disclosure of personal information.

## F.  Operational Requirements

As with any new area of development, there are known requirements and unknown areas to explore. Providing quick and consistent guidance regarding operational requirements will make implementation and ongoing use feasible for large and small users alike. Security questions remain regarding strength of authentication; when, with whom, and how to use digital credentials, and types of transactions to be authenticated.

Critical to efficient execution in the U.S. is intra- and inter- state consistency through mechanisms such as uniform laws, model acts, regulatory action, and reciprocity laws.  One source for U.S. uniformity is the National Health Information Network (NHIN) DURSA agreement.  The NHIN DURSA agreement provides standardized language related to responsibilities regarding privacy and security controls linked to malicious software; privacy and security rules; breach notification and action; oversight of technology, and compliance with laws.

International workgroups such as the Joint Initiative on SDO Global Health Informatics Standardization continue to develop standards and address issues that arise with the shift to increased health IT. The council aims for international standardization and to make all standards available through the ISO 2000 certification process, which is continually updated to meet changing needs and safety concerns. This internationally available certification process for IT systems, similar to the NHIN DURSA agreement in the U.S., encourages consistency for products in the market. However, these standards meet the challenges of enforceability and adhering to a broad range of country laws.

# 4  Discussion

In the U.S., the technical architecture and capability to address privacy and security issues exists and is being actively addressed. Health IT implementation, in any country, also demands the technical capacity to identify and separate sensitive health information, and to differentiate information according to type, data source and patient. The ability to segment and manage data is technically feasible; however, the demands on technology are complex, costly, and dependent on the granularity (consent by data type) required. For example, in current U.S. systems, access controls can be based on different variables (user, role, location, and group) or be rule-based. The rule-based provides greater flexibility moving forward, but it also requires a complete understanding and agreement on the legal and policy framework, the technical and operational business rules and guidance, and sufficient human and financial resources to assure correct implementation and ongoing compliance.

Implementation additionally involves the more difficult task of developing systems that may potentially integrate on an international scale, while concurrently assessing more local policies and challenges. An example of a current health IT challenge in the U.S. is that due to existing U.S. laws, the most difficult population to address is adolescents. To assure their health care needs are not ignored or disenfranchised, health IT infrastructure must have the ability to address variations in state laws regarding minor consent and definitions of "emancipated". The system must also segment adolescent health records to avoid unauthorized disclosure through tagging all data related to a procedure to which a minor has consented, recording the related minor consent status in a structured field, and transmitting minor consent status and information tags. To add to the complexity, providers serving teens in foster care may release "confidential" HIV-related information to an authorized foster care agency, without permission, but are not required according to existing law.[11] Foster care agencies, however, must release any HIV-related medical information to prospective foster or adoptive parents, but also safeguard this information from disclosure to others. Similar to perplexities created by U.S. laws established prior to the expansion of health IT, other countries may have also or will soon need to reassess existing laws and standards when implementing health IT practices. It is anticipated that countries positive, and negative, experiences may be shared to provide examples of practices to avoid or implement while developing health IT systems.

# 5   Conclusion

As health IT evolves and the U.S. health care reform moves forward, decisions will need to be made on when to enforce existing or create new policies, especially those guiding privacy and security. Providers must adjust workflow related to obtaining and managing consent and data systems. Consumers and patients will need to understand the vast changes to their own health care delivery and administration, and conflicting interests of stakeholders will need to be balanced to get to a sustainable, reformed health care and information technology system. Throughout these advancements, patient privacy and security must remain at the forefront of every decision as they are essential to keeping the system credible, trusted and operating. The current experiences of the U.S. health IT evolution and lessons learned from challenges such as reviews of privacy and security laws, consent and related legal issues, use of data for treatment and beyond and identity management, combined with other international experiences, can help guide future formation of international health IT standards related to privacy and security.

# References

[1]  Berwick, D.: Achieving Better Care, Lower Costs: Dr. Berwick's Message. Center for Medicare and Medicaid Services [Video file] Video posted to,
      http://www.youtube.com/watch?v=YvTAyGoBe7Q (April 21, 2011)
[2]  American Recovery and Reinvestment Act. Public Law 111-5 (2009)
[3]  Patient Protection and Affordable Care Act. Public Law 111-148 & 111-152 (2010)
[4]  Confidentiality of Alcohol and Drug Abuse Patient Records, 42 C.F.R. pt. 2 (2009). These regulations were promulgated pursuant to the Comprehensive Alcohol Abuse and Alcoholism Prevention, Treatment and Rehabilitation Act of 1970, Pub. Law 91-616, 84 Stat. 1848, and the Drug Abuse Office and Treatment Act of 1972, Pub. L. No. 92-255, 86 Stat. 65. The rule-making authority granted by both statutes relating to confidentiality of records can now be found at 42 U.S.C. § 290dd-2 (2006)
[5]  The Family Educational Rights and Privacy Act (FERPA), 20 U.S.C. § 1232g; 34 CFR pt. 99 (1974)
[6]  Gramm-Leach-Bliley Financial Modernization Act. Public Law 106–102 (1999)
[7]  E-Government Act, H. R. 2458—48 (2002)
[8]  Genetic Information Nondiscrimination Act (GINA), § 102, 201, 203, 122 Stat. 894, 908-909 (codified at 42 U.S.C.A. § 300gg-1, 2000ff-2 (West 2009))
[9]  Public Welfare. 45 C.F.R. § 160.103 (2009)
[10]  Health Insurance Portability and Accountability Act. Public Law 104-191 (1996)
[11]  Five Rivers Child Care Ltd. Privacy Statement No. 49242 (2010), Accessed from, http://www.five-rivers.org/privacy-policy.asp

# Integrating Patient-Related Entities Using Hospital Information System Data and Automatic Analysis of Free Text

Svetla Boytcheva[1], Galia Angelova[1], Zhivko Angelov[1],
Dimitar Tcharaktchiev[2], and Hristo Dimitrov[2]

[1] Institute of Information and Communication Technologies (IICT),
Bulgarian Academy of Sciences, Sofia, Bulgaria
[2] University Specialised Hospital for Active Treatment of Endocrinology
"Acad. I. Penchev" (USHATE), Medical University Sofia, Bulgaria

**Abstract.** The article presents research in secondary use of information about medical entities that are automatically extracted from the free text of hospital patient records. To capture patient diagnoses, drugs, lab data and status, four extractors that analyse Bulgarian medical texts have been developed. An integrated repository, which comprises the extracted entities and relevant records of the hospital information system, has been constructed. The repository is further applied in experiments for discovery of adverse drug events. This paper presents the extractors and the strategy of assigning time anchors to the entities that are identified in the patient record texts. Evaluation results are summarised as well as application scenarios which make use of the extracting tools and the acquired integrated repository.

**Keywords:** automatic information extraction, secondary use of patient records, temporal aspects of data integration.

## 1 Introduction

Electronic Health Record (EHRs) are viewed as the basic source of patient-related data, keeping all important medical information about each patient and (in a longer run) providing access to the complete patient history. The idea to re-use the EHR content beyond the direct health care delivery is relatively recent (published in 2007, its implementation is still in its infantry according to [1]). EHR data can facilitate the clinical research and reduce substantially the cost of clinical trials as they provide an enormously large resource for statistical observations, comparative studies, quality evaluation, monitoring the effectiveness of public health services and so on. By default the Information Technologies (IT) are the only means to cope with the large data volumes, moreover EHRs are to be supported within IT environments which provide secure, confidential, and private data access. Therefore, it is important to design research prototypes where secondary EHR use demonstrates the potential of novel, IT-enabled developments for improving the clinical practice.

This ambitious and challenging objective, however, faces the incompleteness, fragmentariness, inconsistency and vagueness of expressions in the established

A M. Tjoa et al. (Eds.): ARES 2011, LNCS 6908, pp. 89–101, 2011.

medical practices, which rely on domain and/or implicit knowledge to support the information interpretation. Patient-related data are recorded in various formats, encoded by numerous medical nomenclatures and classifications, with heterogeneous terminologies, specific national traditions to shape the patient record texts and so on. Much EHR information is presented as free text so the Natural Language Processing (NLP) is often viewed as an embedded technology that helps to extract structured knowledge chunks from the EHR texts. Current tasks related to secondary EHR use seem to be mainly focused on the extraction activities; there are fewer integration attempts which aim at the exploitation of the accumulated information.

This paper presents an experimental integration of patient-related clinical data in order to construct a repository for identification of Adverse Drug Events (ADE) in the PSIP project (Patient Safety through Intelligent Procedures in Medication) [2]. Components for automatic extraction of entities from free text have been developed since much information is documented in Bulgarian hospitals as unstructured text. The article discusses specific solutions regarding time anchoring and harmonisation of data units while the automatically extracted entities are integrated with the Hospital Information System (HIS) records to form a unified patient case.

The article is structured as follows. Section 2 overviews related research. Section 3 presents the background of our experiment. Section 4 considers our approach to integration of all recognised entities, which are available as structured HIS values or are extracted by the text analysers. Event sequencing is important and we present our empirical strategy for assignment of temporal markers to all findings. Section 5 considers the evaluation results and discusses feasible application scenarios of the integrated repository given that it inevitably contains some inconsistencies and certain percentage of erroneous assignments. Section 6 contains the conclusion.

## 2   Related Work

Data quality issues, related to secondary EHR use, are discussed in [3]. The authors consider three categories of data quality: *(i) incompleteness* – missing information; *(ii) inconsistency* – information mismatch between various or within the same EHR data source; and *(iii) inaccuracy* – non-specific, non-standards-based, inexact, incorrect, or imprecise information. The article [3] reports about inconsistencies which are common to many data collections, e.g. 48% of the patients did not have corresponding diagnoses or disease documentation in the pathology reports. The suggestion is to develop software tools for automatic data validation and flexible data presentation in order to support information integrity. This recent article encourages us to continue our experiments despite the negative data quality findings in our training corpus; we apply the data quality categories introduced in [3].

Rule-based automatic approaches for data extraction and integration ensure the state-of-the-art achievements in the construction of large scale resources (over 300 millions rows of data from three institutes are currently included in the Biomedical Translational Research Information System [4]). The mapping rules are created manually based on human analysis, using a large dictionary of medical terminology. Predefined queries are developed in the system to respond information needs. This article discusses various kinds of (potential) application of such an integrated resource which however is difficult to obtain as it requires long years of data collection.

Modelling of timelines is considered in [5] which overviews the six state-of-the-art systems related to visualisation of temporal information in EHRs. Most of these systems operate on readily available lists of type- and time-tagged events. One of the systems identifies pre-defined classes of entities (e.g. diseases, investigations, problems, drugs, etc.) and semantic relationships between them (e.g. investigation indicates problem) in natural language texts [6]. Searching useful information with self-service visual query tool is implemented in repositories containing preliminary indexed full-text documents, e.g. the system STRIDE works on a clinical data warehouse containing information about over 1,3 million patients [7].

As our extractors perform free text analysis on the raw texts in the USHATE HIS, we briefly overview the recent achievements in the area.

We deal with the automatic assignment of ICD-10 diagnoses to free text phrases in Bulgarian language (ICD-10 is the International Classification of Diseases, version 10 [8]). A recent review [9] summarises achievements in the automatic coding of English medical texts. The authors note that software tools for automating coding are "available but currently not widely used, most likely because the systems are still in development and their performance in production is unproven". Various evaluation metrics are summarised and the best result reported is 98% coding accuracy. We note that systems coding English medical texts are developed since more than 20 years; results for other natural languages are less precise; e.g. for French the agreement between the automatic procedure for assignment of ICD 10 codes and the EHR content is 21%, which is partly due to the fact that the diagnoses encoded in the hospital information systems often reflect financial considerations [10].

Another important extraction task is the automatic recognition of drugs and dosages, which occur in the patient record texts. State-of-the-art results reported for English are: sensitivity/recall for drug names 88,5% and for dosage 90,8%; precision for drug names 91,2% and for dosage 96,6% [11]. A measure that combines the sensitivity (recall) and the precision is their harmonic mean f-score; another highly successful extraction system is MedEx [12] which extracts drug names with f-score 93,2%, and achieves f-scores 94,5% for dosage, 93,9% for route and 96% for frequency. The French Multi-Terminology Indexer *F-MTI* [10] achieves very good results in drug extraction as well. Codes from the ATC (Anatomical Therapeutic Chemical) classification [13] are automatically assigned to the extracted drug names. The extraction of ATC codes from the free text of French discharge letters is performed with f-score 88% when compared to the manual extraction; however, compared to the Hospital Pharmacy content, the f-score is 49%. These figures are the baseline for assessment of our results in the automatic recognition of drugs in Bulgarian patient record texts.

The performance of information extraction from clinical texts gradually improves and exceeds 90% accuracy [14]. In our experiments we have also developed different modules which focus on various text entities: patient status and values of clinical tests and lab data. These modules were implemented within a period of two years with progressive collection of the corresponding lexical and grammatical resources, leading to progressive improvement. The extractors were trained via specific procedures and can be applied as separate text analysis components. Our results are comparable to the state-of-the-art achievements in the area, see section 5.

## 3   Research Context

Our experiments in secondary use of EHR content are performed on training and testing corpora which contain anonymised hospital Patient Records (PRs).

### 3.1   USHATE - Clinical Settings

USHATE belongs to the oldest and largest Medical University in Bulgaria and is specialised mostly for treatment of endocrine and metabolic disease. Usually patients with such type of diseases have many complications and accompanying illnesses. In this way many patients arrive to the hospital with drugs prescribed elsewhere (in some other hospital, for instance, or at the ambulatory care, or from their GPs). Statistical observations show that the average number of drugs, discussed in a patient discharge letter in USHATE, is 5,4 drugs per hospital record. However, according to the Computerised Physician Order Entry (CPOE), there are fewer medications given to the patients: 1,9 per hospital record. The drugs for accompanying and chronic diseases, which are not prescribed via the Hospital Pharmacy, are entered in the discharge letters as free text. Thus, much information about the treatment is presented as unstructured descriptions. Similar comments can be made concerning the clinical examinations and lab tests: often the patients bring their test results on paper; the practice is not to repeat recent tests. Whenever the clinical test is made in USHATE, the lab data are stored automatically in the Laboratory Information System (LIS) which is a part of the HIS. However the values of clinical tests, made outside USHATE, are re-typed to the discharge letter for all examinations that are relevant to the present hospitalisation. Another particularity is due to the fact that reimbursements by the Bulgarian National Health Fund are based on clinical pathways; often the USHATE experts diagnose formally the principal disease which is sufficient to associate the patient to the desired pathway. But the hospitalised patients usually have specific, complex history cases. Statistical observations show that the average number of diagnoses per patient is 4,32 in contrast of only 1 diagnose recorded in HIS. Thus accompanying illnesses and complications, which are not formally encoded by the USHATE HIS, might be enumerated in the text paragraphs of the discharge letters. In this way the integrated picture of the patient diseases, history, status, lab data and treatment is presented only in the discharge letters of USHATE patients.

Therefore the secondary use of the hospital PRs in USHATE requires: *(i)* obligatory *text analysis* – to identify in the text the drugs, diagnoses, values of clinical tests, lab data as well as patient status attributes; *(ii)* strategies for *integration* of the various information fragments and *(iii)* maintenance of *incomplete information* – including timing of various events which are not precisely dated in the free text.

### 3.2   Specific Text Features of Bulgarian Discharge Letters

Discharge letters in all Bulgarian hospitals have mandatory structure, which is published in the Official State Gazette within the legal Agreement between the Bulgarian Medical Association and the National Health Insurance Fund [15]. The letters contain: *(i)* personal data; *(ii)* diagnoses; *(iii)* anamnesis; *(iv)* patient status; *(v)* lab data; *(vi)* medical examiners comments; *(vii)* discussion; *(viii)* treatment; and *(ix)* recommendations. This structure provides appropriate contextualization of the

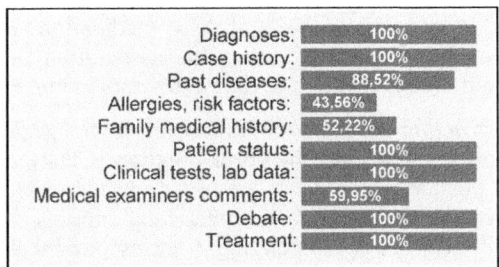

**Fig. 1.** Availability of discharge letter zones

```
... Диабетес мелитус - типус 1. Ретинопатиа диабетика пролиференс.
Статус пост ALC. Полиневропатиа диабетика. Хипертония артериалис гр.
I. ...

... Консултация с офталмолог: VOD= 0,8; VOS= 0,6-0,7; двуочно 0,9-1,0
със собствена корекция. Angiosclerosis vas. retinae hypertonica.
Retinopathia diabetica simplex. макули без рефлекс...
```

**Fig. 2.** Excerpts of hospital PRs in USHATE

extracted entities although it is often neglected because the authoring experts merge sections, omit empty sections, skip subsections, enter incomplete information and so on. Fig. 1 shows the percentage of existing sections in a training corpus of 1,300 anonymised PRs. After our studies in literature dealing with biomedical NLP for other languages, we note that the relatively established format of Bulgarian discharge letters is a significant advantage in the development of automatic analysis for Bulgarian.

Finally we briefly present some specific particularities of the Bulgarian medical language. In the hospital PRs, medical terminology is recorded in both Bulgarian and/or Latin language. There is no preferred language for the terminology so the two forms are used like synonyms. Sometimes Latin terms are written by Cyrillic letters especially when the medical expert prefers to avoid keyboard switching. In general the mixture of Latin and Bulgarian terms is traditionally established and commonly accepted, including in official documents. In this way the automatic identification of a term in the hospital PR texts is a tricky task which requires more than a simple string match. Fig. 2 shows some original excerpts of PR diagnoses: Latin names of diseases are transliterated by Cyrillic letters but alternatively might be given in Latin as well. The measurement units of clinical test are often entered with Latin symbols.

## 4   Integration of Entities Encountered in Hospital PRs

For our PSIP experiment, all entities automatically extracted from the hospital PRs should be integrated as complementary data to the information, contained in the HIS (including the LIS, the CPOE and the Hospital Pharmacy). Therefore we need to design the time framework which unifies and harmonises all events encountered in every particular discharge letter.

The dates (beginning and end of the hospital stay) are set in the HIS of USHATE for each patient. The admission day is referred to as 'Day 0'. All drug prescriptions and lab data, stored in the HIS, are marked by respective dates and hours within the hospital stay interval so the time markers of these medication and examination events are delivered by the HIS. Fig. 3 illustrates the association of time anchors to the entities, extracted from the PR text by the four extractors in our experiment:

(i)   *Diagnoses extraction module* – automatically extracts diagnoses from the PR zone "Diagnoses", associates the corresponding ICD-10 codes and stores them in the PSIP repository;

(ii)  *Drug events extraction module* – automatically extracts drug names, recognised as "current treatment of accompanying diseases", and their dosage. The module automatically associates ATC codes to these drugs. In case they are not prescribed by the Hospital Pharmacy, the extractor relates them to Day 0 (and for chronic diseases like e.g. hypertonia, to each day spent in the hospital day). Then these drugs are stored for the current patient in the PSIP repository;

(iii) *Clinical data extraction module* - automatically analyses the clinical examinations and tests, made outside USHATE (e.g. hormonal tests), anchors the to Day 0 and stores them in the PSIP repository;

(iv)  *Status extraction module* – automatically extracts the patient status' attributes, which by default reflect the patient characteristics at Day 0.

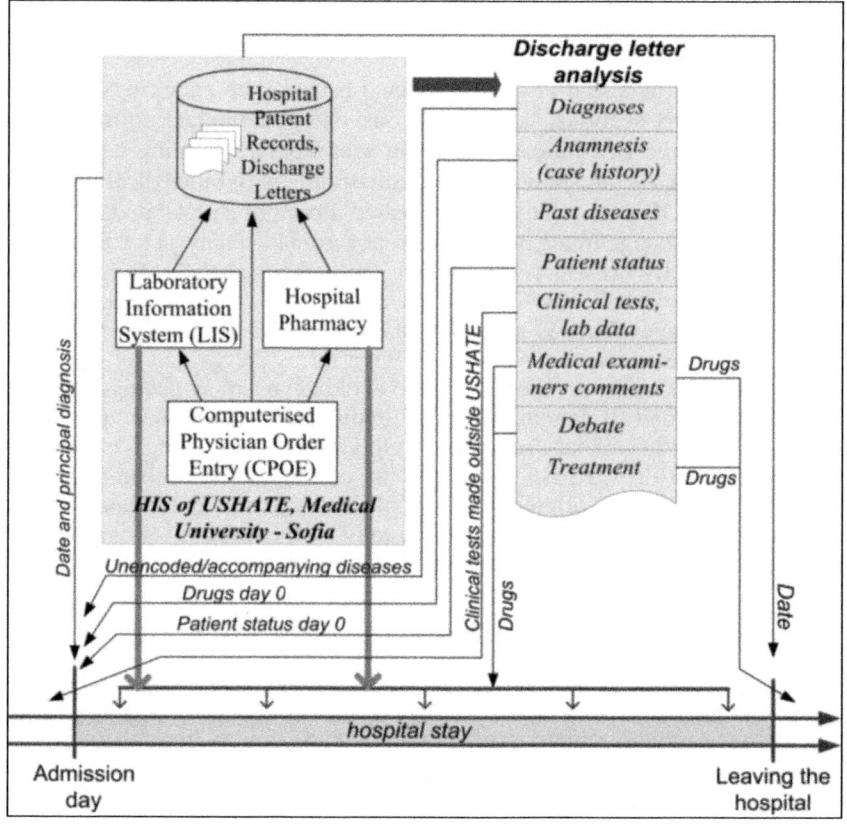

**Fig. 3.** Integration of data and events stored in the Hospital Information System of USHATE and in the free texts of discharge letters

The clinical treatment usually starts at Day 1, so we have made experiments to discover automatically the drugs taken at Day 0. Only the text paragraphs in the *Anamnesis* were considered because this is the PR zone where drugs are listed, with comments that some drugs are taken at the hospitalisation moment. Dosage is often specified explicitly as definition of the admission medication status. The experiment was carried out with the corpus of 6,200 PRs and all 1,537 drugs in our lexicons. In general there are many drugs presented in the *Case history* (30,190 drug name occurrences in 6,194 *Anamneses*). Some 4,088 occurrences (13,5%) were automatically recognised as "current medication" in 3,191 PRs, which means that 51% of the PRs contain explicit statements concerning the "current medication" in the *Anamnesis* text. More than one drug can be specified as a "current" one.

Most often the text expression, signalling the treatment at Day 0, is the phrase "at the admission" (*при постъпването*). This phrase occurs with slight variations in 2,122 PRs (34%). On average 25% of all drugs in the *Case history* are recognised as "Day 0 medication". There are PRs, however, for which up to 45% of the medication events listed in the *Case history* are "current". A sample PR excerpt is: "therapy at the admission novorapid 14+14+14E, insulatard 24E at 22h" (*терапия при постъпването новорапид 14+14+14E, инсулатард 24E в 22ч*)".

The second preferred text expression which signals "Day 0 medication" is "*at the moment*" (*в момента...* ). It occurs in 908 PRs from the test set of 6,200 PRs; in 703 PRs (11%) the phrase refers to explicitly specified drugs in the local context. These 703 cases were encountered after manual inspection of automatically prepared summarising sheets for occurrences of drug names in the *Anamneses*. On average, 14,5% of all drugs in the 703 PRs *Case history* are recognised as "Day 0 medication". Sample usages of this phrase are: "at the moment takes dostinex 2x2 t weekly" (*в момента на достинекс 2x2 т седмично*) and "at the moment treated with physiotens 0,4mg, lorista 1t, isoptin 2x80mg with satistactory effect".

The above-listed drugs are considered as Day 0 only after careful training of the extracting components and evaluation of the erroneous recognitions. Please note that the expressions "*at the admission*" and "*at the moment*" can be used in other phrases as well, like "*therapy at the admission: none*", "*at the moment without complains*" and "*aged X, at the moment 93 kg*".

As an example of integrated entities, we present the Patient Case with ID 26137: *(i)* the principle diagnose in the USHATE HIS is E668 '*Other obesity*', and the extractor discovers in addition E898 '*Postprocedural adrenocortical (-medullary) hypofunction*' and E289 '*Other ovarian dysfunction*'; *(ii)* there is only one entry found in the Hospital Pharmacy (*Metamizole*) and the drug extractor delivered eight records for taking *Metfodiab* for eight days; *(iii)* there are 22 lab data entries in the USHATE HIS but the mining component adds seven more values at Day 0 mostly for hormones.

## 4.1 Automatic Extraction of ICD-10 Codes to Diagnoses

The PRs in our corpus often contain diagnoses expressed as free text (despite the fact that the present USHATE HIS offers menu choice for ICD-10 diagnoses). For the corpus of 6,200 PRs, some 495 different ICD-10 codes were identified in the PR zones *Diagnoses*. Fortunately the zones themselves are presented as major discharge letter paragraphs and can be recognised automatically with almost 100% accuracy. However, in the PR text we find terms, phrases and paraphrases which might differ significantly from the ICD disease labels. The number of diagnoses per patient varies from 1 to about 30; most PRs contain from one to seven diagnoses. The nomenclature ICD-10 with Bulgarian terms is used as an external resource and lexicon for this module.

The main obstacle for the automatic assignment of ICD codes is that the correspondence between the PR diagnoses and ICD-10 disease names is "many to many". There are generally formulated phrases in the PR text which correspond to several ICD-10 diagnoses (like e.g. *hypothyroidism*). Some phrases can be matched exactly to one ICD-10 disease (for instance, *diabetic polyneuropathy*). Major difficulties for the linguistic analysis are caused by transliterations and paraphrases: *(i)* there are Latin names of the illness, transliterated by Cyrillic letters, which differs from the Bulgarian labels included in the ICD-10, for instance, *'Диабетес мелитус'* (*Diabetes Mellitus*) in the PR text vs *'Захарен диабет'* in ICD; *(ii)* the PR texts contain syntactical paraphrases of disease names, often with mixture of Bulgarian-Latin writing, and/or join of various diseases and symptoms in conjunctive nominal phrase, for instance *'полиневропатия ет нефропатия диабетика в стадий на микроалбуминурия'* (*polyneuropathy et neuropathy diabetica in the stage of microalbuminuria*); *(iii)* the PR texts contain sophisticated syntactic constructions, e.g. splitting the components of complex ICD-10 terms and presenting them into various levels of a joint syntactic structures.

For solving this task a machine learning algorithm was especially designed and implemented. A smaller training corpus of 600 PRs was used for manual association of corresponding ICD-10 codes to diagnoses as they are presented in the text. Further the algorithm is automatically trained on 1,300 PRs. More details about the automatic coding of ICD-10 diagnoses in Bulgarian are given in [16].

## 4.2  Automatic Extraction of Drugs

The list of drugs in the USHATE's Hospital Pharmacy is supported with Bulgarian drug names even for drugs produced abroad (in this case the foreign words are transliterated by Cyrillic letters). However, the official list of registered drugs, published by the Bulgarian Drug Agency [17], contains the ATC codes and the drug names in Latin alphabet even for drugs produced in Bulgaria. It is worth mentioning that all the *Application instructions* in the Bulgarian Drug Agency site [17] are written in Bulgarian and the drug names are given there by Cyrillic letters. Note that the ATC classification is not available for drug names in Bulgarian language; therefore we have selected about 2000 drug names (covering the drugs relevant for the USHATE patients in the PSIP corpus) and have (semi-)manually assigned ATC codes to drug names in Bulgarian. In the process of resource compilation for the corpus of 6,200 discharge letters, it became clear that the USHATE patients take 355 drugs during the hospitalisation period, which are not prescribed via the Hospital Pharmacy. The drug extractor is focused on identification of these drugs when they are taken during the hospitalisation period. The information extraction task is accomplished by a rule-based algorithm that uses over 50 regular expressions for drug events recognition.

Recognising drug names is based on string matching which is difficult due to many reasons. Drugs have various names that might be referred to in the PR texts: e.g. brand and generic names. There are variants in writing names, especially for names consisting of several strings. Actually multi-word drug names might occur in the PR text as a single wordform because the other name parts are omitted. Additionally, drug names in the PR might be written with Cyrillic letters, for Bulgarian names and transliterated Latin names, and with Latin alphabet. In order to capture all names during the text processing phase, we need a comprehensive vocabulary of drug names in both languages and both alphabets (as well as the ATC codes).

Due to the highly inflectional Bulgarian language, some drug names might appear in the PR texts with various wordforms. This lexical variety, which prevents the exact match of drug names from the PR texts to the lexicon items, occurs mostly for plural and singular forms. In 1,300 PRs, some 43 grammatical forms of 23 drug names were automatically found by our morphological analysers. Another obstacle in string matching might be due to the typos. In principle spelling errors prevent the correct recognition of all text entities in the PR texts (and need to be tackled by automatic correctors). For 1,300 PRs, 4,042 drug name occurrences of 239 drugs were automatically identified. Some 100 PRs were manually studied for typos. The erroneous occurrences are 59 (1,5%) and the errors appeared in the names of 21 drugs.

The lexicons of our drug extracting component contain 1,182 drug names, which are prescribed via the USHATE Hospital Pharmacy, and another 355 drugs that occur in the USHATE hospital PRs but are not prescribed via the Hospital Pharmacy (the latter are taken by the patients to cure additional/chronic illnesses). Tokens which are part of drugs names occur in the whole PR text; in fact drug names participate even in the zone *Diagnoses* (e.g. 'deficiency of Vitamin D'). In this way our procedure for automatic recognition of drug names finds words, signaling potential drug treatments, everywhere in the PRs. More details about the drug extraction component can be found in [18]. The contextualisation of medication events (i.e. to recognise the drugs admitted during the hospitalisation period) is further discussed in [19]. In section 5 we present new evaluation results concerning the extraction of "current" medication events from the unstructured texts of the PR *Anamnesis*.

### 4.3   Automatic Extraction of Values of Clinical Tests and Lab Data

Fig. 1 shows that the lab data are presented in a specific PR zone which is practically always available and can be automatically identified with almost 100% accuracy despite the variety of section titles and subtitles. The values are listed without predetermined order, using measurement units and their abbreviations both in Bulgarian and Latin. These measurement units are compliant to the LOINC (Logical Observation Identifiers Names and Codes) [20] classification and often enable the recognition of the corresponding indicator which might be referred to without explicit and standardised indicator name. The lab data extractor identifies the tested attribute and its value. The units and reference intervals are desirable features to recognise, and the time, condition and explanation of further details are optional features. The extraction algorithm is based on rules and pattern matching; the rules are acquired after manual training on 1,300 PRs and recorder in different versions to cope with various delimiters and blank spaces, which might occur in the text [16].

## 5   Evaluation Results and Discussion

The automatic extractors were run on 6,200 anonymised PRs. The accuracy for the automatic extraction of diagnoses, drugs, and clinical tests data is presented in Table 1. These events were integrated with the HIS data to constitute the PSIP repository [16]. Recently the repository was used for discovery of USHATE-specific ADEs.

**Table 1.** Number of extracted items from 6,200 PRs

|  | **Extracted entities from the PRs text** | **Precision** | **Recall** | **F-Measure** |
|---|---|---|---|---|
| **Diagnoses** | 26 826 | 97.30% | 74.69% | 84.50% |
| **Drug names** | 160 892 | 97.28% | 99.59% | 98.42% |
| **Laboratory Test Results** | 114 441 | 98.20% | 99.99% | 99.04% |

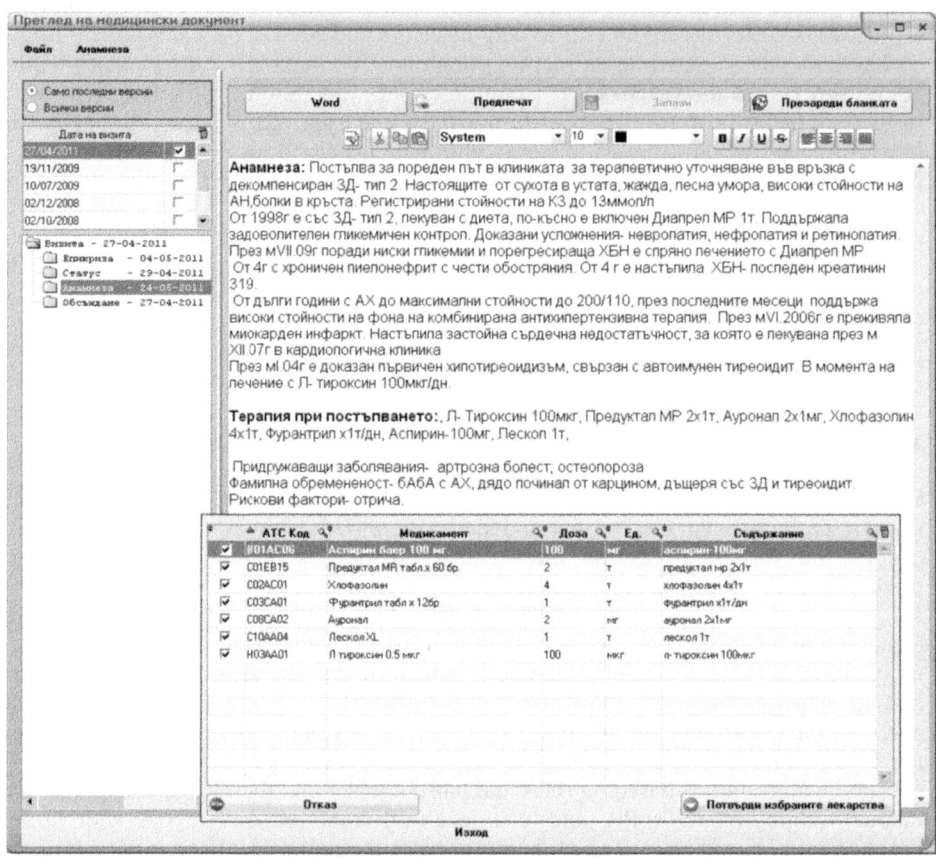

**Fig. 4.** Integration of the drug extractor into on-line validation interface in USHATE

The medication events occurring during the hospitalisation are recognised with f-score 90.17% for 355 drugs [19]. The over-generation is 6%, i.e. some drugs are wrongly classified as "admitted during the hospital stay". These erroneous decisions are made for phrases like *"… to continue the treatment with drug X …"* in the *Debate* section, which communicate incomplete information and are ambiguous for human being as well. In all cases of overlapping descriptions the HIS data are preferred as more exact and reliable. In general the automatically extracted entities have mostly statistical meaning in the procedure of data analysis and ADE discovery for USHATE.

Recently an experimental validation of the PSIP Scorecards [21, 22] in USHATE has been accomplished. Actually the extractors, developed for the Bulgarian PR texts, provided interoperability between the USHATE PRs and the PSIP data formats: once structured information is extracted from the free texts, it can be recorded in various databases using ATC and ICD codes. The validating doctors were quite positive about the experimental integration of the drug extractor as an on-line analyser in the HIS (see Fig. 4). It delivers automatically the drugs taken at Day 0 whenever the *Anamnesis* is recorder in the HIS, which provides structured data in a convenient format that can be further used for prescriptions. Validating the PSIP approach, some situations at risk were found in the experimental USHATE repository (hypo- and hyperkalemia, hypo- and hyperglycemia, leucopenia, renal failure). The integrated repository of patient data, prepared using the technologies presented in this article, is an example of resource which explicates the potential of secondary EHR use.

## 6  Conclusion

This article presents a research effort in automatic extraction of structured information from hospital PRs, performed in order to integrate a repository for experimental discovery of ADEs. We have described our empirical strategy to assign time anchors to the entities encountered in the PR free texts. The integrated repository for USHATE is relatively small but relatively sophisticated as it comprises the HIS data as well as the results of four automatic extractors.

The information extraction approach is to identify entities of interest and to implement software tools which perform partial analysis of the text fragments that contain words of interest. The remaining part of the PR texts is disregarded. Our experience shows that via a rapid development process, one can achieve good performance in several automatic extraction tasks within 2-3 years. To some extent the extraction accuracy reported here is implied by the established structure of the discharge letters in Bulgarian hospitals The negative results (including over-generation) are an inevitable aspect of the NLP performance but they are partly due to the inconsistency, incompleteness and fragmentariness of the medical documentation per se; these shortcomings become obvious in the computer age when ambitious goals like secondary use of EHR data are set. The false positive indications might be dangerous for further use but in our case the small percentage of false positive entities is statistically insignificant and practically negligible (we note that human recognition of medical entities in clinical narratives and data preparation might also include some erroneous choices).

We also note the stable medical tradition to type in textual descriptions even when the HIS stores the prescriptions. Medical experts document carefully information about the therapy and its changes during the hospital stay. These practices make the NLP technology a valuable component in the secondary use of EHR data.

**Acknowledgment.** The research tasks leading to these results have received funding from the EC's FP7 ICT under grant agreement n° 216130 PSIP (Patient Safety through Intelligent Procedures in Medication) as well as from the Bulgarian National

Science Fund under grant agreement n° DO 02-292 EVTIMA (Efficient Search of Conceptual Patters with Application in Medical Informatics).

# References

[1]  Prokosch, H., Ganslandt, T.: Perspectives for medical informatics. Reusing the electronic medical record for clinical research. Methods Inf. Med. 48(1), 38–44 (2009)

[2]  PSIP (Patient Safety through Intelligent Procedures in Medication), http://www.psip-project.eu

[3]  Botsis, T., Hartvigsen, G., Chen, F., Weng, C.: Secondary Use of EHR: Data Quality Issues and Informatics Opportunities. AMIA Summits Transl. Sci. Proc., 1–5 (2010)

[4]  Cimino, J., Ayres, E.: The clinical research data repository of the US National Institutes of Health. Stud. Health Technol. Inform. 160(Pt 2), 1299–1303 (2010)

[5]  Roque, F., Slaughter, L., Tkatchenko, A.: A Comparison of Several Key Information Visualisation Systems for Secondary Use of EHR Content. In: Proc. NAACL HLT 2nd Louhi Workshop on Text and Data Mining of Health Documents, pp. 76–83 (June 2010)

[6]  Hallett, C.: Multi-modal presentation of medical histories. In: IUI 2008: Proc. 13th Int. Conf. on Intelligent User Interfaces, pp. 80–89. ACM, New York (2008)

[7]  Lowe, H., Ferris, T., Hernandez, P., Weber, S.: STRIDE - An integrated standards-based translational research informatics platform. In: AMIA Annual Symp. Proc. 2009, pp. 391–395 (2009)

[8]  International Classification of Diseases (ICD), WHO, http://www.who.int/classifications/icd/en/

[9]  Stanfill, M., Williams, M., Fenton, S., Jenders, R., Hersh, W.: A systematic literature review of automated clinical coding and classification systems. JAMIA (17), 646–651 (2010)

[10] Merlin, B., Chazard, E., Pereira, S., Serrot, E., Sakji, S., Beuscart, R., Darmoni, S.: Can F-MTI semantic-mined drug codes be used for Adverse Drug Events detection when no CPOE is available? Stud. Health Technol. Inform. 160(Pt 1), 1025–1029 (2010)

[11] Halgrim, S., Xia, F., Solti, I., Cadag, E., Uzuner, Ö.: Extracting medication information from discharge summaries. In: Louhi 2010: Proceedings of the NAACL HLT 2010 Second Louhi Workshop on Text and Data Mining of Health Documents, pp. 61–67 (2010)

[12] Xu, H., Stenner, S.P., Doan, S., Johnson, K.B., Waitman, L.R., Denny, J.C.: MedEx: a medication information extraction system for clinical narratives. JAMIA 17, 19–24 (2010)

[13] ATC drugs classification, http://www.whocc.no/atc_ddd_index/

[14] Meystre, S., Savova, G., Kipper-Schuler, K., Hurdle, J.F.: Extracting Information from Textual Documents in the Electronic Health Record: A Review of Recent Research. IMIA Yearbook of Medical Informatics, 138–154 (2008)

[15] National Framework Contract between the National Health Insurance Fund, the Bulgarian Medical Association and the Bulgarian Dental Association, Official State Gazette no. 106/30.12.2005, updates no. 68/22.08.2006, and no. 101/15.12.2006, Sofia, Bulgaria, http://dv.parliament.bg/

[16] Tcharaktchiev, D., Angelova, G., Boytcheva, S., Angelov, Z., Zacharieva, S.: Completion of Struc-tured Patient Descriptions by Semantic Mining. Stud. Health Technol. Inform. 166, 260–269 (2011)

[17] Bulgarian Drug Agency, http://www.bda.bg/index.php?lang=en

[18] Boytcheva, S.: Shallow Medication Extraction from Hospital Patient Records. Stud. Health Technol. Inform. 166, 260–269, 119–128 (2011)

[19] Boytcheva, S., Tcharaktchiev, D., Angelova, G.: Contenxtualisation in Automatic Extraction of Drugs from Hospital Patient Records. In: The Proc. of MIE 2011, the 23th Int. Conf. of the European Federation for Medical Informatics, Norway, August 28-31. IOS Press, Amsterdam (to appear, 2011)

[20] Logical Observation Identifiers Names and Codes (LOINC®), http://loinc.org/

[21] Marcilly, R., Chazard, E., Beuscart-Zéphir, M.-C., Hackl, W., Baceanu, A., Kushniruk, A., Borycki, E.: Design of Adverse Drug Events-Scorecards. In: Proc. Int.l Conf. Information Technology and Communications in Health (ITCH), Victoria, CA (2011)

[22] Koutkias, V., Kilintzis, V., Stalidis, G., Lazou, K., Collyda, C., Chazard, E., McNair, P., Beuscart, R., The PSIP Consortium, Maglaveras, N.: Constructing Clinical Decision Support Systems for Adverse Drug Event Prevention: A Knowledge-based Approach. In: AMIA Annu. Symp. Proc., pp. 402–406 (2010)

# A Methodological Approach for Ontologising and Aligning Health Level Seven (HL7) Applications[*]

Ratnesh Sahay[1], Ronan Fox[1], Antoine Zimmermann[2],
Axel Polleres[1,3], and Manfred Hauswirth[1]

[1] Digital Enterprise Research Institute (DERI), NUIG
IDA Business Park, Lower Dangan, Galway, Ireland
`firstname.lastname@deri.org`
[2] INSA-Lyon, LIRIS, UMR5205, F-69621, France
`firstname.lastname@insa-lyon.fr`
[3] Siemens AG Österreich, Siemensstrasse 90,
1210 Vienna, Austria

**Abstract.** Healthcare applications are complex in the way data and schemas are organised in their internal systems. Widely deployed healthcare standards like Health Level Seven (HL7) V2 are designed using flexible schemas which allow several choices when constructing clinical messages. The recently emerged HL7 V3 has a centrally consistent information model that controls terminologies and concepts shared by V3 applications. V3 information models are arranged in several layers (abstract to concrete layers). V2 and V3 systems raise interoperability challenges: firstly, how to exchange clinical messages between V2 and V3 applications, and secondly, how to integrate globally defined clinical concepts with locally constructed concepts. The use of ontologies for interoperable healthcare applications has been advocated by domain and knowledge representation specialists. This paper addresses two main areas of an ontology-based integration framework: (1) an ontology building methodology for the HL7 standard where ontologies are developed in separated global and local layers; and (2) aligning V2 and V3 ontologies. We propose solutions that: (1) provide a semi-automatic mechanism to build HL7 ontologies; (2) provide a semi-automatic mechanism to align HL7 ontologies and transform underlying clinical messages. The proposed methodology has developed HL7 ontologies of 300 concepts in average for each version. These ontologies and their alignments are deployed and evaluated under a semantically-enabled healthcare integration framework.

**Keywords:** Health Level Seven (HL7), Semantic Interoperability, Ontology Building Methodology, Ontology Alignment.

---

[*] This work is partly funded by Science Foundation Ireland (SFI) project Lion-2 (SFI/08/CE/I1380).

A M. Tjoa et al. (Eds.): ARES 2011, LNCS 6908, pp. 102–117, 2011.

# 1    Introduction

In a large domain like healthcare, knowledge is represented in information models, clinical repositories (databases), ontologies for terminologies, vocabularies, etc. Considering the impact of this domain, standardisation bodies play a crucial role in defining all entities (*e.g.*, terminologies, codes, vocabularies, information models) related to the construction and exchange of clinical messages. Health Level Seven (HL7)[1] is the most widely deployed healthcare standard, which develops information models and schemas for constructing and exchanging clinical information across healthcare stakeholders. There are two major HL7 versions, HL7 Version 2 and HL7 Version 3, later on called V2 and V3. The majority of HL7 applications comply with V2. V3 is emerging and advocated by medical domain experts for greater consistency and interoperability of healthcare applications. Interoperability of HL7 versions is crucial to bridge the gap between two major types of deployments across the healthcare industry [1]. The lack of interoperability between standards (*e.g.*, HL7, openEHR[2], CEN[3] TC/251 13606), and also within two versions of the same standard (*e.g.*, V2 and V3) result in a severe interoperability problem in the healthcare domain. Heterogeneity between V3 applications is usually less critical than between V2 applications because of the presence of a centralised information model in V3 that controls all the vocabularies and terminologies shared by the users. The presence of different healthcare standards, large scale applicability, and limitations of syntactic integration solutions, motivated the application of Semantic Web (SW) technologies and ontologies to resolve heterogeneity in a formal and consistent way.

In order to provide semantic interoperability for HL7-based applications, the initial development stage starts with important questions: how to build ontologies for such a vast and complex standard? Is there any methodological support available for building healthcare ontologies? Unfortunately, traditional ontology building methodologies have several limitations in dealing with concrete applications [7]: (i) more emphasis is given to build a central ontology and (ii) greater effort is invested at requirement gathering stage, that is, consensus building. However, the HL7 standard itself is an agreement between HL7 users. Therefore, the priority shifts from requirement gathering to the reuse of HL7 resources published in various formats and arrangements of global and local ontologies.

In addition to building global and local ontologies, the next issue is to resolve ontological heterogeneity using ontology alignment methods. In this paper we propose the Plug and Play Electronic Patient Records (PPEPR) methodology for ontologising the HL7 standard. The PPEPR methodology is based on our experiences in developing and managing the PPEPR framework [16]. The structure of this paper is as follows: first we identify three HL7-specific features for ontology building and introduce the PPEPR methodology. We describe semi-automatic approaches for ontologising HL7 resources. Finally, we introduce our approach for

---

[1] http://www.hl7.org/

[2] http://www.openehr.org/

[3] http://www.cen.eu/

aligning HL7 ontologies from different versions as well as different local information models. The PPEPR methodology is focused around using and arranging global and local ontologies.

## 2  Ontology Building Methodology

The proposed methodology is scenario-based where ontology engineers first identify an application scenario. All resources and entities identified within the application scenario set the guidelines for further development phases. This scenario-based approach makes the proposed methodology application-dependent. While developing the PPEPR methodology, we considered it important to provide guidance to ontology engineers, healthcare engineers and domain experts as fine-grained as possible to make the sequence of development steps concrete and reproducible. We have identified three HL7-specific features/properties lacking within existing ontology building methodologies: (i) reusability of existing non-ontological knowledge sources such as XML schemas specifications, (ii) layering of ontological knowledge bases, for example, V3 has a globally consistent conceptual model as well as locally designed messaging schemas that enable exchange of clinical messages, (iii) adaptation of local knowledge sources with the upper or global conceptual model.

### 2.1  The PPEPR Methodology

The PPEPR methodology is grounded on existing methodologies and domain experiences. We took inspiration where ever possible from existing methodologies (Enterprise Ontology [18], METHONTOLOGY [6], On-To-Knowledge [17], and DILIGENT [13]).

Additionally, we introduce HL7-specific guidelines for carrying out development phases and steps. The EU project RIDE[4] consortium have suggested a semantic-based roadmap for the interoperability of different healthcare standards and systems. From our RIDE experiences, we obtained a preliminary set of requirements and guidelines for the use of semantics and making healthcare applications interoperable. Fig. 1 presents the PPEPR methodology which consists of four phases: (i) the **scoping phase** establishes the purpose of ontology building and identifies resources that can support the ontology building process; (ii) the **implementation phase** evaluates Semantic Web languages and supporting tools that can fulfill requirements of the scoping phase; (iii) the **modelling phase** provides detailed guidelines for constructing ontologies; finally (iv) the **testing phase** ensures the consistency and correctness of ontologies with respect to previous phases and requirements. Development steps are allocated to each phase, which indicates the order in which the activities should be performed. In this paper, we primarily focus on the modelling phase responsible for ontologising HL7 specifications, which we present along with the respective development steps.

---

[4] http://www.srdc.metu.edu.tr/webpage/projects/ride/

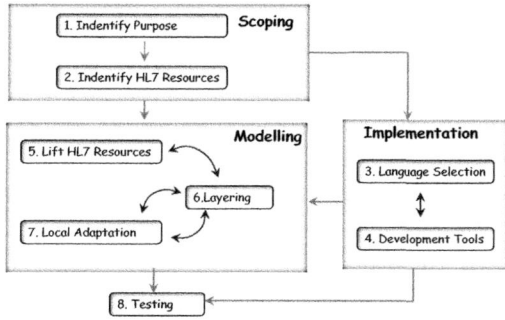

**Fig. 1.** PPEPR Ontology Building Methodology

## 2.2   The Modelling Phase

The modelling phase starts with the task of lifting HL7 resources and ends with the local adaptation of ontologies. The overall goal of this phase is to build HL7 ontologies that have greater conformance with the standard as well as the deployed applications.

**Lifting HL7 Resources.** The Lifting step takes as **input:** HL7 resources in XML; and produces as **output:** HL7 global ontologies (by lifting *coreSchemas*[5]) and message ontologies (by lifting local message schemas).

We have categorised HL7 resources in two types, (i) the conceptual model: artefacts that commonly apply to underlying applications and (ii) message schemas: generated from local applications. The V3 conceptual model consists of vocabularies and datatype definitions available as UML and XML Schema specifications, while V2 has datatype, segment and field specifications published as XML Schemas. Ontology engineers can take two possible routes to ontologise V3:

**Route 1:** V3 UML models are stored as Model Interchange Format (MIF)[6] files and HL7 tools can export UML models into message schemas.

- **Conceptual model:** one possibility is to convert MIF repositories to corresponding ontologies. UML and ontology languages (such as OWL [8] or WSML [2]) have similar notions (*e.g.*, Class, subClass, Attribute/Property) for knowledge modelling. However, one major hurdle for this conversion is the presence of extensive system level information (*e.g.*, when model was created, who created it, machine configuration) within MIF files. It is hard to filter out a conceptual hierarchy from MIF files. Attempts to convert HL7 MIF to OWL ontologies were reported as a tedious task [11]. To provide greater automation to this task, MIF to OWL conversion can be defined using XSLT-based transformation rules.

---

[5] *coreSchemas* are a set of primary schemas containing HL7 message building blocks.
[6] http://wiki.hl7.org/index.php?title=MIF

– **Message schema:** once the conceptual model is converted, message schemas and instances can be lifted from XML(S)↔Ontology using again XSLT rules.

**Route 2:** the conceptual models of both versions are available as XML Schemas (also known as HL7 *coreSchemas*). These *coreSchemas* are arranged in special ways to represent UML notations (Class/Subclass/Attribute) within the XML structure.

– **Conceptual model:** *coreSchemas* represent conceptual parts of the HL7 messaging framework. Specialised XSLT rules can be defined to lift schema definitions.
– **Message schema:** similar transformation rules can be applied to convert message schemas.

We have taken Route 2 where one set of transformation rules (*i.e.*, XML Schema ↔ Ontology) is used to lift both the conceptual and the message schemas without the intermediate transformation to UML/MIF. In the case of Route 1, two sets of transformation rules (*i.e.*, XML Schema ↔ Ontology and MIF ↔ Ontology) are required. However, the advantage of Route 1 is the similarity between UML and ontology languages, which could reduce overall transformation rules. Fig. 2 presents transformation rules between XML Schema ↔ OWL ↔ WSML. For the PPEPR framework we have developed ontologies in two ontological formats (OWL and WSML). Considering the space limitation in this paper, examples are presented using OWL Manchester syntax[7] only. In Fig. 2, italicised schema elements are HL7 specific and other rules can be applied to general XML Schema↔OWL↔WSML conversions.

Fig. 3 shows the XML Schema type *AD* from V3 (part of the conceptual model). The *AD* datatype represents mailing, home or office addresses of healthcare entities (*e.g.*, patient, physician).

| XML Schema | WSML | OWL |
|---|---|---|
| element\|attribute | attribute | ObjectProperty\|DataProperty |
| element@substitutionGroup | subAttributeOf | SubPropertyOf |
| element@type | Range | Range |
| complexType\|group\|attributeGroup | concept | Class |
| extension@base\|restriction@base *union@memberTypes* *attribute@classCode type=Class* | subConceptOf | SubClassOf |
| @maxOccurs @minOccurs | maxCard.\|minCard. | max\|min |
| sequence choice | (..AND..)\|(..OR..) | and\|or |
| *Annotation@appinfo* *hl7:LongName\|hl7:Type* | annotations | Annotations@label\|comment |

**Fig. 2.** XML Schema↔OWL↔WSML transformation rules

---

[7] http://www.w3.org/TR/owl2-manchester-syntax/

*AD* has a sequence of address parts (*adxp*), such as street or post office box, city, postal code, etc. Similarly, Fig. 3 shows that *AD* extends the base type *ANY* (HL7 *ANY* is similar to *owl:Thing*) and has sequence of elements describing each address part. *AD* is the most commonly used element in clinical message exchanges.

```
<xs:complexType name="AD" mixed="true">
  <xs:complexContent>
  <xs:extension base="ANY">
  <xs:sequence>
  <xs:element name="country" type="adxp.country"/>
  <xs:element name="state" type="adxp.state"/>
  <xs:element name="city" type="adxp.city"/>
</xs:complexType>
```

```
<xsd:complexType name="AD">
  <xsd:sequence>
  <xsd:element name="AD.1" type="AD.1.CONTENT"/>
  <xsd:element name="AD.2" type="AD.2.CONTENT"/>
  <xsd:element name="AD.3" type="AD.3.CONTENT"/>
  </xsd:sequence>

</xsd:complexType>
```

**Fig. 3.** V3 *AD* Datatype (XSD)          **Fig. 4.** V2 *AD* Datatype (XSD)

Fig. 5 shows an ontology snippet transformed from the example shown in Fig. 3. The transformation rules described in Fig. 2 define XSD base extensions as *subClass/subConcept* relations and attributes as *objectProperty*. According to these rules, we achieve transformations as "*concept AD subConceptOf Datatype#ANY*" and "*ObjectProperty: country domain: AD range: Adxp.country*".

```
Class: AD SubClassOf: ANY
ObjectProperty: country Domain: AD Range: Adxp.country
ObjectProperty: state Domain: AD Range: Adxp.state
ObjectProperty: city Domain: AD Range: Adxp.city
```

```
Class: AD
ObjectProperty: AD.1 Domain: AD Range: AD.1.CONTENT
ObjectProperty: AD.2 Domain: AD Range: AD.2.CONTENT
ObjectProperty: AD.3 Domain: AD Range: AD.3.CONTENT
```

**Fig. 5.** V3 *AD* Ontology Snippet          **Fig. 6.** V2 *AD* Ontology Snippet

Similarly, Fig. 4 and Fig. 6 show the V2 Schema for *AD* datatype and the corresponding ontology. We notice that the properties of both *AD* ontologies from V2 and V3 have different naming schemes (*e.g.*, city, AD.3). Such heterogeneity requires alignment of datatype ontologies.

**Layering.** The Layering step takes as **input:** HL7 global and message ontologies; and produces as **output:** layered HL7 global and local ontologies. The PPEPR methodology allows for multiple global ontologies so that local ontologies do not have to commit to one overarching standardised ontology. Local ontologies generally originate from different groups (hospitals, countries) where each group commits to different standards/policies. Alignments at different levels (global and local) enable agreement at the upper layer and the resolution of local differences at a separate level.

The layering task arranges ontologies into global (shared by all HL7 users) and local (used within a particular domain) spaces. Global ontologies for both versions can be created from *coreSchemas*. These upper layers are universally applicable to all deployed HL7 applications. To create local ontologies, we suggest using the XML Schemas of locally created clinical messages. The same transformation rules described in Fig. 2 can be used for converting message schemas to

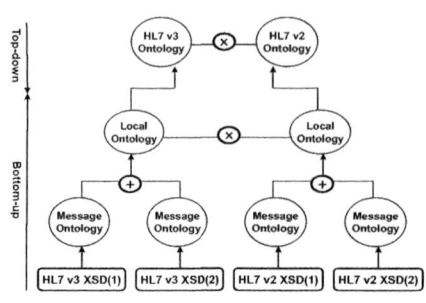

Top-down

Bottom-up

**Fig. 7.** PPEPR Methodology: Layering

```
Class: ObservationOrder.POOB_MT210000UV
SubClassOf: ActObservation
Class: Observer.POOB_MT210000UV
SubClassOf: RoleClass
Class: HemoglobinObservation.POOB_MT210000UV
SubClassOf: ActObservation
```

**Fig. 8.** Lab observation from xsd(1)

```
Class: ObservationRequest
SubClassOf: ActObservation
Class: SpecimenObservation
SubClassOf: ActObservation
Class: Observer SubClassOf: RoleClass
Class: DiabeticType2Observation
SubClassOf: SpecimenObservation
```

**Fig. 9.** Lab observation from xsd(2)

message ontologies. Fig. 7 presents a high level view of arrangement of global and local ontologies. In Fig. 7, a circled plus symbol means that the message ontologies are simply merged to form a local ontology, whereas a circled cross symbol represents the task of ontology alignments where similar concepts and relationships are matched to resolve differences.

The PPEPR methodology aims to reduce the bilateral mappings between local ontologies by using global ontologies: considering the practicalities of HL7 applications and the flexibility that HL7 allows to include/create local vocabularies and codes, it is impossible to completely avoid bi-lateral mappings between local ontologies. Local ontologies are created from message ontologies in a bottom-up way whereas global ontologies are created in a top-down fashion. Two conceptual ambiguities exist between message ontologies: (i) semantically similar concepts are named differently (ii) corresponding concepts are represented at different structural levels. These ambiguities arise because local systems have the flexibility and choices to design clinical messages.

Fig. 8 and Fig. 9 show snippets of message ontologies transformed from *Lab Observation* schemas of two V3 applications. For this paper, we used example message schemas from HL7 ballots (Jan 2007[8] and Jan 2011[9]) and schemas provided by the PPEPR project partners. The different time-line (Jan 2007 and Jan 2011) has been chosen to show heterogeneity between two standard schemas. For example, one difference is the use of codes for *complexType* names (transformed to classes ObservationOrder.POOB_MT210000UV, Observer.POOB_MT210000UV). Codes describe a unique identification of schemas within the HL7 messaging space and they carry a specific meaning. For example, ObservationOrder is a label for the POOB_MT210000UV message where POOB indicates Observation Order, MT stands for Message Type, the number shows the order of message exchanges, and UV is used to denote universal scope. There

---

[8] http://www.hl7.org/v3ballot/html/welcome/downloads/
   v3ballot_schemasexamples_2007JAN.zip

[9] http://www.hl7.org/v3ballot2011jan/html/welcome/downloads/
   v3ballot_schemasexamples_2011JAN.zip

are country-specific codes as well, in that case, UV changes to GB for Great Britain. Our experience suggests that developers use local conventions to name *complexType*, *e.g.*, some use only labels, others use codes, and many use a combination of both like ObservationOrder.POOB_MT210000UV. Another difference between the two schemas is the hierarchy of observation classes. Fig. 8 describes HemoglobinObservation.POOB_MT210000UV as a direct specialisation of ActObservation, while in Fig. 9 SpecimenObservation is a subclass of ActObservation. Diabetic tests require hemoglobin test, however, DiabeticType2Observation is a special test for Diabetic Type 2 patients. It is up to local practices and clinicians in their local contexts (*e.g.*, hospital, lab, country) how they prefer to model any observation.

| |
|---|
| **Class**: ObservationRequest$_s$ **Equivalent To**: ObservationOrder. POOB_MT210000UV$_t$ <br><br>**Class**: Observer$_s$ **Equivalent To**: Observer.POOB_MT210000UV$_t$ <br><br>**Class**: DiabeticType2Observation$_s$ **SubClassOf**: HemoglobinObservation.POOB_MT210000UV$_t$ |

| |
|---|
| **Class**: ObservationRequest **SubClassOf**: ActObservation <br> **Class**: Observer **SubClassOf**: RoleClass <br> **Class**: SpecimenObservation **SubClassOf**: ActObservation <br> **Class**: HemoglobinObservation.POOB_MT210000UV **SubClassOf** : ActObservation <br> **Class**: DiabeticType2Observation **SubClassOf**: SpecimenObservation HemoglobinObservation.POOB_MT210000UV |

**Fig. 10.** Alignment of Fig. 8 and Fig. 9        **Fig. 11.** Merged Local Ontology

A correspondence describing the relationship between two concepts (DiabeticType2Observation, HemoglobinObservation.POOB_MT210000UV) is required to exchange messages. To deal with these two conceptual ambiguities, one option is to provide alignments between message ontologies. However, the maintenance of alignments would be a significant burden. Considering the problem of several small message ontologies and the maintenance of their alignments, we propose a two-step process: (i) merge all message ontologies and alignments into a single local ontology for a domain, which means that each domain is represented by a local ontology; (ii) use alignments to merge semantically similar concepts and properties into a single concept or property. This way, ontologies could be maintained at a reasonable size. This is possible as local systems have more control over their message ontologies than on the global ontology. An additional task is to update references within message instances according to the newly created local ontology.

Fig. 10 shows an alignment between concepts from the message ontologies. The merge can be achieved using general merging tool such as Prompt Suite [10]. When merging is applied to the message ontologies and their alignments, then Fig. 11 shows the output local ontology.

We observe in Fig. 11 that concepts ObservationRequest and ObservationOrder. POOB_MT210000UV are merged into a single concept ObservationRequest. Similarly, concepts Observer and Observer.POOB_MT210000UV are merged to the Observer concept. In case of structural differences, concept DiabeticType2Observation specialises from concepts SpecimenObservation and Hemoglobin Test, such that DiabeticType2Observation is represented at the appropriate level of hierarchy.

**Local adaptation.** The final Local adaptation step takes as **input:** HL7 global and local ontologies; and has as **output:** Extended global and local ontologies meeting local requirements.

The notion of local adaptation was first proposed by DILIGENT [13]. DILIGENT local users adapt the global ontology by introducing local changes and a central board controls the contents of the global and local ontologies. In fact, the HL7 standard works on a similar paradigm where country-specific changes are maintained by respective HL7 groups. A central harmonisation committee (as in the DILIGENT central board) is responsible for introducing local changes within the V2 and V3 conceptual models. Along similar lines, PPEPR global and local ontologies originate from multiple sources, from HL7 standard to locally deployed XML Schemas. The local adaptation step is motivated by normal practices where HL7 applications diverge from the standard guidelines by modifying local XML Schemas and by introducing local vocabularies. The local adaptation phase ensures that: (i) local ontologies are generalised enough to resemble the concepts defined in the global ontology, and (ii) global ontologies are specialised enough to resemble the concepts defined in the local ontologies. Local concepts generally represent the consensus of a local group. Consequently, their understanding is limited to the local environment.

```
Class: ActObservation SubClassOf: Act
Class: ActSpecimenObservation SubClassOf: ActObservation
Class: ActGenomicObservation SubClassOf: ActObservation
Class: ActClinicalTrial SubClassOf: ActObservation
Class: ActCondition SubClassOf: ActObservation
```

**Fig. 12.** Snippet of Global Ontology (V3)

Fig. 12 shows a snippet of the global ontology (V3). The axioms describe top level concepts of the local ontologies shown in Fig. 8 and Fig. 9. For example, "ActObservation" class represents all types of clinical observations possible within a clinical environment and "ActGenomicObservation", "ActClinicalTrial", "ActSpecimenObservation", etc. are specialisations of "ActObservation". Each of the these specialisations requires "lab test order" in different clinical scenarios. The local concept "ObservationRequest" (see Fig. 9) is eligible to inherit from many of these specialisations. In addition to the local adaptation proposed by DILIGENT, the PPEPR methodology suggests three approaches for the adaptation of the local concept "ObservationRequest". These three approaches are refinements of approaches proposed in the Enterprise Ontology [18]:

*Top-Down* extend the global ontology with more specialised concepts that resemble the concepts defined in local ontologies. For example, each of the concepts "ActGenomicObservation" and "ActClinicalTrial" could further be extended with a lab specific concept like "ActClinicalTrialLabObservation" or "ActGenomicLabObservation", to represent that all lab tests specific to clinical trials are denoted by "ActClinicalTrialLabObservation".

*Bottom-Up* extend the local ontology with more generalised concepts that resemble the concepts defined in the global ontology. For example, a super class "ActClinicalTrialLabObservation" for the local concept "ObservationRequest" can be added to the local ontology, so appropriate inheritance like "ActClinicalTrialLabObservation" subClassof "ActClinicalTrial" could be established in the local ontology. For instance, DiabeticType2Observation in Fig. 9 is a local concept and inherited from super class "ActObservation" via "SpecimenObservation".

*Middle-Out* concepts in the global ontology ("ActGenomicObservation" or "ActClinicalTrial") are defined at a higher level of abstraction, which allows local concepts to inherit from all of them. Therefore, instead of specialising or generalising global or local concepts, another approach is to add a specialised class for "Lab Test" on the same level as the above two concepts. For example, Alpha fetoprotein (AFP) is an observation for detecting liver cancer, and V3 (Jan 2011 Ballot) does not include any specialised classes for cancer diseases. It may be appropriate to add "CancerObservation" on a similar level to "ActGenomicObservation" or "ActClinicalTrial", and then extending "CancerObservation" with an "AlphaFetoproteinObservation" concept.

These three approaches could be applied independently or in combinations depending on requirements from different clinical scenarios. Enterprise Ontology suggested the middle-out approach. However, considering the heterogeneities of different clinical scenarios, we intentionally avoid any "fit-for-all" suggestion.

# 3   Aligning HL7 Ontologies

The integration and alignment of ontologies is a well-investigated fundamental problem in the development of Semantic Web techniques. Obviously, just using ontologies instead of XML, does not defeat heterogeneity: it just raises heterogeneity problems to a higher level with a hope for easier integration. Analogous to schema matching and mapping techniques, ontology matching methods have been proposed to deal with ontological heterogeneity. Ontology matching consists of finding the correspondences (*e.g.*, equivalence, subsumption) between elements of ontologies (classes, properties). This is an important task because it helps establishing actual interoperability. It is also a difficult task because (i) independently built ontologies can vary significantly in the terminology they use and the way they model the same entities; and (ii) domain ontologies focus on a particular domain and use terms in a sense that is relevant to the domain and which are not related to similar concepts in other domains.

Most research in the ontology matching [5] area has focused on (semi-) automatically aligning ontologies using approaches based on combinations of syntactic similarity, graph similarity, and using a third upper level ontology. In many cases, linguistic and structural matchings are used in conjunction with an upper level ontology (*e.g.*, CYC[10]) as a common layer for two ontologies to be matched.

---

[10] http://www.cyc.com/

The (semi-)automated approaches of linguistic and structural matchings, typically give an incomplete or incorrect set of correspondences between terms. A human must align the remaining terms and check the machine-built alignments to truly complete the alignment process. Our work places emphasis on exploiting alignment methods to provide valuable insight to the alignment process and improve accuracy. In particular, we want to investigate how "fit" generic ontology alignment methods are for our relatively straightforwardly created HL7 V2 and V3 ontologies: as described in Fig. 8 and Fig. 9, *Lab Observation* concepts are modelled differently within V3. Similarly, Fig. 5 and Fig. 6 show differences in the *AD* datatype of V2 and V3. Fig. 13 shows XSD for the range class (AD.3.CONTENT) of the AD.3 *objectProperty*. The class AD.3.CONTENT is *equivalent* to the class Adxp.city of Fig. 5.

```
<xsd:complexType name="AD.3.CONTENT">
   <xsd:annotation>
     <xsd:appinfo>
       <hl7:Type>ST</hl7:Type>
       <hl7:LongName>City</hl7:LongName>
     </xsd:appinfo>
   </xsd:annotation>
   ...
```

**Fig. 13.** V2 XSD Annotations

We notice that V3 class names (*e.g.*, Adxp.city, Adxp.country, ObservationRequest) are self-descriptive, while V2 class names are coded (*e.g.*, AD.1, AD.1.CONTENT) with descriptions attached as annotations (*e.g.*, hl7:Type or hl7:LongName of Fig. 13). We evaluated three ontology matching tools, namely, Anchor-Prompt [10], Falcon-AO [9], and H-Match [3]. We have selected these three matching tools because we had experience with them and they offer stable and easy testing environments. Matching evaluations are conducted in two categories: (i) finding matches within the same version (*e.g.*, Fig. 8 and Fig. 9 of V3), (ii) finding matches between two versions (*e.g.*, Fig. 5 and Fig. 6 of V3 and V2). Evaluation tests are conducted on full ontologies as well as subparts of ontologies to analyse performance vs. result output.

## 4    Ontology Matching Evaluation

**Anchor-PROMPT** is an ontology mapper that attempts to automatically find semantically similar terms between two ontologies. Anchor-PROMPT uses a graph-based approach where an ontology is taken as a directed labelled graph. Anchor-PROMPT takes as input a set of pairs of related terms, called "anchors", from the source ontologies. These anchors are identified before triggering the matching task; either the user enters them or the system automatically generates them. Based on this set of anchors, Anchor-PROMPT produces a set of pairs of semantically close terms.

**Falcon-AO** is an ontology matching system for finding, aligning and learning ontologies. Falcon-AO is a similarity-based generic ontology mapping system. It consists of two elementary matchers: one is a matcher based on linguistic matching for ontologies, called Linguistic Matching for Ontologies (LMO); the other is a matcher based on graph matching for ontologies, called Graph Matching for Ontologies (GMO). GMO takes the alignments generated by LMO as external input and outputs additional alignments. Linguistic similarity between two entities relies on their names, labels, comments and other descriptions.

**H-Match** performs ontology matching at different levels of depth by deploying four different matching models, namely, *surface, shallow, deep,* and *intensive.* In H-Match a threshold-based mechanism is enforced to set the minimum level of semantic affinity required to consider two concepts as matching concepts. The linguistic affinity function of H-Match provides a measure of similarity between two ontology concepts computed on the basis of their linguistic features (*e.g.*, concept names). For the linguistic affinity evaluation, H-Match relies on a thesaurus of terms and terminological relationships automatically extracted from the *WordNet*[11] lexical system. The contextual affinity function of H-Match provides a measure of similarity by taking into account the contextual features of the ontology concepts. The context of a concept can include properties, relations with other concepts, and property values.

Fig. 14 shows matching results of V2 and V3 ontologies. The second column describes matching between V3 ontologies and the fourth column shows the accuracy of V2 and V3 ontology matching. In the second column, matching ontologies (*i.e.*, local message ontologies for V3) include "common concepts" inherited from the global reference ontology. In the fourth column, global ontologies of different versions (V2 and V3) are matched, which means "common concepts" are irrelevant and concepts are different in terms of their names or structure. The percentage denotes a *precision (p)* and a *recall (r)* measurements for evaluating accuracy of matches discovered. Precision indicates the "correctness" and recall measures the "completeness" of matching results. Both parameters are measured against the reference alignment $R$ with alignment $A$ returned by the matching tools, where $p = \frac{|R \cap A|}{|A|}$ and $r = \frac{|R \cap A|}{|R|}$. In our case the two input ontologies with 310 and 290 concepts have 200 prospective matching concepts (*i.e.*, reference alignment $R$). The third and last columns show the size (*i.e.*, total number of concepts excluding properties) of ontologies and their subparts.

| Method/Tool | HL7 (V3 –V3) precision-recall | Ontology/Subpart HL7V3 | HL7 (V2-V3) precision-recall | Ontology/Subpart HL7 (V2-V3) | Threshold Value |
|---|---|---|---|---|---|
| Anchor-Prompt | 90%-30% | 310/50 | 90%-10% | 290/50-310/50 | Varies |
| Falcon-AO | 70%-50% | 310/50 | 30%-20% | 290/50-310/50 | 0.01 |
| HMatch | 80%-90% | 310/50 | 40%-20% | 290/50-310/50 | 0.5 |
| SPARQL Recipes | 80%-90% | 310/50 | 50%-60% | 290/50-310/50 | |

**Fig. 14.** Matching Evaluation

---

[11] http://wordnet.princeton.edu/

We observe in Fig. 14 that matching results are significantly different between second and fourth columns. For example, Anchor-Prompt has higher $p=90\%$ and lower $r = 30\%$, which indicates that the completeness of alignments is lower. Precision is higher due to obvious matches (the common concepts) from the reference ontology and negligible *false positives* in the alignment between local concepts. Similarly, in the fourth column, Anchor-Prompt recall value is much lower as obvious matches between V2 and V3 are negligible. Precision is higher because of few exact matches between datatypes (*e.g.*, AD of V2 and V3) concepts. The fifth column shows the threshold values for deciding concept equivalent: Anchor-Prompt defines it at run-time, depending on path length and set of anchors; Falcon-AO value (0.01) is fixed by the tool itself; H-Match allows one to select a value between 0 and 1, we opted the default value (0.5). Falcon-AO and H-Match have significantly improved recall for the second column (*i.e.*, 50% and 90%), however, precision falls because of higher *false positives*. H-Match precision and recall ratios are best because it has different levels of matching and we noted the best matches (*intensive* matching). However, *intensive* matching shows greater delays with ontologies of size greater than 50 concepts. This is the reason we have used smaller subparts of ontologies to determine the overall performance and matching results. Unfortunately, the recall measurement for the fourth column is quite low. This is due to the naming scheme (coded for V2 vs. self-descriptive names V3 ontologies). For example, AD of V3 matches with AD, AD.1, AD.1.CONTENT, AD.2.CONTENT concepts of V2, which makes *false positives* within the alignment higher, thus, precision lower.

## 5   SPARQL Recipes

Instead of relying on automated alignments, a simple query-based method for expressing customised and complex alignments between ontologies has been proposed in [14,4] using the SPARQL query language. We have employed this approach specifically to manually match V2 and V3 ontologies.

Surprisingly, a single, generic SPARQL query that matches concept names of the V3 ontology against *LongName* (the label annotations) of the V2 ontology outperforms all automatic mapping attempts. We notice in Fig. 13 that the annotation of *hl7:LongName* ("City") is a substring of the concept named Adxp.city from Fig. 5; this mapping from the annotation in onto the concept name by substrings is a recurring pattern in mappings between V2 and V3. Similarly, HL7 ontologies contain several other "simple patterns" that can guide us in determining correspondences between ontological elements. A domain expert is required to analyse and identify such "simple patterns". Fig. 15 shows a "simple pattern" created as a "SPARQL recipe":

```
CONSTRUCT { ?v3 owl:equivalentClass ?v2 } WHERE { ?v3 rdf:type owl:Class . ?v2 rdf:type owl:Class .
?v2 rdfs:label ?LongName . { FILTER regex(str(?v3), str(?LongName), "i")}}
```

**Fig. 15.** SPARQL Recipe for Ontology Matching

By employing this simple "SPARQL recipe", we observed significant successful matching results for classes that share similarity but are described and modelled differently. SPARQL recipes matching results are similar to H-Match (*precision* 80%, *recall* 90%) for V3 ontologies (second column of Fig. 14) and significantly improved *precision (p)* 50% and *recall(r)* 60% for V2 and V3 ontologies. However, a major limitation of "recipes" is lack of standard matching measures, like threshold, similarity coefficient, etc. Recipes can be created by domain experts after analysing similarities between ontological elements in HL7. As opposed to alignment algorithms that usually just search for simpler alignments, such recipes can express complex correspondences between ontology instances, involving built-in function calls, etc. For example, it allows one to express complex correspondences such as concatenating attributes (*e.g.*, first/last names, dates) and express complex interactions between knowledge of various sources. Similarly, complex correspondences could be expressed in the Rule Interchange Format (RIF)[12], which offers a rich set of built-in functions (*e.g.*, string manipulations), as well as a formal semantics for interoperating with RDF and OWL knowledge bases. RIF has been recently approved as a W3C standard recommendation and we consider it as a prominent candidate to express alignments over ontologies.

## 6   Related Works

The first release of the ANSI normative V3[13] was published in 2003. Since then, ontology engineers have taken initiatives to ontologise V3. To the best of our knowledge, the EU Project Artemis [1] is the only significant contribution for ontologising both V3 and V2. In 2003, Bhavana Orgun has developed V3 ontology using the RDFS language [12]. The main contribution of Orgun's work is to identify important sets of ontological concepts and properties from the V3 artefacts. In 2008, Helen Chan from W3C HCLS IG[14] published V3 ontology. Chan's work has improved Orgun's ontology by covering a broader range of artefacts from the V3. In 2009, Alan Rector [15] proposed to align V3 artefacts with other standard medical vocabularies such as SNOMED[15]. The focus of this work is different from the issue of interoperability between two versions of the HL7 standard and the presence of local applications.

All the approaches mentioned above focus on ontologising upper conceptual models of HL7 standard. None of them consider local applications and related issues. The PPEPR methodology has two development steps that deal with the problem of layered knowledge spaces and how local resources could be adapted with an upper conceptual model. Similarly, none of the related work aimed for (semi-)automatic alignment of HL7 ontologies. Above all, the works mentioned above lack detailed methodology for ontologising HL7 applications.

---

[12] http://www.w3.org/TR/rif-core/
[13] http://www.hl7.org/implement/standards/rim.cfm
[14] http://www.w3.org/wiki/HCLS/ClinicalObservationsInteroperability/HL7CDA2OWL.html
[15] http://www.ihtsdo.org/snomed-ct/

# 7  Conclusion

We have identified three HL7-specific ontology building features (reusability of non-ontological resources, ontology layering, and local adaptation) missing from traditional ontology building methodologies. We propose the PPEPR ontology building methodology for the HL7 standard. The PPEPR methodology extends, refines, and inherits from existing methodologies. We address a key requirement, (semi-)automatic ontology alignment, to resolve ontological heterogeneity. We have tried three ontology matching systems for alignments between different ontologised versions of the HL7, but came to the conclusion that simple manual mapping "recipes" worked better for us. In the future, we plan to extend the evaluation with other matching tools, e.g. from the "anatomy track" of the Ontology Alignment Evaluation Initiative (OAEI)[16]. Our future work also is to extend the PPEPR methodology by introducing mechanisms that may allow interoperation with other prominent healthcare standards and medical vocabularies.

# References

1. Bicer, V., Laleci, G.B., Dogac, A., Kabak, Y.: Artemis Message Exchange Framework: Semantic Interoperability of Exchanged Messages in the Healthcare Domain. SIGMOD Record (ACM Special Interest Group on Management of Data) (2005)
2. de Bruijn, J., Fensel, D., Keller, U., Kifer, M., Krummenacher, R., Lausen, H., Polleres, A., Predoiu, L.: Web Service Modeling Language (WSML), w3C member submission (June 2005)
3. Castano, S., Ferrara, A., Montanelli, S.: Matching Ontologies in Open Networked Systems: Techniques and Applications. In: Spaccapietra, S., Atzeni, P., Chu, W.W., Catarci, T., Sycara, K. (eds.) Journal on Data Semantics V. LNCS, vol. 3870, pp. 25–63. Springer, Heidelberg (2006)
4. Euzenat, J., Polleres, A., Scharffe, F.: SPARQL Extensions for Processing Alignments. IEEE Intelligent Systems 23(6), 82–84 (2008)
5. Euzenat, J., Shvaiko, P.: Ontology Matching. Springer, Heidelberg (2007)
6. Fernández-López, M., Gómez-Pérez, A., Juristo, N.: Methontology: from ontological art towards ontological engineering. In: Proc. Symposium on Ontological Engineering of AAAI (1997)
7. Fernández-López, M., Gómez-Pérez, A.: Overview and analysis of methodologies for building ontologies. Knowl. Eng. Rev. (2002)
8. Hitzler, P., Krötzsch, M., Parsia, B., Patel-Schneider, P., Rudolph, S.: OWL 2 Web Ontology Language Primer W3C Recommendation. Tech. rep., World Wide Web Consortium (W3C) (October 2009)
9. Hu, W., Qu, Y.: Falcon-AO: A Practical Ontology Matching System. Journal of Web Semantics 6(3), 237–239 (2008)
10. Noy, N.F., Musen, M.A.: The PROMPT suite: interactive tools for ontology merging and mapping. Int'l Journal of Human-Computer Studies 59(6), 983–1024 (2003)
11. Oemig, F., Blobel, B.: An Ontology Architecture for HL7 V3: Pitfalls and Outcomes. In: World Congress on Medical Physics and Biomedical Engineering (2009)

---

[16] http://oaei.ontologymatching.org/2010/results/anatomy/index.html

12. Orgun, B.: Interoperabilit In Heterogeneous Medical Information Systems Using Smart Mobile Agents And Hl7 (Emags). Master's thesis, Macquarie University, Australia (2003)
13. Pinto, H.S., Staab, S., Tempich, C.: DILIGENT: Towards a fine-grained methodology for DIstributed, Loosely-controlled and evolvInG Engineering of oNTologies. In: 16th European Conf. on AI (ECAI), pp. 393–397. IOS Press, Amsterdam (2004)
14. Polleres, A., Scharffe, F., Schindlauer, R.: SPARQL++ for mapping between RDF vocabularies. In: Chung, S. (ed.) OTM 2007, Part I. LNCS, vol. 4803, pp. 878–896. Springer, Heidelberg (2007)
15. Rector, A.L., Qamar, R., Marley, T.: Binding ontologies and coding systems to electronic health records and messages. Applied Ontologies 4(1), 51–69 (2009)
16. Sahay, R., Akhtar, W., Fox, R.: PPEPR: Plug and Play Electronic Patient Records. In: Proceedings of the 23rd Annual ACM Symposium on Applied Computing, the Semantic Web and Applications (SWA) Track. ACM, Fortaleza (2008)
17. Staab, S., Studer, R., Schnurr, H.P., Sure, Y.: Knowledge Processes and Ontologies. IEEE Intelligent Systems 16, 26–34 (2001)
18. Uschold, M.: Building Ontologies: Towards a Unified Methodology. In: 16th Annual Conf. of the British Computer Society Specialist Group on Expert Systems, pp. 16–18 (1996)

# Application of Answer Set Programming for Public Health Data Integration and Analysis

Monica L. Nogueira and Noel P. Greis

Center for Logistics and Digital Strategy,
Kenan-Flagler Business School,
The University of North Carolina at Chapel Hill,
Kenan Center CB#3440, Chapel Hill, NC 27713 U.S.A.
{monica_nogueira,noel_greis}@unc.edu

**Abstract.** Public health surveillance systems routinely process massive volumes of data to identify health adverse events affecting the general population. Surveillance and response to foodborne disease suffers from a number of systemic and other delays that hinder early detection and confirmation of emerging contamination situations. In this paper we develop an answer set programming (ASP) application to assist public health officials in detecting an emerging foodborne disease outbreak by integrating and analyzing in near real-time temporally, spatially and symptomatically diverse data. These data can be extracted from a large number of distinct information systems such as surveillance and laboratory reporting systems from health care providers, real-time complaint hotlines from consumers, and inspection reporting systems from regulatory agencies. We encode geographic ontologies in ASP to infer spatial relationships that may not be evident using traditional statistical tools. These technologies and ontologies have been implemented in a new informatics tool, the North Carolina Foodborne Events Data Integration and Analysis Tool (NCFEDA). The application was built to demonstrate the potential of situational awareness—created through real-time data fusion, analytics, visualization, and real-time communication—to reduce latency of response to foodborne disease outbreaks by North Carolina public health personnel.

**Keywords:** data integration, answer set programming, public health, food safety, ontology.

## 1 Introduction

Even though the U.S. food supply is one of the safest in the world, each year thousands of foodborne illness cases still occur causing irreversible human harm and extensive economic damage [1, 2]. The total cost of food contamination in the U.S. alone was recently estimated to be $152 billion, including health and human welfare costs as well as economic damage to companies and entire industries [3]. Surveillance and response to foodborne disease suffers from a number of systemic and other delays that hinder early detection and confirmation of emerging contamination situations. At the onset of an outbreak it is often impossible to link isolated events that may be related to other

A M. Tjoa et al. (Eds.): ARES 2011, LNCS 6908, pp. 118–134, 2011.

events reported by the same or by other data sources. In addition, it is often difficult to link events that may have a spatial relationship that is not immediately apparent from the data. For example, records from patients of different counties within the same state will only be reviewed by their respective local health departments. Once distinct events are suspected to be related, public health officials create a cluster and look for confirmatory evidence as part of a lengthy investigatory process. Latencies in the process could be reduced by the earlier availability and synthesis of other confirmatory information, including spatial information, often outside formal public health channels, including information from private companies and consumers [4].

In practice, local public health departments are usually the first to pick up the signals of foodborne disease. These signals may correspond to reports of illness generated by different types of events, e.g. (E1) a patient with symptoms of gastro-intestinal distress seeking medical attention at a hospital emergency room or a patient's visit to a private physician's office; (E2) laboratory test results for an ill patient which confirm a causative pathogen; and (E3) a cluster of ill patients due to a common pathogen. Routinely, a state's syndromic surveillance system collects data from local health care providers about events of type (E1), (E2) and (E3) on a continuous basis, reporting them to the Centers for Disease Control and Prevention (CDC).

However, other events can signal an emerging foodborne disease outbreak. Many public health authorities and food industry operators, e.g. food manufacturers and grocery stores, maintain complaint hotlines (E4) where consumers report foodborne illness or a suspected adulterated food product. Consumer complaints made directly to public agency hotlines, e.g. local health departments (LHDs), state departments of agriculture or departments of environment and natural resources, are officially recorded and may lead to an investigation, at the discretion of the collecting agency.

A public food recall notification (E5) is another important signal which may be related to existing illness cases. Food manufacturers may voluntarily initiate the recall of one of their food products due to positive test results for foodborne pathogens, unintentional adulteration, mislabeling, and the presence of an allergen or hazardous material in the food product. Recalls may also be advised by authorities after routine inspections and testing conducted by the U.S. Department of Agriculture (USDA), U.S. Food and Drug Administration (FDA), and state agencies.

Food facility inspection reports (E6), which list violations to the food code applicable to such facilities, provide another signal that may inform and help identify the root cause of a contamination situation. Evaluation of the type, severity, and other characteristics of past code violations for a specific facility and the product(s) it manufactures could help link such operations as a probable source of contamination.

Microblogging and social media networks, i.e. Twitter or Facebook, are non-standard data sources that hold the potential, yet to be realized, to provide real-time information about emerging food contamination situations. Bloggers posting microblog messages on a social media network about illness after eating a certain food product or at a particular restaurant can provide timely indication about an emerging problem, referred to as type E7 event.

This paper expands on the work reported in [5], providing more detail and presenting additional work conducted since that paper was written. Our contributions with respect to rule-based event modeling are to: (1) extract relevant information from unstructured text, i.e. web-based recall notifications, to generate events that trigger our rule-based inference engine to "reason" about what it knows in light of the new information encoded by this event; (2) semantically link different types of events by employing (simple) ontologies for food, U.S. geographic regions, North Carolina counties, and foodborne diseases; (3) implement a rule-based inference engine using the Answer Set Programming (ASP) paradigm to identify emerging foodborne disease outbreaks; and (4) reduce latency in outbreak detection by identifying emerging outbreaks when the number of cases falls below the statistical threshold.

The paper is organized as follows. Section 2 discusses the motivation and challenges to represent the food safety domain using the ASP paradigm. Section 3 provides an overview of related work. Section 4 presents our rule-based event model and describes the ASP inference engine developed for our application. An illustrative example of the domain is shown in Section 5. Conclusions and future research directions are discussed in Section 6.

## 2   Motivation and Challenges

Data associated with event types E1–E7 described above are collected by separate information systems and maintained and managed by distinct governmental agencies. Thus, in responding to the twin challenges of early detection of and rapid response to emerging outbreak situations, a central problem is how to access, process and interpret more events more quickly, thus reducing their time, scale, and scope. Framing the problem of outbreak detection as a complex event addresses a major failure of current surveillance methods. Current syndromic surveillance systems utilize statistics-based cumulative sum algorithms, i.e. CUSUM, to detect increases in illness reporting numbers and to determine that a foodborne disease outbreak may be emerging or is on-going. Alerts are normally generated by the system when the number of illness cases assigned to a certain syndrome, e.g. fever, respiratory, or gastro-intestinal distress, exceeds the threshold determined for that particular syndrome for the geographic area originating these events, i.e. county, and the local population baseline. These alerts are typically based solely on reported illness cases, type E1 to E3 events, above. Consideration of event types E4 to E7 aids in the detection of emerging outbreaks before they are sufficiently advanced to rise above the threshold of traditional CUSUM statistical methods.

A recent large foodborne outbreak in Europe provides a clear example of the challenges faced by public health officials worldwide. In May 2011 a new strain of the *Escherichia coli* bacteria, known as *E. coli O104:H4*, sickened more than 3,200 people and caused 36 deaths, mostly in Germany, but the source of contamination has not being confirmed at the time of this writing, on early June 2011 [6, 7]. Initial blame was attributed to raw tomatoes, lettuce and cucumbers but after tests returned with negative results, investigations moved to a new candidate – bean sprouts – with preliminary results still inconclusive. European farmers suffered economic losses amounting to hundreds of millions of euros. This led the European Union Farm Commissioner to propose a €150-million compensation package to aid farmers across Europe, which is being considered insufficient as it corresponds to just one-third of the estimated losses.

To better understand the investigatory processes for outbreak detection, consider the following situation. Two individuals in different but adjoining counties experience severe gastro-intestinal ulceration (GIU) symptoms after eating at their favorite local restaurant chain and seek medical attention at the emergency room of their local hospitals. Two separate illness reports are recorded and entered into the health care system to be reported to the state's public health syndromic surveillance system. First, if the number of reported GIU and foodborne-related cases does not exceed the corresponding threshold for GIU syndrome in the county, then no alert will be generated by the CUSUM algorithm and detection of an emerging situation will be delayed. Second, because CUSUM does not recognize adjoining counties even though the two individuals were made ill but the same pathogen/food no alert will be generated. However, consider that another person falls ill after eating at a different branch of the same food chain and calls a consumer complaint hotline to make a report. Currently, this event will be registered in the receiving agency's database but not automatically passed along to public health syndromic surveillance systems. Consider that another person, also ill after eating at that chain, reports the illness a message on a personal blog or preferred online discussion board. Both these events occur "under the radar" of public health and are not currently picked up as evidence of a possible emerging contamination situation.

## 3   Related Work

The food safety domain is complex, multifaceted and dynamic. Recent high profile food contamination events have led to a surge of new regulations worldwide that provide food safety agencies with broader authority to enable (1) more stringent monitoring of the food supply chain; (2) data sharing among stakeholders; and (3) shifting from a remediation approach to preventive scientific-based risk analysis. But a widely accepted standard for tracking and tracing of food "from farm to fork" is still lacking, as well as computational models and analytical tools that will allow early recognition of emerging issues by fusing data from diverse sources and rapid response to adverse events. Work toward systems to improve identification of emerging food contamination problems is underway both in the U.S. and abroad. A review and classification of existing methods and reactive systems are provided in [8], including:

   *a) Early warning systems/networks* monitor hazards in the food production chain through a centralized database which serves as a platform to communicate with and alert member agencies of emerging hazards, e.g. European Union's Rapid Alert System for Food and Feed (RASFF), European and U.S. Centers for Disease Control and Prevention (ECDC and CDC), International Food Safety Authorities Network (INFOSAN), etc.;

   *b) Combinatorial data systems* monitor food safety data combined with other relevant data sources and advanced algorithms and technologies to identify and analyze associated hazards and risks in the food supply, e.g. Scientific Information and Expertise for Policy Support in Europe (SINAPSE), ECDC Communicable Disease Threat Reports (CDTRs), USDA Center for Emerging Issues (CEI) of the Animal and Plant Health Inspection Service (APHIS);

   *c) Retrospective analysis of reactive systems* evaluate data collected by systems of type *a)* and *b)* above to detect trends that may be associated with the development of food safety issues, e.g. RASFF annual reports, European Food and Veterinary Office (FVO), food inspection agencies;

*d) Proactive methods* involve predictive risk assessment for hazard identification within the food production process and methods for routinely measuring production outcomes, e.g. Hazard Analysis Critical Control Points (HACCP); and

*e) Vulnerability assessment* focuses on the points within the food supply where hazards may be introduced and identification of indicators and countermeasures against potential hazards, e.g. U.S. CARVER-shock methodology.

The application developed and implemented as part of this research is both a combinatorial and retrospective analysis system which provides increased situational awareness to North Carolina's public health officials. Other related work that seeks to identify food safety issues spans different areas. An integrated information system for foodborne disease and food safety focused on pathogen data is discussed in [9]. The system proposed is ontology-driven, and utilizes the semantic web and heterogeneous data sources. Food allergens lead to a large number of food recalls each year as they pose a threat to people's health. Semantic web technologies, i.e. food allergen ontology, are discussed in [10] as bridges that will help promote data sharing and integration among food allergen databases. A new methodology described in [11] utilizes three data mining methods for recognizing patterns linking specific foodborne disease outbreaks with food products and consumption locations. An example of research that addresses the need for methods to trace food products "from farm to fork" can be found in [12]. A comprehensive review of existing methods to select indicators to help identify emerging hazards in the food supply chain appears in [13].

# 4   Application Modeling

Although public health electronic surveillance systems collect and analyze daily massive volumes of data corresponding to patient visits to healthcare providers, it may take days or weeks to detect an emerging foodborne disease outbreak unless it is temporally and spatially localized, e.g. several people attending a banquet fall ill within a few hours and seek medical care at medical facilities located in neighboring geographical regions, e.g. counties. As discussed above, integration of data available to other food safety stakeholders, i.e. governmental agencies, private sector, and consumers, is critical to improve situational awareness and reduce such latencies. In this section we tackle the challenge of achieving data integration by modeling semantically heterogeneous data obtained from food-related events as the first step in developing our food safety application.

## A.   Event Model

An *event* is defined as the acquisition of a piece of information that is significant within a specific domain of interest to the application. In this application the domain of interest is food safety. We distinguish between two different types of events: simple events and materialized complex events. Simple events include both *atomic* events and *molecular* events. Atomic events have a distinct spatio-temporal identity, i.e. they take place at a particular place and time that is relevant to the determination of the complex event. An example of an atomic event would be a single reported case of gastrointestinal illness, an FDA recall, or a consumer complaint. Molecular events can be thought of as atomic events that are "linked together" by evidence, for example that are joined through previous evidence or by public health experts outside the system. Molecular events could include a confirmed cluster of two or more *Salmonella* cases as determined by DNA fingerprinting. An *event stream* is defined as the sequence of simple events received by the complex event processing (CEP) engine that are assigned a timestamp from a discrete ordered time domain and a geostamp consisting of a longitude and latitude geocode. An atomic event has a single timestamp and geostamp; molecular events may have multiple timestamps and geostamps.

A *complex* or materialized event is an event that is inferred by the engine's evaluation of the occurrence of other simple events. For example, in our application the materialized event is a foodborne disease outbreak.

*B. Semantic Model*

Our representation allows for incomplete information which is indicated by a unique reserved symbol of the representation language. Sparse data are an inherent characteristic of the problem, since one of our goals is to detect outbreaks when the number of illness cases has not yet exceeded thresholds employed by traditional statistical methods. The semantic model for the food safety domain is presented in Fig. 1. The events of interest are described by the following concepts.

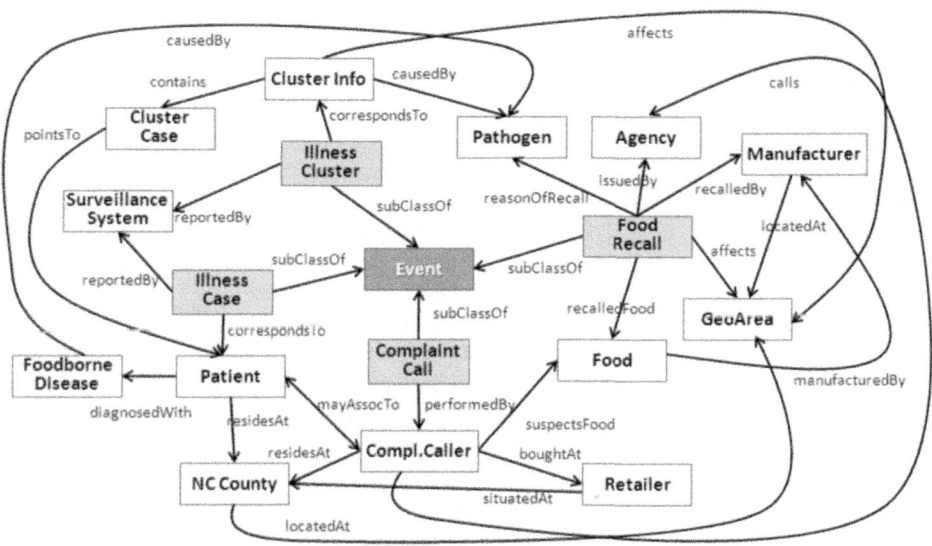

**Fig. 1.** Semantic Model

A patient illness case record corresponding to event type E1 contains information that uniquely identifies a patient in the record generating system, e.g. patient identification code and syndromic surveillance system; patient's county of residence; time and date of the visit to health care provider; syndrome or diagnosis assigned by attending physician, e.g. salmonellosis; and the disease-causing pathogen. This record will be updated to confirm the pathogen identified by a laboratory test when an event of type E2 corresponding to this patient enters the system. A simple ontology of foodborne diseases and related syndromes is employed to enable the semantic link of diagnosis data and pathogen data across different types of events.    In this work, an ontology is a formal explicit description of concepts and individual instances of these concepts, which together constitute a knowledge base [14].

By definition, an illness cluster is formed by a number of patients with a common diagnosis caused by the same pathogen (as identified by laboratory test results or other causal links).    The cluster patient with the earliest disease onset date is referred to as "patient#1." Events of type E3 are represented by two different types of records: (a) a cluster record provides information that uniquely identifies a specific cluster; and (b) a cluster illness case record contains information about a specific patient that is included in the cluster defined by a cluster record. A cluster record contains a unique identification code, the disease-causing pathogen, number of counties affected by the outbreak, number of patients in the cluster, unique identification code of patient#1, and date of patient#1 visit to a health care provider. A cluster illness case record contains the cluster unique identification code, the unique identification code of the patient it represents, and the patient's county of residence. A cluster illness case record acts as a pointer to the more complete patient illness case record of the corresponding patient.

A consumer complaint call, an event of type E4, is represented by three types of records. A complaint caller  record provides a unique call identification code, date and time of call, and information about the caller, e.g. caller's state and county of residence; type of illness codified using the responding agency's medical code; and number of people that fell ill because of the product. A complaint food operator record contains information about the manufacturer and retailer the caller has complained about. A complaint food product record lists the food product as described by the caller and its corresponding FDA food code, date of manufacturing, and other information. A food ontology semantically links recalled food products to those implicated by consumer complaint calls. This ontology differs from existing food ontologies, e.g. [15], in that it closely follows the food categories as determined by FDA's product code which is utilized by industry to codify food shipments.

A recall notification, event of type E5, is represented by two types of records. A recall record contains a unique identification code for this event, the agency issuing the recall, date and time of its release, recalling company, recalled food product, reason for the recall, e.g. mislabeling, presence of allergen, or a specific pathogen, e.g. *Salmonella*, number of illnesses if known, and number of geographic areas affected. U.S. geographic areas are defined by a simple ontology which includes all U.S. states and regions as defined by the U.S. Census Bureau. An associated recall area record is created for each geographic area affected by the recall.

## C.  ASP Rule-Based Inference Engine

In this work, we use a form of declarative programming – Answer Set Programming (ASP) [16], to represent the rule-based CEP of the food safety domain and to search for/detect emerging outbreaks and other information of interest to public health officials. ASP has been applied to industrial problems but, to the best of our knowledge, it has not been used in food safety applications before.

The ASP paradigm is based on the stable models/answer sets semantics of logic programs [17, 18] and has been  shown to be a powerful methodology for knowledge representation, including the representation of defaults and multiple interesting aspects of reasoning about actions and their effects, as well as being particularly useful to solve difficult search problems. In the ASP methodology, search problems are reduced to the computation of the stable models of the problem. Several ASP solvers – programs that generate the stable models of a given problem encoded in the ASP formalism – have been implemented, e.g. ASSAT [19], Clasp [20], Cmodels [21] DLV [22], GnT [23], nomore++ [24], Pbmodels [25], Smodels [26], etc. In what follows we provide the basic syntactic constructs and the intuitive semantics of the ASP language used in this work. A complete formal specification of the syntax and semantics of the language can be found at [18, 22].

A signature $\Sigma$ of the language contains constants, predicates, and function symbols. Terms and atoms are formed as is customary in first-order logic. A literal is either an atom (also called a positive literal) or an atom preceded by $\neg$ (classical or strong negation), a negative literal. Literals $l$ and $\neg l$ are called contrary. Ground literals and terms are those not containing variables. A consistent set of literals do not contain contrary literals. The set of all ground literals is denoted by $lit(\Sigma)$. A rule is a statement of the form:

$$h_1 \vee \ldots \vee h_k \leftarrow l_1, \ldots, l_m, not\ l_{m+1}, \ldots, not\ l_n. \tag{1}$$

where $h_i$'s and $l_i$'s are ground literals, *not* is a logical connective called default negation or negation as failure, and symbol $\vee$ corresponds to the disjunction operator. The head of the rule is the part of the statement to the left of symbol $\leftarrow$, while the body of the rule is the part on its right side. Intuitively, the rule meaning is that if a reasoner believes $\{l_1, \ldots, l_m\}$ and has no reason to believe $\{l_{m+1}, \ldots, l_n\}$, then it must believe one of the $h_i$'s. If the head of the rule is substituted by the falsity symbol $\perp$ then the rule is called a constraint. The intuitive meaning of a constraint is that its body must not be satisfied. Rules with variables are used as a short hand for the sets of their ground instantiations. Variables are denoted by capital letters. An ASP program is a pair of $\{\Sigma, \Pi\}$, where $\Sigma$ is a signature and $\Pi$ is a set of rules over $\Sigma$, but usually the signature is defined implicitly and programs are only denoted by $\Pi$. A stable model (or answer set) of a program $\Pi$ is one of the possible sets of literals of its logical consequences under the stable model/ answer set semantics.

## D.  ASP Program Encoding

Our encoding – the set of rules of program $\Pi$ – contains roughly 100 rules, while event records (in ASP, rules with an empty body, also called "facts") for experiments are in the hundreds. We use the DLV system [22] as our ASP solver. To illustrate the ASP methodology we show below a few (simplified) rules used by our engine to detect emerging clusters. Rule (2) means that if neighboring counties A and B reported a small number of cases of food-related illnesses, due to pathogen P and/or syndrome S, this constitutes evidence for the engine to create a suspected cluster with case records – generated by rules of form (3) – from A and B with illness P and/or S. Then, an emerging outbreak affecting A and B, due to P, is computed by rule (4).

$$suspcluster(A,B,P,S) \leftarrow \tag{2}$$
$$neighbors(A,B),$$
$$min\_reached(A,P,S),$$
$$min\_reached(B,P,S).$$

$$suspcluster\_illness(A,B,Id,P,A) \leftarrow \qquad\qquad (3)$$
$$suspcluster(A,B,P,S),$$
$$P \mathrel{!=} S,$$
$$patient\_illness(Id,H,M,AmPm,Day,Mon,Y,A,Sys,P).$$

$$susp\_outbreak(A,B,P) \leftarrow \qquad\qquad (4)$$
$$suspcluster(A,B,P,\_).$$

To assist public health officials with the task of identifying the food source of the contamination (e.g. fresh vegetable) and its manufacturer (e.g. MyVeggies), our engine seeks to connect a suspected cluster of illnesses to an existing public food recall notice. With rule (5), the engine will link a suspected cluster, occurring in neighboring counties A and B, to a food recall R, if the same pathogen P causing the cluster's illnesses is the reason for R; the area L affected by R encompasses these counties, e.g. L corresponds to the state where A and B are located, and the recall has been issued not too long ago, i.e. within a timeframe that makes the food recalled a probable candidate as the source of contamination for this cluster. By linking the suspected cluster to a food recall, rule (5) allows the inference of the food product causing the contamination, F, and its manufacturer, M.

$$susprecall(R,A,B,F,M,L) \leftarrow \qquad\qquad (5)$$
$$suspcluster(A,B,P,S),$$
$$recall(R,Mon,Y\ M,F,N,P,\_),$$
$$susprecall\_areaOK(R,L),$$
$$susprecall\_dateOK(R,A,B,Mon,Y).$$

It may be possible for a given cluster to be linked to more than one food recall, since it not uncommon to have more than one food product contaminated with a given pathogen at the same time. This is particularly true in ingredient-based outbreaks, where an ingredient, e.g. peanut butter paste, is used in multiple products, e.g. soups and ice cream, which leads to multiple recall notices by various manufacturers. Facts (6)–(11) describe the recall of two different food products, e.g. R1: meat and R2: chicken, due to the same pathogen, *Salmonella*, occurring at the same time, March 2011, with no (zero) officially confirmed illnesses. Recall R1 affects only 3 states, while R2 covers a much larger area, i.e. the whole country.

$$recall(r1,mar,2011,meatfarm,meat,3,salmonella,0). \qquad (6)$$

$$recall\_area(r1,new\_york). \qquad\qquad (7)$$

$$recall\_area(r1,new\_jersey). \qquad\qquad (8)$$

$$recall\_area(r1,north\_carolina). \qquad\qquad (9)$$

$$recall(r2,mar,2011,mama,chicken,1,salmonella,0). \qquad (10)$$

$$recall\_area(r2,nationwide). \qquad\qquad (11)$$

Information about the food product distribution area is frequently provided in food recall notices but is not always specific. A recall may indicate one or more states where the food product has been distributed; cite a whole region, e.g. U.S. Midwest; a county or city, e.g. New York City; or indicate it was distributed "nationwide". In situations where multiple recalls are linked to a cluster due to a causing pathogen, and time and geographical coverage, it may be more efficient for public health officials to focus on recalls whose product distribution is closely related to the cluster's geographical area. Thus, if both recalls R1 and R2 are connected to a local cluster in New York, New Jersey, or North Carolina, these states' public health officials may give higher priority to investigating "MeatFarm's meat" products as the source of contamination instead of "Mama's chicken" products.

We allow users to select if they want to be informed by the engine of all recalls connected to a given suspected cluster, or to be informed only of those recalls that are inferred as "preferred recalls" by the engine due to a more specific geographic link to the cluster. It is ease to express such parametric computations using ASP. In our program, this is accomplished by introducing an atom – prefrecallON – to the set of (truthful) facts to be evaluated by the engine. Preferred recalls can then be inferred by rule (12). Intuitively, this rule says that given two distinct recalls, R1 and R2, already connected to a cluster formed by counties A and B, where area L1 affected by R1 is a subregion of area L2 affected by R2, the engine concludes that R1 is a "preferred recall," of interest to public health officials, unless it can prove – using rule (13) – that there exists another recall, a certain distinct R3, covering a geographical area L3 which is a subregion of L1, and thus more specific to cluster A, B. Notice that if users are not interested that the engine generates "preferred recall" information, they may select not to add atom prefrecallON to the program. The absence of this fact falsifies rules (12) and (13), and no preferred recalls are generated by the engine.

$$pref\_susprecall(R1,A,B,F1,M1,L1) \leftarrow \qquad (12)$$
$$prefrecallON,$$
$$susprecall(R1,A,B,F1,M1,L1),$$
$$susprecall(R2,A,B,F2,M2,L2),$$
$$subregion(L1,L2),$$
$$R1 \: != R2,$$
$$not \: other\_more\_specif(A,B,L1,R2).$$

$$other\_more\_specif(A,B,L1,R2) \leftarrow \qquad (13)$$
$$prefrecallON,$$
$$susprecall(R2,A,B,\_,\_,L2),$$
$$susprecall(R3,A,B,\_,\_,L3),$$
$$subregion(L3,L1),$$
$$R2 \: != R3.$$

The highly expressive power of ASP facilitates the creation of knowledge hierarchies, organization and inference of concepts which are primary requirements for the development of ontologies. We take advantage of the language's expressiveness to represent three (currently simple) ontologies in the following areas: (a) foodborne disease; (b) food; (c) U.S. geographical divisions and North Carolina political divisions. Due to space limitations, only the geographical ontologies are briefly described next.

*E.  Geographical Ontologies in ASP*

The concepts represented in our geographical ontologies are the standards: country, regions, regional divisions, states, territories, counties, and cities. Fig. 2 illustrates the main concepts and relations of these ontologies.  Given that public health officials in the U.S. are mostly interested in solving foodborne disease outbreaks occurring in the country, our data are limited to the United States. In particular, the application developed is to assist North Carolina authorities and thus, at present, county and city data are limited to this state. For implementation purposes, we distinguish the U.S. Ontology from the North Carolina (NC) Ontology, given that the latter includes a neighboring relation among NC counties. The main goals of the geographical ontologies are to enable the engine to infer: (1) preferred food recalls based on their geographic specificity to the state of North Carolina; and (2) clusters of foodborne disease covering a number of neighboring NC counties.

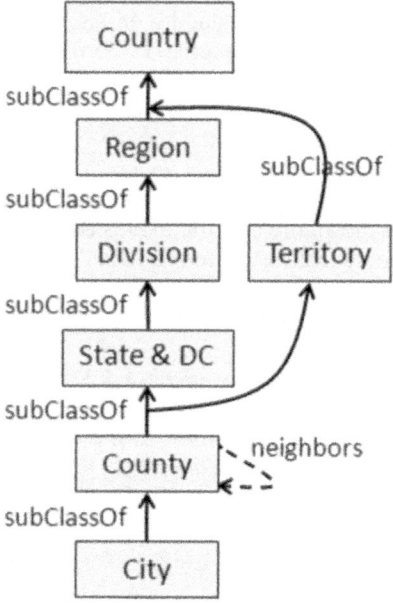

**Fig. 2.** Geographical Ontology

States are represented by facts of type (14), which include the state name, abbreviation, and regional division. We encode 4 U.S. regions which are divided into 9 regional divisions, as adopted by the U.S. Census Bureau. The state of North Carolina is located in the South Atlantic division of the South region, as encoded by (14)–(16). Territories are similarly represented. Part of the food products' distribution information is represented by facts (17)–(21), where "nationwide" is an example of a standard way food recall notices indicate a product has been distributed to the whole country. Rules (22)–(25) are used by rules (12) and (13) to prove that a given recall area, namely L1, is a subregion of another larger area, L2, and therefore information about the recall on-going in L1 is preferred than that on-going in L2.

$$us\_state(north\_carolina, nc, south\_atlantic). \tag{14}$$
$$division(south\_atlantic, south). \tag{15}$$

$$region(R) \leftarrow division(\_, R). \tag{16}$$

$$is\_us\_distr(nationwide). \tag{17}$$
$$is\_us\_distr(R) \leftarrow region(R). \tag{18}$$
$$is\_us\_distr(R) \leftarrow division(R,\_). \tag{19}$$
$$is\_us\_distr(S) \leftarrow us\_state(S,\_,\_). \tag{20}$$
$$is\_us\_distr(S) \leftarrow us\_state(\_, S,\_). \tag{21}$$

$$subregion\ (R, nationwide) \leftarrow region(R). \tag{22}$$
$$subregion(S,R) \leftarrow division(S,R). \tag{23}$$
$$subregion(S,R) \leftarrow us\_state(S,\_, R). \tag{24}$$
$$subregion\ (S,R) \leftarrow us\_state(\_, S, R). \tag{25}$$

To infer new suspected clusters of foodborne illness, rule (2) tries to prove that there are two neighboring counties in the state with at least a minimum number of reported illness cases due to the same pathogen or with a generic GIU diagnosis that may be caused by food contamination. As shown in rule (3), case records inform the patients' county of residence. The simple NC ontology encodes 100 NC counties, e.g. fact (26), more than 100 neighbor relations for these counties, e.g. facts (27)–(30), and around 850 cities distributed throughout these counties, e.g. (31).

$$nc\_county(orange). \tag{26}$$

$$nc\_neighbors(orange, alamance). \tag{27}$$
$$nc\_neighbors(orange, caswell). \tag{28}$$
$$nc\_neighbors(orange, chatham). \tag{29}$$
$$nc\_neighbors(orange, person). \tag{30}$$

$$nc\_city(chapel\_hill, orange). \tag{31}$$

### F.  Evidence Set and Event Evidence Indicator

The set of linked events that provide evidence of the materializing of a complex event is called the *Evidence Set*. An evidence set is associated with a degree of uncertainty as to whether an emerging outbreak event will materialize based on the information in the event data. Rule (32) below exemplifies the computation of elements of the evidence set. Intuitively, the rule meaning is that the engine will conclude that there is evidence that a complaint call C, from county T implicating a food product F1 of type FC per the FDA Code, is connected to a materialized cluster, of illness P affecting neighboring counties A and B, if this call can be linked to an existing recall R of food F2 manufactured by M at location L, if food 2 is also of type FC.

$$
\begin{aligned}
evidence(A,B,P,S,R,F2,M,L,F1,FC,T) \leftarrow & \\
suspcluster(A,B,P,S), nccounty(T), & \\
suspcomplaint(C,A,B,F1,FC,T), & \\
susprecall(R,A,B,F2,M,L), type\_of(F2,FC). &
\end{aligned}
\tag{32}
$$

NCFEDA's engine computes a measure of the strength of the evidence supporting the conclusion of an emerging complex event through a ranking that ranges from 0, or no evidence, to a maximum of 7, highest evidence rating. The computation of the *Event Evidence Indicator* (EVI) is based on the number and strength of the relationships that connect the events in the evidence set and corresponds to the weighted summation of EVI components calculated for the subsets formed when linking pairs of different types of events. For example, we compute the EVI component for the set of all events corresponding to a suspected cluster and incoming recall notification.

## 5   Illustrative Application

The ASP rule-based inference engine was implemented in the North Carolina Foodborne Events Data Integration and Analysis Tool (NCFEDA) shown in Fig. 3. In this system, food-related events are received by the *Events Manager* which consists of two components: (1) a set of databases; and (2) the *Event Trigger Module*. These databases store all food-related events and geocoded datasets across all public and private sector stakeholders contributing to NCFEDA. The Event Manager monitors the databases for new incoming events that are evaluated by the Event Trigger Module for selecting possible triggers. As noted earlier, and in Fig. 3, triggers are events that could include a case related to a foodborne illness or a consumer complaint.

Web scraping techniques are utilized by NCFEDA to obtain information about recalls of food products issued by the FDA and USDA directly from their websites. Given that recall notifications are intended for a human audience, they are written in

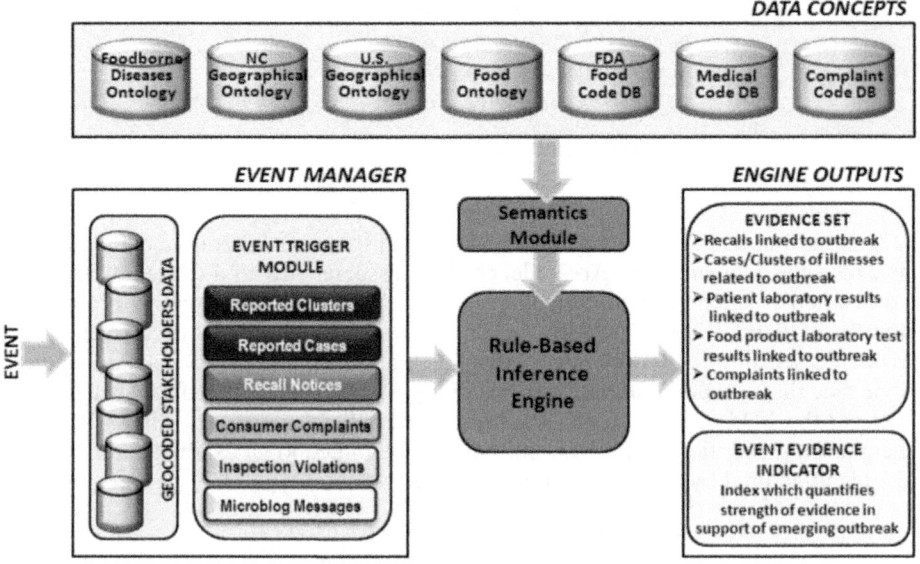

**Fig. 3.** NCFEDA System Architecture

natural language which poses an additional challenge for the extraction of information. A *Semantics Module* enables the extraction of events from unstructured data by automatically parsing recall text and extraction of relevant information.   We utilize a hybrid two-step method to perform the data extraction.  The first step takes advantage of the metadata information contained in the FDA and USDA food recall webpages. Basic pattern matching of single terms is utilized to filter metadata fields of interest, e.g. date a recall was issued.  A second step is required for information contained in the recall notification but not available as metadata, e.g. geographic areas where the food product has been distributed or number of confirmed illness cases attributed to food being recalled. Sequences of alternative patterns based on the ontologies developed are used to perform pattern matching and information extraction.

The Events Manager and Semantics Module work in conjunction with the *Rule-Based Inference Engine* to analyze incoming events and determine their relevance to the current situation(s) being monitored and/or other events previously stored in the system.  NCFEDA databases must be maintained to remain up-to-date with available new information. The bulk of these data constitutes the history of food safety in North Carolina and will be used by the inference engine to support or refute possible conclusions regarding emerging food situations.  Every new event arrival is analyzed and may or may not activate one or more of NCFEDA's inference engine rules. Using knowledge encoded as inference rules, trigger events are processed, together with other possible relevant events, by the Rule-based Inference Engine.  The engine uses rules to "reason" about an existing situation as described by the known facts and encoded rules, and deduces relationships among events to determine whether there is an emerging outbreak event.

The screen shot shown in Fig. 4 illustrates the data integration and analysis capabilities of the application.  The data sources are:  1) all illness cases records reported to the North Carolina Department of Public Health containing among other fields:  the office visit date, probable diagnosis, and a patient's county of residence;  2) all recall notices of food products issued by the FDA stored as records containing:  the recall issuing date, the product recalled, the company recalling the product, the cause for the recall – i.e. pathogen causing the contamination when available, and areas (states) where the product has  been distributed; and 3) all consumer complaint calls implicating a food product including all of the following fields if available:  date of the call, complainant county of residence, product implicated,  retailer/manufacturer/food  service  provider implicated,  complainant medical status (i.e. illness, hospitalization, etc.), diagnosis, and description of the complaint.

In the scenario illustrated, a new small cluster of salmonellosis cases has been detected.  The application searches among incoming consumer complaint calls for any illnesses caused by *Salmonella* or any implicating food products susceptible to this pathogen. The search is narrowed down to a call reporting a hospitalization due to possible consumption of contaminated fruit. The application then searches among both incoming and previously active recall notices to determine whether any potentially relevant *Salmonella* recalls have been reported by FDA and, among those, whether any contaminated product has been shipped to North Carolina. The engine flags an incoming recall of a product to the state of North Carolina and previously restricted to three other states on the West Coast of the United States. The ontologies allow the recognition that cantaloupe is a fruit and that the pathogen causing this

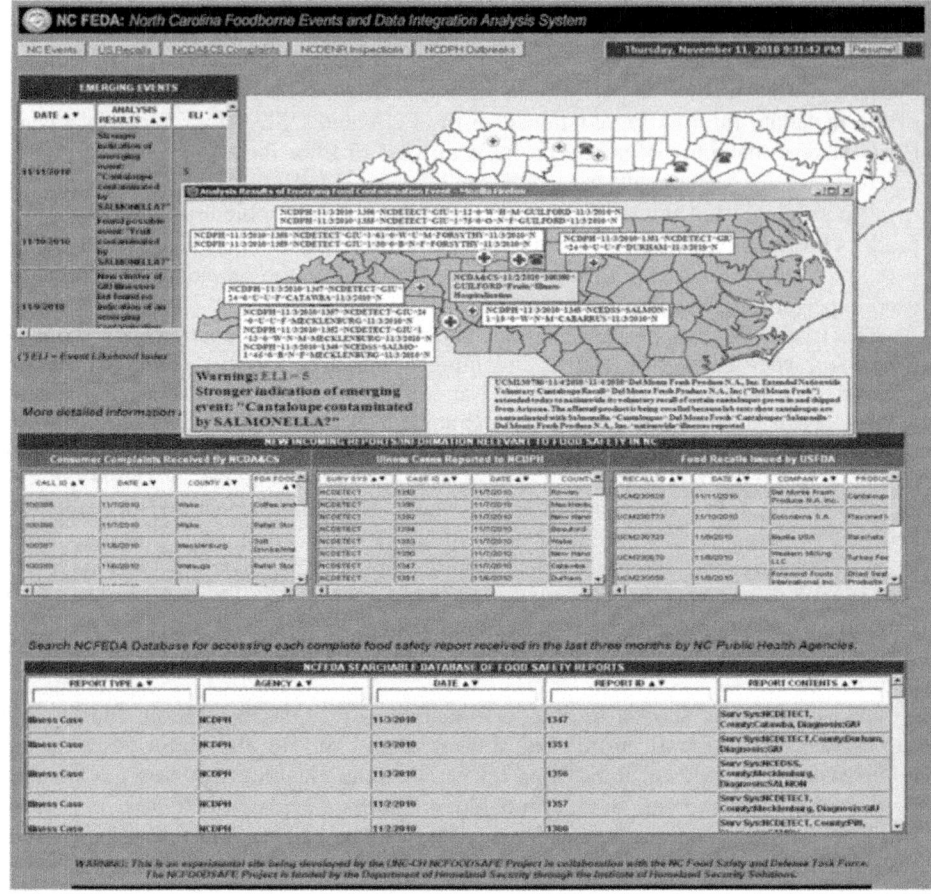

**Fig. 4.** Screenshot of NC Events Page of NCFEDA Use Case Showing A Warning with EVI=5

recall is also the same pathogen causing a reported illness and hospitalization, as reported by a consumer complaint call. Fig. 4 displays the location of all relevant events linked to this threat. When the user hovers the computer mouse over the map icons, detailed information about each reported case/complaint is displayed. The Event Evidence Indicator for the event is computed (EVI=5) and reported on the corner of the pop-up window along with a message relating the illness reports, recalls and consumer complaints, as well as the suspected food product (cantaloupe) and the pathogen (*Salmonella*).

## 6   Conclusions and Future Directions

One of the central challenges in outbreak detection has been the inability to detect signals of an emerging outbreak from cases of illness that may not pass a statistical threshold because they are spatially and temporally dispersed—and for which there are considerable time lags. A primary contribution of this paper has been to frame the outbreak detection problem as a complex event where events include not only structured event data (e.g. case information) but also unstructured event data (e.g. recall or complaint data). We develop semantic models that are able to extract meaningful information from unstructured text data that can serve as event triggers. Using ontologies and rules we are able to discover semantic links between events that provide evidence of an emerging outbreak event. Identification of events that comprise the new suspected clusters of foodborne illness is accomplished using ASP. We successfully implemented these concepts in the NCFEDA prototype. This work is on-going and we are continuing to further develop the rule-based inference engine and we plan to explore the use of the OntoDLV language for our ontology representations [27].

**Acknowledgment.** This project is funded through a subcontract with the Institute for Homeland Security Solutions (IHSS). IHSS is a research consortium established to conduct applied research in the social and behavioral sciences. This material is based upon work supported by the U.S. Department of Homeland Security (DHS) under Contract No. HSHQDC-08-C-00100. Any opinions, findings and conclusions or recommendations expressed in this material are those of the authors and do not necessarily reflect the official policy or position of DHS or of the U.S. Government. The study is approved for public release.

The authors also thank Brett Weed, Compliance and Preparedness Administrator of the Food and Drug Protection Division of the North Carolina Department of Agriculture and Consumer Services, and the members of the North Carolina Food Safety and Defense Task Force for their assistance with this research.

# References

[1] Scallan, E., et al.: Foodborne illness acquired in the United States–Major pathogens. Emerg. Infect. Dis. 17(1), 7–15 (2011)

[2] Morris, J.G.: How safe is our food? Emerg. Infect. Dis. 17(1), 126–128 (2011)

[3] Scharff, R.L.: Health-Related Costs from Foodborne Illness in the United States, The Produce Safety Project at Georgetown University, Washington, D.C (2010)

[4] Greis, N.P., Nogueira, M.L.: Food Safety Emerging Public-Private Approaches: A perspective for local, state, and federal government leaders. IBM Center for The Business of Government (2010)

[5] Nogueira, M.L., Greis, N.P.: Rule-Based Complex Event Processing for Food Safety and Public Health. In: Bassiliades, N., et al. (eds.) RuleML 2011 - Europe. LNCS, vol. 6826, pp. 376–384. Springer, Heidelberg (in press, 2011)

[6] Associated Free Press, Killer bacteria toll rises to 36. AFP, Web, June 13 (2011)

[7] Cowell, A.: Germany Faces Criticism Over E. Coli Outbreak. NYTimes.com, Web, June 7 (2011),
    http://www.nytimes.com/2011/06/08/world/europe/08ecoli.html

[8] Marvin, H.J.P., et al.: A working procedure for identifying emerging food safety issues at an early stage: Implications for European and international risk management practices. Food Control 20, 345–356 (2009)

[9] Yan, X., et al.: From Ontology Selection and Semantic Web to an Integrated Information System for Food-borne Diseases and Food Safety. Software Tools and Algorithms for Biological Systems. In: Arabnia, H.R., Tran, Q.-N. (eds.) Advances in Experimental Medicine and Biology, vol. 696, pp. 741–750 (2011)

[10] Gendel, S.M.: Allergen databases and allergen semantics. Regulatory Toxicology and Pharmacology 54, S7–S10 (2009)
[11] Thakur, M., Olafsson, S., Lee, J.-S., Hurburgh, C.R.: Data Mining for recognizing patterns in foodborne disease outbreaks. J. Food Engineering 97, 213–227 (2010)
[12] Regattieri, A., Gamberi, M., Manzini, R.: Tracebility of food products: general framework and experimental evidence. J. Food Engineering 81, 347–356 (2007)
[13] Kleter, G.A., Marvin, H.J.P.: Indicators of emerging hazards and risks to food safety. Food and Chemical Toxology 47, 1022–1039 (2009)
[14] Noy, N., McGuiness, D.: Ontology Development 101: A Guide to Creating Your First Ontology. Technical Report SMI-2001-0880, Stanford University (2001)
[15] Cantais, J., Dominguez, D., Gigante, V., Laera, L., Tamma, V.: An example of food ontology for diabetes control. In: Proc. of the International Semantic Web Conference 2005 Workshop on Ontology Patterns for the Semantic Web, Galway, Ireland (November 2005)
[16] Marek, V.W., Truszczynski, M.: Stable models and an alternative logic programming paradigm. In: The Logic Programming Paradigm: a 25-Year Perspective, pp. 375–398. Springer, Berlin (1999)
[17] Gelfond, M., Lifschitz, V.: The stable model semantics for logic programming. In: Kowalski, R., Bowen, K. (eds.) International Logic Programming Conference and Symposium, pp. 1070–1080. MIT Press, Cambridge (1988)
[18] Gelfond, M., Lifschitz, V.: Classical negation in logic programs and disjunctive databases. New Generation Computing 9, 365–385 (1991)
[19] Lin, F., Zhao, Y.: ASSAT: Computing answer sets of a logic program by SAT solvers. Artificial Intelligence 157(1-2), 115–137 (2004)
[20] Gebser, M., Kaufmann, B., Neumann, A., Schaub, T.: clasp: A Conflict-Driven Answer Set Solver. In: Baral, C., Brewka, G., Schlipf, J. (eds.) LPNMR 2007. LNCS (LNAI), vol. 4483, pp. 260–265. Springer, Heidelberg (2007)
[21] Lierler, Y.: Cmodels—SAT-based disjunctive answer set solver. In: Baral, C., Greco, G., Leone, N., Terracina, G. (eds.) LPNMR 2005. LNCS (LNAI), vol. 3662, pp. 447–451. Springer, Heidelberg (2005)
[22] Leone, N., Pfeifer, G., Faber, W., Calimeri, F., Dell'Armi, T., Eiter, T., Gottlob, G., Ianni, G., Ielpa, G., Koch, C., Perri, S., Polleres, A.: The DLV System. In: Flesca, S., Greco, S., Leone, N., Ianni, G. (eds.) JELIA 2002. LNCS (LNAI), vol. 2424, pp. 537–540. Springer, Heidelberg (2002)
[23] Janhunen, T., Niemelä, I., Seipel, D., Simons, P., You, J.-H.: Unfolding Partiality and Disjunctions in Stable Model Semantics. ACM Transactions on Computational Logic 7(1), 1–37 (2006)
[24] Anger, C., Gebser, M., Linke, T., Neumann, A., Schaub, T.: The nomore++ System. In: Baral, C., Greco, G., Leone, N., Terracina, G. (eds.) LPNMR 2005. LNCS (LNAI), vol. 3662, pp. 422–426. Springer, Heidelberg (2005)
[25] Truszczynski, M.: Predicate-calculus-based logics for modeling and solving search problems. ACM Transactions on Computational Logic 7(1), 38–83 (2006)
[26] Niemelä, I., Simons, P.: Extending the Smodels System with Cardinality and Weight Constraints. In: Logic-Based Artificial Intelligence, pp. 491–521. Kluwer Academic Publishers, Dordrecht (2000)
[27] Ricca, F., et al.: OntoDLV: An ASP-based System for Enterprise Ontologies. Journal of Logic and Computation 19(4), 643–670 (2008)

# Augmented Reality Approaches in Intelligent Health Technologies and Brain Lesion Detection

Tomasz Hachaj[1] and Marek R. Ogiela[2]

[1] Pedagogical University of Krakow,
Institute of Computer Science and Computer Methods,
2 Podchorazych Ave, 30-084 Krakow, Poland
tomekhachaj@o2.pl
[2] AGH University of Science and Technology,
30 Mickiewicza Ave, 30-059 Krakow, Poland
mogiela@agh.edu.pl

**Abstract.** In this paper authors present their new proposition of system for cognitive analysis of dynamic computer tomography perfusion maps (dpCT). The novel contribution of this article is introducing an augmented reality visualization module that supports real time volume rendering (VR) of derived data. Authors also presents the results of their researches on optimization of VR algorithm memory usage by dynamic computation of volume gradient instead of pre-generation of gradient Authors compare five different discrete gradient computation schemas taking into account image quality and processing speed on two VR algorithms: volume ray casting and texture based visualization with view aligned slices.

**Keywords:** Pattern recognition, cognitive analysis, dynamic brain perfusion, volume rendering, gradient estimation, augmented reality.

## 1 Introduction

The ensuring of patient security during the health care is one of the basic duties of medical personnel [1]. Nowadays many dedicated diagnosis support systems (DSS) emerge on purpose to help physicians in everyday practice. The modern DSS has to satisfy many requirements in order to be accepted in medical society. It has to be not only a reliable tool (low total error rate coefficient) but also quickly generates the support information and has intuitive interface.

In this article authors present their new proposition of system for cognitive analysis of dynamic computer tomography perfusion maps (dpCT) that satisfies all of those requirements.

The proposed solution is the extension of previous works [2], [3], [4]. The novel contribution of this article is introducing an augmented reality visualization module that supports real time volume rendering (VR) of derived data.

Authors also present the results of their researches on optimization of VR algorithm memory usage. The huge amount of GPU memory may be saved by dynamic computation of volume gradient instead of pre-generation of gradient.

A M. Tjoa et al. (Eds.): ARES 2011, LNCS 6908, pp. 135–148, 2011.

Authors compare five different discrete gradient computation schemas taking into account image quality and processing speed on two VR algorithms: volume ray casting and texture based visualization with view aligned slices. Many similar researches on the field of gradient reconstruction for VR were previously reported (for example in [5], [6], [7]). Authors intention was to compare the speed of two most popular VR algorithms with pre-generated and dynamically computed volume gradient on clinical data using different transfer function [8] in order to justify using one (or both) of them in their diagnosis support program. Despite the fact that transfer function is the factor that might highly affect the speed of the VR (especially when rendering algorithms utilizes acceleration techniques like early ray termination or empty-space skipping [9]) we did not found papers in which transfer function was taken into account during dynamic gradient computation. Because of that the presented comparison is also important contribution to state of art of VR visualization.

## 2   Diagnosis Support System Architecture

The authors system enables the quantitative and quality analysis of visualized symptoms like head injuries, epilepsy, brain vascular disease, ischemic and hemorrhagic stroke that changes blood perfusion. The new implementation of the DMD (detection measure and description system [2]) also includes intuitive augmented reality visualization module derived from [10]. The schema of the system is presented in Figure 1.

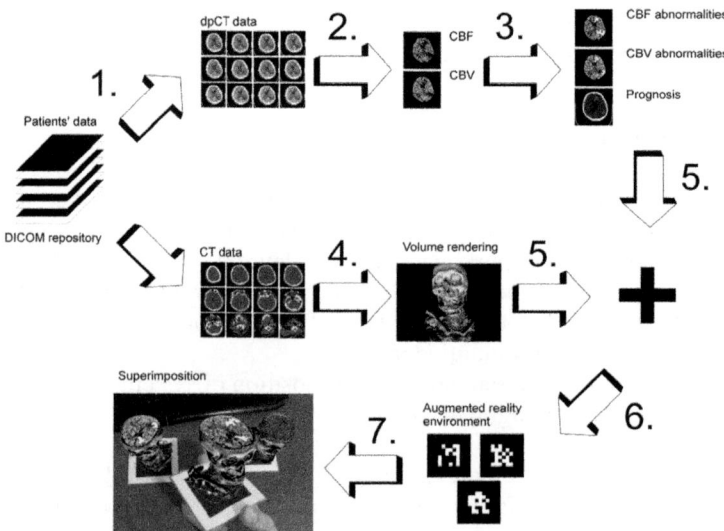

**Fig. 1.** Data flow in DMD system with augmented reality visualization module. Detailed description in text

The patient's data (1) is kept in DICOM repository. It is consisted of neuroradiology images like dpCT, CT (computer tomography) and MR (magnetic resonance). The dpCT is used for generation of perfusion CBF and CBV maps (2). The next step (3) is detection of perfusion abnormalities and generation of ischemia prognosis for infarcted tissues. The CT (or RM) data is processed and visualized with VR algorithms (4). The data from (3) is superimposed into the 3D object (5). The result date is superimposed with augmented reality environment (6) onto image captured by digital camera (7).

## 2.1 Detection of Perfusion Abnormalities

The process of an analysis of dpCT proposed by authors is a fusion of image processing, pattern recognition and image analysis procedures. All of these stages will be described in this paragraph. The input data for the algorithm is cerebral blood flow, cerebral blood volume and CT image.

**Image processing.** Image processing step is consisted of lesion detection algorithm and image registration algorithm. The algorithm used for detection of potential lesions is The Unified Algorithm detailed described in [2]. Lesion detection algorithm finds potentially pathologic tissues (regions of interests - ROI). Image registration algorithm is used for creating of deformable brain atlas in order to make detailed description of visible tissues. Potential lesions are compared with corresponding CT / MR image in order to check its presence there. This process enables proper treatment planning. For registration purpose authors have chosen free-from deformation algorithm proposed in [11]. The detailed (AA based) description of image in authors system has been presented elsewhere [12].

**Image analysis.** Defining the features of entire image after lesion detection step is an easy task. Algorithm measures some important from (medical point of view) features:

- Perfusion in ROI in left and right hemisphere.
- Relative perfusion (perfusion in ROI in left hemisphere divided by perfusion in ROI in right hemisphere and perfusion in ROI in right hemisphere divided by perfusion in ROI in left hemisphere).
- Size of ROI.

The scaling factors between perfusion map and "real brain" can be derived directly from DICOM files.

**Pattern recognition.** In pattern recognition step algorithm determinate what type of lesion was detected and in which hemisphere. In order to do it is necessary to gather medical knowledge about average perfusion values. After image processing step two symmetric regions are detected in left and right hemisphere. Authors' algorithm compares perfusion in left and right (symmetrical) ROI with average perfusion norms and place potential lesion in hemisphere where modulus of difference between average and ROI value is greater. After this it is an easy task to determinate the type of lesion (hemorrhagic or ischemic) simply by checking if perfusion in ROI is greater or smaller than average.

The last step done by the algorithm is to state prognosis for lesion evolution in brain tissues. CBF and CBV have prognostic values in evaluation of ischemic evolution. In many cases simultaneous analysis of both CBF and CBV perfusion parameters enables accurate analysis of ischemia visualized brain tissues and predict its further changes permitting a not only a quality (like CT angiography) but also quantitative evaluation of the degree of severity of the perfusion disturbance which results from the particular type of occlusion and collateral blood.

The algorithm analyze both perfusion maps simultaneously in order to detect:

-    Tissues that can be salvaged (tissues are present on CBF and CBV asymmetry map and values of rCBF did not drop beyond 0.48 [13]).
-    Tissues that will eventually become infracted (tissues are present on CBF and CBV asymmetry map and values of rCBF did drop beyond 0.48 [13]).
-    Tissues with an auto regulation mechanism in ischemic region (decreased CBF with correct or increased CBV).

Summing up, the output data of the algorithm is consisted of: regions of perfusion abnormalities, AA description of brain tissues, measures of perfusion parameters and prognosis for infracted tissues. That information is superimpose onto volumetric CT data and displayed to radiologist.

## 2.2 GPU-Based Volume Rendering

Volume rendering describes a wide range of techniques for generating images from three-dimensional scalar data [8]. These techniques are originally motivated by scientific visualization, where volume data (three dimension arrays of pixels) is acquired by measurement or numerical simulation of natural phenomena. Typical examples are medical data of the interior of the human body obtained by computed tomography (CT) or magnetic resonance imaging (MRI). The scalar data (often monochromatic) is mapped to color space by transfer function that is often implemented as lookup table.

The power of GPUs is currently increasing much faster than that of CPUs. That trend forces many computer programmers to move the burden of algorithm computation to GPU processors. Also the hardware support for interpolation of not only 2D but also 3D texture data enables the rendering of complex volumetric images in real time. Nowadays graphic programmers utilize high-level languages that support implementation of highly parallel algorithms that runs on programmable GPU's shaders. The main obstacle that must be overcome during creation of volume rendering algorithm is the fact that contemporary computer hardware still does not support direct rendering of volumetric data. There are two main groups of the algorithms that support fast visualization of volumetric data with hardware accelerated interpolation. The first group is ray-casting algorithms the second one texture-based algorithms. Both groups are capable to produce almost identical visualization results but they have quite different schemas. Moreover algorithms differs much in performance speed, which is important factor that must be taken into account in case of augmented reality environment [14]. All algorithms described below use tri-linear interpolation hardware support.

**Volume ray-casting algorithms.** In ray-casting process for each pixel in the image to render, algorithm casts a single ray from the eye through the pixel's center into the volume, and integrates the optical properties obtained from the encountered volume densities along the ray. Algorithm uses standard front to back blending equations in order to find color and opacity of rendered pixels:

$$C_{dst} = C_{dst} + (1 - \alpha_{dst}) \alpha_{src} C_{src} \tag{1}$$

$$\alpha_{dst} = \alpha_{dst} + (1 - \alpha_{dst}) \alpha_{src} \tag{2}$$

Where $C_{dst}$ and $\alpha_{dst}$ are the color and opacity values of the rendered pixels and $C_{src}$ and $\alpha_{src}$ are the color and opacity values of the incoming fragment.

The popular approach proposed in [9] includes standard acceleration techniques for volume ray casting like early ray termination and empty-space skipping. By means of these acceleration techniques, the framework is capable of efficiently rendering large volumetric data sets including opaque structures with occlusions effects and empty regions.

**Texture-based algorithms.** The ray casting approach is a classical image-order approach, because it divides the resulting image into pixels and then computes the contribution of the entire volume to each pixel [8]. Image-order approaches, however, are contrary to the way GPU hardware generates images. Graphics hardware usually uses an object-order approach, which divides the object into primitives and then calculates which set of pixels primitive influences.

In order to perform volume rendering in an object-order approach, the resampling locations are generated by rendering proxy geometry with interpolated texture coordinates.

The most basic proxy geometry is a stack of planar slices, all of which are required to be aligned with one of the major axes of the volume (either the x, y, or z axis) [8]. During rendering, the stack with slices most parallel to the viewing direction is chosen. In order to minimize the switching artifacts inter-slice interpolation ought to be included [8].

The more complex proxy geometry is slices aligned with the viewport [8]. Such slices closely mimic the sampling used by the ray-casting algorithm. The sufficient number of slices required for accurate visualization can easily be adjusted during algorithm performance.

## 2.3  Augmented Reality

Augmented reality (AR) is a technology that allows the real time fusion of computer generated digital content with the real world. Unlike virtual reality (VR), that completely immerses users inside a synthetic environment, augmented reality allows the user to see three-dimensional virtual objects superimposed upon the real word [15].

Augmented reality shows its usefulness especially in the field of the medicine [16]. The most notable examples are deformable body atlases, AR surgical navigation systems, interfaces and visualization systems. Pre, intra and post – operative visualization of clinical data is a major source of information for decision making. Augmented Reality aim at lifting this support to a new level by presenting more informative and realistic three-dimensional visualizations [17]. In our system AR is used as intuitive interface that enable easy and reliable manipulation of visualized objects.

Augmented reality environment used by authors utilizes size - known square markers. The transformation matrices from these marker coordinates to the camera coordinates are estimated by image analysis. The details of the algorithm can be found in [15].

## 3 Gradient Reconstructions for VR

Illumination and shading within volume rendering refers to the same illumination models and shading techniques used in polygon rendering. The goal is to enhance the appearance of rendered objects, especially to emphasize their shape and structure, by simulating the effects of light interacting with the object [18].

The most common local illumination model, which calculates light per pixel, is the Phong [19] lighting model. The Phong model is made up of three parts, ambient, diffuse and specular.

$$L = L_{ambient} + L_{diffuse} + L_{specular} \tag{3}$$

$$L_{ambient} = I_{ambient} \cdot K_{ambient} \tag{4}$$

Where $I_{ambient}$ is the constant intensity of the ambient light and $K_{ambient}$ is the coefficient of the ambient reflection of the surface. The ambient term is a constant, which simulates indirect light on the parts of geometry where there is no direct light, they would otherwise be entirely black.

$$L_{diffuse} = \begin{cases} I_{diffuse} \cdot K_{diffuse} \cdot \cos(\alpha), & |\alpha| < 90° \\ 0 & otherwise \end{cases} \tag{5}$$

Where $I_{diffuse}$ is light source intensity, $K_{diffuse}$ is a material constant describing color and $\alpha$ is the angle between light source and surface normal. The diffuse term calculates the reflection of light from a surface without shininess, called a matte surface. The light is reflected at the same angle as it is striking the surface relative to the surface normal.

$$L_{specular} = \begin{cases} I_{specular} \cdot K_{specular} \cdot \cos^{m}(\beta), & |\beta| < 90° \\ 0 & otherwise \end{cases} \tag{6}$$

where $I_{specular}$ is the intensity of the incident light, $K_{specular}$ is the coefficient of specular reflection for the material, $\beta$ is the angle between the reflection vector and the viewing vector and m controls the extension of the highlight. The specular term is added to simulate the shininess of surfaces, it creates highlights, which give the viewer cues of light source positions and geometry details.

An essential part of the illumination model is the surface normal. In VR case a surface normal is replaced by the gradient vector calculated at all points of interest [20].

$$\nabla f(x, y, z) = \left( \frac{df}{dx}, \frac{df}{dy}, \frac{df}{dz} \right) \qquad (7)$$

There are several methods for calculating the gradient vector. The most common are (see Appendix: 3D discrete gradient operators):

- Intermediate difference operator (8) [20].
- Central difference operator (9) [20].
- Neumann gradient operator (10) [20].
- Zucker-Hummel operator (11) [21].
- Sobel operator (12) [18], [22].

Intermediate difference gradient takes as input four neighboring voxels, Central difference gradient takes as input six neighboring voxels, the rest of operators take as input 26 or 27 neighboring voxels. The 26/27 neighbors give usually a better estimation of the gradient, but take more time to calculate. Another disadvantage is that additional smoothing might be introduced [23].

There are two basic methods of gradient computation strategy [7]: pre-generation of volume gradient and passing it to GPU memory by 3D texture or dynamic computation during rendering process. The first method requires large amount of memory (for each volume voxel the three gradient coefficients must be stored). The second method does not require additional memory (that means it uses even four times less memory then pre-generation) but is more expensive computationally as the components are calculated separately. Capacity of GPU memory is still bottleneck in VR algorithm even in visualization of typical medium-sized medical data. The question that we answered in the next paragraph is what is the performance speed of VR algorithms with pre-generated versus dynamically computed volume gradient on typical (off-the-shelf) graphical hardware and if it is sufficient for our needs.

## 4   Results and Discussion

The five gradients calculation methods from the previous paragraph where compared using three volume data (real CT images) of the size 256x256x221, 256x256x212 and 256x256x207 voxels. All of those models were rendered with two transfer function: transfer function with huge amount of semi transparent pixels (Figure 2, top row) and function without semi transparent pixels (Figure 2, bottom row). Those are two boundary cases that might be considered in medicine practice.

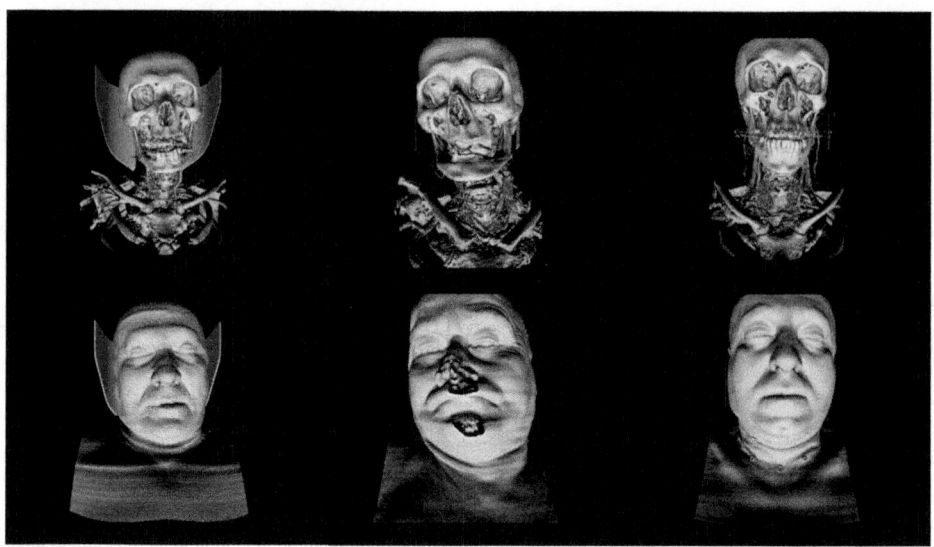

**Fig. 2.** Three different models based on volume CT data. Top row – models with transfer function with semi transparent pixels. Bottom row – same models with transfer function without semi transparent pixels.

For rendering purpose authors used two VR algorithms: volume ray casting (with early ray termination and empty space skipping) and texture based algorithm with view-aligned slices. The algorithms were implemented in .NET C#, XNA Framework 2.0 (Direct X 9.0) with HLSL and executed on Intel Core 2 Duo CPU 3.00 GHz processor, 3.25 GB RAM, Nvidia GeForce 9600 GT graphic card with 32 – bit Windows XP Professional OS.

The performance speed of VR was computed for three volume datasets mentioned above and then averaged. The gradient calculation methods were pre-computation and dynamic computation with 4-points, 6-point and 27-point method. The results are presented in Table 1 and Figure 3.

**Table 1.** Average performance speed (fps) of 3D models as a function of rendering algorithm type, gradient computation method and transfer function

| Rendering algorithm | Gradient computation method | Transfer function | |
|---|---|---|---|
| | | Semi-transparent pixels | No   semi-transparent pixels |
| **View-aligned slices** | Pre-computation | 38.00 | 38.00 |
| | 4 - points | 28.33 | 15.67 |
| | 6 - points | 24.67 | 12.33 |
| | 27 - points | 8.33 | 2.67 |
| **Volume ray casting** | Pre-computation | 29.67 | 54.00 |
| | 4 - points | 12.67 | 32.00 |
| | 6 - points | 11.00 | 28.67 |
| | 27 - points | 2.67 | 9.67 |

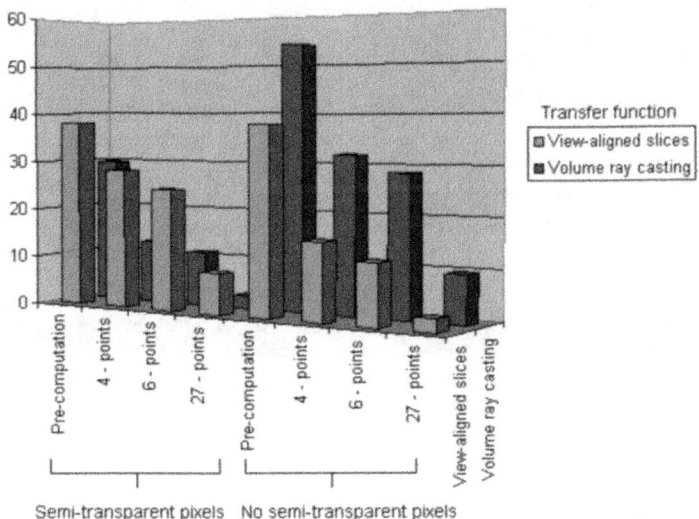

**Fig. 3.** Data from Table 1 presented in the chart. Dependents of average performance speed (fps) of 3D models as a function of rendering algorithm type, gradient computation method and transfer function.

The most time demanding operation is retrieving image data (voxel values) from 3D texture in GPU for computing of a gradient. This is the reason why algorithms with dynamic computed gradients are slower than with their pre-computed versions. The more points are needed for gradient calculation the slower the whole algorithm is. The very important factor that highly affects performance is a transfer function that is used for volume rendering. Volume ray casting is the fastest algorithm if the transfer function do not have many semi-transparent pixels. It is caused by the fact that in that case early ray termination quickly finishes the ray lookup loop. The texture based algorithm has to render all slices no matter if there are visible or not. On the other hand if there are many semi-transparent pixels the empty space skipping and ray termination will not help the ray casting to improve program speed. The number of computation and references to 3D texture memory is higher than in texture-based algorithm, which becomes quicker.

The second factor that we took into account during comparison of gradient computation methods is a quality of gradient reconstruction (Figure 4). The results was similar to those described in [5]. The intermediate difference and central difference operator are good low-pass filters. There are also highly visible quality differences between those two methods: intermediate difference generates much more lighting artifact then the 6-point methods. The Sobel gradient estimation method, as well as other 26/27-pixels gradient estimation approaches, produces less fringing artifacts than other methods. The differences between Sobel, Neumann, Zucker-Hummel are nearly invisible and does not affect the image analysis process. What is more important the differences of quality (when taking into account fringing artifacts)

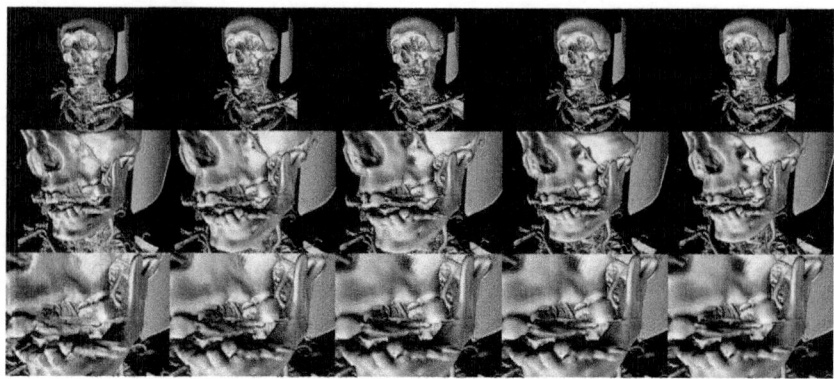

**Fig. 4.** Volume rendering of example model with different methods of gradient estimation. From left to right: intermediate difference, central difference, Sobel, Neumann and Zucker-Hummel.

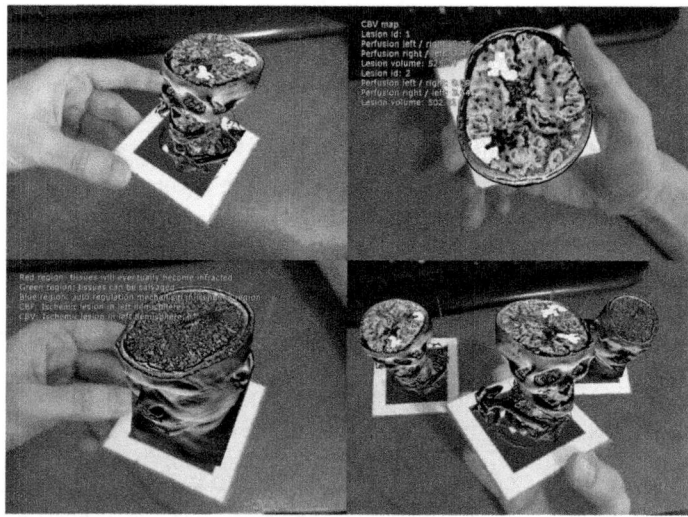

**Fig. 5.** The example visualization of superimposition of dpCT onto volume CT data in AR. (A) CBF map with marked perfusion abnormalities. (B) The detailed view of CBV and prognostic image. In the left top side of each image description done by DMD system. (C) The detailed view of prognostic image. In the left top side of each image description done by DMD system. (D) From left to right: CBV, CBF and Prognostic image.

between central difference and the high order estimation methods do not disqualify the 6-points method. Also visualization with central difference operator is 3 to 4 times faster than with high quality kernels.

Knowing all of those results we decided to use in our solution both visualization algorithms with a dynamic central difference gradient computation method. After determining the transfer function an algorithm decides which of those method runs faster and uses it during session with program. That approach enables the visualization to run with the speed oscillating near 30 fps, which is an accepted value for our needs. The example visualization of superimposition of dpCT onto volume CT data in AR with our program is shown in Figure 5.

## 5   Conclusions and Future Work

This papers presents and summarizes the results of the integration of cognitive image analysis and patter recognition algorithm with a high quality hardware accelerated volume renderer into an augmented reality visualization environment. Augmented reality supplies the system with more informative and realistic three-dimensional visualizations offering very intuitive image manipulation interface. The performance of the presented techniques was demonstrated and evaluated in several experiments by rendering real human CT data with different rendering techniques. The authors also took into account the quality and speed of volume gradient estimation methods considering transfer function type.

There are many important aspects which future work should focus on. Superimposition the dpCT data onto volume CT / MR enables to perform more detailed diagnosis for example taking into account not only dynamic perfusion but also the state of the vascular system (brain angiography). The further researches should also be done in the field of real time large volume visualization that might be needed during superimposition of medical data of several modalities. Our augmented reality system should also be replaced by marker-less solution that would be more convenient for the end user.

**Acknowledgments.** This work has been supported by the Ministry of Science and Higher Education, Republic of Poland, under project number N N516 511939.

## References

[1] Jara, A.J., Zamora, M.A., Skarmeta, A.F.G.: An Initial Approach to Support Mobility in Hospital Wireless Sensor Networks based on 6LoWPAN (HWSN6). Journal of Wireless Mobile Networks, Ubiquitous Computing, and Dependable Applications 2(3), 107–122 (2010)

[2] Hachaj, T., Ogiela, M.R.: CAD system for automatic analysis of CT perfusion maps. Opto-Electronics Review 19(1), 95–103 (2011), doi:10.2478/s11772-010-0071-2

[3] Hachaj, T., Ogiela, M.R.: Computer – assisted diagnosis system for detection, measure and description of dynamic computer tomography perfusion maps. In: Choraś, R.S., Zabłudowski, A. (eds.) Image Processing and Communication Challenges (2009)

[4] Hachaj, T., Ogiela, M.R.: A system for detecting and describing pathological changes using dynamic perfusion computer tomography brain maps. Computers in Biology and Medicine 41, 402–410 (2011)

[5] Bentum, M.J., Lichtenbelt, B.B.A., Malzbender, T.: Frequency Analysis of Gradient Estimators in Volume Rendering. Journal IEEE Transactions on Visualization and Computer Graphics Archive 2(3) (September 1996)

[6] Mihajlovic, Z., Budin, L., Radej, J.: Gradient of B-splines in volume rendering. In: Proceedings of the 12th IEEE Mediterranean Electrotechnical Conference, MELECON 2004 (2004)

[7] Csébfalvi, B., Domonkos, B.: Prefiltered Gradient Reconstruction for Volume Rendering. In: WSCG: The 17th International Conference in Central Europe on Computer Graphics, Visualization and Computer Vision, Pilsen, Czech Republic (2009)

[8] Engel, K., Hadwiger, M., Kniss, J., Rezk-Salama, C., Weiskopf, D.: Real-Time Volume Graphics. CRC Press, Boca Raton (2006)

[9] Krüuger, J., Westermann, R.: Acceleration Techniques for GPU-based Volume Rendering. IEEE Visualization (2003)

[10] Hachaj, T., Ogiela, M.R.: Augmented reality interface for visualization of volumetric medical data. In: Image Processing and Communications Challenges, vol. 2, pp. 271–277. Springer, Heidelberg (2010)

[11] Parraga, A., et al.: Non-rigid registration methods assessment of 3D CT images for head-neck radiotherapy. In: Proceedings of SPIE Medical Imaging (February 2007)

[12] Hachaj, T.: The registration and atlas construction of noisy brain computer tomography images based on free form deformation technique. Bio-Algorithms and Med-Systems, Collegium Medicum - Jagiellonian University, Bio-Algorithms and Med-Systems 7 (2008)

[13] Koenig, M., Kraus, M., Theek, C., Klotz, E., Gehlen, W., Heuser, L.: Quantitative assessment of the ischemic brain by means of perfusion-related parameters derived from perfusion CT. Stroke; a Journal of Cerebral Circulation 32(2), 431–437 (2001)

[14] Kutter, O., Aichert, A., Bichlmeier, C., Traub, J., Heining, S.M., Ockert, B., Euler, E., Navab, N.: Real-time Volume Rendering for High Quality Visualization in Augmented Reality. In: International Workshop on Augmented Environments for Medical Imaging including Augmented Reality in Computer-aided Surgery (AMI-ARCS 2008), USA, New York (September 2008)

[15] Haller, M., Billinghurst, M., Thomas, B.: Emerging Technologies of Augmented Reality: Interfaces and Design. Idea Group Publishing, USA (2006)

[16] Yang, G., Jiang, T.: MIAR 2004. LNCS, vol. 3150. Springer, Heidelberg (2004)

[17] Denis, K., et al.: Integrated Medical Workflow for Augmented Reality Applications. In: International Workshop on Augmented environments for Medical Imaging and Computer-aided Surgery, AMI-ARCS (2006)

[18] Grimm, S.: Real-Time Mono- and Multi-Volume Rendering of Large Medical Datasets on Standard PC Hardware. PhD thesis, Vienna University of Technology, Gaullachergasse 33/35, 1160 Vienna, Austria (February 2005)

[19] Phong, B.T.: Illumination for Computer Generated Pictures. Communications of the ACM 18(6), 311–317 (1975)

[20] Jonsson, M.: Volume rendering, Master's Thesis in Computing Science, October 12 (2005),
http://www8.cs.umu.se/education/examina/Rapporter/MarcusJonson.pdf

[21] Ballard, D.H., Brown, C.M.: Confocal Volume Rendering: Fast Segmentation-Free Visualization of Internal Structures. In: Proceedings of SPIE Medical Imaging 2000 — Image Display and Visualization, SPIE, San Diego, California, February 12-17, vol. 3976, pp. 70–76 (2000)

[22] Chan, M.-Y., Wu, Y., Mak, W.-H., Chen, W., Qu, H.: Perception-Based Transparency Optimization for Direct Volume Rendering. IEEE Transactions on Visualization and Computer Graphics (Proceedings Visualization / Information Visualization 2009) 15(6) (November-December 2009)

[23] Pommert, A., Tiede, U., Wiebecke, G., Hohne, K.H.: Surface Shading in Tomographic Volume Visualization. In: Proceedings of the First Conference on Visualization in Biomedical Computing, vol. 1, p. 19 (1990)

## Appendix: 3D Discrete Gradient Operators

Intermediate difference operator:

$$\nabla f(x_i, y_j, z_k) = \begin{pmatrix} f(x_i+1, y_j, z_k) - f(x_i, y_j, z_k), \\ f(x_i, y_j+1, z_k) - f(x_i, y_j, z_k), \\ f(x_i, y_j, z_k+1) - f(x_i, y_j, z_k) \end{pmatrix} \tag{8}$$

Central difference operator:

$$\nabla f(x_i, y_j, z_k) = \frac{1}{2} \begin{pmatrix} f(x_i+1, y_j, z_k) - f(x_i-1, y_j, z_k), \\ f(x_i, y_j+1, z_k) - f(x_i, y_j-1, z_k), \\ f(x_i, y_j, z_k+1) - f(x_i, y_j, z_k-1) \end{pmatrix} \tag{9}$$

The kernel of Neumann gradient operator:

$$\nabla_x := \frac{1}{52} \begin{pmatrix} \begin{pmatrix} -2 & 0 & 2 \\ -3 & 0 & 3 \\ -2 & 0 & 2 \end{pmatrix} & \begin{pmatrix} -3 & 0 & 3 \\ -6 & 0 & 6 \\ -3 & 0 & 3 \end{pmatrix} & \begin{pmatrix} -2 & 0 & 2 \\ -3 & 0 & 3 \\ -2 & 0 & 2 \end{pmatrix} \end{pmatrix}$$

$$\nabla_y := \frac{1}{52} \begin{pmatrix} \begin{pmatrix} 2 & 3 & 2 \\ 0 & 0 & 0 \\ -2 & -3 & -2 \end{pmatrix} & \begin{pmatrix} 3 & 6 & 3 \\ 0 & 0 & 0 \\ -3 & -6 & -3 \end{pmatrix} & \begin{pmatrix} 2 & 3 & 2 \\ 0 & 0 & 0 \\ -2 & -3 & -2 \end{pmatrix} \end{pmatrix} \tag{10}$$

$$\nabla_z := \frac{1}{52} \begin{pmatrix} \begin{pmatrix} -2 & -3 & -2 \\ -3 & -6 & -3 \\ -2 & -3 & -2 \end{pmatrix} & \begin{pmatrix} 0 & 0 & 0 \\ 0 & 0 & 0 \\ 0 & 0 & 0 \end{pmatrix} & \begin{pmatrix} 2 & 3 & 2 \\ 3 & 6 & 3 \\ 2 & 3 & 2 \end{pmatrix} \end{pmatrix}$$

The kernel of Zucker-Hummel operator:

$$\nabla_x := \begin{pmatrix} \begin{pmatrix} -\dfrac{\sqrt{3}}{3} & 0 & \dfrac{\sqrt{3}}{3} \\ -\dfrac{\sqrt{2}}{2} & 0 & \dfrac{\sqrt{2}}{2} \\ -\dfrac{\sqrt{3}}{3} & 0 & \dfrac{\sqrt{3}}{3} \end{pmatrix} & \begin{pmatrix} -\dfrac{\sqrt{2}}{2} & 0 & \dfrac{\sqrt{2}}{2} \\ -1 & 0 & 1 \\ -\dfrac{\sqrt{2}}{2} & 0 & \dfrac{\sqrt{2}}{2} \end{pmatrix} & \begin{pmatrix} -\dfrac{\sqrt{3}}{3} & 0 & \dfrac{\sqrt{3}}{3} \\ -\dfrac{\sqrt{2}}{2} & 0 & \dfrac{\sqrt{2}}{2} \\ -\dfrac{\sqrt{3}}{3} & 0 & \dfrac{\sqrt{3}}{3} \end{pmatrix} \end{pmatrix} \tag{11}$$

$$\nabla_y := \left( \begin{pmatrix} \dfrac{\sqrt{3}}{3} & \dfrac{\sqrt{2}}{2} & \dfrac{\sqrt{3}}{3} \\ 0 & 0 & 0 \\ -\dfrac{\sqrt{3}}{3} & -\dfrac{\sqrt{2}}{2} & -\dfrac{\sqrt{3}}{3} \end{pmatrix} \begin{pmatrix} \dfrac{\sqrt{2}}{2} & 1 & \dfrac{\sqrt{2}}{2} \\ 0 & 0 & 0 \\ -\dfrac{\sqrt{2}}{2} & -1 & -\dfrac{\sqrt{2}}{2} \end{pmatrix} \begin{pmatrix} \dfrac{\sqrt{3}}{3} & \dfrac{\sqrt{2}}{2} & \dfrac{\sqrt{3}}{3} \\ 0 & 0 & 0 \\ -\dfrac{\sqrt{3}}{3} & -\dfrac{\sqrt{2}}{2} & -\dfrac{\sqrt{3}}{3} \end{pmatrix} \right)$$

$$\nabla_z := \left( \begin{pmatrix} -\dfrac{\sqrt{3}}{\sqrt{3}} & -\dfrac{\sqrt{2}}{2} & -\dfrac{\sqrt{3}}{\sqrt{3}} \\ -\dfrac{\sqrt{2}}{2} & -1 & -\dfrac{\sqrt{2}}{2} \\ -\dfrac{\sqrt{3}}{\sqrt{3}} & -\dfrac{\sqrt{2}}{2} & -\dfrac{\sqrt{3}}{\sqrt{3}} \end{pmatrix} \begin{pmatrix} 0 & 0 & 0 \\ 0 & 0 & 0 \\ 0 & 0 & 0 \end{pmatrix} \begin{pmatrix} \dfrac{\sqrt{3}}{\sqrt{3}} & \dfrac{\sqrt{2}}{2} & \dfrac{\sqrt{3}}{\sqrt{3}} \\ \dfrac{\sqrt{2}}{2} & 1 & \dfrac{\sqrt{2}}{2} \\ \dfrac{\sqrt{3}}{\sqrt{3}} & \dfrac{\sqrt{2}}{2} & \dfrac{\sqrt{3}}{\sqrt{3}} \end{pmatrix} \right)$$

The kernel of Sobel operator:

$$\nabla_x := \left( \begin{pmatrix} -1 & 0 & 1 \\ -3 & 0 & 3 \\ -1 & 0 & 1 \end{pmatrix} \begin{pmatrix} -3 & 0 & 3 \\ -6 & 0 & 6 \\ -3 & 0 & 3 \end{pmatrix} \begin{pmatrix} -1 & 0 & 1 \\ -3 & 0 & 3 \\ -1 & 0 & 1 \end{pmatrix} \right)$$

$$\nabla_y := \left( \begin{pmatrix} 1 & 3 & 1 \\ 0 & 0 & 0 \\ -1 & -3 & -1 \end{pmatrix} \begin{pmatrix} 3 & 6 & 3 \\ 0 & 0 & 0 \\ -3 & -6 & -3 \end{pmatrix} \begin{pmatrix} 1 & 3 & 1 \\ 0 & 0 & 0 \\ -1 & -3 & -1 \end{pmatrix} \right) \quad (12)$$

$$\nabla_z := \left( \begin{pmatrix} -1 & -3 & -1 \\ -3 & -6 & -3 \\ -1 & -3 & -1 \end{pmatrix} \begin{pmatrix} 0 & 0 & 0 \\ 0 & 0 & 0 \\ 0 & 0 & 0 \end{pmatrix} \begin{pmatrix} 1 & 3 & 1 \\ 3 & 6 & 3 \\ 1 & 3 & 1 \end{pmatrix} \right)$$

# Hierarchical Knowledge Structure Applied to Image Analyzing System - Possibilities of Practical Usage

Krzysztof Wójcik

Pedagogical University of Cracow, Institute of Computer Science,
ul.Podchorążych 2, 30-084 Kraków, Poland
krzyw@ap.krakow.pl

**Abstract.** This article describes a proposition and first examples of using inductive learning methods in building of the image understanding system with the hierarchical structure of knowledge. This system may be utilized in various task of automatic image interpretation, classification and image enhancement. The paper points to the essential problems of the whole method: the constructing an effective algorithm of conceptual clustering and creation of the method of knowledge evaluation. Some possible solutions are discussed and first practical results (image filtering) are presented.

**Keywords:** image understanding, pattern recognition, image processing, knowledge engineering, machine learning, cognitive informatics.

## 1 Introduction

The starting point of presented research is the general idea of the image understanding methods (Figure 1). The most important characteristic of that approach is the extraction of the semantic content of the image (or more generally - the phenomenon or event). It is constructed by the automatic reasoning process, according to the knowledge about the images [5]. This scheme can essentially improve the automatic interpretation of the events, but we can also point to some weaknesses. The first one is the assumption that we have a useful model of the phenomena. The process of creating the model of a domain involves both, the definition of concepts and defining the relationships between them [4]. This task is more formally called an ontology building. There are several tools [6] which may support this process but the starting assumptions still depend on the knowledge and intuition of the researcher (i.e. human being) [4]. The created ontology describes one specific reality, so the system is often insufficiently flexible to act in a changing environment. That is the second weakness. Another difficulty is associated with a problem of knowledge acquisition - learning. There is no general methodology of learning [2], we have several methods, but the open problem is how to choose the suitable one and accommodate it to the changing circumstances.

A M. Tjoa et al. (Eds.): ARES 2011, LNCS 6908, pp. 149–163, 2011.

The article describes an attempt to overcome these weaknesses, it explains a simple idea of creating the concept structure according to the visible phenomena. This structure includes the general knowledge about images and may be considered as the model of the phenomena.

The method will be illustrated by the chosen examples - mainly by the method of the removing of obstructions from image. They may be caused by the noise (this is an often effect of image acquiring in extreme poor light condition), by artifacts (as a result of image compression, typically occurs in USB cameras). The obstructions may be also caused by dust or scratches (analyzing of the archive, analog photos).

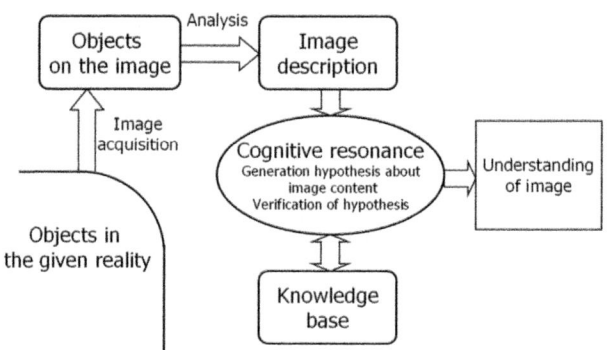

**Fig. 1.** Idea of the image understanding (based on the [5])

## 2    Method Outline

I begin with the problems of ontology creation. Following this approach I will cancel or reduce all initial assumptions about the visible phenomena.

That reduction leads to the statement that the phenomenon consists of a kind of atomic, elementary parts, called primitive objects or instances. They corresponds to the primitive "concepts", called also types or classes. Suffice it to say that concepts are some kind of generalization of objects. The objects are connected by primitive relationships. We will use the following notations:

$$\mathbb{X} \text{ — space of all objects,}$$
$$\mathbf{X_0}, \ \mathbf{X} \subset \mathbb{X} \text{ — sets of objects,}$$
$$\mathbf{C_0}, \ \mathbf{C} \text{ — sets of concepts,}$$
$$\mathbf{D_0}, \ \mathbf{D} \text{ — sets of relationships.}$$

So, at the beginning, we assume that $\mathbf{C_0}, \mathbf{D_0}$ represent primitive concepts and primitive relationships respectively. These sets contain the whole initial knowledge. The main idea is that the general knowledge is included in the structure of concepts. So, the increase of knowledge is possible by creating the new concepts. I consider those concepts as the generalization of objects, therefore the presence of the certain objects in the given reality is a condition of the concept creating. This universal idea is utilized in various kinds of inductive learning and learning based on the observation [1]. The objects which make the creating of the concept possible should be in some way significant. I assume that it will happen if objects are connected by the relationships. A frequent, multiple presence of those objects should strengthen their ability to create concepts, according to the simple rule: *this phenomenon occurs many times, so it must be important.* Now I will be more precise about this.

Let us assume, we can select the primitive objects and recognize them as particular instances corresponding to the certain concepts (classification task). Let us also assume that it is possible to check all prior defined relations between all objects. Consider one of them, indicated by:

$r_i$,        where: $r_i \in \mathbf{D}$, $i \in \mathbf{I}$, $\mathbf{I} = \{1, 2, \dots, u\}$ is a set of indices of relations. Let us presume, $r_i$ has $n$ arguments, so it may be satisfied by some $n$-tuple (ordered sequence of $n$ elements) indicated by:

$t$, $t \in \mathbb{X}^n$        ($n$th Cartesian power of set $\mathbb{X}$)

Of course, this relationship may be satisfied by many other sequence, denoted by:

$t_{ik}$,        where: $i \in \mathbf{I}$, $k \in \mathbf{K}$, $\mathbf{K} = \{1, 2, \dots, m\}$ is a set of indices of tuples, which satisfy $r_i$ relation (the first index of tuple $t_{ik}$, point to $r_i$ relation).

Just according to the selected tuples we will try to create groups (sets) of objects that will allow us to construct the new concept. Let us define the group $\mathbf{G}$ as an ordered set of selected tuples:

$\mathbf{G} = \{t_{ik} : i \in \mathbf{I}, \ k \in \mathbf{K}\}$

(we assume here (see above) that first index of tuple $t_{ik}$ allows us to identify relation which is satisfied).

Let us transform the $\mathbf{G}$ set by the simple replacing of each object in each tuple by the label of object type. We obtain a set, denoted by $\mathbf{S}$, that describes an abstract[1] arrangement of relations in the group. The groups that have identical or similar[2] arrangement will be regarded as similar. Many such groups may appear in the sequence of input images. So, a set of similar groups should be consider:

$\mathbb{G} = \{\mathbf{G}_1, \mathbf{G}_2, \dots, \mathbf{G}_z\}$

The $\mathbb{G}$ set will be used in creation of the new concept. The next chapter presents a simple method of construction of the $\mathbb{G}$ set. Generally, this task should consist of a kind of conceptual clustering[3], in domain of defined above groups. After the clustering process we can obtain a set of groups, which are similar to each other, and according to this we can determine one, most characteristic group. I will use $\mathbf{G}'$ to denote this group, and $\mathbf{S}'$ to denote an arrangement of relations in $\mathbf{G}'$. The whole task of creation of $\mathbf{G}'$ set will be denoted by $\mathbf{FG}$.

---

[1] Depending on the types, not on the particular objects.

[2] Similarity may be defined here in several ways.

[3] We have a $n$-ary relations, that might be represented by the predicate $\mathbb{P}(t)$, $t \in \mathbb{X}^n$. So, the solution of the clustering task may base on the usage of first-order representations and methods of inductive logic programming (ILP) [3].

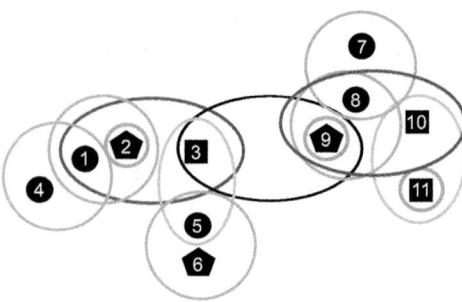

**Fig. 2.** Example of the group structure

Figure 2 shows several indexed objects $x_1, x_2, \dots$ of three types (circle, pentagon, square). The few relationships are also defined ($r_1$ - red oval, $r_2$ - blue, $r_3$ - orange, $r_4$ - green, $r_5$ - black). We can specify several tuples:

$t_{31} = (x_2)$, $t_{32} = (x_9)$, $t_{33} = (x_{11})$ (the $t_{31}$ denotes 1-st tuple of relation $r_3$)

$t_{21} = (x_1, x_4)$, $t_{22} = (x_1, x_2)$, $t_{23} = (x_8, x_9)$, $t_{24} = (x_8, x_7)$

$t_{41} = (x_3, x_5)$, $t_{42} = (x_{10}, x_{11})$,

$t_{11} = (x_1, x_2, x_3)$, $t_{12} = (x_9, x_8, x_{10})$.

So, I can point to two groups "strongly" connected by the relations:
$\mathbf{G_1} = \{t_{31}, t_{21}, t_{22}, t_{11}\}$, $\mathbf{G_2} = \{t_{32}, t_{24}, t_{23}, t_{12}\}$ then $\mathbb{G} = \{\mathbf{G_1}, \mathbf{G_2}\}$ and for example: $\mathbf{G'} = \mathbf{G_1}$

Let us go back to the main problem. As a first approximation, we can say:

$$new\ concept = \mathbf{S'}$$

The new concept is treated as an arrangement of relationships enriched by the information about the types of their arguments. To let us describe the new phenomena more completely, it should contain an additional information. The new object (of a new concept) may be defined as a combination of several sub-objects according to the structure of the group (see next part of this chapter). The new objects may have new attributes (new properties vector). The objects should in some way inherit properties from sub-objects. It may be done for example by the simple copying, calculating a sum or average of given values. More generally, we can imagine the task of calculating the attributes as a combination of certain standard transformation. Let **FA** be a whole process of creating of new properties vector.

There is another significant question. The new objects are the combination of sub-objects, but may they be applied as arguments of old relationships? Or, should the old relationship be rather redefined in order to be applied to the new objects? It depends on how long we require the new objects to inherit a behavior of its parents. To be more precise, it depends on how the attributes are transformed (in the previous **FA** process) and what new interpretation they have. Let **FR** be a process of adapting or creating the new relationships.

Finally, we can consider the concept as a composition of elements:

$$\mathbf{S'}, \mathbf{FG}, \mathbf{FA}, \mathbf{FR}$$

So, the creation of the new concept is performed by the combination of transformations **FG**, **FA** and **FR**. As a result the new concept, new relationships and new objects are obtained. We can join them into the **C**, **D**, **X** sets respectively. The whole process may be operated repetitively. This results in creating a hierarchical structure of concepts and hierarchical structure of new objects, see the Figure 3. The structure of concepts includes the new general knowledge, while the structure of objects contains the knowledge about the particular scene. The structure of concepts may be also treated as a model of given reality. Thanks to hierarchical form, the knowledge may be interpreted, verified, adapted to other systems and finally understood by the man.

Thus, there are two general aspects of learning. First is associated with the process of the creating of the concept structure. It means a building of the model of the reality. The second kind of learning (creating of the structure of objects) deals with the acquisition of knowledge about particular objects (scene).

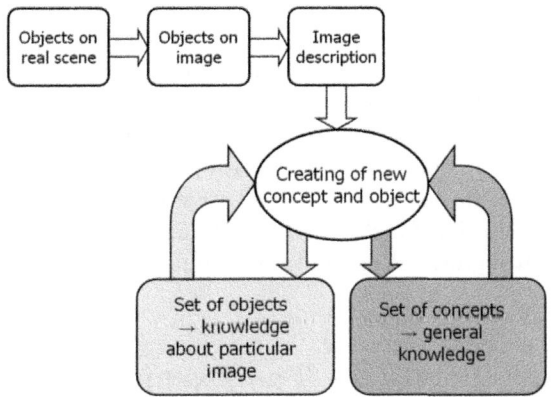

**Fig. 3.** The iterative process of knowledge creation. If the new concepts are not created, the action may be called an "image interpretation".

There still remain two important matters. The first one is associated with the question: is this knowledge really useful? The knowledge evaluation may be performed in several ways:

– By the practical action.
  Let us imagine the system as an agent acting in the certain environment. According to the given scene and its own concept structure the agent can create the structure of objects. Then, the correlation between the existence

of the certain concepts and the agent's ability to make correct decisions (or simple ability to survive) can be computed. We assume that the agent be able to do the correct decisions has the most useful knowledge. This approach may be used especially in evolutionary algorithms.

– By the defined performance function.

The hierarchical knowledge may be interpreted, so a direct method of its evaluation may be defined.

– By the using of the arbiter, teacher (supervised learning).

The second important problem mentioned above, is how to find the best concept structure (i.e. system knowledge). This task may be treated as the task of the optimization of the function in a multidimensional space. It seems to be properly defined; we have the criterion function[4], we can also control the process of creating the concept structure. That suggests that to find the suitable concept structure we can use one of the well-known techniques, for example:

– "Trial and error method".
– Certain kind of evolutionary algorithm (a particular system is considered as an individual).
– Kind of Monte Carlo method.

However, the direct usage of such methods is problematical. The particular concept structure is generated as a result of multiple execution of transformation **FG**, **FA** and **FR**. There are many possible variants of these transformation. The solution is one point of the extremely large hypothesis space. In order to decrease the number of solutions, we can propose some heuristic approach. Assume generally that the selection of each transformations is done with the help of a certain local criterion functions. These functions play a role of a guide that helps searching through the decision tree. The next parts of article provide more details.

## 3    The Simple Solution - The Example of Using the Method in the Image Analysis System

The examples that will be described in the next chapters have been tested in the simple image analyzing system which has been designed mainly as a field of experiments. The first example is trivial, but allows us to point to some important properties of the method.

The first steps refer to defining the initial sets $C_0, D_0$ (primitive concepts and relationships). As a system input is considered a sequence of pictures from CCD camera (I have used figures of animals drawn by a child). By using the segmentation method we can identify sets of pixels which create a simple raster

---

[4] It may be directly the performance function, or some functions that depend on the teacher's decision or effects of the practical action.

figures. These figures may be easily transformed to vectors with properties like: *number of pixels, color, center coordinates, approximate shape*. This structure will be considered as a primitive object. Between such objects some primitive relationships are defined: binary - *neighboring*, and a few unary, for example: *having a small size, having a red color*.

The next steps relate to the **FG**, **FA** and **FR** transformations.

**1.** The **FG** transformation, selection of the $\mathbb{G}$ and $\mathbf{G'}$ sets.

The relationships which hold between the objects in the groups generally refer to any, multi-argument predicates. In this simple case I will take into consideration only one- or two-argument relationships. A group **G** will be created by one main object $o_m \in \mathbf{X}$ and several objects which are connected with it by some relations. That group may be easily determined by checking all possible relationships of the $o_m$ object. In this way we can create groups for all $o_m$ objects. Having the set of groups, a simple clustering can be performed. In this connection we should draw attention to several universal criteria:

1. The basic criterion - number of similar groups. The groups which have identical arrangement of relationships are similar (see previous chapter), and may create a cluster. The number of groups in this cluster indicates how important it is. The arrangement of the groups will be called a "pattern".
2. The validity of objects that create the groups. After a few iterations of the concept creation process we obtain many combined objects. Each object may be evaluated directly basis on the number of objects that were included.
3. The validity of the relationships between the objects of the group. In the simple way it can be expressed by the number of relationships that connect objects in the group. In addition the amount of one-argument relationships that are satisfied by the main $o_m$ object may be respected.
4. The "parent-child" restriction. Let us presume, we create a new group $\mathbf{G_n}$ based on the main object $o_m$. Let $o_m$ (as a combined object) consist of "parent" object $o_p$. Assume that the new group $\mathbf{G_n}$ includes also the $o_p$. Such a "double" object as a redundant should be deleted or, if not, the evaluation of such a group should be decreased.
5. The similarity to old patterns. The similarity between groups on the analyzing scenes is of course a base of clustering. But the similarity between the new groups and groups that was already used to create the concepts is undesirable. It may result in creating a redundant concept.

According to the given rules a sorted list of sets of groups can be made. The best element that may be considered as the $\mathbb{G}$ set will be used to create the concept.

So, the mentioned above criteria play a role of local criterion functions (guide function) that help searching through the decision tree (chapter 2).

**2.** The **FA** transformation, definition of new properties vector.

The calculating of the attributes of the new objects must base on the properties of the component objects. Without going into details, we can calculate the sum (*number of pixels*), average (*color, center coordinate*) and maximum (*shape*).

**3.** The **FR** transformation, process of adapting or creating the relationships. In described case the new concepts inherit all old relationships.

After a description of the **FG**, **FA** and **FR** transformations, we should still explain how we will evaluate the knowledge and which searching algorithm will be used (chapter 2). In our very simple case the evaluation will depend on the "agent's ability to survive". Therefore we use an uncomplicated "trial and error method".

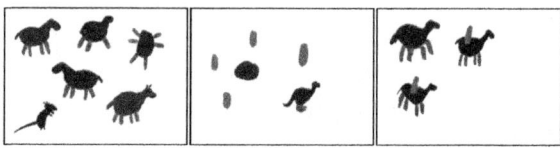

**Fig. 4.** The input sequence of pictures - the figures of animals

Figure 4 shows the sequence of analyzing pictures. The next picture (Figure 5) presents processed images and frames showing the "state" of the system. The green circled item (top right) is an example of a pattern.

1.7 1.7 1.7 1.7 | 3 4 ct 8 ## 3 qqq 10[5]

The list of defined concepts is shown in the left-center frame. The red circled item:

type 10 ct 8 qq 5 pat: 1.7 1.7 1.7 1.7 | 3 4[6]

shows the definition of type 10, that represents something having big, blue body and four green legs. We can consider this as a concept "horse". The bootom frames show the system state after analysis of second and third images presented in the Figure 4. We can identify two another concept:

type 11 ct 0 qq 1 pat: | 5 6

type 13 ct 10 qq 6 pat: 1.11 | 2 4

The first one we consider as a "rider", while the second as a "rider on the horse" (the object of type 11 "rider" is connected to the main object of type 10 "horse"). The creation of the last concept was possible when the concept "horse" was created first. We can say that the proper interpretation of a new phenomenon is possible when the suitable knowledge is available. Without them, it may be understood as a "dragon" with four legs and something red on the top.

---

[5] 1.7 - relation 1 *neighboring*; holds between the main object and four others of type 7, 3 4 - properties of main object *having a blue color, having a big size*, ct 8 - type of the main object (index of concept on the list), ## 3 - number of the group of objects that match the pattern, qqq 10 - value of performance function of pattern.

[6] Type 10 - number of type, ct 8 - type of the main object, qq 5 - value of validity function of that type, pat: 1.7 1.7 1.7 1.7 | 3 4 - the pattern described earlier (objects of type 7 have properties 2,5; *having a green color, having small size*).

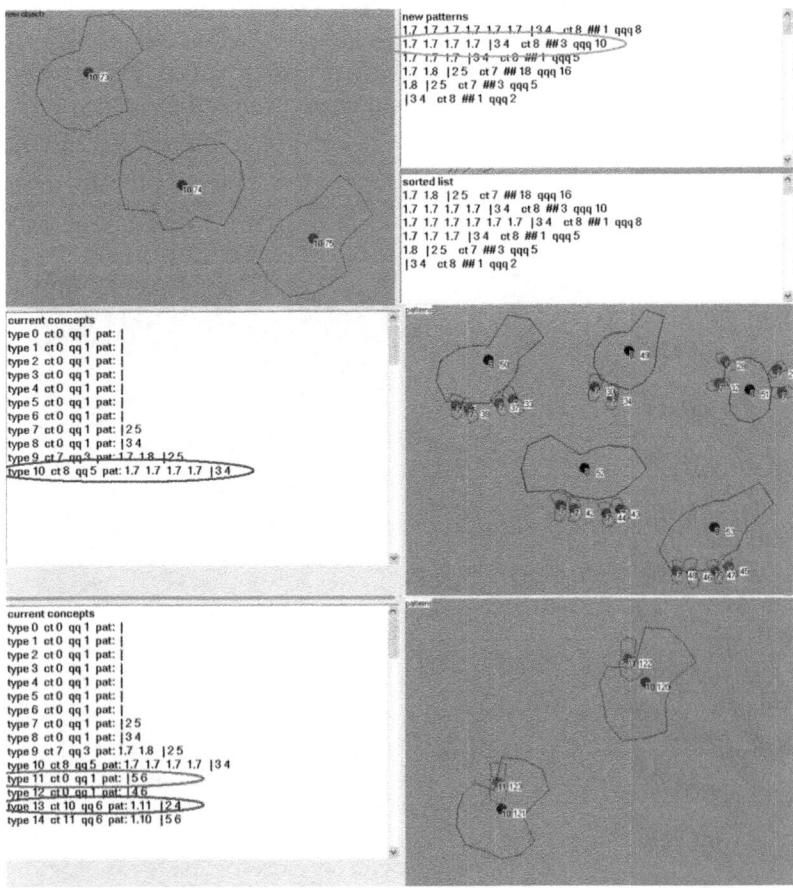

**Fig. 5.** The interface of the image understanding system - the concept definitions

## 4    Image Filtering - Obstruction Removing

The presented above example was an illustration of the method, while the current case may be also applied practically. The task deals with the method of the image quality enhancement. For simplicity, I will only go about the removing of the dust, noise effects or artifacts. The main problem here is how to recognize the little obstructions (artifacts, dust seeds) among other small objects on te picture. The simple image recognition methods consider the properties of the objects, but it is not enough to perform a correct classification. The other small objects have often the same properties. We should also take into consideration relationships between the objects.

As well as in the previous case we have the raster image, so we will also follow analogous steps. The first step corresponds to the definitions of the primitive concepts and primitive relationships (initial sets $C_0, D_0$, chapter 2). Like in the previous example we can obtain (after a segmentation) sets of pixels that represent the objects and then we can calculate the vectors of object properties (identical properties are used: *number of pixels, color, center coordinates, approximate shape*). The figure 6 shows an example of raster image (part A), objects after the segmentation process (part B) and the "map" of primitive objects (part C).

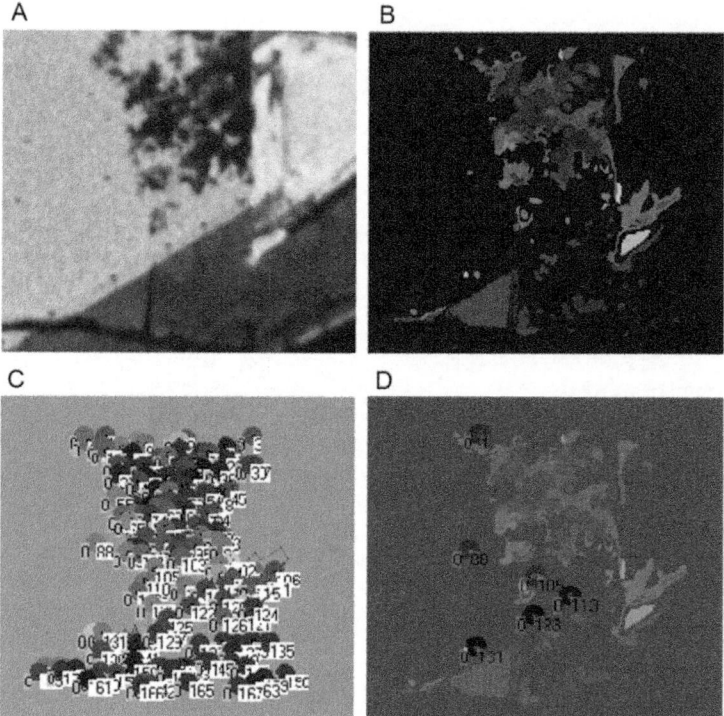

**Fig. 6.** A: example of raster image, that represents a fragment of a house roof. B: objects after the segmentation process (a region growing method was used). C: "The symbolic map" that depicts all object on the picture in the form of symbols (small circles). The unique name tags of objects as well as labels of their type are also displayed. D: Objects of learning strings (see the next chapter).

The definitions of the relationships are also analogous. There are defined unary relations concerning properties like color and size (see chapter 3). In order to better convey the spatial interactions between objects, the binary relationship, *neighboring* (chapter 3) is split into two variants. They are: *neighboring up* (object is above the other one) and *neighboring down*.

Again, also the processes **FG**, **FA** and **FR** will be defined similarly.

In accordance with the our methodology, the next steps should involve two problems:
- the evaluation of the system knowledge,
- the choose of the the optimization method.

## 4.1  Evaluation of Knowledge

A result of the working of the system is an enhancement of the picture quality, so it may be judged by the man. We can imagine thousands of output pictures generated by the systems (having different variants of knowledge). Their evaluation in this way is of course impossible. But remember, we are able to interpret the structure of the concepts (chapter 2). So, we will try to define the performance functions that should evaluate the possibility of usage of the concept structure in the classification task.

Let us divide all concepts which have been created to two parts. Let first of them correspond to the concepts which describe the "normal" objects that may appear in the picture (for example: trees, lives, homes, roofs, chimneys, cats, cat's eyes, dogs, and so one). Let $C_1$ denote that concept set. In contrast, the second part, denoted by $C_0$ corresponds to the obstructions (artifacts, scratches, dust etc.) Additionally, consider the set of primitive objects (denoted in chapter 2 by $\mathbf{X_0}$ ). Based on this set two subset can be created: $S_0, S_1 \subset \mathbf{X_0}$ . Let $S_1$ includes objects which (according to us) may be a part of "normal" objects that belong to concepts from $C_1$. Similarly, $S_0$ will be a set of primitive objects which may create objects of concepts from $C_0$. The $S_0$ and $S_1$ may be considered as training sets (learning sequences), created by the teacher. Our goal is to build such a knowledge (i.e. concept structure) that allows us to good distinguish between objects belonging to concepts from $C_0$ and $C_1$ respectively. If so, any object belonging to concept from $C_1$ set should include (as combined objects) a lot of primitive objects from $S_1$ and very few (or none of them) from $S_0$. Many kinds of functions which have this property can be proposed, for example:

$$f_1(C) = \begin{cases} 0 & \text{if } m_0 > m_1 \text{ or } m_1 = 0 \text{ or } m_0 > 1 \\ \frac{m_1{}^2}{n_1 n} & \text{otherwise} \end{cases} \tag{1}$$

where:
$C \in C_1$
$n$ — number of objects that belong to $C$ concept
$n_1$ — number of elements in $S_1$
$m_0$ — number of primitive objects from $S_0$ that were used to create objects of $C$ concept (the objects have the hierarchical structure, so the usage of the primitive objects may be direct or indirect)
$m_1$ — number of primitive objects from $S_1$ that were used to create objects of $C$ concept

The value of $f_1$ function goes to $1^7$ when concept $C$ includes objects that have been built using many elements of $S_1$. Even if one element from $S_0$ has been used, the value of function is $0^8$.

In the same way a function $f_0$ that evaluates the possibility of recognition of "bad" objects, belonging to concepts from $C_0$ may be defined.

Having the functions:

$f_0(C^j)$, where: $C^j \in C_0, j = 1, 2, \dots$
$f_1(C^k)$, where: $C^k \in C_1, k = 1, 2, \dots$

which evaluate all concepts from $C_0$ and $C_1$ we can propose measure that evaluate the whole knowledge. This function may be based on a calculating of a maximum or weighted average of value of all $f_0(C^j)$ and $f_1(C^k)$. The measure used in our case will be defined later.

Let us note here interesting property of our system: its ability to work correctly without complete knowledge about all objects. The teacher who creates the training set selects such primitive objects, which are, according to him, most relevant and represent "difficult cases". Having such learning sequence the system must build complex structure of concepts, which may precisely interpret such difficult situations. However, a visible image includes a lot of "normal" objects whose components not appear in training set[9]. In that case, the creation of concepts not involves using the evaluation criteria. The created concepts are mostly a small, uncomplicated and even desultory structure. So, automatically created knowledge structure is accurate in the crucial areas, while outside it has more accidental character. Our system may not "know" what is the cat's leg, but it must create the concept "cat's eye" in order to distinguish between small objects that were presented in the strings $S_0$ and $S_1$.

Let us go back to the filtering task. First, with the use of the learning method, introduced above, we should create the set $C_1$. Then, we may propose several variants of filtering procedure. In our case it is defined as follows:

1. Based on the given picture determining the primitive objects.
2. Among them finding the "suspicious" objects, which may be the seed of dust. This is an easy task. Due to the huge number of such objects, system usually creates the concept of "something small". It is also possible to directly choose the small objects from all primitive ones.

---

[7] Normally: $m_1 \leq n$, one object from $C$ concept is created according to only one primitive object from $S_1$, however there may exist object in $C$ which are not be created based on the object from $S_1$. Additionally, what is obvious: $m_1 \leq n_1$.

[8] The construction of the other forms of $f_1$ function involves also the usage of $m_0$ and $m_1$. If it is possible, the function should be independent on absolute value of $n_1$, $n$ and normalized to the chosen range, e.g. $\langle 0, 1 \rangle$.

[9] The optimization method, se the next chapter, creates often many concepts in one route.

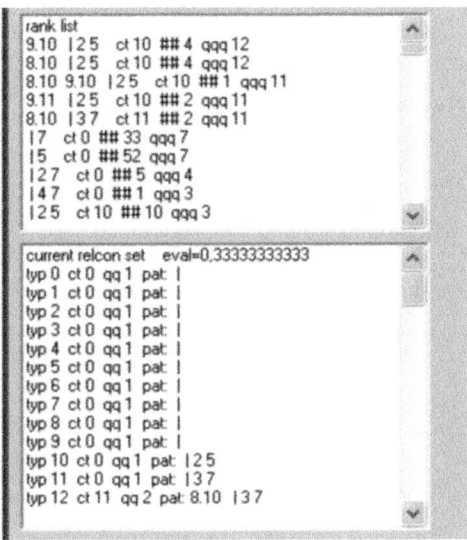

**Fig. 7.** The upper frame: ranking list of the arrangements of the relationships. The bootom frame: set of defined concepts.

3. Creating the objects of all concepts from $C_1$.
4. Removing all suspicious objects which are not a components of the objects of $C_1$ concepts [10].

One remark that only the concepts from $C_1$ are used here, so the function that evaluates the whole knowledge (see above) may be defined very simply:

$$\xi(c_1) = \sum_{k=1}^{m} f_1(C^k), \qquad C^k \in C_1, m - \text{number of elements in } C_1 \text{ set} \quad (2)$$

Figure 6 D. depicts objects of learning strings $S_0$ (red) and $S_1$ (blue) (for the sake of better view they are superimposed on the raster picture). After a process of concepts creation (described in next chapter) a small concept structure was build, depicted in the bottom window of Figure 7. The item:

typ 12 ct 11 qq 2 pat: 8.10 | 3 7

is a definition of a concept that may be interpreted as a small, dark object situated above the brown, big one[11]. The Figure 8 presents two created objects

---

[10] In the complementary method we can create the set $C_0$ (learning utilizes $f_0$ functions). Then, in 4th step we should remove suspicious objects which -are- a components of the objects of $C_0$ concepts.

[11] Type 12 - number of concept, ct 11 - type of the main object, qq 2 - value of validity of that concept, pat: 8.10 - relation 8 - *neighboring up*, holds between the main object and the object of type 10, 3 7 - properties of whole object: *having a brown color, having a big size*, furthermore, typ 10 has properties: 2,5 - *having a blue color, having small size*.

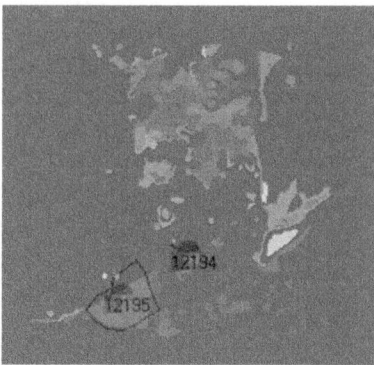

**Fig. 8.** The two instance of concept "rod of the lightning conductor attached to the roof", 12 - number of type (concept), 194,195 - uniqe labels of objects.

of this concept (superimposed on the raster picture). We can identify new concept as the rod of the lightning conductor attached to the roof. The objects of new concept may be distinguished from other objects nearby.

## 4.2   Optimization Method

The whole task of knowledge building may be considered as a task of optimization of a mutli-argument function. The creation of the knowledge (hierarchical concept structure) is a multi-stage iterative process (chapter 2) On each stage we should determine the **FG**, **FA** and **FR** transformation, but in our case the transformation **FA** and **FR** will be always identical. So, we must determine only the **FG** transformations, which corresponds to choosing the groups of tuples. In this problem we will be supported by the heuristic method. On each stage we may rank the groups according to a certain local criterion, which estimates the possibility of the group to make a useful concept[12]. From the best groups we choose a certain number of groups and basing on them we create the concepts. There remains the question which of the groups to choose. The labels of groups on the ranking list on all the stages may be considered as arguments of the function being optimized. The Monte Carlo optimization method has been used here. The concept described in previous point (chapter 4.1) was generated in this way. The figure 7 (upper frame) presents ranking list of the relationship arrangements on the last stage of the crating the hierarchical concept structure. The values of the local criterion functions are displayed on the end of each line.

---

[12] We will not discuss the various forms of this function, its definition may respect the criteria from chapter 3, first of all the number of tuples in the group.

# 5   Conclusions

The conception of knowledge as certain hierarchical structures is relatively simply, but also limited. It not agrees with the many modern ways of understanding the term "knowledge" [2]. Despite this, described approach may be useful in the tasks of the ontology building, knowledge acquisition and interpretation of particular phenomena. This is connected with a prospect of creating of these structure fully automatically. Of course everything depends on the abilities of developing and applying the appropriate methods. So, the most essential challenges are:

- Adapting the existing algorithms of clustering to the task of clustering of groups.
- Finding the methods of evaluating the knowledge.
- Finding the heuristic rules that allow us to accelerate the process of the search of the proper knowledge structure.
- Developing the methods for creating the new objects properties and relationships.

Without a progress in the solving of these problems the method seams to be only a kind of tool to create "something from nothing". The paper provides some solutions of the problem. They should be treated as an incentive to further researches.

# References

1. Michalski, R.S., Steep, R.: Learning from Observation: Conceptual Clustering. In: Michalski, R.S., Carbonell, J.G., Mitchell, T.M. (eds.) Machine Learning: An Artificial Intelligence Approach, vol. 2. Morgan Kaufmann, San Mateo (1986)
2. Michalski, R.S.: Inferential Theory of Learning and Inductive Databases. In: UQAM Summer Institute in Cognitive Sciences, June 30-July 11 (2003)
3. Muggleton, S.H., De Raedt, L.: Inductive logic programming: Theory and methods. Journal of Logic Programming 19(20) (1994)
4. Russell, S., Norvig, P.: Artificial Intelligence: A Modern Approach, 3rd edn. Prentice Hall, Englewood Cliffs (2010)
5. Tadeusiewicz, R., Ogiela, M.R.: Medical Image Understanding Technology. STUDFUZZ, vol. 156. Springer, Heidelberg (2004)
6. Gennari, J., et al.: The evolution of Protégé: An environment for knowledge-based systems development. Int. Journal of Human-Computer Interaction. 58(1) (2003)
7. Wójcik, K.: Inductive learning methods in the simple image understanding system. In: Bolc, L., Tadeusiewicz, R., Chmielewski, L.J., Wojciechowski, K. (eds.) ICCVG 2010. LNCS, vol. 6374, pp. 97–104. Springer, Heidelberg (2010)

# Evaluation of Topological Vulnerability of the Internet under Regional Failures

Wei Peng[1], Zimu Li[2], Jinshu Su[1], and Muwei Dong[1]

[1] School of Computer, National University of Defense Technology,
Changsha, Hunan, 410073, China
{wpeng,sjs,mwdong}@nudt.edu.cn
[2] Network Research Center, Tsinghua University, Beijing, 100084, China
lzm@cernet.edu.cn

**Abstract.** Natural disasters often lead to regional failures which can fail down network nodes and links co-located in a large geographical area. It will be beneficial to improve the resilience of a network by assessing its vulnerability under regional failures. In this paper, we propose the concept of $\alpha$-*critical-distance* to evaluate the importance of a network node in the geographical space with a given failure impact ratio $\alpha$. Theoretical analysis and a polynomial time algorithm to find the minimal $\alpha$-critical-distance of a network are presented. Using real Internet topology data, we conduct experiments to compute the minimal $\alpha$-critical-distances for different networks. The computational results demonstrate the differences of vulnerability of different networks. We also find that with the same impact ratio $\alpha$, the studied topologies have smaller $\alpha$-critical-distances when the network performance is measured by network efficiency than giant component size.

**Keywords:** network topology, vulnerability, regional failure, critical distance, algorithm.

## 1   Introduction

Complex networks like the Internet play an important role in today's world. The society and our lives heavily depend on these networks. For example, most of data communications are accomplished through the Internet. However, as a fast-growing system, the Internet may become vulnerable to intrusions and failures since it integrates more and more components, services and functions. It is generally believed that the current Internet is not so robust or resilient to failures as a critical infrastructure. A breakdown of the Internet for a short while may result in the loss of a large fortune. Considering the importance and the central role of the Internet, its vulnerability has been studied from various aspects.

The topology of a network ranks foremost among all factors which influence the network vulnerability. During the past years, great efforts have been paid in evaluating the vulnerability of a network topology and finding efficient algorithms to enhance the robustness of a network. In most of the works, a network

A M. Tjoa et al. (Eds.): ARES 2011, LNCS 6908, pp. 164–175, 2011.

topology is studied as a pure graph without considering the geographical properties of nodes and links. The network vulnerability is often studied on the logical network topology instead of the physical network topology.

Network nodes or links in a large geographical area may fail to work during the outbreak of electric black-outs and natural disasters like earthquakes, floods and tornadoes. For example, the Taiwan Earthquake in December 2006 damages several undersea cable systems in Asia and the communications between many Asia sites and U.S. sites are disrupted for several ten minutes to hours later. Such regional failures have geographical locations and exhibit strong space correlation among network nodes and links. Therefore, the geographical distribution of a network will have great impact on its vulnerability on regional failures. It has been shown that complex networks including the Internet are resilient to independent random failures, but fragile to intentional attacks [1]. The vulnerability of the Internet under regional failures is still an open issue.

In this paper, we study the vulnerability of the Internet under large-scale regional failures using its city-level topology. A large-scale regional failure means that a significant number of network nodes or links located in a geographical area become unavailable due to natural disasters, electrical black-outs or terroristic attacks. By studying the vulnerability of the Internet in geographical space, we can understand the impact of the geographical properties of the Internet on regional failures. It also helps to identify not only the critical nodes and links, but also the critical area in the network. By the study, we will evaluate the importance of network nodes under regional failures and explore the necessary failure impact range to incur a certain level of degradation of network performance.

To achieve the goal, we develop a binary disk-shape regional failure model as a start. Then the concept of $\alpha$-critical-distance is introduced where $\alpha$ is a given failure impact ratio. The properties of the mapping function from failure impact range to failure impact ratio is analyzed. Based on the properties, a polynomial time algorithm is proposed to calculate the minimal $\alpha$-critical-distance given the impact ratio $\alpha$ and a network topology. We collects topology data sets from the Internet and annotate network nodes with geographical locations. Using the real topology data, we evaluate and compare the network vulnerability of several countries. The experimental results reveal the differences among the studied topologies. We also find that smaller failure impact distances are required when the network efficiency [2] is used as the network performance metric than the giant component size.

The rest of the paper is organized as follows. Section 2 presents a short survey on the related work. Section 3 describes the vulnerability model and the algorithm to find the minimal $\alpha$-critical-distance. The experimental results using real topology data are presented in section 5. We conclude the paper at last.

## 2    Related Work

Numerous efforts have been devoted to the study of the network vulnerability, including proposing vulnerability measures and methods to evaluate the vulnerability of a network, proposing measures and methods to find critical nodes and links in a network. However, few works have explored the network vulnerability issues under geographical correlated failures.

Basic network vulnerability measures are derived from global graph properties like the number of nodes and edges, the lengths of pairwise shortest paths. These measurement criteria include average or characteristic path length, giant component size, network efficiency [2], N-Q measure [3], algebraic connectivity and natural connectivity [4]. Based on these measures, the vulnerabilities of networks with different characteristics are investigated. For example, the giant component size is widely used in the research of complex networks. It is shown that scale-free complex networks including the Internet is vulnerable to intentional attacks with their power-law features [1]. The algebraic connectivity is used to study the robustness of networks of three types subject to random node and link failures [5]. Dinh et al. [6] investigated the measure called *pairwise connectivity* and formulate the vulnerability assessment problem as a *NP-complete* problem and present pseudo-approximation algorithms to detect the set of critical nodes and critical edges.

To assess the importance of nodes on the vulnerability of a network, local nodal measures are proposed, including degree centrality, betweenness centrality and closeness centrality [7]. In [8], a distributed algorithm for locating critical nodes is proposed based on spectral analysis. Kermarrec et al. [9] propose a measurement called *second order centrality* and use random walk to assess node criticality in a distributed manner. Arulselvan et al. [10] have shown that the *critical node problem* in a graph is a *NP-complete* problem and proposed a heuristic algorithm for it. Other approaches consider logical network attacks [11] and the role of humans in system security models [12].

All above approaches aim at the logical network topology, without considering the geographical properties and correlated regional failure effects.

Hansen et al. [13] studied the network resilience under regional failures at routing layer. Grubesic et al. [14] Studied the *Node Removal Impact Problem* in the geographical context. In [15], the vulnerability of networks is assessed in geographical space by modeling the physical network as a bipartite graph. The location of geographical disasters that maximize the capacity of disconnected links is studied. Specifically, a polynomial time algorithm for finding the location of a vertical line segment cut is proposed. The problem is further studied by applying geometric probability techniques to calculate network performance measures on a random line-cut [16]. Agarwal et al. [17] establish a probabilistic geographical failure model and use computational geometric tools to identify vulnerable points within a network. Their algorithms are applied in three optical WDM networks within the continental USA. In [18], both nodes and links located in failure impact area are assumed to be down after a regional failure. Using the European network COST-239 as test network, the authors present some preliminary results by simulating regional failures with three impact ranges.

The previous works try to find the optimal location of geographical failures that maximize the failure impact with a given failure impact range. In contrast with these works, we try to find the optimal regional failure area or the weakest portion of a network that decreases the network performance to a threshold value.

# 3   Vulnerability Evaluation Method

## 3.1   Regional Failure Model

Regional failures belong to the category of multiple-failure scenarios and a large-scale regional failure often occurs in a geographical area where nodes or links may crash or fail to work. A regional failure can affect only a small part of the network, but it can also damage the network severely if it happens in a crucial area and affects enough number of network nodes or links. The area where a regional failure takes effects is defined as the failure area. A regional failure is described by its failure area and the failure probability of nodes and links in the area.

The failure area of a regional failure can be in any shapes. For simplicity, we define a *binary disk-shape failure model* which is characterized by its epicenter position and the failure impact range in a 2-dimension space.

**Definition 1:** The binary disk-shape failure model is defined as $(L0, r)$, where $L0$ is the location of the failure center and $r$ is the failure impact range. For node $i$, if its distance to the failure center is measured by $dd_i$, the state of node $i$ after the failure will be:

$$s_i = \begin{cases} 0 & , & dd_i \leq r \\ 1 & , & else \end{cases} \tag{1}$$

The state 0 means that the node is down while the state 1 represents that the node is still up.

The failure model defined above is deterministic, while one could use more complex models like the probability failure model in [17]. In many cases, a simple model with less complexity can provide enough information for network operators, so we focus on the binary disk-shape failure model in this paper. Our model is similar to that in [18] and the difference is that we do not consider links traversing the failure area.

## 3.2   Vulnerability Measurement

Many statistical metrics have been proposed to quantify the failure impact. In this paper, we consider the following performance metrics:

- $S$: giant component size, which is the number of nodes in the largest connected sub-graph after a failure;
- $E$: network efficiency [2], which is defined as the sum of inverse values of all shortest path lengths in a graph. Given a graph $G$, its network efficiency is defined as

$$E(G) = \frac{1}{n(n-1)} \sum_{i \neq j \in G} \frac{1}{d_{i,j}} \tag{2}$$

where $n$ is the number of nodes in $G$ and $d_{i,j}$ is the shortest path length from node $i$ to node $j$.

The giant component size is widely used in assessing the robustness of complex networks under random failures and intentional attacks. It can characterize network partitioning to some extent. However, if the network remains connected after a failure, it will fail to quantify the impact of the failure. Comparatively, the change of network topology can be revealed by the network efficiency since it will decrease with the increasing of path lengths after a failure. So it is better to assess the performance degradation using network efficiency than giant component size if the computational complexity is bearable.

Given the parameters of a failure and a network topology, we can calculate the performance metrics before and after the failure. The evaluation of the vulnerability of a network is the reverse problem. That is, we need to find the minimal failure impact range to break down a network and the crucial portion of the network. The weakest area in a network is the Achilles' heels of the network.

To achieve the goal, we introduce the concept of $\alpha$-critical-distance which is the minimal impact range in a regional failure when the network performance metric is reduced to $\alpha$ times of the initial value before the failure. $\alpha$ $(0 \leq \alpha \leq 1)$ is called the *impact ratio*. Like the approach in [18], we assume that the epicenter is the location of one node in the network. For node $i$, we use the mapping $F^i$ to define the relationship between the impact ratio $\alpha$ and the impact range $r$. Formally,

$$\alpha = F^i(r) \tag{3}$$

The reverse mapping of $F$ is denoted as $F^{i(-1)}$.

**Definition 2:** Given $\alpha$, the $\alpha$-critical-distance of node $i$ is the minimal impact range $r_i^\alpha$ when node $i$ locates at the epicenter. That is,

$$r_i^\alpha = \min F^{i(-1)}(\alpha) \tag{4}$$

The mapping $F^i$ of node $i$ has the following properties.

**Property 1:** For any $r > 0$, $0 \leq F^i(r) \leq 1$.

**Property 2 (Monotonicity):** If $r_1 > r_2$, then $F^i(r_1) \leq F^i(r_2)$.

**Property 3:** If the maximal distance from node $i$ to any other nodes in the network is $d_i^{max}$, then for any $r \geq d_i^{max}$, $F^i(r) = 0$.

The property 3 means that all nodes will go down if the failure impact range covers all nodes in the network. The network performance is measured as zero when all nodes go down or isolated and the network is totally unavailable.

Let the distance from node $i$ to node $j$ be $d_{i,j}$, $1 \leq j \leq n$, $j \neq i$. We sort the distances from node $i$ to other nodes in ascending order. Let the sorted distances be $d_{i,k_1} \leq d_{i,k_2} \leq \ldots \leq d_{i,k_{n-1}}$. And we assume that nodes co-located with node $i$ on the same position will be down when the failure impact range $r = 0$.

**Property 4:** (1) If $d_{i,k_j} \leq r < d_{i,k_{j+1}}$, $1 \leq j \leq (n-2)$, then $F^i(r) = F^i(d_{i,k_j})$; (2) if $0 \leq r < d_{i,k_1}$, then $F^i(r) = F^i(0)$; (3) if $r \geq d_{i,k_{n-1}}$, then $F^i(r) = F^i(d_{i,k_{n-1}}) = 0$.

Based on the property 4, we can get the conclusion that there will be at most $n$ distinct values of $\alpha$ for each $F^i$.

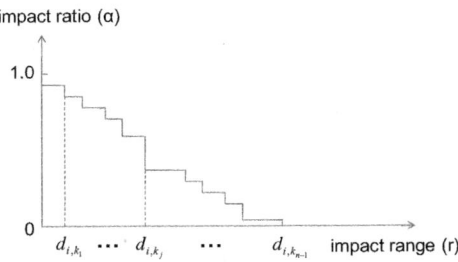

**Fig. 1.** Illustration of Property 4 and 5

**Property 5:** if $p > q$, $F^i(d_{i,k_p}) \leq F^i(d_{i,k_q})$.

Figure 1 is an example to illustrate the Property 4 and 5. In fact, the mapping $F^i$ is a monotonic step-decreasing function of failure impact range $r$.

For node $i$, let $F_p^i = F^i(d_{i,k_p})$ for short. Based on the sorted distances $(d_{i,k_1}, d_{i,k_2}, \ldots, d_{i,k_{n-1}})$, we define $E_p^i$ as the sequence of node $i$ followed by its $p$ nearest nodes.

**Definition 3:** The *p-node-sequence* of node $i$ is defined as $E_p^i = (i, k_1, k_2, \ldots, k_p)$. The *complementary p-node-sequence* is defined as $CE_p^i = (k_{p+1}, \ldots, k_{n-1})$.

If a node $v$ is in the $p$-node-sequence, it is denoted as $v \in E_p^i$. If for any $v \in E_p^i$ and any $u \in E_p^j$, $u \in E_p^i$ and $v \in E_p^j$, then we say $E_p^i = E_p^j$. In such a case, the regional failure centered at node $i$ with the impact range $d_{i,k_p}$ will take the same effects on the network as the failure centered at node $j$ with the impact range $d_{j,k_p}$.

**Property 6:** For any $p$, $1 \leq p \leq (n-1)$, if $E_p^i = E_p^j$, then $F_p^i = F_p^j$.

**Property 7:** If the complementary $p$-node-sequence $CE_p^i$ and $CE_p^j$ have the same node sequence, then for any $m$, $(p+1) \leq m \leq (n-1)$, $F_m^i = F_m^j$.

**Property 8:** For any node $i$ and $j$, $\max\{0, (r_j^\alpha - d_{i,j})\} \leq r_i^\alpha \leq (r_j^\alpha + d_{i,j})$ and $\max\{0, (r_i^\alpha - d_{i,j})\} \leq r_j^\alpha \leq (r_i^\alpha + d_{i,j})$.

**Property 9:** For any node $i$, $\max\limits_{1 \leq j \leq n}\{0, (r_j^\alpha - d_{i,j})\} \leq r_i^\alpha \leq \min\limits_{1 \leq j \leq n}(r_j^\alpha + d_{i,j})$.

Property 7 is a special case of Property 6, because if $CE_p^i$ and $CE_p^j$ have the same node sequence, then for any $m$, $(p+1) \leq m \leq (n-1)$, $E_m^i = E_m^j$. Property 8 relates the $\alpha$-critical-distances of two nodes with the distance between them. Property 9 can be induced from Property 8 directly.

For different values of $\alpha$, a node will have different $\alpha$-critical-distance values. Given the value of $\alpha$, we can assess the importance of the location of a node with its $\alpha$-critical-distance. Smaller the $\alpha$-critical-distance is, more important the node location is. Therefore, we evaluate the vulnerability of a network by finding the node with the smallest $\alpha$-critical-distance in the network.

### 3.3   Finding Minimal $\alpha$-Critical-Distance

Under regional failure scenarios, the node having the minimal $\alpha$-critical-distance is called the *critical node* of the network. The problem of finding the critical node of a network can be described as:

Given a network $G$ and $\alpha$, find $i$

s.t. $r_i^\alpha = \min\left\{r_j^\alpha, 1 \leq j \leq n\right\}$

Because a node has $n$ distinct values of $\alpha$ at most, the $\alpha$-critical-distance of node $i$ can be computed by enumerating all $n$ possible cases. The time complexity of computing $r_j^\alpha$ will be $O(n*T)$ and the worst time complexity of the problem would be $O(n^2*T)$. Here $T$ is the time complexity to calculate the mapping $F^i(r)$ with given failure impact range $r$. The time to compute the giant component size is $O(m)$ where $m$ is the number of edges in the graph. The time to compute the network efficiency is $O(n^3)$. Thus, the worst time complexity of the problem would be $O(mn^2)$ and $O(n^5)$, respectively.

**Table 1.** Variables of Algorithm 1

| Input Variable | Description |
| --- | --- |
| $G$ | network represented by an undirected graph |
| $n$ | the number of nodes in $G$ |
| $\alpha$ | impact ratio of the network performance |
| $K$ | the number of minimal $\alpha$-critical-distances |

| Output Variable | Description |
| --- | --- |
| $M$ | the vector of $\alpha$-critical-distances, $M[i]$ is the $i$-th $\alpha$-critical-distance |

| Temporary Variable | Description |
| --- | --- |
| $d_{i,j}$ | geometric distance between node $i$ and node $j$ |
| $d_{min}$ | minimal value of $\alpha$-critical-distance of a node |
| $d_{max}$ | maximal value of $\alpha$-critical-distance of a node |
| $rset$ | the set of candidate values of $\alpha$-critical-distance |

For large-scale networks, it will be time-costly to find critical nodes in a network. Because the $\alpha$-critical-distance of a node is related to others according to Property 8, we can use the results computed in previous steps to reduce the time complexity. Here we propose a fast algorithm to find $K$ minimal $\alpha$-critical-distance values. The input and output variables are summarized in Table 1.

The algorithm calculates the $\alpha$-critical-distance for each node iteratively. In step 2 and step 3, the algorithm finds the lower bound and the upper bound of $\alpha$-critical-distance that node $i$ can take. According to Property 9, the lower and upper bounds can be computed with the $\alpha$-critical-distances of other nodes found in previous steps. Then the set of candidate values of $\alpha$-critical-distance is generated by selecting nodes which distances fall into the bounds. The procedure $sortCandidateDistances(rset)$ sorts the candidate distance set $rset$ in ascending order. The procedure $binarySearch(G, i, rset)$ finds the $\alpha$-critical-distance of node $i$ by applying the *binary search* method on the candidate distance set $rset$. After the $\alpha$-critical-distance values of all nodes are found, the procedure $sortCriticalDistances(M, K)$ sorts the values in ascending order and outputs the first $K$ values.

By using the *binary search* method, the time complexity to find the $\alpha$-critical-distance of a node can be reduced from $O(n*T)$ to $O(log_2 n * T)$. Both the step 8 and step 11 have the worst-case time complexity of $O(n^2)$, e.g., if the Quicksort algorithm is applied. Thereby, the time complexity of the algorithm will be $O(mnlog_2 n + n^3 + n^2))$ and $O(n^4 log_2 n + n^3 + n^2)$, if the giant component size and the network efficiency are used as performance metrics respectively.

---

**Algorithm 1.** Find $K$ minimal $\alpha$-critical-distances

---

1: **for** $i = 1$ **to** $n$ **do**

2:     $d_{min} = \max\limits_{1 \leq j \leq (i-1)} \{0, M[j] - d_{i,j}\};$

3:     $d_{max} = \min\limits_{1 \leq j \leq (i-1)} \{M[j] + d_{i,j}\};$

4:     $rset = \emptyset;$

5:     **for** $j = 1$ **to** $n$ **do**

6:         **if** $d_{min} \leq d_{i,j} \leq d_{max}$ **then**

7:             $rset = rset \cup \{d_{i,j}\};$

8:     **end for**

9:     $sortCandidateDistances(rset);$

10:    $M[i] = binarySearch(G, i, rset);$

11: **end for**

12: $sortCriticalDistances(M, K);$

---

## 4  Computational Results

### 4.1  Data Sets

To study the vulnerability of the Internet topology and evaluate the algorithm proposed in the above section, we collect some online data sets. Since an autonomous system (AS) may span across a large geographical area, the AS-level Internet topology is not appropriate for the purpose of this study. The router-level Internet topology is ideal for the study. However, there are few available data sets and a lot of links are missing in the public data sets due to privacy issues and limitations of network measurement methods. Instead, we use the city-level Internet topology in this paper.

The data sets come from DIMES [19]. In the city-level topology data sets given by DIMES, the data set of July 2009 has the largest number of nodes and links. We extract the city-level topology from it for several countries, including United Kingdom (UK), Japan (JP), India (IN) and China (CN). The location information for each city in the original data of DIMES lacks precision, so we assign each city with the longitude and latitude looked up from the data provided by MaxMind [20]. Because many cities in the original topology have the same coordinates, we merge them into one city and make the resultant city-level topology compact. We use abbreviation of the country name to name the topology data set for each country. The basic attributes of the topology data sets are shown in Table 2. It should be noted that the topology data set is just a snapshot of the Internet's dynamic structure and the degree of incompleteness may vary greatly for different countries.

**Table 2.** Basic Attributes of Topology Data Sets

| Data Set | Node Number | Edge Number | Average Degree | Average Path Length |
|---|---|---|---|---|
| UK | 1085 | 4044 | 7.454378 | 2.371940 |
| JP | 117 | 856 | 14.632479 | 1.915119 |
| IN | 349 | 1101 | 6.309456 | 2.225933 |
| CN | 922 | 2002 | 4.342733 | 2.900891 |

## 4.2 Evaluation of the Proposed Algorithm

We evaluate the proposed algorithm at first. The giant component size is used as the performance metric. To demonstrate the efficiency of the optimization operations using distance bounds (step 2-9 in algorithm 1), we compare the algorithm with and without the optimization steps. If the optimization steps are not applied, all distance values will be used in step 10, e.g., $rset=\{d_{i,j}, 1 \leq j \leq n\}$. Since computing the impact ratio with a given failure area takes the longest time, we use the number of function calls to evaluate the algorithm performance. The *performance improved ratio* (PIR) is defined as:

$$PIR = \frac{C^{orig} - C^{opt}}{C^{orig}} \tag{5}$$

where $C^{orig}$ is the number of function calls without optimization steps and $C^{opt}$ is that with optimization.

Figure 2 demonstrates the performance of the algorithm. It is shown that the algorithm performance can be improved with the optimization steps for different network topologies. Normally, about half of the function calls can be saved, while 45% function calls can be saved in the worst case. Besides, when the impact ratio ($\alpha$) is approaching its extreme value (0 or 1), the algorithm have better performance than the case when $\alpha$ is in the middle of its value range.

## 4.3 Evaluation of the Topologies

We use the proposed algorithm to find the $\alpha$-critical-distances for different values of $\alpha$. Figure 3 shows that with the increasing of $\alpha$, the $\alpha$-critical-distance

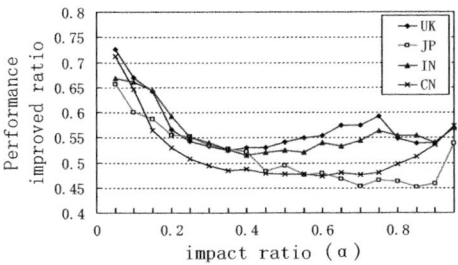

**Fig. 2.** Improved ratio with optimization

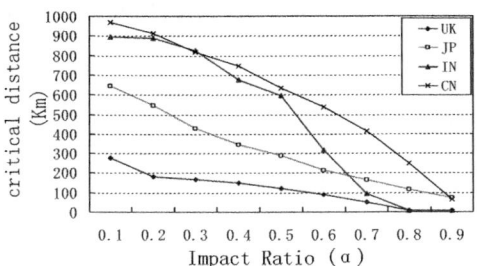

**Fig. 3.** α-critical-distance vs Impact Ratio

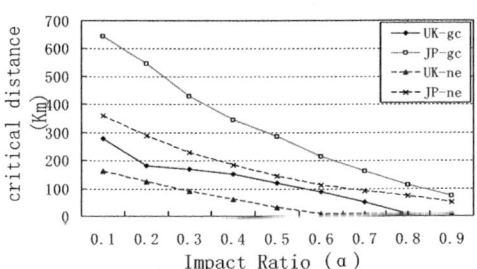

**Fig. 4.** α-critical-distance with Different Metrics

decreases. For different countries, different failure impact ranges are required to get the same impact ratio. When α is less than 0.6, India and China have the greater α-critical-distance values than UK and Japan. It is reasonable since large failure impact ranges are required for countries with large acreage. Japan has longer critical distances than UK for the same impact ratio. Sice the topology snapshot of Japan has less nodes but higher node degrees than the topology of UK, the former is more resilient to disk-shape regional failures than the latter.

Table 3 shows the top 10 minimal α-critical-distances when α=0.5. It is shown that a regional failure with a radius of 120 Kilometers in UK may lead to half of network nodes disconnected to others.

**Table 3.** Top 10 Critical Distances (Km) ($\alpha$=0.5)

| rank | UK | Japan | India | China |
|------|------------|------------|------------|------------|
| 1 | 119.014675 | 284.910063 | 594.922675 | 633.075876 |
| 2 | 119.082917 | 286.358551 | 596.185520 | 634.302529 |
| 3 | 119.086647 | 287.783538 | 605.273073 | 640.487066 |
| 4 | 119.300718 | 291.704459 | 606.387328 | 645.156163 |
| 5 | 119.467601 | 293.769890 | 606.453596 | 646.118720 |
| 6 | 119.510586 | 301.692601 | 607.552635 | 647.432880 |
| 7 | 119.889240 | 301.952568 | 613.332279 | 647.609953 |
| 8 | 120.036688 | 313.328128 | 617.205720 | 649.372846 |
| 9 | 120.250490 | 317.550703 | 619.813512 | 649.941193 |
| 10 | 120.422221 | 319.867304 | 622.285994 | 652.425884 |

With network efficiency as the performance metric, the algorithm finds the $\alpha$-critical-distances for networks of UK and Japan. The results are shown in Figure 4. The suffix '-gc' and '-ne' are used to differentiate the curves using giant component size and network efficiency as the performance metrics respectively. Noteworthy differences can be observed. When the network efficiency is used, the network performance degrades even when regional failures have a small impact range. For example, in the worst case, a regional failure with an impact range of 29Km can lead to the network efficiency of UK's network reduced to half of the normal performance. According to the definition of the network efficiency, it is more sensitive to the change of a network topology than the giant component size. Thus, in the context of regional failures, it is easy to harm the network efficiency of a network with small failure impact range.

## 5   Conclusion

In this paper, we introduce the concept of $\alpha$-critical-distance for the purpose of evaluating vulnerability of networks under regional failures. We define a binary disk-shape regional failure model and study the properties of the mapping from failure impact range to failure impact ratio. It is shown that the mapping is a monotonic step-decreasing function. Based on the theoretic analysis, we propose an algorithm to compute the $\alpha$-critical-distance for a given network topology and $\alpha$. Using real topology data sets, we run the algorithm to evaluate the vulnerability of city-level Internet topologies for several countries. The computational results reveal the differences of network vulnerabilities among different countries and the differences when different network performance metrics are used.

Our work provides a new way to assess the network vulnerability under large-scale regional failures. The future work includes studying the network vulnerability under regional failures which take effects both on nodes and edges, correlated analysis of critical distances and node densities, and so on.

**Acknowledgments.** The work is supported by the grants from the National Natural Science Foundation of China under grant No.61070199 and 60873214, and the National 973 Grand Fundamental Research Program 2009CB320503.

# References

1. Doyle, J.C., Alderson, D., Li, L., Lowet, S., et al.: The 'Robust Yet Fragile' Nature of the Internet. PNAS 102(41) (2005)
2. Latora, V., Marchiori, M.: Efficient Behavior of Small-World Networks. Phys. Rev. Lett. 87, 198–701 (2001)
3. Nagurney, A., Qiang, Q.: A Network Efficiency Measure with Application to Critical Infrastructure Networks. J. Glob. Optim. 40, 261–275 (2008)
4. Wu, J., Barahona, M., Tan, Y.-J., Deng, H.-Z.: Natural Connectivity of Complex Networks. Chinese Physical Lett. 27(7), 078902 (2010)
5. Jamakovic, A., Uhlig, S.: Influence of the network structure on robustness. In: 15th IEEE Int. Conf. on Networks (ICON), Adelaide, Australia, pp. 278–283 (2007)
6. Dinh, T.N., Xuan, Y., Thai, M.T., Pardalos, P.M.: On New Approaches of Assessing Network Vulnerability: Hardness and Approximation. IEEE/ACM Trans. on Networking, under revision (2011)
7. Borgatti, S.P., Everett, M.G.: A graph-theoretic perspective on centrality. Social Networks 28(4), 466–484 (2006)
8. Wehmuth, K., Ziviani, A.: Distributed Algorithm to Locate Critical Nodes to Network Robustness based on Spectral Analysis. CoRR abs/1101.5019 (2011)
9. Kermarrec, A.-M., Merrer, E.L., Sericola, B., Trédan, G.: Second order centrality: Distributed assessment of nodes criticity in complex networks. Computer Communications 34, 619–628 (2011)
10. Arulselvan, A., Commander, C.W., Elefteriadou, L., Pardalos, P.M.: Detecting Critical Nodes in Sparse Graphs (2009)
11. Crescenzo, G.D., Ghosh, A., Kampasi, A., Talpade, R., Zhang, Y.: Detecting Anomalies in Active Insider Stepping Stone Attacks. J. Wireless Mobile Networks, Ubiquitous Computing, and Dependable Applications 2(1), 103–120 (2011)
12. Pieters, W.: Representing Humans in System Security Models: An Actor-Network Approach. J. Wireless Mobile Networks, Ubiquitous Computing, and Dependable Applications 2(1), 75–92 (2011)
13. Hansen, A.F., Kvalbein, A., Čičić, T., Gjessing, S.: Resilient Routing Layers for Network Disaster Planning. In: Lorenz, P., Dini, P. (eds.) ICN 2005. LNCS, vol. 3421, pp. 1097–1105. Springer, Heidelberg (2005)
14. Grubesic, T.H., Murray, A.T.: Vital Nodes, Interconnected Infrastructures, and the Geographies of Network Survivability. Annals of the Association of American Geographers 96(1), 64–83 (2006)
15. Neumayer, S., Zussman, G., Cohen, R., Modiano, E.: Assessing the Impact of Geographically Correlated Network Failures. In: IEEE MILCOM 2008 (2008)
16. Neumayer, S., Modiano, E.: Network Reliability With Geographically Correlated Failures. In: IEEE INFOCOM 2010, San Diego, CA, pp. 1–9 (2010)
17. Agarwal, P.K., Efrat, A., Ganjugunte, S., Hay, D., Sankararaman, S., Zussman, G.: The Resilience of WDM Networks to Probabilistic Geographical Failures (2011)
18. Bassiri, B., Heydari, S.S.: Network Survivability in Large-Scale Regional Failure Scenarios. In: $C^3S^2E$2009, Montreal, QC, Canada (2009)
19. The DIMES project, http://www.netdimes.org/
20. MaxMind GeoLite City, http://www.maxmind.com/app/geolitecity/

# VMBLS: Virtual Machine Based Logging Scheme for Prevention of Tampering and Loss

Masaya Sato and Toshihiro Yamauchi

Graduate School of Natural Science and Technology, Okayama University,
3-1-1 Tsushima-naka, Kita-ku, Okayama, 700-8530 Japan
m-sato@swlab.cs.okayama-u.ac.jp, yamauchi@cs.okayama-u.ac.jp

**Abstract.** Logging information is necessary in order to understand a computer's behavior. However, there is a possibility that attackers will delete logs to hide the evidence of their attacking and cheating. Moreover, various problems might cause the loss of logging information. In homeland security, the plans for counter terrorism are based on data. The reliability of the data is depends on that of data collector. Because the reliability of the data collector is ensured by logs, the protection of it is important problem. To address these issues, we propose a system to prevent tampering and loss of logging information using a virtual machine monitor (VMM). In this system, logging information generated by the operating system (OS) and application program (AP) working on the target virtual machine (VM) is gathered by the VMM without any modification of the OS. The security of the logging information is ensured by its isolation from the VM. In addition, the isolation and multiple copying of logs can help in the detection of tampering.

**Keywords:** Log, security, virtualization, virtual machine monitor, digital forensics.

## 1 Introduction

The countermeasure for terrorism is one important topic in homeland security. In the field of counter-terrorism, enormous quantity of data is gathered and analyzed for the planning of countermeasures. Computers and networks are used to gather and analyze data, computer science is deeply committed to homeland defence and security. In the field of computer science, countermeasures are considered for cyber terrorism as an activity in homeland security. Recently, information technology is used as a tool to control infrastructures. Cyber terrorism is able to cause critical damage on infrastructures in low cost. Thus, the countermeasure for cyber terrorism have been discussed.

The countermeasures might be weakened by attacking on the data gathered for homeland security. Therefore, the protection of the data is important. The protection of the logs of the APs is also necessary to ensure the validity of gathered information.

The computer terrorism has two characters: anonymity and the lack of evidences of attacks. In computer terrorism, it is difficult to acquire the information

A M. Tjoa et al. (Eds.): ARES 2011, LNCS 6908, pp. 176–190, 2011.

that specifies the attacker. Because there are no evidences left on attacks using network, the logs that records the behavior of the systems are important. For this reason, the protection of the information is necessary for the prevention and investigation of computer terrorism.

Digital forensics is a method or technology for addressing these problems. This is a scientific method or research technology for court actions, which allows us to explain the validity of the electronic records. Many researchers are working in this area of the protection of logging information[2,4,8,10,11].

Syslog is commonly used as a logging program in Linux. In this case, the logging information generated by the AP (user log) and kernel (kernel log) is gathered by syslog. Syslog writes logs to file according to the policy, so attackers can tamper with logs by modifying the policy. Moreover, if the syslog program itself is attacked, the log files written are not reliable. In addition, the kernel log is stored in a ring buffer, and therefore, since the kernel log is gathered on a regular schedule, if many logs are generated and stored in the ring buffer before the next gathering time, old logs may be overwritten by new logs. As described above, the user log and kernel log can be tampered with or lost.

In this paper, we propose a logging system to prevent tampering and loss of logs with the virtual machine monitor (VMM). In this system, the OS that should be monitored (monitored OS, MOS) works on the virtual machine (VM). Logs in the MOS are gathered by the VMM without any modification of the MOS's kernel source codes. The VMM gathers user logs by hooking the system calls invoked in the MOS. Because the system gathers logs just after the output of logs, any possibilities for tampering are excluded. The VMM gathers current kernel logs from the buffer before new kernel logs have accumulated. Therefore, the system can gather current kernel logs in conjunction with the accumulation of new ones. Thus, no logs are lost through the buffer being overwritten by new kernel logs.

As mentioned above, the system gathers logs using the VMM. The VMM is independent of and invisible to the MOS, so it is difficult to detect and attack this system. Thus, the system itself is secure. In addition, because the logs gathered by the system are copied to the logging OS (LOS), it is easy to determine which part has been modified by attackers. Moreover, with the isolation of logs, any attacks on the MOS have no effects on the logs gathered by the system. These features mean that this system provides secure logging.

The contributions of this paper are as follows:

(1) The logging scheme for prevention of tampering and loss of logging information using VMM is proposed. The scheme can solve the problems in existing schemes and researches described in Section 2. The implementation has no modification of guest OSes and easy to introduce in existing systems.

(2) Evaluations are described and they show that the system is effective on protection of logs. The measurement of the performance with the system shows the overheads in the system calls that are related to logging is $50\mu s$, and are not related to logging is only $2\sim5\mu s$.

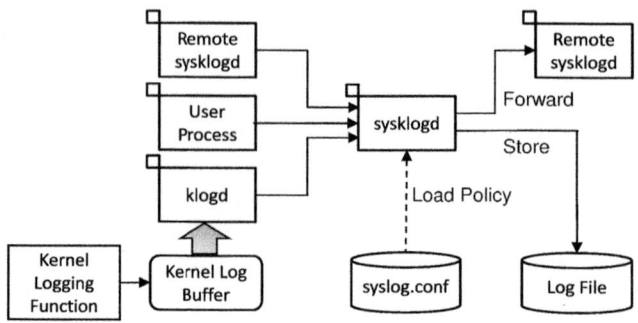

**Fig. 1.** Architecture of syslog

## 2   Existing Logging Schemes

This section describes the architecture and problems of existing logging schemes. Section 6 also refers to these schemes, the comparisons between these schemes and our proposed system are in there.

### 2.1   Syslog

*Syslog* is a protocol for system management and security monitoring standardized by Internet Engineering Task Force (IETF)[6]. Syslog consists of a library and a daemon. The syslog library provides interfaces for logging, and the syslog daemon gathers logs and stores them as a file. Figure 1 shows the architecture of syslog. User and kernel logs are gathered as follows.

The syslog library provides functions for user program to send log messages to the syslog daemon. The syslog function sends messages to /dev/log with the **send** or **write** system call, and the syslog daemon gathers logs from /dev/log with the **read** system call.

The kernel accumulates logs in internal buffer (kernel log buffer). The kernel logging daemon (klogd) gathers logs from the kernel log buffer, and afterwards, klogd similarly sends logs to the syslog daemon.

Syslog also has a filtering function. Its policies are described in the configuration file (syslog.conf).

Syslog has the following problems:

(1) The behavior of the syslog daemon can be modified by tampering with the configuration file. In addition, if the syslog daemon itself is tampered with, its output can be unreliable.
(2) Users who have permission to access logs can tamper with them intentionally.
(3) Kernel logs in Linux are accumulated in the ring buffer and are gathered at fixed intervals. Thus, if the logs are not gathered for a long time, old logs can be overwritten by new ones. Old logs will also be overwritten if many logs are accumulated in a time that is shorter than the gathering interval.

Although improved syslog daemons have been developed (e.g., rsyslog, syslog-ng), these problems have not been addressed.

## 2.2   Protection of Logs

Some research has been carried out on the protection of files by the file system. The system NIGELOG has been proposed for protecting log files [10]. This method has a tolerance for file deletion. It produces multiple backups of a log file, keeps them in the file system, and periodically moves them to other directories. By comparing the original file and the backups, any tampering with the log file can be detected. Moreover, if any tampering is detected, the information that has been tampered with can be restored from these backups.

The protection of files with the file system is still vulnerable to attacks that analyze the file system. Therefore, a log-protection method using virtualization has been proposed [11]. This method protects logs by saving them to another VM, so it is impossible to tamper with the logs from other VM. However, this method aims to protect the log of a journaling file system, so the scope of the protection target is different from that in our research.

The hysteresis signature is used to achieve the integrity of files. However, it is known that the algorithm of the hysteresis signature has a critical weak point. Although the hysteresis signature can detect the tampering and deletion of files, it cannot prevent tampering and deletion. Moreover, the manager of the signature generation histories can tamper with the histories and files. Therefore, a mechanism to solve this problem using a security device has been proposed [2]. This method constructs a trust chain from the data in the tamper-tolerant area of the security device, the source of the trust chain is protected from attackers. Nevertheless, this method is not versatile because it uses the special device.

## 2.3   Protection of Syslog

The methods mentioned above are protecting log files. However, they cannot protect logs before storing of them. Thus, a method to guarantee syslog's integrity has been proposed [4], which uses a Trusted Platform Module (TPM) and a late launch by a Secure Virtual Machine (SVM) to ensure the validity of syslog. The validated syslog receives logs and sends them to a remote syslog.

## 2.4   Original Logging Method

An original logging method, independent of syslog, has been proposed for audit [8]. This method uses Linux Security Modules (LSM) to gather the logs, and Mandatory Access Control (MAC) to ensure their validity. The system also uses SecVisor [9], and DigSig [1]. SecVisor ensures the security of the logging framework, and DigSig prevents rootkit from making modifications to access permissions. DigSig adds a signature to a program, and prevents the execution of an unknown program by verifying its signature. This method gathers logs in its own way, but the method modifies the kernel source codes. In general, kernel modification is difficult and complex, so the method lacks versatility. And the method uses variety of mechanisms, the overheads arising from them have large effect on daily operations on computers.

### 2.5   Problems of Existing Logging Schemes

From the descriptions above, we find that there are three problems for logging:

(1) Attacks on logging information.
(2) Attacks on logging mechanism.
(3) Loss of kernel log.

The security of logging information is the main focus of the current research, and is of utmost important in digital forensics. However, this is not enough to ensure secure logging. For the protection of logging information, it is necessary to protect the logging mechanism itself. The reliability of logs generated by a program is determined by the reliability of the generator, so the security of the logging mechanism is also important. The third problem depends on the architecture of the Linux kernel log buffer. We currently assume that the guest is Linux, and so this problem needs to be addressed.

## 3   VMBLS: Virtual Machine Based Logging Scheme

### 3.1   Requirements and Approaches

To address problems in Section 2, we propose a system to prevent tampering and loss of logging information. There are three requirements for addressing the problems:

(1) Detection of all outputs of log (user log and kernel log).
    We need to detect and gather all logs to keep them secure. Where we support only user logs and kernel logs. We do not support logs not sent to syslog.
(2) Isolation of log.
    In order to secure a log, we obtain a copy of the log and isolate it from the MOS. Since the protection method using the file system is not secure, we isolate the logs in the LOS, assuming that the working environment is on a VM. As the LOS are isolated, attacks on the working environment have no effect on the logs. This isolation also enables us to detect loss of and tampering with logging information, because a comparison between copied logs and original ones will show any differences arising from such attacks.
(3) Security of logging mechanism.
    To achieve security of the logging mechanism, we use a VMM. Since the VMM is independent of the VM, it is generally difficult to detect its existence and to attack it from the VM. A logging method in kernel space (e.g., LSM or kernel modification) is weakly defended from attacks. If attackers obtain root privileges, they can use bugs in kernel or APs to attack some programs and tamper with the logs to hide their activities. Thus, the isolation of the logging mechanism provides greater security than the methods in kernel.

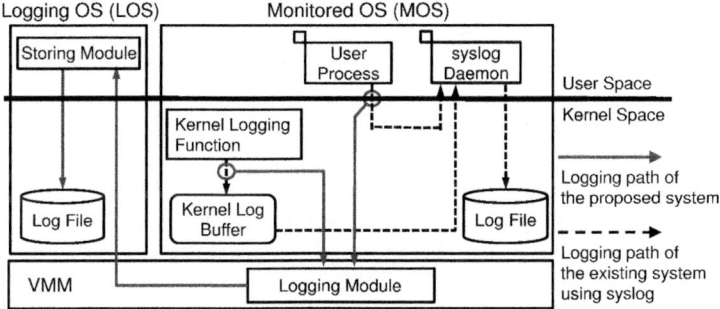

**Fig. 2.** Architecture of the proposed system

Furthermore, simplicity and ease of introduction is demanded. The mechanism using a VMM makes our proposed system easier to introduce. The original logging method and security mechanism with kernel modification is difficult to apply to a new version of the kernel because of the kernel's complexity. The VMM, for which no modification of the kernel of the MOS is required, makes our method more flexible than methods that need kernel modification. Thus, we choose the use of a VMM as our method for the protection of logging information.

### 3.2 Architecture

Figure 2 shows the architecture of the proposed system. The MOS and LOS work on the VM. The LOS is a guest OS for storing logs gathered by the logging module. The logging module works in the VMM, and its details are described below. It gathers logs and sends them to the LOS, which then stores them in files.

### 3.3 Logging module

**User log collector.** The collector acquires logs when the requirement for sending logs occurs. As shown in Fig. 2, the VMM hooks the system call that was invoked for sending logs from the user process to the syslog daemon.

The procedures for user log collection are detailed below:

(1) Detect a connect system call for a socket of /dev/log
(2) Determine the socket number from the first argument of the connect system call invoked at (1)
(3) Detect a send system call for the socket used at (2)
(4) Acquire the string as the log specified in the second argument of the send system call invoked at (3)

To send logs, the user process creates a socket and invokes a connect system call for /dev/log. The user log collector detects this connect system call and specifies the socket number that will be used to send the logs. Finally, the user log collector acquires logs by detecting the send system call for that socket.

However, the collector cannot recognize the process that sends the logs. To address this issue, the collector uses CR3 control register to determine the process; CR3 stores a unique value for each process since it shows the page directory.

**Kernel log collector.** The collector acquires logs when the kernel logging function is called in a guest OS. Typically, the VMM cannot detect a function call in a guest OS. To solve this problem, the system sets a breakpoint in the guest OS. Breakpoint exception occurs when some process reaches this breakpoint. In the proposed system, since the guest OSes are fully virtualized, breakpoint exception is processed by the VMM. Using the exception as an opportunity to acquire logs, the VMM can gather kernel logs.

When the processing is brought to the VMM, the logging module checks the state of the kernel log buffer of the MOS. If new logs have been accumulated in the buffer, the logging module gathers them. After that, the VMM returns the processing to the guest OS. Since these processes have no effect on the state of the guest OS, the guest OS can continue to write the kernel log.

In this method, since kernel logs are gathered when a kernel logging function is called, old logs are never overwritten by new ones.

### 3.4   Storing Module

The storing module stores logs gathered by the logging module. The storing module is an AP working on the LOS, and stores the logs as log files. The storing module actively gathers logs from the buffer of the VMM.

## 4   Implementation

### 4.1   Environment

We implement the system with Xen [3] as the VMM and Linux as the MOS. This version of Xen supports full virtualization. We did not modify the kernel source codes. However, the system needs the System.map file of the MOS, so this information must be provided beforehand. The reason for the system requiring this System.map information is that the system uses the address of the kernel log buffer and the kernel logging function. Because of the need for full virtualization, we prepared a CPU that supports virtualization extension.

### 4.2   Detecting a System Call

The user log collector detects the invoking of system calls; such a mechanism is necessary because the proposed system is implemented with a VMM.

Therefore, in the proposed system, we applied a mechanism that causes a page fault when a system call is invoked [5]. In a fully virtualized environment, if a page fault occurs on the VM, then the VMM is raised (VM exit) [7]. After the VMM has been raised, the logging module acquires the user logs and hides the occurrence of the page fault. Finally, the VMM raises the guest OS, which works as if no event has occurred.

In this method, to cause a page fault, we modified some registers of the MOS. A system call using the sysenter (fast system call) refers the value in sysenter_eip_msr and jumps to its address to execute the system call function (sysenter_eip_msr is one of the machine-specific register (MSR)). Through modification of this value to another address to which access is not permitted from the MOS, a page fault is made to occur when a system call is invoked.

### 4.3   Setting a Breakpoint

In the proposed system, we set a breakpoint in the kernel logging function of the MOS to gather kernel logs. The breakpoint is realized by embedding of a INT3 instruction. VM exit appears if a breakpoint exception occurs in the MOS, and the VMM gathers kernel logs with this exception.

In the following, we detail the procedure for setting breakpoints and gathering kernel logs. Here, we assume that the first INT3 instruction is already embedded.

(1) Breakpoint exception occurs and switches to the VMM.
    Kernel logs are gathered after the processing is switched to the VMM.
(2) Embed INT3 instruction to the next one.
(3) Restore the value at the address at which the exception occurred.
(4) Restart the processing from the restored instruction.
(5) Breakpoint exception occurs and switches to the VMM.
(6) Embed INT3 instruction to the firstly embedded address
(7) Restore the value on the address at which the exception occurred.
(8) Execute instruction from restored point.

## 5   Evaluation

### 5.1   Simplicity and Ease of Introduction

We implemented a prototype of the proposed system by modifying the Xen hypervisor. The total amount of source codes that we added and modified on Xen are only about 1,000 lines. The source codes of the MOS is not modified.

### 5.2   Purposes and Environment

We evaluated the system from two points of view: the prevention and detection of tampering, and the loss of logging information. This paper also describes the overheads of the system. Table 1 details the environment used for this evaluation.

### 5.3   Prevention of Tampering

A log gathered by the proposed system is kept in a place where it is independent of the MOS. Thus, with the MOS working on a VM, it is difficult for attackers to tamper with the log even if they obtain root privileges.

**Table 1.** Environment used for evaluation.

| OS | Domain0 | Linux 2.6.18-xen |
|---|---|---|
| | Fully virtualized domain | Linux 2.6.26 |
| VMM | | Xen 3.4.1 |
| syslog | | rsyslogd 3.18.6 |
| CPU | | Intel Core 2 Duo E6600 |
| Memory | Physical | 2,048 MB |
| | Domain0 | 1,024 MB |
| | Fully virtualized domain | 1,024 MB |

```
Aug 19 20:09:25 debian sendlog: Logging test:0. ⎤
Aug 19 20:09:25 debian sendlog: Logging test:0. ⎬  Logs before the modification of the log.
Aug 19 20:09:25 debian sendlog: Logging test:1. ⎥
Aug 19 20:09:25 debian sendlog: Logging test:1. ⎦
Aug 19 20:10:24 debian sendlog: Logging test:0. ⎤  — Restart of the syslog daemon.
Aug 19 20:10:24 debian sendlog: Logging test:1. ⎦  Logs after the modification of the log.
```

**Fig. 3.** A user log gathered by syslog

### 5.4   Prevention of Loss

**Loss of user log.** We assume that an attacker tampers with the policy of syslog to suppress some parts of the log. We show that the proposed system can gather logs even if the policy has been tampered with. Figure 3 shows the logs gathered by syslog, and Fig. 4 shows those gathered by the proposed system. We compared both logs around the time when the policy was manipulated, as shown in Fig. 5. In the logs gathered by syslog, the logs decreased after the manipulation of the policy because of the exception of the mail facility. On the other hand, there are no changes in the logs gathered by our proposed system around the time of the manipulation of the policy. Thus, it is proved that the proposed system gathers logs regardless of the behavior of syslog.

**Loss of kernel log.** We show that the proposed system can gather logs under the condition of a massive output of kernel logs even if the existing system cannot.

The size of the kernel log buffer of the standard kernel on Debian 5.0.3 is 131,072 bytes. To exhaust this buffer, the program outputs logs with a total size greater than that of the buffer by printk (kernel logging function). One output has a size of 21 bytes, whereas in printk format, the size of the output is 38 bytes. Thus, in order to exhaust the buffer, the program needs to output the log 3,450 times. In this experiment, we compared the logs gathered by the existing system and our proposed system after 4,000 outputs of the log.

Figure 6 shows the log in the MOS, and Fig. 7 shows the log gathered by the proposed system. In the third row of Fig. 6, the log is unusual because something has been lost through overwriting. In contrast, Fig. 7 shows that the proposed

```
(XEN)  send:[<14>Aug 19 20:09:25 sendlog: Logging test:0.] ┐
(XEN)  send:[<22>Aug 19 20:09:25 sendlog: Logging test:0.] │  Logs before the modification
(XEN)  send:[<14>Aug 19 20:09:25 sendlog: Logging test:1.] │  of the policy.
(XEN)  send:[<22>Aug 19 20:09:25 sendlog: Logging test:1.] ┘
(XEN)  send:[<85>Aug 19 20:09:49 sudo:    ****** : TTY=console ;
       PWD=/home/******/****** ; USER=root ;
       COMMAND=/usr/bin/vim /var/log/user_and_mail.log]⟵━━━━━━┐Checking the log.
(XEN)  send:[<85>Aug 19 20:10:04 sudo:    ****** : TTY=console ;
       PWD=/home/******/****** ; USER=root ;
       COMMAND=/usr/bin/vim /etc/rsyslog.conf]⟵━━━━━━━━━┐Modifying the policy.
(XEN)  send:[<85>Aug 19 20:10:18 sudo:    ****** : TTY=console ;
       PWD=/home/******/****** ; USER=root ;
       COMMAND=/etc/init.d/rsyslog restart]⟵━━━━━━━━━━━━┐Restart of the syslog daemon.
(XEN)  send:[<14>Aug 19 20:10:24 sendlog: Logging test:0.] ┐
(XEN)  send:[<22>Aug 19 20:10:24 sendlog: Logging test:0.] │  Logs after the modification
(XEN)  send:[<14>Aug 19 20:10:24 sendlog: Logging test:1.] │  of the policy.
(XEN)  send:[<22>Aug 19 20:10:24 sendlog: Logging test:1.] ┘
```

**Fig. 4.** A user log gathered by the proposed system

```
user,mail.*    -/var/log/user_and_mail.log
        ⬇ Disable the policy for mail.*.
user.*         -/var/log/user_and_mail.log
```

**Fig. 5.** Manipulation of configuration

```
Nov 29 20:12:42 debian kernel: [   17.398956] lp0: using parport0 (interrupt-driven).
Nov 29 20:12:42 debian kernel: [   17.419593] ppdev: user-space parallel port driver
Nov 29 20:14:24 debian kernel: th world.
Nov 29 20:14:24 debian kernel: [  118.900091] Hello   51th world.
Nov 29 20:14:24 debian kernel: [  118.900098] Hello   52th world.
```

**Fig. 6.** A kernel log gathered by the existing system

```
(XEN) KERNLOG:<6>[   17.398956] lp0: using parport0 (interrupt-driven).
(XEN) KERNLOG:<6>[   17.419593] ppdev: user-space parallel port driver
(XEN) KERNLOG:<4>[  118.899567] Hello    0th world.
(XEN) KERNLOG:<4>[  118.899567] Hello    1th world.
(XEN) KERNLOG:<4>[  118.899567] Hello    2th world.
                        ⋮
(XEN) KERNLOG:<4>[  118.900085] Hello   50th world.
(XEN) KERNLOG:<4>[  118.900091] Hello   51th world.
(XEN) KERNLOG:<4>[  118.900098] Hello   52th world.
```

**Fig. 7.** A kernel log gathered by the proposed system

system has correctly gathered all the logs with no interruption. Whereas the existing system could not gather logs before the fiftieth output, the proposed system gathered all the logs. Thus, we have shown that the proposed system can gather all logs, even if they are lost by the existing system.

## 5.5   Detection of Tampering and Loss

The comparison of logs gathered by the existing and proposed systems enables us to detect any tampering with or loss of logs. Therefore, we show that it is possible to detect tampering by comparing these logs.

In preparation, we tamper with the log file. After that, we compare the logs gathered by the existing and proposed systems. This comparison indicates that the proposed system is able to detect tampering.

For this comparison, we use sudo as a program that uses syslog to output user logs. If a command is executed with sudo, the user name, tty, and the name of the command are sent to the syslog daemon. At this point, the information in the log gathered by the existing system and the proposed system is the same.

To hide the executed command, we modify the name of the command in a log in the existing system. Now, comparison between the logs allows a difference in the name of the command to be detected.

As a result, it is seen that tampering with a log in the MOS has no effect on the logs in our proposed system. Moreover, the experiment shows that a part tampered with in the MOS can be detected through comparison between the logs in the MOS and in the proposed system.

## 5.6   Overheads

The user log collector hooks all system calls in the MOS. In this mechanism, the VMM is raised upon each system call, and therefore, the processing time of the system call increases. To determine the overheads of the system, we measured the overheads in some of the system calls that are mainly invoked in the syslog function and the function itself. The results are shown in Tables 2 and 3.

Table 2 shows the overheads of connect and write system calls that were invoked in syslog function. To show the overhead when switching between the MOS and VMM, we also measured the overhead of the getpid system call. From the margin between the overhead of getpid and other system calls, it is found that switching between the VMM and MOS takes about 2 $\mu$s. In invoking a connect system call, our system decides the target of the connect system call. The measurement shows that this decision takes about 3 $\mu$s. In the write system call, the proposed system takes about 47 $\mu$s. This overhead derives from copying of the message between the MOS and the VMM.

In addition, since the difference between the overhead in the syslog function in Table 3 and the write system call is 5 $\mu$s, it can be concluded that the main reason for the overhead in the syslog function is the write system call. Table 3 also shows the overheads of the kernel log collector. The overhead of the proposed system in the printk function is 57 $\mu$s. This result is similar to that for the syslog function. The reason is thought to be that the printk function copies data to the memory in the same way as the syslog function. It can be estimated that the 10 $\mu$s overhead derives from the breakpoint exception.

From these measurements, such overheads have little effect on performance.

**Table 2.** Overheads in the proposed system when a system call was invoked ($\mu$s)

|            | connect | | write | | getpid | |
|------------|---------|----------|--------|----------|--------|----------|
|            | ave     | overhead | ave    | overhead | ave    | overhead |
| unmodified | 1.16    | –        | 92.90  | –        | 0.23   | –        |
| modified   | 6.55    | 5.39     | 142.20 | 49.30    | 2.23   | 2.00     |

**Table 3.** Overheads in the proposed system when a syslog and printk are invoked ($\mu$s)

|            | syslog | | printk | |
|------------|--------|----------|--------|----------|
|            | ave    | overhead | ave    | overhead |
| unmodified | 102.39 | –        | 9.89   | –        |
| modified   | 156.56 | 54.17    | 67.34  | 57.45    |

# 6 Discussion

## 6.1 Opportunity for Gathering Kernel Logs

The proposed system sets a breakpoint at the starting point of the kernel logging function for the opportunity to gather kernel logs. Thus, the system gathers old logs just before the output of current logs, the logs are older than current ones.

In order to acquire the latest logs, it is necessary to set the breakpoint immediately after the output. The current implementation uses the starting address of the kernel logging function from the System.map. Starting points of functions are described here, so it is easy to set a breakpoint. In order to gather logs immediately after the output of a kernel log, we need the returning point of the function. But to acquire the point, we need to analyze the kernel. Although the method can gather latest logs, there is a problem in terms of analyzing the kernel each time it is updated. The method of the proposed system only requires System.map, so there is no difficulty arising from kernel updates.

## 6.2 Security of Logs in Logging Path

To guarantee the integrity of a log, it is necessary to ensure the security of the logging path from its output to the time it is stored in a file. Here, we compare the security of the logging paths of the existing and proposed systems.

Firstly, we analyze the logging path of a user log. A user log might be attacked at the following points:

(1) The time when a user process generates a log
(2) The time between the sending of a log and its receipt by syslog
(3) The time between the receipt of a log and storing it to a file
(4) After the output of a log

The existing system cannot detect and prevent tampering or the loss of logging information at any time. In the proposed system, time (1) is the only possible time when attacks might be suffered. An example of an attack at time (1) would be someone tampering with the program itself. To protect the logs from tampering in this case, it is necessary to ensure the integrity of all programs that generate logs. DigSig [1] is a method that ensures the integrity of a program by assigning a signature to the program. However, this method does not satisfies our demand because it modifies the kernel codes. Moreover, the method causes a large overhead. For time (2) to (4), some research has been carried out, but those methods do not satisfy our demand. The method ensures the integrity of syslog has proposed [4], but the method needs logging server, so if the network is down, it is unavailable. For time (4), hysteresis signature enables us to detect tampering with a log, but it has a problem mentioned in Section 2. In addition, to prevent such tampering, protection methods using the file system already exist [10]. However, these methods modify the source codes of the kernel, so our demand is not satisfied.

Secondly, we analyze the logging path of a kernel log. A kernel log might be attacked at the following moments:

(1)  The time to generate a kernel log in a kernel
(2)  The time to output the log to a kernel log buffer
(3)  While stored in the kernel log buffer
(4)  The time during which a kernel logging daemon gathers a log
(5)  While the kernel logging daemon sends the log to syslog
(6)  While syslog stores the log to a file
(7)  Afther the output of a log

In the existing system, it is impossible to protect a log from an attack by a rootkit at any time. Furthermore, there is a possibility of attack similar to the logging of a user log if the kernel is safe. The proposed system gathers a log at time (2). We can consider tampering with the kernel logging function as an example of an attack at time (2). However, the log gathered by the proposed system is the previous one. Therefore, the logs might be attacked at time (3). Thus, the proposed system can address attacks on and after time (4). The improvement of the proposed system for gathering a log immediately after its output enables it to address time (3) as well.

However, to prevent attacks before time (3), it is necessary to modify the parts related to kernel logging. In this situation, our demand is not satisfied. SecVisor [9] is a technology that ensures the integrity of the kernel, and is effective for the prevention of attacks at times (1) and (2). However, it is impossible to prevent attacks after time (3) with SecVisor alone. Thus, since the proposed system can prevent attacks on or after time (4), the security of logging is ensured unless the kernel logging function itself is attacked.

## 6.3   Applicability for Other OSes

No modification of the kernel code in the MOS is necessary because the proposed system is implemented in a VMM. For this reason, the system can be applied to any kind of OS. Furthermore, if an OS fulfills the following requirements, the proposed system can be applied to an OS that is not open-source software. Here, we discuss the possibility of applying the system to other OSes.

Regardless of how the system is constructed in terms of the logging and storing modules, the storing module is independent from the MOS. Thus, in the adaption of the system, we need to consider the requirement for implementing the logging module. Considering the case of Windows, a widely used OS, the following requirements can be noted:

(1) Use of sysenter instruction in invoking a system call.
(2) Identification of the system call is used in logging.
(3) Identification of the starting address of the kernel logging function.
(4) Identification of the area of the kernel log buffer.

Requirements (1) and (2) are necessary for the gathering of user logs, and (3) and (4) for the gathering of kernel logs.

In Windows XP or later, system calls are generally implemented with sysenter. Moreover, since the identifier of the system call is stored in the EAX register in Windows, the detection of a system call for logging is available with its value. Requirements (3) and (4) can be achieved by analyzing the kernel.

On the basis of these considerations, it is concluded that the proposed system can be applied to various OSes (e.g., Windows) if the requirements are fulfilled.

# 7   Conclusion

This paper describes a logging system with a VMM to prevent log tampering and loss. In the user log collector, the VMM detects an output of the log of the MOS and gathers it before it is gathered by syslog. Because the proposed system gathers logs immediately after the logging request, there is no opportunity for tampering. Also, because the kernel log collector gathers logs in conjunction with the kernel log's output, the system can prevent the loss of logging information caused by the overwriting of old kernel logs. These functions enable the VMM to gather logs of the MOS with no modification of its source codes. Moreover, the system is independent of the MOS because it is implemented as a VMM. Thus, it is difficult to attack the proposed system.

This paper also presents an evaluation of the proposed system, assuming that tampering and loss of logging information occurs. Considering the results of these evaluations, it is proved that it is possible to detect and prevent tampering with log files. Furthermore, the proposed system can address the problem caused by the structure of the kernel log buffer.

This paper also describes the evaluation of the overheads caused by the system. The results show that the overheads associated with the proposed system is only about $50\mu s$ at most.

**Acknowledgements.** This research was partially supported by Grant-in-Aid for Scientific Research 21700034 and a grant from the Telecommunications Advancement Foundation (TAF).

# References

1. Apvrille, A., Gordon, D., Hallyn, S., Pourzandi, M., Roy, V.: Digsig: Runtime authentication of binaries at kernel level. In: Proceedings of the 18th USENIX Conference on System Administration, pp. 59–66 (2004)
2. Ashino, Y., Sasaki, R.: Proposal of digital forensic system using security device and hysteresis signature. In: Proceedings of the Third International Conference on International Information Hiding and Multimedia Signal Processing (IIH-MSP 2007), vol. 02, pp. 3–7 (2007)
3. Barham, P., Dragovic, B., Fraser, K., Hand, S., Harris, T., Ho, A., Neugebauer, R., Pratt, I., Warfield, A.: Xen and the art of virtualization. In: Proceedings of the 19th ACM Symposium on Operating Systems Principles, pp. 164–177 (2003)
4. Bock, B., Huemer, D., Tjoa, A.: Towards more trustable log files for digital forensics by means of "trusted computing". In: 24th IEEE International Conference on Advanced Information Networking and Applications, pp. 1020–1027 (2010)
5. Dinaburg, A., Royal, P., Sharif, M., Lee, W.: Ether: malware analysis via hardware virtualization extensions. In: Proceedings of the 15th ACM Conference on Computer and Communications Security, pp. 51–62 (2008)
6. IETF Syslog Working Group: IETF Syslog Working Group Home Page, http://www.employees.org/~lonvick/index.shtml
7. Intel: Intel 64 and IA-32 Architectures Software Developer's Manual Volume 3B: System Programming Guide, Part 2 (2009), http://www.intel.com/Assets/PDF/manual/253669.pdf
8. Isohara, T., Takemori, K., Miyake, Y., Qu, N., Perrig, A.: Lsm-based secure system monitoring using kernel protection schemes. In: International Conference on Availability, Reliability, and Security, pp. 591–596 (2010)
9. Seshadri, A., Luk, M., Qu, N., Perrig, A.: Secvisor: a tiny hypervisor to provide lifetime kernel code integrity for commodity oses. In: Proceedings of 21st ACM SIGOPS Symposium on Operating Systems Principles, pp. 335–350 (2007)
10. Takada, T., Koike, H.: Nigelog: Protecting logging information by hiding multiple backups in directories. In: International Workshop on Database and Expert Systems Applications, pp. 874–878 (1999)
11. Zhao, S., Chen, K., Zheng, W.: Secure logging for auditable file system using separate virtual machines. In: IEEE International Symposium on Parallel and Distributed Processing with Applications, pp. 153–160 (2009)

# Augmenting Surveillance System Capabilities by Exploiting Event Correlation and Distributed Attack Detection

Francesco Flammini[1], Nicola Mazzocca[2], Alfio Pappalardo[1,2],
Concetta Pragliola[1], and Valeria Vittorini[2]

[1] Ansaldo STS, Innovation & Competitiveness Unit,
Via Argine 425, Naples, Italy
[2] University of Naples "Federico II",
Department of Computer & Systems Engineering,
Via Claudio 21, Naples, Italy
{francesco.flammini,concetta.pragliola}@ansaldo-sts.com,
{nicola.mazzocca,alfio.pappalardo,valeria.vittorini}@unina.it

**Abstract.** In recent years, several innovative security technologies have been developed. However, many of the novel sensing technologies (e.g. video analytics) do not always feature a high level of reliability. Very often, they need to be precisely tuned to fit specific installations and provide acceptable results. Furthermore, in large installations the number of surveillance operators is low with respect to the number of sensing devices, and operators' tasks include facing critical events, possibly including strategic terrorist attacks. In such human-in-the-loop systems, ergonomics and usability issues need to be carefully addressed to increase system performance in terms of detection probability and low rate of false/nuisance alarms. This paper describes a multi-sensor event correlation approach for augmenting the capabilities of distributed surveillance systems. The aim is to provide advanced early warning, situation awareness and decision support features. The effectiveness of the framework is proved considering threat scenarios of public transportation systems.

**Keywords:** Physical Security, Surveillance Systems, Situation Awareness, Event Correlation.

## 1 Introduction

In modern society, the assurance of a secure environment has become an issue of paramount importance. Infrastructure protection against potential threats is usually performed by surveillance systems that are more and more large, distributed and heterogeneous [1]. The cyber-physical and human-in-the-loop nature of this field requires a set of multidisciplinary activities to be performed in order to adopt appropriate and effective protection mechanisms. Due to the variety of natural and malicious threat scenarios, a growing set of different sensing technologies are required. However, many of the developed novel innovative technologies (e.g. video analytics) do not always provide adequate reliability (see e.g. [2], [3]). Many

A M. Tjoa et al. (Eds.): ARES 2011, LNCS 6908, pp. 191–204, 2011.

automatic and intelligent detection subsystems generates unnecessary warnings, which can be classified as false alarms or nuisance alarms. Therefore, with regard to the decision support feature of surveillance systems (e.g. for triggering countermeasures), it is very important to control the rate of these alarms [4]. The integration of information coming from different sources, as sensor networks, is the key for new generations of multi-modal surveillance systems, where many different media streams (video, audio, sensor signals) concur to provide a greater situational awareness and a better decision support [5].

So far, the potential capabilities of the traditional systems are limited by their low capabilities in data analysis and interpretation and hence in real-time prevention and reaction. Since a few human operators are usually employed in security surveillance, human-factors related issues also need to be carefully addressed, including cognitive ergonomics in human-machine interaction [6]. Therefore, the real need is for distributed surveillance systems, acting not only as supporting platforms, but as the concrete core of real-time data comprehension process [7], in such a way to achieve advanced early warning and situation awareness capabilities. These requirements are increasingly important in many application domains, like Homeland Security, environmental sensing, crisis management and other information-rich domains, where a large number of dynamic objects are engaged in complex spatial-temporal relations [8].

This paper describes how to augment the capabilities of an existing integrated surveillance system (briefly presented in Section 2) by means of a complex event correlation framework (briefly presented in Section 3). The details of the integration are provided in Section 4, while Section 5 presents some application examples. Finally, Section 6 draws conclusions and some hints about future developments.

## 2   A Surveillance System for Railway Protection

The Security Management System (SMS) is a multimedia surveillance system used to improve the security of critical infrastructures, in particular the ones used for rail transportation [9]. It integrates intrusion detection and access control, intelligent video-surveillance and intelligent sound detection devices. The system may also integrate CBRNe (Chemical Biological Nuclear Radiological explosive) sensors to improve detection of terrorist attacks.

The SMS architecture (Fig. 1) is distributed and hierarchical; a dedicated network provides reliable communication among the sites and an integrated management system collects the alarms and supports decision making. In case of emergencies, the procedural actions required to the operators involved are orchestrated by the SMS.

Data gathered from the heterogeneous sensing devices are processed by subsystems which generate the alarm events. Those alarms are first collected by peripheral control centers (Peripheral Security Places, PSP, positioned in the stations) and then centralized in line control centers (Central Security Places, CSP, close to the traffic management center). Every security place (peripheral or central) can be provided with a SMS operator interface.

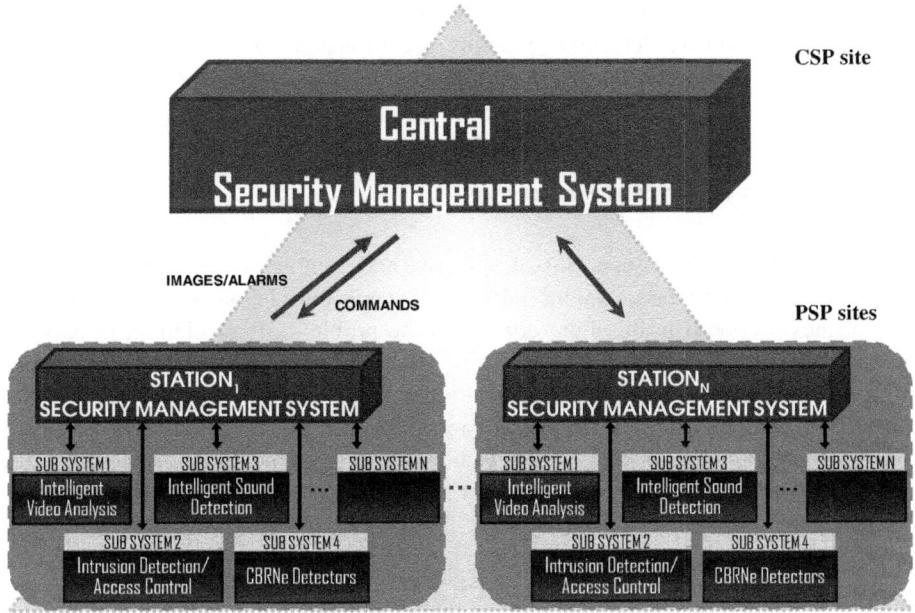

**Fig. 1.** SMS architecture

The events detected by the available sensorial subsystems are stored in appropriate repositories, both at the PSPs and CSP sites. A simplified schema of the stored data, also named *Event History* in the following, is shown in Table 1.

**Table 1.** Schema of Event History

| Field Name | Field Description | Field format (example) |
|---|---|---|
| IDev | Event Identifier | E*x* (e.g. E8) |
| IDs | Sensor Identifier | S*x* (e.g. S4) |
| IDg | Sensor Group Identifier | G*x* (e.g. G7) |
| Tp | Timestamp | *yyyy-mm-dd hh:mm:ss* (e.g. 2010-10-01 23:56:09) |

In practice, the Event History is a database containing the list of basic events detected by sensors or cameras, tagged with a set of relevant attributes including detection time, event identifier, sensor identifier, etc. The detection time is a timestamp related to the event occurrence time, which should be a sensor timestamp (when a global clock is available for synchronization). A more detailed description of SMS and its sub-components is reported in [4].

The SMS is a highly heterogeneous security system, providing automatic event detection based on multi-sensor data. Advanced mechanisms for event correlation and for the detection of possibly complex threat scenarios could greatly augment SMS capabilities to improve detection reliability and to enable early warning and decision support. The same holds for many similar and SCADA-like[1] distributed monitoring systems.

## 3  Detection of Threat Scenarios

In order to detect threat scenarios of any type and complexity, the SMS needs to be enriched with an expert system providing event correlation mechanisms. Many approaches proposed in literature cope with the problem of correlation, in particular of different alerts signals [10]. However, they are generally suitable to computer network monitoring systems. In physical security monitoring applications, it is more difficult to find systems that include advanced correlation features. To the best of our knowledge no existing physical security monitoring system features a scenario-based detection approach like the one described in this paper. This section briefly describes in particular the DETECT (DEcision Triggering Event Composer & Tracker) approach, which was firstly introduced in [11] and [12].

Threats scenarios are described in DETECT using a specific Event Description Language (EDL) and stored in a  Scenario Repository. In this way we are able to store permanently all scenario features in an interoperable format (i.e. using XML). A high level architecture of the framework is depicted in Fig. 2.

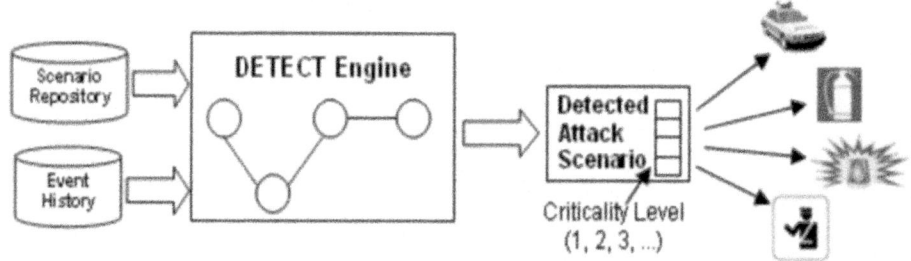

**Fig. 2.** The DETECT framework

A threat scenario expressed by EDL consists of a set of basic events detected by the sensing devices (primitive events) which occur in a predictable sequence (with possible variants). The approach supposes an a-priori knowledge about the possible threats that are coded by a set of scenarios: they are identified during Vulnerability Assessment, which is a fundamental phase of Risk Analysis for critical infrastructures.

---

[1] SCADA stands for *Supervisory Control And Data Acquisition*. It generally refers to a system that collects data from various sensors, and then manages and controls them. They are often used to monitor and control industrial, infrastructure, or facility-based processes.

Generally speaking, an event is a happening that occurs at some location and at some point in time. In the considered context, events are related to sensor data variables (i.e. variable $x$ greater than a fixed threshold, variable $y$ in a fixed range, etc.). Events are classified as *primitive events* and *composite events.*

A primitive event is a condition on a specific sensor which is associated to some parameters (i.e. event identifier, time of occurrence, etc). A composite event is a combination of primitive events by means of proper operators.

Each event is denoted by an *event expression*, whose complexity grows with the number of involved events. Given the expressions $E_1, E_2, ..., E_n$, every application on them through any operator is still an expression. Event expression are represented by *event tree*, where primitive events are at the leaves, while internal nodes represent EDL operators.

According to the context in which a multimedia surveillance system – like the SMS described in previous section – works, the possible threat scenarios to be addressed can be more or less complex on the basis of the number of basic events that is necessary to correlate to detect them. In addition, to improve the detection reliability of such systems, two major techniques are typically adopted: *redundancy* (i.e. the use of more sensors than the ones strictly required) and *diversity* (i.e. the use of detection devices based on different technologies or working principles). Thus, depending on the circumstances, the side effect of these techniques may be a further explosion in the number of involved events in the expressions, and so in the event trees. This possible complexity is to be managed properly, by means of an ad-hoc complex event correlation framework, like the DETECT platform proposed in this section.

DETECT is able to support the composition of complex events in EDL through a *Scenario GUI* (Graphical User Interface), used to draw threat scenarios by means of an intuitive formalism and a user-friendly interface.

Furthermore, in the operational phase, a model manager macro-module has the responsibility of performing queries on the Event History database for the real-time feeding of detection models corresponding to the scenarios, according to predetermined policies. The latter are named *parameter contexts* and are used to set a specific consumption mode of the occurrences of the events collected in the database, as described in the following.

The EDL used in the event correlation framework to build event trees is based on the Snoop event algebra [13]. The tree construction is carried out according to the following Snoop operators: $OR, AND, ANY, SEQ$. Once the trees are built, the related detection models are ready to be inserted in the correlation engine. After that, the engine is fed by the primitive events gathered by the sensorial subsystems on site, and so it is able to recognize the partial or total matching with the known attack scenarios. Fig. 3 shows a sample event tree, where the leafs $E_1, E_2, E_4, E_6$ are primitive events and the operators are internal nodes. This tree represent the composite event $((E_1 \ OR \ E_2) \ AND \ (E_2 \ SEQ \ (E_4 \ AND \ E_6)))$.

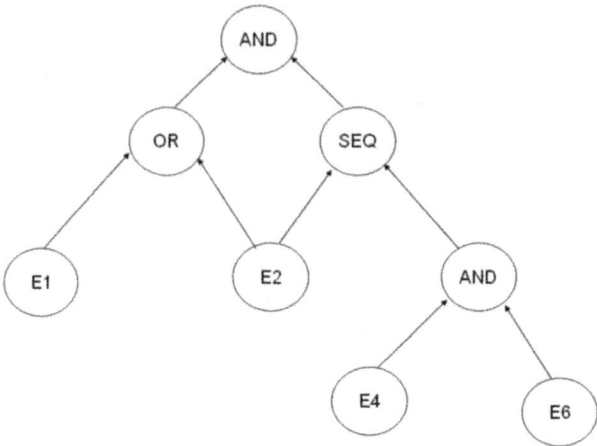

**Fig. 3.** A sample event tree

The semantics of the Snoops operators is the following:

- **OR**. Disjunction of two events $E_1$ and $E_2$, denoted $(E_1\ OR\ E_2)$. It occurs when at least one of its components occurs.
- **AND**. Conjunction of two events $E_1$ and $E_2$, denoted $(E_1\ AND\ E_2)$. It occurs when both events occur (the temporal sequence is ignored).
- **ANY**. A composite event, denoted $ANY(m, E_1, E_2, ..., E_n)$, where $m \leq n$. It occurs when $m$ out of $n$ distinct events specified in the expression occur (the temporal sequence is ignored).
- **SEQ**. Sequence of two events $E_1$ and $E_2$, denoted $(E_1\ SEQ\ E_2)$. It occurs when $E_2$ occurs provided that $E_1$ has already occurred. This means that the time of occurrence of $E_1$ has to be less than the time of occurrence of $E_2$.

Furthermore, *temporal constraints* can be specified on operators, in such a way to consider that the logic correlations could loose meaningfulness when the time interval between component events exceeds a certain threshold. The aim is to define a validity interval for the composite event.

In order to take into account appropriate event consumption modes and to set how the occurrences of primitive events are processed, four parameter contexts are defined. Given the concepts of *initiator* (the first constituent event whose occurrence starts the composite event detection) and *terminator* (the constituent event that is responsible for terminating the composite event detection), the four different contexts are described as follows.

- *Recent*: only the most recent occurrence of the initiator is considered.
- *Chronicle:* the (initiator, terminator) pair is unique. The oldest initiator is paired with the oldest terminator.

- *Continuous:* each initiator starts the detection of the event.
- *Cumulative*: all occurrences of primitive events are accumulated until the composite event is detected.

The effect of the operators is then conditioned by the specific context in which they are placed.

When a composite event is recognized, the output of DETECT consists of:

- the identifier(s) of the detected/suspected scenario(s)[2];
- the temporal value related to the occurrence of the composite event (corresponding to the event occurrence time *tp* of the last component primitive event, which should be a sensor timestamp);
- an alarm level, associated to scenario evolution (used as a progress indicator and set by the user at the time of construction of composite event);
- the component event occurrences which have determined the recognition of the detected/suspected scenario(s);
- possibly other information depending on the detection model (e.g. likelihood of attack in case of heuristic detection, currently not yet implemented);

Fig. 4 shows an example screenshot of the output of DETECT when the correlation engine is activated.

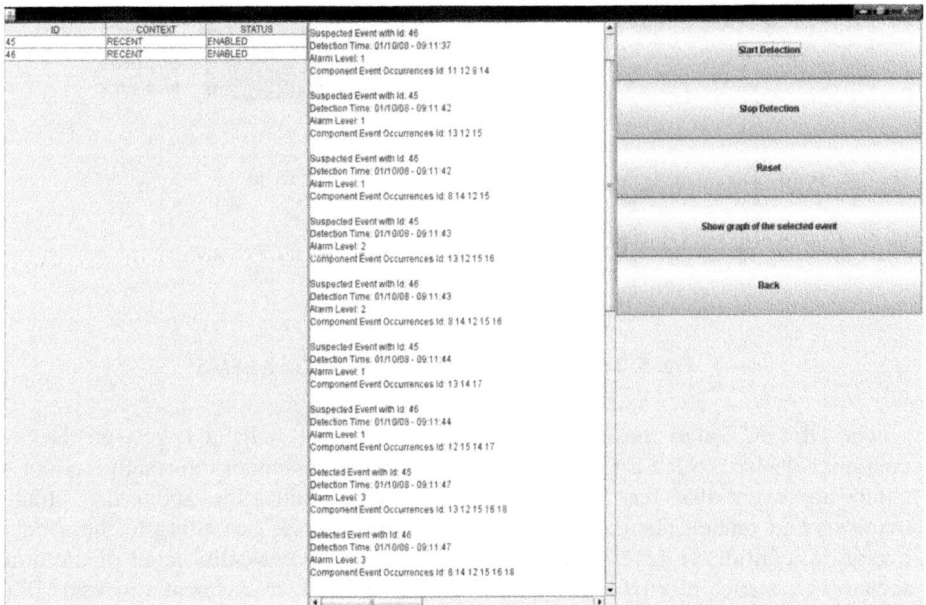

**Fig. 4.** An example screenshot of the output of DETECT

---

[2] The difference between detected and suspected scenario depends on the partial or total matching between its tree and the known attack scenarios.

## 4   An Integrated System for the Detection of Distributed Attacks

This section provides some details about the integration of the SMS with DETECT, in order to enrich the surveillance system with basic but effective reasoning capabilities.

In the integrated environment (see Fig. 5), DETECT and SMS share the Event History database and communicate by exchanging alert messages (from DETECT to SMS) and possibly commands (from SMS to DETECT). The commands consist of specific feedback from human operators which can be used to refine or update the detection models handled by DETECT.

On the one hand, SMS collects all alarms detected by the heterogeneous sensorial subsystems and store them into the shared database. On the other hand, the engine of DETECT is fed by each new entry in the Event History. The interface mode with the database can be synchronous (i.e. by means of queries performed periodically) or asynchronous (i.e. by event-based queries). In the first case, it is necessary to choose an appropriate time interval representing a good trade-off between the response time (short inter-query times are better) and the network/server load (long inter-query times are better).

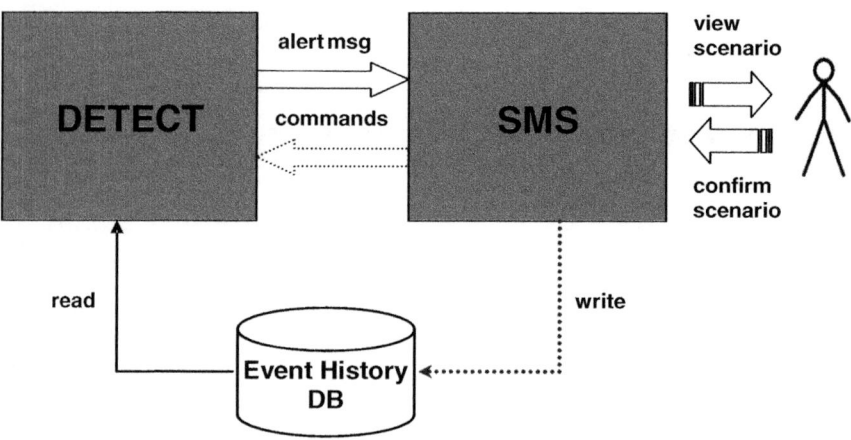

**Fig. 5.** The integration between DETECT and SMS

The DETECT alert message need to be shown on a dedicated view on the SMS operator interface. Such a view gives to the security personnel information about the composite event that has been detected: semantic indication about the situation (explosive in tunnel, chemical attack, etc.), current phase according to the scenario evolution, confidence level of the alarm (if available), criticality level of the attack scenario (a static information obtained during the risk assessment process). If the detected scenario includes primitive events that have been already notified, SMS can drop them from the list of the alarms after confirmation by the operator. The composite event can then be stored in the Event History.

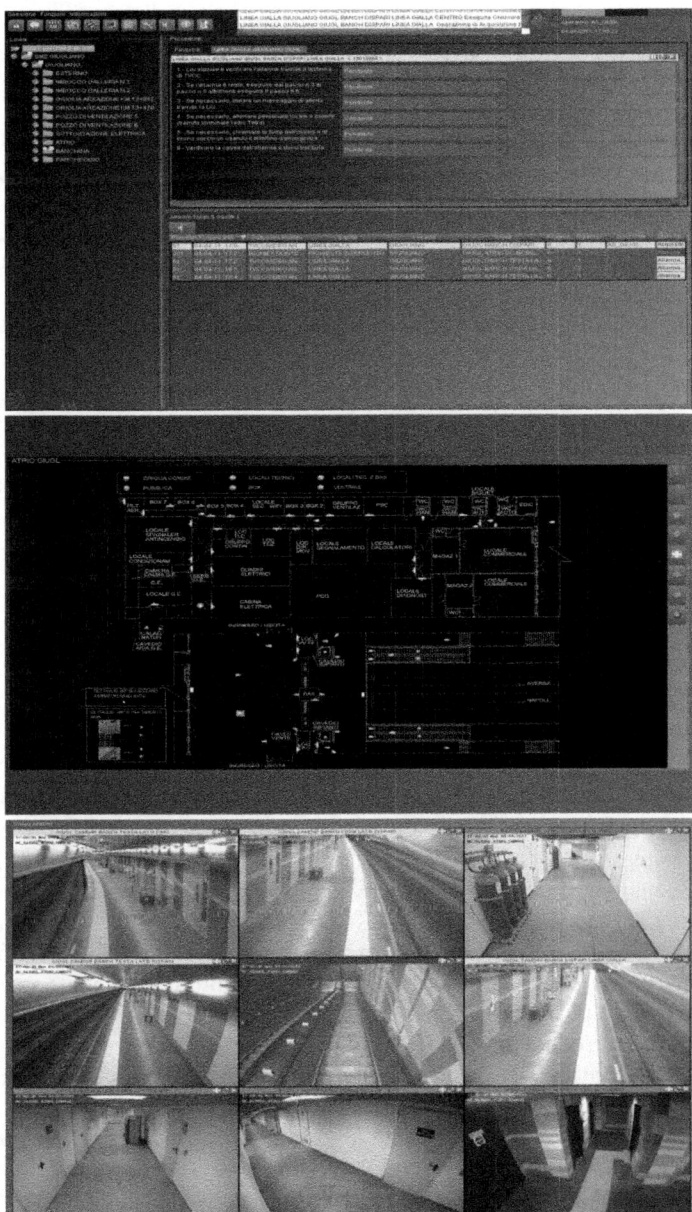

**Fig. 6.** An example of operator interface of the integrated system.

Depending on the specific user configuration required, primitive events can continue to be shown in a hierarchical or tree structured view (e.g. by double clicking on the scenario). According to the static (e.g. criticality level) and dynamic (e.g. evolution level) parameters of the attack scenario, the DETECT alarm may activate specific SMS procedures that will override procedures possibly associated with primitive alarms. In fact, featuring an intrinsic lower level of reliability, alarms from single sensors need to be verified more carefully by the operator, while composite events could even trigger automatic countermeasures, as it will be shown in the example of the following section. Fig. 6 shows an example of an operator interface including different screenshots of the integrated system. In particular, they show: the list of alarms with relative procedures (up), a vector graphics map which helps the operator to localize the source of the alarms (middle), the video streams automatically activated when an alarm is generated by smart-cameras or other sensors (down). The additional screenshot regarding the list of detected/suspected composite events is already showed in Fig. 4.

As stated previously, the SMS architecture is distributed and hierarchical. This configuration can be repeated also for the DETECT architecture in order to make possible the detection of simultaneous and distributed attack, which could not be recognized otherwise. In fact, only having a global view on the current status of all peripheral sites, it is possible to consider specific critical events. As a matter of fact, although they may be unlikely and/or apparently not meaningful from a local viewpoint, they may assume a different and concrete importance from a global viewpoint. This is especially true in case of a simultaneous occurrence of the same event in more places.

## 5   An Example Scenario

This section reports an example of application of the overall approach to a case-study in a metropolitan railway environment. Historically, these mass transit systems, being easy to access public places, are vulnerable to many threats of various kind and seriousness. In fact, they can be theater of criminal acts, aggressions, vandalism as well as sabotages and terrorist strikes. The following is a description of how to detect complex scenarios of terrorist attacks by exploiting heterogeneous sensing devices.

As already mentioned, modern smart-surveillance systems suitable for the protection of metro railways are made up by several non fully reliable sensorial subsystems. When single alarms are not reliable, automatic countermeasures cannot be activated and operators response is slowed down. Mechanisms of alarm correlation can contribute to reduce the FAR (False Alarm Rate) and at the same time improve the POD (Probability of Detection). Improvements in detection reliability can be achieved adopting two main techniques: redundancy and diversity.

Through complex computer vision algorithms, the video analytics allows for the detection of events of different complexity, like intrusions in critical areas, abandoned objects, abnormal behaviors (person running or loitering, downfalls, etc). Since the detection of an event can suffer from the intrinsic reliability of the algorithm, as well as from issues due to environmental conditions (e.g. changes of lighting, presence of reflective materials, occlusions), **redundancy** in cameras dislocation can improve detection reliability and overall system resiliency against both accidental and intentional faults. For example, assuming the use of more intelligent cameras with overlapped views from different viewpoints to detect an abnormal behavior in a platform, the events detected by each camera can be combined with a simple AND logic.

However, the most interesting application of redundancy is when it is used in combination with **diversity**, by exploiting devices based on different technologies. In the assumption that the abnormal behavior includes screaming, which is detectable by means of appropriate audio sensors, the information coming from the microphone and the cameras installed in the platform can be combined using a more complex approach, based on the use of advanced logical and temporal operators.

Let us suppose to address a chemical attack, similar to what happened in the Tokyo subway on March 20, 1995 using Sarin gas. Sarin is a chemical warfare agent (CWA) classified as a nerve agent. It is a clear, colorless, odorless, and tasteless liquid in its pure form, and can evaporate and spread in the environment very quickly.

The current available technologies to identify the contaminated areas, for example include Ion Mobility Spectroscopy (IMS), Surface Acoustic Wave (SAW), Infrared Radiation (IR), etc. They are employed in ad-hoc standoff detectors and each of them is characterized by different performances. One of the most accurate device, the automatic scanning, passive, infrared sensor can recognize a vapor cloud from several kilometers with an 87% detection rate [14]. Thus, to improve sensitiveness and reduce the number of false alarms, different technologies are often integrated in the same standoff detector (for example, the IMS and SAW detection are typically combined). More in general, it is possible to combine heterogeneous detectors and to correlate their alarms (e.g. IMS/SAW and IR detectors), in such a way to get an early warning system for the detection of chemical agents. Exploiting the redundancy and diversity also of these devices, increasingly complex correlations (logic, temporal, and spatial) can be implemented.

A likely scenario consists of a simultaneous drop of CWAs in many subway platforms in the rush hour. Let us suppose that dynamic of events is the following:

1.    the attackers stay on the platforms, waiting for the simultaneous drop of CWA;
2.    the first contaminated people fall to the floor;
3.    the people around the contaminated area run away and/or scream;
4.    the CWA quickly spread in the platform level and reach the escalators to the concourse level.

In each subway site, it is possible to address the attack scenario by means of two intelligent cameras positioned at platform end walls, a microphone between them, two standoff detectors for CWAs positioned on the platform and on the escalator.

The scenario can be formally described by means of the notation "sensor description (sensor ID) :: event description (event ID)":

**Intelligent Camera (S1) :: Fall of person (E1)**
**Intelligent Camera (S1) :: Abnormal running (E2)**
**Intelligent Camera (S2) :: Fall of person (E1)**
**Intelligent Camera (S2) :: Abnormal running (E2)**
**Audio sensor (S3) :: Scream (E3)**
**IMS/SAW detector (S4) :: CWA detection (E4)**
**IR detector (S5) :: CWA detection (E4)**

Given the scenario described above, the composite event **drop of CWA in platform** can be represented by the event tree in Fig. 7, built using the DETECT framework.

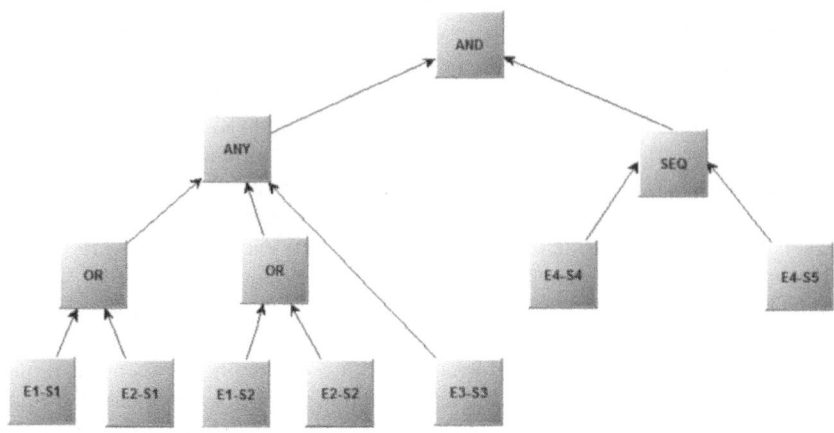

**Fig. 7.** Event tree associated to "drop of CWA in platform"

A partial alarm level (e.g. 1) can be associated to the scenario evolution in case of occurrence of the ANY event (at the left of tree). The $m$ parameter of ANY is set to 2 (trough the Scenario GUI) , this means that when 2 out of 3 distinct events detected by intelligent cameras and/or microphone occur, the monitored situation is considered abnormal (in fact each of the single events: person who falls, runs or scream, can not represent a meaningful state of alert). Besides, a temporal constraint can be set on ANY operator, in such a way to catch real alarm conditions: e.g. if fall and scream are detected at a distance of time of 30 minutes, that could not represent an alert condition for the specific scenario. In the specific example, it could be set to 5 minutes to take into account the latency of both gas propagation and intoxication symptoms.

An higher alarm level (e.g. 2) can be associated to the scenario evolution in case of occurrence of SEQ event (at the right of tree). The use of the sequence operator is due to the different assumed locations of the CWA detectors: IMS/SAW detector at platform level, IR at escalator or concourse level, in such a way to detect correctly the spread of CWA. If IR detector gives a warning before the one based on IMS/SAW detection, this could be an abnormal condition due to a false alarm and should not cause the activation of a warning. To further avoid false alarms, also a temporal constraint should be set. In this case, it can be set to 10 minutes to be conservative while taking into account the movement of air flows between different environments.

Finally, it is necessary to set the parameter context to regulate the consumption mode of the occurrences of events in feeding the detection engine. In this case, the assumption is that only the most recent occurrence of each event is meaningful. Thus, parameter is set to "recent context".

The use of many alarm levels can be useful to trigger countermeasures properly: e.g. the alarm level 1 can trigger the opening of the turnstiles; at level 2 an appropriate ventilation strategy can be activated; finally, the detection of the whole composite event can be associated to actions like: evacuation message from public address, stop trains from entering the station, and emergency call to first responders.

Assuming the simultaneous use of the correlation engine in each peripheral sites and in the main control center, it is possible to address strategic terrorist attacks (which often feature simultaneous strikes). In the considered example, if the control center detects the simultaneous (possibly partial) evolution of the above described scenario in different subway platforms, then the evacuation of the involved stations and the block of train traffic could be triggered immediately. This approach can enable an advanced situation awareness, early warning and decision support. Accordingly it is possible to improve the impact of countermeasures in a significant way. As stated in previous section, this is the key to detect simultaneous and distributed attacks, which could not be recognized otherwise, and to react promptly. The hierarchical architecture of the integrated monitoring system, including both SMS and DETECT, is functional for this purpose.

## 6 Conclusions and Future Work

The paper describes an approach to augment the capabilities of distributed surveillance systems in order to better support security operators in responding to threats. The approach is based on the DETECT framework, which implements a model-based detection engine, currently limited to Event Trees but suitable to accommodate different detection models. The decision making of the operators is supported by indications of suspect scenarios with increasing alarm levels in order to better and quickly discriminate between false and real alarms. Operators can then bias their behavior accordingly, guided by custom event management procedures.

In particular, further efforts are going towards the enrichment of the framework with stochastic extensions, by associating sensor events with reliability parameters (e.g. probability of false alarms) and automatically computing the reliability of composite events. That would help the operators to also be aware of the real level of reliability of the detected scenario.

## References

1. Garcia, M.L.: The Design and Evaluation of Physical Protection Systems. Butterworth-Heinemann, Butterworth (2001)
2. Goldgof, D.B., Sapper, D., Candamo, J., Shreve, M.: Evaluation of Smart Video for Transit Event Detection. Project #BD549-49, FINAL REPORT (2009),
   http://www.nctr.usf.edu/pdf/77807.pdf (last access January 6, 2010)
3. Martin, P.T., Feng, Y., Wang, X.: Detector Technology Evaluation (2003),
   http://www.mountain-plains.org/pubs/pdf/MPC03-154.pdf
   (last access January 6, 2010)
4. Bocchetti, G., Flammini, F., Pragliola, C., Pappalardo, A.: Dependable integrated surveillance systems for the physical security of metro railways. In: IEEE Procs. of the Third ACM/IEEE International Conference on Distributed Smart Cameras (ICDSC 2009), pp. 1–7 (2009)

5. Zhu, Z., Huang, T.S.: Multimodal Surveillance: Sensors, Algorithms and Systems. Artech House Publisher, Boston (2007)
6. Wickens, C., Dixon, S.: The benefits of imperfect diagnostic automation: a synthesis of the literature. Theoretical Issues in Ergonomics Science 8(3), 201–212 (2007)
7. Cucchiara, R.: Multimedia Surveillance Systems. In: Proceedings of the Third ACM International Workshop on Video Surveillance & Sensor Networks (2005)
8. Flammini, F., Gaglione, A., Mazzocca, N., Moscato, V., Pragliola, C.: Wireless Sensor Data Fusion for Critical Infrastructure Security. Advances in Intelligent and Soft Computing 53, 92–99 (2009)
9. Flammini, F., Gaglione, A., Ottello, F., Pappalardo, A., Pragliola, C., Tedesco, A.: Towards Wireless Sensor Networks for Railway Infrastructure Monitoring. In: Proc. ESARS 2010, Bologna, Italy, pp. 1–6 (2010)
10. Pouget, F., Dacier, M.A.: Alert correlation: Review of the state of the art. Technical Report RR-03-093
11. Flammini, F., Gaglione, A., Mazzocca, N., Pragliola, C.: DETECT: a novel framework for the detection of attacks to critical infrastructures. In: Martorell, et al. (eds.) Safety, Reliability and Risk Analysis: Theory, Methods and Applications, pp. 105–112 (2008); Procs. of ESREL 2008
12. Flammini, F., Gaglione, A., Mazzocca, N., Moscato, V., Pragliola, C.: On-line integration and reasoning of multi-sensor data to enhance infrastructure surveillance. Journal of Information Assurance and Security (JIAS) 4(2), 183–191 (2009)
13. Chakravarthy, S., Mishra, D.: Snoop, An expressive event specification language for active databases. Data Knowl. Eng. 14(1), 1–26 (1994)
14. Davis, G.L.: CBRNE - Chemical Detection Equipment. eMedicine (2008), http://emedicine.medscape.com/article/833933-overview

# Shifting Primes: Extension of Pseudo-Mersenne Primes to Optimize ECC for MSP430-Based Future Internet of Things Devices

Leandro Marin, Antonio J. Jara, and Antonio F.G. Skarmeta

Computer Science Faculty,
University of Murcia, Murcia, Spain
{leandro,jara,skarmeta}@um.es

**Abstract.** Security support for small and smart devices is one of the most important issues in the Future Internet of things, since technologies such as 6LoWPAN are opening the access to the real world through Internet. 6LoWPAN devices are highly constrained in terms of computational capabilities, memory, communication bandwidth, and battery power. Therefore, in order to support security, it is necessary to implement new optimized and scalable cryptographic mechanisms, which provide security, authentication, privacy and integrity to the communications. Our research is focused on the mathematical optimization of cryptographic primitives for Public Key Cryptography (PKC) based on Elliptic Curve Cryptography (ECC) for 6LoWPAN. Specifically, the contribution presented is a set of mathematical optimizations and its implementation for ECC in the 6LoWPAN devices based on the microprocessor Texas Instrument MSP430. The optimizations presented are focused on Montgomery multiplication operation, which has been implemented with bit shifting, and the definition of special pseudo-Mersenne primes, which we have denominated "shifting primes". These optimizations allow to implement the scalar multiplication (operation used for ECC operations) reaching a time of $1,2665$ seconds, which is $42,8\%$ lower of the reached by the state of the art solution TinyECC ($2,217$ seconds).

**Keywords:** Security, 6LoWPAN, ECC, pseudo-Mersenne primes, shifting prime, Internet of Things.

## 1 Introduction

Security is one of the major issues for the current digital society. The evolution of hardware technologies with the development of new devices such as wireless personal devices, embedded systems and smart objects, and the evolution of the services with the definition of cloud computing, online services, and ubiquitous access to the information are defining an extension of the capabilities of the current Internet, what make feasible to connect to Internet the objects and devices which are found surround us, it is the so-called Internet of things (IoT). IoT allows that systems can get a total control and access to another systems

A M. Tjoa et al. (Eds.): ARES 2011, LNCS 6908, pp. 205–219, 2011.

for leading to provide ubiquitous communication and computing. Thereby a new generation of smart and small devices, services and applications can be defined.

These small and smart things with connectivity and communication capacity from the IoT are what can be found, since some years ago, in the Low-power Wireless Personal Area Networks (LoWPANs). IETF 6LoWPAN working group has defined, in the RFC4944 [1], the standard to support IPv6 over that LoW-PANs (6LoWPAN), in order to provide the technological basis for extending the Internet to small devices. 6LoWPAN offers to the LoWPANs advantages from the Internet Protocol (IP) such as scalability, flexibility, ubiquity, openness, and end-to-end connectivity. It could be considered that 6LoWPAN devices are also empowered with derived IP protocols, i.e., protocols for mobility such as MIPv6, management such as SNMP, and security such as IPSec. However it is not feasible, since 6LoWPAN nodes are highly constrained in terms of computational capabilities, memory, communication bandwidth, and battery power.

Therefore, with the mentioned constrains, it is a challenge to implement and use the cryptographic algorithms and protocols required for the creation of security services. Nowadays, 6LoWPAN security is based on Symmetric Key Cryptography (SKC) which is directly supported by specific hardware in the microprocessor. SKC is suitable to offer local solutions, such as were originally designed these personal area networks and local solutions such as location [2], but for the future internet, it is required a higher scalability. For that reason, Public Key Cryptography (PKC) needs to be supported, Specifically, our research is focused on Elliptic Curve Cryptography for 6LoWPAN devices based on MSP430.

The MSP430 has been chosen since it is one of the most extended microprocessors in the Internet of Things devices and embedded systems. It is used for 6LoWPAN devices such as the Tmote Sky, for active Radio Frequency Identification (RFID) [3], and new hybrid technologies such as DASH7 [4].

The mathematical optimization of cryptographic primitives has been widely mentioned from a general point of view, and also for constrained devices. An overview of the state of the art is carried out in Section 2. From all the related works, TinyECC [9] is one of the most relevant references about ECC implementations for devices such as the based on MSP430. TinyECC chose Barret algorithm for reduction modulo $p$, but it has been demonstrated, in our previous work [16], that Montgomery multiplication is more suitable for these devices.

In this paper is presented an evolution of the mentioned previous work with the inclusion of special primes, which reduce almost to the half the cycles needed for Montgomery multiplication. The selection of special primes is a very extended technique, for example in FIPS 186-3 are recommended special primes for elliptic curve, called generalized Mersenne numbers, for which modular arithmetic is optimized for processors that use 32 or 64 bits operations, see [18, Section D.2]. Our advance has been to determinate the ideal primes for Montgomery multiplication based on the optimizations defined for 16-bits microprocessors.

In conclusion, this paper proposes an implementation of multiplication operation for ECC based on bit shifting, presented in Section 3, instead of the microprocessor's multiplication operation for microprocessor, which has not hardware support for multiplication operation such as MSP430. In addition, this has defined specific pseudo-Mersenne primes, which offer a simplification of the Montgomery multiplication implementation based on bit shifting, which have been denominated shifting primes, presented in Section 4. Finally, all the optimizations are implemented in Section 5, and evaluated in Section 6.

## 2   Related Works

The usual solutions for WSNs are based on Symmetric Key Cryptography (SKC), but it is not suitable for the Future Internet of Things, since it is not scalable. SKC requires that both the origin and destination share the same security credential (i.e. secret key), which is utilized for both encryption and decryption. As a result, any third-party that does not have such secret key cannot access the information exchange. The majority of WSNs, included 6LoWPAN, are based on the IEEE 802.15.4 standard, which offers three levels of security: Hash Functions, Symmetric Key Cryptography and both [8].

This work is focused on Public Key Cryptography (PKC), also known as asymmetric cryptography, which is useful for secure broadcasting and authentication purposes, and this satisfies the scalability requirements from the Future Internet of Things. It requires of two keys: a key called secret key, which has to be kept private, and another key named public key, which is publicly known. Any operation done with the private key can only be reversed with the public key, and vice versa. These primitives provide the confidentiality, integrity, authentication, and non-repudiation properties.

Public Key Cryptography was considered unsuitable for sensor node platforms, but that assumption was a long time ago. The approach that made PKC possible and usable in sensor nodes was Elliptic Curve Cryptography (ECC), which is based on the algebraic structure of elliptic curves over finite fields. Some studies has been carried out about RSA in reduced chips [12], but it was non-viable. Therefore, PKC for small and smart devices is mainly focused on ECC, since ECC presents lower requirements both in computation and memory storage, due to its small key sizes and its simpler primitives [13].

The related works of the implementation of an efficient cryptographic algorithm for constrained devices have been focus on the optimizations of the multiplication operation, since it is the most expensive operation in RSA and ECC algorithms. ECC implementation can be over either $GF(2^m)$ or $GF(p)$, we have focused on modular arithmetic, i.e. $GF(p)$, since this has similar nature to the arithmetic of the micro-controller used in the 6LoWPAN devices. However, some interesting approaches have been defined for ECC implementations over $GF(2^m)$, for example [14] has showed that field multiplication is faster over $GF(2^m)$ than in $GF(p)$ for new suggested hardware implementations, where the instructions set and arithmetic of the micro-controller are closer to $GF(2^m)$.

Some of the most known software implementations over modular arithmetic for ECC are TinyECC [9,10] and NanoECC [11], which implement ECC-based operations. TinyECC adopted several optimization techniques such as optimized modular reduction using pseudo-Mersenne primes, sliding window method, Jacobian coordinate systems, in-line assembly and hybrid multiplication in order to achieve computational efficiency. Realise, that the computational and memory requirements of these algorithms are not small (e.g. signature requires 19308 bytes ROM and 1510 bytes RAM for the MICAz, generating a signature in 2 seconds. and verifying it in 2.43 seconds), although the implementation of these primitives is constantly evolving and improving.

## 3   Mathematical Optimization Based on Bit Shifting Instead of Microprocessor's Multiplication Operation

There is an important literature about the advantages of the Montgomery's representation for this calculation [16,5,6]. For that reason, it is used for both solutions i.e. based on bit shifting and multiplication operation. The original details of the Montgomery's representation for can be found in [7], although many other books or papers refer to it. Our solution is based on ECC, which requires an integer size $(k)$ of 160-bits, i.e. $k = 160, R = 2^{160}$).

Montgomery representation has been chosen instead of other solutions, such as the Barrett reduction used in TinyECC [9], since in Montgomery representation, the representation of the numbers $a$ and $b$, which are going to be multiplied, are $aR$ and $bR$ mod $n$ ($n$ is a prime for ECC). Addition and subtraction operations with these numbers do not cause problems since $R$ is common factor. The problem is coming with the multiplication operation, when $aR$ and $bR$ is multiplied, the result is $abR^2$, but what is required is $abR$. Therefore, it needs to be reduced by factor $R$. The great advantage of Montgomery representation is to carry out the reduction of the factor $R$ during multiplication,

The multiplication operation is what consumes the higher part of the time, since it is repeated thousands of times. For that reason, it is the part optimized and discussed more in detail in the next subsections.

### 3.1   Bit Shifting

Let $a$ and $b$ two integers in Montgomery representation. Then, $aR$ and $bR$ mod $n$ between 0 and $n-1$. They are stored in binary representation, i.e. $aR = \sum_i a_i 2^i$ and $bR = \sum_i b_i 2^i$.

It is calculated $(aR)(bR)R^{-1} = (ab)R$, therefore it is required to carry out $k$ right bit shifting (with $k = 160$).

Since that, modulus $n$ is odd, because it is a prime in ECC. Thus, when it is divided by 2 mod $n$, two options are defined: either it is even number and it can be directly shifted, or it is odd number and consequently needs to add $n$, in order to reach 0 in the least significant bit, in order to be able to shift it.

Multiplication process requires a variable to accumulate the current result, we will call to that variable $P$, whose digits are $P = \sum_i P_i 2^i$. Each one of the digits $B_i$ is multiplied by $\sum_i A_i 2^i$ and divided by 2. As initially $P$ is 0, if $B_i = 0$

for some initial values, it can be ignored. Therefore, this starts directly by the digit in the position $i_0$, such that $B_{i_0} = 1$, and copy the value of $A_i$ in $P_i$.

From the position $i_0$, we can find in the next steps: $B_i = 0$ or 1. On the one hand, when $B_i = 0$, it divides $P$ by 2, and add $n$ when $P$ is odd. On the other hand, when $B_i = 1$, then it adds the value of $aR$ to $P$, before it is divided by 2.

To make a first estimation of the time, we consider that the probability to find $B_i = 1$ or 0 is the same, i.e. $0, 5$. Therefore, for each $k$ bits of $B_i$, when it is 1, it needs to carry out an addition of $k$ bits (i.e. addition of $a_i$) and a division by 2 of $P$. Otherwise, when it is 0 only one right bit shifting is required. Therefore, $k$ divisions by 2 and $k/2$ additions. Since, each division by 2 is always a shifting and, with probability 0.5, is also an addition of $n$. Therefore, the total time is:

$$k(d + s/2) + (k/2)s = k(d + s),$$ where $d$ is the time for $k$ right bit shifting, and $s$ is the time for $k$ bits addition.

Microprocessor MSP430 offers 16-bits operations. Therefore, additions and bits shifting are carried out in blocks of 16 bits. $\alpha$ is the time for 16-bits additions and shifting (usually 1 to 4 CPU cycle for bit shifting and 1 to 6 cycles for additions, depends on access to memory and registers). The final time is:

$$2\alpha k^2/16 = \alpha k^2/8.$$

The program code of the bit shifting algorithm is presented in the Algorithm 1. This has been programmed in assembler code with the other presented optimizations. The assembled code is based on MSPGCC.

## 3.2   Microprocessor's Multiplication Operation

Let an instruction from the microprocessor's set of instructions to carry out multiplication operation, which operates 2 registers of 16-bits and save the 32-bits of the result in two registers of 16-bits. This instruction is simulated in MSP430 chip, in [17, page. 478-480]. It is called $\mu$ to the time spent by that operation, and $\alpha$ for the time of 16-bits additions and 16-bits shifting.

Let the next numbers to apply the multiplication $aR = \sum_j \overline{A}_j 2^{16j}$ and $bR = \sum_j \overline{B}_j 2^{16j}$. In this case, $j$ values are between 0 and $k/16$, instead of between 0 and $k$. Therefore, for each multiplication of $k$ bits, it needs to carry out $k/16$ 16-bits multiplications and $2k/16$ additions, getting the results in a variable of $k + 16$-bits. Therefore, the time is equal to: $(\mu + 2\alpha)k/16$.

For each step of the multiplication of $aR$ and the digits of $\overline{B}_i$, since multiplication is carried out in blocks of 16-bits, this needs to add the current result with the previous one i.e. an addition of (a sum of two numbers $k$ bits and 16 bits. Thus, $\alpha(k + 1)/16$ additions), then it needs to divide it by $2^{16}$ mod $n$. It is called $\delta$ to the time used for the division by $2^{16}$.

The total time for each one of the 16 bits blocks ($k/16$ blocks, $\overline{B}_i$) is $(\mu + 2\alpha)k/16 + \alpha(k + 1)/16 = \frac{\mu k + \alpha(3k+1)}{16}$, and addition $\delta$, i.e. the total time is:

$$\frac{\mu k^2 + \alpha(3k+1)k}{256} + \frac{k\delta}{16}.$$

Division of a number of $k + 16$ bits by $2^{16}$ mod $n$ is carried out adding $n$ until that the result is multiple of $2^{16}$. If the last digit of $n$ in base $2^{16}$ is 1 the process is simple, since the number of times to subtract $n$ is indicated by the last digit of the number to be divided by $2^{16}$ mod $n$. Therefore the total time is:

$$\delta_t = \frac{(\mu + 3\alpha)k + \alpha}{16}.$$

$\delta_t$ is the ideal time, when $n$ has been chosen such that its last digit is equal to 1, in order to carry out in a simple way the division. In a general case, it cannot be assumed that the value of the last digit of $n$ is equal to 1, thus this estimation is not realistic. But, Extended Euclidean algorithm can be used, in order to fix the process pre-calculating the modular multiplicative inverse of the last digit of $n$ mod $2^{16}$ and it can be used with the last digit of $p$. Therefore, it is reached a more realist time:

$$\delta = \tfrac{k}{16}(\mu + 3\alpha) + 2\mu + 2\alpha.$$

This can be simplified considering that terms without $k$ are not highly relevant for the total time. Therefore $\delta_t$ and $\delta$ are very similar, in the order of $\frac{k}{16}(\mu + 3\alpha)$. Therefore, based on that expression and reducing terms that do not have $k^2$, the total time for microprocessor's multiplication operation is:

$$M \simeq \frac{\mu k^2}{256} + \frac{(\mu + 3\alpha)k^2}{256} = \frac{(2\mu + 3\alpha)k^2}{256}.$$

---

**Algorithm 1.** Code based on Bit shifting

---

```
accumulator = 0
for i = 0 to k do
    if B_i equals 1 then
        accumulator = accumulator + A
    end if
    if accumulator is odd then
        accumulator = (accululator + p)/2
    else
        accumulator = accumulator/2
    end if
end for
```

---

### 3.3 Comparative between Bit Shifting and Microprocessor's Multiplication Operation

The comparative between bit shifting and microprocessor's multiplication operation shows us that in a general way bit shifting is better than microprocessor's multiplication operation, when the following equation is true:

$$\frac{\alpha k^2}{8} < \frac{(2\mu + 3\alpha)k^2}{256} \Rightarrow 32\alpha < 2\mu + 3\alpha \Rightarrow \frac{29}{2} < \frac{\mu}{\alpha}.$$

In conclusion, when the number of cycles to carry out microprocessor's multiplication operation is more than 15 times the cycles to carry out addition or bit shifting, it is preferable bit shifting solution. Since, MSP430 microprocessor's multiplication operation requires a big amount of clock cycles (150 cycles in the MSP430), while the bit shifting and additions only needs between 1 and 4 cycles for bit shifting and 1 and 6 cycles for addition, this depends on the access to registers and memory, i.e. $rrcR4$, i.e. bit shifting for registers is just 1 cycle, but $rrc0(R1)$, which is bit shifting in the memory address with value $R1$ are 4 cycles. The evaluation has presented that bit shifting is better than microprocessor's multiplication operation with a relation of when its cost is 15 times or less than multiplication i,e, $\mu < 15\alpha$, and MSP430 has a $\mu/\alpha$ between 38 and 150.

## 4   Shifting Primes

Shifting primes are special pseudo-Mersenne primes for bit shifting Montgomery multiplication. They have been defined under this work to optimize them for the bit shifting implementation presented in the Section 3. The shifting primers are formally defined as:

**Definition 1.** *It is said that $p$ is a shifting prime (of type $\alpha$ and $\lambda$), if $p$ is a prime and exists $u$ such that: $p = u \cdot 2^{\lambda-\alpha+1} - 1$ and $2^{\alpha-2} < u < 2^{\alpha-1}$.*

The parameter $\alpha$ denotes the length of the word for addition and $\lambda$ the length of the prime number. Our work is focused on the case $\alpha = 16$ and $\lambda = 160$, i.e. ECC with 160-bits key length in our MSP430-based 16-bits microprocessor. Notice that if $2^{\alpha-2} < u < 2^{\alpha-1}$ then $2^{\alpha-2+\lambda-\alpha+1} - 1 < p < 2^{\alpha-1+\lambda-\alpha+1} - 1$. Therefore, $2^{\lambda-1} - 1 < p < 2^{\lambda} - 1$ and then $p$ is $\lambda$-bits length.

The number of shifting primes depends on $\lambda$ and $\alpha$. For example, for $\alpha = 8$ and $\lambda = 160$ there is only one (with $u = 100$). For $\alpha = 16$ and $\lambda = 160$ there are 288 shifting primes.

The basic operations based on these special primes (shifting primes) for the Montgomery multiplication presented in the Section 3 are presented in the next subsection.

### 4.1   Basic Operations

In order to implement the basic operations, it has been considered, in addition to the mentioned, the next optimizations.

On the one hand, the points and coordinates, for an elliptic curve $E$ over a field is a nonsingular cubic curve, are defined over the projective plane. It has been considered the field $\mathbb{Z}_p$ with $p$ a 160 bits prime, and $E$ in Weierstrass normal form, $E : y^2 = x^3 + ax + b$. It has been considered the special case with $a = -3$, which reduces the amount of operations. There are different coordinate systems that can be used to represent the points. We consider the mixed coordinate system considered in [6] for which the basic time for scalar multiplication is $1610.2M$ with $M$ the time for a basic 160 bits modular multiplication mod $p$, our focus in our research is optimize modular multiplication, since scalar multiplication is based on this.

On the other hand, all the operations are implemented in assembler, where one of the main decisions has been to use 10 registers to store a number (called the accumulator) in which we make the basic bit shifting and additions. This decision makes that only 2 registers are available for other operations, but it is worth, since operations with the accumulator are very fast, and when the accumulator is combined with the shifting primes, the result is also very quick.

Following the same methodology defined in the Section 3, there are three main operations in Montgomery multiplication:

**Division by 2.** The most basic operation for Montgomery multiplication is $x \mapsto x \cdot 2^{-1}$ in $\mathbb{Z}_p$. Suppose $x = x_0 + x_1 \cdot 2^{16} + \cdots + x_9 \cdots 2^{16 \cdot 9} < p$.

The usual algorithm for this operation is as follows:

**if** $x$ is even **then**

    *result* is shifting $x$ one position to the left.

**else**

    *result* is $x + p$ shifted one position to the left.

**end if**

Even when is being used the accumulator, it is needed 3 cycles to check if $x$ is odd and jump depending on it. Once we have decided that, it is needed 10 cycles to shift the accumulator in the best case, and 30 cycles to add a general prime $p$ and shift. This makes that this algorithm for a general prime requires between 13 and 33 cycles with an optimal programming.

The algorithm for shifting primes is:

shift $x$

**if** no carry (i.e. if $x$ was even) **then**

    jump to (END), because the result is already in $x$.

**end if**

ignore the carry and add $u$ to the most significant word of $x$.

(END) The result is in $x$

The result is clear when $x$ is even. In case $x$ is odd, if this shifts $x$, then this gets $(x - 1)/2$ and this requires $(x + p)/2$. But, if $u$ is added to the most significant word of $x$, then the result reached is

$$(x - 1)/2 + u \cdot 2^{\lambda - \alpha} = \frac{x - 1 + u \cdot 2^{\lambda - \alpha + 1}}{2} = \frac{x + p}{2}$$

It is exactly the result required. This is the advantage from the shifting primes.

The number of cycles for this operation with this optimization is equal to: 10 cycles to shift $x$, 2 cycles for the jump, and another 2 cycles in case that it is required to add $u$. Realise, that when $x$ is between 0 and $p$, then $(x + p)/2$ is also between 0 and $p$, and consequently it is not required any additional correction. The total number of cycles is 12 in the even case and 14 in the odd case. This reduction is significant because this operation should be done $\lambda$ times for a

Montgomery multiplication. Since, the probability for odd $x$ is 0.5 the usual algorithm would give $13 \cdot 0.5 + 33 \cdot 0.5 = 23$ cycles and the one with shifting primes 13 cycles. Therefore, a reduction of the $43, 47\%$ of the cycles is reached.

**Addition and correction modulo $p$.** Montgomery multiplication algorithm requires to add the second operand to the accumulator depending on the value of the bits of the first operand. In order to to keep the result between 0 and $p - 1$, when the addition is over this quantity, it is required to make a correction, i.e. subtract $p$, to offer the result inside the range.

Adding a $\lambda$-bits variable to the accumulator requires a lot of cycles, because the variable should be in memory. Specifically, it is required 10 additions add(c).w mem,reg, where for each addition are required 3 cycles. Therefore, the whole addition 30 cycles.

The correction for a general prime requires to compare the result with the prime. In order to do it, this compares the significant word of the accumulator with the most significant word of the prime (2 cycles), and then a jump (2 cycles) is carried out to different places, depending on the result. There are two cases in which the problem is clear (if the numbers are not equal). If they are equal, then it needs to check the following values, since it is possible to require a correction or not.

The mentioned correction is simpler in the case of shifting primes since:

**Proposition 1.** *Let $p$ be a shifting prime $p = u \cdot 2^{\lambda - \alpha + 1} - 1$ and $a = \sum_{i=0}^{\lambda/\alpha - 1} a_i 2^{\alpha i}$ the accumulator after a partial sum in the Montgomery multiplication of $x$ and $y$. Then:*

1. *$a$ cannot be exactly $p$.*
2. *$a$ needs no correction if and only if the most significant word of $a$ is under $2u$.*

*Proof.*

1. In Montgomery multiplication, the accumulator has partial products $h \cdot y$. If $y \neq 0$ the partial products cannot be 0 (or $p$, that is the same element in $\mathbb{Z}_p$) and in case $y$ is 0, the partial result would be always 0, not $p$.
2. The accumulator needs correction if and only if $a \geq p$, that using (1) is equivalent to $a > p$. Let $k = \lambda/\alpha - 1$. Then:

$$a = \sum_{i=0}^{k} a_i 2^{\alpha i} = a_k 2^{\lambda - \alpha} + \sum_{i=0}^{k-1} a_i 2^{\alpha i}$$

$$p = 2u2^{\lambda - \alpha} - 1$$

The number $\sum_{i=0}^{k-1} a_k 2^{\alpha i}$ is between 0 and $2^{\lambda - \alpha} - 1$ because it is written with $k - 1$ words. Therefore:

$$a > p \Leftrightarrow a_k 2^{\lambda - \alpha} + \sum_{i=0}^{k-1} a_i 2^{\alpha i} > 2u2^{\lambda - \alpha} - 1$$

$$\Leftrightarrow (a_k - 2u)2^{\lambda-\alpha} > - \left( \sum_{i=0}^{k-1} a_i 2^{\alpha i} + 1 \right)$$

The number $- \left( \sum_{i=0}^{k-1} a_i 2^{\alpha i} + 1 \right)$ is negative, therefore if $a_k - 2u \geq 0$ we have $a > p$. Conversely, if $a_k - 2u < 0$ then $a_k - 2u \leq -1$. Therefore:

$$(a_k - 2u)2^{\lambda-\alpha} \leq -2^{\lambda-\alpha} \leq - \left( \sum_{i=0}^{k-1} a_i 2^{\alpha i} + 1 \right).$$

This has been proved that the result needs correction if $a > p$ and this is equivalent to $a_k \geq 2u$. Then correction is required if and only if $a_k < 2u$.

**Addition with shifting and correction modulo $p$.** Following the Montgomery multiplication algorithm, this requires after the addition, a shifting for the following loop. It is usually better to consider both operations together because we can reduce the number of cycles avoiding a partial correction.

Suppose $a$ is the accumulator and it required to calculate $(a + w)2^{-160}(p)$. The algorithm is the following:

add $w$ to $a$ from right to left
shift $a$ from left to right with carry without previous correction.
**if** no carry **then**
   jump to (END)
**end if**
compare $u$ with the most significant word of $a$.
**if** $u$ is less than it **then**
   add $u$ to the most significant word of $a$ and jump to (END)
**end if**
sub $u$ to the most significant word of $a$ and add 1 to the final result.

## 4.2   Assembler Implementation and Execution Times

The previous algorithms and optimizations are implemented in the MSP430 with the following conventions: It is used the register R5 for $u$, R4 for the address of the operand, and 10 registers for the accumulator R6, R7, ..., R15.

DIV2

```
RRC.w R6
RRC.w R7
RRC.w R8
RRC.w R9
RRC.w R10
RRC.w R11
```

```
RRC.w R12
RRC.w R13
RRC.w R14
RRC.w R15
JNC end
ADD.w R5,R6
end:
```

In DIV2 it is needed that the carry flag is 0 before executing these instructions. Therefore, an extra instruction CLRC is required to clear the carry bit. The execution time is 12 cycles, when no carry and 13 cycles in the other case (probability 0.5). Therefore, this code needs 12.5 cycles.

In modADD R4, it is needed 30 cycles for the addition to the accumulator, 2 cycles to check if there is carry overflow. The probability of correction is around 0.5, therefore we are going to calculate both cases. If there is no correction, then it compares R6 with $2u$ (2 cycles) and jump to the end (2 cycles). This is equal to $30 + 2 + 2 + 2 = 36$ cycles. Otherwise, when correction is required, the highest probability if that carry bit is active after the addition, in that case, it is needed $30 + 2 + 1 + 2 + \epsilon = 35 + \epsilon$ cycles, where $\epsilon$ is a part of the code with very low probability. In conclusion, the average cycles needs for this code are 36 cycles.

modADD R4

```
ADD.w  18(R4),R15        reqC:   SUB.w 2u,R6
ADDC.w 16(R4),R14           ADD.w #1,R15
ADDC.w 14(R4),R13           JNC end
ADDC.w 12(R4),R12           ADD.w #1,R14
ADDC.w 10(R4),R11           ADDC.w #0,R13
ADDC.w 8(R4),R10            ADDC.w #0,R12
ADDC.w 6(R4),R9             ADDC.w #0,R11
ADDC.w 4(R4),R8             ADDC.w #0,R10
ADDC.w 2(R4),R7             ADDC.w #0,R9
ADDC.w 0(R4),R6             ADDC.w #0,R8
JC reqC                     ADDC.w #0,R7
CMP.w R6,2u                 ADDC.w #0,R6
JL end                   end:
```

modADD+DIV2 R4

```
ADD.w  18(R4),R15        JNC end
ADDC.w 16(R4),R14        CMP.w R5,R6
ADDC.w 14(R4),R13        JNC pre
ADDC.w 12(R4),R12        SUB.w R5,R6
ADDC.w 10(R4),R11        ADD.w #1,R15
ADDC.w 8(R4),R10         JNC end
ADDC.w 6(R4),R9          ADD.w #1,R14
ADDC.w 4(R4),R8          ADDC.w #0,R13
ADDC.w 2(R4),R7          ADDC.w #0,R12
ADDC.w 0(R4),R6          ADDC.w #0,R11
RRC.w R6                 ADDC.w #0,R10
RRC.w R7                 ADDC.w #0,R9
RRC.w R8                 ADDC.w #0,R8
RRC.w R9                 ADDC.w #0,R7
RRC.w R10                ADDC.w #0,R6
RRC.w R11                JMP end
RRC.w R12                pre:    ADD.w R5,R6
RRC.w R13                end:
RRC.w R14
RRC.w R15
```

In conclusion, it is required addition and shift. If the accumulator is even (probability is 0.5), then it is required 42 cycles, else it is 4 cycles in case that is required to add $p$ and $7 + \epsilon$ in case that it has that subtracts $p$. Therefore, the final cost is $42 + 0.5(4 + 0.5(3 + \epsilon)) \equiv 45$ cycles.

## 5   Bit Shifting and Shifting Primes

The Section 4 has described the advantages for the Montgomery multiplication with the defined shifting primes. This section describes the union of the presented bit shifting implementation in the Section 3 and the mentioned shifting primes. Finally, some additional optimizations have defined for the whole process.

The operations on elliptic curves have been studied extensively and optimized for very different architectures. The basic operation with elliptic curves is the scalar multiplication $n \times P$, where $P$ is a point on the curve, and $n$ is a number of large size. This operation is deeply analysed in [6], where is defined that the cost of the scalar multiplication for primes of 160-bits requires $1610, 12$ modular multiplications of 160-bit numbers. Therefore, modular multiplication is what is being optimized in this work.

Such as mentioned in the related works, Section 2, there are several alternatives for the implementation of the modular multiplication. For example, TinyECC solution is based on Barrett reduction [9]. For our solution, it has been chosen Montgomery representation, since this is more suitable to exploit the advantages from the shifting primes.

Let $x$ and $y$, which are the multiplication operands and $p$, a shifting prime for a determined $u$.

A basic implementation of the Montgomery multiplication with the shifting primes requires the following steps:

1. Traverse bit by bit the operand $x$.
2. If it is found a bit with value equal to 0, then the accumulator is rotated, i.e. (operation DIV2).
3. Otherwise, if it is found with value equal to 1, then $y$ is added to the accumulator and the accumulator is also rotated (operation modADD+DIV2).

The cost of the operations DIV2 and modADD+DIV2 have been already mentioned in the Section 4.

For traversing $x$ bit by bit has been used the next registers:

- 10 registers to store the accumulator, R6,R7,...,R15.
- 1 register to store $u$.
- 1 register to read the word of which is being traversed of $x$. Notice, that $x$ is composed by 10 words of 16 bits.
- In order to access to the right word of $x$, it is stored in the stack memory the address of the last word which has been access of $x$ increased in 2 memory units, in order that it is pointing to the next word of $x$.
- In addition, it is also stored in the stack memory the address from the first word of $x$.
- At the beginning of the loop to traverse the operand $x$, it is stored in the register R5 the address of the first word of $x$, and then is used the following code.

```
MOV.w  0(R5),R5
SETC
RRC R5
```

This code introduces a bit of control, which allows us to rotate the register until that the result is equal to 0. When, the result is 0, that bit is ignored, since it was introduced by us, with the presented code. Then, it is read the next word of $x$. This technique allows to avoid the use of a counter to control when the register has been fully traversed.

For example, an example where is used that method is the next code, which shows how to find the first bit which is equal to 1 of $x$.

```
        ADD.w  #18,R5
        PUSH.w  R5
        SUB.w  #20,R5
        PUSH.w  R5
next0 : MOV.w  2(R1),R5
        CMP.w  R5,0(R1)
        JZ  end0
        SUB.w  #2,2(R1)
        MOV.w  0(R5),R5
        SETC
Loop0 : RRC R5
        JNC  Loop0
        JZ  next0
```

The jump to end0 is defined to finish returning the value 0, since it has read all the operand and it has not been found any bit set to 1. The total number of cycles is until 17 cycles for jumping to another word, considering that this operation is required for each new word (i.e. each 16 bits), it can be considered that is introduced 1.7 cycles by each bit of the operand.

Considering that the probability to find a bit set to either 1 or 0 are equal to 0.5, it is obtained the following time:

1. If the bit is 1, then it is required 3 cycles to check it. In addition, it needs to be checked the control bit, i.e. 2 additional cycles, and carry out an addition with rotation, which are 45 cycles. In total 50 cycles with probability 0.5.
2. Otherwise, if the bit is 0, it is also required 3 cycles to check it, and 15.5 cycles to rotate it. In total 18.5 cycles with probability 0.5.
3. Therefore, the mean number of cycles per bit is equal to $25 + 9.25 = 34.25$.
4. To the mentioned mean number of cycles needs to be added a jump, and the checking of end of world. In total is equal to 38.
5. This mean number of cycles per bit needs to be multiplied by 160 bits. Therefore, this results 6080 cycles, in addition this requires some pre-calculus and function callings, that we have estimated in 6293 cycles. This results with a clock speed equal to 8 Mhz from the MSP430,

$$1610 \cdot 6293/8 \cdot 10^6 - 1.2665 \ seconds.$$

This implementation offers better results than other implementations based on other types of primes. For example, notice that this operation with TinyECC has a cost to encrypt or decrypt, where is used the scalar multiplication of $3,271$ seconds and $2,217$ seconds respectively. These operations can be carried out with our implementation in around $1,2665$ seconds with shifting primes.

## 6    Results and Evaluation

The evaluation of the algorithms optimized has been initially simulated over our own developed simulator, which verifies the results with the cryptographic library LiDIA, and finally evaluated over real motes, specifically over Tmote Sky with the Contiki 2.4 OS, where is defined a set of functions with assembler code inline.

The quickest ECC algorithm is based on *Montgomery + window method*, see [6,16]. This has been optimized for MSP430 with bit shifting in assembler language for the Montgomery multiplication of 160 bits and for the arithmetic advantages from the defined shifting prime. Modular Montgomery multiplication is carried out in 6293 cycles, and consequently scalar Montgomery in around 1610 times the modular Montgomery multiplication. The time reach, considering the 8 Mhz MSP430 microprocessor found in the Tmote Sky, is:

$$1610 \cdot 6293/8 \cdot 10^6 = 1.2665 \; seconds.$$

In order to reach this solution, we have used 10 microprocessor's registers to keep the 160 bits variable (the accumulator) with the partial multiplication results, with this optimization we have reduced almost the 40% of the total number of cycles, since $rrc$ operation for bit shifting, and $add$ operation for addition spend 1 cycle and 3 cycles respectively, instead of 4 and 6. In addition, loops have been unrolled in order to optimize more the final assembler code. Finally, such as mentioned special primes have defined in order to optimize the modular Montgomery multiplication, moving from a number of cycles for 12480 following the optimization from the Section 3 to 6293 cycles, i.e. from around $2, 5$ seconds similar to TinyECC, which lower time is $2, 217$ seconds to $1, 2665$ seconds which is a $42, 8\%$ lower than TinyEcc and our previous work [16].

## 7   Conclusions and Future Work

Future Internet of Things is defining a new set of challenges in order to offer security support, since technologies such as 6LoWPAN offers Internet connectivity to small and smart devices with highly constrained resources. Therefore, it is necessary to provide efficient, scalable, and suitable security mechanisms. For that reason, it is required Public Key Cryptography (PKC). This work has evaluated and optimized Elliptic Curve Cryptography (ECC) implementation for Future Internet of Things devices based on the Texas Instrument MSP430 microprocessor, which is used for several Future Internet of Things devices.

The optimizations for ECC are based mainly on bit shifting implementation of the modular Montgomery multiplication, and in a special type of primes (shifting primes) defined under this work, which offer a set of arithmetic advantages for the implementation of the bit shifting based modular Montgomery multiplication.

The result reached with the mentioned optimizations is $1, 2665$ seconds for the scalar Montgomery multiplication, which reduces a $42, 8\%$, with respect to the TinyECC implementation which offers a result of $2, 217$ seconds. Therefore, it can be concluded, that with the reached time, ECC is suitable for the Future Internet of Things.

Finally remark, selection of special primes is a very well-known technique, which does not mean any vulnerability or weakness for our systems, e.g. standards such as FIPS 186-3 recommends specific elliptic curves for which modular arithmetic is simpler for 32 and 64 bits microprocessors. Therefore, our advance has been to determinate the ideal primes for Montgomery multiplication based on bit shifting operations and the 16-bits MSP430 microprocessor.

Ongoing work is focused on carry out additional optimizations based on reduction of the number of additions accessing to blocks of 4 bits in each step, instead of bit by bit, and the use of pre-calculated values.

# References

1. Montenegro, G., Kushalnagar, N., Hui, J., Culler, D.: Transmission of IPv6 Packets over IEEE 802.15.4 Networks. RFC 4944 (2007)
2. Nobles, P., Ali, S., Chivers, H.: Improved Estimation of Trilateration Distances for Indoor Wireless Intrusion Detection. Journal of Wireless Mobile Networks, Ubiquitous Computing, and Dependable Applications 2(1) (2011) ISSN: 2093-5374
3. Zampolli, S., Elmi, I., et al.: Ultra-low-power components for an RFID Tag with physical and chemical sensors. Journal of Microsystem Technologies 14(4), 581–588 (2008)
4. Norair, J.P.: DASH7: ultra-low power wireless data technology (2009)
5. Cohen, H., Miyaji, A., Ono, T.: Efficient Elliptic Curve Exponentiation. In: Han, Y., Quing, S. (eds.) ICICS 1997. LNCS, vol. 1334. Springer, Heidelberg (1997)
6. Cohen, H., Miyaji, A., Ono, T.: Efficient Elliptic Curve Exponentiation Using Mixed Coordinates. In: Ohta, K., Pei, D. (eds.) ASIACRYPT 1998. LNCS, vol. 1514, pp. 51–65. Springer, Heidelberg (1998)
7. Montgomery, P.: Modular Multiplication Without Trial Division. Math. Computation 44, 519–521 (1985)
8. 802.15.4-2003, IEEE Standard, Wireless medium access control and physical layer specifications for low-rate wireless personal area networks (May 2003)
9. Liu, A., Ning, P.: TinyECC: A Configurable Library for Elliptic Curve Cryptography in Wireless Sensor Networks. In: 7th International Conference on Information Processing in Sensor Networks, SPOTS Track, USA, pp. 245–256 (2008)
10. Seo, S.C., Han, D.G., et al.: TinyECCK: Efficient Elliptic Curve Cryptography Implementation over GF(2m) on 8-bit MICAz Mote. IEICE Transactions on Info and Systems E91-D(5), 1338–1347 (2008)
11. Szczechowiak, P., Oliveira, L.B., et al.: NanoECC: Testing the Limits of Elliptic Curve Crytography in Sensor Networks. In: UNICAMP, Brasil (2008)
12. Gura, N., Patel, A., et al.: Comparing Elliptic Curve Cryptography and RSA on 8-bit CPUs. In: Workshop on Cryptographic Hardware and Embedded Systems (2004)
13. Hitchcock, Y., Dawson, E., et al.: Implementing an efficient elliptic curve cryptosystem over GF(p) on a smart card. ANZIAM Journal (2003)
14. Uhsadel, L., Poschmann, A., Paar, C.: Enabling Full-Size Public-Key Algorithms on 8-bit Sensor Nodes. In: European Workshop on Security and Privacy in Ad hoc and Sensor Networks (2007)
15. Hodjat, A., Batina, L., et al.: HW/SW Co-Design of a Hyperelliptic Curve Cryptosystem using a Microcode Instruction Set Coprocessor Integration. VLSI Journal 40(1), 45–51 (2007)
16. Ayuso, J., Marin, L., Jara, A., Skarmeta, A.F.G.: Optimization of Public Key Cryptography (RSA and ECC) for 8-bits Devices based on 6LoWPAN. In: 1st International Workshop on the Security of the Internet of Things, Tokyo, Japan (2010)
17. Bierl, L.: MSP430 Family Mixed-Signal Microcontroller Application Reports, pp. 478–480 (2000), http://focus.ti.com.cn/cn/lit/an/slaa024/slaa024.pdf
18. Locke, G., Gallagher, P.: FIPS PUB 186-3: Digital Signature Standard (DSS). National Institute of Standards and Technology (2009)

# Semantic Modelling of Coronary Vessel Structures in Computer Aided Detection of Pathological Changes

Mirosław Trzupek

AGH University of Science and Technology, Institute of Automatics,
30 Mickiewicza Ave, 30-059 Kraków, Poland
mtrzupek@agh.edu.pl

**Abstract.** In the paper, the author discusses the results of his research on the opportunities for using selected artificial intelligence methods to semantically analyse medical images. In particular, he will present attempts at using linguistic methods of structural image analysis to develop systems for the cognitive analysis and understanding of selected medical images, and this will be illustrated by the recognition of pathological changes in coronary arteries of the heart. The problem undertaken is important because the identification and location of significant stenoses in coronary vessels is a widespread practical task. The obtained results confirm the importance of the proposed methods in the diagnosis of coronary heart disease.

**Keywords:** Intelligent medical image processing and understanding, spatial modelling of coronary vessels, computer-aided diagnosis.

## 1 Introduction

Coronary Heart Disease (CHD) is the leading cause of death in developed countries and at the same time constitutes a crucial diagnostic problem of the $21^{st}$ century. Every year, over 19 million people globally suffer sudden, severe coronary incidents. Early diagnosis and risk assessment are widely accepted strategies to combat CHD [1]. The impressive technological progress in medical image diagnostics and the wide opportunities for 3D visualization of human organs have significantly improved the efficiency of medical diagnostic tasks. The 3D reconstructions of examined medical structures [2] obtained by rendering make it possible to truly represent the selected organ (including the changes in its texture), allowing its external and internal morphology to be observed precisely. Such high technologies of image processing [3] are today used in almost all types of diagnostic examinations based on digital technologies and of surgical jobs performed with the use of medical robots. As a result, it has become possible to identify a greater number of qualitative parameters of the examined structure which may be significant for making the correct diagnosis, and which could not be identified if the examination was made using a conventional method (2D imaging) [4]. However, all these achievements in the visualization technology field offer limited opportunities for automating the interpretation of the diagnostic images acquired. This is mainly due to the difficulties which informatics encounters in formally describing and modelling complex thought processes taking

A M. Tjoa et al. (Eds.): ARES 2011, LNCS 6908, pp. 220–227, 2011.

place in the human mind which enable the semantic interpretation of analyzed medical images. Such intelligent IT systems supporting the thought processes of a physician analyzing complex cases simply have not been developed yet. There are, however, tools which support the work of a diagnostician by making quantitative measurements of pathologies depicted in the image [5], [6], which obviously makes his/her work easier, but only understanding the essence of the disease process allows the appropriate diagnosis to be made and the correct therapy to be prescribed.

## 2  The Problem of Analysis and Understanding of Medical Images

One of the main difficulties in developing universal, intelligent systems for medical image diagnostics is the huge variety of images, both healthy and pathological, which have to be taken into account when intelligently supporting physicians interpreting them. In particular, the aforementioned varied shapes of morphological elements make it difficult to create a universal pattern defining the model shape of a healthy organ, or a pathological one. On the other hand, a computer using the well-known and frequently used techniques of automatic image recognition needs such a pattern to be provided to it. This is because the information technologies applied rely to a significant extent on intuition to determine the measure of similarity between the currently considered case and such an abstract pattern. These technologies frequently fail if there are unexpected changes to the shapes of analysed organs caused by the disease process or individual variability. All of this means that attempts to effectively assess the morphology using computer software are very complicated and frequently outright impossible, because there are too many cases that would have to be analysed to unambiguously determine the condition of the structure being examined. For this reason it is necessary to use those advanced artificial intelligence techniques and computational intelligence techniques that can generalize the recorded image patterns. What is particularly important is to use intelligent description methods that would ignore individual characteristics of the patient examined and characteristics dependent on the specific form of the disease unit considered, while at the same time making it possible to locate significant morphology changes and also to interpret and determine their diagnostic significance. Such methods, aimed at focusing the image description on diagnostically significant properties to the maximum extent can then be used in intelligent computer-aided diagnostics systems.

## 3  Methodology

Research work was conducted on images from diagnostic examinations made using SOMATOM Sensation Cardiac 64 tomograph [7] in the form of animations saved as AVI (MPEG4) files with the 512x512 pixel format. Such sequences were obtained for various patients and present in a very clear manner all morphologic changes of individual sections of arteries in any plane. Coronary vessels were visualized without the accompanying muscle tissue of the heart. Since image data has been saved in the form of animations showing coronary vessels in various projections, for the further analyses should be selected the appropriate projection which will show the examined coronary vessels in the most transparent form most convenient for analysis. In the research work, attempts were made to automate the procedure of finding such a projection by using selected geometric transformations during image processing. Using the fact that the spatial layout of an object can be determined by projecting it onto the axes of the Carthesian coordinate system, values of horizontal Feret diameters [8], which are a measure of the horizontal extent of the diagnosed coronary artery tree, are calculated for every subsequent animation frame. The projection for which the horizontal Feret diameter is the greatest is selected for further analyses.

To help represent the examined structure of coronary vascularisation with a graph, it is necessary to define primary components of the analyzed image and their spatial relations, which will serve to extract and suitably represent the morphological characteristics significant for understanding the pathology shown in the image. It is therefore necessary to identify individual coronary arteries and their mutual spatial relations. To ease this process, the projection selected for analyzing was skeletonised by the Pavlidis skeletonising algorithm [9] (it leaves the fewest apparent side branches in the skeleton and the lines generated during the analysis are only negligibly shortened at their ends). This gives us the skeleton of the given artery which is much thinner than the artery itself, but fully reflects its topological structure (fig. 1.). Skeletonising is aimed only at making it possible to find points where artery sections intersect or end in the vascularisation structures and then to introduce an unambiguous linguistic description of individual coronary arteries and their branches. These points will constitute the vertices of a graph modelling the spatial structure of the coronary vessels. The next step is labelling them by giving each located informative point the appropriate label from the set of vertex labels (this set comprises abbreviated names of arteries found in coronary vascularisation). If a given informative point is a branching point, then the vertex will be labelled with the concatenation of names of the vertex labels of arteries which begin at this point. This way, all initial and final points of coronary vessels as well as all points where main vessels branch into lower level vessels have been determined and labelled as appropriate. After this operation, the coronary vascularisation tree is divided into sections which constitute the edges of a graph modelling the examined coronary arteries. This makes it possible to formulate a description in the form of edge labels which determine the mutual spatial relations between the primary components, i.e. between subsequent arteries shown in the analysed image.

Mutual spatial relations that may occur between elements of the vascular structure represented by a graph are described by the set of edges. The elements of this set have been defined by introducing the appropriate spatial relations: vertical - defined by the set of labels $\{\alpha, \beta,..., \mu\}$ and horizontal - defined by the set of labels $\{1, 2,..., 24\}$ on a hypothetical sphere surrounding the heart muscle. These labels designate individual final intervals, each of which has the angular spread of $15°$. Then, depending on the location, terminal edge labels are assigned to all branches identified by the beginnings and ends of the appropriate sections of coronary arteries (fig. 1). The presented methodology draws upon the method of determining the location of a point on the surface of our planet in the system of geographic coordinates, where a similar cartographic projection is used to make topographic maps. This representation of mutual spatial relations between the analysed arteries yields a convenient access to the unambiguous description of all elements of the vascular structure. At subsequent analysis stages, this description will be correctly formalised using ETPL(k) (Embedding Transformation-preserved Production-ordered k-Left nodes unambiguous) graph grammar G defined in [10], [11], supporting the search for stenoses in the lumen of arteries forming parts of the coronary vascularisation. Grammar G generates the language L(G) in the form of IE (indexed edge-unambiguous) graphs which can unambiguously represent 3D structures of heart muscle vascularisation visualised in images acquired during diagnostic examinations with the use of spiral computed tomography. Quoted below (1) is the formal definition of the IE graph [10], [11].

$$H=(V, E, \Sigma, \Gamma, \Phi) \tag{1}$$

where:
V is a finite, non-empty set of graph node with unambiguously assigned indices
$\Sigma$ is a finite, non-empty set of node labels
$\Gamma$ is a finite, non-empty set of edge labels
E is a set of graph edges in the form of $(v, \lambda, w)$, where $v, w \in V$, $\lambda \in \Gamma$ and the index v is smaller than the index w
$\varphi : V \rightarrow \Sigma$ is a function of node labelling

After applying the presented methodology, a graph model representing the coronary arteries on the CT images was obtained (fig. 1.).

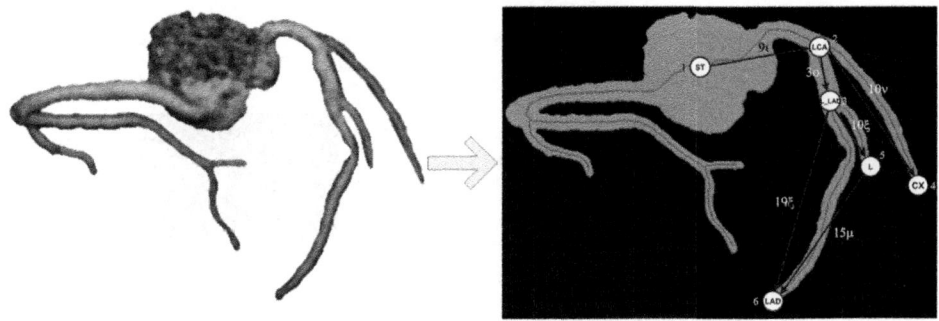

**Fig. 1.** The representation of the left coronary artery using IE graph

Due to the fact that in obtained during diagnostic examination visualisations of coronary vascularisation, we can distinguish three different types of topologies, characteristic for these vessels, therefore, for each of the three types of topology, appropriate type of ETPL(k) graph grammars can be proposed. Each grammar generate IE graphs language, modelling particular types of coronary vascularisation. This representation was then subjected to a detailed analysis, to find the places of morphological changes indicating occurrence of pathology. This operation consists of several stages, and uses, among others context-free sequential grammars, used successfully for the detection of lesions in coronary planar images [12]. Next steps in the analysis of the example coronary artery are shown in fig. 2. Artery with the vertices $L\_LAD_3$ – $LAD_6$ represented by the edge $19\xi$ of the IE graph has been subjected to the operation of the straightening transformation [12], which allows to obtain the width diagram of the analyzed artery, while preserving all its properties, including potential changes in morphology. In addition, such representation allows to determine the nature of the narrowing (concentric or eccentric). Concentric stenoses occur on a cross-section as a uniform stricture of the whole artery (this symptom is characteristic for a stable disturbance of heart rhythm), whereas eccentric stenoses occur only on one vascular wall (an unstable angina pectoris) [13]. Analysis of morphological changes was conducting based on the obtained width diagrams, and using context-free attributed grammars [12]. As a result of carried out operations the profile of the analyzed coronary artery with marked areas of existing pathology, together with the determination of the numerical values of their advancement level was obtained (fig. 2). Methodology presented above was implemented sequentially to the individual sections of coronary vascularisation represented by the particular edges of the introduced graph representation.

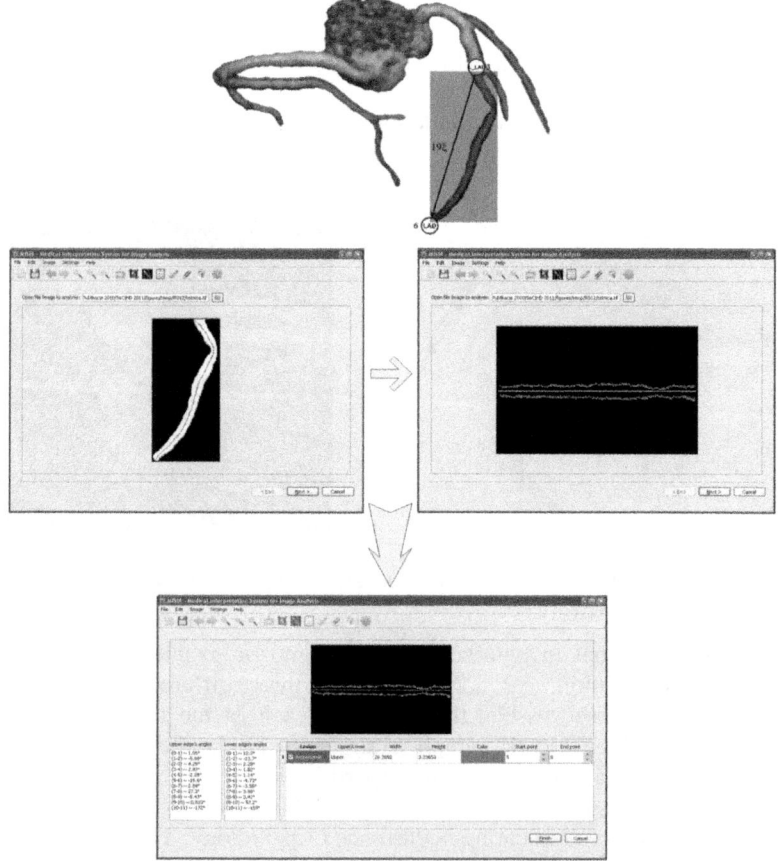

**Fig. 2.** Next steps in the analysis and recognition of pathological changes occurring on the example of the left coronary artery

# 4 Results

The set of test images, which has been used to determine the efficiency of the proposed methods consisted of 20 complete reconstructions of coronary vascularisation obtained during diagnostic examinations of various patients, mainly suffering from coronary heart disease at different progression stages. These images were obtained during diagnostic examinations with 64-slice spiral computed tomography. Due to the different types of topologies of coronary vascularisation, the set of analyzed images consisted of three basic types (balanced artery distribution, right artery dominant, left artery dominant). Structure of the coronary vascularisation was determined by a diagnostician at the stage of acquisition of image data. This distinction was intended to obtain additional information about the importance of providing health risks of the patient depending on the place where pathology occurs in the type of coronary vascularisation. The test data also consisted of visualisations previously used to construct the grammar and the syntactic analyser. To avoid analysis of images that were used to construct the set of grammatical rules, from the same sequences frames were selected that were several frames later than the projections used to construct the set of grammatical rules, and these later frames were used for the analysis. The above set of image data was used to determine the percentage efficiency of correct recognitions of the stenoses present, using the methodology proposed here. The recognition consists in identifying the locations of stenoses, their number, extent and type (concentric or eccentric). For the research data included in the experiment, 85% of recognitions were correct. This value is the percentage proportion of the number of images in which the occurring stenoses were correctly located, measured and properly interpreted to the number of all analysed images included in the experimental data set. No indication of major differences in the effectiveness evaluation, depending on the structure of the coronary vascularisation is noticed. In order to assess whether the size of the stenosis was correctly measured, comparative values from the syngo Vessel View software forming part of the HeartView CI suite were used. This program is used in everyday clinical practice where examinations are made with the SOMATOM Sensation Cardiac 64 tomograph [7]. In order to confirm or reject the regularity of the stenosis type determination (concentric or eccentric) shown in the examined image, a visual assessment was used, because the aforementioned programs did not have this functionality implemented. As the set of test data was small the results obtained are very promising. Further research on improving the presented analysis techniques of lesions occurring in the morphology of coronary vessels might bring about a further improvement in the effectiveness and the future standardisation of these methods, obviously after they have first been tested on a much more numerous image data set.

# 5 Conclusions

The obtained results show that graph languages for describing shape features can be effectively used to describe 3D reconstructions of coronary vessels and also to formulate semantic meaning descriptions of lesions found in these reconstructions [14], [15]. Such formalisms, due to their significant descriptive power (characteristic especially for graph grammars) can create models of both examined vessels whose morphology shows no lesions and those with visible lesions bearing witness to early or more advanced stages of the ischemic heart disease. In addition, by introducing the appropriate spatial relations into the coronary vessel reconstruction, it is possible to reproduce their biological role, namely the blood distribution within the whole coronary circulation system, which also facilitates locating and determining the progression stage of lesions. The research also has shown that one of the hardest tasks leading to the computer classification and then the semantic interpretation of medical visualisations is to create suitable representations of the analysed structures and propose effective algorithms for reasoning about the nature of pathologies found in these images. Visualisations of coronary vascularisation are difficult for computers to analyse due to the variety of projections of the arteries examined. Problems related to automating the process of generating new grammars for cases not included in the present language remain unsolved in the on-going research. However, it is worth noting that generally, the problem of deriving grammatical rules is considered unsolvable, particularly for graph grammar. It can appear if the image undergoing the analysis shows a coronary vascularisation structure different from the so far assumed three cases of vessel topologies occurring the most often, i.e. the balanced distribution of arteries, the dominant right artery or the dominant left artery. In those cases it will be necessary to define a grammar taking this new case into account. The processes of creating new grammars and enriching existing ones with new description rules will be followed in further directions of research on the presented methods.

**Acknowledgments.** This work has been supported by the Ministry of Science and Higher Education, Republic of Poland, under project number N N516 478940.

# References

1. Yusuf, S., Reddy, S., Ounpuu, S., Anand, S.: Global burden of cardiovascular diseases, Part I. General considerations, the epidemiologic transition, risk factors, and impact of urbanization. Circulation 104, 2746–2753 (2001)
2. Lewandowski, P., Tomczyk, A., Szczepaniak, P.S.: Visualization of 3-D Objects in Medicine - Selected Technical Aspects for Physicians. Journal of Medical Informatics and Technologies 11, 59–67 (2007)
3. Sonka, M., Fitzpatrick, J.M.: Handbook of Medical Imaging. Medical Image Processing and Analysis, vol. 2. SPIE, Belligham (2004)
4. Katritsis, D.G., Pantos, I., Efstathopoulos, E.P., et al.: Three-dimensional analysis of the left anterior descending coronary artery: comparison with conventional coronary angiograms. Coronary Artery Disease 19(4), 265–270 (2008)
5. Wang, Y., Liatsis, P.: A Fully Automated Framework for Segmentation and Stenosis Quantification of Coronary Arteries in 3D CTA Imaging. In: Dese, Second International Conference on Developments in eSystems Engineering, pp. 136–140 (2009)
6. Oncel, D., Oncel, G., Tastan, A., Tamci, B.: Detection of significant coronary artery stenosis with 64-section MDCT angiography. European Journal of Radiology 62(3), 394–405 (2007)
7. SOMATOM Sensation Cardiac 64 Brochure.: Get the Entire Picture. Siemens medical (2004)

8.  Tadeusiewicz, R., Korohoda, P.: Computer Analysis and Image Processing. Foundation of Progress in Telecommunication, Kraków (1997) (in Polish)
9.  Pavlidis, T.: Algorithms for graphics and image processing. Computer Science Press, Rockville (1982)
10. Tadeusiewicz, R., Flasiński, M.: Pattern Recognition. PWN, Warsaw (1991) (in Polish)
11. Skomorowski, M.: A Syntactic-Statistical Approach to Recognition of Distorted Patterns. Jagiellonian University, Krakow (2000)
12. Tadeusiewicz, R., Ogiela, M.R.: Medical Image Understanding Technology. Springer, Heidelberg (2004)
13. Faergeman, O.: Coronary Artery Disease. Elsevier, Amsterdam (2003)
14. Ogiela, M.R., Tadeusiewicz, R., Trzupek, M.: Picture grammars in classification and semantic interpretation of 3D coronary vessels visualisations. Opto.-Electronics Review 17(3), 200–210 (2009)
15. Trzupek, M., Ogiela, M.R., Tadeusiewicz, R.: Image content analysis for cardiac 3D visualizations. In: Velásquez, J.D., Ríos, S.A., Howlett, R.J., Jain, L.C. (eds.) KES 2009. LNCS, vol. 5711, pp. 192–199. Springer, Heidelberg (2009)

# Pose and Expression Recognition Using Limited Feature Points Based on a Dynamic Bayesian Network

Wei Zhao[1], Goo-Rak Kwon[2], and Sang-Woong Lee[1]

[1] Department of Computer Engineering
[2] Department of Information and Communication Engineering,
Chosun University,
Gwangju, Korea 501-759
brandyzhao@gmail.com,
{grkwon,swlee}@chosun.ac.kr

**Abstract.** In daily life, language is an important tool during the communications between people. Except the language, facial actions can also provide a lot of information. Therefore, facial actions recognition becomes a popular research topic in Human-Computer Interaction (HCI) field. However, it is always a challenging task because of its complexity. In a literal sense, there are thousands of facial muscular movements many of which have very subtle differences. Moreover, muscular movements always occur spontaneously when the pose is changed.

To address this problem, firstly we build a fully automatic facial points detection system based on local Gabor filter bank and Principal Component Analysis (PCA). Then the Dynamic Bayesian networks (DBNs) are proposed to perform facial actions recognition using junction tree algorithm over a limited number of feature points. In order to evaluate the proposed method, we have applied the Korean face database for model training, and CUbiC FacePix, FEED, and our own database for testing. Experiment results clearly demonstrate the feasibility of the proposed approach.

**Keywords:** DBNs, Pose and expression recognition, limited feature points, automaticly feature detection, Local Gabor filters, PCA.

## 1 Introduction

Facial actions can provide information not only about affective state, but also about cognitive activity, psychopathology and so on. However, this is always a tough task because of the essence of facial actions. Thousands of distinct nonrigid facial muscular movements have been observed and most of them only differ in a few features. For example, spontaneous facial actions are usually in the term of slight appearance changes. What is more, different facial actions can happen simultaneously. All of these make the recognition difficult. Many methods are proposed by researchers in order to solve this problem. The Facial Action Coding

A M. Tjoa et al. (Eds.): ARES 2011, LNCS 6908, pp. 228–242, 2011.
© IFIP International Federation for Information Processing 2011

System (FACS) [1] is one of the most popular methods to analyze the facial actions. In FACS system, nonrigid facial nuscular movement is described by a set of facial action units (AUs).

In this paper, we focus on the methods based on DBNs. Many researchers have attempted to build different DBNs to solve this problem. In [2], a unified probabilistic framework is built to recognize the spontaneous facial actions based on DBNs. The authors assume there are coherent interactions among rigid and nonrigid facial motions. According to this idea, facial feature points can be organized into two categories: global feature points and local feature points. By separating these 28 feature points into two groups, they realize the interactions between pose and expression variables. In this paper, the pose is considered in only pan angle and divided into three state: left, frontal and right. The expression is analyzed by FACS. In another paper [3], a probabilistic measure of similarity is used instead of standard Euclidean nearest-neighbor eigenface matching. The advantage of this improved method is demonstrated by the experiments. In paper [4], the authors use BN for face identification. Some other researchers use hierarchical DBNs for human interactions [5]. In our case, we use DBNs to handle the pose and expression recognition using only 21 feature points on human face. We assume that pose and expression can only be considered as a kind of distribution of the feature points.

The paper is organized as follows: Section 2 illustrates a novel facial features detection method. Section 3 briefly introduces the theories of BN and DBNs. In section 4, our model will be introduced in detail and experiment results will be given too. Section 5 gives the conclusions.

## 2    Facial Feature Point Detection

Generally, a whole facial actions system includes the detection system and recognition system. The facial feature detection system is very crucial. It decides the performance of the recognition system and the whole system. Here we proposed a low-dimensional facial feature detection system.

### 2.1    Facial Feature Points Extraction Based on Local Gabor Filter Bank and PCA

For feature points extraction, there are many popular methods such as Gabor filter-based method, Active Shape Model(ASM), Active Appearance Models (AAM) and so on. ASM performs well in experiments [6]. However, ASM is a statistical approach for shape modeling and feature extraction. In order to train the ASM model, a lot of training data is necessary. AAM [7] has the same problem as ASM. In order to realize the fully automatic feature point detection, several other methods appear. One of the most popular methods is to detect feature points using Gabor filter [8]. Gabor filter is a powerful tool in computer vision field. Gabor filters with different frequencies and orientations can serve as excellent band-pass filters and are similar to human visual system. The Gabor filter function can be written as in equation (1):

$$g(x, y, f, \theta) = \frac{1}{ab} exp[-\pi(\frac{x_r^2}{a^2} + \frac{y_r^2}{b^2})][exp(i2\pi f x_r)] \tag{1}$$

where

$$x_r = x \cos\theta + y \sin\theta$$
$$y_r = -x \sin\theta + y \cos\theta$$

In paper [9], the concept of local Gabor filter bank has been proposed and compared with traditional global Gabor filter bank. Both the theoretical analysis and the experiment results show that the local Gabor filter bank is effective. In our experiments, we choose 4 orientations and 3 frequencies from the original 8 orientations and 6 frequencies according to the method introduced in [9]. The 12 Gabor filters are combined together to form a local Gabor filter bank as shown in Fig. 1.

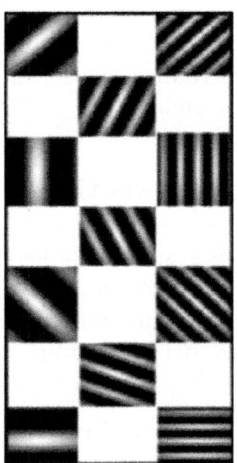

**Fig. 1.** Local Gabor filter bank with 4 orientations and 3 frequencies

Pupils are the significant features on human faces. Firstly, we apply the method introduced in [10] to detect the pupils and nostrils. Then we take the pupils and nostrils as the reference points to separate the face into several areas. In each small area, we build up the feature vector for each point. The feature vector is extracted from a $11 \times 11$ image patch which centered on that point. The image patch is extracted from 12 Gabor filters and the original gray scale image. Thus 1573 ($11 \times 11 \times 13 = 1573$) dimensional vector is used to present one point. In order to describe the method better, we give an example of the feature vector. As shown in Fig. 2 and Fig. 3, there are 12 images each of which is a $11 \times 11$ image patch. We can reshape these patches into a vector. This vector represents the point 6 as marked in Fig. 4. In Fig. 2, features of point 6 extracted from two different persons are given. The Fig. 3 shows the features of point 6 and another point. The Gabor filter used in this example is the global Gabor filter. We can also figure out the necessity of using the local Gaobr filter because some patches are similar with each other in these images. The proposed method is similar with the feature extraction method introduced in [8]. However, because we use the local Gabor filter here, the dimension of the feature vector (1573) is much lower than the dimension in [8] which is 8281.

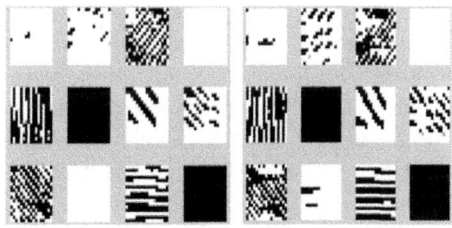

**Fig. 2.** Features of points 6 from two different persons

**Fig. 3.** Features of two points. The left figure is the features of point 6 as marked in Fig.4. The right figure is the features of another point.

In order to reduce the dimension further, Principal Component Analysis (PCA) is applied. Considering a set of N images $(x_1, x_2, ..., x_N)$, each image is represented by t-dimensional Gabor feature vector. The PCA [9] [11] can be used to transform the t-dimensional vector into a f-dimensional vector, where normally $f \ll t$. The new feature vector $y_i \in \Re^f$ are defined by

$$y_i = W_{pca}^T x_i \quad (i = 1, 2, ..., N) \tag{2}$$

where $W_{pca}^T$ is the linear transformations matrix, $i$ is the number of sample images.

In our case, each feature point is represented by 1573-dimensional feature vector. Then we apply PCA to reduce the dimension to a lower dimension. After dimension reduction, calculate the Euclidean distances among tested points and the trained points, we can decide which point is the feature point.

## 2.2   Experiments and Results of Feature Points Detection

The facial feature points detection method proposed here is trained and tested on the Korea Face database. For our study, we use 60 Korea Face database samples. In Korea Face database, there are several different images for one person which are taken under different illuminations or expressions. We choose the images with natural expressions here. The 60 images are divided into two groups. 20 images are used for training and the 40 images are used for testing. To evaluate the performance of our system, the located facial points were compared to the true points which are got manually. If the distance between automatically detected point and the true point is less than 2 pixels, the detection is defined as a success. Table 1 gives the results of 17 facial feature points' detection result based on Korea Face database. Table 2 gives the results of pupils and nostrils detection results using the method introduced in [10]. From the result table, we can find that the corner points are more easier to be detected while the bottom points like point 8 and point 16 are missed more frequently. This is because the characters of corner points are obvious and stable. The feature points described in Table 1 and Table 2 are shown in Fig. 4. Also Fig. 4 gives an example that the feature points are successfully detected and Fig. 5 shows some general mistakes in experiments.

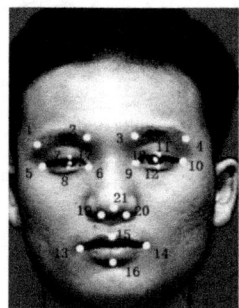

**Fig. 4.** An example of successfully detected points and the feature points described in Table 1 are marked here too

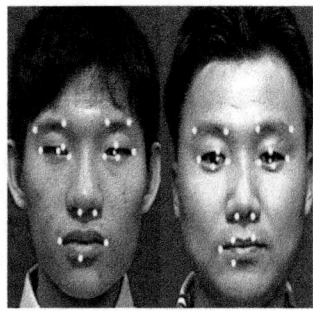

**Fig. 5.** The points 8,15,19 are missed in the left image and the points 14,15,16 are missed in the right image

**Table 1.** Facial Feature Point Detection Results Based On Korea Face database

| 16 feature points detection results | |
| --- | --- |
| Detected point | Accurate Rate |
| 1: left corner of left eyebrow | 95% |
| 2: right corner of left eyebrow | 93% |
| 3: left corner of right eyebrow | 90% |
| 4: right corner of right eyebrow | 90% |
| 5: left corner of the left eye | 98% |
| 6: right corner of the left eye | 98% |
| 7: top of the left eye | 90% |
| 8: bottom of the left eye | 86% |
| 9: left corner of the right eye | 93% |
| 10: right corner of the right eye | 95% |
| 11: top of the right eye | 93% |
| 12: bottom of the right eye | 90% |
| 13: left corner of mouth | 93% |
| 14: right corner of mouth | 90% |
| 15: top of the mouth | 86% |
| 16: bottom of the mouth | 80% |
| 21: center of the nose | 90% |
| Average accurate rate of first 16 points | 90.625% |

**Table 2.** Pupils and nostril Detection Results using the method introduced in [10]

| Pupils and nostril detection | |
| --- | --- |
| Detected point | Accurate Rate |
| 17: left pupil | 98% |
| 18: right pupil | 98% |
| 19: left nostril | 92% |
| 20: right nostril | 90% |
| Average accurate rate of first 16 points | 94.5% |
| Average accurate rate of all points | 92.87% |

# 3    The Preliminary of Bayesian Network and Dynamic Bayesian Networks

## 3.1    An Brief Introduction of BN

A BN was firstly proposed by Pearl[14]. The BN represents the joint probability distribution over a set of random variables in a directed acyclic graph(DAG). The links between these variables represent the causality relationships.

More formally, we can define $Pa(X_i)$ as the parents of variable $X_i$ and the joint probability $P(x)$ over the variables is given by the following equation:

$$P(x) = \prod_{i=1}^{n} P(X_i|Pa(X_i)) \tag{3}$$

where $i$ is the index of variables and $n$ is the total number of variables. From equation (3), we can tell that a BN consists of two crucial respects: the structure and the parameters. So how to learn the structure and the parameters from a actual problem becomes an important issue in BN. We only consider the parameter learning issue here because the structure of BN has already been decided. Parameter learning can be classified into 4 types, depending on the goal is to compute full posterior or just a point, and all the variables are observed or some of them are hidden. In our case, the goal is point estimation and the hidden nodes exist. Hence, Expectation-Maximization(EM) algorithm is applied here.

After parameter learning, the Bayesian network has been fixed. The next work is to infer the result from evidences. Inference is another important task in BN. In this paper, we use Junction Tree Algorithm as our inference engine. Junction Tree algorithm is a very popular algorithm and can perform exact inference in both directed and undirected graphical models.

## 3.2    An Brief Introduction of DBNs

A DBN can be defined as $B = (G, \Theta)$ where G is the model structure, and $\Theta$ represents the model parameters like the CPDs/CPTs for all nodes. There are two assumptions in the DBN model: First, the system is first-order Markovian. Second, the process is stationary which means that the transition probability $P(X^{t+1}|X^t)$ is the same for all t. Therefore, a DBN can be also defined by two subnetworks: the static network $B_0$ and $B_\rightarrow$ as shown in Fig. 6. The static distribution $B_0 = (G_0, \Theta_0)$ captures the static distribution over all variables $X^0$. The transition network $B_\rightarrow = (G_\rightarrow, \Theta_\rightarrow)$ specifies the transition probability for all t in finite time slices T.

Given a DBN model, the joint probability over all variables can be factorized by unrolling the DBN into an extended static BN, whose joint probability is computed as follows:

$$P(x^0, ..., x^T) = P_{B_0}(x^0) \prod_{t=0}^{T-1} P_{B_\rightarrow}(x^{t+1}|x^t) \tag{4}$$

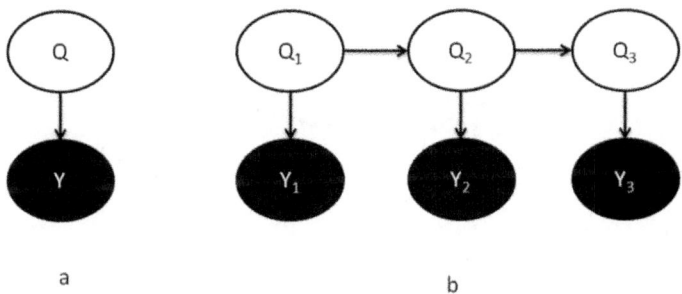

a                                                    b

**Fig. 6.** The left image is a static network $B_0$ and the right image is the transition network $B \rightarrow$

and transition network $B_\rightarrow$ can be decomposed as follows based on the conditional independencies encoded in the DBN:

$$P_{B_\rightarrow}(x^{t+1}|x^t) = P_{B_0}(x^0) \prod_{i=1}^{N} P_{B_\rightarrow}(x_i^{t+1}|pa(x_i^{t+1})) \tag{5}$$

## 4  Pose and Expression Recognition Based on the Proposed BN and DBNs

### 4.1  Introduction of the Proposed BN and DBNs

We build a BN and then extend it to DBNs. We first build a two-layer BN. The first layer contains two discrete variables: pose and smile. Generally, three kinds of angles are used to represent the pose: pan,tilt and roll.

In this paper, we only consider the pan angle. For human being's head, pan angle means turn left or right. Here pan angle is separated into 5 groups according to the angle of the head pose: frontal, left, more-left, right and more-right which are corresponding to five discrete states in BN( Pan angle $\in \{1, 2, 3, 4, 5\}$). As described, we separate left- turn and right-turn angle into two groups. Usually, if the angle is around or larger than $45°$, it will be clustered to the more-left or more-right group. If the angle is between $15°$ and $45°$, it will be clustered to left or right group. Of course, the interval here is general.

The second layer consists of four continuous variables: eyebrow, eye, nose and mouth. Each variable is presented by a vector with different length. The joint probability of the first two layers of BN in Fig. 7 is factored into conditional probabilities and prior probabilities as in equation (6). For better expression, we denote P for node pose, S for smile, B for eyebrow, E for eye, N for nose and M for mouth.

$$P(B, E, N, M, P, S) = P(B, E, N, M|P, S) \times P(P, S) \tag{6}$$
$$= P(B|P, S)P(E|P, S)P(N|P, S)P(M|P, S)P(P)P(S)$$

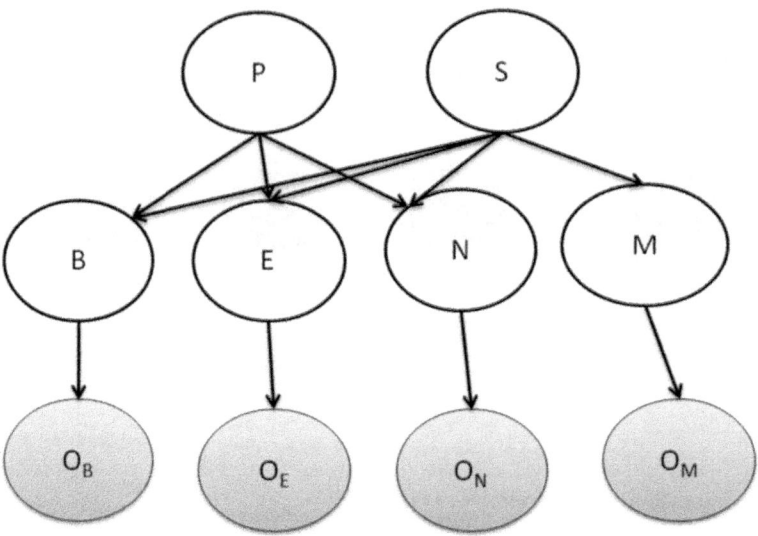

**Fig. 7.** A simplified Bayesian network of proposed model

Our aim is to estimate the belief of Pose and Smile nodes given the evidences of the second layer:

$$P(P, S | B, E, N, M) = \frac{P(B, E, N, M, P, S)}{\sum_{pose} \sum_{smile} P(P, S, B, E, N, M)} \qquad (7)$$

where the summation is over all possible configurations of the values on the node Pose and Smile.

Then the third layer is built. In this layer, the observation of the second-layer nodes are defined. According to this definition, the nodes in this layer are

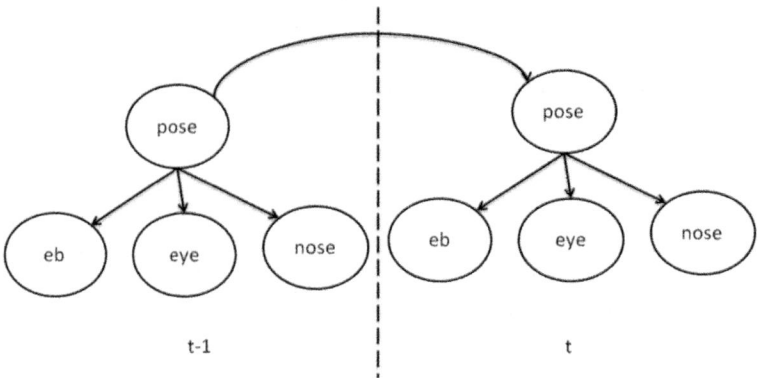

**Fig. 8.** DBN of pose recognition

continuous too. The second and third layers reflet the uncertain relationship between the observations and the real values. The nodes on the third layer can be denoted by $O_B, O_E, O_N, O_M$. The joint probability of the nodes from these two layers can be calculated by formula (8):

$$P(B, E, N, M, O_B, O_E, O_N, O_M) = P(B, O_B)P(O_B)P(E, O_E)P(O_E)P(N, O_N)P(O_N)P(M, O_M)P(O_M) \quad (8)$$

According to the definition of DBNs, we unroll the original BN in finite time slices as shown in Figure 8.

## 4.2  Parameter Learning of the Proposed Bayesian Network

We only take 21 points on human face as feature points which are shown in Fig 4. When training the BN and DBNs, we choose 50 people from Korea Face database. Each person contains 5 poses and 1 expression. After parameter learning, we can verify the success by sampling some data from the BN and compare them with the training data. From Fig. 9 and Fig. 10, we can figure out that after learning, the similarity of the two figures dramatically increase. This similarity implies the success of parameter learning of BN.

The parameter learning of DBNs can also be verified in the same way. Now we have already get a whole BN and DBNs. Next work is to test this network in experiments.

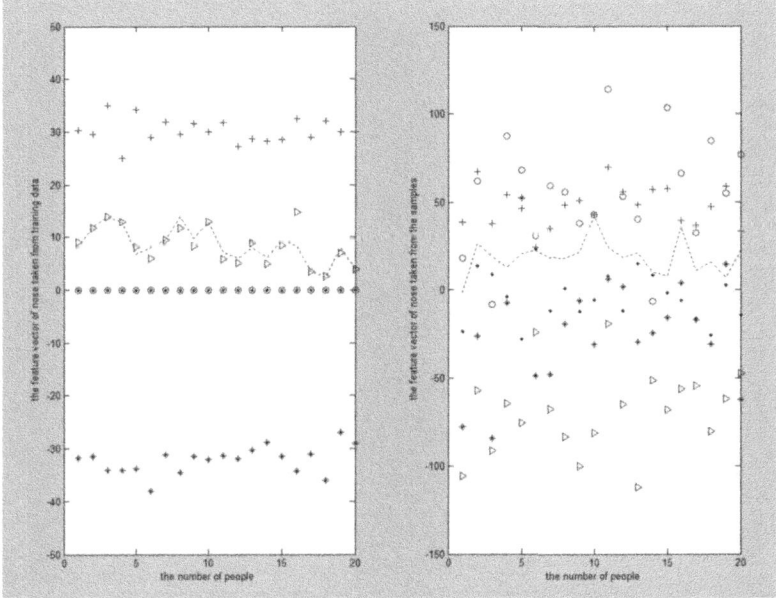

**Fig. 9.** The left image is from training data of nose. Because the length of nose vector is 6, there are 6 lines in the figure. The right image is the data sampled from model before parameter learning.

## 4.3    Experimental Results of Pose and Expression Recognition Based on BN

**Evaluation on CUbiC FacePix(30) Database and Our Own Database**
CUbiC FacePix(30) is a face image database [12][13]created at the Center for Cognitive Ubiquitous Computing (CUbiC) at Arizona State University. It contains face images of 30 people. There are 3 sets of face images for each of these 30

**Table 3.** Pose recognition with five levels

| Pose recognition | | |
|---|---|---|
| Pose | The group this pose belong to | Accurate Rate |
| Right(15°) | right | 100% |
| Right(30°) | right | 100% |
| Right(45°) | more-right | 100% |
| Left(15°) | left | 93% |
| Left(30°) | left | 100% |
| Left(45°) | more-left | 100% |
| Images from video | uncertained | 95% |

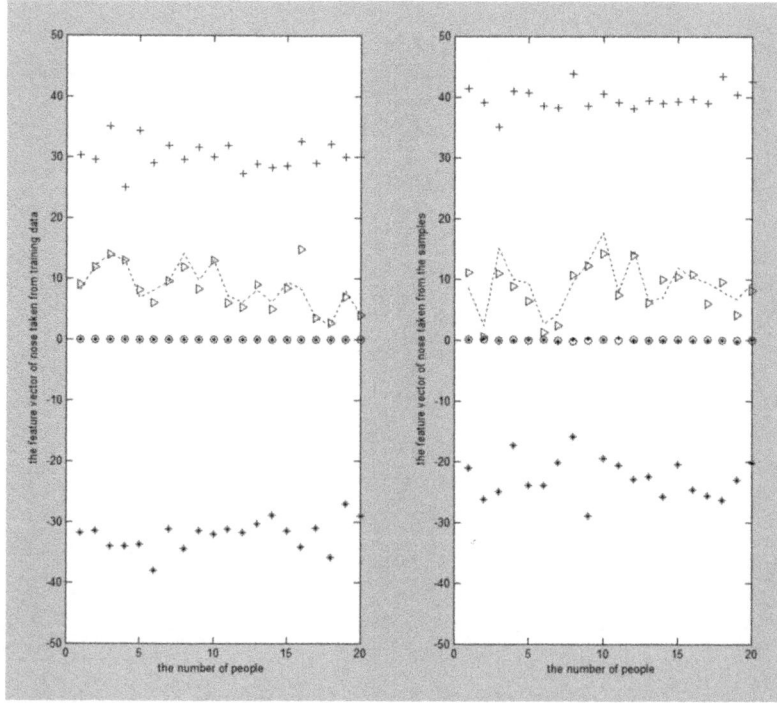

**Fig. 10.** The left image is training data. The right image is the data sampled from model after parameter learning.

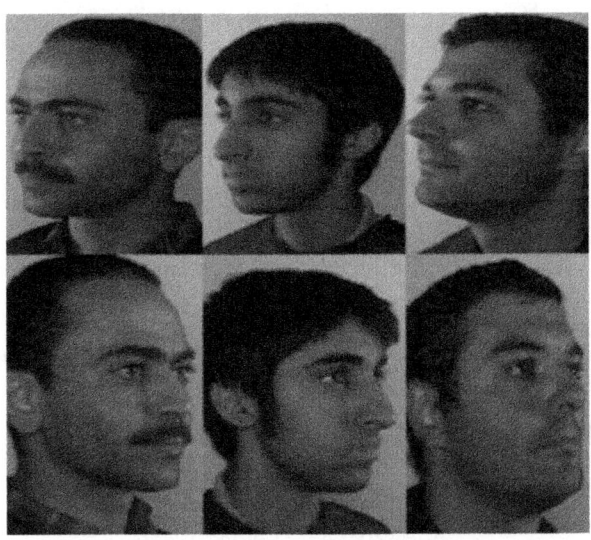

**Fig. 11.** An example of the test data from CUbiC FacePix(30) database [12] [13] we used in Bayesian Network. The first row is left–turn pose( 45 degree). The second row is right–turn pose(45 degree).

people (each set consisting of a spectrum of 181 images) where each image corresponds to a rotational interval of 1 degree, across a spectrum of 180 degrees. We use the first set here. In this set, images are taken from the participant's right to left, in one degree increments. Fig. 11 shows some examples from CUbiC FacePix(30) database. We evaluate pose recognition of our system on this database. Firstly, 45 images are picked from database randomly. These 45 images include 6 different angles: right turn $(15°, 30°, 45°)$ and left turn $(15°, 30°, 45°)$. The experiment results are shown in Table 3.

After evaluating the network based on CUbiC FacePix(30) database, we generate a small database ourselves. This database is extracted from some short videos in order to evaluate the pose recognition accurate rate in spontaneous situation.

**Evaluation on FEED Database.** In order to evaluate the expression recognition of our system, we use the FEED Database(Facial Expressions and Emotion Database) [15]. This Database with Facial Expressions and Emotions from the Technical University Munich is an image database containing face images showing a number of subjects performing the six different emotions. The database has been developed in order to assist researchers who investigate the effects of different facial expressions. We use the images with happy expressions as shown in Fig 12.

**Fig. 12.** The images with happy expression from FEED Database [15]

The experiments results based on FEED Database are shown in Table 4.

**Table 4.** Smile recognition based on the FEED Database

| Smile recognition | |
| --- | --- |
| Expression | Smile(front) |
| Accurate Rate | 100% |

## 4.4 Experiment Result of Pose and Expression Recognition Based on DBNs

We give the results of pose recognition and smile recognition separately. For each recognition, we define some simple action elements. Firstly, we define four action elements of head pose in two time slices. The definitions are given in Table 5. We choose 50 persons from Korea Face database for training the DBNs. Each person's images contain variety of head poses. We use other 30 persons to test the head pose recognition. Table 5 also gives the results of recognizing these four motions.

**Table 5.** The definition of action elements

| $T = t-1$ | $T = t$ | The name of action elements | Accurate rate |
| --- | --- | --- | --- |
| left | left | keep left | 90% |
| left | right | turn right | 93% |
| right | right | keep right | 100% |
| right | left | turn left | 90% |

For smile recognition, we define four smile's action elements in two time slices whose definitions are given in Table 6. For evaluating the smile recognition, we apply the FEED Database which has introduced previously. We choose 30 persons to train the DBNs and 20 persons to test. The results are shown in Table 6 too.

**Table 6.** The definition of action elements

| $T = t - 1$ | $T = t$ | The name of action elements | Accurate rate |
|---|---|---|---|
| smile | smile | keep smile | 75% |
| smile | normal | finish smile | 90% |
| normal | smile | smile | 95% |
| normal | normal | keep normal | 90% |

# 5  Conclusions and Future Work

In this paper, we propose a whole system for facial actions recognition. There are some conditions for using this method. Firstly, the poses and expressions must have clear and unique feature points' distributions. Secondly, the distribution can reflect the main and universal characters of the poses and expressions we are going to recognize.

Firstly, we build a facial points detection system. The proposed method decreases the dimensions of features dramatically and speed up the system. This method can realize the fully automatic feature detection. However, it is not a realtime method. In practice, it can be used to prepare the training data for other realtime tracking methods like ASM and AAM.

Secondly, we introduce our BN and DBNs for facial actions recognition without 3D information. In BN, The different poses and expressions are presented by different distributions of feature points. Some researchers reconstruct 3D face from 2D images and then project the feature points to a 2D plane. However, sometimes it is difficult to get 3D information. Through these experiments, we find that for inexact pose recognition, 2D information can be applied directly and the results are satisfied.

Extending the BN into DBNs, a set of simple gestures are defined and recognized in experiments. These gestures recognized here are defined between two adjacent time slices. In practice, some gestures can appear instantaneously and disappear suddenly. In order to catch these gestures, the interval between two time slices must be tiny. This requires a very fast feature tracking system. What is more, in order to guarantee the performance, more other features should be added.

Future research directions are realtime face tracking and more other kinds of facial actions recognition. Finally, we want to realize the realtime communication between human and computer.

# References

1. Donato, G., Bartlett, M.S., Hager, J.C., Ekman, P., Sejnowski, T.J.: Clasifying Facial Actions. IEEE Transactions on Pattern Aanlysis and Machine Intelligence 21(10) (October 1999)
2. Tong, Y., Chen, J., Ji, Q.: A Unified Probabilistic Framework for Spontaneous Facial Action Modeling and Understanding. IEEE Transactions on Pattern Aanlysis and Machine Intelligence 32(2) (February 2010)

3. Moghaddam, B., Jebara, T., Pentland, A.: Bayesian face recognition. Pattern Recognition 33, 1771–1782 (2000)
4. Heusch, G.: Bayesian Networks as Generative Models for Face Recognition. IDIAP RESEARCH INSTITUTE
5. Park, S., Aggarwal, J.K.: A hierarchical Bayesian network for event recognition of human actions and interactions. Department of Electrical and Computer Engineering, The University of Texas at Austin, Austin, TX 78712, USA
6. Dang, L., Kong, F.: Facial Feature Point Extraction Using A New Improved Active Shape Model. In: 3rd International Congress on Image and Signal Processing, CISP 2010 (2010)
7. Tu, C.-T., Lien, J.-J.J.: Automatic Location of Facial Feature Points and Synthesis of Facial Sketches Using Direct Combined Model. IEEE Transactions on Systems, Man, and Cybernetics Part B: Cybernetics 40(4) (August 2010)
8. Vukadinovic, D., Pantic, M.: Fully Automatic Facial Feature Point Detection Using Gabor Feature Based Boosted Classifiers. In: IEEE International Conference on Systems, Man and Cybernetics Waikoloa, Hawaii, October 10-12 (2005)
9. Deng, H.-B., Jin, L.-W., Zhen, L.-X., Huang, J.-C.: A New Facial Expression Recognition Method Based on Local Gabor Filter Bank and PCA plus LDA. International Journal of Information Technology 11(11) (2005)
10. Majumder, A., Behera, L., Subramanian, V.K.: Automatic and Robust Detection of Facial Features in Frontal Face Images. In: 2011 UKSim 13th International Conference on Modelling and Simulation (2011)
11. Duda, R.O., Hart, P.E., Stork, D.G.: Pattern Classification. Wiley, New York (2001)
12. Black, J., Gargesha, M., Kahol, K., Kuchi, P., Panchanathan, S.: A framework for performance evaluation of face recognition algorithms. In: ITCOM, Internet Multimedia Systems II, Boston (July 2002)
13. Little, G., Krishna, S., Black, J., Panchanathan, S.: A methodology for evaluating robustness of face recognition algorithms with respect to changes in pose and illumination angle. In: ICASSP 2005, Philadelphia (March 2005)
14. Pearl, J.: Probabilistic Reasoning in Intelligent Systems: Networks of Plausible Inference. Morgan Kaufmann, San Francisco (1988)
15. Wallhoff, F.: Facial Expressions and Emotion Database. Technische University, Mnchen (2006), http://www.mmk.ei.tum.de/~waf/fgnet/feedtum.html

# Extended Spatio-temporal Relations between Moving and Non-moving Objects

Chang Choi[1], Junho Choi[1], Juhyun Shin[1],
Ilsun You[2], and Pankoo Kim[3,*]

[1] Dept. of Computer Engineering, Chosun University,
375 Seosuk-dong Donggu, Gwangju 501-759, South Korea
enduranceaura@gmail.com, xdman@paran.com,
jhshin@chosun.ac.kr
[2] School of Information Science, Korean Bible University,
16 Danghyun 2-gil, Nowon-gu, Seoul 139-791, South Korea
isyou@bible.ac.kr
[3] Dept. of CE, Chosun University, South Korea
pkkim@chosun.ac.kr

**Abstract.** During the last decade, the emerging technology for video retrieval is mainly based on the content. However, semantic-based video retrieval has become more and more necessary for the humans especially the naive users who can only use the human language during retrieval. In this paper, we focus on semantic representation using topological and directional relations between non-moving and moving objects for security using CCTV(closed-circuit Television). In this paper, we propose new spatio-temporal relation to extend previous work using topological and directional relations and investigate spatio-temporal predicates which propose our models. In the experiment part, we compared retrieval results using TSR(Tangent Space Representation) with those using rules represented by the proposed model.

**Keywords:** Spatio-temporal Relation, Motion Recognition, Motion Predicates.

## 1 Introduction

During the last decade, the emerging technology for video retrieval is mainly based on the content. However, semantic-based video retrieval has become more and more necessary for the humans especially the naive users who can only use the human language during retrieval. So, semantic-based video retrieval research has caused many researchers' attentions.

Since the most important semantic information for video is based on video motion research which is the significant factor for video event representation, there has been a significant amount of event understanding research in various application domains[12]. One major goal of this research is to accomplish the automatic extraction of feature semantics from a motion and to provide support for

---

* Corresponding author.

A M. Tjoa et al. (Eds.): ARES 2011, LNCS 6908, pp. 243–254, 2011.

semantic-based motion indexing, retrieval and management. Most of the current approaches to activity recognition are composed of defining models for specific activity types that suit the goal in a particular domain and developing procedural recognized by constructing the dynamic models of the periodic pattern of human movements and are highly dependent on the robustness of the tracking.

Spatio-temporal relations are the basis for many of the selections users perform when they formulate queries for the purpose of semantic-based motion retrieval. Although such query languages use natural-language-like terms, the formal definitions of these relations rarely reflect the language people would use when communicating with each other. To bridge the gap between the computational models used for spatio-temporal relations and people's use of motion verbs in their natural language, a model of these spatio-temporal relations was calibrated for motion verbs.

In the previous works, the retrieval using spatio-temporal relations is similar trajectory retrieval, it's only the content-based retrieval but not semantic-based. Therefore, we propose a novel approach for motion recognition from the aspect of semantic meaning in this paper. This issue can be addressed through a hierarchical model that explains how the human language interacts with motions and we evaluate our new approach using trajectory distance based on spatial relations to distinguish the conceptual similarity and get the satisfactory results. In the experiment and application part, we apply the proposed approach to semantic recognition of motions and trajectory retrieval. Extending our novel motion verbs model with more abundant motion verbs for gapping the chasm between high-level semantics and low-level video feature is our further consideration. Finally, we can apply a security using CCTV through this study.

## 2   Related Works

The trajectory of a moving object is a presentation of spatio-temporal relationship between moving objects and an important element in video indexing for content-based retrieval. In Temporal relation, John Z. Li et al.[14] represented the trajectory of a moving object as eight directions – North(NT), Northwest(NW), Northeast(NE), West(WT), Southwest(SW), East(ET), Southeast(SE) and Southwest(SW). There are many researches on spatial relations of moving objects. Martin Erwig[2] is defined spatio- temporal predicates and Our previous work[3] was proposed Hierarchical relation modeling about moving object. Lee[4][13] have proposed relations such as 3D C-string for the various extensions of the original representations of 2D and W Ren, M Singh and S Singh[7] proposed to combine directional relations with topological relations by specifying six spatial relationships: 'Left', 'Right', 'Up', 'Down', 'Touch', and 'Front'. Pei-Yi Chen[8] measure velocity similarity by six possible velocity trends. The SMR scheme by Chang et al.[5][6] makes use of fifteen topological operators to describe the spatial relationships between moving object and non-moving object and also makes a new scheme to identify objects. Egnehofer and Franzosa[1] that proposed eight topological spatial relationships including 'equal', 'inside', 'cover', 'overlap', 'touch', 'disjoint', 'covered-by' and 'contains'. This model is the most famous study.

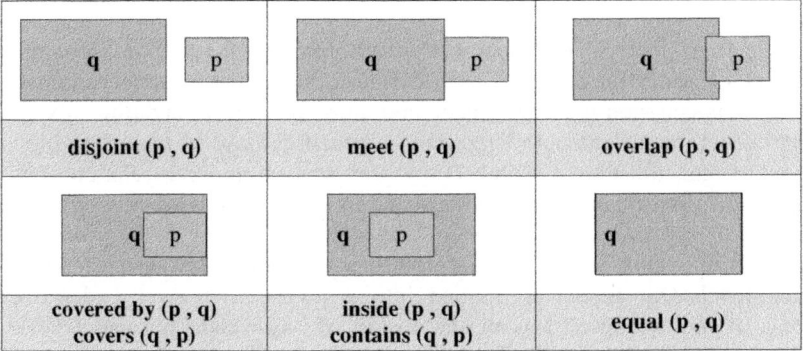

**Fig. 1.** Topological Relation of Egnehofer and Franzosa

For example, if two regions are disjoint and later they overlap, then there must have been a topological situation where both regions have met each other and they cannot move directly such as, from disjoint to equal in the fig. 2.

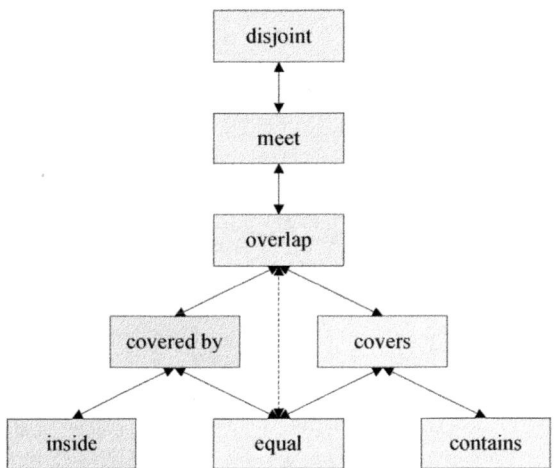

**Fig. 2.** Conceptual neighborhood graph

However, Most of study represents motion between 2 moving objects and some study is not sufficient to provide a complete representation of the semantic motion based on directional relations by ignoring topological relations and describing the concept or semantics motion. Therefore, we represent the semantics between moving object and non-moving object through topological relations that we make elements of motion. We also match motion verbs so that they don't have direction features for intrusion detection using CCTV[15][16].

## 3  Previous Work

In the previous work[3], we propose a novel approach for motion recognition from the aspect of semantic meaning. We define 5 basic elements to represent spatial relations between non-moving object and moving object, and then expand them through a hierarchical model. Therefore, it specifies how to give definitions to the motions of general moving objects by the spatio-temporal relation, and match between the definition of moving objects and motion verbs in the vocabulary.

The fig. 3 shows hierarchical semantic relations[11] for motion verbs, in other words, motion verbs and visual information map from low-level features to the semantic-level. Our model is divided into 3 levels. The level 1 describes basic elements of motion, level 2 is the extension of basic elements and level 3 shows combination of level 2. And, we represent semantic relation between motions and motion verbs for each element. For example, '*go into*' and '*go out*' are subclasses of motion word '*go through*' which was set with 'Part_of ' relation and '*go_to*'('*come up*) can be inserted into '*go_through*', it also has a relation of antonym between '*go_out*'(*depart*) and '*enter*'. Even if each motion verb is different in directional and spatial relations, the semantic relation is the same.

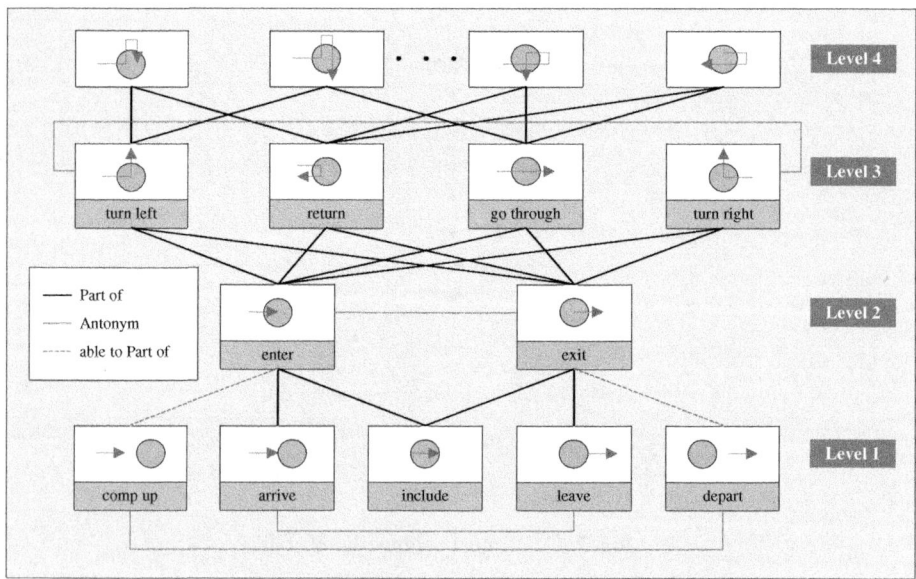

**Fig. 3.** Hierarchical relation modeling about moving object

However, it's difficult to distinguish semantics only using topological relations in level 3, which contains trajectories in the same topological relation. That is, we have to consider directional relations. We introduce proposed new spatio-temporal relation in next section and measure trajectory similarity using TSR which is represented moving distance and angle.

# 4 Building of Extended Spatio-temporal Relation

In this section we divided non-directional relation and directional relation.

## 4.1 Modeling of Non-directional Relation Motion

In the fig. 3 is cannot representation of all of Motion so we extended our spatio-temporal relation using Egenhofer's model and our previous work. Firstly, we define motion using initial and final topological relation. For example, if initial topological relation is *Disjoint* and Final topological relation is *Disjoint* or *Meet* fallowing fig. 2, table 1 is shown motion. For the motion, we considered the number of all cases.

**Table 1.** Representation of Topological Relation about *disjoint*

| No. | Initial | | Final | | Motion |
|---|---|---|---|---|---|
| | Topology | position | Topology | position | |
| 1 | disjoint | 1 | disjoint | 1 | go to |
| 2 | disjoint | 1 | disjoint | 1 | surround |
| 3 | disjoint | 1 | disjoint | 1 | go by |
| 4 | disjoint | 1 | meet | 1 | arrive |
| 5 | disjoint | 1 | disjoint | 2 | around |
| 6 | disjoint | 2 | disjoint | 2 | depart |
| | disjoint | 1 | overlap | 1 | X |
| | disjoint | 1 | covered by | 1 | X |
| | disjoint | 1 | covers | 1 | X |
| | disjoint | 1 | inside | all | X |
| | disjoint | 1 | contains | 1 | X |
| | disjoint | 1 | equal | all | X |

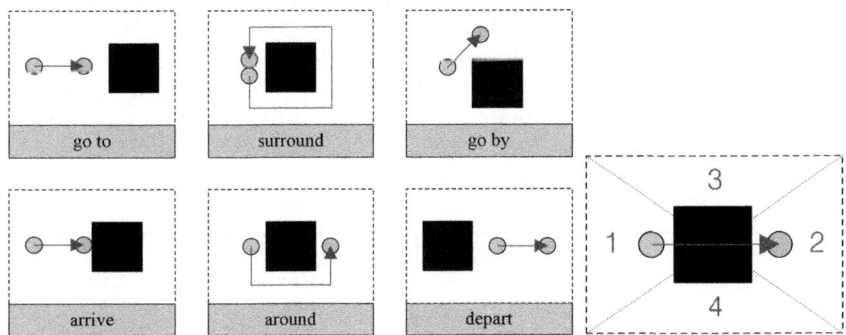

**Fig. 4.** Motion and Topological Position

Fig. 4 is shown motion and motion verbs also the position is shown in the table 1. Actually, *Disjoint* is can move the *disjoint and meet* but it cannot move the others such as *overlap, inside* and etc. from fig. 2. And *disjoint* can represent *go to, surround, go by, arrive, around* and *depart* from initial and final position. Table 2 is the representation of topological relation about others.

**Table 2.** Representation of Topological Relation about others

| No. | Initial | | Final | | Motion |
|---|---|---|---|---|---|
| | Topology | position | Topology | position | |
| 7 | meet | 1 | disjoint | 1 | leave |
| 8 | meet | 1 | meet | 1 | contact |
| 9 | meet | 1 | overlap | 1 | enter |
| 10 | overlap | 1 | meet | 1 | exit |
| 11 | overlap | 1 | overlap | 1 | contact |
| 12 | overlap | 1 | covered by | 1 | enter |
| 13 | overlap | 1 | covers | 1 | include |
| 14 | overlap | 1 | equal | 1 | same |
| 15 | covered by | 1 | overlap | 1 | exit |
| 16 | covered by | 1 | covered by | 1 | included by |
| 17 | covered by | 1 | inside | all | included by |
| 18 | covers | 1 | overlap | 1 | exit |
| 19 | covers | 1 | covers | 1 | include |
| 20 | covers | 1 | contains | 1 | include |
| 21 | inside | all | covered by | all | included by |
| 22 | inside | all | inside | all | included by |
| 23 | contains | all | covers | all | include |
| 24 | contains | all | contains | all | include |
| 25 | equal | - | overlap | all | exit |
| 26 | equal | - | equal | - | same |

We get 14 motions from table 1 and 2. Some motion verb is including several motions. Even if initial position changed, it is not a problem because we consider all of one way direction. This means if initial position changed, final position also changed. Other case is combination of motion we can solve using combination and it made a new model such as fig. 5. For example DJ_OL from table 3(For example, if initial topological relation is DJ and Final topological relation is also DJ, we'll represent DJ_DJ) is can be representation using fig. 2 but we need this case so we combine DJ_ME with ME_OL. In this case 2DJ is a sufficient condition for DJ_OL.

**Table 3.** Representation of Topological Relation

| Representation | Topological Relation | Representation | Topological Relation |
|---|---|---|---|
| DJ | Disjoint | CD | Covered by |
| ME | Meet | CR | Covers |
| OL | Overlap | IN | Inside |
| EQ | Equal | CN | Contains |

Finally, we define 51 motions it doesn't consider object size. It means that some motion represent covered by or covers between moving object size and non-moving object size so except this case we get 51 motions.

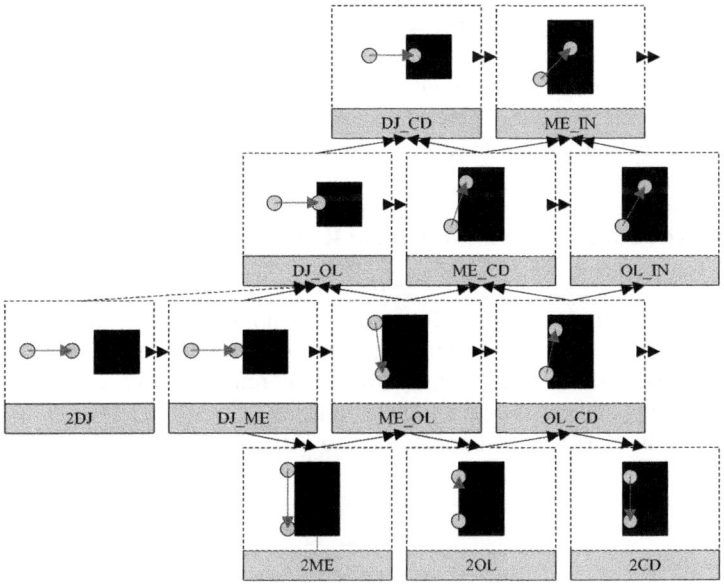

**Fig. 5.** Part of Proposed Motions

## 4.2   Modeling of Directional Relation Motions

Some case gets a directional relation such as table 4 and fig. 6. They represent a different motion following final position. In this paper, we just consider 4 directions such as fig. 4.

**Table 4.** Topological Relation including Directional Relation

| No. | Initial | | Final | | Motion |
|-----|---------|----------|----------|----------|--------|
|     | Topology | position | Topology | position | |
| 1 | disjoint | 1 | disjoint | 1 | return |
| 2 | disjoint | 1 | disjoint | 2 | go through |
| 3 | disjoint | 1 | disjoint | 3 | turn left |
| 4 | disjoint | 1 | disjoint | 4 | turn right |

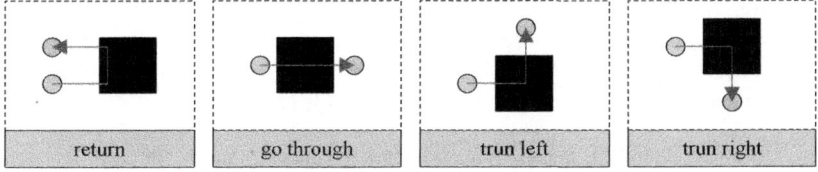

**Fig. 6.** Motions including Directional Relation

## 5 Similarity Measure between Motions

In this section, we introduce the method of similarity measure non-directional relation and directional relation. Similarity Measure Non-Directional Relation model is using our proposed section 4 and Directional Relation model is using TSR(Tangent Space Representation).

### 5.1 Similarity Measure Non-directional Relation Model

We proposed spatio-temporal relation in previous section. This relation is continuously moving of object following temporal relation. In fig 7, similarity (distance) is 9 from DJ1_DJ1 (number is position of table 1 and 2) to DJ2_DJ2 and it is 10 from DJ1_DJ1 to go through(directional relation). We can get a similarity between moving objects. For example similarity is 5 from CD1_IN to CD2_OL2. Another case, similarity is 3 from DJ1-DJ1 to ME1_IN.

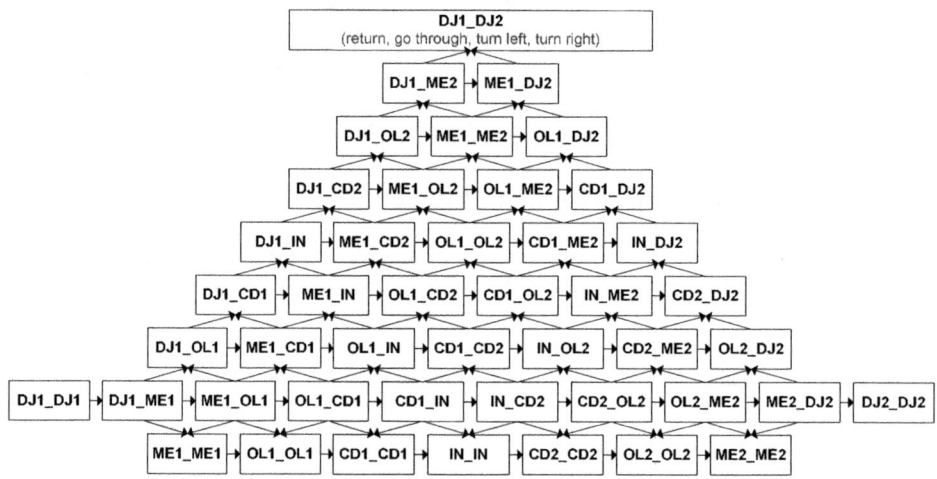

**Fig. 7.** Proposed Spatio-temporal Relation

For the similarity, we are using the LCM (Least Common Multiple). For example, let's get a similarity between ME1_IN and DJ1_DJ1. ME1_IN can be divided ME1_CD1 and OL1_IN. Also ME1_CD1 is can be divided ME1_OL1 and OL1_CD1 such as fig. 8. OL1_IN is a union between OL1_CD1 and CD1_IN. DJ1_DJ1is a basic element and cannot divide. Using this, we can get a 3 distance – 2, 3 and 4 (between ME1_OL1 and DJ1_DJ1, between OL1_CD1 and DJ1_DJ1, between CD1_IN and DJ1_DJ1). Therefore similarity is 1/3(2+3+4) = 3.

$$ME1\_IN = ME1\_OL1 + OL1\_CD1 + CD1\_IN$$

$$DJ1\_DJ1 = DJ1\_DJ1 + DJ1\_DJ1 + DJ1\_DJ1$$

$$Similarity = 1/3 ( 2 + 3 + 4 ) = 3$$

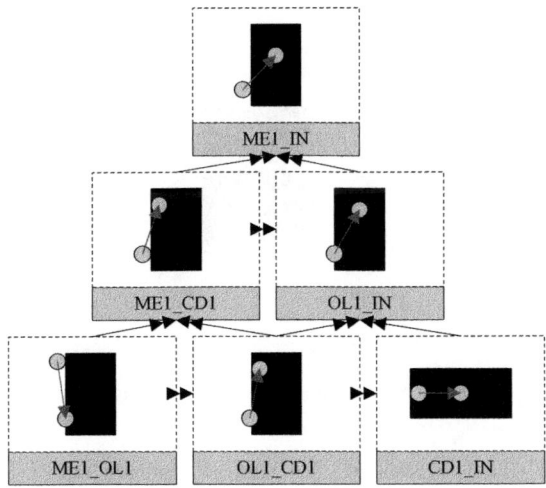

**Fig. 8.** Proposed Spatio-temporal Relation

## 5.2 Similarity Measure Directional Relation Model

TSR(Tangent Space Representation)[9][10] is a kind of method to measure similarity about a object's shape in two or three dimensions. Actually, polygonal shapes consist of lines and the line also contains points, so we used TSR for measuring similarity between trajectories. In the figure 9, *Object A* and *Object B* is a same shape. The right graph is TSR about *Object A* and *Object B*. The abscissa is sum of distance about lines and the ordinate is sum of angle between lines. In this graph, there isn't difference about area so they are same shape. In this way, we applied to measure similarity between trajectories using TSR.

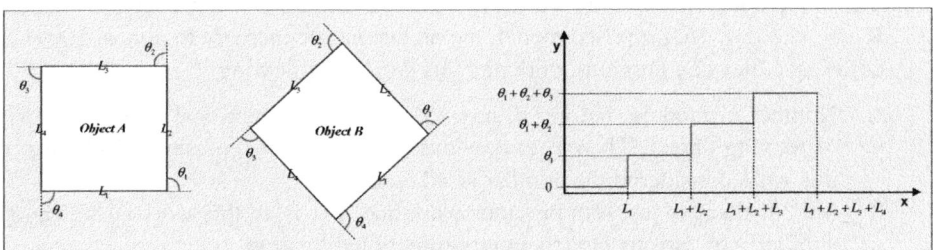

**Fig. 9.** Similarity Measure Methods of Object Shape

In the figure 10, the left part shows sample motions about '*turn_left*'. The Rusult(table 5) is that they are the same semantic so the right figure shows the same graph about a group of '*turn_left*'. We get the value after measuring similarity between trajectories. In this study, if two trajectories are the same, the similarity between those is 0. In other words, similarity is in inverse proportion to measured value. The sample trajectory is the most similar with '*turn left*' in table 5.

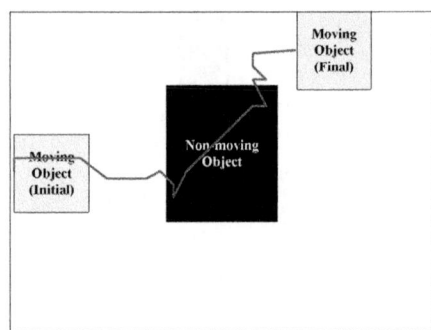

**Fig. 10.** Sample trajectory of moving object

**Table 5.** Similarity Measure using sample trajectory

|  | go_through | **turn_left** | return |
|---|---|---|---|
| Similarity | 51.26031 | 30.4637 | 97.0059 |

## 6  Experiment

We experiment on semantic-based trajectory retrieval with the proposed method. For the experiment, we make 100 coordinate set (non-moving object's coordinate set and moving object's trajectory) using simulator. The result is 97% (3% is simulator error) because is not a real video data. This paper is a just proposed Extended Spatio-temporal relation so we did use a real video data because problem of object detection and trajectory extraction. Therefore the result doesn't have a any meaning. It just checks our model. In previous work[3], we got a 92.857% using previous model + TSR and when we use proposed model, the precision rate increase to almost 100%.

Difference between previous work and this work as following :

A.  Number of models (before: 6, now: 51) – except directional relation and size of moving object. Therefore, previous model cannot represent all of case but this work considered the number of all cases.
B.  Max distance is just 4 in previous work and it is 10 in this work so we can get similarity of various models in non-directional relation.
C.  This research is inserted initial and final position so it's better than before work for the retrieval of motions such as intrusion detection using CCTV.

## 7  Conclusion and Future Works

In this paper, we proposed new spatio-temporal relation. Previous work, we cannot representation all of models but we considered the number of all cases in this study.

Increasing number of models, we limit a mapping between motions and motion verbs so we define motion verb about the 14 basic model and others are representation using topological relation and position. We be sure when applying intrusion detection system, get a good result therefore next study we will apply this using real video data and CCTV.

**Acknowledgments.** This work was supported by the Korea Science and Engineering Foundation (KOSEF) grant funded by the Korea government (MEST) (No. 2009-0064749) and by the National Research Foundation of Korea (NRF) grant funded by the Korea government (MEST) (No. 2010-0011656).

# References

1. Egenhofer, M., Franzosa, R.: Point-set topological spatial relations. International Journal of Geographical Information Systems 5(2), 161–174 (1991)
2. Erwig, M., Schneider, M.: Spatio-Temporal Predicates. IEEE TKDE 14(4), 881–901 (2002)
3. Cho, M., Choi, C., Choi, J., Yi, H., Kim, P.-K.: Trajectory Annotation and Retrieval Based on Semantics. In: Boujemaa, N., Detyniecki, M., Nürnberger, A. (eds.) AMR 2007. LNCS, vol. 4918, pp. 251–264. Springer, Heidelberg (2008)
4. Lee, A.J.T., Chiu, H.-P., Yu, P.: Similarity Retrieval of Videos by using 3D C-String knowledge Representation. Journal of Visual Communication & Image Representation, 749–773 (2005)
5. Chang, J.W., Kim, Y.j., Chang, K.J.: A Spatial Match Representation Scheme for Indexing and Querying in Iconic Image Databases. In: ACM International Conference on Information and Knowledge Management, pp. 169–176 (November 1997)
6. Chang, J.-W., Kim, Y.-J.: Spatial-Match Iconic Image Retrieval with Ranking in Multimedia Databases. In: Proceedings of Advances in Web-Age Information Management: Second International Conference (July 2001)
7. Ren, W., Singh, M., Singh, S.: Image Retrieval using Spatial Context. In: 9th International Workshop on Systems, Signals and Image Processing (November 2002)
8. Chen, P.-Y., Chen, A.L.P.: Video Retrieval Based on Video Motion Tracks of Moving Objects. In: Proceedings of SPIE, vol. 5307, pp. 550–558 (2003)
9. Baek, S., Hwang, M., Cho, M., Choi, C., Kim, P.: Object Retrieval by Query with Sensibility based on the Kansei-Vocabulary Scale. In: Huang, T.S., Sebe, N., Lew, M., Pavlović, V., Kölsch, M., Galata, A., Kisačanin, B. (eds.) ECCV 2006 Workshop on HCI. LNCS, vol. 3979, pp. 109–119. Springer, Heidelberg (2006)
10. Hwang, M., Baek, S., Kong, H., Shin, J., Kim, W., Kim, S., Kim, P.: Adaptive-Tangent Space Representation for Image Retrieval based on Kansei. In: Gelbukh, A., Reyes-Garcia, C.A. (eds.) MICAI 2006. LNCS (LNAI), vol. 4293, pp. 828–837. Springer, Heidelberg (2006)
11. Cho, M., Song, D., Choi, C., Choi, J., Park, J., Kim, P.-K.: Comparison between Motion Verbs using Similarity Measure for the Semantic Representation of Moving Object. In: Sundaram, H., Naphade, M., Smith, J.R., Rui, Y. (eds.) CIVR 2006. LNCS, vol. 4071, pp. 281–290. Springer, Heidelberg (2006)
12. Aghbari, Z.A.: Studies on Modeling and Querying Video Databases. Degree of Doctorate of Philosophy, Kyushu University (2001)

13. Lee, S.Y., Hsu, F.J.: Spatial reasoning and similarity retrieval of images using 2D C-String knowledge representation. Pattern Recognition 25(3), 305–318 (1992)
14. Li, J.Z., Ozsu, M.T., Szafron, D.: Modeling of Moving Objects in a Video Data-base. In: Proceedings of the International Conference on Multimedia Computing and Systems, pp. 336–343 (1997)
15. Pieters, W.: Representing Humans in System Security Models: An Actor-Network Approach. Journal of Wireless Mobile Networks, Ubiquitous Computing, and Dependable Applications 2(1), 75–92 (2011)
16. Sun, J., Wang, Y., Si, H., Yuan, J., Shan, X.: Aggregate Human Mobility Modeling Using Principal Component Analysis. Journal of Wireless Mobile Networks, Ubiquitous Computing, and Dependable Applications q(2/3), 83–95 (2010)

# A Handover Security Mechanism Employing Diffie-Hellman PKDS for IEEE802.16e Wireless Networks

Fang-Yie Leu, Yi-Fu Ciou, and Yi-Li Huang

Department of Computer Science, Tunghai University, Taiwan
leufy@thu.edu.tw, stevennick@gmail.com, yifung@thu.edu.tw

**Abstract.** In this paper, we propose a handover authentication mechanism, called handover key management and authentication scheme (HaKMA), which as a three-layer authentication architecture is a new version of our previous work Diffie-Hellman-PKDS-based authentication method (DiHam for short) by improving its key generation flow and adding a handover authentication scheme to respectively speed up handover process and increase the security level for mobile stations (MS). AAA server supported authentication is also enhanced by involving an improved extensible authentication protocol (EAP). According to the analyses of this study, the HaKMA is more secure than the compared schemes, including the PKMv2 and DiHam.

**Keywords:** HaKMA, DiHam, PKM, WiMax, IEEE802.16, Wireless security.

## 1 Introduction

Recently, wireless networks due to their popularity and the characteristics of convenience and high access speed have been a part of our everyday life. Through wireless systems, people can surf web contents, send emails and watch video program outdoors anytime anywhere. To satisfy the requirements of high-speed mobile wireless networks, the IEEE 802.16 Working Group in 2005 developed the IEEE 802.16e standard, known as the WiMax system, which is an extended version of IEEE 802.16 by adding mobility management and handover scheme so as to provide users with mobile broadband wireless services.

To prevent malicious attacks, the IEEE802.16 standard employs a key management and authorization mechanism called privacy key management (PKM) to authenticate users and wireless facilities [1, 2]. However, several problems have been found [1], like lacking mutual authentication, and having authorization vulnerabilities and key management failures. Also, the high complexity of its authentication mechanism and the involvement of designing errors [1] make the PKM fail to effectively protect a wireless system. To solve these problems, the IEEE Network Group proposed PKMv2 in 2005 to fix the defects of PKMv1 by adding mutual authentication and EAP support. But this enhancement also makes PKMv2 more complicated and difficult to maintain

A M. Tjoa et al. (Eds.): ARES 2011, LNCS 6908, pp. 255–270, 2011.
© IFIP International Federation for Information Processing 2011

than PKMv1if someday new shortcomings are found. On the other hand, Leu et al. [3] proposed a Diffie-Hellman-PKDS-based authentication method (DiHam) to improve some of the defects. However, the scheme does not guarantee full security since it only considers the initial network entry without providing handover and user authentication.

Therefore, in this paper, we propose a handover authentication mechanism, called handover key management and authentication system (HaKMA for short), which is an extended version of the DiHam by improving the key generation flow and adding a handover authentication scheme to respectively speed up handover process and increase the security level for mobile stations (MSs). It also enhances the AAA server authentication by employing an improved version of extensible authentication protocol (EAP). To meet different security levels of wireless communication, two levels of handover authentication are proposed. The analytical results show that the HaKMA is more secure than the DiHam, and the PKMv2.

## 2     Background and Related Work

### 2.1     The WiMax Network Architecture

Fig. 1 shows a modern multi-layer wireless network configuration. The ASN-GW is connected to a network service provider (NSP) backbone network, and BSs are directly linked to their ASN-GWs. An ASN-GW can not only communicate with other ASN-GWs via the backbone network through R3 reference points, but also directly communicate with other ASN-GWs with direct links via R4 reference points [4]. An NSP may provide many ASN-GWs to serve users. The MS may currently link to a BS, or hand over between two BSs under the same ASN-GW, called Intra-ASN-GW handover, or different ASN-GWs, called Inter-ASN-GW handover. In this study, due to limited pages, we only discuss the Intra-ASN-GW handover.

### 2.2     Privacy Key Management Protocol

The PKM protocol first specified by the IEEE 802.16-2004 provides device authentication (also known as facility authentication), and PKMv2 proposed in the IEEE 802.16e-2005 is a new version of PKM protocol by correcting designing errors for security found in PKMv1 [4] and supporting user authentication.

**PKMv2.** PKMv2 uses X.509 digital certificates together with either a RSA public-key encryption algorithm or a sequence of RSA device authentication to authenticate communication facilities. After that, an EAP method is employed to further authenticate users. The encryption algorithms used by PKMv2 for key exchange between MS and BS are more secure than those used by PKMv1. According to IEEE802.16 standard, the optimized handover can skip the security sublayer operation and reuses old keys, such as TEKs [2, 4], or provide handover support through mobile IPv6 with other proposed scheme [5, 6].

PKMv2, allowing mutual authentication or unilateral authentication, also supports periodic re-authentication/re-authorization and key renew. All PKMv2 key derivations are performed based on the Dot16KDF algorithm defined in IEEE802.16e standard.

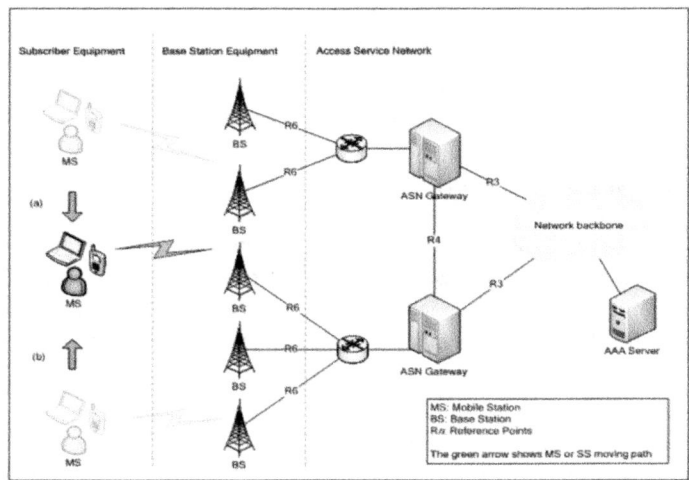

**Fig. 1.** The WiMax network security architecture in which MS may perform an Inter-ASN-GW handover and an Intra-ASN-GW handover

### 2.3    Diffie-Hellman PKDS-Based Authentication

The DiHam [3] was developed based on PKMv1 by improving the key exchange flow and providing different data security levels. Basically, its key exchange process consists of two phases, authentication phase and TEK exchange phase.

In the authentication phase, AK is individually generated by BS and MS after the delivery of the Authentication-Request message and Authentication-Reply message [3]. In the TEK exchange phase, three security levels of TEK generation processes are proposed to meet users' different security requirements. This phase starts when MS sends a TEK-Exchange-Request message to BS, and ends when BS replies a TEK-Exchange-Reply message.

However, the DiHam as stated above only considered initial network entry, without dealing with handover network re-entry. If it is involved by a handover procedure, the whole process needs to be fully performed on each handover, consequently causing serious service disruption time (SDT).

## 3    The Proposed Security System

The HaKMA, besides retaining the advantages of DiHam's Key Exchange and AK Generation processes [3], also involves an enhanced version of an EAP method to authenticate users. A handover support to make the HaKMA more suitable for wireless environment is added as well. The HaKMA architecture consists of three isolated processes: CSK Generation process in which ASN-GW and MS mutually authenticate each other, User Authentication process in which AAA server authenticates users, and TEK Generation and Renew process in which TEKs are produced to encrypt data messages. The three processes together are called the HaKMA authentication scheme. As a layered architecture, the changing on one of the three processes does not affect the functions of others, consequently making us easier to develop a new authentication process for IEEE802.16 wireless networks when some functions in one of the three processes need to be modified. The outputs of the three processes are sequentially CSKs, MSK and CSKs, and TEKs. In this study, we move Authenticator from BS to ASN-GW to simplify the HaKMA architecture and its handover process.

## 3.1 Initial Process of Network Entry

With the HaKMA, if MS has successfully completed one or two previous processes, but fails in an underlying process, the failed process is resumed from its beginning, instead of re-initiating the CSK Generation process. Of course, if the CSK Generation process fails, the HaKMA authentication scheme should be restarted. Table 1 lists the terms and functions used in this study.

**Table 1.** The terms and functions used in this study

| Term or function | Explanation |
|---|---|
| $P$ | A strong prime number |
| $g$ | The primitive root of $P$ |
| $RS_i$ and $RA_i$, $i = 1, 2$ | Private keys generated by MS and Authenticator |
| $P_{RSi}$ and $P_{RAi}$, $i = 1, 2$ | Public keys generated by MS and Authenticator |
| $CSKi$, $i = 1,2$ | Common secret keys |
| EXOR$(x, y)$ | Exclusive OR function, i.e., $x \oplus y$ |
| SEXOR$(key, data)$ | Stream exclusive OR function, repeating $key$ content to match the length of $data$, and performing exclusive OR bit by bit |
| Certfun(a, b, ...) | Modulus function, i.e., $g^{a+b+\cdots} \bmod P$ |
| Encrypt($PubKey, message$) | The standard RSA-OEAP-Encryption function for encrypting $message$ into $ciphertext$ with given public key $PubKey$ |
| Decrypt($PrivKey, ciphertext$) | The standard RSA-OEAP-Decryption function that decrypts $ciphertext$ into plaintext with given private key $PrivKey$ |
| ADR(a, b) | A binary adder, but ignoring the carry of the greatest significant bit |

**CSK Generation process.** The main objective of the CSK Generation process is to perform mutual authentication between Authenticator and MS, and produce two CSKs.

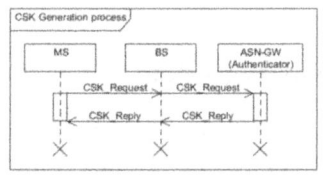

**Fig. 2.** Sequence chart of the CSK Generation process. BS only relays messages for MS and Authenticator.

Fig. 2 shows the sequence chart. It first establishes a secure communication channel between MS and Authenticator, and completes the following steps for initial network entry. MS and Authenticator first mutually check each other's X.509 certificate, and perform a DiHam-like process to generate CSKs which are only known to MS and Authenticator, and with which both sides encrypt those messages exchanged in User Authentication process and TEK Generation process. BS recognizes a message received by accessing its OP_Code, and relays messages for MS and Authenticator without providing any authentication functions. This process can be further divided into two phases: Authenticator-CSK phase and MS-CSK phase.

## (1)   Authenticator-CSK phase

In this phase, MS first sends a CSK_Request message, of which the format is shown in Fig. 3, to Authenticator.

$$\text{OP\_Code}|\text{NS}_{MS}|\text{Cert}(MS)|P_{RM1}|P_{RM2}|\text{Capabilites}|\text{SAID}|\text{HMAC}(PubKey(MS))$$

**Fig. 3.** Format of a CSK_Request message sent by MS to Authenticator

In this message, $RM_1$ and $RM_2$, two random numbers, are private keys generated by MS, $P_{RM1}$ and $P_{RM2}$ are two public keys where

$$P_{RMi} = g^{RM_i} \bmod P, 1 \le i \le 2 \tag{1}$$

$\text{NS}_{MS}$, the nonce, is a timestamp indicating when this message is created, capabilities field lists the security configurations acceptable by MS, the SAID field contains MS's primary SAID that is currently filled with the basic CID, and the hash-based message authentication code (HMAC) function produces a message signature by inputting all fields of the message as its plaintext and $PubKey(MS)$ as the encryption key. Authenticator on receiving the message checks to see whether the message signature calculated by itself by using $PubKey(MS)$ retrieved from $\text{Cert}(MS)$, and the $\text{HMAC}(PubKey(MS))$ sent by MS are equal or not. If not, implying the message has been altered, the Authenticator discards this message. If yes, it randomly selects two random numbers $RA_1$ and $RA_2$ as private keys to generate the corresponding public keys $P_{RA1}$ and $P_{RA2}$ where

$$P_{RAi} = g^{RA_i} \bmod P, 1 \le i \le 2, \tag{2}$$

produces two CSKs, i.e., $CSK1$ and $CSK2$, where

$$CSKi = P_{RMi}^{RA_i} \bmod P, 1 \le i \le 2 \tag{3}$$

and calculates the certificate function $\text{Certfun}(PubKey(MS), CSK1, CSK2)$. After that, Authenticator sends a CSK_Reply message of which the format is shown in Fig. 4 to MS. To make sure that the message is securely delivered, the HMAC which is generated by involving all other fields of the message as the inputs and the authenticator's certificate public key (i.e., PubKey(Authenticator)) as the encryption key is also added.

$$\text{OP\_Code}|\text{NS}_{MS}|\text{NS}_{Authenticator}|\text{Cert}(Authenticator)|$$

$$\text{Encrypt}(PubKey(MS), P_{RA1}|P_{RA2})|\text{Certfun}(PubKey(MS), CSK1, CSK2)|$$

$$\text{HMAC}(PubKey(Authenticator))$$

**Fig. 4.** Format of a CSK_Reply message sent by Authenticator to MS

## (2)  MS-CSK phase

MS on receiving the CSK-Reply message checks to see whether the message has been maliciously modified or not by comparing not only the HMAC value calculated and the value received from the CSK_Reply message, but also $\text{NS}_{MS}$ retrieved from the message with previous nonce involved in CSK_Request message. They should be individually equal. Otherwise, the message is discarded. MS further records $\text{NS}_{Authenticator}$ for later authentication, and checks to see whether the Authenticator is trustable or not by comparing the authenticator's certificate Cert($Authenticator$) with the certificate list provided by a trustable network provider and pre-installed in the MS. If yes, MS retrieves the public key $P_{RA1}$ and $P_{RA2}$ by performing RSA decryption function with its own private key, calculates CSKs, i.e., $CSK1$ and $CSK2$, and the certificate function Certfun($PubKey(MS), CSK1, CSK2$), and then compares the calculated Certfun() value with the one conveyed on CSK_Reply message sent by Authenticator where

$$CSKi = P_{RAi}{}^{RM_i} \bmod P, 1 \leq i \leq 2 \tag{4}$$

If two values are equal, the CSK Generation process terminates. MS starts the User Authentication process. Otherwise, MS discards the message and the calculated CSKs, and waits for a valid CSK-Reply message for a predefined time period. If MS cannot receive a reply from the Authenticator after timeout, it assumes the CSK Generation process fails and then restarts the process by sending a CSK-Request message to Authenticator.

**User Authentication process.** In this process, MS and the Authenticator first negotiate with each other to choose an EAP method. After that, Authenticator communicates with AAA server to check to see whether the user is authorized to access requested services or not.

However, EAP was originally designed for wired networks. When it is applied to wireless networks, hackers can intercept and decrypt sensitive information. To solve this problem, in this study, CSKs are involved to encrypt messages exchanged between MS and Authenticator. In fact, some EAP methods do not provide security mechanism (e.g., EAP legacy methods). Involving our encryption scheme can ensure the security of the originally insecure EAP communication between MS and BS so that hackers cannot easily decrypt sensitive information, even though an insecure EAP authentication method is used. Further, we employ EAP-AKA [7] as an EAP example, and suggest involving EAP-authentication based AK generation flow to balance handover performance and the security of the concerned system. Basically, our modular design strategy results in the fact that any authentication methods designed for wireless authentication [7] can substitute EAP-AKA to perform user authentication. A general EAP authentication process can be found in [2].

Before this process starts, the MS first generates a 160-bits random number $RAND$, and derives the EAP encryption key

$$\text{EAP Encryption Key} = \text{ADR}(\text{EXOR}(CSK1, RAND), CSK2) \tag{5}$$

which is generated individually by MS and Authenticator and used to encrypt and decrypt EAP messages by involving a streamed Exclusive OR method/function $\text{SEXOR}(EAP\ Encrypt\ Key, EAP\text{-}messages)$ . Fig. 5 illustrates our User Authentication process in which MS sends a PKMv2-EAP-Start message, of which the format is shown in Fig. 6, to notify Authenticator the start of the process. Authenticator on receiving the message extracts $RAND$ by using its private key, derives the EAP encryption key, and replies an EAP-Request/Identity message to start security negotiation and EAP authentication.

If user is authenticated, AAA server after checking the correctness of the MAC and the RES received sends a Radius-Access/Accept message which contains an MSK 512 bits in length to Authenticator. Authenticator delivers an EAP-Success message to MS [7], indicating the user is authenticated.

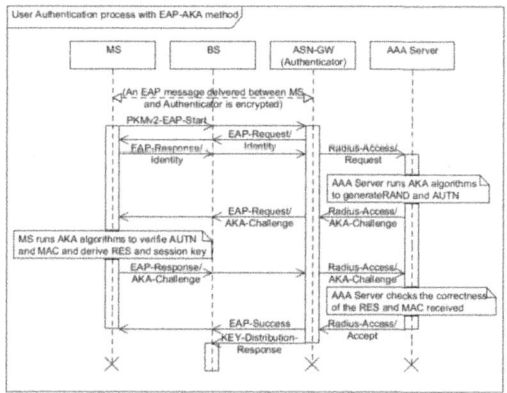

**Fig. 5.** The HaKMA's User Authentication process with EAP-AKA method

$$\text{OP\_Code}|\text{NS}_{Authenticator}|\text{NS}_{MS}|\text{Encrypt}(PubKey(Authenticator), RAND)|$$
$$\text{HMAC}(PubKey(Authenticator))$$

**Fig. 6.** The format of PKMv2-EAP-Start message sent by MS to Authenticator

**Key Distribution in the Initial Network Entry.** In the HaKMA, we design a key distribution message, prefixed by KEY-Distribution, to deliver keys from a former process to current process and among serving BS, target BS and Authenticator. Authenticator sends a KEY-Distribution-Response message which contains MSK and CSKs to BS (see Fig. 5). Fig. 7 shows the format of this message. Note that both TEK_Lifetime and TEK_Count are zeros since TEKs have not been generated. Their usage will be described later. BS on receiving this message extracts MSK and CSKs from this message, and starts its TEK Generation and Renew process. Currently, both BS and MS own MSK and CSKs.

$$\text{OP\_Code}|\text{BSID}|\text{SAID}|\text{CSK1}|\text{CSK2}|\text{MSK}|\text{BS-Random}|$$

$$\text{TEK\_Lifetime}|\text{TEK\_Count}|\text{TEK1}|\text{TEK2}$$

**Fig. 7.** The format of a KEY-Distribution-Response message sent by Authenticator to BS

**TEK Generation and Renew process.** Like that in the DiHam, TEKs are individually generated by MS and BS by involving required key parameters supplied by Authenticator. Fig. 8 shows the process which starts when MS sends a TEK-Request message, of which the format is shown in Fig. 9, to BS. Both MS and BS invoke the Dot16KDF algorithm, which accesses the first 160 bits of MSK, to individually derive AK, where

$$AK = \text{Dot16KDF}("AK", 2, \text{TRUNCATE}(MSK, 160), 160) \qquad (6)$$

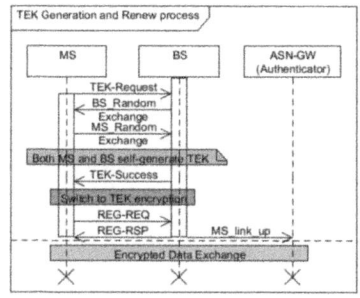

**Fig. 8.** Sequence chart of the TEK Generation and Renew process

$$\text{OP\_Code}|\text{NS}_{MS}|\text{SAID}|\text{HMAC}(\text{ADR}(\text{CSK1}, \text{CSK2}))$$

**Fig. 9.** The format of the TEK-Request message sent by MS to BS

BS (MS) self-generates a random number called *BS_Random* (*MS_Random*) which is also 160-bits in length. BS_Fingerprint (MS_Fingerprint) is then generated by encrypting *BS_Random* (*MS_Random*) with CSKs and AK, and delivered to MS (BS) through wireless channels. The propose is to protect the random number from being intercepted by hackers where

$$BS\_Fingerprint = ADR(EXOR(BS\_Random, CSK1), AK) \qquad (7)$$

and

$$MS\_Fingerprint = ADR(EXOR(MS\_Random, CSK2), AK) \qquad (8)$$

After that, a BS_Random_Exchange message, of which the format is shown in Fig. 10 and which carries BS_Fingerprint, OP_Code, and lifetime of TEKs, denoted by Key-lifetime, is sent by BS to MS.

$$OP\_Code|NS_{MS}|NS_{BS}|BS\_Fingerprint|Key\text{-}lifetime|HMAC(ADR(CSK1,CSK2))$$

**Fig. 10.** The format of the BS_Random_Exchange message sent by BS to MS

MS on receiving the message decrypts the *BS_Random* by using one of the following formulas:

$$BS\_Random = \begin{cases} (BS\_Fingerprint - AK)\oplus CSK1 & , \text{if } BS\_Fingerprint \geq AK \\ (BS\_Fingerprint + \overline{AK} + 1)\oplus CSK1 & , \text{if } BS\_Fingerprint < AK \end{cases} \qquad (9)$$

After that, MS sends MS_Random_Exchange message, of which the format is shown in Fig. 11, to BS.

$$OP\_Code|NS_{BS}|NS_{MS}|MS\_Fingerprint|HMAC(ADR(CSK1,CSK2))$$

**Fig. 11.** The format of the MS_Random_Exchange message sent by MS to BS. Note that Key-lifetime is not involved since it is determined by BS.

Following that, MS generates TEKs where

$$TEK_i = EXOR(ADR(EXOR(MS\_Random, AK),BS\_Random), CSK_i), 1 \leq i \leq 2 \qquad (10)$$

BS on receiving the MS_Random_Exchange message retrieves the MS-Random number, and generates TEKs with same formula where *MS_Random* is calculated by using one of the following formulas:

$$MS\_Random = \begin{cases} (MS\_Fingerprint - AK)\oplus CSK2 & , \text{if } MS\_Fingerprint \geq AK \\ (MS\_Fingerprint + \overline{AK} + 1)\oplus CSK2, & \text{if } MS\_Fingerprint < AK \end{cases} \qquad (11)$$

Now both sides own the TEKs. A TEK-Success message shown in
Fig. 12 is sent by BS to inform MS the success of the TEK generation. MS registers its terminal device with BS by sending a REG-REQ message, and BS replies a REG-RSP message to finish this process. The data exchange can now be started.

$$\text{OP\_Code}|NS_{BS}|NS_{MS}|\text{HMAC(ADR(TEK1,TEK2))}$$

**Fig. 12.** The format of the TEK-Success message sent by BS to MS

## 3.2 Handover Process of Network Re-entry

The main objective of a handover process is minimalizing the handover delay by key reuse and pre-distribution in the employed security scheme. If a user is authenticated in the initial network entry, as stated above, we assume that he/she is still authenticated after handover. This means we can reuse MSK and CSKs generated in previous processes to avoid the latency of re-authentication. For security reason, we can also renew TEKs on each handover. That means each time when MS moves to a target BS, new TEKs are required to substitute the two TEKs used by the serving BS, called previous TEKs (prev_TEKs for short to avoid confusing with the term pre_TEKs used in PKMv2).

In this study, two security levels of handover are proposed to meet different security requirements. With Level-1 handover, before prev_TEKs expires, the target BS after MS's handover reuses the same TEKs to encrypt data messages so as to shorten SDT. With Level-2 handover, on each handover, target BS temporarily reuses prev_TEKs to communicate with MS, generates new TEKs, and encrypts data messages with the new TEKs.

**Summary of Key Distribution in the Network Re-entry.** To deliver key information between MS and Authenticator, the KEY-Distribution-HOInfo message shown in Fig. 13 is designed to provide MS with handover support. In this message, the TEK_Count indicates the number of generated TEK pairs, and the TEK_Lifetime shows TEKs' remaining time in minutes.

$$\text{OP\_Code}|\text{Serving\_BSID}|\text{Target\_BSID}|\text{SAID}|\text{CSK1}|\text{CSK2}|\text{MSK}|$$

$$\text{TEK\_Lifetime}|\text{TEK\_Count}|\text{TEK1}|\text{TEK2}$$

**Fig. 13.** The format of the KEY-Distribution-HOInfo message sent by a serving BS to Authenticator or Authenticator to another Authenticator.

| SAID | BSID | CSK1 | CSK2 | MSK | TEK_Lifetime | TEK_Count | TEKs |
|------|------|------|------|-----|--------------|-----------|------|

**Fig. 14.** The fields of an AK Table. TEKs field stores TEKs

Before MS hands over to the target BS, serving BS sends a KEY-Distribution-HOInfo message to its Authenticator. Authenticator stores the concerned keys in the MS's corresponding tuple in its Authentication key table (AK Table), a table used to keep authentication keys including MSK and CSKs for the authenticator's subordinate MSs. AK Table is indexed by SAID to identity which MS the concerned keys belong to. Fig. 14 shows the fields of this table. Authenticator further checks to see whether or not the target BS that it should newly associate with is in its BS Table, a table for recording the BSIDs of the authenticator's subordinate BSs, including those of its own and those subordinated by all its successor Authenticators, implying Authenticators are organized as a hierarchy. The table has only one field BSID. If yes, a KEY-Distribution-Response message that carries CSKs, MSK, and prev_TEKs is then sent to the target BS. If not, Authenticator needs to relay the KEY-Distribution-HOInfo message to other ASN-GW that subordinates the target BS.

The AK table should be updated dynamically each time when MS performs network entry or re-entry, MS is going to hand over, and MS key's lifetime expires. When MS initially enters a network, AK Table is updated when MS completes the User Authentication process. Authenticator saves MS's keys, leaving the TEKs field empty. The field will be filled after Authenticator receives KEY-Distribution-HOInfo message from its BS and then stores them in its AK Table. In fact, when MS is going to hand over, Authenticator extracts MS's TEKs from KEY-Distribution-HOInfo message received from serving BS and stores them in the AK Table. Finally, if the TEK_Lifetime expires, the TEK Generation and Renew process should be reinitiated to reproduce TEKs. After that Authenticator replaces the TEKs with the new TEKs in its AK Table.

**Summary of TEK Generation and Renew process on Handover.** Both process of the two handover security levels start when MS sends a HO_IND message to its serving BS (see Fig. 15). The serving BS then sends a MSHO_link_down message to inform ASN-GW to start transferring data messages received from MS's corresponding node (CN) to both the serving BS and the target BS, and delivers a KEY-Distribution-HOInfo message, which contains MS security attributes, such as CSKs, MSK and TEKs that serving BS currently uses, to its Authenticator.

Authenticator stores the keys in its AK Table if the target BS is under the Authenticator. Otherwise, it sends the keys to another ASN-GW during MS handover. No matter on which case, the Authenticator delivers a KEY-Distribution-Response message to the target BS. The target BS on receiving the message retrieves security keys and saves them for future use. Now, data message transfer can be resumed before TEK Generation and Renew process starts, i.e., target BS can relay data messages to MS before new random number exchange, i.e., exchanging new *MS_Random* and *BS_Random*, is completed.

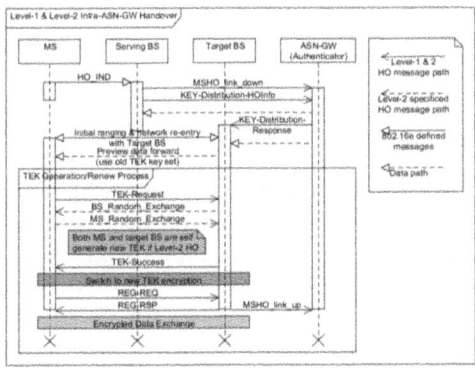

**Fig. 15.** The process of Level-1 & Level-2 Intra-ASN-GW handover

After the completion of the TEK Generation and Renew process, an MSHO_link_up message will be sent by target BS to its Authenticator to terminate sending data messages to serving BS, and the transmission of encrypted data messages can be continued.

**Summary of Level-1 Intra-ASN-GW Handover: TEK reuse mode.** Once MS chooses Level-1 handover, the KEY-Distribution-Response message sent to target BS by Authenticator includes TEKs used by serving BS. Target BS then waits for MS to complete its network re-entry, and it on receiving the TEK-Request message sent by MS as shown in Fig. 15 delivers a TEK-Success message to MS, indicating the success of TEK reuse mode. MS then sends a REG-RSP message to register itself with the BS. BS replies a REG-RSP message and sends an MSHO_link_up message to inform the ASN-GW the termination of the handover service.

**Summary of Level-2 Intra-ASN-GW Handover: TEK regeneration mode.** If MS selects Level-2 handover, the steps with which MS completes the network re-entry are the same as those of Level-1 Intra-ASN-GW handover. The following steps are a little different. The target BS generates a new **BS-Random**, extracts CSKs and MSK from KEY-Distribution-Response message received from Authenticator, uses Dot16KDF algorithm to generate AK, and then sends a BS_Random_Exchange message containing a newly generated **BS-Fingerprint** (See Eq.(7)) to MS. MS then generates a new MS-Random and sends a MS_Random_Exchange message which contains a newly generated MS-Fingerprint (See Eq.(8)) to the target BS. The BS and MS individually generate new TEKs by using the new **MS-Random** and the **BS-Random**. After that, MS and the target BS which is now MS's serving BS communicate with each other by using the new TEKs. The following steps are the same as those of Level-1 handover. Now, previous serving BSs can no longer communicate with MS since the prev_TEKs are out of date.

# 4    Security Analyses and Performance Analyses

## 4.1    Message Integrity and Replay Attack Avoidance

Message integrity is to ensure that a message has not been changed during its delivery. In this study, all authentication messages are unchangeable once they are sent. The receiving end on receiving a message uses HMAC function to detect data tampering, retrieves the nonce conveyed on the message and saves it. The output of HMAC code conveyed on a message received can act as a verification code for that message. If at least one parameter has been changed, including the nonce, the HMAC code varies. The message will be discarded. If HMAC code passes the verification, we further verify the nonce.

The first time a message is sent, the receiving end $R$ records the nonce contained in the message. If $R$ receives the same or similar message again, it confirms that this is not a replay attack by comparing the nonce previously saved and the one retrieved from the message. If the nonce received is smaller than the one saved, then the message is considered as an illegal one and will be discarded. All messages delivered in the CSK Generation process and TEK Generation and Renew process are detected by this method. The DiHam scheme provides key integrity, rather than message integrity [3]. All messages exchanged in the authentication phase and TEK generation phase could be maliciously altered, but the receiving end cannot discover the change. The DiHam also lacks the involvement of nonce. Hence, it cannot discover replay attacks issued by resending an intercepted Authentication-reply message. The PKMv2 uses cipher-based message authentication code (CMAC) or HMAC to authenticate authentication messages, and detects replay attacks by employing CMAC_KEY_COUNT after the success of EAP authentication or re-authentication. However, due to involving no nonce, it cannot avoid replay attacks during the EAP authentication session.

## 4.2 Confidentiality

In our scheme, we analyze the confidentiality by checking to see whether exchanged information can be decrypted easily or not, and estimating the probability that a concerned message is cracked.

**CSK Confidentiality.** The HaKMA uses the key exchange process of the DiHam to produce two CSKs. In this process, two public keys should be exchanged between MS and Authenticator for each CSK. However, only the MS public keys $P_{RM1}$ and $P_{RM2}$ will be transferred through wireless channels (see Fig. 3), the Authenticator public keys $P_{RA1}$ and $P_{RA2}$ have been encrypted by using MS's certificate public key $PubKey(MS)$ (see Fig. 4) which can only be decrypted by using MS's certificate private key $PrivKey(MS)$. Therefore, hackers who only know $P$ and $P_{RMi}$ cannot easily derive $CSK1$ and $CSK2$ where

$$CSK_i = x \bmod P = P_{RMi}{}^y \bmod P, 1 \leq i \leq 2 \qquad (12)$$

in which $x - P_{RAi}{}^{RMi}$ (see Eq.(4)) and $y = RA_i$ (see Eq.(3)) are known and need to be determined, thus

$$x = P_{RMi}{}^y, 1 \leq i \leq 2 \qquad (13)$$

and the possible combinations of $x$ and $y$ pair are infinite. Due to the difficulty of determining the real values for $x$ and $y$, hackers can only generate CSKs by other methods, e.g., the brute-force method.

However, the number of possible 160-bit CSK values is $2^{160} \approx 1.4615 \times 10^{48}$. The probability of successfully guessing the CSK on one trial is $1/2^{160}$ which approaches to zero. However, two CSKs are used in the HaKMA. The probability will be one second of that when only one CSK is employed. Therefore, CSK confidentiality is high.

**EAP Encryption Key Confidentiality.** In this study, we use the EAP encryption key to encrypt and decrypt messages exchanged between MS and Authenticator. Since this encryption key is static and may be illegally decrypted, we involve the random number *RAND*, which is encrypted by Authenticator's public key (see Eq.(5)) during its delivery to generate encryption keys. Hackers cannot directly access *RAND*. Hence, it is hard to derive the EAP encryption key. Furthermore, each EAP encryption key is used only by one session, i.e., it is not used again, making hackers more difficult to collect EAP messages, and then accordingly decrypt the key. Therefore, our scheme has high EAP encryption key confidentiality.

**TEK Confidentiality.** Since TEKs are used to encrypt data messages, we need to keep it secure. TEKs are self-generated by MS and BS. Two random numbers *BS_Random* and *MS_Random* are also involved in the key generation process. To prevent hackers from collecting random numbers so as to derive TEKs, the two random numbers are encrypted to BS_Fingerprint and MS_Fingerprint. Since our TEK generation scheme involves ADR function [3] (see Eq.(10)), which ignores the carry, to calculate TEKs from BS_Fingerprint and MS_Fingerprint, hackers have to face four different mathematical equations (see Eq.(9) and Eq.(11)). Since each equation has up to $2^{160} \approx 1.4615 \times 10^{48}$ solutions, and all the four equations involve *AK, CSK1* and *CSK2* as parameters which are unknown to hackers, the possible parameter combinations for each equation is $2^{160 \times 3} \approx 3.1217 \times 10^{144}$. Thus, we can conclude that the TEK confidentiality is high.

If hackers try to decrypt data messages, they must find the two correct TEKs for uploading and downloading streams. If we assume that the time required to try a possible TEK is only one instruction, which takes about $1.4573 \times 10^{29}$ years on a 159,000 MIPS machine. In other words, the HaKMA is a secure and safe system.

### 4.3     Forward and Backward Secrecy on Handover

The forward (backward) secrecy means key $K_n$ used in session $n$ cannot be used in session $n + 1$ (session $n - 1$). In Level-1 Intra-ASN-GW Handover, we reuse TEKs during and after the handover, implying Level-1 Intra-ASN-GW Handover does not provide the forward and backward secrecy. In the Level-2 Intra-ASN-GW Handover, we temporarily reuse TEKs for shortening the SDT, and generate new TEKs random numbers exchanged between MS and BS, this handover by involving the process provide the forward and backward secrecy.

PKMv2, due to considering performance optimization on Fast BS Switch (FBSS) and reusing all security attributes including TEKs does not provide the forward and backward secrecy. The DiHam process due to providing no handover support does not have forward and backward secrecy.

### 4.4     Man-in-the-Middle Attack Avoidance

Man-in-the-middle attack means hackers can stay between valid MS and Authenticator to act as a legitimate Authenticator and MS. In the CSK Generation process and User Authentication process, MS and Authenticator exchange device certificate and determine whether the other side is legitimate or not. But in the CSK Generation process, we use MS's and Authenticator's public keys to encrypt important keys, such as $P_{RA1}$ and $P_{RA2}$ in the CSK_Reply message (see Fig. 4), and *RAND* in the PKMv2-EAP-Start message (see Fig. 5). Receiving end needs its own private key to decrypt those encrypted messages and keys. Now we assume that a hacker, *M*, is standing between valid MS and Authenticator and wishes to steal EAP user passwords by eavesdropping EAP messages. *M* also needs to act as an Authenticator so that it can get the valid CSK to continue the following User Authentication process since our EAP messages are all encrypted by using CSKs and other parameters, like *RAND*. To complete the CSK Generation process, *M* besides relaying MS's and Authenticator's certificates also needs to replace the Authenticator certificate with its own so that it can decrypt *RAND* for User Authentication process. However, if *M* replaces the certificate with its own, this illegal certificate will not be recognized by MS and this session will be terminated. On the other hand, if *M* continues using the real authenticator's certificate, it will not be able to decrypt the *RAND* carried on the next PKMv2-EAP-Start message sent by MS since this value can only be decrypted by Authenticator's private key that *M* currently does not have, and the User Authentication process is still secure because all EAP messages are encrypted with both the CSKs and *RAND*. As a result, our scheme can prevent man-in-the-middle attacks.

### 4.5    Performance Analysis on Key Generation

Generally, in a Diffie-Hellman based authentication method, exponential operations dominate decisive performance differences [3]. In this study, two CSKs are individually generated by MS and Authenticator, and only Diffie-Hellman based public keys, with which the strong security is ensured based on the difficulty of solving discrete logarithm problem [8], are transmitted through wireless channels. In the DiHam, Diffie-Hellman style keys are widely used, e.g., the generation of the CSK, AK and TEK. These keys provide a very secure method to protect the communication system, but the cost of key calculation is high.

Others important algorithms employed in HaKMA and PKMv2 are HMAC, CMAC and Dot16KDF. But since those algorithms perform fast operations, their costs which are very smaller than those of exponential operations can be ignored. Table 2 summarizes the costs of the evaluated schemes. We can see that the cost of the HaKMA operations is between those of PKMv2 with EAP-AKA method and DiHam with level-1 TEK.

**Table 2.** Lists of modular operations for different security schemes

| Security scheme | Exponential operations | | | |
|---|---|---|---|---|
| | CSK | EAP | TEK | Total |
| DiHam with level-1 TEK | 7 | - | 1 | 8 |
| DiHam with level-2 TEK | 7 | - | 6 | 13 |
| DiHam with level-3 TEK | 7 | - | 76 | 83 |
| PKMv2 with EAP-AKA | - | 2 | - | 2 |
| HaKMA with EAP-AKA | 5 | 2 | - | 7 |

# 5    Conclusions and Future Work

In this paper, the HaKMA security scheme which provides fast and secure key generation process, mutual authentication and EAP based user authentication is proposed. The three-layer architecture simplifies key generation flows compared to those proposed in the DiHam and PKMv2. It further provides a fast and secure key renew process for handover. We also introduce two levels of handover processes to minimize SDT, give connections between MS and BS forward and backward secrecy and analyze the HaKMA's security and performance. From which we can conclude that the HaKMA provides low-cost and effective handover, and its authentication approach is more secure than those of the DiHam and PKMv2.

In the future, we would like to enhance the HaKMA by developing its error handling capability. In the handover support, we will design a flexible MS keys' routing scheme to deliver keys between/among Authenticators, and develop behavior and reliability models so that users can predict the HaKMA's behavior and reliability before using it. The handover authentication between two heterogeneous networks, such as IEEE 802.11 or 3GPP LTE, will also be developed. Those constitute our future research.

# References

1. Johnston, D., Walker, J.: Overview of IEEE 802.16 security. IEEE Security & Privacy 2, 40–48 (2004)
2. WiMAX Forum Network Architecture. Stage 2: Architecture Tenets, Reference Model and Reference Points - Part 2, pp. 167. WiMAX Forum (2009)
3. Leu, F.Y., Huang, Y.F., Chiu, C.H.: Improving Security Levels of IEEE802.16e Authentication by Involving Diffie-Hellman PKDS. In: Conference Improving Security Levels of IEEE802.16e Authentication by Involving Diffie-Hellman PKDS, pp. 391–397 (2010)
4. Ergen, M.: Mobile broadband including WiMAX and LTE. Springer Science+Business Media, LLC, Boston (2009)
5. Bernardos, C.J., Gramaglia, M., Contreras, L.M., Calderon, M., Soto, I.: Network-based Localized IP mobility Management: Proxy Mobile IPv6 and Current Trends in Standardization. Journal of Wireless Mobile Networks, Ubiquitous Computing, and Dependable Applications 1, 16–35 (2010)
6. Yan, Z., Zhou, H., You, I.: N-NEMO: A Comprehensive Network Mobility Solution in Proxy Mobile IPv6 Network. Journal of Wireless Mobile Networks, Ubiquitous Computing, and Dependable Applications 1, 52–70 (2010)
7. Arkko, J., Haverinen, H.: Extensible Authentication Protocol Method for 3rd Generation Authentication and Key Agreement (EAP-AKA). RFC. Internet Engineering Task Force: Network Working Group (2006)
8. Elgamal, T.: A Public Key Cryptosystem and a Signature Scheme Based on Discrete Logarithms. IEEE T. Inform Theory 31, 469–472 (1985)

# Securing Location-Aware Services Based on Online/Offline Signatures in VANETs*

Chul Sur[1], Youngho Park[2], Takashi Nishide[1],
Kouichi Sakurai[1], and Kyung Hyune Rhee[2,**]

[1] Graduate School of Information Science and Electrical Engineering,
Kyushu University, Japan
{chulsur,nishide,sakurai}@itslab.csce.kyushu-u.ac.jp
[2] Department of IT Convergence and Application Engineering,
Pukyong National University, Republic of Korea
{pyhoya,khrhee}@pknu.ac.kr

**Abstract.** In this paper, we propose a novel privacy-preserving location assurance protocol for secure location-aware services over vehicular ad hoc networks (VANETs). In particular, we introduce the notion of location-aware credentials based on "hash-sign-switch" paradigm so as to guarantee the trustworthiness of location in location-aware services while providing conditional privacy preservation which is a desirable property for secure vehicular communications. Furthermore, the proposed protocol provides efficient procedures that alleviate a burden of computation for location-aware signature generation and verification on vehicles in VANETs. In order to achieve these goals, we consider online/offline signature scheme and identity-based aggregate signature scheme as our building blocks. Finally, we demonstrate experimental results to confirm the efficiency and effectiveness of the proposed protocol.

**Keywords:** VANETs, Location Assurance, Privacy Preservation, Location-Aware Credential, Online/Offline Signatures.

## 1 Introduction

Vehicular ad hoc networks (VANETs) have emerged as a promising research field to provide significant opportunities for the deployment of a variety of applications and services as well as intelligent transportation systems to users. A VANET mainly consists of on-board units (OBUs) and roadside units (RSUs), where OBUs are installed on vehicles to provide wireless communication capability, while RSUs are deployed to provide access point to vehicles within their radio coverage. By this organization, the VANET enables useful functions, such

---

* This work was supported by the National Research Foundation of Korea Grant funded by the Korean Government(Ministry of Education, Science and Technology). [NRF-2010-357-D00223].
** Corresponding author.

A M. Tjoa et al. (Eds.): ARES 2011, LNCS 6908, pp. 271–285, 2011.

as cooperative driving and probe vehicle data, that increase vehicular safety and reduce traffic congestion, and offer access to location-aware service applications.

A location-aware service on a VANET is to provide time-sensitive and higher-level services that distribute on-demand information such as traffic conditions, weather, and available facilities (e.g., gas station or restaurant) for a certain geographic area of interest by taking advantage of vehicular communications [4]. For the sake of supporting such a useful service, Dikaiakos et al. [4] proposed the development and deployment of location-aware service infrastructure on top of emerging VANETs based on a vehicular information transfer protocol (VITP) [5] which is an application layer communication protocol specifying the syntax and the semantics of messages for a VANET service. However, VITP does not provide built-in security features although it is necessary to develop a suit of elaborate and carefully designed security mechanisms before all other implementation aspects of VANETs [17].

Upon taking security design for viable location-aware service applications into consideration, location assurance is a fundamental security requirement from user's perspective because location information is an indispensable aspect for guaranteeing a reliable and trustworthy location-aware service. Recent advances in localization technologies enable accurate location estimation of vehicles based on transmission signal properties such as signal strength and direction. Prior location verification schemes [11,16,18] in the literature focused on secure packet forwarding in geographic routing protocol to identify a false node, which fakes its position, by verifying whether a neighbor node physically resides within a communication range. However, this approach is different from our protocol, and further, cannot support location assurance from the view of location-aware service.

On the other hand, sensitive information such as the identity and location privacy of a vehicle should be preserved from being illegally traced by a global eavesdropping attacker through vehicular communications [17]. To satisfy the requirement of privacy preservation, a variety of privacy-preserving authentication protocols have been proposed on the basis of digital signature including group signature schemes and anonymous certificates using pseudonyms of vehicles to conceal the real identities of vehicles [12,13,15]. However, those protocols cannot fulfill the location assurance requirement in our mind. Moreover, the requirement of location assurance seems to conflict with location privacy.

**Our Contribution.** In this paper, we propose a novel and efficient privacy-preserving location assurance protocol that addresses the conflicting goals of privacy preservation and location assurance for location-aware services over VANETs. Even though ordinary digital signature schemes are sufficient to guarantee the authenticity of a message including location information, it is insufficient to guarantee the semantics that the message was responded from a vehicle that passed through the claimed location since there is no binding between the signature function and the location information. Consequently, we introduce the notion of location-aware credential which is a signature on a trapdoor hash value [10] under geographic location information and can be transformed into location-aware signatures on location-aware messages by applying "hash-sign-switch" paradigm [20] without violating location privacy of vehicles through vehicular communications. Moreover, the proposed protocol gains merit from the performance point of view by providing efficient signature generation and even verification on vehicles. In order to achieve these goals, we elaborately incorporate online/offline signatures [3] with an identity-based aggregate signature scheme [19] to generate location-aware credentials and signatures for location assurance, and make use of pseudonym-based anonymous authentication for privacy preservation.

## 2   System Model

### 2.1   Architecture

In this section, we describe our system model, in which communication nodes are either the trusted authority (TA), RSUs, or OBUs. The detailed description of system components is as follows:

- **TA** is public agencies or corporations with administrative powers in a specific field; for example, city or state transportation authorities. The TA is in charge of the registration of RSUs and vehicles deployed on a VANET, and issues cryptographic quantities through initial registration. In addition, the TA should be able to trace the real identity of a message originator by law enforcement when a problematic situation occurs.
- **RSUs** are subordinated to the TA and responsible for issuing location-aware credentials to each vehicle within RSUs' geographic areas. They assist the TA to resolve dispute cases and may not disclose any inner information without the authorization of the TA.
- **OBUs** are installed on the vehicles. They communicate with other OBUs for sharing location-aware information, and with RSUs for requesting the location-aware credentials used to generate signatures for a secure location-aware service.

To define architectural model more clearly, we make the following assumptions:

- RSUs are able to establish a secure channel with the TA by the Internet or any other reliable communication links with high bandwidth.
- Vehicles are equipped with an embedded computer, a GPS receiver, a wireless network interface compliant to standards like 802.11p incorporated with dedicated short range communications (DSRC) [21].
- A number of roadside service facilities (e.g., gas stations, coffee shops, restaurants, etc) are also equipped with short-range wireless interfaces and participate in the VANET.
- The TA can inspect all RSUs at high level and maintain the compromised entities list.

Since the main goal of this paper is to design security protocol, we do not describe the process of location-aware service transactions in detail. Instead, we assume the functionalities of the VITP [5] for our underlying location-aware service on VANETs. Multi-hop message delivery can be supported by geographic routing protocol such as GPSR [8], which forwards messages toward their geographic destination.

## 2.2   Security Objectives

Here we clarify our security objectives in order to provide secure and trustworthy location-aware services among vehicles in VANET environments. The concerns of our design are summarized as follows:

- **Location Assurance.** A location-aware service should guarantee the semantics that the information about a certain location of interest is related to the claimed target location. That is, it must be possible for a requesting vehicle to verify that a response message was actually originated from a vehicle within the target location area.
- **Authentication.** Only legitimate entities should take part in the VANETs. In addition, the origin of the messages should be authenticated to guard against the impersonation and message forgery attacks.
- **Location Tracking Avoidance.** The real identity and location privacy of a vehicle should be preserved from illegal tracing through a vehicular communication even though location assurance is supported.
- **Traceability.** The authority should be able to trace the originator of a message by revealing the real identity in case of any disputed situation such as liability investigation. That is, privacy preservation protocols in a VANET must be conditional by way of precaution against problematic situations.

## 3   Proposed Protocol

In this section, we present an efficient privacy-preserving location assurance protocol consisting of system setup, OBU and RSU registration, location-aware credential issuance, and location-aware signature generation and verification. To design the protocol, we consider identity-based authenticated key agreement scheme [2] for mutual authentication between an OBU and an RSU, and online/offline signatures [3] and identity-based aggregate signature scheme [19] for efficient location-aware signature generation and verification, respectively. Especially, the essence of our protocol is to use location-aware credentials based on "hash-sign-switch" paradigm [20] for providing reliable and trustworthy location-aware services without violating the location privacy of OBUs. Table 1 describes the notations used in the proposed protocol.

**Table 1.** Notations

| Notation | Description |
|----------|-------------|
| $params$ | public system parameters |
| $sk_i, vk_i$ | signing/verification key pair of entity $i$ |
| $ok_i, rk_j$ | identity-based secret keys for OBU$_i$ and RSU$_j$, respectively |
| $HK_i, TK_i$ | hash key and trapdoor key for OBU$_i$, respectively |
| $\Sigma_{i,j}$ | location-aware credential for OBU$_i$ issued from RSU$_j$ |
| $H_1, H_2, H_3, H_4, H_5$ | cryptographic hash functions |
| $\mathcal{L}_j$ | location information of RSU$_j$ |
| $T$ | valid time period |
| $MAC_k$ | MAC function under the key $k$ |
| $Enc_k, Dec_k$ | symmetric encryption and decryption functions under the key $k$, respectively |
| $KDF$ | key derivation function |

### 3.1 System Setup

The TA generates the required groups and public system parameters according to [2,3,19]. The TA chooses a multiplicative group $\mathbb{G}$ of the prime order $p$ and bilinear map groups $(\mathbb{G}_1, \mathbb{G}_2)$ of the same prime order $q$, then random generators $g \in \mathbb{G}$, $P \in \mathbb{G}_1$. Let $e : \mathbb{G}_1 \times \mathbb{G}_1 \to \mathbb{G}_2$ be a bilinear map. The TA picks random $\gamma \in \mathbb{Z}_p^*$, $\alpha \in \mathbb{Z}_q^*$ as the master keys for identity-based cryptography and sets $g_0 = g^\gamma$, $P_0 = \alpha P$ as the corresponding public keys, respectively. The TA also chooses cryptographic hash functions which are defined as $H_1 : \{0,1\}^* \to \mathbb{G}_1$, $H_2 : \{0,1\}^* \to \mathbb{Z}_q^*$ and $H_3, H_4, H_5 : \{0,1\}^* \to \mathbb{Z}_p^*$.

In addition, the TA chooses a collision resistant one-way hash function $h$ and a secure symmetric encryption algorithm $Enc$, then defines a key derivation function $KDF$ built on the hash function $h$. Finally, it publishes the public system parameter $params = \{\mathbb{G}, \mathbb{G}_1, \mathbb{G}_2, g, g_0, e, P, P_0, H_1, H_2, H_3, H_4, H_5, Enc, KDF\}$.

### 3.2 OBU and RSU Registration

In our system, all OBUs and RSUs need to be registered from the TA and pre-loaded with their own secret quantities before joining a VANET. Fig. 1 describes the procedure of initial registration with respect to OBUs and RSUs, respectively.

If the registration entity is an OBU$_i$, it submits its own real identity ID$_i$ to the TA. Then the TA first checks its validity. If the identity ID$_i$ passes the check, it derives a pseudo identity PID$_i = Enc_K(\text{ID}_i)$ under the secret key $K$ from OBU$_i$s real identity ID$_i$, then computes $ok_i = \alpha H_1(\text{PID}_i)$ as OBU$_i$'s identity-based secret key used for mutual authentication with RSUs. The TA transmits $\langle params, \text{PID}_i, ok_i \rangle$ to OBU$_i$ and registers $\langle \text{ID}_i, \text{PID}_i \rangle$ as a legitimate entity in secure storage.

---

**Registration for OBU$_i$**

1. Generate PID$_i$ = $Enc_K(\text{ID}_i)$ as OBU$_i$'s pseudo identity.
2. Compute $ok_i = \alpha H_1(\text{PID}_i)$ as OBU$_i$'s identity-based secret key.
3. Issue $\langle params, \text{PID}_i, ok_i \rangle$ to OBU$_i$.

**Registration for RSU$_j$**

1. Compute $rk_j = \alpha H_1(\mathcal{L}_j || T)$ as RSU$_j$'s identity-based secret key.
2. Choose $s_j \in \mathbb{Z}_p^*$ and compute $\Delta_j = g^{s_j}$.
3. Set $sk_j = s_j + \gamma H_3(\mathcal{L}_j || T || \Delta_j) \pmod{p}$ as RSU$_j$'s signing key.
4. Issue $\langle params, rk_j, sk_j, \Delta_j \rangle$ to RSU$_j$.

---

**Fig. 1.** Initial registration for OBUs and RSUs by the TA

On the other hand, if the registration entity is an RSU$_j$, the TA computes $rk_j = \alpha H_1(\mathcal{L}_j || T)$ and $sk_j = s_j + \gamma H_3(\mathcal{L}_j || T || \Delta_j) \pmod{p}$ using the location information $\mathcal{L}_j$ in which RSU$_j$ is located together with the valid time period $T$. At this step, $rk_j$ is an identity-based secret key used for mutual authentication with OBUs and $sk_j$ is a signing key which is used for issuing location-aware credentials for assuring location-aware services in VANETs, respectively. Then the TA issues $\langle params, rk_j, sk_j, \Delta_j \rangle$ to the RSU$_j$.

*Remark 1.* According to [4], a location information $\mathcal{L}$ can be represented as two-value tuples [road-ID, segment-ID], where road-ID is a unique key representing a road and segment-ID is a number representing a segment of that road [14]. Given that the movement of vehicles is constrained within the road system, we can assume that the geographic areas of interest are restricted to roads and road segments. Therefore, those representations can be used as identifiers for our key generation.

*Remark 2.* The valid time period $T$ used in our protocol makes fine-grained revocation possible with respect to RSU$_j$'s identity-based secret quantities. For instance, if the TA sets the valid time period $T$ as current date to generate $rk_j = \alpha H_1(\mathcal{L}_j || T)$ and $sk_j = s_j + \gamma H_3(\mathcal{L}_j || T || \Delta_j)$, the vulnerability window of RSU$_j$ is restricted to the end of the day since RSU$_j$'s secret keys are inherently useless after current date. Moreover, the process of secret key renewal on the TA is insignificant operation since only hash function, 1 point multiplication of $\mathbb{G}_1$ and 1 modular exponentiation of $\mathbb{Z}_p^*$ are used in our protocol and pre-computations are also possible.

### 3.3   Location-Aware Credential Issuance

When an OBU$_i$ wants to get a new location-aware credential for joining secure location-aware service from the RSU$_j$ located in the OBU$_i$'s geographic area, the $OBU_i$ and the $RSU_j$ perform a location-aware credential issuance protocol. The proposed protocol is composed of two phases. One is mutual authentication between the $OBU_i$ and the $RSU_j$ using their identity-based secret keys, and the other is a location-aware credential generation by the $RSU_j$. The detailed steps are as follows.

**Step 1.** The $OBU_i$ picks a random $a \in \mathbb{Z}_q^*$ to compute $X = aP$ and generates $Q_i = H_1(PID_i)$, then sends $\langle X, Q_i \rangle$ to the $RSU_j$ as a request.

**Step 2.** Upon receiving the request, the $RSU_j$ picks a random $b \in \mathbb{Z}_q^*$ and computes $Y = bP$. The $RSU_j$ establishes $k = e(bQ_i, P_0) \cdot e(rk_j, X)$ and computes $\pi_j = MAC_{k_0}(Q_i, X, Y, \mathcal{L}_j, T)$, where $k_0 = KDF(k||0)$. Then the $RSU_j$ sends $\langle Y, \mathcal{L}_j, T, \pi_j \rangle$ to the $OBU_i$ as a response.

**Step 3.** The $OBU_i$ also establishes $k = e(ok_i, Y) \cdot e(aQ_j, P_0)$ and checks that $\pi_j \overset{?}{=} MAC_{k_0}(Q_i, X, Y, \mathcal{L}_j, T)$ to authenticate the $RSU_j$, where $Q_j = H_1(\mathcal{L}_j||T)$ and $k_0 = KDF(k||0)$. If it holds, the $OBU_i$ chooses a random $x_i \in \mathbb{Z}_q^*$ as a trapdoor key $TK_i$ and sets $HK_i = x_iP$ as the corresponding hash key, respectively. Finally, the $OBU_i$ computes $C_i = Enc_{k_1}(PID_i, HK_i)$, where $k_1 = KDF(k||1)$ and $\pi_i = MAC_{k_0}(PID_i, Q_i, X, Y, HK_i, \mathcal{L}_j, T)$, then transmits $\langle C_i, \pi_i \rangle$ to the $RSU_j$.

**Step 4.** First, the $RSU_j$ decrypts $C_i$ under $k_1 = KDF(k||1)$ to obtain OBU's pseudo identity $PID_i$ and hash key $HK_i$. Then it looks up the up-to-date revocation list retrieved from the TA to check the validity of the given $PID_i$. If the $PID_i$ is revoked one, the $RSU_j$ refuses to issue a location-aware credential. Otherwise, it checks that $\pi_i \overset{?}{=} MAC_{k_0}(PID_i, Q_i, X, Y, HK_i, \mathcal{L}_j, T)$. If the check holds, the $RSU_j$ chooses a random $\lambda_i \in \mathbb{Z}_q^*$ and computes the trapdoor hash value $\xi_i = \lambda_i HK_i$. The $RSU_j$ also picks a random $r \in \mathbb{Z}_p^*$, then generates a location-aware credential $\Sigma_{i,j} = (\Delta_j, U_i, V_i)$:

$$\begin{cases} U_i = g^r \\ V_i = r\psi_{i,0} + sk_j\psi_{i,1} \pmod{p} \end{cases}$$

where $\psi_{i,0} = H_4(\xi_i||\mathcal{L}_j||T||U_i||\Delta_j)$ and $\psi_{i,1} = H_5(\xi_i||\mathcal{L}_j||T||\psi_{i,0}||U_i||\Delta_j)$. Finally, the $RSU_j$ computes $C_j = Enc_{k_1}(\lambda_i)$ and $\pi_j' = MAC_{k_0}(\lambda_i, \Sigma_{i,j})$, then transmits $\langle C_j, \Sigma_{i,j}, \pi_j' \rangle$ to the $OBU_i$. In addition, $RSU_j$ stores $\langle PID_i, HK_i \rangle$ in its local credential list for assisting the TA by way of provision against a liability investigation. Note that, in location-aware credential generation, no identity-related information is included in $\Sigma_{i,j}$.

**Step 5.** The $OBU_i$ retrieves the secret value $\lambda_i = Dec_{k_1}(C_j)$, then checks $\pi_j' \overset{?}{=} MAC_{k_0}(\lambda_i, \Sigma_{i,j})$. If the check is valid, the $OBU_i$ sets $sk_i = \langle TK_i, \lambda_i \rangle$ as its singing key and $vk_i = HK_i$ as its verification key, respectively.

*Remark 3.* The location-aware credential $\Sigma_{i,j} = (\Delta_j, U_i, V_i)$ for $OBU_i$ is an identity-based signature on the trapdoor hash value $\xi_i$ under the geographic location $\mathcal{L}_j$ and the valid time period $T$. Moreover, the location-aware credential $\Sigma_{i,j}$ can be re-used whenever OBU$_i$ wants to sign a location-aware message during the specific time period $T$.

### 3.4   Location-Aware Signature Generation and Verification

Fig. 2 depicts the message structure used for a secure location-aware service. The type field represents either request or response. The target and source fields contain location area of interest that specifies the road and segment identifiers, as retrieved by an on-board navigation and positioning system. Hash_key and signature fields contain message originator's hash key and a digital signature on the message under location information and valid time period, respectively.

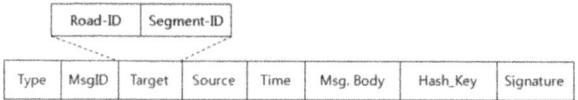

**Fig. 2.** Message structure

As aforementioned, since we assume an underlying VANET routing protocol, we just present how location-aware credential lead to location-aware signature generation and verification on the message for a secure and trustworthy location-aware service as shown in Fig. 3. For a given location-aware service message $m$, any entity in a VANET is able to convert a location-aware credential $\Sigma$ into a location-aware signature $\sigma$ on the message $m$ by using its own trapdoor key $TK$ during the valid time period $T$.

---

**Signature Generation** for given location-aware service message $m$ and credential $\Sigma_{i,j}$, an OBU$_i$ performs as follows:

1. Choose a random $c \in \mathbb{Z}_q^*$ and compute $\kappa = cP$.
2. Compute $\omega = \lambda_i - \delta c x_i^{-1} \pmod{q}$, where $\delta = H_2(m||\kappa)$.
3. Set $\sigma = (\kappa, \omega, \Sigma_{i,j})$ as a signature on $m$.

**Aggregate Verification** for $n$ pairs $(m_i, \sigma_i)$ where $i \in [1, n]$, the receiver performs as follows:

1. Compute $\delta_i = H_2(m_i||\kappa_i)$ and $\xi_i = \delta_i \kappa_i + \omega_i H K_i$ for $i \in [1, n]$.
2. Compute $\psi_{i,0} = H_4(\xi_i||\mathcal{L}_j||T||U_i||\Delta_j)$ and $\psi_{i,1} = H_5(\xi_i||\mathcal{L}_j||T||\psi_{i,0}||U_i||\Delta_j)$ for $i \in [1, n]$.
3. Check that $g^{\sum_{i=1}^n V_i} \overset{?}{=} \prod_{i=1}^n U_i^{\psi_{i,0}} \cdot \prod_{i=1}^n \Delta_j^{\psi_{i,1}} \cdot g_0^{\sum_{i=1}^n \psi_{i,1} H_3(\mathcal{L}_j||T||\Delta_j)}$.

---

**Fig. 3.** Location-aware signature generation and verification

The consistency of the location-aware signature verification can be proved as follows:

- For the trapdoor hash value $\xi_i$, we have that

$$
\begin{aligned}
\xi_i &= \delta_i \kappa_i + \omega_i HK_i \\
&= H_2(m_i \| \kappa_i) \kappa_i + \omega_i HK_i \\
&= H_2(m_i \| c_i P) c_i P + (\lambda_i - H_2(m_i \| c_i P) c_i x_i^{-1}) \cdot x_i P \\
&= \lambda_i HK_i
\end{aligned}
$$

- For the verification check, we have that

$$
\begin{aligned}
g^{\sum_{i=1}^n V_i} &= g^{\sum_{i=1}^n r_i \psi_{i,0} + \sum_{i=1}^n sk_j \psi_{i,1}} \\
&= g^{\sum_{i=1}^n r_i \psi_{i,0}} \cdot g^{\sum_{i=1}^n sk_j \psi_{i,1}} \\
&= \prod_{i=1}^n (g^{r_i})^{\psi_{i,0}} \cdot g^{\sum_{i=1}^n (s_j + \gamma H_3(\mathcal{L}_j \| T \| \Delta_j)) \psi_{i,1}} \\
&= \prod_{i=1}^n U_i^{\psi_{i,0}} \cdot \prod_{i=1}^n \Delta_j^{\psi_{i,1}} \cdot g_0^{\sum_{i=1}^n \psi_{i,1} H_3(\mathcal{L}_j \| T \| \Delta_j)}
\end{aligned}
$$

The proposed protocol is highly efficient in terms of signature generation and even verification since only 1 point multiplication of $\mathbb{G}_1$, and 2 point multiplications of $\mathbb{G}_1$ and 4 modular exponentiations of $\mathbb{Z}_p^*$ are required in signature generation and verification phases, respectively. Moreover, for $n$ messages with signatures $\sigma_i$ ($1 \leq i \leq n$) replied from $n$ vehicles, the receiver aggregately verifies the $n$ signatures to significantly reduce the computational costs.

## 4   Security Analysis

In this section, we analyze how the proposed protocol satisfies the security objectives stated in Section 2.2.

- **Location Assurance.** This goal can be satisfied by the location-aware credential $\Sigma$ which is a signature under a location information $\mathcal{L}$ and a time period $T$. If the location-aware credential in a location-aware signature $\sigma$ is verified as valid by using the location information $\mathcal{L}$ and the time period $T$ specified in a location-aware message, then the verifier can be convinced that the message was responded by an OBU that passed through the claimed location $\mathcal{L}$ for given time period $T$ because the location-aware credential for the OBU is issued by the RSU physically located in the target geographic area. Moreover, since the location-aware credential is generated by an identity-based aggregate signature scheme [19] which was proven to be secure against adaptive chosen message attacks, no adversary can launch a forgery attack against the location-aware credential.

- **Authentication.** The authenticity of entities that participated in a VANET can be assured by the identity-based secret keys issued through the initial registration in the protocol. That is, only the RSU possessing a valid $rk$ corresponding to its location and the OBU possessing a valid $ok$ derived from its pseudo identity can be authenticated to each other. Therefore, when we assume the security of the underlying identity-based cryptography, no one can launch an impersonation attack unless the entity is registered to the TA. To forge location-aware signatures based on online/offline signatures [3], and further, an adversary should find collisions of the trapdoor hash value $\xi$ given the corresponding hash key $HK$. However, this implies the adversary can solve the discrete logarithm problem in $\mathbb{G}_1$, which is computationally infeasible.
- **Location Tracking Avoidance.** In our protocol, message senders and receivers are specified by their hash keys. The distribution of hash key $HK$ is computationally indistinguishable from uniform distribution in $\mathbb{G}_1$ if the probability over the choice of $x$ is uniformly distributed in $\mathbb{Z}_q^*$. Therefore, indistinguishability of hash keys can prevent an adversary from identifying OBUs. In addition, since the hash key is renewed whenever an OBU enters into different geographic areas, an attacker cannot match the originators between observed messages from different locations. As a result, unlinkability of hash keys at different locations can prevent a global eavesdropper from tracking movement of an OBU.
- **Traceability.** In dispute case, the TA is involved in tracing the originator of the message. Given a message formed as shown in Fig. 2, the TA first retrieves the location information $\mathcal{L}_j$ and originator's hash key $HK_i$ from the message. Then the TA requests the pseudo identity $\mathsf{PID}_i$ corresponding to the hash key $HK_i$ to the $\mathrm{RSU}_j$ located in $\mathcal{L}_j$. On TA's demand, the $\mathrm{RSU}_j$ searches the $\mathsf{PID}_i$ from its local credential list and responds with the $\mathsf{PID}_i$. Finally, the TA can recover the real identity $\mathsf{ID}_i$ by decrypting the $\mathsf{PID}_i$ under TA's secret key $K$.

## 5    Performance Evaluation

In this section, we evaluate the performance of the proposed protocol in terms of RSU location-aware credential issuance, message processing rate of a responding vehicle, and message processing delay for reply messages. In order to evaluate the processing time of location-aware credential issuance protocol, and location-aware signature generation and verification, we considered PBC library [23] for implementing bilinear pairing and modular operations with 1024 bits security level on Pentium IV 3GHz.

Table 2 shows the measures to estimate the proposed protocol. Since the computations of a bilinear pairing $t_p$, a point multiplication $t_m$ and a modular exponentiation $t_e$ are much time consuming operations, we did not account any other negligible computation such as cryptographic hash functions.

**Table 2.** The number of cryptographic operations and the processing time

|  | RSU | OBU | Time(ms) |
|---|---|---|---|
| Credential issuance | $2t_p+3t_m+1t_e$ | $2t_p+3t_m$ | 37.3 |
| Msg. signing | - | $1t_m$ | 1.9 |
| Msg. verifying | - | $2t_m+4t_e$ | 12.2 |

### 5.1 Processing of RSU Location-Aware Credential Issuance

The main operation of an RSU is to issue location-aware credentials to vehicles on requests within RSUs valid coverage range $R_{rng}$. Hence, RSU's performance always depends on vehicles density $d$ and speed $v$ within the coverage range. The RSU valid serving ratio $S_{RSU}$, which is the fraction of the number of actually issued credentials to the number of requests [13], can be defined by

$$S_{RSU} = \begin{cases} 1, & \text{if } \frac{R_{rng}}{T_k \cdot v} \cdot \frac{1}{d \cdot \rho} \geq 1; \\ \frac{R_{rng}}{T_k \cdot v} \cdot \frac{1}{d \cdot \rho}, & \text{otherwise.} \end{cases}$$

where $\rho$ is the probability for each vehicle to request a location-aware credential and $T_k$ is the execution time of location-aware credential issuance protocol.

Fig. 4 depicts the RSU valid serving ratio with different vehicle density and different vehicle speed for $R_{rng} = 500m$, and the probability $\rho = 0.8$ and $\rho = 1.0$, respectively. From the results, we can observe that RSU can sufficiently deal with the location-aware credential requests in most practical scenarios even though RSU cannot fully process credential issuance protocol if more than 320 vehicles request their location-aware credentials with the probability greater than 0.8 at the same time. Thus, we conclude that the proposed location-aware credential issuance protocol is feasible.

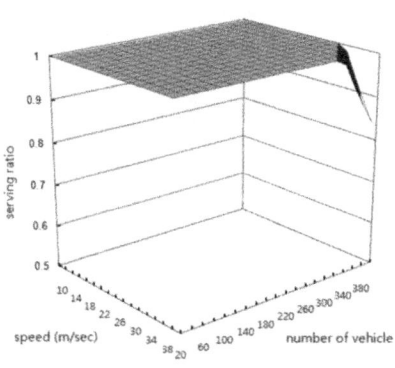
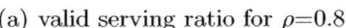

(a) valid serving ratio for $\rho$=0.8

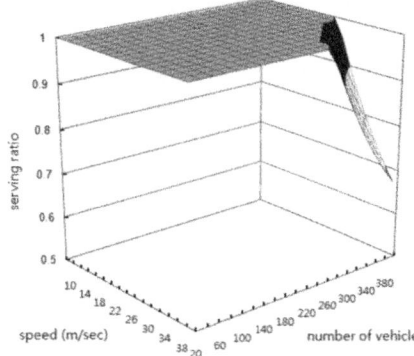

(b) valid serving ratio for $\rho$=1.0

**Fig. 4.** RSU valid serving ratio for location-aware credential issuance

## 5.2    Processing of Responding Vehicle

Within a target location area, the valid response processing ratio of a responding vehicle is estimated as the fraction of the actually processed location-aware responses to the number of received requests while the responding vehicle goes through the area after obtaining a location-aware credential. A serving duration $T_D$ for the vehicle passing the target area can be computed as $T_D = (R_{rng}/v) - T_k$. Let $T_s$ and $T_v$ be the processing times for signature generation and verification, respectively. Since the responding vehicle requires a signature verification for a request message and a signature generation for a response message, the number of response $N_{res}$ which the responding vehicle can deal with is measured by $N_{res} = T_D/(T_s + T_v)$. Let $N_r$ be a request message rate per second, and $V_n$ be the average number of requesting vehicle for a target area. Then, the number of request $N_{req}$ received while passing the target area is $N_{req} = (R_{rng}/v) \cdot N_r \cdot V_n$, and then the response ratio $S_{res}$ can be evaluated as $N_{res}/N_{req}$.

$$S_{res} = \begin{cases} 1, & \text{if } \frac{T_D/(T_s+T_v)}{(R_{rng}/v) \cdot N_r \cdot V_n} \geq 1; \\ \frac{T_D/(T_s+T_v)}{(R_{rng}/v) \cdot N_r \cdot V_n}, & \text{otherwise.} \end{cases}$$

Fig. 5 depicts serving ratio of a responding vehicle with 20m/s speed in 300m segment area depending on the number of requesting vehicles and message rates. From the results, if a message rate is higher than two messages per second and more than 32 vehicles send request messages, the responding vehicle cannot fully process the all requests. However, location-aware service is an on-demand service and the VITP puts a longer time interval than one second as considering the replying phase processing delay. Consequently, the proposed protocol can practically process almost all location-aware requests in a secure manner.

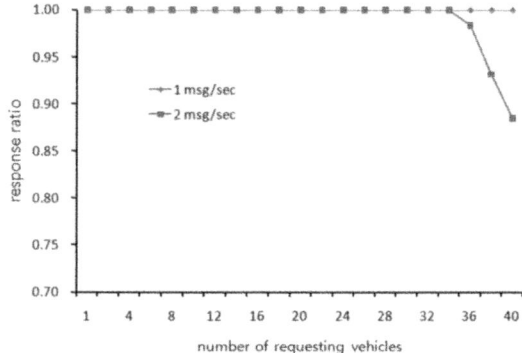

**Fig. 5.** Serving ratio of a responding vehicle in a target area depending on query message rate

## 5.3   Simulation Result

To evaluate the performance for the proposed secure location-aware message query and response over VANETs, we simulated vehicular communications considering highway-traffic scenario by using NS-2 simulator. We used the GPSR [8] as a geographic routing protocol provided by [9] and IEEE 802.11p wireless interface configuration [22] with 11Mbps bandwidth and 250m nominal transmission range.

In our highway-traffic scenario, we deployed vehicles on 5km-long road with 3 lanes to each direction, and fixed target road segment range to 300m. Then, we estimated the message processing delay by varying the query distance to the target area and inter-vehicle space on the road, respectively.

The left part in Fig. 6 shows the message processing delays to the query distance from 500m to 2,500m and $n$ response messages within 300m target road segment, where $n = 5, 10, 15$. The delay was measured by end-to-end round-trip time and location-aware signature generation and verification time. However, we did not take into account message loss suffered from routing failure. In addition, the right part in Fig. 6 shows the message processing delays depending on a vehicle density to 2,000m query distance. To measure the processing delay, we varied the inter-vehicle space from 50m to 150m, respectively. From the result, we can observe that the longer inter-vehicle space, which means sparse density, increases the message transmission delay due to much routing processing time.

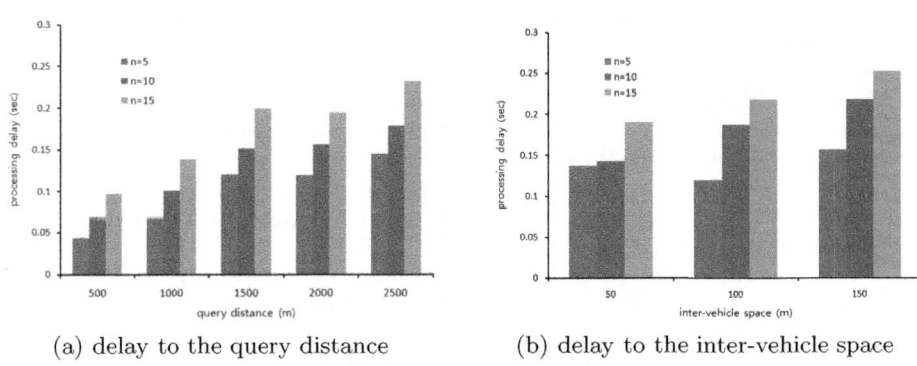

(a) delay to the query distance          (b) delay to the inter-vehicle space

**Fig. 6.** Message processing delay depending on the query distance and the inter-vehicle space with the number of response messages

## 6   Conclusion

In this paper, we have proposed a novel and efficient privacy-preserving location assurance protocol for providing reliable and trustworthy location-aware services as well as privacy preservation in VANETs. In particular, we have introduced the notion of location-aware credential based on online/offline signatures and "hash-sign-switch" paradigm to guarantee the trustworthiness of location without violating location privacy. Furthermore, the proposed protocol provides efficient procedures for location-aware signature generation and verification to effectively alleviate computational costs on vehicles in VANETs. We have provided comprehensive analysis to confirm the fulfillment of the security objectives, and the efficiency and effectiveness of the proposed protocol.

# References

1. Bellare, M., Rogaway, P.: Random oracles are practical: A paradigm for designing efficient protocols. In: ACM CCS 1993, pp. 62–73 (1993)
2. Chen, L., Chen, Z., Smart, N.P.: Identity-based key agreement protocols from pairings. International Journal of Information Security 6(4), 213–241 (2007)
3. Chen, X., Zhang, F., Susilo, W., Mu, Y.: Efficient generic on-line/off-line sinatures without key exposure. In: Katz, J., Yung, M. (eds.) ACNS 2007. LNCS, vol. 4521, pp. 18–30. Springer, Heidelberg (2007)
4. Dikaiakos, M.D., Florides, A., Nadeem, T., Iftode, L.: Location-aware services over vehicular ad-hoc networks using car-to-car communication. IEEE Journal on Selected Areas in Communications 25(8), 1590–1602 (2007)
5. Dikaiakos, M.D., Iqbal, S., Nadeem, T., Iftode, L.: VITP: An information transfer protocol for vehicular computing. In: 2nd ACM Internationial Workshop on Vehicular Ad Hoc Networks (VANET 2005), pp. 30–39 (2005)
6. Galindo, D., Garcia, F.D.: A Schnorr-like lightweight identity-based signature scheme. In: Preneel, B. (ed.) AFRICACRYPT 2009. LNCS, vol. 5580, pp. 135–148. Springer, Heidelberg (2009)
7. Gentry, C., Ramzan, Z.: Identity-based aggregate signature. In: Yung, M., Dodis, Y., Kiayias, A., Malkin, T. (eds.) PKC 2006. LNCS, vol. 3958, pp. 257–273. Springer, Heidelberg (2006)
8. Karp, B., Kung, H.: Greedy perimeter stateless routing for wireless networks. In: 6th Annual ACM/IEEE International Conference on Mobile Computing and Networking (MobiCom 2000), pp. 243–254 (2000)
9. Kiess, W., Füßler, H., Widmer, J., Mauve, M.: Hierarchical location service for mobile ad-hoc networks. ACM Sigmobile Mobile Computing and Communications Review 8(4), 47–58 (2004)
10. Krawczyk, H., Rabin, T.: Chameleon signatures. In: Symposium on Network and Distributed Systems Security (NDSS 2000), pp. 143–154 (2000)
11. Leinmuller, T., Schoch, E., Kargl, F.: Position verification approaches for vehicular ad hoc networks. IEEE Wireless Communications 13(5), 16–21 (2006)
12. Lin, X., Sun, X., Shen, X.: GSIS: A secure and privacy preserving protocol for vehicular communications. IEEE Transactions on Vehicular Technology 56(6), 3442–3456 (2007)
13. Lu, R., Lin, X., Zhu, H., Ho, P.H., Shen, X.: ECPP: Efficient conditional privacy preservation protocol for secure vehicular communications. In: IEEE INFOCOM 2008, pp. 1229–1237 (2008)
14. Nadeem, T., Dashtinezhadd, S., Liao, C., Iftode, L.: Trafficview: Traffic data dissemination using car-to-car communication. ACM Sigmobile Mobile Computing and Communications Review 8(3), 6–19 (2004)
15. Park, Y., Sur, C., Jung, C., Rhee, K.H.: An efficient anonymous authentication protocol for secure vehicular communications. Journal of Information Science and Engineering 26(3), 785–800 (2010)

16. Pathak, V., Yao, D., Iftode, L.: Securing location aware services over VANET using geographical secure path routing. In: IEEE International Conference on Vehicular Electronics and Safety (ICVES), pp. 346–353 (2008)

17. Raya, M., Hubaux, J.-P.: Securing vehicular ad hoc networks. Journal of Computer Security 15(1), 39–68 (2007)

18. Ren, Z., Li, W., Yang, Q.: Location verification for VANETs routing. In: IEEE International Conference on Wireless and Mobile Computing, Networking and Communications, pp. 141–146 (2009)

19. Selvi, S.S.D., Vivek, S.S., Shriram, J., Rangan, C.P.: Efficient and provably secure identity based aggregate signature schemes with partial and full aggregation. Cryptography ePrint Archive, Report 2010/461 (2010)

20. Shamir, A., Tauman, Y.: Improved online/offline signature schemes. In: Kilian, J. (ed.) CRYPTO 2001. LNCS, vol. 2139, pp. 355–367. Springer, Heidelberg (2001)

21. Dedicated Short Range Communications (DSRC),
    http://www.leearmstrong.com/dsrc/dsrchomeset.htm

22. Overhaul of IEEE 802.11 Modeling and Simulation in NS-2,
    http://dsn.tm.uni-karlsruhe.de/Overhaul_NS-2.php

23. Pairing-Based Cryptography Library, http://crypto.stanford.edu/pbc

24. Simulation of Urban Mobility, http://sourceforge.net/projects/sumo

# A Novel Secure Image Hashing Based on Reversible Watermarking for Forensic Analysis

Munkhbaatar Doyoddorj[1] and Kyung-Hyune Rhee[2]

[1] Dept. of Information Security, Pukyong National University
[2] Dept. of IT Convergence and Application Engineering, Pukyong National University,
Busan, Republic of Korea
{d_mbtr,khrhee}@pknu.ac.kr

**Abstract.** Nowadays, digital images and videos have become increasingly popular over the Internet and bring great social impact to a wide audience. In the meanwhile, technology advancement allows people to easily alter the content of digital multimedia and brings serious concern on the trustworthiness of online multimedia information. In this paper, we propose a new framework for multimedia forensics by using compact side information based on reversible watermarking to reconstruct the processing history of a multimedia data. Particularly, we focus on a secure reversible watermarking to make the image hash more secure and robust. Moreover, we introduce an algorithm based on Radon transform and scale space theory to effectively estimate the parameters of geometric transforms and to detect local tampering. The experimental results show that the quality of the embedded image is very high and the positions of the tampered parts are identified correctly.

**Keywords:** Secure Image hashing, Radon transform, Reversible Watermarking, Forensic Analysis.

## 1 Introduction

Emerging and future communications are going much beyond dealing with one pair of sender and receiver. We have witnessed growing trends of communications involving multiple users in a heterogeneous environment such as peer-to-peer and wireless networks to deliver content rich audio-visual data.

However, the digital nature of multimedia data and the advancement of multimedia processing technologies have made it easy to modify the digital content. Multimedia data can be intentionally altered to create a forgery and convey a different meaning. For example, objects can be removed from or inserted into an image, and multiple pieces of content may be combined into new creation. As such, it is critical to evaluate the trustworthiness of multimedia information and reveal its complete processing history in order to achieve better decision and usage of online multimedia information. Forensic hash is a short signature attached to an image before transmission and acts as side information for analyzing the processing history and trustworthiness of the received image.

There are two traditional techniques to evaluate image trustworthiness and authenticity, namely, robust image hashing [1-2] and blind multimedia forensics [3].

A M. Tjoa et al. (Eds.): ARES 2011, LNCS 6908, pp. 286–294, 2011.

Robust image hashing is an extension from traditional cryptography hash. A cryptography hash is used to evaluate authenticity of text or binary data and is sensitive to a single bit difference, while image hash is designed to evaluate similarity between visually similar images that may have undergone some allowable operations but sensitive against malicious tampering. The distance between two image hashes is compared with a threshold to determine whether the received image is authentic.

The research objective of multimedia forensics is to provide tools for analyzing the origin, processing history, and trustworthiness of multimedia information. Recent research in multimedia forensics can determine whether a received image or video has undergone certain operations without knowing any information about the original data. This is accomplished by analyzing intrinsic traces left by devices and processing, and by identifying inconsistencies in signal characteristics. Thus, it is difficult to trace history of some operations such as cropping and rotation without any side information about the original image. Many signal statistics and traces left by image operations may be removed or altered by further post-processing. A considerable amount of computational complexity is also involved in most blind forensic analyses.

## 1.1 Background and Organization

Conventional image hashing only provides a binary authentication answer using simple distance comparison, and non-intrusive blind forensics techniques have limitations in terms of the scope of questions that can be answered and the computational complexity. We use the FASHION (Forensic hash for information assurance) framework to bridge these two research and combine their benefits. The FASHION [8] framework uses side information called forensic hash to assist forensic analysis. The relation between two other research areas is shown in Figure 1.

In this paper, in order to achieve a good accuracy performance as well as ensuring the security of image features, we propose a novel secure image hashing based on FASHION for forensic analysis by using side information captured in a secure hash representation. Combined construction of two forensic analyses can provide robust estimation of geometric transform such as rotation and scaling.

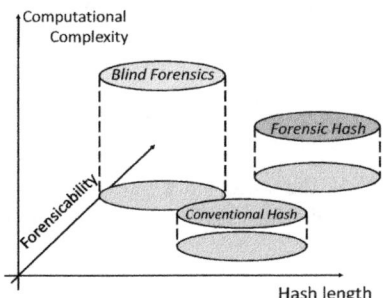

**Fig. 1.** Forensic hash as compared to image hashing and blind forensics

The rest of this paper is organized as follows: Section 2 provides the requirements of reversible embedding method; the backgrounds of Radon transform and scale space theories are described. In Section 3, the proposed scheme of a new secure image hashing based on FASHION model is introduced in detail. Section 4 introduces a detection and localization of image tampering. Experimental results are presented and analyzed in Section 5. Finally, we conclude the paper in Section 6.

## 2  Preliminaries

### 2.1  Reversible Data Embedding by Using Difference Expansion

This method can be applied to digital image, audio and video as well that employs an integer wavelet transform to losslessly remove redundancy in a digital image to allocate space for watermark embedding [4]. One basic requirement of digital watermarking is its imperceptibility, embedding a watermark will inevitably change the original content. Even a very slight change in pixel values may not be desirable, especially in sensitive imagery, such as military and medical data. In such scenario, every bit of information is important for forensic analysis.

Let's assume a sequence of pairs of grayscale values $(x_1, y_1), (x_2, y_2), \cdots, (x_n, y_n)$, where $x_i, y_i \in \mathbf{Z}$, $0 \leq x_i, y_i \leq 255$, $1 \leq i \leq n$. We can embed the payload $b = \{b_1, b_2, \cdots, b_n\}$, where $b_i \in \{0, 1\}$, $1 \leq i \leq n$, by repeating the above process,

$$l_i = \left[\frac{x_i + y_i}{2}\right], \qquad h_i = x_i - y_i, \qquad 1 \leq i \leq n.$$

For each difference number $h_i$, whose binary representation as:

$$h_i = r_{i,0}\, r_{i,1} \cdots r_{i,j(i)},$$

where $r_{i,o} = 1$, is the MSB, $r_{i,m} \in \{0,1\}$, for $1 \leq m \leq j(i)$, with $j(i) + 1$ as the bit length of $h_i$ in its binary representation. Then we could embed $b_i$ into $h_i$ by

$$h'_i = r_{i,0}\, \boldsymbol{b_i}\, r_{i,1} \cdots r_{i,j(i)}.$$

Finally, we compute the grayscale values, based on the new difference number $h_i$ and original average number $l$,

$$x' = l + \left[\frac{h' + 1}{2}\right], \qquad y' = x' - h', \quad 1 \leq i \leq n.$$

From embedded pair $(x', y')$, the watermark detector (or authenticator) can extract the embedded bit $b$ and get back the original pair $(x, y)$ by a similar process as the embedding.

### 2.2  Radon Transform and Scale Space Theory

The radon transform [5] of a two-dimensional function $I(x, y)$ is defined as

$$R(\rho,\theta) = \int_{\infty}^{\infty} \int_{\infty}^{\infty} I(x,y)\delta(\rho - x\cos\theta - y\sin\theta)\,dxdy \tag{1}$$

The Radon transform has useful properties about rotation and scaling as outlined in equation (2)-(3).

Rotation by $\emptyset$:

$$I(\rho,\theta)\{I(x\cos\theta + y\sin\theta, -x\cos\theta + y\sin\theta)\} = R(\rho,\theta + \emptyset) \tag{2}$$

Scaling:

$$I(\rho,\theta)\left\{I\frac{x}{s},\frac{y}{s}\right\} = sR(\frac{\rho}{s},\theta) \tag{3}$$

Here, $R(\rho,\theta)$ is the Radon transform of $I(x,y)$, $s$ is the scaling factor and $\emptyset$ is the rotation angle.

Radon transform is a line integral of an image alone certain directions. Such line integral captures salient information about the image alone particular directions, and is robust to small variations in the image content, which may come from noise, moderate cropping, local tampering, and content preserving operations. We use a compact summarization along the orientation axis in the transform domain for rotation estimation and use scale space theory to identify scale-resilient features along projections at different directions for scaling estimation.

**Rotation Estimation.** The direction of image edges can reveal information about image orientation. Given test image $I'(x,y)$ is obtained from original image $I(x,y)$ by rotating $\alpha$ degrees. First, we compute its edge map $E'(x,y)$. Radon transform is then applied to the edge map. $R_{E'}(\rho,\theta) = R_E(\rho,\theta + \alpha)$. Thus, in the transform domain, rotation becomes a shift along the angle axis. This property of Radon transform has been exploited in the image registration and authentication literature, where a 1-D summarization of Radon transform along the angle axis is used to estimate the rotation angle. Accordingly, 1-D summarization is derived as $m'(\theta) = max_{\rho}\left(R_{E'}(\rho,\theta)\right)$. For representation, quantization and sub-sampling are applied to $m'(\theta)$. Since down-sampling may cause aliasing, we first pass the signal $m'(\theta)$ through a low-pass filter $f(\cdot)$ to obtain $\widehat{m}'(\theta) = f(m'(\theta))$. If $n$-byte alignment component is desired, we downsample the signal $\widehat{m}'(\theta)$ to obtain the image hash $h'(\emptyset) = \{h'(1), ..., h'(n)\}$ with

$$h'(i) = \widehat{m}'\left(\left[(i - 1)\cdot\frac{180}{n}\right] + \emptyset\right), \quad \emptyset \in \{0, 1, ..., 179\}.$$

To further compress the image hash, we can store only the rank order information of $h$, $rank(h) = \{r(1), ..., r(n)\}$, where $r(i) \in \{1,...n\}$ is the rank of $h(i)$. $h$ is recovered SIFT (Scale-Invariant Feature Transform) features from image hash in each block of the original image $I$.

Our defined $h'(\emptyset)$ of $I'$, its rank order information is denoted by $rank(h'(\emptyset)) = \{r'(1), ..., r'(n)\}$. The shift amount that minimizes the $L$ distance between $rank(h)$ and $rank(h'(\emptyset))$ will be estimated rotation angle between two images $I$ and $I'$.

$$\alpha = argmin \sum_{i=1}^{n} |r(i) - r'(i + \emptyset)|, \qquad \emptyset \in \{0, 1, ..., 179\}.$$

The rotation estimation using rank order information gives comparable performance to estimation using cross-correlation, and a proper fusion of the two similarity metrics can lead to even better estimation accuracy.

**Scaling estimation.** Scale space theory [6] is a technique for analyzing signals at different scales, which makes it useful for automatic scale selection and scale invariant image analysis. Given projection $f'(\rho) = s \cdot f(s \cdot \rho)$ of the scaled image, we generate its scale space representation $L(\rho; t)$ by convolving $f'(\rho)$ with a 1-D discrete Gaussian filter $g(\rho; t)$ at scale $t$:

$$L(\rho; t) = g(\rho; t) * f'(\rho), \text{ where } g(\rho; t) = \frac{1}{\sqrt{2\pi t}} e^{-\rho^2 / (2t)}$$

The scale space representation is a 2-D signal with higher value of $t$ indicating coarser scale. With $L(\rho; t)$ computed, we then locate the space extrema of $L(\rho; t)$ at each scale $t$ by detecting the zero-crossing positions of $\partial L(\rho; t)/\partial t$ for each $t$.

Given the extrema positions of the two signals $f(\rho)$ and $f'(\rho) = s \cdot f(s \cdot \rho)$, we randomly choose two extrema $x, y$ from $f(\rho)$ and two extrema $x', y'$ from $f'(\rho)$. An estimate $\hat{s}$ of the true scaling factor $s$ is given by the ratio of $|x' - y'|/|x - y|$.

By computing the Radon projections of the original image along both the vertical and horizontal directions, we can obtain the scaling factors along these two directions using the above method.

## 3   Proposed Approach

We proposed a secure image hashing based on reversible watermarking method, which is properly designing image hash that captures important side information from the original image. First, the original image is split into non-overlapping blocks. The SIFT points with higher contrast values are typically more stable against such image operations as rotation, scaling, and compression. The SIFT points of each blocks are extracted with contrast values above a certain threshold $\tau$, and then utilizes a reversible data embedding by using difference expansion with an encryption by secret key $k$. In forensic analysis, the image hash is extracted through a decryption with a received secret key $k$ and a reversible data extracting method, as shown in Figure 2. Cryptographic one-way hash function is very sensitive to changes in the input signal. Generally, single-bit change will produce a completely different hash, therefore transmission analysis can detect whether the recovered secure hash altered or not.

The extracted image hash is to be securely attached along with the transmitted image and assist the forensic analysis on the received image.

The role of the post-processing block is applied a property of Radon transform to change the content of the image. For example, when the image is being distributed through different types of networks, to various receiving devices, some adaptations to the image format and content may occur, such as the image may resized and cropped for different screen sizes; logos may be inserted to the image corners.

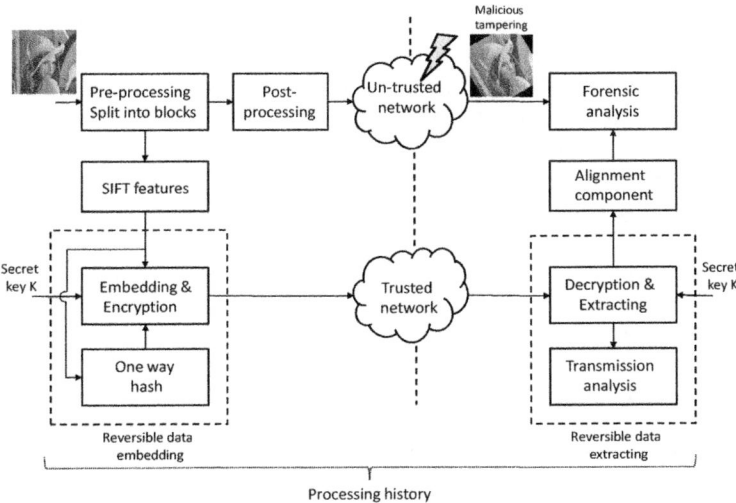

**Fig. 2.** Pipeline of the proposed method

Forensic analysis block is evaluated using a geometric transforms, such as rotation and scaling. More details introduced in the Section 2.

# 4  Detection and Localization of Image Tampering

In this section, we describe how the above proposed alignment component of the image hash can enable image cropping detection and tampering localization.

**Cropping Estimation.** Cropping can be used by an attacker to remove important part on the boundary of an image. We can use the image hash containing stable extrema proposed above to estimate the amount of cropping.

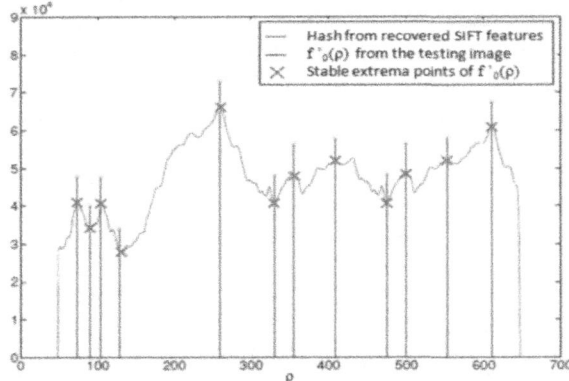

**Fig. 3.** Cropping estimation by aligning extrema from original and testing images

Given testing image $I'$, is split into $n$ blocks. We compute its Radon projections along the vertical and horizontal directions to obtain $f_o'(\rho)$ and $f_1'(\rho)$, respectively. The positions of the most stable extrema of $f_o'(\rho)$ and $f_1'(\rho)$ are also computed. Then, we can align the extrema which is recovered the SIFT features from image hash, with the extrema from $f_o'(\rho)$ and $f_1'(\rho)$ such that the number of matched extrema is maximized, as described in Section 2. An example of the alignment is shown in Fig. 3. Once the two signals are properly aligned, the amount of cropping can be obtained by comparing the distance between the boundaries of two different signals.

Thus, the accuracy of cropping estimation depends on the accuracy of the geometric estimation, since the testing image needs to be aligned with the original image through rotation and scaling.

**Tampering localization.** An adversary can modify local regions of an image and alter its original content by operations such as cut and paste. In this approach, the two images need to be properly aligned before comparison. Comparison for tampering localization based on consistencies in image statistics, as used in blind multimedia forensics, which consistencies can achieve more efficient and more accurate tampering localization. A tampered part of the image usually has significant difference from the original in term of their gradient information.

# 5   Experimental Results

In this section, we evaluate the performance of our proposed approach. All of our experiments are carried out on a PC machine 1.80 GHz Dual CPU with 2GB RAM. Also all of the simulation was carried out using Matlab version R2008a.

We test the integrity check component, rotation and scaling estimation accuracy of the proposed image hash on 50 images selected from the Corel database [7]. The image size is either 256x384 or 384x256. To evaluate the robustness of geometric transform estimation, we perform 15 operations for each of the 50 images, which give us a database of 750 images. The operations are listed in Table 1.

For the local tampering operation, we randomly select and swap two blocks within the image, where the block sizes are 50x50, 100x100. For each of 50 original images, we generate an image hash; composed of both alignment component, and integrity check component, and then evaluate the forensic analysis performance over 750 modified images. The confidence of geometric transform is computed both among same images and between different images. We show the discrimination performance in Figure 4, where all the hashes have roughly the same length, around 700 bits.

**Table 1.** List of image operations

| Operations | Operation parameter |
|---|---|
| Rotation | 5, 15, 45 degrees |
| Scaling | Scaling factor = 0.5, 0.8, 1.2, 1.5 |
| Cropping | 20%, 40% of entire image |
| Local tampering | Block size 50x50, 100x100 |
| Various combinations of rotation, scaling, cropping and local tampering ||

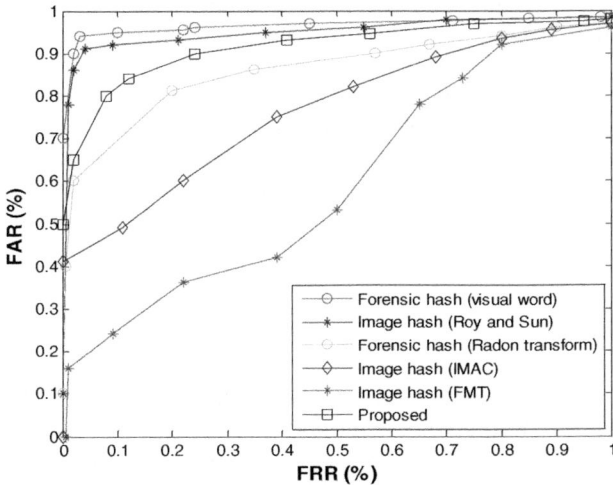

**Fig. 4.** Comparison of the discrimination performance

The quality of the embedded image is measured by Peak-Signal-to-Noise Ratio (PSNR) which is shown as follows:

$$PSNR = 10\log_{10}\frac{255^2}{MSE}\,, \qquad MSE = \frac{1}{mn}\sum_{i=0}^{m-1}\sum_{j=0}^{n-1}[I(i,j)-I'(i,j)]^2\,;$$

where *MSE* is the mean square error between the original image and the corresponding embedded image. Generally, it is acceptable if typical values for the *PSNR* in lossy image and video compression are between 30 and 50 db, where higher is better. Table 2 shows the effects of the embedded images. The quality of each embedded image is achieved very high ratio.

**Table 2.** The qualities of embedded images

| Quality of embedded images | |
|---|---|
| The original images | PSNR of the embedded images |
| Lena | 43.605 |
| Beach | 46.320 |
| Architecture | 43.021 |
| Flower | 42.253 |
| Chemical-plant | 45.468 |

**Table 3.** Geometric transform estimation accuracy

| Threshold values ($SIFT > \tau$) | 170 | 180 | 190 | 200 | 210 | 220 |
|---|---|---|---|---|---|---|
| Length of hash (bpp) | ~1116 | ~668 | ~535 | ~394 | ~241 | ~99 |
| Rotation angle ($\alpha$) | $1.41^o$ | $1.64^o$ | $1.93^o$ | $2.56^o$ | $3.74^o$ | $8.41^o$ |
| Scaling factor ($s$) | 1.1% | 1.3% | 1.8% | 2.2% | 2.6% | 6.8% |

In geometric transform estimation, we calculate the average estimation error for rotation and scaling over the 750 images using the alignment component as shown in Table 3.

The 1-D summarization of Radon transform of the image is down-sampled to assist rotation estimation, but the stable extreme in the Radon projection along horizontal and vertical directions are used for scaling estimation. By increasing the length of image hash, more stable points and extrema can be included to improve the estimation performance. The length of the image hash depends on contrast values above a certain threshold $\tau$.

## 6  Conclusion

In this paper, we proposed a novel secure image hashing based on reversible watermarking for forensic analysis. Our proposed method is order to achieve a good accuracy performance, as well as ensuring the security of image features. Compared to prior work, the proposed image hash can achieve more robust and accurate forensic analysis at the same hash length. The geometric transform offered by the image hash serves an important building block for further tampering localization using block based features.

**Acknowledgment.** This research was supported by Basic Science Research Program through the National Research Foundation of Korea (NRF) funded by the Ministry of Education, Science and Technology (Grant No. 2011-0012849).

## References

1. Venkatesen, R., Koon, S.M., Moulin, P.: Robust image hashing. In: Proc. of IEEE International Conference on Image Processing, vol. 3, pp. 664–666 (2000)
2. Mao, Y., Wu, M.: Robust and secure image hashing. IEEE Trans. on Information Forensics and Security 1(2), 215–230 (2006)
3. Delp, E., Memon, N.: Special issue on forensics analysis of digital evidence. IEEE Signal Processing Magazine 26(2) (March 2009)
4. Tian, J.: Reversible data embedding using a difference expansion. IEEE Trans. on Circuit and Systems for Video Technology 13, 890–896 (2003)
5. Peiling, C., Junhong, L., Hongcai, Z.: Rotation and scaling invariant texture classification based on Radon transform and multi-scale analysis. Pattern Recognition Letters 27, 408–413 (2006)
6. Lindeberg, T.: Scale space theory in computer vision. Kluwer Academic Publishers, Dordrecht (1994)
7. Corel test set, http://wang.ist.psu.edu/~jwang/test1.tar
8. Lu, W., Varna, A.l., Wu, M.: Forensic hash for multimedia information. In: Proc. of SPIE Media Forensic and Security, p. 7541 (2010)

# Learning Web Application Firewall - Benefits and Caveats

Dariusz Pałka[1] and Marek Zachara[2]

[1] Pedagogical University of Cracow, Poland
dpalka@up.krakow.pl
[2] University of Science and Technology (AGH) Cracow, Poland
mzachara@agh.edu.pl

**Abstract.** The paper discusses selected issues related to the implementation and deployment of the Web Application Firewall that protects the target application by verifying the incoming requests and their parameters through matching them against recorded usage patterns. These patterns in turn are learned from the traffic generated by the users of the application. Since many web applications, including these operated by the government, are prone to exploits, there is a need to introduce new easily implementable methods of protection to prevent unauthorized access to sensitive data. A Learning Web Application Firewall offers a flexible, application-tailored, yet easy to deploy solution. There are certain concerns, however, regarding the classification of data that is used for the learning process which can, in certain cases, impair the firewall ability to classify traffic correctly. These concerns are discussed on the basis of reference implementation prepared by the authors.

**Keywords:** web, firewall, learning, security.

## 1 Introduction

According to a recent survey [27], 72% of the interviewed companies had their web sites/applications hacked during the preceding 24 months. Most of the successful attacks happen on the application layer (Layer 7 of OSI model [12]) - as this is still the most vulnerable area. Even though lower levels are not ultimately secure, over the years the network protocols have been hardened to the point where hacking them is extremely difficult and few vulnerabilities emerge. Also, the operating systems, web servers, and encryption engines are relatively secure, as they usually come from only a few vendors and each has a large enough user base to identify vulnerabilities early and get them fixed quickly.

Web applications, however, are the opposite - they are usually unique (even if they use portions of a common code - e.g. some framework) and usually maintained by or for a single client only. This results in both lower average security of the code (as the specialized knowledge is less available for each company in such fragmented market) and fewer chances to spot the vulnerability before it is exploited. This is why web application vulnerabilities still outnumber browser/operating system vulnerabilities by the ratio of 1:10 [17].

A M. Tjoa et al. (Eds.): ARES 2011, LNCS 6908, pp. 295–308, 2011.
© IFIP International Federation for Information Processing 2011

Many web applications have vulnerabilities that are extremely easy to exploit. According to the research by Web Application Security Consortium [30], "More than 13% of all reviewed sites can be completely compromised automatically. About 49% of web applications contain vulnerabilities of high risk level (Urgent and Critical) detected during automatic scanning. However, detailed manual and automated assessment by a white box method allows to detect these high risk level vulnerabilities with the probability reaching 80-96%".

Unfortunately, governmental web sites and applications are no exception. Although there are no specific statistics available for the vulnerability ratios of such sites, they are subject to successful hacking attempts. For example, a recent news item has reported a large number of these sites hacked with access details available for sale on the black market [10]. It is important to note that governmental sites attract not only regular cyber-crime, but also the attention of hostile governments. With incomparably larger resources that can be committed to find/exploit a vulnerability and also cover the actions, this is a significant threat that cannot be ignored. In recent years there have been a number of accusations of such actions circulating the media, yet for obvious reasons no hard proof has been presented to the public.

## 2   Common Attack Methods

There are numerous methods in which an attack on a web application can be conducted. Yet, there are a few distinct categories that group most of them. Some of them are explained in greater detail below. These are the types of attack that can be (to various extent) prevented with the use of the dynamic parameter evaluation described in this paper. What is important to note, however, is that the list includes all most common vulnerabilities according to SANS Top 25 CWE list [1]. More in-depth explanation, also reffering to other categories, can be found in [9].

*Script injections,* especially *SQL Injections* are attack vectors that attempt the execution of an arbitrary code on the target machine. In its simplest form, such vulnerability exists if a user-supplied parameter is inserted into a predefined query and sent to the target interpreter. Vulnerability to this kind of attack is usually the result of insufficient validation of input, which neither sanitizes nor rejects harmful parameter values.

*Parameter tampering* is a general term for modifying the parameters sent to the server with a request, usually assigning them values not expected by the server. The objective of this action is to push the application servicing the request off its usual working pattern, possibly making it behave in an unpredictable way. Script injections are an example of parameter tampering, but the attack may also center on application/server failure (DoS) or identity theft.

*Forceful browsing* is a method of directly accessing available server's resources by requesting specific URL's instead of following links and forms provided by the application. This way a potential attacker can get access to pages/files outside normal execution path or can bypass poorly designed authentication procedures.

*Cross-site scripting* refers to a specific code injection technique, where the goal of the attacker is not to attack the server itself but other users that are (or will be) connected to it. If the web application allows for user-supplied content and does not validate that content properly before making it available to other users, the attacker can post a harmful code that can be presented by the server to other users - and executed on their PCs. As a result, the attacker may gain access to confidential information - including users' session identification.

For the sake of fairness, it should be noted that there are also various other threats/attack vectors that are not affected by the methods presented in this paper. The major ones that have to be considered are:

*Buffer overflows* that exploit stack/heap or other limited memory allocation pools by trying to overwrite the program's data with their own code. Even though they are a serious threat in general, they usually do not affect web applications. Although theoretically possible, they would be extremely difficult to conduct because of primarily two reasons: most web applications are written in relatively 'safe' languages that implement boundary controls, and also the web applications are often customized or custom made - forcing the attacker to act 'blindly'. Because of this, it is much easier to conduct this type of attack against other components of the system - the web server, database, or even a WAF - since these are widely available components that the attacker can investigate prior to the attack.

*Man in the middle* is a technique that involves listening to (or modifications of) the data in transit between a client and the server. The goal is to either get access to privileged information (e.g. user's credentials) or to change it before it reaches the server (e.g. change the account number for wire transfer). So far the primary protection against this threat is an encrypted transmission with verification of digital certificates. Unfortunately, if the user's operating system is compromised, there is hardly any way to protect them against such threat.

*Session hijacking, cookies tampering* and other methods that target user-side data in order to gain access to user's resources (e.g. by exploiting the Session ID) are only affected if the attack vector utilizes a cross-site action (as described above). Otherwise, they are unaffected by a WAF. Generally, WAF's task is to protect the server, while the user protection granted by possible rejection of cross-site scripting attempts is an additional bonus.

*Denial of Service (DoS) and Distributed DoS (DDoS)* are attacks that intent to prevent a web service (a web application) from functioning. This can be achieved by either exploiting a system bug or vulnerability (e.g. shutting down the service by a means of sending special command to the server), or by utilizing system resources (e.g. saturating the bandwidth) to the point where the system becomes unresponsive. While a WAF can protect against the former scenario, little can be done to prevent the latter. Also, in most cases, the protection against resources overloading should rather be done on a lower, network level.

## 3    Attack Prevention Measures

Most companies live in a delusional comfort of superficial protection. According to CSI/FBI 2006 study [4]: "97% of interviewed companies and administrations were using an anti-virus, 98% have a network firewall, 69% have intrusion detection systems. However ... 65% of these organizations have undergone a viral or spyware attack, 32% have experienced unauthorized access to their internal data and even 15% have suffered from network intrusions"

To fend off attacks, two broad categories of methods are used, namely *prevention* and *detection*. Prevention is the 'first line of defense' - its task is to block harmful attempts from reaching a vulnerable spot. Prevention usually works by blocking certain user's activities on the basis of prior knowledge - considering them either harmful or unnecessary for the use of the service. Detection, on the other hand, is used to identify attack attempts that get past the blockade, usually by monitoring the traffic and identifying certain behavioral patterns. These patterns can be in turn compared to a fixed database of known types of malicious behavior (which is in a way similar to the design of most anti-virus programs), or some heuristics which identify unusual circumstances can be implemented (this is the domain of Intrusion Detection Systems [21]).

Unfortunately, the flexibility offered by heuristic solutions comes at a price of false alarms being raised in unusual, but not attack-related circumstances. A system ability to detect an unknown (undefined) attack pattern is usually a trade-off for a number of legitimate users being reported as abusers. With increased sensitivity of such a system, the number of false positive reactions increases, making it unacceptable to allow it to act (e.g. block certain users from accessing the application) on its own. Therefore, such alerts are usually forwarded to a human supervisor for a decision. On the other hand, lowering the sensitivity, which would allow for the elimination of human supervision, results in a possibly higher number of real attacks passing unnoticed.

Focusing on securing a web application, it must be noted that this is a multi-objective task. It includes secure architecture and data handling, secure implementations and securing of external systems and libraries used by an application (e.g. an external database). It is postulated by many professionals, including Microsoft [7], to treat security as a process spanning through the application life cycle rather than a single task, yet in reality it rarely happens. Corporate management prefer to have 'security/penetration tests' checked off somewhere on the way and to move to the next tasks in a project.

This increases the importance of well-defined specific solutions that would address the security issues, while being understandable and manageable by project managers in organizations. As far as web applications are concerned, the Web Application Firewall (WAF) [28] [29] is probably the most universal solution which limits the risk of exploiting the application, yet it is rarely used. This is due to several reasons:

- Difficulty in configuring a WAF - which needs to cover every aspect of interactions between the users and the protected application - the parameters passed from the user, the logic of the page flow, etc.
- Duplication of protection rules that should be implemented in the application itself. This implies acknowledging that the application may not be secure.
- Constant adjustment of WAF rules as the web application grows and evolves to match the new usage scenarios.

The combination of these conditions, especially the need of constantly adjusting a WAF to mirror the changes in the application, theoretically makes the application developers best suited for the task - at least from the organizational/management point of view. However, this leads to the situation when they are loaded with extra work based solely on an assumption that their core work (the application) is insecure. Naturally, their reaction will be to convince the management that a WAF is not really necessary and it is better to direct the available resources towards the development to achieve better quality and functionality. Personal experience of the authors confirms that WAF adoption is very limited in commercial environments, even for critical systems like Internet banking.

## 4    Adaptive Web Application Firewall

As it was already mentioned, the complexity and number of rules needed for setting up a WAF is probably the most important obstacle preventing its wider adoption. Therefore, a natural approach would be to try generating a rule set from a sample of legitimate traffic. In other words, to equip a WAF with the ability to learn.

Before discussing the methods of creating WAF rules, it is important to outline how a HTTP request is processed. A typical request looks like this:

```
POST /service/admin/base?p=submit&type=normal HTTP/1.1
User-Agent: Mozilla/5.0
Accept: text/html,application/xhtml+xml,application/xml,*/*
Accept-Language: en-us,en;q=0.5
Accept-Encoding: gzip,deflate
Accept-Charset: ISO-8859-1,utf-8;q=0.7,*;q=0.7
Keep-Alive: 115
Connection: keep-alive
Referer: http://server.domain/service/admin/login
Cookie: PHPSESSID=12345678901234567890
Content-Type: application/x-www-form-urlencoded
Content-Length: 42

42
email=manitou@some.server&password=try_me!
```

As can be noticed, this request carries four parameters:

- *p* and *type* inside the URL
- *email* and *password* as POST data content.

The request also includes other pieces of important information:

- the target web page: */service/admin/base*[1]
- the previous URL visited: *http://server.domain/service/admin/login*

Storing and analyzing this information for each target page over a period of time can lead to valuable conclusions:

*Page flow of the webservice:* By comparing the current Referrer URL against the statistics of the Referrer URLs collected for the page, it can be determined whether the current client's behavior matches the usual usage patterns. If the Referrer URL has not been observed before, or has been observed extremely rarely, it can be assumed that the client is not behaving correctly, i.e. can be doing something undesirable. Such request can then be rejected, providing the application with the protection against the *Forceful browsing* exploit scenario.

*Parameters range for the page:* Having a large enough set of values for each parameter supplied by clients for the page, it can be deducted whether the currently supplied value falls within what can be considered as a 'normal' range. This is a typical classification task [5] with a potential for simplification, as described later. By controlling and rejecting parameter values which do not match normal behavior patterns, the application can be protected against all kinds of *Parameter tampering* attacks, including *SQL injections* and *Cross-site scripting*.

Of course, the effectiveness of these methods rely heavily on the quality of the statistics which in turn rely on the number of data samples collected and the ratio of malicious or erroneous attempts against all events. This issue will be discussed in greater detail in the following section.

## 5   Concerns and Implementation Issues

Despite obvious benefits of a self-learning WAF, there are still certain issues that prevent market adoption and will need to be addressed. These can be divided into two major categories.

### 5.1   Data Collection

Apart form purely engineering issues of gathering the HTTP traffic, there are several major issues that have been encountered during the design and implementation of the self-learning WAF. These are related to the amount of data collected, the storage of the data and the application context considered for the parameter analysis.

---

[1] If an URL parsing module is used (e.g. Apache's mod_rewrite), some parameters may be passed as part of the target URL path.

*Data scope.* One of the primary decisions that impact a WAF ability to correctly deal with incoming parameter values is the scope of historical (reference) data that is used for evaluation. Too little data and a WAF may reject legitimate values that just did not make it into the reference scope, too much data and a WAF will be a subject to over-training that impairs generalization (similarly to the effect observed in neural networks). The data retention time (DRT), over which the data is analyzed, depends primarily on clients' usage patterns that may e.g. change on a weekday basis. There seems to be no sound scientific model that could help estimate the DRT, leaving it to the experience of the system administrators. It is important to note that the shorter DRT is, the quicker a WAF will adjust itself to a changed application, yet it will also be more vulnerable to an attack that will flood the server with forged requests.

*Parameter context.* From the user's point of view, a web application (or parts of its functionality) is a stateful machine with its behavior and state depending on user's actions. This implies that in some cases the range or number or valid parameter's values depend on the current state. A typical example could be a money transfer, where a logged user can supply the target account number as a parameter value, but a user who is doing so without being logged will be denied. As with the data scope, the optimal context may depend on specific application needs, yet in most real cases the target page is used as the context, optionally with the referrer URL and/or session ID presence flag.

*Data storage.* A WAF processes the same information which is sent by a user to the target web application. This means that it also receives sensitive personal data, including authorization data (login names and passwords). However, if a WAF is to have the ability to check the incoming values against the historical knowledge, it must retain the data over a period of time. This leads to a critical issue of storing the values on the server that contains sensitive data. Since a WAF does not know in advance which data might be sensitive, it should apply the same rules to all analyzed parameters. One possible solution is to encrypt all the data stored with a key (preferably supplied from outside a WAF on runtime). The other is to keep all the retained data in RAM only. The former solution puts a tremendous overhead on computational power required as data needs to be encrypted and decrypted constantly. The latter implies loosing all protective knowledge on each server restart - leaving a potential attack window open until enough new data is collected. A practical, yet not elegant solution is to specify parameters that contain sensitive data manually - and only these parameters are e.g. encrypted - or most often an arbitrary value pattern is defined for them by the system administrator.

## 5.2   Learning Patterns

As far as data collection and analysis are concerned, there are two distinct work regimes that can be discussed. One is a triggered learning (TL) scenario, and the other is a continuous learning (CL) scenario. The TL scenario requires a

WAF administrator to specifically trigger on and off the learning mode. In this mode, parameter values are collected - and are either stored as reference values or possibly generalized into a reference pattern or a value set. After the learning stage is completed, a WAF is switched into 'working' mode where the learned patterns are not adjusted, only the incoming parameter values are compared against the learned knowledge. This scenario has several important benefits:

- There is no need to consider the data retention period size. The data considered for pattern evaluation is all the data gathered during the learning process.
- There is no need to store all historical data. At the end of the learning period, all the data can be transformed into a matching pattern or a value set. This also eliminates the sensitive data storage concerns described earlier.
- A WAF is resistant to attacks targeting its learning process.

However, there are also considerable drawbacks:

- The learning process must be complete; i.e. include all possible usage patterns - and since all these actions must be performed by the staff, it may incur additional costs. However, as most commercial deployment of web applications include acceptance tests - which usually cover all of the application usage scenarios, this work can be utilized to train a WAF.
- A WAF must be manually re-trained after each change introduced to the protected application. Again, in the commercial environment such changes usually trigger some acceptance tests that can be used for this purpose.

To summarize, this scenario is preferable for a commercial deployment, especially of web applications that do not change frequently over time (e.g. Internet banking). It may be difficult to apply to very dynamic web services (e.g. a web portal).

The CL WAF offers somehow less precise protection at the benefit of much less manual input being required. In this case, as described above, the data is collected from user-supplied input over a defined constantly moving time window. The data from the recent window is used to verify incoming parameters. The major issues implied by this scenario are as follows:

- A WAF will only accept parameter values that match recent users' behavior patterns. If these patterns change over longer periods of time, there will be a high number of false positive reports by a WAF
- The firewall may be susceptible to specially engineered attacks that target its learning process (e.g. supplying malicious data slowly over a period of time in order to make a WAF accept it as a valid pattern).

## 5.3   Statistical Data Significance

The following considerations apply to the CL scenario only, since in the TL scenario all the learning data is considered to be valid and legitimate. Gathered data retained by a CL WAF may, however, include incorrect or even harmful parameter values - since it is collected from unknown, usually anonymous users. For a WAF to function correctly the following assumption must be met: *the amount of incorrect parameter values must be an insignificantly small portion of all the analyzed values.*

The reason behind this requirement is obvious: the significant amount of incorrect data will train a WAF to accept them as valid input. What is not obvious is how to set the level of 'insignificance' for a certain data set. As of now, there has not been specific research targeting the distribution and grouping/classification of web services parameter values, hence there are no clear guidelines. In most cases, this significance level will be set by the system administrator based on his experience, expected traffic and knowledge about the application.

There is, however, a certain characteristic of the parameter values that can be exploited for the benefit of classification. Based on authors' experience, a significantly large number of parameters have values that fall into one of the following groups:

- *Numerical values.* A large portion of users' input is numerical. Moreover, numerical values are used to control the state of the application, to point at certain database records, etc.
- *Selection values.* These are usually tied to users' selection options. As a result, only a very limited number of values is observed.

These two groups are relatively easy to detect using simple heuristic methods. Therefore, adding appropriate algorithms to the parameter evaluation provides significant engineering benefits, although there are still parameters which will not fall into these groups (e.g. addresses), and which are at the same time a popular target for hacking attempts.

## 5.4    Reference Implementation

A Learning Web Application Firewall has been implemented as a module for the Apache HTTP Server. The Apache HTTP Server was selected because it is free, open source, modular and powerful software. It is also the most widely used web server - as shown by Netcraft [18], Apache is used by over 61% of 312 693 296 sites investigated in the survey. The main components of the proposed Learning WAF are presented in Fig.1. Request Data Validator is an Apache module which registers and analyzes incoming requests from web server clients. It is located in the input filter chain right after the SSL filter which is responsible for decoding incoming SSL requests. The Request Data Validator extracts a request context and values of all request GET and POST parameters from incoming requests. The extracted data are then sent to the Data Collector and Data Validator subsystems.

The Data Collector sends request data to the Data Store, but due to security reasons discussed above, all request parameters must first be encoded. Request data from the Request Data Validator is also checked by Data Validator to detect and prevent web attacks. If a potential attack is detected, it can be logged and

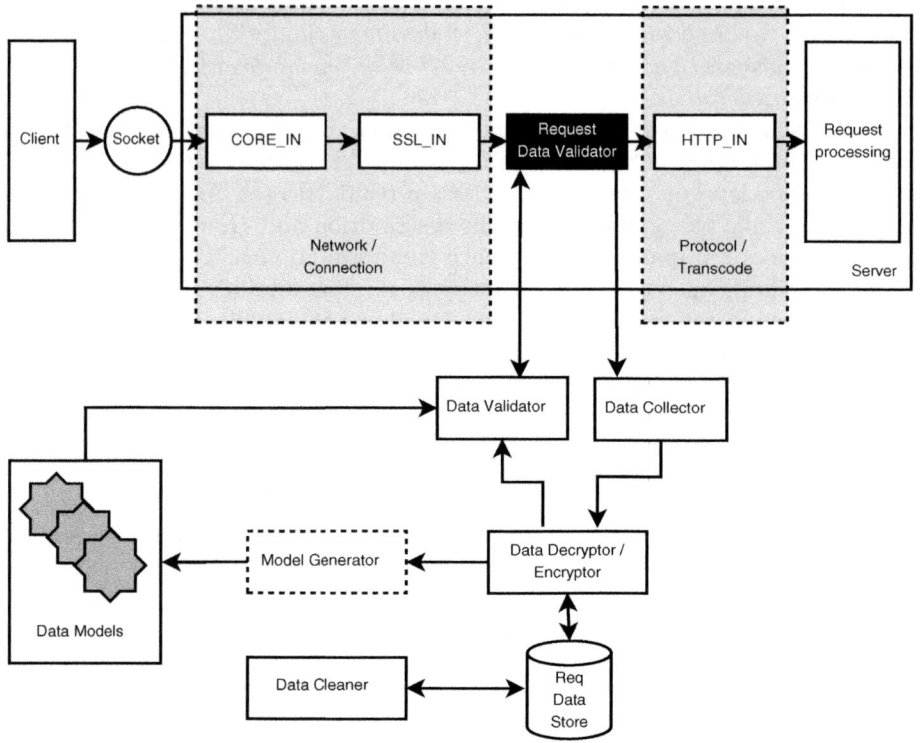

**Fig. 1.** The Learning Web Application Firewall components

the request may be rejected. Apart from the Request Data Validator module there are also other external processes working with Request Data Store, e.g. Data Cleaner whose task is to remove old parameter values (that are past data retention window). This cleaning process prevents excessive growth of the data store.

The most important of those external processes is Model Generator whose task is to create models for the data collected from requests. If the data in the incoming request do not match the current model, an anomaly score is assigned for this request. The request with an anomaly score that exceeds an assumed threshold is treated as an attack attempt. The Models for the request data are based on the following characteristics:

- the length of parameter values
- the character distribution of parameter values
- belonging to one or more predefined classes (such as numerical value, email address, URL)
- belonging to an enumerated type

The models mentioned above (as well as others) can be found in [14], however unlike [14], the method proposed in this paper can utilize a continuous learning (CL) scenario for creating the models.

In case of some attacks, the models described above are not sufficient to detect anomalies in parameter values; in such cases a model of parameter structure can be useful. To create such model it is assumed that parameter values are words belonging to a language L generated by an unknown grammar G. On the basis of those words (positive examples) grammar inference is conducted and grammar G obtained in this process is treated as a data model. Because of the complexity of the process, it is assumed that in order to describe parameter values, the simplest (in Chomsky's understanding) hierarchy regular grammar [11], [13], [14] is enough. In the worst case however, learning only from positive examples is known to be NP-complete [8]. Because of this, instead of identifying grammar G, other methods are used including: inference of Deterministic Finite Automaton (DFA), Nondeterministic Finite Automaton (NFA) or Hidden Markov Models (HMMs), which might be treated as probabilistic generalization of NFA. There is extensive literature on learning regular languages [2], [3], [6], [19], [22], [25], [26].

Due to a stochastic character of the sample data (incoming requests), it was decided to base the grammar inference on HMMs and use Baum-Welsh algorithm [23]. It should be noted, however, that creating a model based on grammar inference is time-consuming, which means that using it in a CL scenario is limited.

# 6   Conclusions and Future Work

The article discusses potential benefits of introducing a Learning Web Application Firewall for the purpose of detecting and eliminating malicious users' behavior. Making use of learning processes for the benefit of computer security is recently gaining audience among researchers [14], [11], and, with the growing number and sophistication of the web attack attempts, it appears to be a logical approach to address these problems. The obvious benefit of such a WAF is the ability to fend off a large class of dangerous attack patterns directed at the web application, with a very limited set-up time.

## 6.1   Comparison against Existing WAFs

Certainly, WAFs are not an absolute novelty. They have been available on the market for several years and there are many vendors (e.g. Cisco, Barracuda, F5) offering their commercial hardware/software products (a larger list of sample vendors is available in [28]). There is also an open source Apache ModSecurity project that can be used to provide that functionality. Yet, all of these solutions are based on fixed rule sets, which need to be configured manually for a custom web application. The vendors often provide templates for typical services or applications, but if a custom made application is to be secured, it usually requires a lot of manual setup and on-going maintenance as described earlier in this paper. On the other hand, commercial solutions, especially those that include vendor's hardware, come with additional features, e.g. load balancing, effective SSL support, and so on.

There are other systems which might be helpful in securing Web Applications, e.g. signature scanning intrusion detecting system (IDS), such as SNORT [24] or Bro [20]. However, such signature based methods require frequent updates of the attack signature databases by security experts and tuning it to reduce false positive alarms. These systems also cannot detect novel (zero day) attacks.

There are also anomaly based systems which treat web servers as generic network services, and in such systems incoming and outgoing data are modelled as a stream of bytes or discrete packets. The anomaly detection can be based on packet headers [15] or on matching patterns in the first few packets of connection [16]. In those systems no rules need to be written and they can detect novel (zero day) attacks.

The Learning WAF presented in this paper resembles the approach proposed in [13] and [14], however, it has been implemented as the Apache module located in the input filter chain (not as a log analyzer as in [13] and [14]), and, as a result, it has access to all parameters transferred through GET and POST. Additionally, it can block requests identified as attack attempts, and not only report detected threats. Another significant difference between these two approaches is the fact that instead of triggered learning used in [13] and [14], our learning WAF can also utilize a continuous learning process.

## 6.2   Fields of Use

The primary advantage of a Learning WAF is its ability to secure custom applications with none or little extra setup involved. Companies that utilize commonly used products or components may be able to get a pre-defined templates for a WAF that will protect their applications, but organizations that run unique or highly customized web applications need to take care of the protective rule sets on their own.

In such cases, a Learning WAF may be the best option - providing a customized protection without much manual work required. The best environment for such a WAF is either one with high traffic, and/or where complete acceptance tests are part of the deployment. Sample types of organizations that could be considered for this solutions are:

- Portals and other high traffic, frequently changed web sites.
- Banks and institution with high financial exposure to Internet threats (but they also have a very thorough acceptance tests).
- Governmental institutions - last but not least, they almost always use unique/ custom web applications while often not employing security professionals to protect them (with a notable exception of military). With these applications often having access to very sensitive data (e.g. individual tax reports), they are attractive targets for crooks and the enemies of the state alike.

The major concern for the deployment of a Lerning WAF into the production environment is the quality and completeness of the data used to train a WAF before it can reliably be used to control incoming traffic. In case of a TL WAF, the only concern remaining is the completeness of the training data, as all of it comes presumably from a trusted source. A CL WAF, however, poses a much greater challenge, as it requires automated evaluation and classification of unknown data coming from untrusted sources. This does not mean that such a CL WAF would not protect the application, but it must be taken into account that it may not provide a complete protection and, under certain circumstances, might allow malicious attacks to pass through. This type of WAF thus requires further research.

# References

1. CWE/SANS Top 25 Most Dangerous Software Errors (2010), http://cwe.mitre.org/top25/archive/2010/2010_cwe_sans_top25.pdf
2. Angluin, D., Smith, C.: Inductive Inference: Theory and Methods. ACM Computing Surveys 15(3), 237–269 (1983)
3. Cicchello, O., Kremer, S.C.: Inducing grammars from sparse data sets: a survey of algorithms and results. Journal of Machine Learning and Research 4, 603–632 (2003)
4. CSI/FBI Computer Crime and Security Survey (2006), http://i.cmpnet.com/gocsi/db_area/pdfs/fbi/FBI2006.pdf
5. Duda, R.O., Hart, P.E., Stork, D.G.: Pattern Classification. Wiley, New York (2001) ISBN: 978-0-471-05669-0
6. Fernau, H.: Algorithms for Learning Regular Expressions. In: Jain, S., Simon, H.U., Tomita, E. (eds.) ALT 2005. LNCS (LNAI), vol. 3734, pp. 297–311. Springer, Heidelberg (2005)
7. Gallagher, T., Jeffries, B., Landauer, L.: Hunting Security Bugs. Microsoft Press, Redmond (2006) ISBN: 978-0-7356-2187-9
8. Gold, E.: Complexity of automaton identification from given data. Information and Control 37(3), 302–320 (1978)
9. Hope, P., Walther, B.: Web Security Testing Cookbook. O'Reilly Media, Sebastopol (2008) ISBN: 978-0-596-51483-9
10. Imperva Data Security Blog: Major websites (gov,mil,edu) are Hacked and Up for Sale, http://blog.imperva.com/2011/01/major-websites-govmiledu-are-hacked-and-up-for-sale.html
11. Ingham, K., et al.: Learning DFA representations of HTTP for protecting web applications. Computer Networks 51, 1239–1255 (2007)
12. ISO/IEC standard 7498-1:1994, http://standards.iso.org/ittf/PubliclyAvailableStandards/s020269_ISO_IEC_7498-1s_1994E.zip
13. Kruegel, C., Vigna, G.: Anomaly detection of web-based attacks. In: Proceedings of the 10th ACM Conference on Computer and Communications Security, pp. 251–261. ACM Press, New York (2003)
14. Kruegel, C., Vigna, G., Robertson, W.: A multi-model approach to the detection of web-based attacks. Computer Networks 48(5), 717–738 (2005)
15. Mahoney, M.V., Chan, P.K.: Learning nonstationary models of normal network traffic for detecting novel attacks. In: Proceedings of the Eighth ACM SIGKDD International Conference on Knowledge Discovery and Data Mining, pp. 376–385. ACM Press, New York (2002)

16. Mahoney, M.V.: Network traffic anomaly detection based on packet bytes. In: Proceedings of the 2003 ACM Symposium on Applied Computing, pp. 346–350. ACM Press, New York (2003)
17. Microsoft Security Intelligence Report, Key Findings, http://www.microsoft.com/security/sir/keyfindings/default.aspx
18. Netcraft, Web Server Survey (April 2011), http://news.netcraft.com/archives/2011/04/06/april-2011-web-server-survey.html
19. Oliveria, A.L., Silva, J.: Efficient search techniques for the inference of minimum sized finite automata. In: Proceedings of the Fifth String Processing and Information Retrieval Symposium, pp. 81–89. IEEE Computer Press, Los Alamitos (1998)
20. Paxson, V.: Bro: A System for Detecting Network Intruders in Real-Time. In: Proceedings of 7'th USENIX Security Symposium Lawrence Berkeley National Laboratory, San Antonio TX, January 26-29 (1998)
21. Pietro, R., Mancini, L. (eds.): Intrusion Detection Systems. Springer, Heidelberg (2008) ISBN: 978-0-387-77265-3
22. Pitt, L.: Inductive Inference, DFAs, and Computational Complexity. In: Jantke, K.P. (ed.) AII 1989. LNCS, vol. 397, pp. 18–44. Springer, Heidelberg (1989)
23. Rabiner, L.: A Tutorial on Hidden Markov Models and Selected Applications in Speech Recognition. Proc. IEEE 77(2), 257–286 (1989)
24. Roesch, M.: Snort Lightweight Intrusion Detection for Networks. In: Proceedings of 13th Systems Administration Conference, LISA 1999, pp. 229–238 (1999)
25. Sakakibara, Y.: Recent Advances of Grammatical Inference. Theor. Comput. Sci. 185(1), 15–45 (1997)
26. Stolcke, A., Omohundro, S.: Best-first model merging for Hidden Markov Model induction, Technical Report TR-93-003. International Computer Science Institute, Berkeley, Ca (1993)
27. The State of Web Application Security (2011), http://www.barracudanetworks.com/ns/downloads/White_Papers/Barracuda_Web_App_Firewall_WP_Cenzic_Exec_Summary.pdf
28. Web Application Firewall, https://www.owasp.org/index.php/Web_Application_Firewall
29. Web Application Firewall Evaluation Criteria, http://projects.webappsec.org/w/page/13246985/Web-Application-Firewall-Evaluation-Criteria
30. Web Application Security Statistics (2008), http://projects.webappsec.org/w/page/13246989/Web-Application-Security-Statistics

# A Novel Chaining Approach to Indirect Control Transfer Instructions

Wei Chen, Zhiying Wang, Qiang Dou, and Yongwen Wang

School of Computer, National University of Defense Technology,
Changsha 410073, Hunan, China
chenwei@nudt.edu.cn

**Abstract.** Both dynamic binary translation systems and optimization systems store the translated or optimized code in the software maintained code cache for reuse. The performance of the code cache is crucial. Translated code is usually organized as code blocks in the code cache and each code block transfer control to the next one through a control transfer instruction. As the target address of a control transfer instruction is in the form of its source program counter, the conventional code cache system has to check the address mapping table for the translated target address to find the required target code block, which will cause considerable performance degradation. Control transfer instructions can be divided into two categories as direct control transfer instructions and indirect control transfer instructions. For indirect control transfer instructions, the target address is hold in the register or memory element whose content can be changed during the execution of the program. It is difficult to chain the indirect control transfer instructions with a fixed translated target address through pure software approaches. A novel indirect control transfer chaining approach is proposed in this paper. The principle of the technique is to insert custom chaining instructions into the translated code block while translating the indirect control transfer instructions and execute those chaining instructions to implement dynamical chaining. Some special hardware and software assists are proposed in this paper. Evaluation of the proposed approach is conducted on a code cache simulator. Experiment results show that our hardware assisted indirect control transfer instruction chaining approach can improve the performance of the code cache system dramatically.

**Keywords:** code cache, indirect control transfer instruction, dynamic chaining, simulator.

## 1 Introduction

Software maintained Code Cache Systems (CCS) [1] have been widely used by many binary translation or optimization systems (optimization system is a kind of translated system in which translation is performed between the same instruction set architecture; in the rest of the paper, the translation system includes the optimization system if not especially declared) to store the translated or optimized code for reuse. As more and more translation systems have been proposed and developed, the

A M. Tjoa et al. (Eds.): ARES 2011, LNCS 6908, pp. 309–320, 2011.

performance of the code cache systems becomes a hot topic in both the industry and academic fields, especially for those virtual computing environments.

In the code cache, the translated code is organized in terms of code blocks. Each code block ends with a control transfer instruction which switches control flow between different code blocks. When a source code block is translated the first time, its target code block may have not been translated most of the time. Thus, the translated code block always keeps the target address of the control transfer instruction in terms of its original Source Program Counter (SPC). The conventional code cache system always maintains an Address Mapping Table (AMT) [2] for recording the code block's SPC and its corresponding Translated Program Counter (TPC). During the execution, CCS finds the required translated target code block by looking up AMT as Fig. 1(a) [2] shows.

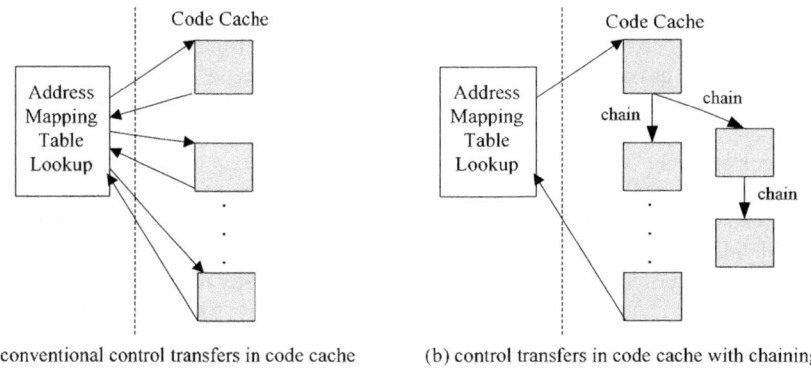

(a) conventional control transfers in code cache    (b) control transfers in code cache with chaining

**Fig. 1.** Control flow changes among code blocks in the code cache

When executing within a code block, the execution/control flow is straight-line. However, transitions from one code block to another may cause performance degradation because the control flow is changed and costly address mapping table lookup mechanism must be invoked. In our code cache simulator, an AMT lookup may cost 15~25 local instructions while a context switch may cost about 40 local instructions. Therefore, if the control transfer instruction can be chained directly to the translated target address (as Fig. 1(b) shows), the performance of the code cache system may be dramatically improved as table lookup and context switch operations can be avoided.

Control transfer instructions can be divided into two categories as direct control transfer instructions and indirect control transfer instructions. For direct control transfer instructions, the target address always appears as an immediate value in the instruction itself. So, no matter the immediate value indicates an address or an offset, the target address of a direct control transfer instruction can be calculated from the instruction itself and is fixed during execution. Thus, the SPC of the direct control transfer instruction can be placed with its TPC through software mechanisms. We have proposed an effective solution to this problem in our previous work [2].

For indirect control transfer instructions, the target address is saved in a register or a memory element. The indirect control transfer instruction figures out its target address by reading the register or the memory element. During execution, the content of the register or memory element can be changed, which means that the target address of the indirect control transfer instruction is not fixed. Therefore, it is difficult to fix the indirect control transfer instruction's target address with a fixed TPC. At present, as we know, there is not a pure software approach which can solve this problem effectively.

In this paper, a hardware assisted Indirect Control Transfer Chaining (IDCTC) method is proposed for the indirect control transfer instruction. The principle of IDCTC is: (1) while translating the source code block, inserting custom chaining instructions into the translated code block which contains indirect control transfer instructions, (2) during execution, executing the inserted chaining instructions to dynamically determine the translated target address. Special hardware/software assists are occupied by IDCTC. The key of IDCTC is a hardware assist called indirect transfer target buffer, which saves most frequently accessed indirect control transfer instructions.

To evaluate the efficiency of IDCTC, we conduct experiments on a code cache simulator and the experiment results show that IDCTC can dynamically chain the indirect control transfer instructions and dramatically improve the performance of the code cache system.

The rest of the paper is organized as follows. Section 2 introduces some related works. Section 3 introduces the hardware and software assists occupied by IDCTC. Section 4 describes the process of our indirect control transfer chaining approach. Section 5 presents the evaluation of IDCTC and section 6 concludes this paper.

## 2  Related Work

Code cache systems are the critical part in a binary translation system or optimization system. All the translated codes are cached in the code cache system for reuse. Transmeta Crusoe [3] use the Code Morphing Software (CMS) to translate x86 binaries into Very Long Instruction Word (VLIW) forms. The translated VLIW instructions are stored in the code cache as superblocks. IBM DAISY [4] translates PowerPC binary codes into its VLIW version as "tree regions", which are cached in the code cache for reuse. IA-32 EL [5] translates IA-32 instructions into Itanium instructions. It is a two-stage translator that begins with a simple basic block translator and invokes an optimizing translator once hotspot code is detected. Both the basic code blocks and superblocks are stored in the code cache. The well-known optimization system HP Dynamo [6] optimizes the hotspot of the source code and stores the highly optimized code in the code cache in terms of trace. Other successful translation /optimization systems which employ code caches include: FX!32 [7], UQDBT [8], Strata [9], DELI [10], et al.

As the performance of the code cache system has great impact on the translation system and optimization system, quite a few researchers put their interests on the approaches to improving the performance of the code cache system. Kim works on the code cache management schemes and proposed a generational code cache based code cache management algorithm [1]. This algorithm categorizes code traces based on their expected lifetimes and groups traces with similar lifetimes together in separate storage areas. Using this algorithm, short-lived code traces can easily be removed from a code cache without introducing fragmentation and without suffering the performance penalties associated with evicting long-lived code traces.

A software prediction approach is proposed in [11] to predict the target address of the indirect control transfer instructions. The principle of the prediction based approach is to compare the content of the register of the indirect control transfer instruction with the pre-defined target SPC, which is most likely to be the real target SPC. If the value of the register matches with the predicted SPC, the control flow can be easily transferred to the required TPC which is corresponding to the pre-defined SPC. The software prediction based approach actually provides a kind of chaining of the indirect control transfer instruction and is easy to be implemented. The prediction depth can be configured flexibly. The shortage of this approach is that a large number of instructions should be inserted into the translated codes in order to implement the prediction. This means considerable code expansion which may offset the performance improvement. Especially in the case that the prediction is failed after several times of comparing, the software approach will cause extra overhead.

In our previous work, we proposed a software implemented Direct Control Transfer instruction Chaining (DCTC) [2] approach to chain the direct control transfer instructions. The principle of DCTC is to replace the target address of the direct control transfer instruction with its TPC, in order to reduce the context switching and the address mapping table lookup operations. DCTC adopts an address mapping table and a special direct control transfer target address mapping table to assist the chaining process. DCTC has been demonstrated its efficiency in chaining the direct control transfer instructions. If the indirect control transfer instructions can be chained effectively, the performance of a code cache system can be further improved.

In this paper, we focus on improving the performance of the code cache through chaining the indirect control transfer instructions.

## 3   Software and Hardware Support for IDCTC

### 3.1   Hardware Support for IDCTC

It is difficult to chaining the indirect control transfer instructions through only software approaches. Thus, in this paper, we propose a novel hardware support called Indirect Transfer Target Buffer (ITTB) to support chaining the indirect control transfer instructions to their translated targets.

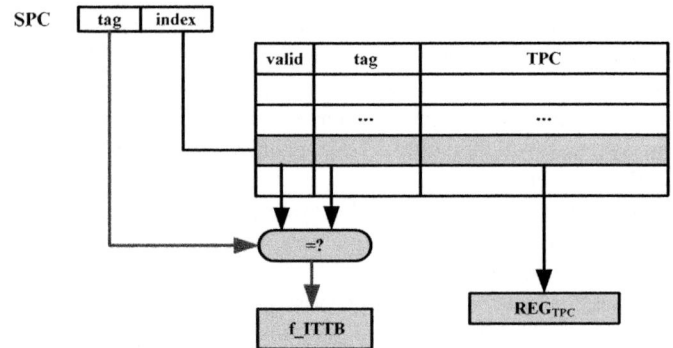

**Fig. 2.** Infrastructure of indirect transfer target buffer

**Table 1.** Special purpose registers custom designed for ITTB

| Register | Description |
|---|---|
| REG$_{TPC}$ | Register used to store address of the translated code block |
| f_ITTB | Status flag indicting whether ITTB is hit or not; f_ITTB can be implemented using reserved bit of the status flag register of the microprocessor as most modern microprocessors have reserved status bits and it can also be implemented through custom individual status flag register |

ITTB is implemented as a high speed buffer on chip which can provide one read/write operation in one clock cycle. ITTB is used to store the frequently accessed target address of the control transfer instructions. Obviously, ITTB provide a copy of AMT. As ITTB is a hardware approach, target address can be looked up quickly. The principle of ITTB is similar to Translation Look-aside Buffer (TLB) [12] used in the management of virtual memory space. Fig. 2 shows the infrastructure of ITTB.

ITTB stores the corresponding TPC of indirect control transfer instructions, and is accessed by the SPC of the indirect control transfer instructions. SPC is divided into tag and index, while ITTB use valid bit and tag to check whether the required SPC is matched in ITTB. ITTB can be implemented as a cache, which can be organized with multi-way associativity and replacement policies. The ITTB accessing result will update the flag f_ITTB, if it is hit, this flag will be set as 1, or it will be cleared. If it is hit in ITTB, the required TPC will be written into the special purpose register REG$_{TPC}$, which is custom designed in the microprocessor for ITTB. Table 1 gives out the description of f_ITTB and REG$_{TPC.}$

As ITTB is custom designed hardware, it should be accessed via custom designed instructions as "search_ITTB, reg" and "store_ITTB, <SPC, TPC>" which are added to the instruction set of the microprocessor.

- Search_ITTB, reg: this instruction looks up ITTB according to the content of the register '"reg", which is corresponding to the register used by the register control transfer instructions. The value of "reg" is the SPC of the target address.
- Store_ITTB, <SPC, TPC>: this instruction update the corresponding ITTB element related to SPC with the value of TPC.

The above two instructions are custom designed for ITTB access. Furthermore, the ITTB checking result will be used by other two instructions which should also be provided in the microprocessor as "JMP REG$_{TPC}$" and "JITTB, imm". The former transfers control to the address indicated by REG$_{TPC}$ while the latter checks the status of flag f_ITTB. Detailed description of the custom instructions can be found in Table 2.

In some microprocessors, the instruction set architecture may not support the instruction format that one instruction consists of two immediate values. In that case, "strore_ITTB" can be implemented through several register-register instructions. First, write SPC and TPC into two registers, and then execute "strore_ITTB, reg1,

**Table 2.** Custom designed instructions for using ITTB

| Instruction | Description |
|---|---|
| Search_ ITTB, reg | Lookup ITTB according to the value of register "reg"; if it is hit, write TPC into $REG_{TPC}$, if not, clear flag f_ITTB |
| Store_ITTB, <SPC, TPC> | Write TPC into the ITTB element according to the SPC |
| JMP $REG_{TPC}$ | Jump to the address indicated by $REG_{TPC}$ |
| JITTB, imm | Check if ITTB access is hit. If it is hit, transfer control to the instruction whose address has an offset of "imm" with the current instruction, if not, then execute the next instruction. |

reg2" like instruction. How to implement "store_ITTB, <SPC, TPC>" depends on the instruction set architecture of the target microprocessor.

## 3.2 Software Support for IDCTC

Besides the hardware support, DBT systems should also maintain some software data structures to assist the chaining of the indirect control transfer instructions. One is the Address Mapping Table [2] which stores the SPC and TPC of the code blocks. The other is called T-SPC, which is a hash table used to save any possible source programming counter (SPC) of the target address of the indirect control transfer instructions. T-SPC will be updated under two situations:

● During profiling, any time an indirect control transfer instruction is executed, the value (SPC of the target address) of the register or memory used by the indirect control transfer instruction should be written into T-SPC.

● When a translated code block transfers the execution to VMM because of the fact that the indirect control transfer instruction at the end of the code block has not been chained, VMM should write the target SPC of the indirect control transfer instruction into T-SPC.

T-SPC is used to update ITTB when a new code block is translated.

# 4   Indirect Control Transfer Instruction Chaining

Based on the hardware and software assists introduced in section 3, we propose a novel indirect control transfer instruction chaining approach. The basic principle is: 1) to insert specific instructions which will directly chain the indirect control transfer instructions when translating the source code block; 2) to execute these specific chaining instructions before executing the indirect control transfer instructions during the execution of the translated code block.

## 4.1  Insert Chaining Instructions

The first step is to insert custom chaining instructions and update the AMT, ITTB and T-SPC, when generating the translated code block which contains indirect control transfer instructions.

Though, different indirect control transfer instructions may require different sequence of chaining instructions, the translating process or the inserting process is similar. Thus, we take the indirect jump instruction for example. The indirect jump instruction stores the target address in a register. When translating the source indirect jump instruction, IDCTC has to insert those custom chaining instructions at the place where the translated indirect jump instruction should appear. Fig. 4 indicates how to insert the chaining instructions in details. $TPC_{cur}$ represents the address of the indirect jump instruction itself in the code cache. $LEN_{JITTB}$ represents the length/bytes of the JITTB instruction. Similarly, $LEN_{save\ register\ content}$ represents the total length/bytes of the instructions which are used to save the content of the register in the indirect jump instruction.

---

Insert custom chaining instructions during translation

---

1. Update AMT, write SPC and TPC of the current code block into AMT;
2. Insert chaining instructions into the current translated code block at the place where the indirect control instruction should appear;
3. Lookup T-SPC according to the SPC of the current code block;
4. if the required SPC exists in T-SPC
5.     Execute "Store_ITTB,<SPC,TPC>" instruction to update ITTB;
6.     Update T-SPC, delete the SPC from T-SPC;
7. endif

---

**Fig. 3.** Insert custom chaining instructions and update related software/hardware assists

---

**Insert chaining instructions for indirect jump instruction**

---

1. Generate "Search_ITTB, reg" instruction at the address of $TPC_{cur}$ (reg points to the register used by the indirect jump instruction)
2. Generate "JITTB, $LEN_{JITTB}+LEN_{save\ register\ content}+LEN_{stub\ code}$" instruction
3. Generate the instructions that save the content of the register used by the indirect jump, i.e. save the target SPC
4. Generate stub code
5. Generate "JMP REG$_{TPC}$" instruction
6. Return

---

**Fig. 4.** Insert chaining instructions for indirect jump instruction

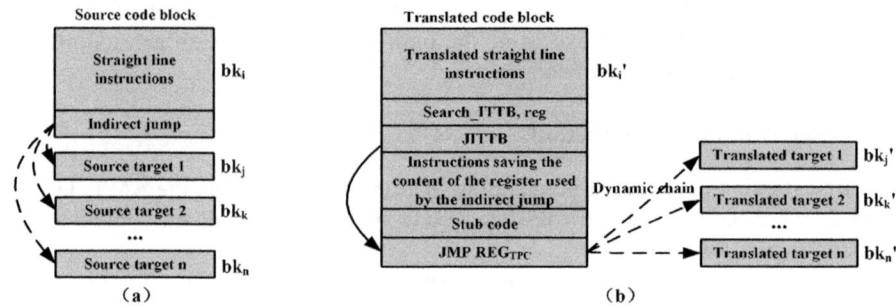

**Fig. 5.** The status of the source code block ends with an indirect jump and the status of the corresponding translated code block

Fig. 5 (a) shows the status of the source code block ends with an indirect jump. Fig. 5(b) shows the status of the corresponding translated code block. It shows that the translated code block has been inserted with the custom chaining instructions. The source indirect jump instruction has not been translated to a local indirect jump in the translated code.

In this paper, we only introduce register indirect control transfer instructions, for memory indirect control transfer instructions, the chaining approach is the similar. The difference is that the content of the memory element should be first moved into a register so as to execute the "Search_ITTB, reg" instruction. Thus, this paper focuses on the chaining of the register indirect control transfer instructions. Moreover, the source target address may need to be calculated by adding the value of the register/memory with a certain offset. In this case, we only need to calculate the source target address by following the source target address calculation rule and then write the source target address into a certain register and then execute the "Search_ITTB, reg" instruction.

Stub code is used when the chaining of the indirect control transfer instruction is failed. The stub code saves the execution context and turns the control back to VMM that the corresponding VMM routine looks up the AMT according to the value hold in the register of the indirect control transfer instruction. If it is hit in AMT, write the related SPC and TPC into ITTB. This is based on the fact that ITTB is a copy of AMT, as the capacity of ITTB is limited, there may be some indirect control transfer instructions whose SPC and TPC have not been saved in ITTB. Hence, if it is hit in AMT, the SPC and TPC of the current indirect control transfer instruction should be written into ITTB.

Other indirect control transfer instructions include indirect branch, indirect sub-routine call, and return. Similar operations can be performed on these instructions to insert chaining instructions.

### 4.2 Executing Chaining Instructions

Though the chaining instructions are inserted into the translated code block, the chaining of the indirect control transfer instruction is finally finished during execution of the translated code block.

The "Search_ ITTB, reg" instruction looks up ITTB according to the content of the register (SPC) of the indirect control transfer instruction, in order to quickly check whether the required TPC is already existed. If the TPC is existed, which means the corresponding TPC has been automatically written into $RRG_{TPC}$, the "JMP $REG_{TPC}$" instruction will be executed so as to transfer the control to the target TPC. If the required TPC is not existed, stub code will be executed that the control will be transferred to VMM so as to lookup AMT or perform the interpretation or translation.

Obviously, the novel chaining approach we proposed is a dynamically chaining method based on ITTB.

# 5  Evaluation

## 5.1  Evaluation Environment

The experimental infrastructure is based on a Code Cache Simulator (CCS) [2]. We construct CCS to evaluate the control transfer instruction chaining performance. CCS is a two-stage simulator which consists of a profiler, a trace constructor, a code cache and a control unit. In the first stage, CCS runs the source code and the profiler collects the execution information. The trace constructor reorganizes the frequently executing source code into traces and stores the reorganized code blocks in the code cache. In the second stage, CCS runs the code blocks in the code cache instead of the source code while executing the hotspots. Detailed information of the simulator can be found in [2].

The benchmarks (gzip, gap, parser, vortex) we use are selected from SPEC INT 2000 [13]. In [2], we have demonstrated that for these benchmarks, a small number of code blocks may cause huge number of control transfers as hot code blocks are frequently executed. Obviously, without chaining, control transfers are costly because of the large number of AMT looking up operations and context switching overhead.

## 5.2  Performance Evaluation of IDCTC

In the experiments, we first let CCS run the benchmarks without chaining, then use IDCTC to chain the code blocks which contain the indirect control transfer instructions.

**Chaining efficiency of IDCTC**
Indirect control transfer instructions realize fast dynamic chaining through accessing ITTB. The target code block may not have been translated when the indirect control transfer instruction is translated the first time and some of the target address is untranslatable instructions [14], this will cause the IDCTC failed. But, the capacity limit of ITTB is the main reason which causes the failure of the chaining of the indirect control transfer instruction. However, because of the principle of locality [12], most of the time, when indirect control transfer instruction accesses ITTB, the required information can be found in ITTB. Fig. 6 shows the chaining success rate of different benchmarks when using direct mapping ITTB with 64 elements, 128 elements and 256 elements. For the ITTB which contains 256 elements, the average success chaining rate achieves 92.5%. Obviously, the hardware ITTB can dynamically assists to chain the indirect control transfer instructions high efficiently. As a result, the chaining efficiency indicates that most of the table lookup operation and context switching overhead can be avoided.

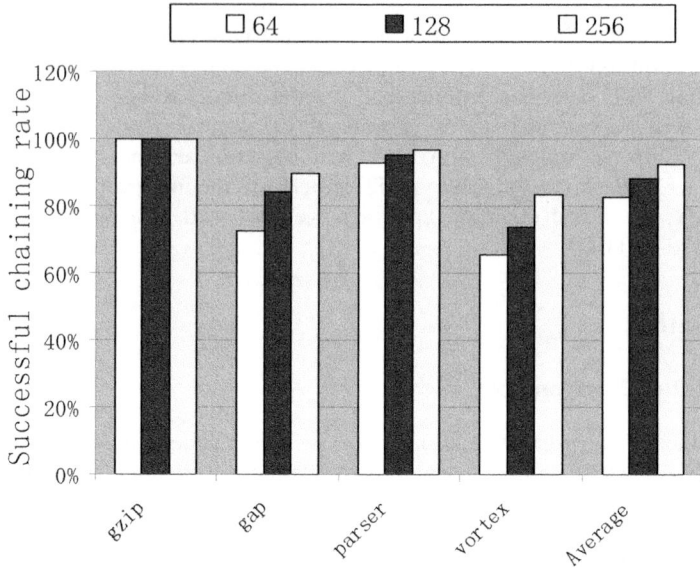

**Fig. 6.** Successful chaining rate of indirect control transfer instructions

Fig. 6 indicates that the successful chaining rate is sensitive to the size of the ITTB. For gap and vortex, the chaining rate is lower, because the locality of the target address of the indirect control transfer instruction is not so centralized in these two benchmarks. However, the increase of the ITTB size can fit the address changing character of these benchmarks.

Though, there are still some instructions can not be chained, they only occupy quite a few portion of all the (dynamic) indirect control transfer instructions.

**Performance improvement of the code cache**

Because most of the indirect control transfer instructions can be chained, the performance of the code cache could be improved. Fig. 7 shows the performance improvement of each benchmark. The y-axis is the performance speedup caused by IDCTC compared to the original execution without chaining.

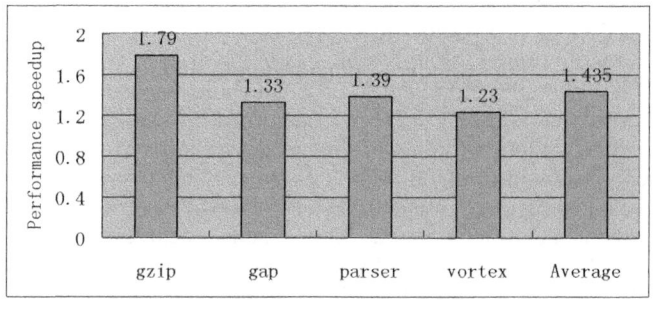

**Fig. 7.** Performance speedup caused by IDCTC

The average speed up is 1.435. This demonstrates the efficiency of our indirect control transfer instruction chaining approach. The performance improvement is determined by the chaining efficiency. As a result, IDCTC performs most powerfully for gzip, but still shows dramatic improvement for other benchmarks.

# 6 Conclusions

Code Cache systems are the key element of the binary translation system and the optimization system. Translated/optimized codes are saved in the code cache in terms of code blocks which ends with control transfer instructions. Conventional code cache systems look up the address mapping table to find the translated target code block according to the source target address. The table lookup operation is considerably costly. Chaining the control transfer instruction with their translated target address can avoided most of the table lookup overhead. The target address of the indirect control transfer instructions are saved in the register or memory and can be changed during execution. It is difficult to chain the indirect control transfer instructions through pure software approaches. In this paper, we propose an indirect transfer target buffer which is implemented as a high speed buffer on chip. ITTB is used to store the frequently accessed target address of the control transfer instructions. Based on ITTB, we propose a novel indirect control transfer instruction chaining method which inserts custom chaining instructions into the translated code block instead of translating the indirect control transfer instructions. During execution, the chaining instructions access ITTB to find the required TPC of the target address. Because of the principle of locality, most of the required target of the indirect control transfer instructions can be found in ITTB. IDCTC is a dynamic chaining approach, in which chaining is performed during execution instead of translation. Evaluation of IDCTC is conducted on a code cache simulator. The experiment results show that IDCTC can bring dramatic performance improvement for the code cache system.

In the future work, we will use CCS to run more benchmarks to further evaluate the efficiency of IDCTC. Further more, in the future work, we will try to merge the chaining approaches of both direct control transfer instructions and indirect control transfer instructions so as to further improve the performance of the code cache systems as well as those binary translation systems and optimization systems.

**Acknowledgments.** This work is supported by National Basic Research Program under grant No.2007CB310901. This work is also supported by the National High Technology Research and Development Program of China, under grant No.2009AA01Z101.

# References

1. Cettei, K.H.: Code Cache Management in Dynamic Optimization Systems. Phd. Thesis. Harvard University, Cambridge, Massachusetts (2004)
2. Xu, W., Chen, W., Dou, Q.: A Novel Chaining Approach for Direct Control Transfer Instructions. In: The IEEE International Workshop on Digital Computing Infrastructure and Applications, in Conjunction with the 16th International Conference on Parallel and Distributed Systems, pp. 664–669. IEEE Press, New York (2010)

3. Dehnert, J.C., Grant, B.K., Banning, J.P., Johnson, R., Kistler, T., Klaiber, A., Mattson, J.: The Transmeta Code MorphingTM Software: Using Speculation, Recovery, and Adaptive Retranslation to Address Real-Life Challenges. In: 1st Annual IEEE/ACM International Symposium on Code Generation and Optimization (CGO 2003), pp. 15–24. IEEE Press, New York (2003)

4. Ebcioglu, K., Altman, E.R.: DAISY: Dynamic Compilation for 100% Architectural Compatibility. In: 24th International Symposium on Computer Architecture (ISCA 1997), pp. 26–37. ACM Press, New York (1997)

5. Baraz, L., Devor, T., Etzion, O., Goldenberg, S., Skaletsky, A., Wang, Y., Zemach, Y.: IA-32 Execution Layer: a two-phase dynamic translator designed to support IA-32 applications on Itanium®-based systems. In: 36th International Symposium on Microarchitecture (MICRO 2003), pp. 191–204. IEEE Press, Washington, DC (2003)

6. Bala, V., Duesterwald, E., Banerjia, S.: Dynamo: A Transparent Dynamic Optimization System. In: The ACM SIGPLAN Conference on Programming Language Design and Implementation (PLDI 2000), pp. 1–12. ACM Press, New York (2000)

7. Hookway, R.J., Herdeg, M.A.: Digital FX!32: Combinning Emulation and Binary Translation. Digital Techncal Journal 9(1), 3–12 (1997)

8. Ung, D., Cifuentes, C.: Machine-Adaptable Dynamic Binary Translation. In: The ACM SIGPLAN Workshop on Dynamic and Adaptive Compilation and Optimization (DYNAMO 2000), pp. 41–51. ACM Press, New York (2000)

9. Kevin Scott, N., Kumar, S., Velusamy, B., Childers, J.W., Davidson, M.L.: Soffa: Retargetable and Reconfigurable Software Dynamic Translation. In: The International Symposium on Code Generation and Optimization, pp. 36–47. IEEE Press, New York (2003)

10. Desoli, G., Mateev, N., Duesterwald, E., Faraboschi, P., Fisher, J.A.: DELI: A New Run-Time Control Point. In: The 35th International Symposium on Microarchitecture, pp. 257–268. IEEE Press, New York (2002)

11. Kim, H.-S.: A Co-Designed Virtual Machine for Instruction Level Distributed Processing. Ph.D thesis. University of Wisconsin Madison, USA (2004)

12. Hennessy, J.L., Patterson, D.A.: Computer Architecture: A Quantitative Approach, 3rd edn. Morgan Kaufman Publishers, San Francisco (2002)

13. SPEC CPU2000, http://www.spec.org/cpu

14. Chen, W.: Research on Dynamic Binary Translation Based Co-Designed Virtual Machine. Ph.D thesis. National University of Defense Technology (2010)

# A Study on Context Services Model with Location Privacy

Hoon Ko[1], Goreti Marreiros[1], Zita Vale[2], and Jongmyung Choi[3]

[1,2] Institute of Engineering Polytechnic of Porto, GECAD,
Rua Dr. Antonio Bernardino de Almeida, 431, 4200-072 Porto, Portugal
{hko,goreti}@isep.ipp.pt, zav@isep.ipp.pt
[3] Mokpo National University,
Muangun, Jeonnam, S. Korea
jmchoi@mokpo.ac.kr

**Abstract.** A lot of smart context-aware services would be adopting location information as context information. However, the location information is also very important information to be protected for users' privacy, security, and safety. In this paper, we propose One Time Password (OTP) in the communication between users' devices and network devices such as APs. By using this approach, APs does not keep user specific information but OTP values, so that attackers cannot get user information even though they access to the log files in APs. We also introduce context-aware service scenario and context information for the service.

**Keywords:** Context-Aware, Context-Services, Location Privacy, OTP (One Time Password), Security.

## 1 Introduction

Micle Altschul, a corporate lawyer of Cellular Telecommunications & Internet Association (CTIA), which is an international association of Wireless Communication Enterprise and Wireless Services Provider, warned the privacy problem in mobile communication. He advised not to use commercial mobile services through open Wi-Fi hotspots such as Starbucks WiFi [1]. This is because the policies and technologies for privacy protection are different among the service providers. The simple use of WiFi can reveal some user's privacy information such user's location. Actually, Sky Hook developed software that can calculate user's location in 20 meters radius using triangulation method of WiFi hotspots [1]. Another example is WaveMarket. This company has cooperated with wireless service providers and has been providing the location-based services which tracks the locations where family members or friends area. The most popular method for protecting location privacy is to use informed consent policies, in which companies let users know what information they get about users and users' locations and get consent for that. Although they try to use these policies, some arguments have been continually being issues, because disobedience of these policies may break all the privacy protection. The problem is that they have hardly mentioned technical issues for location privacy in WiFi. Assume that attackers get and analyze log files or configuration files in network devices, and then they can get users' information including user locations and their routes [2].

A M. Tjoa et al. (Eds.): ARES 2011, LNCS 6908, pp. 321–329, 2011.
© IFIP International Federation for Information Processing 2011

In this paper, to solve location privacy problems, we propose a method of using One Time Password (OTP) in the communication between a user's device and network devices. Once the user moves from one place to other place, all user information will be erased in the log files, and only OPT values are left. This approach is totally different from the existing systems, in which all information is kept in their log files. Therefore, if attackers look inside the log files, they cannot get user specific privacy information. The only information they can get is the OTP values. If network devices have some troubles, the administrator can check the log files and the OTP values to find out the causes of the troubles, but he/she cannot identify users from the OTP values, either. The remainder of the paper is organized as follows. In Section 2, we discuss other research that is closely related to our work. Then we define the location privacy in context-aware systems in Section 3. After that we show some discussion issues for the location privacy in context-aware systems in Section 4. Finally, we reveal the conclusions of our work in Section 5.

## 2     Related Work

John Krumm [1] explains location privacy problem of services which provide user location information. In his paper, he defines that protecting from let other users know where user is and where path user had can be function and availability. He suggests some solutions to solve using anonymity, spatial / temporal degradation, specialized queries, and configuration privacy. However he does not consider encryption and access control. Therefore, if attackers access the log files, they can get user information rather easily. Hulsebosch et al. [2] introduce location privacy problem from anonymous accesses for users and user contexts on ambient context. In their paper, they suggest a process distinction at user location through a security level definition.

Garreti Brown and Travis Howe [3] propose a solution of social network and context-aware spam.

In their work, they mention problems of the location based service of Facebook user, and they argue unnecessary context named context spam receiving problem, by exposing of the user location. Those three researches introduce location privacy problems by their own approaches [8], but they have a common assumption, which is that if users do not leave their information in network devices such as servers and access points (APs), then users' routes or their location privacy do not matter. However, during the process for mobile communication, the mobile devices have to get helps from APs and network devices around users, and these requests cause privacy information to be open [9]. Currently, most of smart mobile devices such as iPhone and iPad are connected to the network via wireless APs and other network devices in the public area, and the users' location may be revealed by analyzing the log files of these network devices.

## 3     Location Privacy in Context-Aware System

### 3.1     Location-Based Context-Aware Service Scenario

Context-aware systems provide intelligent services, and most of them adopt user location as context information. In our work, we introduce a context-aware service which uses location information, and we show location privacy protection method.

## A.    One-Time Password (OTP)

A OTP is a password which is valid for only one login session or transaction. OTP usually avoids a number of shortcomings that are associated with traditional and static passwords. The most important shortcoming that is addressed by OTP is that, they are not vulnerable to replay attacks. This means that if a potential intruder manages to record an OTP that was already used to log into a service or to conduct a transaction; he or she will not be able to abuse it since it will be no longer valid. On the downside, OTPs are difficult for human beings to memorize. Therefore they require additional technology in order to work [13]. OTP generation algorithms typically make use of randomness. This is necessary because otherwise it would be easy to predict future OTPs from observing previous ones. Concrete OTP algorithms vary greatly in their details. Various approaches for the generation of OTPs are listed below.

- Based on time-synchronization between the authentication server and the client providing the password (OTPs are valid only for a short period of time)
- Using a mathematical algorithm to generate a new password based on the previous password (OTPs are, effectively a chain and must be used in a predefined order).
- Using a mathematical algorithm where the new password is based on a challenge (e.g., a random number chosen by the authentication server or transaction details) and/or a counter.

There are also different ways to make the user aware of the next OTP to use. Some systems use special electronic tokens that the user carries and that generate OTPs and show them using a small display. Other systems consist of software that runs on the user's mobile phone. Yet other systems generate OTPs on the server-side and send them to the user using an out-of-band channel such as SMS messaging. Finally, in some systems, OTPs are printed on paper that the user is required to carry with them [13]. Step (1) of OTP application in Location Hide Algorithm (LHA) in Section 4.2 points this method which connects OTP value to devices ID.

## B.    Scenario

*Before Shella goes to bed, she inputs her tomorrow's plain in her device: 1) to wake up at 7 am, 2) to visit a cafe at 8 am near her house, 3) to meet her friend at 9 am, 4) to buy a Jacket in black in A shop, a brown boots in B shop, and 5) to visit C book store and check some books which have been published recently.* [6][7] [Figure 1].

In the scenario, we have three things to consider as shown below.  Case 1 and 2 show some context-aware services using location information, and Case 3 shows location privacy issues in these services.

**Case 1:** Shop A and Shop B are able to send new information to Shella as soon as she shows up near their stores. Furthermore, they can recommend some products to her based on her purchase history at their stores.

**Case 2:** Book store C also sends the new book list to her according to her book purchase history and her favorite genre.

**Case 3:** Location Privacy: Shella uses wireless network by connecting to wireless APs when she is in a cafe, on Outlet Street, and in bookstore. And this wireless connection enables her to get smart services from stores. However, attackers can get her locations and her movement route by analyzing data stored in APs.

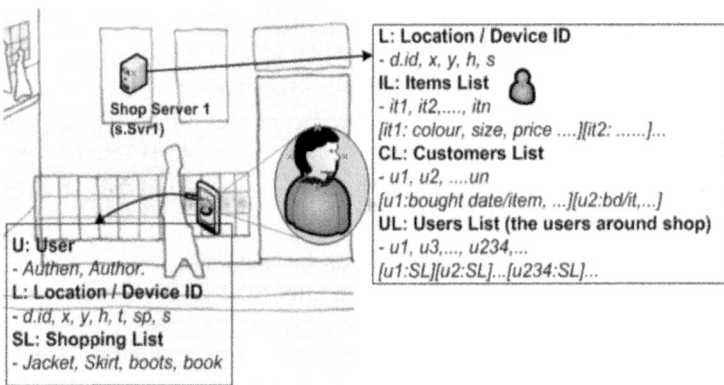

**Fig. 1.** Service Scenario. Shella tries to put that item (Jacket) on her AVATAR in her device without her directly wearing in that shop (one part-Book Store C and Shop B are in another area not in figure).

Fig.1 shows the service scenario in detail, and context information for the services. In that figure, Shella moves from one place to new place near AP *pn2,* and she gets services from stores near her location. Before she arrives at *pn2*, she got services from other *pn#*, and then servers and AP *pn#* keep her information in their log files or database. In this situation, if attackers access to the log files or database, then they can trace her location and s.

## 3.2   Context Classification

In context-aware systems, context determines service contents, and/or triggers event driven services. In Fig. 1 service scenario, context for the service consists of user location and other information such as user's purchase history and user's favorite genre. For the service, all context information is not only stored in her device, but also stored in all network devices around her [5][7]. At present location, she references Shop A, Shop B, Shop C, *pn2* and user contexts. As we see Fig. 2, *pn2* keeps all information about near around shops. Also, all shops have user's purchase history information (CLs in Shop A, B and C), and the purchase information is represented as `u1:bought date/item` in Shop A. This information is used to evaluate her purchase intention, and to recommend suitable goods to her on her visit [7]. She can also get some similar information by sharing or publishing her interests in goods of Shop A, B, and C. At this time, *pn2* are keeping information of Shop A, B and C. Also, it already has users' information that is in area (present information) or was in area (past information). Finally all shops can reference them.

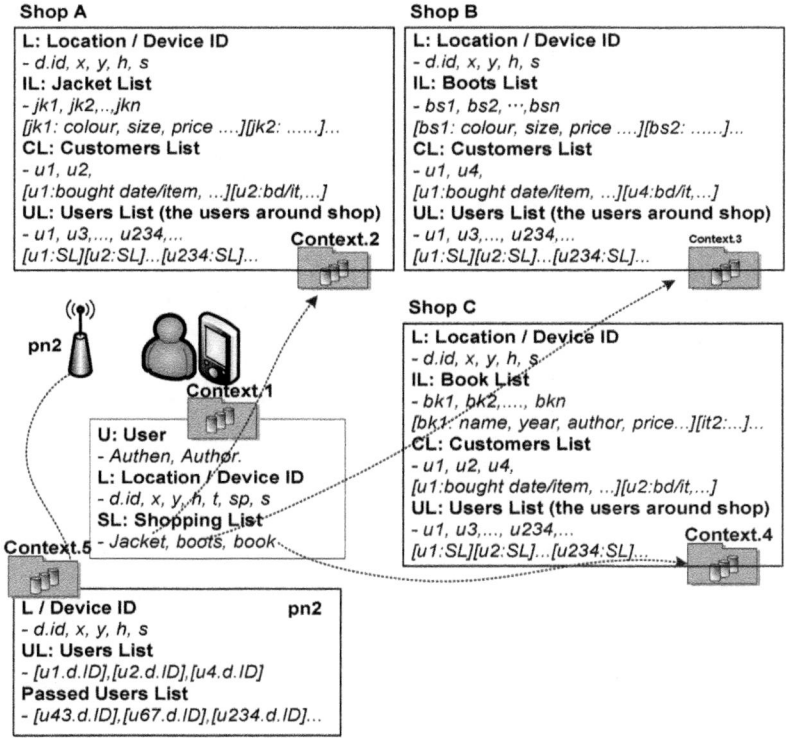

**Fig. 2.** Context Information for Service Scenario

## 4   Discussion

In section 4, we show seven UML sequence diagrams which define what actions are conducted while she moves around. Fig. 3 shows the sequence diagrams according to service scenario.

### 4.1   Sequence Diagrams

Fig. 3-(a) shows how her device is connected to the wireless network. Undoubtedly, it uses information in *pn2*. Fig. 3-(b) is the diagram that she adds her plan and her interesting goods to look for and to buy; usually she takes it before she goes out. Fig. 3-(c) shows her location.

Fig. 3-(d) illustrates how to evaluate Shella's preference based on her purchase history and it also shows how to recommend goods to her according to her preference information.   Fig. 3-(e) is about to get detailed information about a specific goods. Fig. 3-(f) is the step to optimize the promotion for a specific user; it helps some users to organize SNS with them who are going to buy the same goods in future. At last, in Fig. 3-(g), she puts her buying goods on cyber character in her device, after that, she catches how good that before she buys.

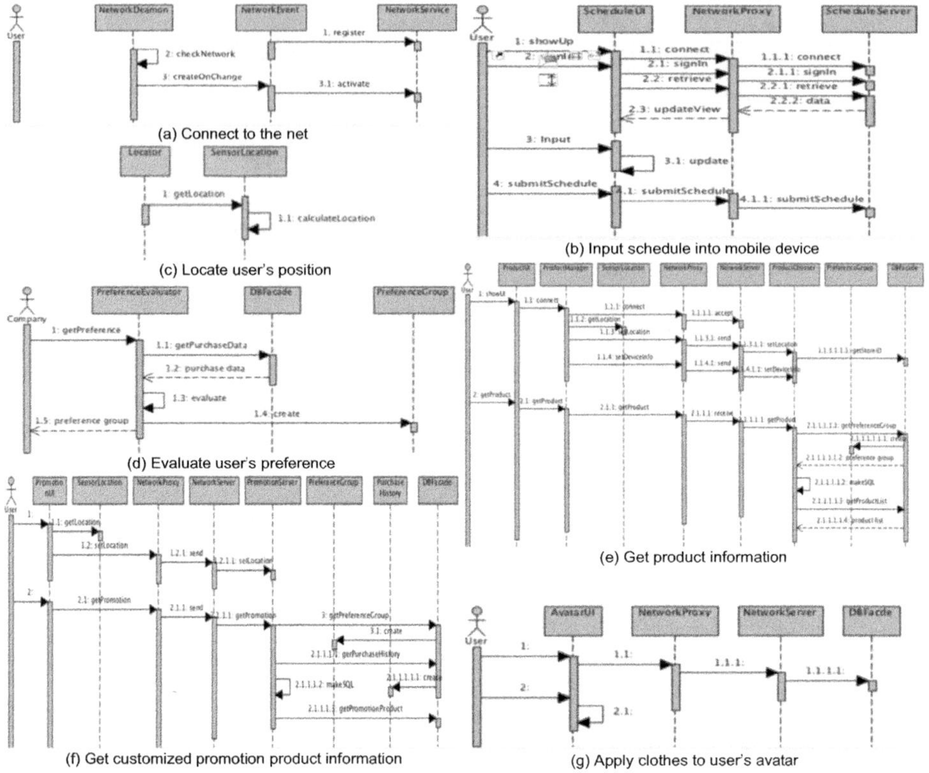

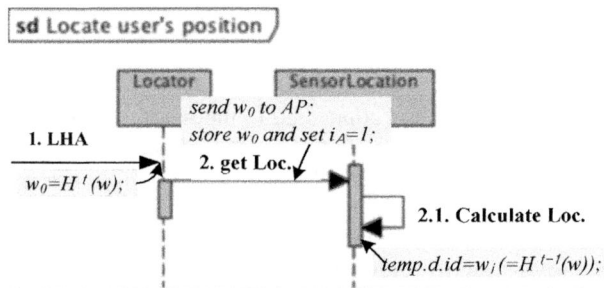

**Fig. 3.** Service Sequence Diagrams

## 4.2    Location Hide Algorithm (LHA)

Fig. 4 explains an algorithm named Location Hide Algorithm (LHA), which protects user's location and their routes with location hide flow [1].

**sd Locate user's position**

send $w_0$ to AP;
store $w_0$ and set $i_A=1$;

1. LHA

$w_0=H^t(w)$;

2. get Loc.

2.1. Calculate Loc.

$temp.d.id=w_i(=H^{t-1}(w))$;

**Fig. 4.** Location Hide Flow

A user's location can be known by analyzing stored information in network devices or  pn# which has provided services to users. In Fig. 4, the device information, *d.id,* is registered to *pn2*, and attackers usually use *d.id* information to figure out from what *pn#* the user receives services. Finally they get privacy information, for example, what paths or what *a pn#* she has to get there etc. LHA connects user device information (*d.id*) and temporary registration information (*w_i*), and registers them. After then, *pn* sends all services to *w_i*, and it forwards them to *d.id* which is pending. Finally, it avoids the exposure of user's location by defining *d.id.w_i*. And although the user moves to other area, it is difficult to get the user's routes and present location because *d.id* is deleted in *pn#*.

The below algorithm defines LHA steps that we propose. In step (1) – step (2), it shows how it gets the value (*w_i*) by OTP, from step (3), it takes to connect both *d.id* and *w_i* which are gotten from step (1) through (2). That is, while the user moves, he/she is supposed to get services from *pn2*. At that time, *pn2* keeps *d.id.w_i* information. Because of this process, no matter how attackers analyze log files in *pn2* and get *w_i*, they cannot know whose *w_i* it is. Finally, attackers cannot get his/her routes and where he/she is now.

---

*// Location Hide Algorithm (LHA)*
*Initial Secret(W), HashFunction(H);*
*compute $w_0 = H^t(w)$;*                          *(1)*
       *send $w_0$ to AP;*
       *store $w_0$ and set $i_A = 1$;*
       *output temp.d.id=$w_i$(=$H^{t-1}(w)$);  //send A, i, $w_i$*
    *process $H(w_i)=w_{i-1}$;*
*set $i_A <- i_A + 1$;*                               *(2)*
*put $w_i$ to d.id;*                                  *(3)*
*define d.id.$w_i$; //d.id-real device ID, $w_i$ is temporal d.id*

---

### 4.3 Recommending Items

Fig. 5 shows the simulation implementation result of context service model that we proposed using jContext[12][13], which is a java-based framework for context-aware systems. In the simulation, Shella moves through (i) Fashion Shop -> (ii) Café -> (iii) Book Store, also, before she leaves from home, she puts her interesting goods to buy today into her device.

*Assume: pn2 provides all services to (i) Fashion Shop, (ii) Café and (iii) Book Store.*

In first place, (i) Fashion Shop, the shop server detects her from *pn2*, as soon as detecting her, it references all registering goods information that she had put before she leaves from her home. After that, servers in shops send the relevant notices such as recommendation of Blue Jacket and Leather Jacket. In next area, (ii) Café, that server will not recommend any coffee, because of her physical condition which had already added it by her. In last place area, (iii) Book Store, she gets recommendation book list: Black cat and White hand, because the bookstore evaluates her favorite genre as mystery based on her purchase history. Through those steps, she usually gets them step by step.

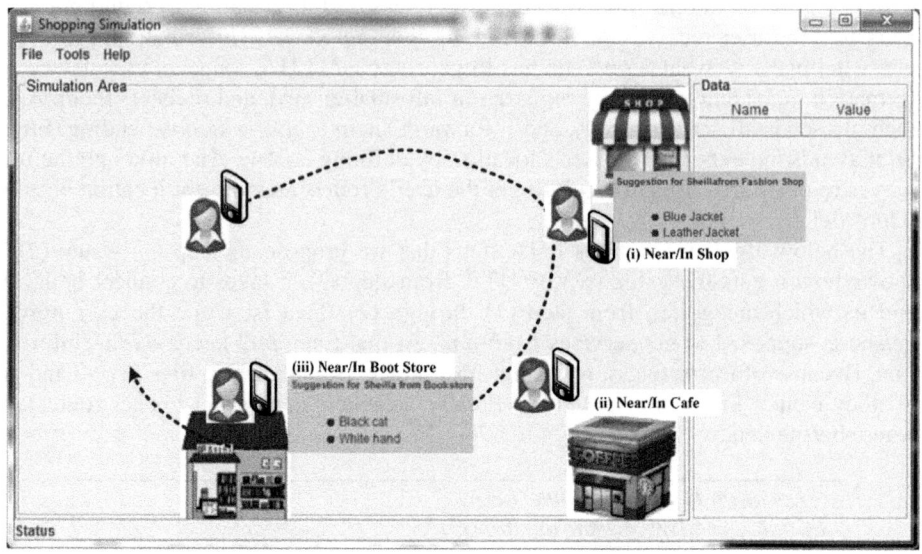

**Fig. 5.** Recommending Items near each area

## 5    Conclusions

In this paper, we studied context-aware services with hiding user location information. To avoid exposure of user devices information ($d.id$) and location ($w_i$), we used OPT, and then we tried to connect both $d.id$ and $w_i$. By building and analyzing a simulation implementation, a user, Shella, can get her interesting notices according to her location which registered already before she goes out. Finally, she gets the relevant information from Fashion Store, Café and Book Store with $d.id$ *(hidden)* and $w_i$ *(open)* which set for service and for user location protection. In the future, we will add social network concept to this systems so that users who are in same area and have similar purpose communicate each other in ad hoc manner. Also, we will study some service scenarios illustrated in Fig. 3 in detail.

**Acknowledgment.** This work is partially supported under the support of the Portuguese Foundation for Science and Technology (FCT) in the aims of Ciência 2007 program for the hiring of Post-PhD researchers.

## References

1. Krumm, J.: A survey of computational location privacy. Pervasive Ubiquitous Computing (13), 391–399 (2009)
2. Hulsebosch, R.J., Salden, A.H., Bargh, M.S., Ebben, P.W.G., Reitsma, J.: Context sensitive access control. In: Proceedings of the Tenth ACM Symposium on Access Control Models and Technologies, SACMAT 2005, pp. 111–119 (2005)

3. Brown, G., Howe, T., Ihbe, M., Prakash, A., Borders, K.: Social Networks and Context-Aware Spam. In: CSCW 2008, San Diego, California, USA, November 8-12 (2008)
4. Dey, A.K.: Understanding and Using Context. Journal Personal and Ubiquitous Computing 5(1), 4–7 (2001)
5. Sadok, D.H., Souto, E., Feitosa, E., Kelner, J., Westberg, L.: RIP-A robust IP access architecture. Computer & Security, 1–22 (February 2009)
6. Yoneki, E.: Evolution of Ubiquitous computing with Sensor Networks in Urban Environments. In: Ubiquitous Computing Conference, Metapolis and Urban Life Workshop Proceedings, pp. 56–59 (September 2005)
7. Fetzer, A.: Recontextualizing context. In: Proceedings of Context Organiser Workshop, Manchester, UK, April 9-1 (1997)
8. Pieters, W.: Representing Humans in System Security Models: An Actor-Network Approach. Journal of Wireless Mobile Networks, Ubiquitous Computing, and Dependable Applications 2(1), 75–92 (2011)
9. Nobles, P., Ali, S., Chivers, H.: Improved Estimation of Trilateration Distances for Indoor Wireless, Intrusion Detection. Journal of Wireless Mobile Networks, Ubiquitous Computing, and Dependable Applications 2(1), 93–102 (2011)
10. Bunt, H.: Context and aialogue control. In: Proceedings of CONTEX 1997 (1997)
11. Connolly, J.H.: Context in the study of human languages and computer programming languages: A comparison. In: Akman, V., Bouquet, P., Thomason, R.H., Young, R.A. (eds.) CONTEXT 2001. LNCS (LNAI), vol. 2116, p. 116. Springer, Heidelberg (2001)
12. Coutaz, J., Rey, G.: Recovering foundations for a theory of contextors. Presentation delivered at the 4th International Conference on Computer-Aided Design of User Interfaces, Valenciennes, France (May 2002)
13. One-Time Password (OTP),
    http://en.wikipedia.org/wiki/One-time_password
14. jContext, http://sourceforge.net/projects/jmcontext/
15. Choi, J.: jContext: A Toolkit for Context-aware Systems Using Java Reflection and Method Overloading. Journal of KIISE (April 2011) (submitted, in Korean)

# Digital Profiling: A Computer Forensics Approach

Clara Colombini[1,*] and Antonio Colella[2,**]

[1] External researcher at University of Milan, Italy
cmcolombini@email.it
[2] Lieutenant Colonel Italian Army, Rome, Italy
colella@acm.org

**Abstract.** Nowadays investigations have become more difficult than in the past. It is already clear that, in modern crime scene, a vast amount of evidence are in the electronic or digital form and that the computer system or network have a paramount role in researching of indicators and evidence. The correct analysis of log file and the data saved in the system memory, in this new scenario, are crucial for understanding the criminal actions. Moreover, in order to transform these new elements in evidence, it is important, as well, do not lose sight of the goal of the investigative process and namely identify the perpetrator, even in the cases in which the association of the criminal and of the computer, where crime has been committed, is difficult.

This paper, under this prospective, aims to recognize an alternative investigation approach to traditional criminal profiling. Starting from digital evidence left on the computer system, this research suggests an analytic methodology useful to draw a compatible user digital profile in conjunctions to the evidence left on the system.

**Keywords:** Hacking profiling, modus operandi, data mining, criminal behaviour, hackers signature.

## 1 Introduction

The development of modern technology has led to an evolution in the role of digital devices that, now, turned from data containers to a sort of "digital diaries".

The software is being implemented on a growing number of digital devices with a high level of personalization: the agendas of meetings, access to chat rooms, blogs, forums, social networks, etc.., have now turned the phone, MP3 player, game console, satellite navigation, in real custodians of the lifestyle of the individual who normally uses it.

The Digital Profiling, in this scenario, offers a new tool to digital investigation. It analyses the digital memory through specific technical and intelligence profiling, in order to obtain information with which it is possible to reconstruct the user fingerprint and description of its *modus operandi*.

---

\* Digital Forensics Consultant for the Italian Prosecutor's Office, Italy and member of IISFA Italian Chapter, International Information System Forensics Association (http://www.iisfa.it).

\*\* Criminologist and Computer Forensics Expert, Professor at Master of Art in Forensics Science, University of Rome La Sapienza and member of IISFA Italian Chapter, International Information System Forensics Association (http://www.iisfa.it).

A M. Tjoa et al. (Eds.): ARES 2011, LNCS 6908, pp. 330–343, 2011.

The process starts from research and analysis of all the information that can be gathered from "digital footprints" left on PC. The computer is a machine and its user tends to customizes the electronic environment, as well as, normally he do in the real world. Thus, user cannot avoid to leave, even unconsciously, evidences that can be detected, recognized and compared.

## 2  Techniques of Digital Profiling Analysis of a Computer System

The process of Digital Profiling that has been developed in this research includes six steps:

1) identify the goal: what to look for in relation with the type of problem;
2) collect and assess targeted data from mass memory;
3) selection of relevant information and extraction of *indicators*;
4) information matching of data *(indicators)*;
5) collection of information (previously compared) and develop a *"digital profile"*;
6) interpretation of the result in comparison to the initial goal.

## 3  The Method

The Digital Profiling is based on a method that includes mining, comparison and recognition of digital profiles of a user digital device. Identification is done through the comparison of a digital basic profile, built with those data collected from PC and directly attributable to subject under investigation, and all possible profiles extracted from other digital devices on which crimes were committed. It should be noted that the method, upon which is based, is a two-way method, that means you can also start from user digital profile "anonymous" of the device, for comparison with profiles of other devices (also not involved in the offence) attributed with certainty to particular subjects. It can also extract a digital profile of a modus operandi (e.g. cyber attack) to compare with others in order to recognize and identify the author.

The method comprises the following steps which describe a cycle that can be repeated whenever new information is added:

- extrapolation of a basic user digital profile established as "standard profile";
- extrapolation of the users profiles from the digital devices in any other analysis;
- comparison of the profiles in order to highlight convergence-divergence;
- quantitative and qualitative analysis of the convergence-divergence among the profiles for identification of the subject.

## 4  The Model

The creation of model starts from the study of information characterizing the detected files on a PC and the devices based on the memory capacity, and for high degree of customization allowed by all available applications.

The model describes the elements, the profiles, the features and functions of the elements, the sequence of operations to create the digital profile, the comparison, the evaluation of the result.

## 5   The Characteristics and Functions of the Elements

### 5.1   D - Digital Device

Digital device "$D_i$ " means:

- any digital device provided with permanent memory capable of storing files. Example: PC, mobile phone, navigation system, etc..;
- data storage device. Example: Hard drive, smart card, USBpen, etc..);
- remote data storage area created by users;
- virtual machine containing an operating system;
- set of data file access. Example: log file.

### 5.2   Feature - f

For feature "$f_i$" is defined the single basic hardware or software feature, derived from the files stored inside the device and selected on the basis of objective investigation, describing the "digital behaviour" of the user, that cannot be broken down further more in the context of the study. It may consist of:

- file properties (metadata type);
- content of the file (type of information);
- a file may contain one or more feature: they are considered basic features, depending on the purpose of the investigation:
- *Filename*. Example: texts, photographs, music, movies, videos, etc...;
- *Path*. Example: some files seem identical, this feature indicates if this file has the same location in the folder tree with respect to another one (same folder name or set of folders);
- *MD5* (or other hash algorithm).The features provides the mathematical certainty of coincidences among the same files found on various devices;
- *Date of creation, modification, deletion*. These three features provide a history of saving, editing, deleting the same files found on other devices;
- Any type of information relevant to the target can be taken from its content.

### 5.3   Area of File - A

The file that can potentially be considered as feature inside device memory called generically D, is divided in specific areas with expression $A_i$ (D), according to typology and in order to better identified them.

$$\bigcup_i A_i (D) \subset D \tag{1}$$

It defines the $A_i(D)$ as the homogeneous subset of D that contains all the different kind of files that may contain features relative to the device D.

## 5.4  Classification of Areas of File A

Each device has its own specific line mapping file that contains features and available applications. This is a generic classification of the basic areas related to PC. The number of research areas of this feature is flexible and depends on the type of research and applications on the device.

*$A_1$ – Registry File: system users.*
*$A_2$ - Registry File: hardware installation.*
*$A_3$ - Registry File: software installations.*

It is considered as "personal files" all those files stored on the user device, excluding the installed programs, which may contain information that characterize the "digital behaviour" of the users. The area of personal files has been divided by type of file in the following categories:

*$A_4$ - Text personal file*  - Text files were written by the user (notes, memoranda, personal letters, etc..) (file doc, docx, txt, rtf, odt, pdf, xls, etc...) that reveal the writing style. Their analysis can highlight several features. In addition to information that can provide through metadata analysis, other features can be detected by the content of the following files: signature, nickname, proper name, password to access, idiom, misspelling, typing mistakes, reference to a specific event, reference to a particular person, reference to a given object, reference to a place, particular phrases, email address, etc.

*$A_5$ - Personal email messages* (except for newsletters, advertising, etc.).
*$A_6$ – Chats.*
*$A_7$ - Images ((bmp, jpg, tif, etc.)* - Photographs taken from cameras, cell phones, etc.
*$A_8$ - Graphic images (jpg, tif, dwg, etc.).-* Collections  of graphic images, such as DVD covers, CD, thematic collections of pictures, art, comics, etc.
*$A_9$ - Movies video (Mpg avi., etc..)* - Movies made by video cameras, cell phones, etc..
*$A_{10}$ - Audio files (wav, mp3, etc. )* - Collection of audio files stored by the user.
*$A_{11}$ – URL –* Connection logs to personal webpages, FTP connections, etc.

## 5.5  Collection of Feature - F

The analysis of the different areas, points out a set of basic features. However, with Feature F is defined a set of all the individual background characteristics analysed in a digital device.

$$F = \{f_1 (A_i)(D_i), f_2(A_i)(D_i), ... f_n(A_i) (D_i)\} \tag{2}$$

## 5.6  Minimum Feature - m

Once you fix the set of the maximum possible feature detectable from the device, it must be reduced to the features actually present on the device under analysis, according to the specific requirements of the investigation. For a particular device the order is compose an initial selection of features, , which restricts the number to form the minimum set of features. Therefore, the $m_i$ is a consistent feature, which belongs to all the basic features, selected in relation with the specific investigation.

$$m_i(A_i)(D_i) \in F(D_i) \tag{3}$$

The name of this minimal feature is therefore: $\mathbf{m_i(A_i)(D_i)}$   where:
$\mathbf{m_i}$ - identifies the minimum feature;
$\mathbf{A_i}$ - identifies the area belonging to the source file;
$\mathbf{D_i}$ - identifies the digital device from which it was extracted.

### 5.7  Minimum Set of Features - M

A subset $S(D_i)$ in relation to the individual case under investigation is defined as the minimum set of features.

$$M(D_i) \in F(D_i)$$
$$M(D_i)= \{m_1(A_i)(D_i)\{m_2(A_i)(D_i),... \{m_n(A_i)(D_i)\} \tag{4}$$

The set of features is the minimum set of filters applying to the files for the extraction of characteristic information *(indicators)* that will make the digital profile.

### 5.8  Indicator - s

The indicator represents the "single information" collected and analysed in the context of study for the purpose of profiling. It is obtained from the files selected by the application of minimum features filter $\mathbf{m_i}$, during the generation of the digital profile. It is defined as $i_i(l_i)(A_i)(D_i)$ information, in a specific area $(A_i)$ of a device $\mathbf{D_{(i)}}$. $(l_i)$ identifies the file from which the indicator has been extracted. The indicator is a *digital evidence* and can be detected, recognized and compared as well.

### 5.9  Set of Indicators - I

It is defined as the set of indicators $\mathbf{I(D_i)}$:

$$I(D_i)= \{i_1(l_i)(A_i)(D_i) \ i_2(l_i)(A_i)(D_i) \ ... \ i_n(l_i)(A_i)(D_i)\} \tag{5}$$

The set of indicators that characterize all the information is collected from the files. It describes the user device "*digital behaviour*" under analysis.

### 5.10  File That Contains Indicators - k

$\mathbf{k_i(A_i)(D_i)}$ uniquely identifies every file that contains one or more indicators, when:

- $(A_i)$ identifies the area where you found the file;
- $(D_i)$ identifies the device.

The file that contains one or more indicators is the *"source of digital evidence"* confirming the source of the indicator.

## 5.11  Set of Files Containing the Indicators - K

$K (D_i)$ defines the set of files that contain information related to a specific device ($D_i$).

$$K (D_i) = \{k_1(A_i)(D_i) \ \ k_2(A_i)(D_i) \ ... \ k_n(A_i)(D_i)\} \tag{6}$$

# 6  The Sequence of Operations Useful for the Creation of Digital Profile

The sequence of operations includes the following extrapolation of five profiles from a PC:

(1)  the profile obtained from the log files,

(2)  the profile obtained from the files in the user folder ,

(3)  the profile obtained from the files in the remaining areas of memory .

From which are derived :

(4)  the user profile, formed by their union;

(5)  the model profile, which matches with the user profile, but refers to a device selected as the *"sample"* for the comparison with others. From the sample profile are drawn: the indicators or the information characterizing to be used for comparison with other profiles for user identification and the file containing them (test wells).

Having in mind that a PC can identify the presence of multiple users, the above mentioned explanation of the method,  presents an example of the digital profile of a personal computer referred to a single user, in relation to a Microsoft Windows operating system.

## 6.1  Profile System - Ps

Starting point is the log files (Area $A_1$), providing all the information *(indicators)* about the user machine configuration. They will form the profile of system $Ps_i(D)_i$, where ($D_i$) identifies a specific device.

$$Ps_i(D_i)= I (Ps_i)(D_i) \ \cup \ \ K (Ps_i)(D_i) \tag{7}$$

where:

- the set of indicators collected from the log files, called $I (Ps_i)(D_i)$ where:

  ○ $I$     - all the indicators measured;

  ○ $Ps_i$  - identifies the specific profile of system;

  ○ $D_i$   - identifies the specific device.

- the set of files that contains them, called **K** **(Ps$_i$)(D$_i$)** where:
  - o  **K**          - set of files;
  - o  **Ps$_i$**     - Identifies the specific profile of system;
  - o  **D$_i$**      - Identifies the specific device.
    in which:
  - o each indicator consists of a single information  which cannot  be further decomposable;
  - o each indicator refers to one or more files;
  - o each file can contain one or more indicators.

## 6.2  User Profile Folder - Pc

The Second step is the analysis of files stored in folders created by the operating system for each user. In fact, they contains the most "personalized files" made by the user. This creates a profile called PC (D$_i$) (user profile folder), based on the analysis of files in the folder you created on the operating system of the device D$_i$.There is a PC for every user  folder found in the PC memory.

*(e.g, D$_1$.PC OS Windows XP: c: \ Documents and Settings \ SuperPippo \ ...).*

If there are multiple operating systems (including OS contained in virtual machines), each of them should be treated as a separate device. The user profile folder **Pc$_i$(D$_i$)** is defined as:

$$Pc_i(D_i)= I(Pc_i)(D_i) \cup K(Pc_i)(D_i) \tag{8}$$

where:
- **I(Pc$_i$)(D$_i$)** is the set of indicators collected by the files in your user folder, where:
  - o **I$_i$**     - set of indicators collected
  - o **Pc$_i$**    - identifies the user profile folder
  - o **D$_i$**     - identifies the device
- **K(Pc$_i$)(D$_i$)** is the set of files that contains them, in which
  - o **K**        - set of file
  - o **Pc$_i$**    - identifies the user profile folder
  - o **D$_i$**     - identifies the device
  in which:

  - o  each indicator consists of a single information  which cannot  be further decomposable,
  - o  each indicator refers to one or more files,
  - o  each file can contain one or more indicators.

## 6.3  Device Profile - Pd

The creation of the user profile folder is not sufficient to delineate the entire profile of the user machine, since other features can be detected from files stored in areas not included in the user folders. The Device Profile includes those files, for example, contained in directory on other partitions, on additional hard disks, including also deallocated files, etc. .. A second round is done so that, using the feature of all M (minimum feature), which aims to highlight all those feature file containing stored outside the user folders. The Device Profile $Pd_i(D_i)$ is defined as:

$$Pd_i(D_i) = I (Pd_i)(D_i) \cup K (Pd_i)(D_i) \tag{9}$$

where:

. the set of indicators drawn from the files contained in your user folder, called $I_i$ **$(Pd_i)(D_i)$**, where:

   - ○ **I**        - all the indicators measured
   - ○ **$Pd_i$**    - identifies the device profile
   - ○ **$D_i$,**    - identifies the device
- all the file that contains them, called **$K_i(Pd_i)(D_i)$**, where:
   - ○ **K**      - set of files
   - ○ **$Pd_i$**   - identifies the device profile
   - ○ **$D_i$,**   - identifies the device

   in which:
   - ○ each indicator consists of a single information which cannot be further decomposable;
   - ○ each indicator refers to one or more files;
   - ○ each file can contain one or more indicators.

## 6.4  User Profile - Pu

The profiles that are extrapolated so far (see **Fig. 1**) consist of all the elements necessary for creating the user profile called $Pu(D_i)$. It is the digital behavioural model that describes the user interaction with the digital device under analysis. It is therefore composed of:

- all the characterizing information *(indicators)* that are recognized on the entire machine during the analysis,
- all files that contain them.

The user profile Pu $(D_i)$ is then defined by:

$$Pu (D_i) = I (Pu) (D_i) \cup K (Pu) (D_i) \tag{10}$$

where:
- **I (Pu) $(D_i)$** - derive from the union of the three sets of indicators reported:
$$I (Ps) (D_i) \cup I (Pc) (D_i) \cup I (Pd) (D_i)$$
- **K (Pu) $(D_i'$** - all derive from the union of three sets of files:
$$K (Ps) (D_i) \cup K (Pc) (D_i) \cup K (Pd) (D_i).$$
   in which each indicator is no further information from a single piece:
   - ○ each indicator refers to one or more files;
   - ○ each file can contain one or more indicator.

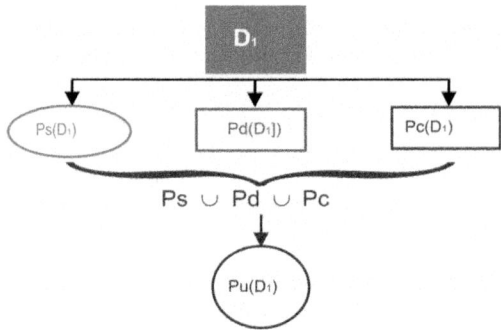

**Fig. 1.** - The user profile Pu

The follow table summarize the coincident indicators detected by the comparison of profiles.

**Table 1.** Sample summary of coincident indicators detected by the comparison of profiles.

| Reference files (sources) | FEATURE (filter applied) | Indicator |
|---|---|---|
| | m8($A_1$) -- computer name | $i_1$($k_1$) ($A_1$)($D_1$) - PC_SuperPippo |
| $k_1$($A_1$)($D_1$) - SAM | m9($A_1$) -- user system name | $i_2$($k_2$) ($A_1$)($D_1$) - SuperPippo |
| $k_2$($A_1$)($D_1$) - SYSTEM.DAT | m10($A_1$) - name of installed hardware | $i_3$($k_3$) ($A_1$)($D_1$) - USBpen Trust |
| | m14($A_1$) - hardware installed-serial | $i_4$($k_4$) ($A_1$)($D_1$) - A01234567 |
| | m13($A_1$) - software installed: nome | $i_5$($k_5$) ($A_1$)($D_1$) - AVAST v1.34 |
| $k_3$($A_1$)($D_1$) - SOFTWARE.DAT | m14($A_1$) - software installed: serial | $i_6$($k_6$) ($A_1$)($D_1$) - AD1234DC1234 |
| $k_4$ ($A_2$)($D_1$) - XXX.DOC | $m_1$ ($A_2$) - Nome file | $i_7$ ($k_4$)($A_2$)($D_1$) - xxx.doc |
| | $m_6$ ($A_2$) - Path | $i_8$ ($k_4$)($A_2$)($D_1$) - c:\Documents and Settings\SuperPippo\Desktop\XXX\ |
| | $m_{16}$($A_2$) - nickname | $i_9$ ($k_4$)($A_2$)($D_1$) - ilgiaguaro |
| | $m_7$ ($A_2$) - MD5 | B1E5CBE1E019E12E5B73EB4AFB619B5A |
| $k_5$ ($A_2$)($D_1$) - NOTAMIA.TXT | $m_1$ ($A_2$) - Nome file | $i_{10}$ ($k_5$)($A_2$)($D_1$) - Notamia.txt |
| | $m_{16}$($A_2$) - nickname | $i_{11}$ ($k_5$)($A_2$)($D_1$) - superpippo |
| | $m_6$ ($A_2$) - Path | $i_{12}$ ($k_5$)($A_2$)($D_1$) - c:\Documents and Settings\SuperPippo\Desktop\XXX\ |
| | $m_7$ ($A_2$) - MD5 | $i_{13}$ ($k_5$)($A_2$)($D_1$) - C1E5CBE1E019E12E5B73EB4AFB619B5A |
| $k_6$ ($A_3$)($D_1$) - message01.eml | $m_{28}$ ($A_3$) -- email address | $i_{14}$ ($k_6$)($A_3$)($D_1$) - superpippo@lamiaposta.com |
| | $m_{28}$ ($A_3$) - email address | $i_{15}$ ($k_6$)($A_3$)($D_1$) - ilgiaguaro@jahoo.com |
| $k_7$ ($A_3$)($D_1$) - message02.eml | $m_{28}$ ($A_3$) - email address | $i_{16}$ ($k_7$)($A_3$)($D_1$) - superpippo@lamiaposta.com |
| | $m_{28}$ ($A_3$) - email address | $i_{17}$ ($k_7$)($A_3$)($D_1$) - ilgiaguaro@jahoo.com |
| $k_8$ ($A_3$)($D_1$) - message03.eml | $m_{28}$ ($A_3$) - email address | $i_{18}$ ($k_8$)($A_3$)($D_1$) - superpippo@lamiaposta.com |
| | $m_{28}$ ($A_3$) - email address | $i_{19}$ ($k_8$)($A_3$)($D_1$) - ilgiaguaro@jahoo.com |
| $k_9$ ($A_4$)($D_1$) - 0261f112b3f57021.dat | $m_{19}$($A_4$) - idiomatic expression | $i_{20}$ ($k_9$)($A_4$)($D_1$) - ola hombre |
| | $m_{16}$($A_4$) - Nickname | $i_{21}$ ($k_9$)($A_4$)($D_1$) - ilgiaguaro |
| | $m_{16}$($A_4$) - Nickname | $i_{22}$ ($k_9$)($A_4$)($D_1$) - superpippo |
| | $m_{27}$($A_4$) - particolar phrase | $i_{23}$ ($k_9$)($A_4$)($D_1$) - non mi hai lasciato le sigarette nel solito posto ieri |
| | $m_{24}$($A_4$) - reference to an object | $i_{24}$ ($k_9$)($A_4$)($D_1$) - sigarette |
| | $m_{25}$($A_4$) - reference to a place | $i_{25}$ ($k_9$)($A_4$)($D_1$) - solito posto |
| | $m_{26}$ ($A_4$) - reference to a data | $i_{26}$ ($k_9$)($A_4$)($D_1$) - 24/12/2009 |
| | $m_{22}$($A_4$) - reference to an event | $i_{27}$ ($k_9$)($A_4$)($D_1$) - mancata consegna |
| | $m_{23}$($A_4$) - reference to a person | $i_{28}$ ($k_9$)($A_4$)($D_1$) - giaguaro |
| $k_{10}$ ($A_5$)($D_1$) - DSC_0001.jpg | $m_1$($A_5$) - file name | $i_{29}$ ($k_{10}$)($A_5$)($D_1$) - DSC_0001.jpg |
| | $m_6$($A_5$) - path | $i_{23}$ ($k_{10}$)($A_5$)($D_1$) - c:\Documents and Settings\SuperPippo\101ND040\ |
| | $m_{32}$($A_5$) -- image of a specific object | $i_{30}$ ($k_{10}$)($A_5$)($D_1$) - yellow car with palate nr. MI01234567 |
| | $m_{24}$($A_5$) - reference to an object | $i_{31}$ ($k_{10}$)($A_5$)($D_1$) - yellow car |
| | $m_{24}$($A_5$) - reference to an object | $i_{32}$ ($k_{10}$)($A_5$)($D_1$) - targa MI01234567 |
| | $m_7$($A_5$) - MD5 | $i_{33}$ ($k_{10}$)($A_5$)($D_1$) - D1E5CBE1E019E12E5B73EB4AFB619B5A |
| $k_{11}$ ($A_6$)($D_1$) - Dvd01.tif | $m_1$($A_6$) - nome file | $i_{34}$ ($k_{11}$)($A_6$)($D_1$) - Dvd01.tif |
| | $m_6$($A_6$) - path | $i_{35}$ ($k_{11}$)($A_6$)($D_1$) - Dvd01.tif c:\Documents and Settings\SuperPippo\Desktop\XXX\copertine dvd\ |
| | $m_7$($A_6$) - MD5 | $i_{36}$ ($k_{11}$)($A_6$)($D_1$) - A2E5CBE1E019E12E5B73EB4AFB619B5A |

**Table 1.** (*continued*)

| $k_{12}$ ($A_6$)($D_1$) - Dvd02.tif | $m_1(A_6)$ - nome file | $i_{37}$ ($k_{12}$)($A_6$)($D_1$) - Dvd02.tif |
|---|---|---|
| | $m_6(A_6)$ - path | $i_{38}$ ($k_{12}$)($A_6$)($D_1$) - c:\Documents and Settings\SuperPippo\Desktop\XXX\copertine dvd\ |
| | $m_7(A_6)$ - MD5 | $i_{39}$ ($k_{12}$)($A_6$)($D_1$) - A3E5CBE1E019E12E5B73EB4AFB619B5A |
| $k_{13}$ ($A_6$)($D_1$) - Dvd03.tif | $m_1(A_6)$ - nome file | $i_{40}$ ($k_{13}$)($A_6$)($D_1$) - Dvd03.tif |
| | $m_6(A_6)$ - path | $i_{41}$ ($k_{13}$)($A_6$)($D_1$) - c:\Documents and Settings\SuperPippo\Desktop\XXX\copertine dvd\ |
| | $m_7(A_6)$ - MD5 | $i_{42}$ ($k_{13}$)($A_6$)($D_1$) - B6E5CBE1E019E12E5B73EB4AFB619B5A |
| $k_{14}$ ($A_6$)($D_1$) - La cumparsita.mp3 | $m_1(A_6)$ - nome file | $i_{43}$ ($k_{14}$)($A_6$)($D_1$) - La cumparsita.mp3 |
| | $m_6(A_6)$ - path | $i_{43}$ ($k_{14}$)($A_6$)($D_1$) - c:\Documents and Settings\SuperPippo\Desktop\XXX\miomp3\ |
| | $m_7(A_6)$ - MD5 | $i_{44}$ ($k_{14}$)($A_6$)($D_1$) - C3E5CBE1E019E12E5B73EB4AFB619B5A |
| $k_{15}$ ($A_6$)($D_1$) - El dindondero.mp3 | $m_1(A_6)$ - nome file | $i_{45}$ ($k_{14}$)($A_6$)($D_1$) - El dindondero.mp3 |
| | $m_6(A_6)$ - path | c:\Documents and Settings\SuperPippo\Desktop\XXX\miomp3\ |
| | $m_7(A_6)$ - MD5 | $i_{46}$ ($k_{14}$)($A_6$)($D_1$) - E6E5CBE1E019E12E5B73EB4AFB619B5A |
| $k_{16}$ ($A_6$)($D_1$) - History.dat | $m_{40}(A_9)$ - URL | $i_{47}$ ($k_{16}$)($A_6$)($D_1$) - http://www.facebook.com/superpippo2345cdk0945.php |
| | $m_{40}(A_9)$ - URL | $i_{48}$ ($k_{16}$)($A_6$)($D_1$) - http://www.ilmiosito.com/ superpippo234sdfgoap43.php |
| | $m_{37}(A_9)$ - URL | $i_{49}$ ($k_{16}$)($A_6$)($D_1$) - http://www.lamiaposta.com/superpippo3456asdf567.php |
| $K_{17}$ ($A_2$)($D_1$) - carved[123456789].doc | $m_{16}(A_2)$ - nickname | $i_{50}$ ($k_{17}$)($A_2$)($D_1$) - superpippo |
| | $m_{18}(A_2)$ - password | $i_{51}$ ($k_{17}$)($A_2$)($D_1$) - piùvelocedellaluce |
| | $m_{26}(A_2)$ - indirizzo email | $i_{52}$ ($k_{17}$)($A_2$)($D_1$) - superpippo@lamiaposta.com |
| | $m_{26}(A_2)$ - riferimento a un dato | $i_{53}$ ($k_{17}$)($A_2$)($D_1$) - 339123456 |
| | $m_7$ ($A_2$) - MD5 | $i_{54}$ ($k_{17}$)($A_2$)($D_1$) - D1E9ABE1E009E12E5B23EB4DFB689B5E |
| $K_{18}$ ($A_6$)($D_1$) - carved[123456749].j | $m_{32}(A_6)$ – image of an object | $i_{55}$ ($k_{17}$)($A_6$)($D_1$) - credit card Bankamericard |
| | $m_{26}(A_2)$ - reference to an object | $i_{56}$ ($k_{17}$)($A_2$)($D_1$) - Bankamericard |
| | $m_{26}(A_2)$ - reference to a data | $i_{57}$ ($k_{17}$)($A_6$)($D_1$) - 4935 1500 4556 5784 |
| | $m_7$ ($A_2$) - MD5 | $i_{58}$ ($k_{17}$)($A_6$)($D_1$) - A1E5CBE1E019E12E5B23EB4AFB619B5A |
| $K_{18}$ ($A_6$)($D_1$) - carved[123451049].3gp | $m_{30}$ ($A_2$) – person image | $i_{59}$ ($k_{17}$)($A_6$)($D_1$) - Rossi Mario |
| | $m_{23}$ ($A_2$) - reference to a person | $i_{60}$ ($k_{17}$)($A_2$)($D_1$) - Rossi Mario |
| | $m_7$ ($A_2$) - MD5 | $i_{61}$ ($k_{17}$)($A_2$)($D_1$) - B1E5CBE1E019E13E5B73EB4AFB619B5D |
| ORGANIZATION FILES: Organization of personal files and folders of user "SuperPippo" in $D_1$:<br>c:\Documents and Settings\SuperPippo\Desktop\XXX\<br>c:\Documents and Settings\SuperPippo\Desktop\XXX\copertine dvd\<br>c:\Documents and Settings\SuperPippo\Desktop\XXX\miomp3\<br>c:\Documents and Settings\SuperPippo\101ND040\ | | |

### 6.5   User Profile Sample - Puc

The user profile sample Puc ($D_i$) matches with the user profile Pu ($D_i$) which differs only by definition because it is set as a benchmark for comparison with other devices. In fact , the indicators collected will be used as filters to search for information within the overlapping memories of other devices.

## 7   The Comparison

Once you have the sample profile Puc ($D_1$) from a device, the indicators collected are used as filters for the detection of the same profile on other devices, to detect connections and/or differences. The follow describe the comparison of the coincident indicators in the two different devices.

The final step, if necessary, is the comparison between the dates of creation / modification / deletion of files extracted by the two devices in order to reconstruct the history of user actions on devices over time. The example of **Table 2** illustrates how the search for indicators, are extrapolated from the device $D_1$. The files stored in the device $D_2$ have 30 information characterizing the user, share (75% of filters applied). They show that both devices were used by the same subject. However, this type of comparison is one way: the search characteristic information is performed based on the indicators found in a single device, called "sample", leaving out the analysis and therefore the search for possible indicators on other devices. To work around this problem you can take an additional step of refining the profiles through the cross referencing, which is based on the contents of memory to all devices.

**Table 2.** Comparison of the coincident indicators in the two devices

| Nr. | Feature | Indicator | D₁ | D₂ |
|-----|---------|-----------|-----|-----|
| 1 | organization folders | ... \ SuperPippo \ Desktop \ XXX \ | ● | ● |
| 2 | organisation folders | ... \ SuperPippo \ Desktop \ XXX \ dvd covers \ | ● | ● |
| 3 | organization folders | ... \ SuperPippo \ Desktop \ XXX \ miomp3 \ | ● | ● |
| 4 | path file | ... \ SuperPippo \ Desktop \ dvd covers \ Dvd01.tif | ● | ● |
| 5 | path file | ... \ SuperPippo \ Desktop \ dvd covers \ Dvd02.tif | ● | ● |
| 6 | path file | ... \ SuperPippo \ Desktop \ XXX \ miomp3 \ The cumparsita.mp3 | ● | ● |
| 7 | path file | ... \ SuperPippo \ Desktop \ XXX \ miomp3 \ dindondero.mp3 | ● | ● |
| 8 | personal file | Dvd01.tif | ● | ● |
| 9 | personal file | Dvd02.tif | ● | ● |
| 10 | personal file | The cumparsita.mp3 | ● | ● |
| 11 | file personal | dindondero.mp3 | ● | ● |
| 12 | sender email | superpippo@lamiaposta.com | ● | ● |
| 13 | email recipient | ilgiaguaro@jahoo.com | ● | ● |
| 14 | nickname sender skype | SuperPippo | ● | ● |
| 15 | skypenickname | recipient'sfriend jaguar | ● | ● |
| 16 | skype password | piùvelocedellaluce | ● | ● |
| 17 | idiomatic expression | ola hombre | ● | ● |
| 18 | nickname | ilgiaguaro | ● | ● |
| 19 | particular sentence | you left me no cigarettes in the same place yesterday | ● | ● |
| 20 | in reference cigarettes | sigarette | ● | ● |
| 21 | to risereference | usual place | ● | ● |
| 22 | referenceat the date | 24/07 / 2010 | ● | ● |
| 23 | object reference | Bankamericardns 4935 1500 4556 5784 | ● | ● |
| 24 | reference no phone | 339123456 | ● | ● |
| 25 | refers to vehicles | with yellow number plate Car MI01234567 | ● | ● |
| 26 | url | http://www.facebook.com/superpippo2345cdk0945.php | ● | ● |
| 27 | url | http://www.ilmiosito.com/superpippo234sdfgoap43.php | ● | ● |
| 28 | url | http://www.lamiaposta.com/superpippo3456asdf567.php | ● | ● |
| 29 | hardware | USBpen Trust sn A01234567 | ● | ● |
| 30 | software | v1.34 sn AVAST AD1234DC1234 | ● | ● |

## 8  Cross Comparison

The step consists of crossing the analysis of all the information gathered for each device (see **Fig. 2**). Its implementation involves the following steps:

1. Puc sample extrapolation of user profiles of all devices in the analysis, each of which will consist of:
   - union of the three sets of indicators reported: $I(Ps)(D_i) \cup I(Pc)(D_i) \cup I(Pd)(D_i)$;
   - union of three sets of files:  $K(Ps)(D_i) \cup K(Pc)(D_i) \cup K(Pd)(D_i)$.
2. extraction of the indicators **I (Pu) (D_i)**  and its files **K(Pu) (D_i)**  from each profile;
3. the application of each set of filters drawn from the indicators **I(Pu)(D_i)**  to each of the devices;
4. update individual profiles to new indicators identified.

The procedure, though having the disadvantage of lengthening lead times, may prove useful in cases where the information obtained from the analysis of a single device are not very significant because it allows  to analyse the data in all devices,  increase the number of indicators obtained and make  more consistent the user profiles. It's also allows to detect any additional users.

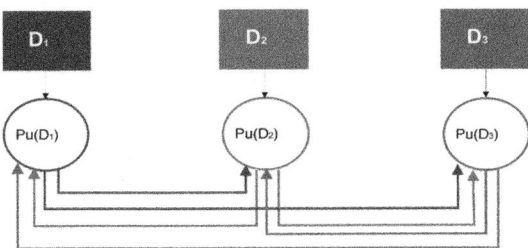

**Fig. 2.** Comparison of cross

# 9  Multi-user Devices

A more complex case (see **Fig. 3**) can occur if the same device $D_i$ is used by more than one person (e.g. PC). Then, a profile for each user can be extrapolated according following rules:

1. build a profile Pc for each user (ie $Pc_1, Pc_2$ etc..) on each of the user folders;
2. build a system profile Ps (eg, $Ps_1, Ps_2$ etc..) for each user;
3. build a unique profile Pd;
4. cross compare each Pc and Pd that produces so many profiles as there are user devices Pu Pc User Profiles folder;
5. each user profile $Pu_i(D_i)$ will be defined as:

$$Pu_i(D_i)= Pc_i(D_i) \quad \cup \quad Pd(Pc_i)(D_i) \quad \cup \quad Ps(Pc_i)(D_i) \tag{11}$$

The comparison between different user profiles folder Pc device profile and Pd are designed to:

- identify their own indicators in the areas of memory included in the device profile;
- extract the files containing them and add them to your **Pdu,** formed by:
  - o   the set of indicators in common with the PC;
  - o   all files that contain them.
- create many profiles **$Pu_i(D_i)$**  how many user folders (not empty) comprising:
$$Pc_i(D_i) \quad \cup \quad Pdu_i (Pc_i)(D_i) \quad \cup \quad Ps_i(D_i) \tag{12}$$
- decrease the size of the Pd profile that will ultimately be composed of these indicators (and related files) are not included in different user profiles.

The end result is:

- *n*   user profiles - the set of characteristic information that describes the behaviour of digital users found on the machine;
- No 1 anonymous Pda Device Profile (if any) - that is, a set of information characterizing not related to those users, which will also include that information on configuring the system does not give users found.

This last profile is not deleted, but is listed as anonymous profile because it contains information that may be useful for the identification of other entities by comparison with other devices in subsequent analysis.

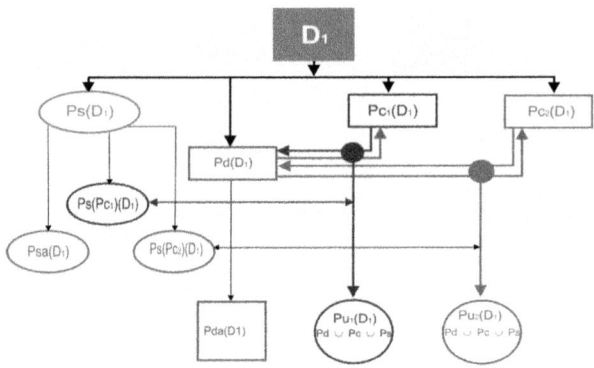

**Fig. 3.** Process of detection of n. 2 profiles in a multi-user device

# 10    Evaluation of Results

The evaluation of the result (operation of close relevance investigator), is carried out both in a quantitative sense (ie, considering the number of coincident indicators measured), which in a qualitative sense (ie, the veracity of information), as even a only information can be found as the solution of the problem posed by the analysis goal.

## 10.1    The Quantitative Assessment

It is carried out in statistical way by calculating the percentage of coincident indicators found by comparing the total of those used as a filter.

*EXAMPLE:* Quantitative assessment of the results obtained by simple comparison (on the case presented in Table 1):

Task 1 - Create User Profile sample PCU ($D_1$).
N. filters applied: ....44        RESULT: indicators extracted............40
Task 2 - Research using filters of the indicators on the device $D_2$.
            N. filters applied: ....40        RESULT:    coincident indicators found.......30

On the total of nr. 40 indicators/filter applied by simple comparison has been detected Nr 30 coincident indicators, which is 75%.

## 10.2    The Qualitative Assessment

This analysis gives to the information obtained (indicators) a value of "relevance" based of the individual indicators in relation to their degree of usefulness for the target. In consideration of the digital nature of the analysis, the sources are not assessed: if properly extracted and verified by hashing algorithms, they are to be considered *"completely reliable."*

With regard to the *information* obtained in the case presented here, it shows no qualitative assessment (under responsibility of the investigator, in the survey), as the specific research described by the example given here was aimed solely to collecting coincident (ie in possession of only two values: *match / no match*), which could bring with certainty the identity of the same subject in question.

## 11  Conclusions

The digital profiling is a new computer investigation tool with the aim of extracting information from memory of  digital devices and assist computer investigator in their analysis and help them to identify a possible user/criminal digital profile.  This type of analysis is suitable to all the devices: to all personal computers, mobile phones, smartphones, tablets etc.

However, embedded devices are not excluded of this methodology: to give just one example, a GPS navigator, even though it may seems at first glance that may not contain data useful to find a solution of a crime, can  provide valuable information on the movements of a subject, such as places where has gone, the usual route that, if compare with the position of his home, may help to delineate the aim of its activities.

Digital profiling techniques can also be applied to the contents of storage areas provided in remote provider and data streams selected for example in a certain time on a computer attack.

At the end, this technique is particularly useful in operations against organized crime, anti-terrorism operations, intelligence operations, where it can be interfaced with the statistical study in the prediction and prevention of criminal events.

**Acknowledgments.** This work was supported by IISFA Italian Chapter, International Information System Forensics Association (http://www.iisfa.it), and does not reflect the official policy or position of the University of Milan and Italian Army General Staff.

## References

1. Casey, E.: Digital evidence & computer crime, 2nd edn. Elsevier Academic Press, Amsterdam (2004)
2. Loia, V., Mattiucci, M., Senatore, S., Veniero: Computer Crime Investigation by Means of Fuzzy Semantic Maps, M. Web Intelligence and Intelligent Agent Technologies (2009)
3. Picozzi, M., Zappalà, A.: Criminal Profiling, dall'analisi della scena del delitto al profilo psicologico del criminale. McGraw-Hill, New York (2002)
4. Turvey, B.: Deductive Criminal Profiling: Comparing Applied Methodologies Between Inductive and Deductive Criminal Profiling Tecniques. Knowledge Solutions Library (January 1998)

# New Steganographic Techniques for the OOXML File Format

Aniello Castiglione[1,*], Bonaventura D'Alessio[1]
, Alfredo De Santis[1], and Francesco Palmieri[2]

[1] Dipartimento di Informatica "R. M. Capocelli"
Università degli Studi di Salerno, I-84084 Fisciano (SA), Italy
Tel.:+39089969594; Fax: +39089969594
castiglione@{ieee,acm}.org, bdalessio@dia.unisa.it, ads@dia.unisa.it
[2] Dipartimento di Ingegneria dell'Informazione
Seconda Università degli Studi di Napoli, I-81031 Aversa (NA), Italy
francesco.palmieri@unina.it

**Abstract.** The simplest container of digital information is the file and among the vast array of files currently available, MS-Office files are the most widely used. The "Microsoft Compound Document File Format" (MCDFF) has often been used to host secret information. The new format created by Microsoft, first used with MS-Office 2007, makes use of a new standard, the "Office Open XML Formats" (OOXML). The benefits include that the new format introduces the OOXML format, which lowers the risk of information leakage, as well as the use of MS-Office files as containers for steganography.

This work presents some new methods of embedding information into the OOXML file format which can be extremely useful when using MS-Office documents in steganography. The authors highlight how the new methods introduced in this paper can also be used in many other scenarios, not only in MS-Office documents. An evaluation of the limits of the proposed methods is carried out by comparing them against the tool introduced by Microsoft to sanitize MS-Office files. The methods presented can be combined in order to extend the amount of data to be hidden in a single cover file.

**Keywords:** Steganography, OOXML Format, Stegosystem, Document Steganography,Microsoft Office Document, Information Hiding, Document Metadata, Covert Channel.

## 1 Introduction

The MS-Office suite is, without a doubt, the most widely used word-processing tool for preparing and writing documents, spreadsheets and presentations [13]. Therefore, the possibility to hide information inside them is a challenge that probably concerns many different parties. Starting with the 2007 version (MS-Office 2007), Microsoft has completely changed the format of its files increasing,

---

* Corresponding author

A M. Tjoa et al. (Eds.): ARES 2011, LNCS 6908, pp. 344–358, 2011.
© IFIP International Federation for Information Processing 2011

among other things, the level of security and thus making it more difficult to hide information inside them. In fact, it has gone from using the old binary format to the new OOXML [5], which uses XML files. In addition to guarantee a significantly high level of "privacy and security", it has also introduced the feature *Document Inspector*, which makes it possible to quickly identify and remove any sensitive, hidden and personal information. It is therefore evident that the old methodologies of Information Hiding that exploit the characteristics of the binary files of MS-Office are no longer applicable to the new XML structures. However, the steganography techniques that take advantage of the functions offered by the Microsoft suite( [7], [8], [9], [10]), are still valid, and therefore independent from the version used. The new format offers new perspectives, as proposed by Garfinkel et al. [6] as well as Park et al. [15]. Both authors describe methodologies which use characteristics that do not conform to the OOXML standard and therefore can be characterized by searching for abnormal content type that is not described in the OOXML specifications inside the file.

This study proposes and analyzes four new steganography techniques for MS-Office files, with only the first not taking advantage of characteristics that do not conform to the OOXML standard.

The remaining of this paper is structured as follows. Section 2 introduces the OOXML standard and the features of the Document Inspector. Section 3 discusses the methodology that takes advantage of the possibility to use different compression algorithms in generating MS-Office files. Section 4 highlights how it is possible to hide data in the values of the attribute that specifies a unique identifier used to track the editing session (revision identifier). In Section 5 a methodology, that uses images not visualized by MS-Office, but present in the file, is analyzed in order to hide information. Section 6 illustrates how the macro of MS-Office can be used to hide information. In Section 7 the methodologies are compared, verifying the overhead introduced as well as the resulting behavior of save actions.

## 2   The OOXML Format

Starting with the 2007 version, Microsoft has adopted the OOXML format based on XML (XML-based file format). In fact, Microsoft has begun the transition from the old logic, that saw the generation of a binary file format, to a new one that uses XML files. The Extensible Markup Language (XML) is used for the representation of structured data and documents. It is a markup language and, thus, composed of instructions, defined as tags or markers. Therefore, in XML a document is described, in form and content, by a sequence of elements. Every element is defined by a *tag* or a pair *start-tag/end-tag*, which can have one or more attributes. These attributes define the properties of the elements in terms of values. The OOXML format is based on the principle that even a third party, without necessarily owning product rights, can extract and relocate the contents of the MS-Office file by only using standard transformation methods. This is possible because XML text is clearly written and therefore visible and modifiable with any text editor. Moreover, OLE attachments are present in the source file format and therefore can be visualized with any compatible viewer.

Distinguishing documents produced in this new format is easy due to the file extensions being characterized by an "*x*" at the end, with the file Word, Excel and PowerPoint respectively being *.docx, .xlsx, .pptx.* An additional feature is that a macro is not activated unless specified by the user. In this case, the extension of the files changes by adding "*m*" rather than "*x*" and thus become *.docm, .xlsm, .pptm.* The new structure of an OOXML file, which is based on the ECMA-376 standard [3], uses a container, a ZIP file, inside of which there are a series of files, mostly XML, and are opportunely organized into folders, that describe both the content as well as the properties and relationships of them. It is highly likely that the ZIP standard was chosen because it is the most commercially well-known, in addition to having characteristics of flexibility and modularity that allow for any eventual expansions in future functionalities [16]. There are three types of files stored in the "container", that can be common to all the applications of MS-Office or specific for each one (Word, Excel, PowerPoint):

– XML files, that describe application data, metadata, and even customer data, stored inside the container file;
– non-XML files, may also be included within the container, including such parts as binary files representing images or OLE objects embedded in the document;
– relationship parts that specify the relationships between the parts; this design provides the structure for an MS-Office file.

For example, analyzing a simple Word document, the structure [4] of the folders and files in a ZIP container will be like that shown in Fig. 1.

Therefore, beginning from version 2007, the MS-Office documents:

– are files based on the ZIP standard;
– contain XML files;
– have common characteristics and formats to those of generic MS-Office files (character format, cell properties, collaborative document, etc.);
– may contain OLE objects (images, audio files, etc.);
– conform to the ECMA-376 standard, opportunely customized.

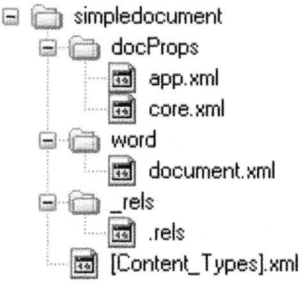

**Fig. 1.** Structure of a simple Word document

Another key concept related to the OOXML format is the modularity, either inside the files or among files, which allows for either the easy addition of new elements or the removal of old ones. For example, the addition of a new JPEG image inside a Word file could be simply performed by:

- copying the file with the *.jpg* extension in the folder named *media* within the ZIP container;
- adding a group of elements in the *document.xml* file (it contains the XML markup that defines the contents of the document) in order to describe the insertion methods within the page;
- adding, in several files of the relationship, some XML lines which declare the use of an image.

The OOXML format gives new opportunities to the community, as indicated by Microsoft [5]. In fact with the new standard:

- it is possible to show only the text of the document. If the file is a Word document, for example, only the file *document.xml* will be analyzed without necessarily opening all the files which contain the remaining information about the document;
- the files are compressed, and consequently are shorter and easy to manage;
- it is simpler to scan for viruses or malicious contents thanks to its textual form instead of the old binary format;
- the new format does not allow to have macro inside it, thus guaranteeing a satisfactory level of security;
- if some of the files in the ZIP container are damaged, the integrity of the entire document could be preserved, and in some cases the main document could be reconstructed starting from the remaining "untouched" files.

MS-Office 2010, also known as Office 14, maintains formats and interfaces that are similar to the 2007 version. The substantial difference between the two suites is that MS-Office 2010 is much more web-oriented than the previous one. The new suite, for example, sends the user an alert message when transmitting sensitive information via e-mail. It is also able to translate documents and deal with different languages, as well as transform presentations into clips. It makes possible to present a PowerPoint "slideshow" to users connected to the Internet. In [11] Microsoft analyzes, describing some of their characteristics, all the new features introduced in the new version, highlighting the updated parts with respect to the old version.

The management flexibility offered by the new OOXML format has obvious implications when dealing with security. On one hand, the clear-text offers the seeming impossibility to hide information. While, on the other, it offers the possibility to malicious parties to read its content and eventually freely manipulate it. It is also well-known that MS-Office files contain data that can reveal unwanted personal information, such as people who have collaborated in the writing of the document, network parameters, as well as devices on which it has been edited. In current literature, there are several papers which describe how to extract and reconstruct different types of information from such documents. Castiglione et al. [1] introduced a steganography system which can be applied to all versions before MS-Office 2007. Furthermore, authors analyzed the information leakage issue raised prior of MS-Office 2007 documents.

In order to guarantee a higher level of security and privacy, Microsoft (starting from MS-Office 2007 for Windows) have introduced the feature called Document Inspector which makes it possible to find and remove, quickly, personal, sensitive and hidden information. More details on the Document Inspector can be found in [12].

# 3   Data Hiding by Different Compression Algorithm of ZIP

Taking advantage of the characteristic that OOXML standard produces compressed files, it is possible to hide information inside a ZIP structure without taking into account that the same file will be interpreted by MS-Office as a document produced by its own application. The ZIP format is a data compression and archive format. Data compression is carried out using the DeflatS format [2], which is set as default, with it being possible to set a different compression algorithm. For example, by using WinZip (ver. 14.5 with the command-line add-on ver. 3.2) it is possible to choose one of the compression algorithm indicated in Table 1.
Therefore, by inserting in the command

```
wzzip [options] zipfile [@listafile] [files...]
```

one of the options indicated in Table 1, the desired algorithm compression will be applied. It is worth noting that, in a ZIP container, all the files contained can be compressed with a different algorithm. In MS-Office files, that are ZIP containers, it is possible to set various compression algorithms.

Not all the algorithms listed in Table 1 are correctly interpreted by MS-Office. In fact, after some tests, it has been possible to ascertain that only the 5 algorithms present in Table 2 are supported by MS-Office. Initially, the tests has

**Table 1.** Compression options in the ZIP format

| Algorithm | Acronym | Option |
|---|---|---|
| maximum ($PPMd$) | $PPDM$ | $ep$ |
| maximum ($LZMA$) | $LZMA$ | $el$ |
| maximum ($bzip2$) | $BZIPPED$ | $eb$ |
| maximum (enhanced deflate) | $EnhDefl$ | $ee$ |
| maximum (portable) | $DeflateX$ | $ex$ |
| normal | $DeflateN$ | $en$ |
| fast | $DeflateF$ | $ef$ |
| super fast | $DeflateS$ | $es$ |
| best method for each file (based on the file type) | | $ez$ |
| no compression | $Stored$ | $e0$ |

**Table 2.** Association character-algorithms

| Algorithm | Option | *Char* |
|---|---|---|
| DeflatF | *ef* | 0 |
| DeflatN | *en* | 1 |
| DeflatX | *ex* | 2 |
| DeflateS | *es* | 3 |
| Stored | *e0* | 4 |

been performed on a .docx file, which has been compressed by using the different compression algorithms. It has been determined that both MS-Office 2007 and MS-Office 2010 do not correctly handle file compressed with the following compression switches: *eb, ee, el, ep, ez*. In such a case, it is shown an error message stating that the ZIP format is not supported. MS-Office uses by default the compression algorithm named *DeflateS*.

The proposed steganographic technique considers different compression algorithms as different parameters of source encoding. More precisely:

– hidden data is codified with an alphabet of 5 elements, the 5 different values that indicate the compression algorithm used;
– the codes obtained through the previous point are hidden in ZIP files associating a character to every file present in the container;
– the compression algorithm applied to the single file corresponds to the value of the character to be hidden.

*Example 1.* Consider the binary string $(10101011011111111001000100001)_2$ to be hidden in a Word document which has just been created and has no characters. This document is made up of 12 files, as listed in the first column of Table 3.

**Table 3.** Decoding table

| File | Algorithm | *Char* |
|---|---|---|
| $[Content_Types].xml$ | DeflatS | 3 |
| $\backslash docProps \backslash app.xml$ | DeflatS | 3 |
| $\backslash docProps \backslash core.xml$ | DeflatX | 2 |
| $\backslash word \backslash document.xml$ | DeflatF | 0 |
| $\backslash word \backslash fontTable.xml$ | DeflatN | 1 |
| $\backslash word \backslash settings.xml$ | DeflatS | 3 |
| $\backslash word \backslash styles.xml$ | Stored | 4 |
| $\backslash word \backslash stylesWithEffects.xml$ | DeflatS | 3 |
| $\backslash word \backslash webSettings.xml$ | DeflatX | 2 |
| $\backslash word \backslash theme \backslash theme1.xml$ | Stored | 4 |
| $\backslash word \backslash \_rels \backslash document.xml.rels$ | DeflatN | 1 |
| $\backslash \_rels \backslash .rels$ | DeflatS | 3 |

The files are listed in alphabetical order in relation to their "absolute" name (comprehensive of the path). Thus, there is an univocal sequence on which it codifies or decodes. In order to hide the binary string, it has to be first converted into a number in base 5. The base 5 representation of the number $(101010110111111001000100001)_2$ is a string of 12 numbers: $(332013432413)_5$. It is assumed that the values indicated in Table 2 can be associated to the various compression algorithms. In order to obtain the stego-text, every file will be simply compressed with the corresponding algorithm associated to the character to be hidden (see Table 3). □

If the MS-Office file contains $M$ files, the proposed technique allows to hide

$$\log_2 5^M = M \cdot \log_2 5 \cong M \cdot 2.32$$

bits of information. $M$ is at least 12, but usually is greater.

## 4    Data Hiding by the Revision Identifier Value

The second proposed method of hiding information in MS-Office documents, which is only applicable to Word files, is to use the value of several attributes that are in XML. The revision identifier *rsid* is a sequence of 8 characters which specifies a unique identifier used to track the editing session. An editing session is defined as the period of editing which takes place between any two subsequent save actions. The *rsid*, as an attribute of an XML element, gives information on the part of code contained in the same element. The types of revision identifier, usable in the OOXML standard, are listed in the specifications of the ECMA-376. These attributes, defined as the *ST_LongHexNumber* simple type, are strings of 8 hexadecimal characters:

$$(x_0x_1x_2x_3x_4x_5x_6x_7) : x_i \in \{0, 1, 2, 3, 4, 5, 6, 7, 8, 9, A, B, C, D, E, F\}$$

All the revision identifier attributes, present with the same value in a document, indicate that the code in the element has been modified during the same editing session.

An example element which contains 3 *rsid* attributes is:

```
<w:p w:rsidR="000E634E" w:rsidRDefault="008C3D74" w:rsidP="00463DF8">
```

It is worth noting that there are three sequences of 8 characters, that represent the unique identifier associated to the attributes: *rsidR*, *rsidRDefault* and *rsidP* (see pp. 243-244 of the ECMA-376 specifications [3]).

The methodology proposed in this section consists of replacing the values of the *rsid* attributes with the data to be hidden, codified in hexadecimal. Thus, if $T$ is the number of occurrences of these attributes in the MS-Office files, the maximum number of bits that can be hidden will be:

$$\log_2 16^{T \cdot 8} = 32 \cdot T$$

due to every attribute being composed of 8 hexadecimal characters. If the information to be hidden exceeds the maximum number of bits that can be contained in the MS-Office document, it is possible to add to the XML file further elements with *rsid* attributes. Furthermore, one more trick is required to avoid the detection of hidden data by a stego-analysys inspection. MS-Office records in the file setting.xml all the *rsid* values that have been used in different versions of the file document.xml. To perform such an activity, MS-Office uses the XML element <w:rsid w:val="002A31DF">. Consequently, when, to hide information, it is used the methodology presented in this section, after having modified the *rsid* values in the file document.xml, it is necessary to insert the same values even in the file setting.xml. In fact, the presence of *rsid* values in the file document.xml which are not present in the file setting.xml is a strange situation that could raise suspicion.

Among the various functionalities available in MS-Office, there is the possibility to track the changes of a document. By using such feature, MS-Office keeps track of all the modifications performed in a document (deleted, inserted or modified text), of the date when they have been made and of the user who has carried out such modifications. Those information, even though can be partially reconstructed by the analysis of the *rsids*, are traced by using two XML elements. Such elements, delimited by a pair of *start-tag* and *end-tag*, are different if used to track a deletion (with the tag <w:del ...> </w:del>) or an insertion (with the tag <w:ins...> </w:ins>).

This element has the following 3 attributes: identification code (*id*), author who modified the document (*author*) as well as time and date in which the change (*date*) occurred (this is an optional attribute). Consequently, all the modifications performed by the same author within the same editing session will be placed in the XML file between the *start-tag* and *end-tag* of the "change-tracking" element.

For example, if the user PCCLIENT would have deleted the text "one" at 09:23:00 GMT of October 11, 2010, the code excerpt will be like:

```
<w:del w:id="0" w:author="PCCLIENT" w:date="2010-10-11T09:23:00Z">
    <w:r w:rsidRPr="00111111" w:rsidDel="00333333">
        <w:rPr>
            <w:lang w:val="en-US"/>
        </w:rPr>
        <w:delText xml:space="preserve">one</w:delText>
    </w:r>
</w:del>
```

That being stated, the methodology presented in this section will continue to work even though the change tracking is activated in MS-Office. Enabling the change tracking means that personal information is inserted into the document. Therefore, the Document Inspector signals the presence of the change tracking as an anomaly and proceeds to eliminate this information from the document.

*Example 2 (Coding with rsid).* As an example, it can be considered that the document under scrutiny has 19 occurrences of the *rsid* values:

```
<w:p w:rsidR="00463DF8" w:rsidRDefault="00463DF8" w:rsidP="00463DF8">
<w:r w:rsidRPr="0074047B">
<w:p w:rsidR="00463DF8" w:rsidRDefault="00463DF8" w:rsidP="00463DF8">
<w:r w:rsidRPr="008C3D74">
<w:r w:rsidRPr="0074047B">
<w:p w:rsidR="00463DF8" w:rsidRPr="008C3D74" w:rsidRDefault="00463DF8" w:rsidP="00463DF8">
<w:p w:rsidR="000E634E" w:rsidRPr="00463DF8" w:rsidRDefault="00463DF8">
<w:sectPr w:rsidR="000E634E" w:rsidRPr="00463DF8" w:rsidSect="009B2A88">
```

Thus, it has 152 (19x8) characters to store information (see Table 4).

Let the message *"this message is hidden in a word document"* (41 characters) to be hidden. The first step is to replace every character of the message with the 2 characters that are the relative representation of the ASCII code (see Table 5).

A sequence of 82 characters is obtained, with a further 70 symbols "0" attached. Thus, a string of 152 symbols is obtained (see Table 6).

**Table 4.** Sequence of *rsid* values

| | | | | |
|---|---|---|---|---|
| 00 46 3D F8 | 00 46 3D F8 | 00 46 3D F8 | 00 74 04 7B | 00 46 3D F8 |
| 00 46 3D F8 | 00 46 3D F8 | 00 8C 3D 74 | 00 74 04 7B | 00 46 3D F8 |
| 00 8C 3D 74 | 00 46 3D F8 | 00 46 3D F8 | 00 0E 63 4E | 00 46 3D F8 |
| 00 46 3D F8 | 00 0E 63 4E | 00 46 3D F8 | 00 9B 2A 88 | |

**Table 5.** Coded message

| t h i s | m e s | s a g e | i s | h i d d |
|---|---|---|---|---|
| 74 68 69 73 | 20 6D 65 73 | 73 61 67 65 | 20 69 73 20 | 68 69 64 64 |
| e n i n | n a | w o r d | d o c | u m e n |
| 65 6E 20 69 | 6E 20 61 20 | 77 6F 72 64 | 20 64 6F 63 | 75 6D 65 6E |
| t | | | | |
| 74 | | | | |

**Table 6.** Sequence of *rsid* values with hidden data

| | | | | |
|---|---|---|---|---|
| 74 68 69 73 | 20 6D 65 73 | 73 61 67 65 | 20 69 73 20 | 68 69 64 64 |
| 65 6E 20 69 | 6E 20 61 20 | 77 6F 72 64 | 20 64 6F 63 | 75 6D 65 6E |
| 74 00 00 00 | 00 00 00 00 | 00 00 00 00 | 00 00 00 00 | 00 00 00 00 |
| 00 00 00 00 | 00 00 00 00 | 00 00 00 00 | 00 00 00 00 | |

Finally it will be enough to replace, in an XML file, the string of symbols in Table 6 to the values of the *rsid* attributes in order to complete the steganography process.

```
<w:p w:rsidR="74686973" w:rsidRDefault="206D6573" w:rsidP="73616765">
<w:r w:rsidRPr="20697320">
<w:p w:rsidR="68696464" w:rsidRDefault="656E2069" w:rsidP="6E206120">
<w:r w:rsidRPr="776F7264">
```

```
<w:r w:rsidRPr="20646F63">
<w:p w:rsidR="756D656E" w:rsidRPr="74000000" w:rsidRDefault="00000000" w:rsidP="00000000">
<w:p w:rsidR="00000000" w:rsidRPr="00000000" w:rsidRDefault="00000000">
<w:sectPr w:rsidR="00000000" w:rsidRPr="00000000" w:rsidSect="00000000">
```

Obviously the message to be hidden would be preferably encrypted before embedding it (see Section 7).                                                                    □

## 5   Data Hiding by Zero Dimension Image

The methodology proposed in this section uses an OLE-object (of type "image"), inserted into a MS-Office document in order to contain the information to be hidden. This object, which is totally compatible with the OOXML standard, will:

- be located in the upper-left position and placed in any of the pages that make up the document;
- have both the height and width equal to zero;
- be placed "behind the text".

These properties will make it possible to hide the image during the visualization or modification of the document. It is worth noting that the file associated to OLE-object, even if declared as "image", can in reality be any type of file (text, audio, etc.) with a appropriate extension (.jpg, .bmp, etc.). Therefore, this methodology can be used in order to hide data of a different nature, and is not only limited to images. The identification of the OLE-object and the decoding of the hidden text make it more difficult to associate files of reduced dimensions and encrypt the message to be hidden.

A simple and fast method to hide information using this methodology is the following:

- rename the file which contains the hidden message with an extension compatible with an image type;
- insert the image introduced in the previous step into the Word, Excel or PowerPoint document;
- modify the layout of the text related to the image, setting the "Behind the text" style;
- move the image to the upper-left position;
- from the menu "Dimension and position" set both the height and width of the image to 0.

The folder where to copy the OLE-object associated to the file varies according to the type of MS-Office document worked on, with it being *word\media* for Word files, *xl\media* for Excel files, and *ppt\media* for PowerPoint files.

Another way of applying such methodology is to work directly on the XML files. In this case, it is necessary – besides copying the file containing the message to hide in the proper directory (of the ZIP container) – to insert in the XML files the elements to:

- relate to the image;
- declare the presence of the image;
- set the position of the image on the upper-left;
- set the image placed behind the text;
- set the dimensions of the image equal to zero.

In order to set the dimensions of the image to zero, the XML `extent` attribute will have to be worked on (see pp. 3173-3176 in the ECMA-376 specifications [3]). This element, in fact, defines the dimension of the bounding box that contains the image. Therefore, reducing the height and width of the bounding box to zero, will obtain the desired effect. Two examples of the `extent` element, respectively for Word and Excel files, are the following:

```
<wp:extent cx="0" cy="0" />
<a:ext cx="0" cy="0" />
```

Where attributes `cx` and `cy` are, respectively, the width and height of the bounding box. In Excel files, among the elements used to describe the image inserted in the spreadsheet, there are:

```
<xdr:from>
    <xdr:col>0</xdr:col>
    <xdr:colOff>9525</xdr:colOff>
    <xdr:row>0</xdr:row>
    <xdr:rowOff>28575</xdr:rowOff>
  </xdr:from>
<xdr:to>
    <xdr:col>0</xdr:col>
    <xdr:colOff>161925</xdr:colOff>
    <xdr:row>0</xdr:row>
    <xdr:rowOff>28575</xdr:rowOff>
  </xdr:to>
```

These elements identify the box of cells that contains the image (see pp. 3516-3517, 3523-3524 and 3532-3533 of the ECMA specifications [3]). The coordinates (line, column) are relative to the two cells situated respectively in the upper-left and lower-right corners. Therefore, in order to reduce the dimensions of the image to zero, it is sufficient to reduce the box of cells that contains it (`<xdr:col>0` and `<xdr:row>0`) to zero. Thus, there is no need to place the image in the upper-left position due to it already being not in a selectable position: the cell with the coordinates (0,0).

In order to set the image in the upper-left corner position of the page, for Word files, it will be necessary to operate on the `position` element (see pp. 3480-3483 of the ECMA specifications in [3]). This element indicates the position of the image with respect to a part of the document (page, column, paragraph). Therefore, placing the image at a distance 0 of the "page" will obtain the desired effect. An example of how the block of elements on which the modification operates, is the following:

```
<wp:positionH relativeFrom="column">
<wp:posOffset>1685925</wp:posOffset>
<wp:positionV relativeFrom="page">
<wp:posOffset>967105</wp:posOffset>
```

The attribute `relativeFrom` indicates the part of the document in relation to which the position will be calculated while `posOffset` is the position. Therefore, upon placing the image on the left, the following elements will be modified:

```
<wp:positionH relativeFrom="page">
<wp:posOffset>0</wp:posOffset>
<wp:positionV relativeFrom="page">
<wp:posOffset>0</wp:posOffset>
```

In order to place the image in the upper-left position, the `<a:off x="0" y="0"/>` element cannot be used due to the position indicated by the $x$ and $y$ coordinates referring to the paragraph and not to the page.

There is a problem for PowerPoint files, where the image, also if reduced to dimension zero and placed in the upper-left corner position, could still be selected by using the "Select Area" function. Moreover, it is not possible to insert an image outside a slide. In fact, the image would be interpreted as an anomaly by the Document Inspector. This methodology, therefore, is not really suitable for PowerPoint files.

## 6    Data Hiding by Office Macro

A macro is a group of commands which make it possible to obtain a series of operations with a single command [14]. Thus, a macro is a simple recording of sequence of commands which are already available in a software. For this reason, there would seem no need for a programming language. However, macro has acquired a programming language that, in the event of MS-Office, is Visual Basic. The new format of MS-Office, as previously stated, in order to guarantee a greater level of security does not allow macro to be saved inside the file. When using macro in documents, it is necessary to enable this function as well as modify the extension of the name file, which will be: *.docm, .xlsm, pptm*, etc.. The structure of the files with macro (e.g. *example.docm*) and without (e.g. *example.docx*) is different. This is evident when carrying out a simple test: changing the extension of the file from *.docm* to *.docx* and displaying the document, the system gives an error message indicating that the format is not the one expected. However, MS-Office can open the file, recognizing it as a document with macro and processing it as a normal *.docm* file.

Thus, it is possible to consider using MS-Office macro as a channel to transmit hidden information. In fact, macro can be seen as a function $F(x)$ with $x \in X$, where $X$ is the set of the inputs. Therefore, it is possible to hide information:

- in the description of the function $F(x)$;
- in the value associated to the function $F(k)$, where $k \in K$ and $K \subseteq X$ is the set of stego-key that are highly unusual inputs.

In the first case, the information to be hidden will be stored inside the macro. For example, it is possible to insert the data to be hidden as a comment to the code or as a value assigned to a variable.

In the second case, as consequence of specific input, the macro has a behavior which generates an output that makes the hidden data visible. As an example, in a Word document, a macro given a word as input, searches for it in the text and highlights it in yellow. There could be another routine in the macro, that can only be executed if the searched word is the stego-key, than highlights several characters in the document in yellow. These characters, read in sequence, are the hidden information. In this case:

- the macro will be recognized as reliable by a user as it carries out the task for which it has been realized;
- inside the code, the characters of the hidden message will not be explicitly present but only the coordinates of the corresponding position in the document;
- only who knows the right stego-key will know the secret.

This methodology does not place limits on the amount of information that can be hidden. In fact, a macro does not pre-exist but is created or modified according to the data to be hidden.

## 7    Methodologies Compared

The Document Inspector, as indicated in Section 2, is the tool supplied by Microsoft to search for and remove any eventual information hidden in MS-Office files. Thus, for an Information Hiding methodology to be considered good, it has to pass the controls of this tool. All four methodologies presented in this paper pass the analysis of the Document Inspector. In addition to controlling and removing hidden information with the Document Inspector, MS-Office also carries out a type of optimization and normalization of the ZIP container every time the file is saved. These operations consist of eliminating everything that it is not recognized as valid for the application (e.g. files attached without a link) as well as reorganizing the elements that reorganize the XML code according to a predetermined layout. As a consequence, the techniques presented in Sections 3 and 4 are vulnerable. In fact, as a result of a save action, MS-Office compresses all files in a ZIP container using the default algorithm (DeflateS) and assigns new values to the rsid attributes. Therefore, in order to avoid that the hidden information is removed as a result of an "involuntary" save action (e.g. automatic saving), it is worthwhile marking the document as the "final version".

Let us make some considerations about the overhead of the proposed methods. In the method discussed in Section 3, the overhead is a function of the compression ratio of the different algorithms. Therefore, the dimension of the file can either increase, remain unchanged or diminish. On the other hand, the method presented in Section 4 has a null overhead if the text to be hidden is less than $32 \cdot T$. In other words, it is necessary to increase $T$ by adding XML lines, in order to host longer secret information. The overhead introduced by the solution proposed in Section 5 is a function of two values: the size of the attached image file, that contains the hidden data and the elements added in the XML files by the technique. Finally, in the case discussed in Section 6, the overhead introduced is a function of the size of the macro code. The four methods discussed in this paper can all be applied simultaneously to the same document. In conclusion, in order to obtain confidentiality, the data to be embedded should be encrypted using a symmetric key algorithm.

## 8    Conclusions

MS-Office documents are the most used file type around the Internet. This makes such file format the ideal candidate for implementing an effective steganographic scheme. This paper proposes four new methods for hiding data in MS-Office documents. The common feature of all the methods is that they pass the Document Inspector analysis. The first technique exploits the chance to use several compression algorithms when creating/managing MS-Office documents. The second technique uses the possibility to conceal information in the values of some special attributes which are normally used to specify unique identifiers when tracking different editing sessions. Using the third method it is possible to hide data by using special sized images embedded in a MS-Office document. The fourth and last technique takes advantages from the adoption of macros for implementing data hiding. In order to increase the information to be concealed in a MS-Office document, all the four methods can be used together.

## References

1. Castiglione, A., De Santis, A., Soriente, C.: Taking advantages of a disadvantage: Digital forensics and steganography using document metadata. Journal of Systems and Software 80(5), 750–764 (2007)
2. Deutsch, P.: DEFLATE Compressed Data Format Specification version 1.3 (May 1996), http://www.ietf.org/rfc/rfc1951.txt
3. ECMA International: Final draft standard ECMA-376 Office Open XML File Formats - Part 1. In: ECMA International Publication (December 2008)
4. Erika Ehrli, M.C.: Building server-side document generation solutions using the open xml object model (August 2007), http://msdn.microsoft.com/en-us/library/bb735940%28office.12%29.aspx
5. Frank Rice, M.C.: Microsoft MSDN. Introducing the Office (2007) Open XML File Formats (May 2006), http://msdn.microsoft.com/it-it/library/aa338205.aspx
6. Garfinkel, S.L., Migletz, J.J.: New xml-based files implications for forensics. IEEE Security & Privacy 7(2), 38–44 (2009)
7. Hao-ran, Z., Liu-sheng, H., Yun, Y., Peng, M.: A new steganography method via combination in powerpoint files. In: 2010 International Conference on Computer Application and System Modeling (ICCASM), vol. 2, pp. V2-62–V2-66 (October 2010)

8. Jing, M.Q., Yang, W.C., Chen, L.H.: A new steganography method via various animation timing effects in powerpoint files. In: 2009 International Conference on Machine Learning and Cybernetics, vol. 5, pp. 2840–2845 (July 2009)

9. Lin, I.C., Hsu, P.K.: A data hiding scheme on word documents using multiple-base notation system. In: 2010 Sixth International Conference on Intelligent Information Hiding and Multimedia Signal Processing (IIH-MSP), pp. 31–33 (October 2010)

10. Liu, T.Y., Tsai, W.H.: A new steganographic method for data hiding in microsoft word documents by a change tracking technique. IEEE Transactions on Information Forensics and Security 2(1), 24–30 (2007)

11. Microsoft Corporation: Compare office professional plus 2010, and the 2007 suite, http://office.microsoft.com/en-us/professional-plus/professional-plus-version-comparison-FX101871482.aspx (visited May 2011)

12. Microsoft Corporation: Remove hidden data and personal information from office documents, http://office.microsoft.com/en-us/excel-help/remove-hidden-data-and-personal-information-from-office-documents-HA010037593.aspx (visited May 2011)

13. Microsoft Press Release: Microsoft office 2010 now available for consumers worldwide, http://www.microsoft.com/presspass/press/2010/jun10/06-152010officelaunchpr.mspx (visited May 2011)

14. MSDN Library: Introduction to macros, http://msdn.microsoft.com/en-us/library/bb220916.aspx (visited May 2011)

15. Park, B., Park, J., Lee, S.: Data concealment and detection in microsoft office 2007 files. Digital Investigation 5(3-4), 104–114 (2009)

16. Wikipedia: ZIP (file format), http://en.Wikipedia.org/wiki/ZIP_file_format (visited May 2011)

# Automated Construction of a False Digital Alibi

Alfredo De Santis[1], Aniello Castiglione[1,*], Giuseppe Cattaneo[1]
Giancarlo De Maio[1], and Mario Ianulardo[2]

[1] Dipartimento di Informatica *"R.M. Capocelli"*
Università degli Studi di Salerno, I-84084, Fisciano (SA), Italy
Tel.: +39089969594; Fax: +39089969594
{ads,cattaneo,demaio}@dia.unisa.it, castiglione@{ieee,acm}.org
[2] Computer Crime Lawyer, Italy
marioianulardo@codicieleggi.it

**Abstract.** Recent legal cases have shown that *digital evidence* is becoming more widely used in court proceedings (by defense, accusation, public prosecutor, etc.). Digital tracks can be left on computers, phones, digital cameras as well as third party servers belonging to Internet Service Providers (ISPs), telephone providers and companies that provide services via Internet such as YouTube, Facebook and Gmail.

This work highlights the possibility to set up a false digital alibi in a fully automatic way without any human intervention. A forensic investigation on the digital evidence produced cannot establish whether such traces have been produced through either human activity or by an automated tool. These considerations stress the difference between digital and physical - namely traditional - evidence. Essentially, digital evidence should be considered relevant only if supported by evidence collected using traditional investigation techniques. The results of this work should be considered by anyone involved in a Digital Forensics investigation, due to it demonstrating that court rulings should not be based only on digital evidence, with it always being correlated to additional information provided by the various disciplines of Forensics Sciences.

**Keywords:** Digital Evidence, Digital Investigation, Digital Forensics, Anti-Forensics, Counter-Forensics, False Digital Evidence, Automated Alibi, False Alibi, Digital Alibi, False Digital Alibi.

## 1 Introduction

### 1.1 The Digital Evidence

The use of digital technology is rapidly growing. The number of Internet users in the world is almost 2 billion, with a penetration of 28.7% of the world population [1]. As a consequence, more and more crimes are performed on the Internet or have something to do with digital equipment. For these reasons, there is an increase in the amount of digital evidence being used in courtrooms around the

---

[*] Corresponding author.

A M. Tjoa et al. (Eds.): ARES 2011, LNCS 6908, pp. 359–373, 2011.
© IFIP International Federation for Information Processing 2011

world. Consequently, courts are now becoming concerned about the admissibility and probative value of digital evidence. Even if digital devices have not been directly used by an individual who has been indicted for a crime, they can be subject to forensic investigations in order to collect useful traces about the suspect activities, in order to be either cleared or charged with an offense. The elements required to determine the liability for having committed a crime often consist of files stored in a PC memory, photos on a digital camera, information on a mobile phone, as well as on many other digital devices.

Digital traces are *ubiquitous*: they can be located anywhere in the world. In fact, digital traces can be retrieved on mobile devices (phones, PDAs, laptops, GPSs, etc.) but especially on servers that provide services via Internet, which often register the IP addresses and any other information concerning the connected clients. These servers can be located in remote countries, with different national laws being an obstacle for the acquisition of digital evidence during the investigation.

Digital traces are also *immaterial*. It is well known that all digital data present on a device are mere sequences of one and zero. These data can be modified by anyone who has enough privileges on that device.

## 1.2   The Digital Alibi

Computers cannot only be involved in, as well as contain, the proof of crimes, but they can also be an *alibi* for the defense of anyone who is under accusation. In the Latin the word *alibi* is an adverb meaning "in or at another place". According to the Merriam-Webster online dictionary [14], alibi is "the plea of having been at the time of the commission of an act elsewhere than at the place of commission".

There are several examples of legal proceedings in which digital evidence has been considered an alibi that contributed to exonerating the accused. These include the interesting case of Rodney Bradford [2], [3], accused of armed robbery and released thanks to his digital alibi, consisting of activities on his Facebook account. The Erb Law Firm, a corporation of lawyers in Philadelphia, emphasized that "Facebook Can Keep You Out of Jail" [21]. Another example is the Italian case of "Garlasco" [4], in which the proceedings of the first instance ended with the acquittal of Alberto Stasi, the main suspect in the murder of his girlfriend Chiara Poggi. Digital evidence of the work activity left on his laptop during the committing of the crime confirmed his digital alibi.

Identifying the true originator of digital evidence is a very hard task. In fact, it is possible to trace the owner of a digital device, but the digital evidence itself does not contain any information on *who* or *what* has produced it.

This work shows that it is possible to set up a series of automated actions in order to produce digital traces that are *post-mortem indistinguishable* from those left by a person, and how such evidence could be claimed in a court to forge a valid alibi. The direct consequence of this result is that the forensic analysis in legal cases should focus not only on the retrieval and analysis of digital evidence, but also on the identification of its author.

The paper is organized as follows: in Section 2 various approaches of forging a false digital alibi are discussed. In Section 3 the methodology of forging a false digital alibi creating a fully automated tool is presented and analyzed. In Section 4 a case study on Microsoft Windows systems is reported, while in Section 5 some considerations on the use of a digital alibi in a Court are examined. Finally, this paper ends with the authors conclusions in Section 6.

## 2    Creation of a False Digital Alibi

In this work it is assumed that there is a particular device (e.g. PC, smartphone, etc.) used to produce evidence. Moreover, there are some trusted companies providing services (e.g. online social networks, mailboxes and so on) that record traces about their users, such as access date, session duration, which can be considered trusted in a legal case scenario. In order to forge a digital alibi based on these assumptions, it is possible to follow different strategies. A simple technique is to engage an accomplice which produces digital evidence on behalf of another person (e.g. accessing his mailbox, leaving messages on Facebook, etc.). This technique does not require any particular skill. However, the presence of another person could produce unwanted non-digital (e.g. biological) evidence which can be revealed by traditional forensic investigation techniques.

In this work two new approaches, which do not require any human accomplice, are presented: remotization and automation.

- *Remotization.* In order to forge a digital alibi by themselves, it is necessary to produce evidence at some trusted entities during the same timeline of the alibi. To accomplish this task, it is possible to remotely control a device by means of an IP connection (e.g., over the Internet), using a KVM device or a Remote Control software. However, this technique requires the interaction with another device (the controller) while producing the evidence.
- *Automation.* The automation method consists of forging a digital alibi using a fully automated software tool. This approach does not require any interaction with the device while producing the digital evidence.

### 2.1    Remotization

In this section two techniques to forge an alibi by using a personal computer to be remotely controlled are discussed.

**Remote Connection by Means of KVM Over IP**   An individual who intends to create an alibi can use a KVM over IP switch (iKVM) [15] to control his PC remotely. This technique does not require any suspicious software to be installed. However, the individual must take some precautions to limit the amount of unwanted traces. For example, he should configure the iKVM with a static IP address in order to avoid that requests to the local DHCP server are recorded. While assuming that he could take all reasonable precautions to avoid suspicious evidence, an accurate investigation at the ISP side can reveal the unusual IP connection persisting for the overall duration of the alibi.

**Remote Connection Through Remote Control Software** Someone looking for an alibi can use a Remote Control software. To limit suspicious traces, he can use a portable software from a USB flash drive (e.g. TeamViewer Portable for Windows), but traces of such softwares on the host computer may also be found. However, as in the previous case, the IP connection to the Remote Control software produces non-removable unwanted evidence at the ISP side as well as on the routers along the network path. In both cases, in order to try to fool a digital investigator, an unwary person should obfuscate the auxiliary hardware such as the iKVM switch and the USB flash drive in order to not raise any suspicion.

## 2.2    Manual vs Automation

The production of digital evidence for an alibi can be considered an Anti-Forensics activity. Following the "manual" approach, an individual can forge his alibi generating digital evidence a-priori or a-posteriori to the alibi timeline. For example, he can manually modify the access time of a file in order to pretend he was writing a document at the time of the crime. This can be considered the "classic" Anti-Forensic approach. However, this approach produces evidence that is "local" to the system of the suspected person and should not always be considered trusted by the Courts.

With respect to manual techniques, the automation can act "at the same time" (or "during") as the crime being committed. It determines that the forged evidence can be *validated* by trusted third parties. For example, an automation can activate the Internet connection and access the Facebook account of an individual, so that both the ISP and Facebook will record its logon information. These records can subsequently be claimed as evidence.

## 3    Undistinguishable Automated Production of Digital Evidence

In this paper the production of digital evidence by means of automated tools is discussed. It is also shown how this evidence is undistinguishable, upon a post-mortem forensic analysis, from that produced by the human behavior and therefore can be used in a legal case to claim a digital alibi. The typical actions performed by a human on a PC, which may be simulated by automated tools, are mouse clicks, the pressing of keyboard keys, the writing of texts, the use of specific software, which are all separated by random timings.

There are several automation tools used to avoid boring, manual, repetitive, and error-prone tasks. They speed up otherwise tedious, time-consuming tasks, thus avoiding the possibility of errors while doing them. Applications of automation tools include data analysis, data munging, data extraction, data transformation as well as data integration.

In this paper, a new potential application of automation tools for the construction of a digital alibi is introduced. Some automation tools generally have the possibility to perform simple operations such as simulate keystrokes and mouse gestures, manage windows (e.g., activation, opening, closing, resizing), get information on (and interact with) edit boxes, check boxes, list boxes, combos, buttons, status bars, control time for operation (e.g., choose time to schedule each operation or choose time delay between consecutive tasks).

Automation tools usually provide much powerful functions, but the basic and simple operations listed above are sufficient to automate tasks for the purpose of constructing a digital alibi. The list of tasks includes:

- *Web navigation.* Opening new tabs, new windows, new URLs. Inserting username, password, text. Uploading or downloading files. These include interacting with online social networks, and popular web sites such as Picasa, Dropbox, Gmail.
- *Files and folders.* Processing specific files, renaming them, working with folders.
- *Photos and images.* Processing photos, cropping images, creating thumbnails.
- *Music and audio files.* Playing an audio file, adjusting audio controls, converting audio to text.
- *Compound files.* Creating new text files, modifying (inserting and deleting) them, saving them. These include Office documents being processed by Word, Excel and Powerpoint.
- *Computer applications.* Launching any application. For example, launching a browser or using email by opening unread messages and sending new messages with attachments.
- *Phone calls.* While it would be easy to simulate a phone call using IP Telephony like Skype/VoIP, it is possible to make a phone call over the PSTN circuit or GSM mobile network by using additional hardware, as well as send a text message. For example, AT commands can be sent to a modem connected with a PC.

## 3.1   Digital Evidence of an Automation

An individual who intends to create an alibi should identify unwanted evidence that the deployed program leaves on the system, then implement a technique to avoid or remove such traces. The evidence of the automation strongly depends on the OS in which it is executed. As discussed later in this section, there are two categories of unwanted traces that should be removed: execution traces and logon traces.

**Execution Traces** For any OS, the *process* is considered as the basic execution unit [19], and even the simplest OS provides mechanisms to trace the execution of each process it runs saving data such as executable name, the time it was started, the amount of CPU allocated during the execution, maximum resident size for virtual memory and so on. These records are generally referred to as "accounting data". Depending on the OS, the execution of an automation generated with tools such as AutoIt also leaves this kind of trace. For example, Windows stores accounting data in the Registry. In Linux, application logs are stored in the `/var/logs` directory and the memory map of the processes is maintained in `/proc`. Most of the more recent OSes implement techniques such as "Virtual Memory Allocation" and "Prefetch", which also store data about programs on the filesystem.

**Logon Traces.** Besides the data related to the process execution, another specific OS module is in charge of storing each user access to the system *logon data*. Normally, this is done during login-logout phases and the module is supposed to record data such as local login time, local logout time, source address of the connection (if the operation was performed through a network connection) or the `tty` (the "serial" line) the user used to connect to the terminal both for local or modem access. Although it is possible to modify the files containing such records, there are several Digital Forensics tools that can verify the integrity of such files and, in this case, they should be considered meaningful.

### 3.2    Different Approaches to Unwanted Evidence Handling

The use of an automation tool produces some unwanted traces that can be detected by digital forensics analysis. In order to forge an alibi all this evidence should be removed. There are basically two approaches that can be adopted to accomplish this task.

**Avoid Evidence a-priori.** The individual can take several precautions in order to avoid as much unwanted evidence as possible. Sometimes, when it is not possible to completely delete some evidence, an *a-priori obfuscation* strategy could be used in order to avoid any logical connection between the evidence and the automation process, in a way that it could have been the result of "normal" operations within the system. For example, it is possible to disable some OS-specific mechanisms that record data about process execution. The fact that such mechanisms have been disabled could depend on either a direct user operation or an optimization software which is very common to speed-up the operating system.

**Remove Evidence a-posteriori.** It is possible to adopt wiping techniques in order to remove the unwanted traces left by the automation on the system drive(s). Sometimes it is not possible to wipe all unwanted data, which makes an *a-posteriori obfuscation* strategy necessary in order to avoid logical connections between these data and the automation tool.

The most productive approach to avoid that a digital forensics analysis reveals suspicious evidence about an automation is to design it in a way that leaves as less unwanted traces as possible. However, even using this approach, a separate solution should be adopted to address the problem of removing (or obfuscating) the file(s) implementing the automation itself. There are some OS-specific precautions that can be taken in order to avoid unwanted evidence. They mostly regard OS configuration. For example, in Windows it is possible to disable the Virtual Memory and the Prefetch mechanisms in order to avoid that data about processes is stored on the filesystem, as well as application logging being possible to disable in Linux.

Some OS-independent tricks can be also adopted to avoid unwanted traces, for example running the automation executable from a removable device avoiding to copy it onto the hard disk. This approach could address the problem of obfuscating the file(s) implementing the automation. However, an external drive can leave traces regarding its use. Generally, it is not possible to completely avoid the accounting data. For example, in Windows it is not possible to disable the recording of program execution paths in the Registry. It is not possible to avoid that memory maps of processes are stored on the filesystem in Linux. In such cases, traces that cannot be avoided should be wiped or obfuscated. Moreover, if the automation program is stored on the hard disk, it is itself unwanted evidence that must be deleted.

### 3.3   Removing Unwanted Digital Evidence of an Automation

Evidence of automation can be removed employing three different approaches.

**Manual Deletion.** The individual who intends to generate an alibi can manually remove the unwanted evidence from the system. In particular, he/she has to delete all the system information regarding the automation. For example, in Windows it includes Registry entries, while in Linux the memory map files. The file(s) constituting the automation itself must be removed using wiping techniques.

**Semi-Automatic Method.** It is possible to further minimize the unwanted data that will be left on the drive running the automation executable by using a removable device (e.g. an USB flash drive or a CD-ROM). Using this approach, the person does not have to wipe the file(s) of the automation from the drive. However, he/she should also remove all suspicious evidence "recorded" by the OS about its execution. Moreover, the trace left by the use of the removable device should be considered.

**Automatic Method.** The deletion process of unwanted evidence can itself be part of the automation. It requires that the individual who prepares the automation is skilled enough to create a shell script that firstly runs the automation part, then deletes all unwanted traces about its execution "recorded" on the OS, and eventually wipes itself. This work deals with the semi-automatic deletion method, due to it being considered the simplest. An analysis of the automatic method for the deletion of digital evidence has been carried out in [18].

### 3.4   Automation Development and Testing

The construction of an automation consists of two iterative phases: the development of the automation and the testing on the system. Along with the implementation of the automation, it is necessary to identify the unwanted evidence that the automation leaves on the system. It is possible to forge a digital alibi only if all (or at least the most suspicious) unwanted traces are detected and removed/obfuscated. First of all, the documentation about the OS and the used filesystem should be consulted and considered. However, the lack of documentation makes the use of software tools to identify unwanted evidence sometime necessary. For example, useful tools for this purpose are:

- *Process monitoring tools*. Some utilities to monitor the activities of the automation at execution time can be used. For example, Process Monitor [13], which is an advanced monitoring tool for Windows that shows real-time filesystem, Registry and process/thread activity could be very useful.
- *Digital forensic tools*. Digital forensic tools can be used in a post-mortem fashion in order to analyze the system drive(s) and detect traces left by the execution of the automation.

**Design of the Automation.** The automation itself must be developed and tested to verify if it acts correctly and does not leaves suspicious traces on the target system. In most cases, the automation must be extensively tested before being used for such a sensible task, which is the creation of a false digital alibi. In fact, an automation created using software tools is strictly connected to the running environment. For example, when using AutoIt under Microsoft Windows, the mouse movements and clicks must be specified using absolute coordinates $(x, y)$, therefore the different positions of an element on the screen result in a different behavior of the automation. Due to these considerations, the automation must be tested on a system that has the same appearance as the target system (screen resolution, windows position, desktop theme, icon size, etc.).

The automation must also be extensively tested in order to identify (and consequently minimize) all the unwanted traces left on the system by its execution, using the methodologies discussed above. Moreover, it is necessary to verify the effectiveness of the deletion method used to remove the automation from the system after its execution.

**Unwanted Evidence of the Automation Development.** The preparation of the automation can leave some unwanted traces. The OS, in fact, typically records recently opened files and applications. For example, Microsoft Windows stores this information in the Registry, which can only be modified by the Administrator, with some of the modifications taking effect only after a system reboot.

It is possible to employ some workarounds to avoid most of the suspicious traces about the development phase.

- *Virtual machine*. A virtual machine running an identical copy of the OS of the target system can be used in order to test the automation. This technique does not leave unwanted traces on the target system except for the files containing the virtual machine image and traces that the virtual machine itself has been powered on.

- *Live OS.* A live CD/USB version of the target OS can be used in order to develop and test the automation. This technique does not leave any unwanted traces on the hard disk because the live OS only uses the central memory for all its operations.
- *Another system.* The automation can be simply developed and tested on another PC running the same OS with a similar configuration. Subsequently, the program responsible for the automation can be copied onto a removable media and launched directly from there. In this case, the entire secondary PC must be obfuscated in order to avoid any forensic analysis on it.
- *External device.* It is possible to use portable software in order to implement and test the automation from an external (local or remote) device. In this case, it is possible to configure the OS in order to avoid that it records meaningful unwanted evidence, such as accounting data of the used programs. Following this approach, the development of the automation takes place on the same system where it will be deployed.

### 3.5   Additional Cautions

A recent paper [7] explains how it is possible to recognize who has used a computer analyzing the bacteria left by their fingertips on the keyboard and mouse. The imprint left by the bacteria on the keys and mouse persists for more than two weeks. This is potentially a new tool for a forensic investigation. Obviously, investigators should use gloves before examining any device. This kind of analysis can be exploited by an individual to validate his digital alibi. If the suspect made sure of being the only one to use the computer, the defending lawyer can request a forensic analysis within two weeks, which will confirm that bacterial traces on the keyboard and mouse are those of the suspect.

People have their habits and follow a predictable pattern. For example, it may be usual for the suspect to connect to the Internet during the morning, access his mailbox, browse some web sites and work on his thesis. In practice, the behavior of the suspect inferred from his digital alibi must be not very different from his typical behavior. Suspicious traces must not be discovered by an Anomaly Detection analysis. The testing phase of the automation can already give regularity to the behavioral pattern of the suspect and therefore may be useful in order to guard against eventual Anomaly Detection analysis [11] [9].

## 4   Case Study

In this section a case study is analyzed with it being the development of an automation to produce a digital alibi in Microsoft Windows XP with Service Pack 3 and Microsoft Windows Vista. The script language chosen to implement the automation is AutoIt v3 for Windows [8]. AutoIt has been chosen for this experiment due to it being a powerful and easy-to-use tool which does not require a detailed knowledge of programming languages, and therefore can be used by unskilled users.

## 4.1   AutoIt

AutoIt is a freeware automation language for Microsoft Windows. The syntax of AutoIt is similar to BASIC language. An AutoIt automation script can be compiled into a compressed, stand-alone executable which can be run on computers that do not have the AutoIt interpreter installed. A very basic knowledge of the AutoIt scripting language is required in order to create a fully-fledged automation program. The main functions used in the experiment are listed below:

- *Run("path/to/external/program")*   Runs an external program;
- *Send("sequence_of_keys")*   Sends simulated keystrokes to the active window;
- *MouseClick("mouse_button", x_coordinate, y_coordinate, number_of_clicks)*
  Performs a mouse operation, simulating the pressure of a mouse button;
- *WinWaitActive("title")*   Pauses until the requested window is active;
- *Sleep(delay)*   Pauses the script for *delay* milliseconds.

## 4.2   AutoIt Script Example

Several AutoIt scripts have been created as proof of concept, which implement a different number of actions and alibi timelines. The scripts have been compiled into standalone executables and do not require that the AutoIt interpreter is installed on the target system. Generally, for a sample source script of 300 lines the resulting executable file is about 200Kb.

In order to show how simple is the construction of an automation by using the AutoIt scripting language, a script excerpt which simulates the actions of interacting with the web pages of the BBC and Facebook is presented. The automation opens the Firefox web browser and inserts the URL http://www.bbc.co.uk/ in the location bar, then simulates the pressing of the ENTER key which lets the browser load the web site. After the web page has been loaded, it clicks on a link and simulates the human activity of reading page contents waiting some minutes. Subsequently, the script simulates an access to Facebook loading the http://www.facebook.com/ web site and inserting the access credentials. The main part of the relative source code is listed below:

```
...
Run ("C:\Program files\Mozilla Firefox\
     firefox.exe")
Send ("^t")
Send ("http://www.bbc.co.uk/")
Send ("{ENTER}")
WinWaitActive ("BBC")
MouseClick ("left","295","355","1")
WinWaitActive ("Sport")
Sleep (12940)
...
```

```
...
Send ("^t")
Send ("http://www.facebook.com/")
Send ("{ENTER}")
WinWaitActive("Facebook")
Send ("{TAB}")
Send ("castiglione@ieee.org")
Send ("{TAB}")
Send ("password")
Send ("{ENTER}")
...
```

## 4.3   Unwanted Traces

In the presented case study, the approach of a-priori avoid as much unwanted evidence as possible has been followed (see Section 3.2). In this subsection, the unwanted traces detected in the experiment, and some simple techniques to avoid them, are described. The only trace that remains on the filesystem is the automation executable file, which has to be deleted. For a more complete discussion about deletion see Subsection 4.4.

**Windows Registry.** Microsoft Windows contains significant amounts of digital evidence that enables an investigator to reconstruct the events that took place on the machine before it was seized. The Windows Registry, in particular, contains a wealth of information about the configuration and use of a computer [10]. In details, Windows records in the Registry data relative to programs executed on the system. If an executable is launched using the `File Explorer` mechanism, its complete pathname is recorded in the following Registry keys:

1) `HKEY_CURRENT_USER\Software\Microsoft\Windows\ShellNoRoam\MUICache`
2) `HKEY_USERS\S-1-5-21-2025429265-688789844-854245398-1003\Software`
   `\Microsoft\Windows\ShellNoRoam\MUICache`

Otherwise, if an executable is launched using the DOS command prompt, only the value `x:\windows\system32\cmd.exe` is recorded in the above Registry key number 1).

Due to it not being possible to completely avoid the recording of such evidence, in this experiment the execution of the automation has been *obfuscated* running it from a command prompt. In this case, the string recorded in the Registry (`x:\windows\system32\cmd.exe`) does not reveal any information regarding the automation. In fact, the shell may have been used to launch any other command (e.g., a `ping`). According to the authors' experience, a further digital forensics analysis does not reveal any other meaningful information about the automation in the Registry.

**Filesystem.** Windows XP and subsequent versions implement the Prefetch mechanism [16]. The *prefetcher* is a component of the *memory manager* that attempts to accelerate application and boot launch times respectively by monitoring and adapting to usage patterns over periods of time and loading some files and data into the memory, so that they can be accessed very quickly when needed.

Auxiliary files (with `.pf` extension) containing information about used programs are stored on the filesystem in the directory `x:\WINDOWS\Prefetch`. In the experiment, this mechanism has been disabled in order to avoid that unwanted evidence of the automation program was stored on the hard disk by the *prefetcher*. This has been accomplished by setting to zero the following Registry key value:

3) `HKEY_LOCAL_MACHINE\SYSTEM\CurrentControlSet\Control\SessionManager\`
   `MemoryManagement\PrefetchParameters`

Disabling the *prefetch* mechanism should not be considered a suspicious action. In fact, this configuration can sometimes reduce hard disk utilization and is often used among the Windows users. Moreover, there are many tweaking tools for optimizing the performance of a PC that, among other tasks, disable the *prefetch* feature.

**Virtual Memory.** Another mechanism implemented by Microsoft Windows, which must be disabled in order to avoid unwanted evidence on the filesystem, is the Virtual Memory [19]. In order to free up space in the memory, an operating system with a virtual memory capability transfers data that is not immediately needed from the memory to the hard disk. When that data is needed again, it is copied back into the memory. In Microsoft Windows, there is a specific file on the filesystem used for swapping such data, namely `pagefile.sys`, which could also memorize information relative to the automation.

In this case study, the Virtual Memory mechanism has been disabled by setting the virtual memory size equal to zero in the system properties of Windows using the following navigation: `Control Panel->Advanced->Performance-> Settings->Advanced->Virtual memory`. Disabling the virtual memory can sometimes improve the system performance as well as increase the hard disk space available. Several Windows users employ this customization, with it therefore not being considered suspicious by investigators.

## 4.4   Wiping

In the case study, some Windows-specific settings have been modified in order to avoid that the OS would record meaningful evidence about the execution of the automation script. The only potential unwanted evidence that remains available is the compiled AutoIt script implementing the automation.

It is well-known that deleting a file using the OS-specific functions does not completely remove the file from the drive. In fact, the sectors that were occupied by a file become available for a new writing operation, but the previous data remains on the disk until it is overwritten.

The amount of rewritings necessary to perform secure wiping of data on a drive is a controversial issue [5], [6], [17]. Considering the NIST Special Publication 800-88 [20], which claims that "Studies have shown that most of today's media can be effectively cleared by one overwrite", the approach adopted in this experiment consists of a single rewriting. However, the replacement of this technique with a more paranoid one, consisting of multi-rewritings, can be quite straightforwardly implemented.

In this study, a *semi-automatic* approach for deleting the automation data has been adopted, due to it being easier to carry out by unskilled users. In practice, an USB flash drive has been formatted and almost completely filled with audio and video files, then the automation script has been also copied onto it. The USB flash drive has been plugged into the PC two days before executing the automation. After the automation execution, the script has been deleted (using the "classic" Windows `del` command from the `cmd.exe` shell) and the USB flash drive has been completely filled by copying additional multimedia files onto it. These actions should guarantee that the traces left by the USB flash drive in the Registry are not suspicious as it was plugged in two days before the alibi timeline. Moreover, filling the USB flash drive after the deletion of the script should overwrite all sectors previously occupied by the automation script.

## 5   The Digital Alibi in Court

In some countries, it is a common practice that, in legal proceedings, digital evidence are vetted by digital forensics experts, which assess its trustworthiness according to the *Five Ws Rule* (Who, What, When, Where, Why).

It is well known that a human accomplice could be engaged in order to forge an alibi, but this approach is hazardous since he could avow his actions or even blackmail the suspect. Consequently, if the individual interested in producing the alibi has enough technical skills, he may prefer to use an automation in order to forge a digital alibi. In this case, the absence of accomplices and the creation of ad-hoc digital evidence, undistinguishable post-mortem from those left by ordinary human behavior could produce a "perfect alibi".

In fact, the Court would be in a delicate situation if the digital alibi confirms that the suspect was using his PC while the crime was being committed, which means that:

- if on the *locus committi delicti* (i.e. the crime scene) there is no evidence related to the suspect (biological traces, witnesses, etc.), the Court could consider decisive the probative value of the digital alibi and acquit the suspect;
- on the contrary, if on the crime scene biological traces referable to the suspect have been detected (left, for example, during previous contact with the victim), the probative value of the digital alibi should be carefully weighed.

After this paper, the technical consultants which carry out any form of Digital Forensics analysis should consider the hypothesis that the suspect might have used an automation to forge his digital alibi. A technical consultant, aware of such a possibility, has to carefully analyze the exhibits and look for eventual evidence left by an incorrect implementation of the automation process.

In general, criminal investigation divisions should include Digital Forensics experts who constantly update their knowledge and understanding in order to face the evolution of Anti-Forensics techniques. This is an additional argument on the importance of scientific knowledge for the expert testimony in a Court, according to the rule 702 of the "Federal Rules of Evidence" [23] and to the "Daubert Test" [22].

## 6   Conclusions

A PC may contain lot of information about the people who use it, such as logon data, used applications, visited web sites and so on. As a result, the number of court cases involving digital evidence is increasing. In this paper, it has been shown how simple the set up of digital evidence could be in order to provide an individual with a false digital alibi. In particular, an automated method of generating digital evidence has been discussed. Using this approach, it is possible to claim a digital alibi involving some trusted third parties. In fact, the automation could, for example, activate the Internet connection by means of an ISP, access a Facebook account, send an email and so on, leaving traces on their respective servers. The problem of avoiding unwanted evidence left by the automation has been addressed. Finally, a real case study has been presented in order to demonstrate that the implementation of such methodologies is not a hard task and can even be carried out by unskilled users.

Experiments on various OSes have been and are being conducted in order to prove that the techniques described in this paper really do produce digital evidence that is undistinguishable from those produced by a human. Moreover, a fully automated approach of deleting evidence from a drive is analyzed in [18].

The main goal of this work is to stress the need of an evolution in approaching legal cases that involve digital evidence. Evidently, a legal investigation case should not only rely on digital evidence to pass judgement, but should also consider it to be part of a larger pattern of behavior reconstructed by means of traditional forensics investigations. In conclusion, the plausibility of a digital alibi should be verified *cum grano salis*.

**Acknowledgements.** The authors would like to thank their friends from IISFA (International Information System Forensics Association) for their support, their valuable suggestions and useful discussions during the research phase. In particular to Gerardo Costabile (President of IISFA Italian Chapter), Francesco Cajani (Deputy Public Prosecutor High Tech Crime Unit Court of Law in Milano, Italy), Mattia Epifani and Litiano Piccin of the IISFA Italian Chapter. A warm thank goes to Paolo Iorio for the many discussions during the preparation of his thesis.

# References

1. Internet World Stats, June 30 (2010), http://www.internetworldstats.com/stats.htm
2. Beltrami, D.: The New York Times, I'm Innocent. Just Check My Status on Facebook, November 12 (2009), http://www.nytimes.com/2009/11/12/nyregion/12facebook.html?_r=1
3. Juarez, V.: CNN, Facebook status update provides alibi, November 12 (2009), http://www.cnn.com/2009/CRIME/11/12/facebook.alibi/index.html
4. Xomba, A.: Writing Community, Garlasco, Alberto Stasi acquitted (December 2009), http://www.xomba.com/garlasco_alberto_stasi_acquitted
5. U.S. Department of Defense. DoD Directive 5220.22, National Industrial Security Program (NISP), February 28 (2010)
6. Gutmann, P.: Secure Deletion of Data from Magnetic and Solid-State Memory. In: Sixth USENIX Security Symposium Proceedings, San Jose, California, July 22-25 (1996)

7. Fierer, N., Lauber, C.L., Zhou, N., McDonald, D., Costello, E.K., Knight, R.: Forensic identification using skin bacterial communities. In: Proceedings of the National Academy of Sciences, Abstract (March 2010)

8. Bennett, J.: AutoIt v3.3.6.0, March 7 (2010), http://www.autoitscript.com/autoit3/

9. Di Crescenzo, G., Ghosh, A., Kampasi, A., Talpade, R., Zhang, Y.: Detecting anomalies in active insider stepping stone attacks. Journal of Wireless Mobile Networks, Ubiquitous Computing, and Dependable Applications 2(1), 103–120 (2011)

10. Mee, V., Tryfonas, T., Sutherland, I.: The Windows Registry as a forensic artefact: Illustrating evidence collection for Internet usage. Journal of Digital Investigation 3(3), 166–173 (2006)

11. Chandola, V., Banerjee, A., Kumar, V.: Anomaly detection: A survey. ACM Computing Surveys 41(3), 15:1–15:58 (2009)

12. Shelton, D.E.: The "CSI Effect": Does It Really Exist? National Institute of Justice, Journal No. 259, March 17 (2008)

13. Russinovich, M., Cogswell, B.: Microsoft Sysinternals Process Monitor, April 13 (2011), http://technet.microsoft.com/en-us/sysinternals/bb896645

14. Merriam-Webster Dictionary, http://www.merriam-webster.com/dictionary/alibi

15. Wikipedia, KVM switch, http://en.wikipedia.org/wiki/KVM_switch

16. Carvey, H.: Windows Forensics Analysis, 2nd edn. Syngress (2009)

17. Craig, W., Dave, K., Shyaam, S.R.S.: Overwriting Hard Drive Data: The Great Wiping Controversy. In: Sekar, R., Pujari, A.K. (eds.) ICISS 2008. LNCS, vol. 5352, pp. 243–257. Springer, Heidelberg (2008)

18. Castiglione, A., Cattaneo, G., De Maio, G., De Santis, A.: Automatic, Selective and Secure Deletion of Digital Evidence. In: Proceedings of the Sixth International Conference on Broadband and Wireless Computing, Communication and Applications, BWCCA 2011, Barcelona, Spain, October 26-28 (2011)

19. Silberschatz, A., Galvin, P.B., Gagne, G.: Operating System Concepts, 7th edn. Wiley, Chichester (2004)

20. NIST Special Publication 800-88: Guidelines for Media Sanitization, p. 7 (2006)

21. The Erb Law Firm, Facebook Can Keep You Out of Jail (November 2009), http://www.facebook.com/note.php?note_id=199139644051

22. Berger, M.A.: What Has a Decade of Daubert Wrought? American Journal of Public Health 95(S1), S59–S65 (2005)

23. U.S. House of Representative, Federal Rules of Evidence (December 2006), http://afcca.law.af.mil/content/afcca_data/cp/us_federal_rules_of_evidence_2006.pdf

# IT Issues on Homeland Security and Defense

Kangbin Yim[1] and Ilsun You[2,*]

[1] 646 Eupnae, Shinchang, Asan, 336-745 Korea
yim@sch.ac.kr
[2] 214-32 Dongilro, Nowongu, Seoul, 139-791 Korea
isyou@bible.ac.kr

**Abstract.** This paper surveys remarkable incidents that were related to the Homeland Security and Defense such as terrors, disasters and cyber-attacks and overviews the existing projects given by the department of Homeland Security and Defense of the US government. Through the overview, technological foundations in the projects are extracted and discussed. Additionally, this paper introduces a common framework, as an example, supporting the delivery service for RFID Tracking, Sensor Network, Video Surveillance and Image Screening, which are the major technological foundations in the Homeland Security and Defense. As providing an outline of the technological aspects of the Homeland Security and Defense, this paper is expected a reference for initiators of the related projects.

**Keywords:** homeland security, homeland defense, terror and disaster control, emergency readiness, and cyber threats.

## 1 Introduction

IT convergence is a big topic of conversation these days. Through the convergence, the IT technologies have been applied to various traditional industries. The u-City and similar projects have merged IT framework into the traditional constructions and residential infrastructure and have connected the environment all around to the network. As the results, many private companies and even individual houses have incorporated ubiquitous sensor network connected to the Internet, large scaled intelligent video surveillance network has substituted the CCTV system, and the intelligent secure border wall has fielded sensors on the border fence between countries.

Even though the fundamentals of the Information Technologies are originated from military purposes, the traditional IT technologies developed and used in militaristic field were very confidential not more than twenty years ago. However, penetration of communication technologies into the public domain, such as the RF technologies and network protocols for the cellphones and the Internet for example, had changed the situations in many ways.

Framework of communication is available totally in virtue of the standardization on its protocols and element technologies. However, standardization, in some aspects,

---

* Corresponding author.

A M. Tjoa et al. (Eds.): ARES 2011, LNCS 6908, pp. 374–385, 2011.

makes security very difficult to be achieved. Because of the reason, another or several heavy layers of hardware or software are usually required to closely equalize the standardized results with the same quality of security to the confidential ones. Most of those layers are crypto based and mathematically approved and they are considered to be secure enough. However, lots of problems and subsequent accidents have been found on the real world implementations.

Recent advances and diffusions of Information Technologies as well as communication technologies also introduced a number of new services available to people in the public domain. To meet the requirement in the environment, many infrastructures in various industries and government organizations also have been connected to the Internet. Every local site in a gigantic class factory is monitored on the mobile phone in the public domain through the Internet. Videos for every common spot on the cruise ship can be delivered to public and live views on harbors, ports and docks are anytime available. Especially, many projects are recently involved to deploying unmanned surveillance and defensive systems even for nation-wide and military infrastructures. This means hackers can attack these infrastructures in such a way that was usually found in public domain.

Along with this IT convergence into the significant infrastructures, security problems and the defenses against the homeland are getting focused to consider. In case of the United States, the government reorganized many agencies to form the Department of Homeland Security after the September 11 terror attacks [3]. Other countries also have been focusing on the Homeland Security and Defense. Especially, many Korean researchers have insisted the government to prepare a strategic plan for Homeland Security and Defense because Korea is now a unique divided country in the world.

Even though the effort for the Homeland Security and Defense is getting focused, it could take too much time to have practical results and might miss the adequate time to adopt. Such as in the u-City projects, where there is a large gap in the viewpoints of the financial contributions between the IT industry and the existing industries.

## 2  Homeland Security and Defense

Homeland is defined as the physical region that includes the nation's possessions, territories, and surrounding territorial waters and airspace [1]. Homeland Security is defined as a concerted national effort to prevent terrorist attacks within the nation, reduce its vulnerability to terrorism, and minimize the damage and recover from attacks that occur [2]. Homeland Defense represents the protection of territory, sovereignty, domestic population, and critical infrastructure of a nation against external threats and aggression, or other threats [2]. Although Homeland Defense and Homeland Security are officially defined separately and differentiated from each other as above, they are usually hsaconsidered interchangeable and the term Homeland Security and Defense (HSD) will be used in this paper to represent either or both.

As mentioned, HSD is based on the IT convergence to various existing industries because the industrial foundations are all components of the homeland. Major threats on the homeland components are terrors and natural or pollutional disasters. The terrors are unlawful violence or threat of unlawful violence to inculcate fear intended to coerce or to intimidate governments or societies in the pursuit of goals that are generally political, religious, or ideological [4]. There have been lots of terrors around the world for a long time. One of the most unforgettable terrors would be the September 11 attack in 2001, by which more than 3,500 people from more than 90 countries were killed and more than 60,000 million dollars was economically damaged. For the natural disasters, nobody could forget the recent two severe tsunamis that hit Japan and Thailand. The earthquake at Sichuan, China also killed more than 90,000 people and 370,000 people were wounded. For the pollutional disasters, smog in London, England and toxic chemical at Niagara fall, USA were most serious. The followings are the remarkable terrors since 2001 and disasters during this century.

Different from the disasters, worries about the location in HSD by terrors usually goes to the airports, seaports, plants or logistic flows. Even though these places are dealing with different flows or functions, it is common that the severity would be miserable if they were attacked. Therefore, the focus of HSD has been putted on the facilities on these places.

**Table 1.** Remarkable terrors since 2001

| when | where | how | casualty |
|------|-------|-----|----------|
| 07/2001 | Colombo, Sri Lanka | airport bombings | 43 /16 flights |
| 09/2001 | New York, USA | flight attacks | 3,500 /$60B |
| 04/2002 | Jerba island, Tunisia | gas truck | 20+ /$2M |
| 11/2003 | Istanbul, Turkey | Synagogue bombing | 480 /$10M |
| 03/2004 | Madrid, Spain | train bombings | 2000 /$20M |
| 07/2005 | London, England | subway bombings | 756 /$100M |

**Table 2.** Remarkable natural or pollutional disasters during century

| when | where | why | casualty |
|------|-------|-----|----------|
| 10/1948 | Donora, USA | smog | 20+6,000 |
| 1940-52 | New York, USA | toxic chemical | unknown |
| 12/1952 | London, England | smog | 12,000 |
| 12/1984 | Bhopal, India | toxic gas | 2,800+200,000 |
| 05/2008 | Sichuan, China | earthquake | 90,000+370,000 |
| 12/2004 | Andaman, Thailand | tsunami | 18,000+ |
| 03/2011 | Tohoku, Japan | tsunami | 24,000+ |

**Table 3.** Remarkable cyber threats during decades

| when | from | to | how |
|------|------|-----|-----|
| 1994 | Personal/England | USA | PSTN-Internet |
| 1998 | worldwide | USA | complex |
| 1998 | unknown | India | miwOrm |
| 1999 | Yugo | Nato, USA | Mail bomb, virus |
| 2000 | unknown | Australia | SCADA |
| 2001 | China/USA | China/USA | Info warfare |
| 2003 | unknown | Korea+ | Slammer |
| 2009 | unknown | Korea | 77DDOS |

Besides the problems in HSD, the cyber threats are getting more threatening day by day. The cyber threats based on the terrorism in some cases may deliver more significant damages than practical terrors. People have had performance gain quad times per three years at half price, network bandwidth triple times per year in computing environment and now they gained the data transfer rate 90,000 times for 20 years and reduced the cost to 1% for 30years to process the same unit of data. This means that potential attackers can succeed a cyber-terror at a very low cost. Especially, 77DDOS attack in 2009 in Korea used well designed bot-net and left no footprint even though more than 60,000 personal computers were infected as an agent of the bot-net. In this situation, the DDOS attack is not the major problem and the damage would be more critical than expected because the framework is complete and the agent could equip any functions that were intended other than DDOS.

## 3 IT Projects and Homeland Security and Defense

Department of Homeland Security (DHS) of the United States serves various activities and programs in such fields as Borders and Maritime Security, Chemical and Biological, Command, Control and Interoperability, Explosives, Human Factors and Behavioral Sciences, and Infrastructure and Geophysical. It also founded related entities such as Homeland Security Centers of Excellence, Homeland Security Studies and Analysis Institute, Homeland Security Advanced Research Projects Agency (HSARPA), and Office of National Laboratories (ONL) and published regulations, standards and references such as SAFETY Act, Science & Technology Standards, SECURE, S&T Snapshots, and Tech Solutions.

Especially in the Borders and Maritime Security field, dozens of IT based research projects have been issued. Summary of the projects is helpful to understand the state of the art IT researches and developments related to the HSD. The summary is as the following [5].

- Advanced Container Security Device (ACSD) Project is developing an advanced sensor system for monitoring containers' integrity in the maritime supply chain. The ACSD is a small unit that attaches to the inside of a container to monitor all six sides and report any intrusion. If ACSD detects a symptom, it transmits alarm information through the MATTS to U.S. Customs and Border Protection.
- Marine Asset Tag Tracking System (MATTS) Project is establishing a remote, global communications and tracking network that works with Advanced Container Security Device. MATTS communicates security alert information globally through the use of radio frequency, cellular and satellite technology. In addition, the commercial shipping industry can track and monitor cargo as it moves through the supply chain.
- Advanced Screening and Targeting (ASAT) Project is providing an enhanced risk assessment through development of computer algorithms and software that will provide next-generation risk assessment and targeting tools to complement the CBP Automated Targeting System.
- Air Cargo Composite Container (ACC) Project is expanding upon the composite material developed in the Composite Container Project to determine whether it is effective in the air-cargo supply chain. The air cargo composite container must be comparable to existing aluminum containers and be interoperable with existing aircraft loading infrastructure.

- Automatic Target Recognition (ATR) Project is developing an automated imagery detection capability for anomalous content including persons, hidden compartments, contraband for maritime, land, and air cargo for existing and future Non-Intrusive Inspection (NII) systems.
- Border Detection Grid (BDG) Project is providing a grid of advanced sensors and detection, classification, and localization technologies to detect and classify cross-border movement. This technology will revolutionize border control by providing a way for a single Border Patrol officer to effectively monitor more than 10 miles of border.
- Border Officer Safety (BOS) Project is integrating technologies that will enable border-security and law-enforcement agents to more safely perform their mission. These technologies include Enhanced Ballistic Protection, Automatic Facial Recognition, Hidden Compartment Inspection Device, Pursuit Termination-Vehicle/Vessel Stopping, Covert Officer Safety Transmission System, Gunfire, Less-Lethal Compliance Measure for Personnel.
- CanScan (CS) Project is developing a next-generation NII system that will be used to detect terrorist materials, contraband items, and stowaways at border crossings, maritime ports, and airports. These new systems may provide increases in penetration, resolution, and throughput and will support marine containerized cargo as well as airborne break-bulk, palletized, and containerized cargo.
- Hybrid Composite Container (HCC) Project is developing a next-generation ISO composite shipping container with embedded security sensors to detect intrusions. Composites are stronger than steel, 10-15% lighter than current shipping containers, and are easier to repair.
- Secure Carton (SC) Project develops technology to detect any shipping carton tamper event and transmit an alert to authorities after it leaves the point-of-manufacture to the point that it is delivered in the supply chains. This project provides improved supply chain visibility, chain of custody, and security.
- Secure Wrap (SW) Project provides a transparent, flexible, and tamper-indicative wrapping material to secure and monitor palletized cargo after it leaves the point-of-manufacture to the point-of-delivery in the land, maritime and air-cargo supply chains.
- Sensors/Data Fusion and Decision-Aids (SFDA) Project develops systems to enable law enforcement officers and commanders to have full situational awareness, enabling effective decision making and execution in complex and dynamic operational environments.
- Sensors and Surveillance (SS) Project develops and demonstrates visual and non-visual technologies for monitoring the maritime border. The project includes the technologies such as Affordable Wide-Area Surveillance, Advanced Geospatial Intelligence Technical Exploitation, Port and Coastal Radar Improvement, Small Boat Harbor Surveillance Study/Pilot, Inland Waterway Maritime Security System.
- Situational Awareness and Information Management (SAIM) Project provides information management technology to quickly identify threats at the maritime border and to provide required information to decision makers and security forces.

- Supply Chain Security Architecture (SCSA) Project maps the international supply chain including point-of-stuffing, port-of-entry, shippers, CBP, foreign Customs, and container manifests to provide DHS the framework to incorporate near-term and future container-security technologies into supply chain operations.

Throughout the survey of the projects summarized above, technological aspects or foundations are categorized into two main issues including RFID Tracking and Sensor Network (RTSN), and Video Surveillance and Image Screening (VSIS) as shown in fig. 1. In the RTSN field, interface specification, integrating protocols, power management, routing algorithms, and location privacy problem are considered. In the VSIS field, integrating protocols, object extraction, relation and tracking, image distribution, interoperability, privacy masking and restoration are considered.

For the RTSN, interface includes analog and digital specification of the sensor modules. Analog interface is based on either current loop or voltage level, which is less than several mA in peak and TTL level or CMOS level, respectively. Integrating protocols are related to interoperability between sensor modules and several frames are defined for control, status and data. Power management is important because sensor modules used in HSD framework are almost wireless ones and it is sometimes involved with the routing algorithm, which delivers sensing information all around the sensor modules and unwanted module should be awaken to relay others' information. Location privacy can be achieved by encryption or nebulosity. Encryption and nebulosity cause much overhead respectively in computing and bandwidth and need to be traded off.

For the VSIS, protocols to transfer image information are different among devices and need to be converged. The VSIS is highly involved with image information and object extraction or sometimes object tracking in a video is required to enhance intelligence of the system. To share the information, the distribution function is essential though the devices usually don't support it. Sharing of the image information sometimes causes privacy invasion problem and a privacy masking policy is required. The privacy mask also needs to be stripped in case of criminal investigation.

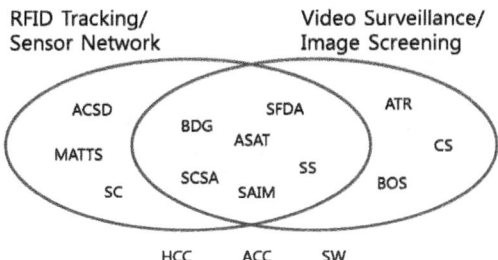

**Fig. 1.** Technological aspects or foundations are classified into two categories: one is for RFID Tracking and Sensor Network (RTSN) and the other for Video Surveillance and Image Screening (VSIS). Some projects are in RTSN, some in VSIS and the others in both.

# 4  Major Topics in Homeland Security and Defense

As mentioned, RTSN and VSIS are major research topics for the HSD. Although the features and characteristics of these categories are far different, their frameworks and architectures to acquire and share the related information are similar to each other. The major differences are on the endpoint interfaces and client software organizations. However, convergence of these differences into a coherent architecture leads a common framework sharable as shown in fig. 2. This chapter introduces a reasonable architecture of the common framework for RTSN and VSIS.

During this couple of decades, video cameras are digitalized and improved to become modernized for the integrated video surveillance system. The video surveillance system originally has been regulated to provide a closed security channel monitoring public violence such as illegal car parking, illegal waste dumping for where there is no security staff hired. However, the communication society required for more digitalized camera connections to many different fields including farmlands, factory assembly lines or disaster sites or even borders between countries.

Even though the traditional CCTV was for closed channel as mentioned above, recent hot issue on the video surveillance system is to provide an integrated framework that is compatible with heterogeneous video formats and protocols along with supporting multiple cameras and clients. During the development of the video surveillance systems, researchers have contributed many efforts to a better protocols and compression algorithms to provide best service connections. However, that approach was considered a failure when they started to connect multiple cameras and multiple clients in an integrated network. The existent performance and bandwidth of a networked camera have proved that they are limited in the number of client connections to a camera. Even more, management and security problems were arisen where the cameras have been installed at remote places and isolated from the regular update and secure environment. Because of the reasons, the centralized management system (CMS) for multiple cameras and multiple clients became required to be deployed within a secure network as a proxy server and integrate the multiple cameras and clients [8].

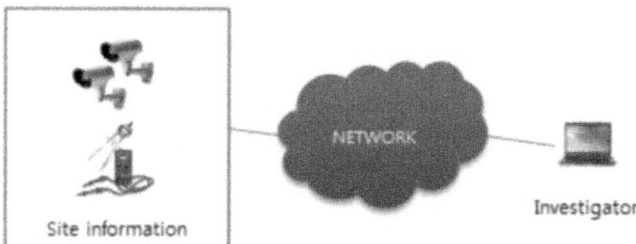

**Fig. 2.** Although the features of RTSN and VSIS are far different, their frameworks are similar to each other and the differences on the endpoint interfaces and client software organizations can converge into a unique framework to share.

For a usual CMS, it is deployed along with a new deployment of a same type of new multiple cameras for a new site. However, to integrate the existing multiple cameras or sites, a new adaptation mechanism is required for different types of cameras from different vendors [9]. Several frontier projects supported by the government yet replaced hundreds of existing cameras each because of the incompatibility. Just a small site seems reasonable to replace them as well as do for sites that have one type of camera dominantly deployed in number. However, new software architecture is required to seamlessly integrate different types of cameras for a globalized intelligent surveillance network, which is required these days.

Originally, networked cameras have been incorporating their own individual protocols and providing dedicated API libraries to give accessibility to users. These protocols were usually designed based on simple socket connections. For this kind of cameras, client software needs to implement all the sequences to request the images directly to the server.

Socket-based individual protocols required to much overhead for client software developers. Subsequently, the architecture of the network camera has changed for easy connections. Therefore, comparatively new models has incorporated HTTP based web server for connection and control and RTP facilities for video streaming [7]. In general, the HTTP is a set of rules for transferring files including text, images, sound, video, and other multimedia files. Because the networked camera deals with several different media, this transfer method has been applied to networked camera communication services.

The HTTP based protocols requires for client software developers only to organize a text based script to connect to the server and enables them easy to develop. However, the message formats for the script were still diverse because the network camera manufactures are quite different in the way of accessibility, control features and image compress methods, such as JPEG, MJPEG, MPEG, and Wavelet. Because of the incompatibility between client software, the administrator should have managed each site by running different client software. Additionally, each client from different manufacture had its own independent modules for connection and decoding, there were much overhead and inflexibility on the user platform running multiple clients. As the result, the government or a large scaled organization has found much difficulty to manage and access different network cameras in remote sites in parallel to servicing the videos for massively multiple users [6].

Generally, camera manufacturers provide API libraries to encourage client software development. Some of the libraries have a part of portable modules for both connection and decoding, which are dynamically inserted into client software. It makes time-to-market very short because several lines of script can assess the dedicated cameras. It is easy to construct a CMS and also helpful when the CMS integrates multiple cameras even from different manufactures if they have detailed specification for the software interfaces only if the server needs to be connected from just one client. In this case, client script simply embeds portable modules that were already published on the server for each camera then the modules will be downloaded and executed on the client platform.

When multiple clients want to connect to the same camera, problems arise. As mentioned, effectively only one connection is allowed to a networked camera. To overcome this limitation, the CMS server needs to distribute the video stream that was gathered from a camera to multiple clients. In this situation, it is very difficult for the CMS to provide the same functionality as was provided on various cameras because heterogeneous connection protocols and media formats are transacted between the CMS server and clients in this approach. Therefore, an architectural framework should be designed to provide a flexible incorporation of various cameras for multiple users.

Instead of emulating camera functionality on the CMS, a unified connection protocol could be designed between the CMS server and clients and an integrated portable module could be distributed to the client software. The CMS server can only be responsible for connection to cameras using connection modules and bypass all the media information from cameras to multiple clients. It is essential for camera manufacturers to provide a separated set of connection and decoding modules for the CMS server and the clients, respectively. In this approach, the CMS server plays a role as a media switch. Even though the CMS server needs to brew connection modules if camera manufactures didn't provide them, it would be simpler than developing a number of camera emulators.

Analyzing basic architecture of the network cameras, their APIs, image compression algorithms and protocols may confuse in many ways. However, it is required to analyze, evaluate, classify the existing features and design a unique coherent architecture for heterogeneous environment.

Several considerations are especially required on designing the decompression module for clients. For the networked camera based on the JPEG compressed images the client could completely decompress an image independently. However, MPEG or modifies Wavelet based images are transacted by components independently from key frame (I-Frame) to delta frame (P-Frame) only if some changes occur on the information. This means that if client didn't received any key frame from the camera, client itself is unable to decompress delta frame image. Therefore, this integrated client need to receive a key frame and keep it until the delta frame is resolved. For the sensor information, the parsing module is prepared. This module restores the data frame into the original format of sensor information.

The CMS server is designed to have six separated functional stages. Internal structures and information flows in the server are shown in fig. 4. For a connection request, it is issued only when a client asked for the camera. Although this type of connection minimizes number of simultaneous connections, it takes too much delay for connection setup. Instead, pre-connection sets up possible connections to cameras and maintains them.

Queuing is required between the server and the client software for each connection to support analogous service. The number of buffers for queuing is determined by the policy of the jitter management. In case of multiple clients to ask for the same video stream from a camera, the video information is copied to multiple queuing buffers on the distribution stage. On the processing stage, several selective functions are provided. These functions include frame rate scaling, privacy masking and encryption. The frame rate scaling is an alternative for the jitter management on the queuing stage. Privacy masking in this stage is post-compression privacy masking and it is sometimes very difficult and gives too much overhead because it needs to find adequate marker codes. Rectangular masks are only possible as well.

Some connection modules are prepared for sensor modules. According to the connection specification of the sensors, these connection modules are designed as a virtual camera connection.

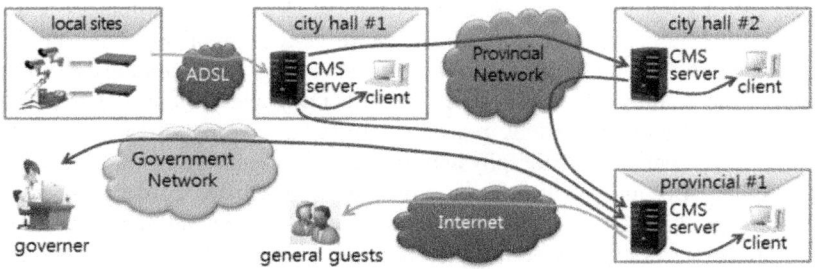

**Fig. 3.** Overall architecture including a common framework and equipment supports heterogeneous information such as video stream, image shot and various types of sensor data

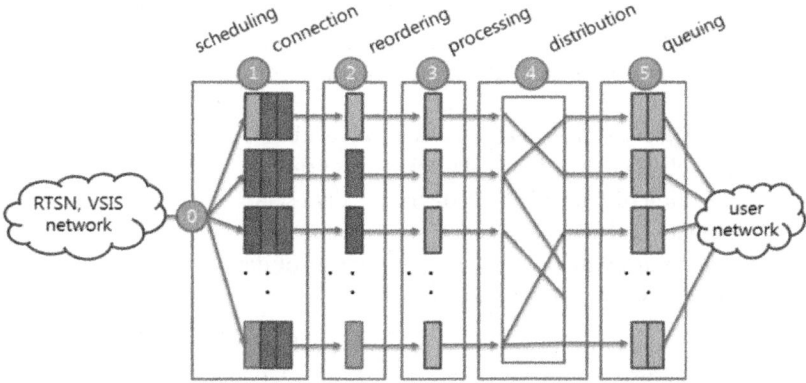

**Fig. 4.** Server software is composed of several stages for different functions including scheduling connections, buffering and reordering packets, processing image or sensor information, and distributing them to multiple clients

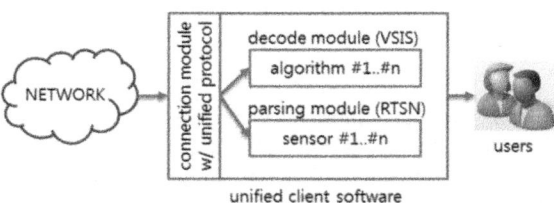

**Fig. 5.** Client software is composed of three different function modules: connection module for unified connection protocol, decode module for decompress or restoration of the images or objects, and parsing module for sensor information

# 5  Conclusions

This paper surveys existing projects, technological foundations in the Homeland Security and Defense and introduces a common framework supporting delivery service for RFID Tracking, Sensor Network, Video Surveillance and Image Screening. Because almost every infrastructure as a component of the homeland is getting connected to the Internet, existing cyber threats are potentially possible to be applied to the framework of the Homeland Security and Defense. If these kinds of threats are tried and realized by possible terrorists, severity of the relevant attacks would be more than that of the physical terrors and the range of the affection would be worldwide. Because of the reason, considerations on the countermeasures to the vulnerabilities and attacks to the infrastructure of the Homeland Security and Defense are required. Especially, research topics required in near future need to be carried on shortly to keep the homeland security infrastructure safer. Several major ones of these topics are as the following.

- Multiple privilege level support for access control to RTSN and VSIS data
- Key management framework for multiple privileges and privacy masking/restoration
- Dynamic privacy masking technology to mask on compressed data, images or videos
- Intelligent object extraction and masking algorithm
- High speed object extraction and tracking algorithm
- Synchronization of multiple heterogeneous data sets
- Secure primary and secondary backup of the integrated data
- Indexing and retrieving policy for image or sensor data
- Real-time support for sensor information

Especially, researches on the dynamic privacy masking, the privacy mask restoration based on multiple privilege levels, and the secure secondary backup storage are now on the way, related to the framework introduced in chapter 4.

**Acknowledgments.** This work (Grants No.00043599) was supported by Business for International Cooperative R&D between Industry, Academy, and Research Institute funded by Korea Small and Medium Business Administration in 2010.

# References

1. Moseley, T.M.: Homeland Operations. Air Force Doctrine Document 2(10), 9–10 (2006)
2. Sharp, W.L.: Homeland Security. JP 3-27 (2007),
   http://www.fas.org/irp/doddir/dod/jp3_27.pdf
3. Martyn, A.: The Right of Self-Defence under International Law-the Response to the Terrorist Attacks of September 11. Australian Law and Bills Digest Group (2002)
4. Ruby, C.L.: The Definition of Terrorism. In: Analyses of Social Issues and Public Policy, pp. 9–14 (2002)
5. Department of Homeland Security, http://www.dhs.gov/index.shtm

6. The Best Source for Digital Video and Network (IP) Security Products,
   http://www.cctvsentry.com/
7. Network camera developments enable live web imaging. White paper, Axis (1999)
8. IKebe, Oqawa, Hatayanma: Network camera system using new home network architure
   with flexible scalability. In: International Conference on ICCE 2005, pp. 151–152 (2005)
9. Lee, K., Yim, K., Mikki, M.: A secure framework of the surveillance video network
   integrating heterogeneous video formats and protocols. Submitted to be Published on the
   Journal of Computers and Mathematics with Applications
10. Lee, K., Yim, K.: Safe Authentication Protocol for Secure USB Memories. Journal of
   Wireless Mobile Networks, Ubiquitous Computing and Dependable Applications
   (JoWUA) 1(1), 46–55 (2010)

# Author Index